❋ Named One of the Best Books of 2013 by *The Economist* ❋
❋ Named One of the 100 Notable Books of 2013 by *The New York Times* ❋

"Pollack has provided a useful briefing for anyone seeking to better understand what drives Iranian policy. Even more, he tackles the nature of the challenge the country poses to the United States. The book proves a valuable tool for pushing back on claims that containment is just a policy of surrender. In making the case here that containment is the worst possible strategy, except for all the others, Pollack has contributed to a smarter, more reality-based Iran policy debate."

—*American Prospect*

"Learned, lucid and deeply sobering."

—*Kirkus Reviews*

"*Unthinkable* is well-organized and clearly written. . . . It reads like an expanded version of what's known in government circles as a policy or decision memo. . . . Pollack argues compellingly for his choice of the 'least bad' option. But even if he fails to persuade, he still renders a valuable service by forcing us to think rigorously about the unthinkable."

—*The Plain Dealer* (Cleveland)

"The great strength of *Unthinkable* is that Pollack includes enough evidence for those who disagree with him to make their case. That is what makes his book not only informative, but an essential contribution to the debate."

—Joel B. Pollak, Breitbart.com

"An engrossing book. . . . Mr. Pollack has produced an account that is mercifully free of swagger. If Congress gets a vote on going to war with Iran, let's hope that this book is on everyone's reading lists. It might just change a few minds."

—*The Economist*

Unthinkable

Iran, the Bomb, and American Strategy

Kenneth M. Pollack

Simon & Schuster Paperbacks

New York   London   Toronto   Sydney   New Delhi

Simon & Schuster Paperbacks
A Division of Simon & Schuster, Inc.
1230 Avenue of the Americas
New York, NY 10020

First Simon & Schuster trade paperback edition September 2014

SIMON & SCHUSTER PAPERBACKS and colophon are
registered trademarks of Simon & Schuster, Inc.

For information about special discounts for bulk purchases,
please contact Simon & Schuster Special Sales at
1-866-506-1949 or business@simonandschuster.com.

The Simon & Schuster Speakers Bureau can bring authors to your live event.
For more information or to book an event contact the Simon & Schuster Speakers
Bureau at 1-866-248-3049 or visit our website at www.simonspeakers.com.

Designed by Ruth Lee-Mui
Jacket design and illustration by Base Art Co.

Manufactured in the United States of America

1   3   5   7   9   10   8   6   4   2

Library of Congress Cataloging-in-Publication Data is available.

ISBN 978-1-4767-3392-0
ISBN 978-1-4767-3393-7 (pbk)
ISBN 978-1-4767-3394-4 (ebook)

For Barry Posen and Stephen Van Evera,

Who taught me how to think

Contents

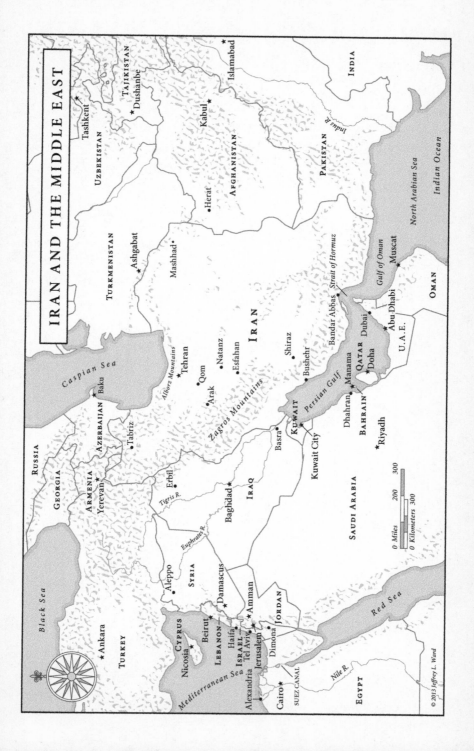

IRAN AND THE MIDDLE EAST

© 2013 Jeffrey L. Ward

Unthinkable

Introduction

COMING TO THE CROSSROADS

Since 2002, when the world learned of Iran's progress toward acquiring a nuclear weapons capability, the United States has endured a protracted crisis with the Islamic Republic. It has been painful and frustrating, as all interactions with the Iranian regime typically prove. There have been moments of success. The United States has helped forge a broad coalition of states that have imposed unprecedented sanctions, isolation, and other forms of punishment on Iran to try to convince it to negotiate an end to its nuclear program, albeit to no avail. Iran today is weaker, poorer, and more friendless than ever. Yet for all its successes, the policy has not achieved its ultimate goal and may never do so. In spite of all the pain Iran has suffered, its leaders remain determined to acquire the capacity for nuclear weaponry—and perhaps to field an arsenal once they have done so. There may still be some options for the United States, short of war, to prevent Iran from crossing the nuclear weapons threshold, but their number is dwindling, as is the likelihood that they will succeed.

This presents us with a dilemma over what to do next. Having tried the easy options and many hard ones, too, it looks increasingly likely that we will soon have to make the hardest choice of all: whether to contain a nuclear Iran or go to war as the final option to prevent one.

That decision is the principal focus of this book.

The debate has already begun. Many on the right have already begun to advocate for an attack on Iran. Others who recognize that America's war-weariness after Iraq and Afghanistan makes it politically impractical to call openly for war with Iran have instead begun to argue that no alternative to war is viable. Meanwhile, many on the left are pleading that war is unnecessary or that it would be disastrous. Some have begun to argue that containment offers a better alternative.

Both sides know the ultimate fork in the road of America's Iran policy is approaching. We are not there yet, but we may be there soon. It is time to begin to consider those choices so that we can make the best one, rather than having one forced upon us. None of the options we have left when it comes to dealing with Iran's nuclear arsenal are good ones. Events overtook the good options long ago, leaving a bunch of difficult long shots. If our last chances all fail, as seems distressingly likely, we will have only the two worst options left: war or containment.

I believe that going to war with Iran to try to prevent it from obtaining a nuclear arsenal would be a worse course of action than containing Iran, even a nuclear Iran. However, I do not believe that the military option is foolish, and I believe that there are much stronger arguments in its favor than was the case even a few years ago. I simply believe that it entails more costs and risks than containment—except in some very specific circumstances. I will explain why in the course of this book.

Although frequently misrepresented, at its heart, containment is a strategy that seeks to prevent Iran from expanding beyond its current borders or destabilizing the Middle East until the regime collapses of its own internal contradictions. It is the strategy that the United States has employed against Iran since the earliest days following the Islamic Revolution. It is not appeasement. It does not mean simply acquiescing to Iran's acquisition of nuclear weapons, let alone to its dominance of the Persian Gulf region. Indeed, there are many varieties of containment, some more passive, some very aggressive. If we continue to pursue containment toward Iran in the future, one of the most important questions we will have to address is when to employ a more assertive brand of containment and when to hold back and focus more on its defensive aspects.

I also recognize that containment is nothing but the less bad of the two final options. Perhaps more important than which option we choose, the worst thing of all we could do would be to refuse to think through our choice beforehand. Frequently, a politically expedient denial of reality has left us unprepared for unfortunate choices. On those occasions, we have stumbled into one policy or another, and the result has often been disastrous.

Many Americans believe that the invasion of Iraq in 2003 was our nation's greatest foreign policy mistake since Vietnam. That war was born of the failure of our efforts to contain Saddam Husayn's Iraq in the 1990s, and that failure was itself the result of our unwillingness to recognize the *need* to contain Saddam's regime for the long term back in 1991. At that moment, at the end of the Persian Gulf War, America's leaders assumed that Saddam would be overthrown by his generals. They designed U.S. policy toward Iraq based on this assumption without any consideration of backups or alternatives. When Saddam survived, the United States was forced into a containment policy for which it had not planned. When that policy crumbled less than a decade later, it left the American people with the worst choices of all and convinced President George W. Bush (and the majority of the American people, who supported him at the time) to invade Iraq. Yet the worst decision was not the decision to invade, but the insistence that it was not necessary to plan or prepare to occupy, secure, and rebuild Iraq. And that mistake stemmed from the Bush 43 administration's willful denial that such a massive undertaking would be necessary.

How we handle Iran is likely to be every bit as consequential as how we handled Iraq. This time, we need to do it right. That can only mean considering our options and preparing to implement them with a clear-eyed resolution, rather than the rose-colored ignorance that plagued us in Iraq.

The Goals of the Book

Defining a new policy toward Iran has two inherent, unavoidable problems. First, there is too much that we do not know. It is too often the case that we just don't know what the Iranians are doing and thinking. It is not that we do not have any information, only that the information is incomplete and open to multiple interpretations. Therefore, much of our decision-making about Iran must of necessity be based on assumptions. And the assumptions we make determine which policy options we favor or dislike. If you assume that the Iranians will use nuclear weapons once they get them, you will prefer war over containment, and vice versa. How we choose to fill the gaps in our knowledge is often more important than the knowledge we have.

The second unavoidable problem in making policy toward Iran is that there is no "best" strategy to pursue. We have tried lots of different approaches to Iran. None has worked and the Iranians are getting close to having the capability to quickly build nuclear weapons—a point that most people believe could change our relationship and our policy options with Iran. Every path we might take, every policy we might adopt, both before and after we reach that point, entails both significant costs and frightening risks. Deciding which strategy the United States should adopt is a matter of deciding which costs and risks are more or less acceptable. And every individual will weigh those costs and risks differently depending on his or her own perspectives, preferences, and assumptions.

This book is meant to serve two purposes. First, it lays out my own thinking about how the United States should handle the current crisis over Iran's nuclear program. I have been thinking about and working on this question for more than twenty-five years, both in government and out, and I have a preference for one course of action—containment.

Second, the book is meant to provide a framework for understanding the current crisis over Iran's nuclear program and to help others make an informed choice regarding what the United States should do about it, whether that means agreeing with my preference for containment or adopting the alternative of war.

My foremost consideration in writing this book has been to try to be as transparent as I can. I have tried to make the best arguments for all the different policy options that the United States might pursue toward Iran, even those with which I disagree. I have also tried to be honest about the drawbacks associated with the policies that I prefer. If you end up agreeing with me, great; but you should only do so in the full knowledge that the course of action I favor carries significant risks and costs, too, if only because they all do. Similarly, if you end up disagreeing with me and preferring a different policy option toward Iran, that's good, too. My hope is only that this book will have helped you to figure out which strategy you prefer and why, and to be ready to accept the costs and risks (and uncertainties) involved in whichever option you prefer.

In the past, my views on various issues have been misrepresented. I tried to write a balanced, nuanced book about Iraq in 2002 only to find it caricatured by people who read nothing but the subtitle—or cherry-picked lines from it. There is only so much I can do to prevent that happening to this book as well, but I am going to do what I can to make it harder this time around. And I want to start by presenting, up front, the basic argument of this book.

So here is a summary of my view:

I believe that U.S. policy toward Iran moving forward should begin by trying a revamped version of the carrot-and-stick strategy Washington has employed at least since 2009 (and arguably since 2006). In particular, we need to lay out more attractive benefits to Iran if it is willing to make meaningful concessions on its nuclear program and other problematic activities. Simultaneously, and as one of the "sticks" to convince Tehran to compromise, the United States should explore how we might better support indigenous Iranian opposition groups seeking to reform or even overthrow the Islamic Republic. I see this latter option as morally right, strategically sensible, and a potentially useful adjunct to a carrot-and stick approach of diplomacy and sanctions. I believe that an Israeli strike on Iran would serve no good purpose and might be disastrous for the United States, Israel, and our other allies. If the carrot-and-stick approach fails and regime change proves impractical, I prefer to see the United States opt for containment of Iran rather than war. I do not see the military option as stupid or reckless, and there are strong arguments in its favor. There are also circumstances in which it could be the best course of action. However, on the whole, I believe that the costs and risks of containment are more acceptable than the costs and risks of starting down the path of war with Iran. I do not believe that the containment of Iran, including potentially a nuclear Iran, will be easy or painless, just preferable to the alternative. Finally, containment does not mean appeasement, or even acceptance, of a nuclear Iran. Containment can take many shapes, some confrontational, some far more passive, and one of the keys to making containment work will be determining how assertive or reserved to be at any time.

The Structure of the Book

The rest of the book will flesh out this perspective while providing the background to the crisis and the key aspects of the different policy options available toward Iran. It is not a history of Iran or of the American relationship with Iran, although I will try to provide all the pertinent history related to the different issues relevant to Iran, its nuclear program, and the wider U.S.-Iranian confrontation.[1]

The book has three parts. Part I addresses the "problems" of Iran. It looks at Iranian goals, personalities, decision-making, and policies, as best we understand them. In particular, I try to highlight what we don't know and the competing explanations for what we do know. It also provides an overview of the Iranian nuclear program. The first part then goes on to discuss the different threats that a nuclear Iran could create for American interests. Taken together, this information should serve as a foundation on which to build a new American policy toward Iran.

Part II looks at the different policy options we might still try to employ to prevent Iran from acquiring a nuclear weapons capability. It starts by discussing the trade-offs involved in these policies and then provides a summary of the progress of the Obama administration's policy so far. It moves on to look at four potential paths forward: revamping the current Dual Track (or carrot-and-stick) strategy, pursuing a form of "regime change" by aiding Iranian opposition groups, allowing Israel to strike Iran's nuclear facilities, or exercising the military option ourselves.

Part III explores containment in much greater depth. It surveys what different versions of containment could look like, what it would require to make them work, and under what circumstances the United States might opt for more or less aggressive versions of containment. It spends as much time on the question of "how to contain" as on "whether" the United States should do so. The strongest argument for war is that containment is impossible, or at least unlikely to work, and therefore choosing between them requires looking much harder at the question of whether containment can work.

I end by laying out how I weigh the different trade-offs, pros and cons, and how I arrive at my conclusion that, left with no other alternative but war, I believe containment of Iran to be the better choice. I do so in the firm belief that, given the many problems that beset either course of action, what matters most today is less what path we as a nation decide to take and far more having an honest, open process to reach that decision. Whatever we conclude, we need to be clear about the price we will pay, the risks we will run, and what it will take to make it work.

In 1962, the Cold War nuclear strategist Herman Kahn wrote a famous book called *Thinking About the Unthinkable.*[2] At that time, what was "unthinkable" was the idea of a nuclear war between the United States and the Soviet Union. Kahn's warning was that we had to think about that "unthinkable" event, because not to do so would leave us unprepared if it ever occurred and so might make it more likely. Today, as we face the challenge of Iran's pursuit of a nuclear weapons capability, I fear that our choices are being narrowed to just two: going to war to prevent Iran from acquiring such a capability, or else learning to live with it. Watching our current public debate over Iran policy, I am struck by how many of our leaders, thinkers, and opinion-makers have deemed both of these ultimate alternatives inconceivable, unimaginable, impossible—unthinkable. Yet, it seems ever more likely that we will have to choose between them. When we do, we are going to wish that we had thought a great deal about them and decided which was the least bad, even though they may both be unthinkable.

Part I

Reality and Hyperbole

1

Iran from the Inside Out

I n many ways, the crisis with Iran begins with the Iranian regime itself. All of the questions about Iran's pursuit of a nuclear weapons capability are bound up with the regime. Why does Tehran want a nuclear capability? Why do Americans (and Israelis, and Saudis, and Turks, and others) fear how Iran would behave once it acquired such a capability—and should they? Can we deter Iran's regime from behaving in an aggressive manner if it were to acquire such a capability? Or must we go to war to prevent it from gaining that capability because we don't believe that we can live with it? In every case, a critical element of the answer lies in understanding the motives and inner workings of the Iranian leadership.

The Iranian regime is often a mystery. If Iran were ruled by a different government, one that we understood better, the answers to those questions would be easier. If it were ruled by a less paranoid, less antagonistic government, we would not be asking these questions at all. But Iran is ruled by the same theocracy that emerged as the victor of Iran's revolution in 1979. That's not to say that the regime has not changed since then.

It has, and in some very important ways. But it has retained many of its most important features—its fears, its pathologies, its ideology, its belligerent insecurity, and its impenetrability.

So all of the questions persist, and we have to try to find answers to them to inform our decision, *whatever* that decision may be, and *uncertain* though it will be. That requires trying, as best we can, to understand the Iranian regime as the starting point for answering the many questions that should help us devise a policy toward Iran.

The Limits to Our Understanding of Iran

It's actually not hard to be an expert on Iran. You only need to know two phrases: "I don't know" and "it depends." For better or worse (mostly worse), those are the answers to most of the questions you will ever be asked about Iran.

It's not just that the Iranians work diligently to prevent outsiders from understanding what is going on in their government, it is also that it is difficult, if not impossible, to know what is going on at the highest levels of Iranian decision-making in real time. Outsiders often fail to understand what decision Tehran made—let alone why the Iranians made that choice—until well after the fact, if ever. This is particularly noteworthy given how fascinated many Iranians are by their own politics, and how much they write about their political affairs.

The fog starts with Iran's culture. In the eloquent and revealing words of Hooman Majd, "No book, article, or essay . . . can ever completely unravel the mystery of Iran for a reader, or fully explain either the country or its people to his or her satisfaction."[1] Iranian society tends to be secretive by nature. Much has been made of the principally Shi'i practice of dissimulation known as *taqiyyah*, which forgives—some would say encourages—believers to mislead others about one's faith and other important information.[2] Iranians are more than 90 percent Shi'a, and Iranians and outside observers alike comment on how the practice of taqiyyah has spread to other aspects of Iranian life, particularly the secrecy of the clerical regime. One of the wisest scholars of Iranian politics and strategy, Shahram Chubin, adds that Iran suffers from "a national narcissism that makes it ignorant, insensitive, or dismissive of others' concerns."[3]

The endemic factionalism of the Iranian system promotes further obscurity as groups attempt to hide their views, their alliances, and their actions from others. Anthropologists have long suggested that mountainous terrain, such as that which dominates Iran's populated areas, tends to breed cultural heterogeneity and individualism, which in turn often produces the kind of factionalism predominant in Iran—and other mountain-dwelling communities from Afghanistan to Lebanon to Switzerland to Appalachia.[4] The great Iranian scholar R. K. Ramazani once famously called the politics of the Islamic Republic "kaleidoscopic" in the sense that the Iranian political scene was divided up into thousands of tiny factions (often just individuals), and every time the matter at hand changed, all of those groups lined up differently.[5] Iran's political mosaic is constantly changing, often in unpredictable ways. Because alliances tend to be ephemeral it is hard for Iranian politicians to sustain big coalitions that can engineer large-scale changes in Iranian policy over time, predisposing the Iranian system to an unhelpful inertia. As many Iranians complain, it is hard to get the Iranian regime to do something it is not already doing, or to get it to stop or change something that it is already doing. Moreover, Iranian political leaders will often hold different beliefs that outsiders see as incompatible (such as a commitment to acquiring nuclear weapons *and* a willingness to repair relations with the West). Depending on the issue, leaders can line up in ways that seem incomprehensible to outsiders.[6]

Beyond the effects of Persian culture, the cloak over Iranian decision-making is spun from a political system that is Byzantine, fragmented, and counterintuitive. More than thirty years after the Iranian Revolution, the Iranian government is a hodgepodge, sporting numerous entities with overlapping and seemingly redundant functions. Iran has institutions that serve purposes only the Iranians seem to understand, with mandates so vague they could be all powerful or utterly powerless. In many cases, several governmental organizations will be responsible for a task, and in other cases, no one is. It has an "Assembly of Experts" that chooses the Supreme Leader, and ostensibly meets every six months to monitor his performance, although it does not seem to do either in practice. It has a "Council of Guardians" that vets candidates for government offices and can nullify legislation for being un-Islamic or unconstitutional—which is not a power entrusted to the judiciary. It also has an "Expediency Discernment Council," created to mediate disputes between Iran's parliament (the Majles) and the Council of Guardians, although it seems to do little of that and mostly just advises the Supreme Leader on subjects unknown.

The Supreme Leader himself is ultimately Iran's chief executive, although the president is nominally the head of government. The Supreme Leader seems to set policy on whatever issues he likes whenever he wants, although the president is responsible for all government activity. Iran has two complete militaries (the Islamic Revolutionary Guards Corps and the Iranian Armed Forces) and multiple internal security organizations. Almost every former senior official stays on as a senior advisor of one kind or another. Moreover, some of them seem to have real influence while others have none. As a result, whenever anyone attempts to produce a wiring diagram of the Iranian government, showing all of its entities and their lines of authority and responsibility, it becomes so labyrinthine and speculative as to be useless.

What matters is often not the formal powers or responsibilities of any government office, but the informal authority of the person who heads it. The government of the Islamic Republic is highly personalized. An office that seemed all-important when one man held it can become irrelevant the moment someone else takes it over. It is often difficult to know which institutions matter unless one understands how the Supreme Leader views the officeholders at that moment—and the Supreme Leader's views of people are constantly changing.

There are only two exceptions to this rule: the Revolutionary Guards and the Supreme Leader himself. The leadership of the Islamic Revolutionary Guard Corps (IRGC, or Sepah-e Pasdaran-e Enqelab-e Islami, in Farsi) has consistently played a critical role in Iranian decision-making from its formation in the wake of the 1979 revolution and subsequent Iraqi invasion of 1980. Today the Guard is one of the most powerful, if not the most powerful, institution in Iran.[7] It plays vital roles in defending the regime from enemies both foreign and domestic, and its leaders and veterans have gone on to hold many other key posts in the Islamic Republic. Almost alone among Iran's high offices, the IRGC commander has been a key policymaker and advisor to the Supreme Leader regardless of who has held either post.

The Supreme Leader (or Rahbar, for "leader" in Farsi), Ayatollah Ali Khamene'i, is the highest manifestation of the personalized functioning of the Iranian regime. Ayatollah Khamene'i is the man in charge of Iran. This was not always the case, and it took at least a decade or more after he was named the Supreme Leader upon Ayatollah Khomeini's death in 1989 for Khamene'i to consolidate his power and emerge as Iran's undisputed authority. But Khamene'i now sits alone atop the Iranian power pyramid. Khamene'i makes all of Iran's most important decisions, including those related to Iran's nuclear program. And Khamene'i may be the deepest of all of Iran's mysteries.

It is rare that outsiders—or even other Iranians—ever know when Khamene'i makes a decision, or if he does, what he has opted to do. He relies on a number of trusted emissaries to convey his decisions. Likewise, when he makes a decision, it is difficult for outsiders and insiders alike to know whose counsel (if any) Khamene'i sought, let alone heeded, to reach his conclusions. To some extent, this limitation is inherent in autocracies because the autocrat's views are decisive and it is never possible to know what is in another person's head. Consider one of the most infamous and closely scrutinized autocrats of all time. Even with two books written by his own hand (or at least dictated by his own mouth), dozens of memoirs written by those who knew him, scores of public speeches, and a welter of documents reflecting his decisions and orders, we still have an imperfect understanding of Adolf Hitler. And we know much less about Khamene'i's views than we do about Hitler's. The Ayatollah speaks in public, but his private views rarely ever reach those beyond his closest circle of confidants—an ever-changing group, never large and often shrinking.

Khamene'i's secretive, personalized method of decision-making appears to stem from both his nature and his environment. He is said to be suspicious and conspiratorial even to the point of paranoia. This may well have been reinforced by his accession to power as a nonthreatening compromise whom few respected at the time. This was followed by a long struggle to become the master of Iran's political circus, during which his position and authority were repeatedly challenged from within the system and without.[8] Yet Khamene'i remains a weak man in a strong position. His unique ability to act to overcome the inertia of the Iranian political system also entails the power to alienate those who do not favor his decisions to do so. Khamene'i has tried to minimize the numbers of people who could be angered by his rulings, often by not deciding at all or by issuing Delphic pronouncements open to widely varying interpretations. Obviously, such decisions reveal little about his true preferences.

For these reasons, we need to respect the limits of our knowledge when it comes to Iran. Unfortunately, that does not excuse us from making hard choices regarding Iran, but we must do so without any false confidence. Churchill famously called Russia a "riddle wrapped in a mystery inside an enigma," but that image seems to fit modern Iran even better.

Our sense of humility regarding our ignorance about Iran should be reinforced by all of the times that we and so many others have gotten Iran wrong over the past three decades. In particular, every time that the United States has tried to influence Iran's internal political processes, we have ended up hurting the people we sought to help. From the Iran-Contra fiasco to President Clinton's failed bid at rapprochement to the Obama administration's Dual Track approach, the United States has tried to help the more moderate voices within the Iranian political system—and there *have* always been real moderates among Iran's political leadership—only to find that far from assisting the moderates, our efforts only undercut them. Our modesty about the limits of our knowledge should also be reinforced by our experiences with Iraq, especially the stunning and terrible realization that Saddam had eliminated his weapons of mass destruction before the 2003 invasion. We (and most of the world, including this author) missed it completely.

Iranian Goals

Our understanding of Iranian goals is imperfect, to say the least. The Islamic Republic has never published an authoritative statement of its goals. Ayatollah Khomeini wrote any number of things about what he hoped Iran would accomplish, but few of these were concrete. Many still seem well beyond Iran's current capacity. Khamene'i and his lieutenants have done little to enlighten the world regarding their ultimate aims. Moreover, we should recognize from the authoritative statements of foreign policy objectives regularly intoned by American officials that even formal enunciations of governmental goals often have little or nothing to do with actual goals. Thus, as always when we think about Iran, we have to acknowledge that when it comes to Tehran's goals, we don't really know and it depends.

Yet Iranian goals and the priority among them are critical to understanding both how we still might prevent Iran from acquiring a nuclear capability (and the extent that that is still a possibility), and how Iran would behave if it were to acquire such a capability. If, for instance, Iran valued spreading its Islamic Revolution even more than the survival of the Iranian state, it would be both difficult to prevent Iran from acquiring a nuclear capability and difficult to deter Iranian aggression once Tehran acquired such a capability. Thus, we have no choice but to try, as best we can, to discern Iran's objectives from their behavior over the years.

PRESERVING THE ISLAMIC REGIME'S CONTROL OVER IRAN. Whether their inspiration is ideological or venal, Iran's leaders are determined to hold on to power. The evidence suggests that this aim is their highest priority, as demonstrated by their willingness to use force (including mass arrests, torture, and large-scale killings) to hold power.

DEFENDING THE IRANIAN NATION FROM HARM. In some ways, it is hard to know if this goal should come before or after preservation of the regime's control over Iran. Doubtless, the Iranian leadership seeks to save Iran and the Iranian people, to keep them safe from harm and to see them prosper. Over the years they have acted to defend Iran and Iranians from external attack. However, just as consistently, the clerical regime has willingly endured tremendous damage—damage to the Iranian nation and the Iranian people—in pursuit of other goals. During the Iran-Iraq War, Iran suffered more than a half million casualties in pursuit of Ayatollah Khomeini's determination to "liberate" Baghdad, Mecca, and Jerusalem.[9] Whether the current leadership would tolerate similar levels of misery inflicted on the Iranian people is uncertain, but it seems less likely. Khomeini is gone and his ideology commands much less reverence from many Iranians. Moreover, in 1988, when the leadership realized how much Iran would have to endure to continue the war, even Khomeini relented.[10]

REGIONAL HEGEMONY. For more than 2,500 years, with only a six-hundred-year interruption for the (Arab) Islamic and Mongol conquests, Iran was the dominant power in southwest Asia. Heralded by Cyrus the Great's defeat of the Medes in 549 BC, the Persian empire became the world's first superpower, the height of political, military, economic, and cultural civilization. The Seleucids, Parthians, Sassanids, Safavids, and Qajars that followed continued to dominate their corner of the world in a way that modern Iranians have been taught was something like the "natural" order. In their view, Iran is the greatest civilization in the region—far above the Turks, Arabs, Afghans, South Asians, and Central Asians, whom Iranians often hold in contempt. Whether by nature or divine provenance, a great many Iranians agree that Iran ought to be the dominant power, the hegemon of the region.

Few Iranians will come right out and say that they seek to be the regional hegemon. Instead they speak endlessly of "respect." Of course, Iranians have difficulty defining what "respect" means to them.[11] Often, when Iranian officials are asked to explain what they mean by "respect," the conversation devolves into puerile assertions that anything Iran does not like is a sign of "disrespect." Obviously, this tack is not helpful and only reinforces the sense of Iran's neighbors that Iranian hegemony would be similarly undefined—and therefore potentially all-encompassing. It resurrects their traditional fears that Iran will want to choose their governments for them, if not control their territory outright.

Despite the ineffable quality of Iranian insistence that it should be the dominant power in the region, it seems unlikely that Iran seeks to conquer any of its neighbors outright—although the small, wealthy Gulf emirates might tempt Tehran if it were within Iran's power to grab them. Instead, it seems more likely that Iran seeks to ensure that all of the region's governments are friendly to it and subservient. That, rather than outright conquest, appears to be Iran's goal in places like Iraq and Lebanon.

What's more, Iran's determination to regain what it sees as its rightful place as the dominant force in southwest Asia extends beyond its immediate neighbors. Tehran appears to be of the opinion that any major event, dispute, or crisis in the Middle East is Iran's concern. Iran continues to insinuate itself into the Arab-Israeli confrontation, Lebanese politics, the Yemeni civil war, and even events in North Africa and the Balkans. Although Iran often has multiple motives for doing so, an important theme appears to be Tehran's determination to assert its importance.

SPREADING THE ISLAMIC REVOLUTION. For the first decade after the fall of the Shah, when Khomeini ruled Iran, spreading his Islamic Revolution may have been Iran's highest priority. Today, for the majority of Iranians, that is no longer the case. Many would like to see less of Khomeini's revolution at home and have no interest in seeing it spread abroad. But Iranian opinion runs a gamut. At least some Iranians continue to see the spread of their Islamic Revolution as not just relevant, but imperative. For them, Iran must be willing to continue to make sacrifices for the sake of spreading the revolution and seeing their vision of God's will enacted.[12] A significant number of influential Iranian policymakers—typically referred to as radical hardliners, principalists, or ultraconservatives—seem to share that view. In Iran's Islamic Revolutionary Guard Corps, this view predominates among the senior officers, as it does with numerous key figures in Iran's parliament (the Majles), judiciary, and intelligence services.[13]

Where things get tricky with this goal, however, is that it is often difficult to distinguish between spreading the Islamic Revolution and the more traditional Iranian (and Persian) goal of regional dominance. Especially for many of Iran's hardliners, the policies they advocate are often consistent with both goals, and they seem to use arguments related to one or the other interchangeably. Iranian hardliners favor aid to the oppressed Shi'a majority of Bahrain as a way to spread the Islamic Revolution, in the expectation that the Bahraini Shi'a will be able to overthrow their king just as the Iranians overthrew the Shah. Yet they also see it as a way of increasing Iranian regional sway, as they expect that a new Shi'i government in Bahrain would be deferential to, and dependent on, Tehran. Which motive is stronger? Do Iranian hardliners recognize a difference between these arguments? We don't know, and it likely varies from hardliner to hardliner.

The Rahbar

In addition to the role Khamene'i plays to obscure the workings of the Iranian regime to outsiders, the Supreme Leader is important to the story of Iran's nuclear program in a number of other ways. In particular, as the most powerful decision-maker in the Iranian system by far, what Khamene'i wants from the nuclear program matters a great deal, and it may be all that matters. Although we don't know a lot about Khamene'i's views at any given time, we do know some. More than that, we have a sense of his general approach to important topics that bear on Iran's nuclear program and how Iran might behave with a nuclear arsenal.

What we do know is helpful, but not hopeful. First off, the evidence suggests that Khamene'i takes a relatively rigid and doctrinaire view of the ideological underpinnings of the Islamic Republic. He opposed the liberalizing tendencies of former presidents Rafsanjani and (especially) Khatami.[14] He even disowned former president Mahmud Ahmadinejad for deviating in small but important ways from his dogma and the system he enforces.[15] The respected Iran scholar Ali Ansari writes, "There is a tight and highly dependent relationship between Khamenei and the [hardline] faction. This is not simply an ideological relationship, but a partnership in the consolidation of power, and it is important to recognize this as one of mutual dependence."[16]

Khamene'i is also determined to make Iran strong, independent, and self-sufficient, in part to eliminate the foreign influences that have been the bugbear of every Iranian leader for more than a century. Like many Iranians, Imam Khomeini was obsessed with foreign influences, believing that they were responsible for all the ills bedeviling Iran. His successor has followed suit, even taking actions that represent the national equivalent of cutting off one's nose to spite one's face. At times, Khamene'i has even claimed that the international sanctions against Iran were a blessing as they forced Iran to further shed its dependence on foreigners and more ardently embrace self-sufficiency. Indeed, only the hermit kingdom of North Korea shares Khamene'i's appreciation of autarky and willingness to suffer to achieve it.[17]

The foreign state that Khamene'i fears and despises most, of course, is the United States. The Supreme Leader has indicated that he sees the United States as determined to remove the Islamic Republic and install a submissive Iranian regime to re-create the relationship the U.S. once had with the Shah. That appears to be the touchstone of all of his thinking about the United States.[18] Karim Sadjadpour, a brilliant expert on Iran, writes that "Khamenei's contempt for the United States has been remarkably consistent and enduring. In over three decades of speeches—first as president and later as Supreme Leader—he has very rarely spoken favorably, in public at least, about the United States or the prospect of restoring relations with the U.S. government. On the contrary, whether the topic of discussion is foreign policy, agriculture, or education, he seamlessly relates the subject matter to the cruelty, greed, and sinister plots of the 'Global Arrogance' [as he calls the United States]." [19]

In recent years, he has increasingly articulated his conspiratorial fears of the United States as an American "soft war" being waged against Iran. He argues that the U.S. government employs all aspects of Joseph Nye's famous conception of "soft power"—propaganda, cultural influence, prestige, media power, political sway, even trade and investment—to undermine the Iranian state. This fear has been a major component of Khamene'i's objection to any agreement with the United States on any issue, including the nuclear standoff. He insists that such agreements would only further American "soft war" subversion while denying Iran the tools it needs to fight back against that threat. [20] Ray Takeyh, one of the most insightful Iran analysts of his generation, writes, "For the supreme leader, the United States was always devious and arrogant, and its policies were mere cover designed to advance its nefarious purposes. To preserve the integrity and authenticity of Iran's Islamic path, one had to resist America's blandishments and forego the rewards that resumed relations might offer. Khamenei made his suspicions clear: 'America appears with a deceitful smile but has a dagger behind its back and is ready to plunder. That is its true nature.' In the end, Khamenei perceived that Iran 'has nothing to talk to them about and no need for them.'" [21]

When it comes to America's allies in the region, Khamene'i's views have tended toward greater moderation, at least by the standards of the Islamic Republic. He seems to share Khomeini's view that the United States implanted Israel into the Middle East to fight the Islamic world, and wishes for the latter's destruction—a commonplace among Tehran's power brokers. He has also repeatedly indicated his willingness to support groups working for the destruction of Israel. But Khamene'i has also gone to some lengths to insist that Iran is not actively and *directly* seeking to destroy Israel, especially after Ahmadinejad's various suggestions to the contrary. [22] Moreover, Khamene'i has also intimated that enmity toward Israel is a secondary consideration of Iranian foreign policy, especially compared to its enmity toward America, going so far as to say that "the Palestine issue is not Iran's jihad."[23]

Khomeini's pan-Islamic revolution famously rejected Saudi Arabia's brand of Salafiyya Islam (literally "fundamentalist" in Arabic, but also known pejoratively as "Wahhabi" Islam, for Muhammad Ibn 'Abd al-Wahhab, who introduced the concept to the Arabian peninsula in the eighteenth century). Khomeini blasted it as a "baseless and superstitious cult" in his final testament.[24] However, his successor has been far more circumspect with the Kingdom. Khamene'i has repeatedly signaled that he is open to improved relations with Riyadh, and portrays aggressive Iranian moves against the Kingdom as having been provoked by Saudi aggression against Iran or Iranian interests, including Saudi support for American policies. He was notably mute after Saudi forces helped crush the mostly Shi'i uprising against the Sunni royal family of Bahrain in 2011. Nevertheless, on his watch, Iran has attempted to help Shi'i revolutionaries overthrow the Bahraini government in 1996; and in 2012, after Saudi Arabia proposed a union with Bahrain, *Kayhan*, a conservative newspaper that frequently reflects the views of Khamene'i, called instead for Iran to annex it.[25]

Although Khamene'i's approach to foreign policy is antithetical to American interests both by ideological design and diplomatic circumstance, he has typically pursued it in a calculated, pragmatic fashion. Khamene'i has repeatedly approved terrorist plots, and has tolerated some considerable risks. But he has also tried hard to avoid recklessness, pulled in his horns when he overstepped, and emphasized defending Iran over attacking its enemies whenever the two have been in conflict. He has never acted irrationally, or even with the same irresponsible belligerence and willful denial of reality as Saddam Husayn. As Israel's greatest scholar of Iran, David Menashri, puts it, "With few exceptions, whenever ideological convictions have clashed with the interests of the state—as prescribed by the clerical ruling elite—state interests ultimately have superseded revolutionary dogma in both foreign relations and domestic politics. The change, noticeable already under Khomeini, became even

more discernible following his death in 1989. Although national considerations were alien to Khomeini's stated desire to expand Islamic influence throughout the Middle East, his regime chose to conduct its policy
primarily from a perception of Iran's state interests. . . . An analysis of
Iran's policies toward its neighbors demonstrates the degree to which actual policies have been primarily shaped by pragmatic, national interests,
rather than ideological convictions." [26]

PRAGMATISM AND FREELANCING. On March 23, 2007, while British
forces were still in Iraq as part of the U.S.-led occupation, fifteen British
sailors and marines were searching a ship suspected of smuggling in the
Shatt al-Arab waterway, which divides southeastern Iraq from southwestern Iran, when a large force of Iranian Revolutionary Guard naval boats
surrounded them. The IRGC personnel boarded the British boats and,
because the local British commander was under orders from London not
to fight back, the Iranians took the British boats and the fifteen personnel
back to Iran. Although this incident could have provoked a war between
Iran and the United Kingdom (and its American ally), the operation apparently was the decision of the local Iranian IRGC navy commander,
Captain Abol-Ghassam Amangah. He acted without conferring with
Tehran. No captain in the U.S. Navy—or any other worth its salt—would
risk provoking a war without first checking with his chain of command.
Remarkably, Tehran rewarded Amangah for his initiative. [27] Similarly, at
various times during the Iran-Iraq War, Iranian naval and air commanders conducted provocative actions and even opened fire on American
armed forces in the Persian Gulf without permission from higher Iranian
political authorities.

This is one of the few instances in which the United States has good
evidence that local commanders took provocative actions on their own.
There may well be others. For instance, in August 1998, Iran deployed
roughly two hundred thousand troops to the Afghan border after the
Taliban government (which then still ruled most of Afghanistan) killed
eleven Iranian diplomats in Mazar-e Sharif. [28] At the time, reports indi-

cated that the IRGC military leadership wanted to invade Afghanistan to punish the Taliban and deployed six divisions to the Mashhad area on its own—only to have Tehran dispatch eight regular army (Artesh) divisions to prevent the IRGC forces from moving on their own. The story is still unconfirmed.

These incidents point to an important and somewhat unique aspect of Iranian governance: the ability of actors to freelance or push the edge of the envelope on important and sensitive policy matters. Throughout his time in office, Khamene'i has often ruled by remaining aloof and not clarifying his edicts, allowing subordinate entities to interpret them as they like, having them take actions, and then deciding which course to take based on how those initial moves pan out. Likewise, he allows some personnel and organizations—particularly his favorites and the powerful Revolutionary Guards, upon whose support his power depends—the ability to take some actions that he has not necessarily sanctioned.

SUCCESSION. The last aspect of Khamene'i's role in the Iranian nuclear saga that bears discussion is his mortality. Khamene'i was born in 1939, at a time when Iran was desperately poor and underdeveloped. He grew up without the benefit of the most advanced health care or nutrition. He is believed to be in good health, and there is no reason to expect that he will die anytime soon. But he will not live forever. The Islamic Republic may outlive him, and if Iran crosses the nuclear threshold on his watch, that capability will live on beyond him. Consequently, the question of who succeeds him as Supreme Leader is also of importance when considering how the United States should treat Iran's potential nuclear capability.

Unfortunately, when it comes to succession, once again, we don't know and it depends. Khamene'i has not identified a successor. The current Iranian constitution does not include provisions for an obvious successor. Khamene'i has probably avoided giving any indication of who his successor might be both to avoid creating a rival to his own authority and to prevent infighting among various Iranian factions over who it should be. His successor might not be chosen until after he is dead, in which case the choice will likely be determined by whichever factions are most powerful at that time. The list of candidates stretches from dangerous ideologues such as Ayatollah Taqi Mesbah-Yazdi, to opportunistic moderates such as Ali Akbar Hashemi Rafsanjani, to middle-of-the-road types such as Guardian Council member Mahmoud Hashemi Sharoudi, to innocuous figureheads like former judiciary chief Mohammad Yazdi.

The first constitution of the Islamic Republic provided for a committee to serve in the capacity of Supreme Leader if no suitable candidate were available. Although that constitution was superseded in 1989, Iran's fragmented political leadership may not be able to agree on a single candidate and may look for a way to revert back to this earlier alternative. Although this may prove difficult, the current constitution provides for a council of the president, the head of the judiciary, and a member of the Guardian Council chosen by the Expediency Council to act "temporarily" in place of the Supreme Leader until a successor can be chosen.[29] In the event of protracted political deadlock—often the norm in Iran, especially on issues of such import—that council might remain in power for some time, possibly even in perpetuity.[30]

Although less likely, this outcome does not appear impossible and it is worth considering as a possibility. Committees have different patterns of behavior from individuals. They tend to be more prone to inertia, caution, and compromise than most individuals. However, committees are not immune to aggressive, dangerous, and even risky behavior, and may be especially prone to them if that is the compromise position among the different members. Committees can sometimes make it easier for a group to compromise with a foreign adversary as no individual is wholly responsible for the blame, but may be unable to summon the courage of a strong leader to compromise when doing so would buck a trend, public desire, or ingrained interests. In short, arguments can be made on both sides regarding Khamene'i's succession and which outcome would be best or worst for American interests as they relate to Iran and its nuclear program.

The Great Purge

In June 2009, Iran and the rest of the world received some unhelpful clarity concerning Iranian decision-making and policy. That month Iranians went to the polls to vote for president, and the incumbent—the infamous Mahmud Ahmadinejad—won reelection with a surprising 63 percent of the vote.

We may never know if Ahmadinejad's election was fair or fraudulent, and if the latter, by how much.[31] There are a lot of reasons to be skeptical—from the uniformity of his vote count across Iran's disparate voting districts to irregularities in several aspects of the vote to the rapidity with which his victory was announced. Indeed, many of the most highly regarded Iran experts are certain that Ayatollah Khamene'i and the hardliners rigged the vote to ensure that they would not face another Mohammad Khatami, the reformist who won the presidency in 1997 and threatened the autocratic rule of the Supreme Leader and the conservative base of the Islamic Republic. Although Ahmadinejad has proven an erratic statesman who has often shot off his mouth in foolish and unhelpful ways, the Supreme Leader saw him at the time of the 2009 election as a committed hardliner who would not challenge his authority or his overarching policies for Iran.[32]

Regardless of what outsiders believed, a great many Iranians concluded that the vote was rigged. They took to the streets to protest, and those protests swelled to numbers and passions not seen since 1979 and the last Iranian revolution. Within a matter of days, hundreds of thousands, even millions of Iranians were pouring into the streets of Tehran and a dozen other cities to protest the stolen election.[33] Most stunning of all, the protests escalated from demanding that the election results be overturned to demanding the overthrow of the regime itself. Although the leaders of the revolt mostly sought only to reform the system, the young people who made up its rank and file demanded a much more radical overhaul. Iranians stood on their rooftops and shouted "death to the dictator" to the night sky, as they had in 1978–79. But this time they meant Khamene'i, not the Shah.

This was no mere wave of protests such as Iran had experienced pe-riodically since the 1990s. It was a determined—if unplanned—effort to bring about a revolution against what had become an oppressive and sclerotic autocracy, anticipating the revolutions of the Arab Spring by two years. The would-be revolutionaries took the name the Green Movement, echoing the "color revolutions" of Eastern Europe that overthrew the communist dictatorships there, but choosing the color of Islam, green, the color of the cloak of the Prophet Muhammad.

The scale and anger of the Green Revolution caught the regime off guard. To find so many sick of their misrule stunned the Iranian leader-ship, and initially split the regime. All of Iran's leaders seemed to recog-nize that they faced the greatest challenge to their power since 1979. But they were divided over how to respond. The more moderate and prag-matic members of the regime, such as former presidents Rafsanjani and Khatami, argued for reform and reconciliation. They urged Khamene'i to reach out to the revolutionaries and make concessions to them, princi-pally by agreeing to greater transparency, representation, and pluralism coupled with reduced political and social strictures. Predictably, this sug-gestion horrified the hardline and conservative wings of the regime. They reportedly warned that giving in to the revolutionaries even a little bit would be opening Pandora's box, placing the regime on a path that would lead to their overthrow. They warned that making concessions, showing weakness as they saw it, was the mistake the Shah had made—and why they now ruled in Tehran rather than the Shah. They argued for a crack-down to crush the incipient revolution.

The debate within the regime appears to have been fierce, but not lengthy. Khamene'i seems to have made his decision within a few days, and he sided with the hardliners.[34] Within a week or so of the dis-puted election, Iran's Law Enforcement Forces (LEF), backed by the government-sponsored goon squad called Ansar-e Hizballah and ele-ments of Iran's Revolutionary Guard and Basij militia, smashed the would-be revolution. They shut down Internet and cell phone service to black out the social networking systems that the Greens had used to coordinate their activities. They arrested all of the opposition leaders along with thousands more; they beat up hundreds, if not thousands, and killed perhaps as many as a hundred for good measure—often at random to drive home to the revolutionaries that anyone involved with the Greens might pay the ultimate price.[35] Within a few more weeks, they had snuffed out the Green Revolution and driven the movement underground.

The public suppression of the Green Movement was only part of the hardline reaction to the events of June 2009. Along with the counter-revolution came the purge. Some have called it a "coup" because it was executed by the Revolutionary Guard leadership and resulted in their political elevation. But it was much more an old-fashioned Stalinist purge than a coup, authorized and encouraged by the Supreme Leader to get rid of a troublesome segment of the Iranian political elite.[36] In an unusual move, the Supreme Leader and his allies in the IRGC, the Majles, and the judiciary moved to root out the moderate and pragmatic elements within the Iranian leadership. Some were stripped of titles and authorities, including even Rafsanjani, who was not reelected as the head of the Assembly of Experts. Others were arrested, placed under house arrest, or had their children (many of whom had joined the Greens) arrested. Still others were excluded from the conversations that mattered within the government—the personalized discourse that is the warp and weft of Iranian governance.[37] When Ahmadinejad submitted the names of his new cabinet in September 2009, seven of the twenty-one ministers named (including the ministers of defense, intelligence, interior, Islamic guidance, and oil) were former IRGC personnel. Many others had ties to Iranian intelligence and security agencies.[38]

As a result, the Iranian leadership that emerged from the fires of the 2009 Green revolt is a far more homogeneous and hardline coven than any since 1981. In Takeyh's words, "In today's Islamic Republic, all moderate voices have been excised from the corridors of power, and the debates of the previous decades have been displaced by a consensus among a narrow cast of militant actors."[39] Or as Sadjadpour has put it, the Iranian political spectrum "now ranges from pitch black to charcoal grey."[40] They still had disputes—it is Iran, after all—particularly between Ahmadinejad and his coterie on the one hand, and the rest of the Iranian political establishment on the other. However, these are now debates between the Iranian right and its far right. Moreover, these have often been disputes about personality and power masquerading as arguments over substance.[41] On issues of policy, particularly foreign policy, the disputes have tended to be over tactics and limits, to the extent there have been any differences at all. For instance, Ahmadinejad had shown an interest in cutting a deal with the Americans on nuclear issues, but only on his terms, and reportedly only to claim that he had tamed the Great Satan when no one else could.

Iranian Foreign Policy Since 2009

Not surprisingly, the triumph of Iran's hardliners since 2009 has been reflected in Iran's foreign policy. However, it has been tempered by Khamene'i's own approach to Iran's external affairs, producing a practice different from what the hardest of the hardliners might have pursued if left to their own devices. As a result, there has been a noticeable shift to the right, but it has been a matter of degree, as Khamene'i remains the consistent polestar of Iranian strategy.

OFFENSIVE DEFENSE OR DEFENSIVE OFFENSE? One of the great unknowns of Iranian foreign policy, especially since the hardline consolidation of 2009, is whether it is an offensive strategy with defensive components, or defensive with offensive components. Is Iran's support for various terrorist groups an effort to weaken its adversaries to allow Iran to make gains at their expense? Or is it meant to weaken Iran's adversaries to hinder them from attacking Iran? Or might it be both? Iranian actions are consistent with both, and different Iranian leaders suggest one or the other—or both—on differing occasions. Nevertheless, the answer is important because it would provide an intimation as to whether Iran seeks a nuclear capability to prevent aggression against it or to enable its own aggression against others.[42]

BATTLING THE GREAT SATAN. One of the defining features of Iran's hardline streak is its abiding hatred of the United States. This hatred is no by-product of other Iranian goals, but a distinct strand. When Khomeini branded the United States the "Great Satan," that rhetoric was not an idle put-down. He meant it. Khomeini had a Manichean philosophy (and it is worth noting that Manes, from whose name the word *manichean* derives, was a Persian who conceived of the world as being divided into good and evil). This worldview characterized human history as a struggle between the forces of God/good and Satan/evil. For Khomeini, the United States was the devil's champion while Iran was God's. To this was added the traditional Iranian mistrust of foreigners, which after World War II and the fall of Prime Minister Mohammad Mosaddeq (toppled in a coup aided by the CIA) became largely focused on the United States as the external force subverting, controlling, and suppressing the Iranian people for its own benefit. These twin strands of ferocious anti-Americanism make up one of the critical pillars of the Islamic Republic's worldview.[43]

This concern may have faded or even been discarded for the moderate and pragmatic elements of the Iranian elite, but for its most zealous adherents, it remains gospel. As Ayatollah Ahmad Jannati, one of the hardest of the hardliners and a member of the powerful Council of Guardians, said in 2007, "When all is said and done, we are an anti-American regime. America is our enemy and we are the enemies of America."[44] It is also clear that the hardliners continue to stoke the fire of anti-Americanism to legitimize their own increasingly autocratic rule. Indeed, Jannati also said in January 2009, "If we are to assure that the Islamic establishment, the revolution and Islam are to stay and the people are to live comfortably, the flag of the struggle against America should always stay hoisted."[45]

Although Khamene'i shares the hatred, fear, and distrust of the United

States, he appears to prefer a more pragmatic policy toward America than others, particularly the leadership of the Revolutionary Guard Corps. The tendency of key actors within the system—particularly the Guard—to freelance appears most often when it comes to Iranian anti-Americanism. This tension makes it hard to sort out just how much consensus there is in Tehran for conducting various attacks on the United States. We know that attacks occur. What we do not know is whether the most provocative attacks are conducted by freelancers or sanctioned by the highest authority, and if the latter, did they represent the farthest that Khamene'i was willing to go, or (as seems likely with the IRGC leaders) was it a compromise position to maintain a consensus with more risk-tolerant elements of the regime? This question may seem esoteric, but it looms large when nuclear weapons enter the mix.

In the fall of 2011, the attorney general of the United States announced the arrest of Mansour J. Arbabsiar, a naturalized U.S. citizen and the cousin of Gholam Shakuri, a high-ranking officer in the Quds force of the Iranian Revolutionary Guards. The Quds force (named for Jerusalem, "al-Quds" in Arabic and Farsi) is the arm of the IRGC that conducts terror attacks, supports terrorist groups and other violent extremists, wages unconventional warfare beyond Iran's borders, and exports the Iranian Revolution abroad. As best we understand the operation, Arbabsiar's cousin asked him to make contact with various Mexican drug cartels to try to hire one of them to kill the Saudi ambassador to the United States, Adel al-Jubeir. Arbabsiar arranged for the Los Zetas cartel to bomb a popular restaurant in Washington, D.C., called Café Milano while Ambassador al-Jubeir was having dinner there. When all of the preparations were in place, his cousin from the Quds force told him to execute the operation. It never happened. Arbabsiar's Los Zetas contact was an informant for the U.S. Drug Enforcement Administration, and the U.S. government caught Arbabsiar with extensive evidence of his guilt.[46] American officials then taped a conversation between Arbabsiar and Shakuri in which the latter told Arbabsiar about killing al-Jubeir, "[j]ust do it quickly, it's late."[47] Ultimately, Arbabsiar confessed and pled guilty to the charges in October 2012.[48]

There is a lot we don't know about the plot. The U.S. government is confident that the operation was ordered by high-ranking officials of the Quds force. However, they have never indicated that they know that the operation was blessed by Iran's highest political leadership (including Khamene'i). In the past, Khamene'i *did* have to approve all terrorist operations abroad, and in 1997, a German court had sufficient evidence to conclude that Khamene'i had ordered the killing of four Iranian Kurdish dissident leaders in a Berlin restaurant (the Mykonos) in 1992.[49] So either the Iranians have gotten better at concealing Khamene'i's involvement in such activities, or the Quds force was freelancing.

Either way, it seems likely that the attempted killing of Ambassador al-Jubeir was in retaliation for the assassination of several Iranian scientists connected to Tehran's nuclear and missile programs.[50] And either way, it represents an important escalation in Iranian attacks on the United States. In the past, Tehran had always steered clear of attacking the U.S. homeland, for fear that doing so would trigger an American conventional military response, which the Iranians fear. During the so-called Tanker War of 1987–88, Iran attempted to block the oil exports of the Gulf emirates for their support of Iraq during the Iran-Iraq War, prompting American air and naval intervention. Iran's naval forces clashed with the U.S. Navy, only to take severe losses in several encounters with only a tiny fraction of America's armed forces.[51] That experience has taught Iran to respect U.S. conventional power. Despite glib assertions to the contrary, Iran has avoided provoking an American military retaliation against Iran since then. At least until the Arbabsiar incident.

What has changed, if anything, remains unclear. Was the Quds force freelancing to provoke a war with the United States and the international community? Was it Khamene'i signaling his desperate fear that his rule was being undermined by America's soft war? Or the belief that the United States was killing his nuclear scientists? And how much did it represent an Iranian assessment that the Obama administration would never retaliate, either because it was seen as weak or so determined to end America's military involvement in the Middle East that it would never start down a path that could end in a full-scale war between the United States and the Islamic Republic? Moreover, why was it not repeated—and is that a sign that it was a rogue operation that won't recur now that the senior leadership is aware of what almost happened? We don't know the answers, but know that they would tell us a great deal if we did.

Meanwhile, Iran continues to battle the United States and its allies across the Middle East. In Syria, Lebanon, and Iraq, the Iranians provide extensive support to various armed groups. In Syria, Iran is among the last backers of Bashar al-Asad's faction, technically still the Syrian government, but in truth just the (Shi'i) Alawi community and other minorities waging a civil war against mostly Sunni opposition forces. In Lebanon, Iran continues to support Hizballah, which, thanks to spillover from the Syrian civil war, is increasingly in conflict again with Sunni (and Maronite Christian) factions supported by Saudi Arabia, Jordan, and the Gulf states. In Iraq, the Iranians back a range of Shi'i groups that employ violence against Sunni Arabs, the Kurds, and one another. Likewise, Iran still supports Hamas and Palestinian Islamic Jihad (although Hamas has distanced itself from Iran since the Arab Spring) in their struggles against Israel and the more moderate Palestinian leadership represented by Fatah. However, with the withdrawal of U.S. troops from Iraq, Iran's only direct confrontation with the United States is in Afghanistan, where the Quds force has provided money, weapons, explosives, and other support to the Taliban and other Afghan groups, albeit not at the same level as it did in Iraq.[52]

UNDERMINING THE STATUS QUO IN THE MIDDLE EAST. So far, Iranian foreign policy has singularly failed to achieve its goal of dominating southwest Asia. Especially before the Arab Spring, when Tehran's leadership looked out at the world, they probably found little solace. Tehran had few friends in the Middle East—or Central or South Asia. Across the Middle East, nearly all of the states of the region, and all of its most powerful states, were not aligned with Iran. They were aligned with the United States. Turkey, Israel, and all of the strongest Arab states (Egypt, Saudi Arabia, Morocco, the United Arab Emirates, Kuwait, Qatar, and Jordan) were American allies. Iran had Syria, Hizballah (which had secured tacit control of Lebanon), and Hamas (which controlled Gaza). Iran had made important inroads in Iraq and was more influential there than the United States by 2011, but Iraq was no Iranian vassal, and Iraqi prime minister Nuri al-Maliki tried to push back on Iranian pressure. The status quo across the region favored the United States and threatened Iran.

Consequently, virtually anything that threatened to overturn the status quo was positive from Tehran's perspective. It seemed that it was impossible for them to imagine that the geopolitics of the region could get worse for them, given that they had almost nothing.

The Arab Spring, when it came, was thus something of a rude awakening for Tehran. Initially, the Iranians embraced it readily, seeing it as the end of the old Middle Eastern status quo and likely to bring to power regimes far more sympathetic to Tehran. The Iranian leadership appeared to believe that the Islamist movements poised to triumph across the Arab world if the dictators and monarchs were pushed out would be sympathetic to Iran's own Islamist regime. Instead, Iran has found that the Sunni Arab Islamists who have taken power in Tunisia, Egypt, and Yemen, and are threatening to do so in Jordan, Syria, Libya, and Kuwait (each in different ways), have no love for the Persian Shi'a.[53]

Moreover, Tehran fears that the Syrian civil war will end with the destruction of their allies, the Alawite regime. Syria is roughly 80 percent Sunni, and the opposition militias are being armed and equipped by the Gulf states and Turkey with more limited assistance from the United States and the Europeans.[54] All of this suggests that the opposition will eventually prevail over the remnants of the regime (really just the Alawite community and several other Syrian minorities, such as the Kurds and Druse, all of whom fear being slaughtered if the Sunnis prevail).

The Syrian conflict has created serious problems for the Iranians even beyond the unpleasant prospect of losing their one real, national ally in the Middle East. The Syrian civil war, coming on top of the Iraqi civil war of 2005–2007, has exacerbated the Sunni-Shi'a split across the region. The animosity has taken a firm hold on the Sunni side, where the Saudis, Jordanians, Moroccans, Gulf emirates, and even Egypt and Tunisia increasingly see the Arab world as besieged by Iranian-backed Shi'i chauvinists (Iraq, Syria, Lebanon) and revolutionaries (Bahrain and the heavily Shi'a eastern province of Saudi Arabia).[55] For the Sunni states, this looks like a region-wide Sunni-Shi'a war, and while Syria may be the main battlefield right now, it is only one of many. The Iranians fear that the emergence of this view is rallying both Sunni governments and populations against them in ways that it had not in the past. Hamas, which is Sunni fundamentalist, has distanced itself from Iran as a result of it, and Hizballah (which is Shi'a) tried hard for many months not to choose a side for fear of galvanizing Lebanon's Sunni and Christian communities into action against them.

SUPPORT FOR TERRORISM AND UNCONVENTIONAL WARFARE. Supporting both terrorist attacks and unconventional warfare campaigns* has been a cardinal element of Iranian foreign policy from the earliest days of the Islamic Republic. At first the regime killed Iranian dissidents living abroad, backed a variety of efforts to overthrow the Iraqi, Saudi, Bahraini, and Kuwaiti governments, and organized various Lebanese Shi'i terrorist and militia groups into Hizballah. Iran has mounted or backed acts of terrorism against Israelis both in Israel and abroad. The regime has attacked American soldiers in Lebanon, Iraq, Saudi Arabia, and Afghani-

---

* Americans frequently group all unconventional attacks under the rubric of "terrorism." However, the vast majority of accepted definitions of terrorism focus on the use of violence for a political purpose against noncombatants. Many of the Iranian attacks against the United States and its allies have used terrorist methods—such as car bombs—but against soldiers. Although they may feel like terrorism to us, they do not meet the definition. They are acts of war, of unconventional war or asymmetric war, not terrorism. To some extent, this distinction is one without real difference since they do engender a similar response; however, there is no question that Americans, and most people, react differently to the killing of women and children in civilian areas than they do to the killing of soldiers, especially soldiers in a war zone. Thus, labeling an attack on American soldiers "terrorism" is often inaccurate and excessively inflammatory. I believe it important to differentiate between these two different forms of political violence.

stan and American diplomats in Lebanon and Kuwait. It has provided assistance to other violent extremist groups across the Middle East, Europe, North Africa, and Asia. It has enabled al-Qa'ida terrorist operations against Americans, Iraqis, Afghans, and Saudis. In recent years, Iran has added another form of covert warfare to its arsenal: cyberwarfare, which it has reportedly employed against American and Gulf Arab institutions.[56]

This persistent campaign serves to defend the regime against its foreign foes and, as the Iranian leadership seems to see it, to prevent their adversaries from threatening them at home. Thus, beginning in 2011, Iran unleashed a new campaign of covert attacks to try to deter and prevent what it perceives as a joint American-Israeli-Gulf Arab campaign to sabotage the Iranian nuclear program through similar methods. As part of this, Iran is believed to have been responsible for terrorist attacks on Israeli officials in Georgia and India, on Israeli tourists in Bulgaria, and for cyberattacks on the United States and the Gulf Arabs.[57] Moreover, as noted above, Tehran typically sees anything that undermines the status quo as beneficial to reorienting the geopolitics of its neighborhood in a favorable way. Overthrowing governments that oppose Iran or ally with the United States (which Tehran often considers the same) and otherwise putting Washington and the conservative Arab states on the defensive can also help prevent them from going on the offensive against Iran.

These points also highlight a common misunderstanding about Iranian support for terrorists, namely that the Iranians always (or even generally) support Shi'i groups. This confusion stems from the misperception that Iran's only goal is to spread the revolution and that Iranian leaders conceive of the revolution as being a Shi'i phenomenon. Neither is correct. Certainly many of Iran's hardline leaders do believe in spreading the revolution, but that is only one of several motives, and the priority that each assigns to that goal seems to vary. Although many Iranian hardliners are Shi'a chauvinists, Khomeini's ideology saw the revolution as pan-Islamist, and therefore embracing Sunni, Shi'a, Sufi, and other, more nondenominational Muslims. More than this, Iran has never allowed ideology to determine which violent extremists to support. Because of

Tehran's emphasis both on defending itself and overturning the regional status quo, Iran has been ecumenical about its support to terrorists and other violent extremists, helping out Shi'a groups (such as Hizballah and Jaysh al-Mahdi in Iraq), Sunni groups (such as Hamas, Palestinian Islamic Jihad, the Taliban in Afghanistan, and even some indirect support to al-Qa'ida itself), secular Marxists (the anti-Turkish PKK and the Popular Front for the Liberation of Palestine), Christians (Armenian guerrillas fighting the Shi'i Azeris), and others.[58]

Iran often finds it easiest to work with Shi'i groups because the Shi'a tend to be more receptive to Iranian offers, but the Iranians have shown a willingness to work with anyone interested in overturning the status quo and damaging the United States and its allies. And it is worth noting that many of the Sunni fundamentalist groups that Iran has provided aid to—including the Taliban—are insanely anti-Shi'a, loathing them as heretics, and spewing far more venom against them than at infidel Christians and Jews. In some cases, the Iranians have even supported non-Muslims fighting Muslims (even fighting Shi'i Muslims), and Sunnis fighting Shi'a (like al-Qa'ida in Iraq). In short, the Iranians are not fussy when it comes to violent extremists. Anyone willing to wreak havoc on the prevailing order is typically good enough for Tehran, regardless of the group's ostensible aims.

HATRED OF ISRAEL. Iran's leadership seems to vary in its feelings about Israel, from passive distaste to genocidal loathing.[59] Ayatollah Khomeini was both anti-Semitic and anti-Zionist, and his beliefs have influenced his followers and successors. Khamene'i and other Iranian leaders fulminate against Israel. At times this posture is an adjunct of their anti-Americanism, treating Israel as the "little Satan" to America's "Great Satan" and deriding the Jewish state as an offense inflicted upon the Muslim world by the United States and the West.[60]

Nevertheless, Iran still has a small Jewish population that is among the largest left in the Muslim world.[61] Other Iranians harbor little animosity toward Israel or Jews in general, and some even speak wistfully of the clandestine Iranian-Israeli relationship that existed during the Shah's era (and led to the Israelis' clandestine agency Mossad helping the Shah to build his fearsome SAVAK intelligence service).[62] For the most part, after the revolution, Iran saw Israel as a distant obscenity rather than an imminent threat. Iran would lash out at Israel whenever it was convenient to do so, and embraced the Arab-Muslim cause against the Jewish state with great vigor for ideological reasons, but also because doing so allowed them to ingratiate themselves with the Arabs and other Muslims. It also gave them a seat at the table of a key Middle Eastern dispute.[63] That the international community did not punish Israel for its acquisition of a nuclear capability has allowed Tehran to cry hypocrisy and claim that the Western campaign against Iran's nuclear program is nothing but a Jewish conspiracy.[64]

Since 2002, however, Tehran's progress toward a nuclear weapon has changed the nature of the Iranian-Israeli relationship. It is not clear how the Iranian leadership saw its acquisition of a nuclear weapons capability affecting its relationship with Israel. However, the Israeli leadership perceived it to be a grave threat to the Jewish state because of Iran's support for terrorism against Israel, its own terror attacks against Israelis, and its ferocious rhetoric against Israel. As Jerusalem demanded international action to prevent Iran from acquiring this capability and threatened to attack Iran's nuclear sites preventively, Tehran's perception of the danger from Israel changed.[65] Still, Iran's senior-most leaders—particularly Khamene'i—have been careful to indicate only that they would retaliate for any Israeli attack, avoiding any indication that they want nuclear weapons to attack Israel. Ahmadinejad's stupid and undisciplined comments are the exceptions that prove the rule.

There is no question that Iran now feels a growing sense of threat from Israel, where formerly Tehran had felt none. The most obvious manifestation of that threat is the covert war going on between Iran and Israel, with both sides conducting terror attacks against the other and both governments lashing out at each other on a regular basis. But the Iranians also appear to believe that the Israelis (and the Saudi Mukhabarat, CIA, and MI6) have been encouraging Iran's unhappy minority groups such as the Baluch, Arabs, and Kurds to resist the regime.[66] It is likely that Iran has been encouraging Hizballah and the various Palestinian terrorist groups to ratchet up their attacks on Israel as well, but all of them now have their own problems created by the Arab Spring and all feel the need to distance themselves or to concentrate on their own internal problems rather than picking a fight with the Israelis.

Iranian Foreign Policy: The Big Picture

Overall, and particularly since 2009, Iranian foreign policy has largely hewed to the hardline perspective, but Iran has mostly pursued its objectives in a pragmatic and even restrained manner. It has continued to defy the international community in pursuit of a nuclear weapons capability, and despite punishing international and multilateral sanctions, it has shown no willingness to improve relations with the United States. It has clung to its ally in the Syrian regime, no matter how many civilians the regime slaughters or how isolated it becomes from other nations. Although Iran does not appear to be courting a sectarian war across the Middle East, neither has it backed down, challenging the Sunni champions of Saudi Arabia, the Gulf emirates, Jordan, Morocco, and Turkey, and supporting Shi'i groups in Syria, Iraq, Bahrain, and Yemen.

Although in some areas Iranian policy toward the United States and its allies has been aggressive (and unprovoked), in other areas it has been passive or merely reactive. To some extent, in the conflict in Afghanistan and before that to a much greater extent in Iraq, Iran went on the offensive, providing support to a variety of groups willing to kill Americans. The Iranian regime can claim perverse responsibility for a considerable number of the 6,500 American military personnel killed in Iraq and Afghanistan. Yet Iran has also been the defender at other times, fending off assassinations, sabotage, and cyberattacks that Tehran believes to have been the work of the United States, Israel, Britain, and Saudi Arabia. Even here, Iran's efforts to retaliate and deter further attacks have shown the mark of its dominant hardline leadership, with the Arbabsiar plot standing out as a serious potential miscalculation. Indeed, the Iranians might have gotten lucky: had they succeeded in blowing up Café Milano, they may have killed dozens and injured scores—on American soil. It seems most likely that, in the post-9/11 United States, it would have been difficult if not impossible for President Obama to have resisted public pressure for massive military retaliation against Iran for a brazen terrorist attack on American soil.

Moreover, what the Arbabsiar plot may highlight is that as much as we may misunderstand the Iranians, they understand us no better, perhaps even less.

In June 2013, Iran surprised the world once again, electing the pragmatic reformer Hassan Rowhani to succeed Ahmadinejad as president. That the majority of Iranians would vote for Rowhani—the most anti-establishment figure among the six candidates—was no surprise. Iranians have consistently voted for whoever offered the greatest prospect for change since 1997, with the obvious exception of the (likely) rigged election of 2009. What was more unexpected was that Khamene'i would allow Rowhani to win given his apparent desire for a submissive president who would not challenge him as both Khatami and Ahmadinejad had.

Whether Rowhani's election will result in any meaningful change is another story entirely. Like his mentor Rafsanjani, Rowhani has expressed a greater interest in rationalizing Iran's economy, easing social restrictions, improving relations with the United States and compromising on aspects of Iran's nuclear program to rebuild foreign economic ties. As president, Rowhani will have some authority within the system to push such agendas, but ultimately he cannot rival the Supreme Leader. Khamene'i crushed both Khatami and Ahmadinejad when they attempted to deviate from his line. This history suggests that Rowhani will run into trouble if he tries to fundamentally alter Iran's domestic or foreign policies. If he does try to do so, he may simply provoke another major internal struggle that will at least be a distraction for the Iranians if not a real threat to the regime's hold on power. Still, Rowhani's unanticipated victory at the polls should serve as a reminder of just how unpredictable Iran is and how we should never assume that any conclusion is foregone in Tehran.

2

The Iranian Nuclear Program

Iran's nuclear program dates back to the days of the Shah. He hoped to build a nuclear power infrastructure and at least toyed with the idea of acquiring nuclear weapons to realize his ambition of having Iran join Russia and America as a third superpower. Most of the Shah's effort, however, was focused on nuclear energy to ensure that Iran's hydrocarbon wealth was available for export and not needed for domestic consumption. Moreover, the Shah appears to have recognized that Iran's size and wealth meant it could develop a conventional military that would allow it to dominate the Persian Gulf region and his acquisition of nuclear weapons was not only unnecessary, but potentially counterproductive if it spurred Iran's neighbors to do the same.[1] Perhaps the best evidence that the Shah chose not to seek nuclear weapons was that he became a charter member of the Nuclear Non-Proliferation Treaty (NPT), signing (even before France and China) in July 1968.[2]

The NPT remains the cornerstone of the modern nonproliferation regime. However, it is also a problematic document, reflecting the naïve assumptions of an earlier time. It is grounded in the notion of "atoms for peace," the early Cold War belief that one could separate civilian from military uses and countries would not use the former as a cover for the latter. Thus, the NPT enables all member states to pursue nuclear energy for civilian purposes, but forbids any that did not possess them in 1968 (that is, the United States, USSR/Russia, China, Britain, and France) from acquiring nuclear weapons. Moreover, the NPT requires all nonweapons states to sign Comprehensive Safeguards Agreements, which obliges them to declare all civilian nuclear facilities and allow them to be inspected by the International Atomic Energy Agency (IAEA).

The revolution of 1978–79 halted all aspects of the Iranian nuclear program. However, at some time during the 1980s, after Iran recognized that Saddam Husayn intended to acquire nuclear weapons himself—and doubtless would have used them to defeat Iran in their vicious eight-year struggle—Tehran reignited its own nuclear drive.[3] The program came under the auspices of the Revolutionary Guard, and it had nothing to do with generating electricity. Yet even after the Iran-Iraq War ended in 1988, Tehran's nuclear program continued to chug along, possibly out of sheer inertia.

Soon thereafter, the Iranian nuclear program received an important boost from Pakistan's Abdul Qadeer Khan. Khan was the father of the Pakistani nuclear program and was later discovered to have run a covert network selling equipment, material, and know-how related to nuclear weapons to many of the worst countries in the world—Libya, North Korea, and Iran among them. Nuclear weapons require solving both complex theoretical physics problems and equally complicated practical engineering problems to manufacture both the radioactive "fissile" material that is the explosive fuel and the mechanical device that causes the fissile material to detonate. Most countries can benefit from the help of others who have already solved these problems, and in the late 1980s, Iran definitely needed help.

There are many ways to produce the fissile material. All of them involve separating trace elements of either uranium or plutonium from

other materials to produce purified concentrations, which when combined in sufficient quantity (a "critical mass") can sustain the chain reaction that produces a nuclear explosion. Saddam's Iraq used giant magnets
to try to do the job—the same technology that the United States used to
produce the Hiroshima bomb in 1945. The North Koreans used a breeder
reactor, which threw off quantities of purified plutonium as a by-product
that can then be collected and reprocessed for weapons. The Iranians,
following the Pakistani lead, chose to use cascades of high-speed centrifuges, which take uranium in gaseous form (uranium hexafluoride) and
spin out the gas to separate the heavier U-238 molecules from the lighter
U-235 (the uranium molecules needed for bombs and energy). Perhaps
as a hedge, the Iranians also set up a plutonium separation facility on the
North Korean model at Arak.

A. Q. Khan began to provide Iran with information related to nuclear
weapons fabrication in 1989. He would go on to provide Iran with the
design for Pakistan's first-generation P-1 centrifuge, and in 1995 he provided Tehran with the plans for a more advanced Pakistani centrifuge,
the P-2. The P-1 design enabled the Iranians to build their own IR-1 centrifuges, which now form the vast majority of Iran's functioning centrifuge inventory. The Iranians also built a small number of advanced IR-2,
-3, and -4 centrifuges modeled on the P-2, which can enrich uranium far
faster than the first-generation models. In January 2013, Iran announced
that it would begin to operate advanced IR-2 centrifuges at its Natanz
uranium enrichment plant.[4] Its IR-3 and -4 versions are not yet fully operational.[5]

Several years after Khan first began providing help, Tehran's nuclear
ambitions received another important boost. Like most things in the
Islamic Republic, the nuclear program was mismanaged and made little
progress for most of its first decade or more in operation. Bizarrely, what
pulled it out of its torpor was the reformist president Mohammad Khatami. There is no evidence to suggest that Khatami was more eager for a
nuclear weapon than his predecessors. In fact, in private communications
with the United States through trusted emissaries, he signaled his willing-

ness to trade away the program in return for American concessions in other areas, such as trade, aid, and investment.[6] There are two versions of what happened. The first version focuses on Khatami's reforms, part of which were intended to remove from power the unqualified clerics and their bureaucratic protégés who had taken over the Iranian government after the revolution and helped run it into the ground. Khatami was determined to repopulate Iran's institutions with competent technocrats. In this version of events, the nuclear program was no exception. The alternative version is that it was not Khatami but Khamene'i himself who cleaned house. The Supreme Leader, annoyed with the glacial pace of Iran's nuclear program, wanted to see it making greater progress.[7] In either version, the end result was the same: Reza Amrollahi, the longtime chief of the Atomic Energy Organization of Iran, was sacked, and replaced with the dynamic former oil minister, Gholamreza Aghazadeh-Khoi. Aghazadeh brought the same energy and efficiency to the nuclear program that he had once brought to Iran's hydrocarbon sector.[8]

As a result, between 1997 and 2002, between the efforts of Khan and Aghazadeh, the Iranian program began to accelerate. In August 2002, the Mujahedin-e Khalq (MEK), an Iranian Marxist-Islamist opposition group, happened upon information indicating that the Iranian nuclear program had made far greater progress than had been previously realized (it is widely rumored that the Israeli Mossad provided the information to the MEK). The MEK revealed to the world the existence of Iran's uranium enrichment facility at Natanz and its plutonium extraction facility at Arak, both in violation of Iran's requirements under its Safeguards Agreement with the IAEA, a critical component of its NPT obligations.

In response to these revelations, the IAEA began a much more intrusive investigation of Iranian nuclear activities. Neither Arak nor Natanz constituted incontrovertible proof of a nuclear weapons program, because it is possible to use either plutonium or enriched uranium in civilian reactors, but the fact that these facilities and other activity had not been declared to the IAEA left the impression that they were for military purposes. Similarly, the Iranians claimed that they were not obligated to inform the IAEA of new nuclear facilities until they were finished—an argument they continue to advance. Not only is this not correct under their Safeguard Agreement with the IAEA, but if the facilities were purely for civilian use, why conceal them at all? In addition, if Iran wanted to acquire nuclear reactors for civilian purposes, they needed neither the capability to enrich uranium domestically nor to extract plutonium. It would have been far cheaper and easier for Iran to have bought fuel from another country, as the vast majority of countries with nuclear energy programs do.[9] The Iranians insisted that they were not trying to acquire nuclear weapons, but they could not provide a plausible explanation either for having concealed the plants or for why they needed such capabilities.[10]

Since then, Iran briefly suspended its enrichment activities in 2003–2005, and may have ended or suspended most or some of its weaponization programs. It has been subject to six binding United Nations Security Council resolutions demanding that it halt its nuclear activities—all enacted under Chapter VII of the UN Charter and therefore superseding the provisions of the NPT under international law. Iran has endured multiple rounds of international and multilateral sanctions that have inflicted enormous damage on the Iranian economy. It has also had its nuclear program attacked by computer viruses and some of its nuclear scientists attacked physically (and some killed). Yet, Iran has persevered. Its program has been slowed but not stopped.

The Evidence

Why does everyone (or almost everyone) think Iran's nuclear program is intended to produce weapons? It's an excellent question. After all, enrichment is (technically) permitted under the NPT and could be related to civilian needs, and most of the hard evidence regarding the Iranian nuclear program relates to its enrichment of uranium. Indeed, Iran insists that its nuclear program is entirely peaceful. So it is worth asking why so many people are so convinced that the Iranian program is really intended to give Tehran the capability to build nuclear weapons.

Iran does not deny that it has an extensive nuclear program—how could it with inspectors monitoring so much of it? However, Tehran insists that the program is meant only for medical uses and civilian energy production.[11] This claim is difficult to square with the available information. The evidence suggests that the Iranian program is intended for military purposes, although it certainly can (and has) produced relatively small amounts of both civilian energy and radioactive material for medical uses. Nevertheless, while the evidence indicates that Iran intends to acquire the capability to build nuclear weapons, it does not definitively indicate that Iran has made the decision to build those weapons and field a nuclear arsenal, and that is where the debate within the international community is currently focused.

First off, for more than a decade and continuing to the present, Iran has lied and concealed information from the IAEA (and various other countries and international organizations) about its nuclear program in contravention of its Safeguards Agreement under the NPT.[12] For instance, the Iranians concealed the assistance they received from Pakistan and A. Q. Khan. When the IAEA inspected the Natanz and Arak sites in 2002, the inspectors found traces of enriched uranium hexafluoride in the centrifuges (the feedstock used for enrichment), indicating that the centrifuges had been used to enrich uranium, which violated Iran's Safeguard Agreement with the IAEA.[13] The Iranians claimed that the enriched uranium had been on the centrifuges when they got them from another country, which they would not name—but which turned out to be Pakistan. The fact that Iran had imported centrifuges without notifying the IAEA was also a violation of its Safeguard Agreement. The inspectors found uranium from two different countries, China and Pakistan. This discovery forced the Iranians to admit that they had acquired nearly two tons of slightly refined uranium (called "yellowcake") from China; uranium hexafluoride and uranium in two other, lesser stages of refinement, from another foreign supplier (Pakistan); and had decided to start mining uranium from their own indigenous sources. The Iranians also admitted to having a Laser Isotope Separation program, yet another way to enrich uranium. Finally, the Iranians told the IAEA that they were building a plant near Esfahan that would convert yellowcake into uranium hexafluoride. Since enriching any uranium hexafluoride would have been yet another violation of their Safeguards Agreement, the Iranians claimed that they had not performed any enrichment or even testing as of 2002. Not even the IAEA found that claim credible.[14]

The list went on and on. The IAEA discovered that Iran had produced polonium-210, a short-lived, unstable element whose only real use is as an initiator for nuclear weapons (although the Iranians claimed it was for nuclear batteries to be used in satellites and deep space exploration vehicles, neither of which they have). The Iranians also continued to dissemble on a range of other issues, and delayed the IAEA from conducting several inspections that hampered its work.

In December 2003, under tremendous international pressure and fearing an American invasion, Iran signed the Additional Protocol to its Comprehensive Safeguards Agreement, a refinement of the NPT that allowed IAEA inspectors much greater access and latitude in conducting inspections and monitoring of Iranian nuclear facilities—and in checking out suspected clandestine nuclear facilities. However, the Iranians have refused to implement the agreement and allow the inspectors the access they promised.[15] As a result of all of Iran's deceptions, in June 2004, the IAEA Board of Governors adopted a resolution condemning Iran for failing to provide the requisite information, for obstructing the inspections, and for not suspending its uranium enrichment process as promised. In a momentous decision, the IAEA referred Iran's nuclear program to the United Nations Security Council for further action. It was only the first of many occasions on which the IAEA found the Iranians unwilling to cooperate or abide by its obligations under the NPT and the UN Charter related to its nuclear program.[16]

Iran's claim that its goal is nuclear power plants for civilian energy needs is ridiculous.[17] An authoritative study by Ali Vaez and Karim Sadjadpour concluded, "No sound strategic energy planning would prioritize nuclear energy in a country like Iran."[18] Building enrichment facilities is expensive, and for that reason, most countries with civilian nuclear energy programs purchase fuel supplies from elsewhere. Although its nuclear program has been in existence for decades, and Iran has insisted the program is intended only for civilian uses at least since 2002, it has belied these claims with the paltry effort it has expended on the construction of civilian nuclear power plants—especially compared to the priority it has placed on developing enrichment capabilities. In 2004, Iranian foreign minister Kamal Kharrazi stated that Iran planned to build the capacity to generate 7,000 megawatts of electricity by 2025, but this statement has never been confirmed or repeated, and Tehran has made no effort to implement it, if it had any official standing at all.[19] Iran has only one functioning civilian nuclear plant, a 1,000-megawatt reactor at Bushehr, which did not come on line till 2011. Iran has announced that it will complete the moribund project to build another (360-megawatt) power plant at Darkhovin in southwestern Iran using an indigenous design, but it appears to have little interest from the Iranian leadership and so is languishing far behind schedule. If Iran wanted nuclear energy, it could have begun by building the power plants, bought fuel from abroad, and explored the cost-effectiveness of enriching its own fuel later. That is what states looking to develop nuclear power do.[20] In fact, in the late 1990s, Iran shifted resources away from getting the Bushehr power plant operational and devoted them to its enrichment program instead.[21] That is what a military program, not a civilian program, looks like.[22]

Iran sits on the second-largest natural gas reserves in the world. Natural gas is a cheaper and easier method of generating power than nuclear.[23] In 2002–2003, when the British, French, and Germans first sat down with the Iranians to discuss the recent revelations about their nuclear program, the Iranians claimed they were pursuing nuclear energy because it was more cost-efficient than natural gas. The Europeans, surprised to hear this claim, requested that the Iranians provide them with the studies they had done that led them to this conclusion. After all, if Iran had found a way to use nuclear plants to produce energy more cost-effectively than natural gas, the whole world would want to know about such a remarkable breakthrough. According to one British official at these talks, the Iranians "looked at each other as if to say, 'studies, what studies?'"[24] Needless to say, the Iranians have never produced any documentation to demonstrate that nuclear plants would be more cost-effective than natural-gas-fired plants, which may explain why they have made so little effort to build nuclear energy plants.

At least as early as 2006, Iran began construction of its Fordow enrichment facility near the Iranian holy city of Qom. The Fordow plant now has a full complement of roughly 2,800 centrifuges, many of which are operational. Several aspects of Fordow seem more consistent with a military facility. First, it was built at a Revolutionary Guards base. Second, it was built at enormous cost deep inside a mountain where it is impervious to Israeli air attack. Even the United States Air Force could have difficulty destroying it with conventional munitions. Third, Iran kept the facility secret (a further violation of its Safeguards Agreement under the NPT) until the United States and European nations revealed its existence in 2009. Fourth, in late 2012, Iran began using it to produce uranium enriched to 19.75 percent purity—which it claims will be for the Tehran Research Reactor (TRR), where it manufactures radioactive products needed in medical procedures such as some cancer treatments. Iran has already produced uranium enriched to 19.75 percent purity, in excess of what the TRR requires, for years to come, but is still producing more.[25] If Iran's goal is a cost-effective civilian energy and medical research program, why pay the massive expenses of building an underground nuclear enrichment facility (especially when you can buy the fuel from Brazil or Argentina at a fraction of the cost)? And why move the highest levels of enrichment to the most bombproof facility? A better way of proving one's innocence would have been to have left the higher-level enrichment at less heavily defended facilities. Moreover, after the exposure of the Fordow facility, President Ahmadinejad announced that Iran planned to build ten more enrichment facilities, all of them inside mountains like Fordow.[26]

There's also evidence that Iran has been working on taking its fissile material and turning it into nuclear bombs and warheads for its ballistic missiles.[27] Iran was forced to admit to having both uranium enrichment and plutonium separation programs (albeit, only after being caught red-handed with enormous secret facilities to do so), two paths to producing the fissile material for nuclear weapons. However, it has never admitted to a weaponization program, the engineering effort to build the mechanical device that causes the fissile material to explode in a nuclear chain reaction. Nevertheless, there is evidence that Iran had an active weaponization program at least until 2003 and has a more clandestine (and possibly smaller) effort to this day. In 2007, the U.S. intelligence community publicly stated that Iran had had an active weaponization program at least up until the fall of 2003.[28] Many European and Middle Eastern intelligence services have echoed this conclusion privately and publicly. The IAEA has posed numerous questions to the Iranian government to ascertain the validity of this evidence, and year after year Tehran has refused to answer those questions. In 2012, Iran agreed to discuss the matter with the IAEA, but when the two sides met in January, the Iranians did not provide any satisfactory answers and instead just claimed (without any proof) that all of the evidence regarding their weapons program was disinformation manufactured by the Americans, Europeans, and Israelis. When the IAEA asked to visit the Parchin military complex, where much of the engineering work on nuclear weapons had reportedly taken place, Tehran again refused. Satellite imagery showed the Iranians performing an industrial cleanup of the areas there where nuclear weapons research work was believed to have taken place.[29] As of early 2013, Iran had still not agreed to allow the IAEA to inspect Parchin despite all of its cleanup efforts.[30]

The IAEA's frustration with Iran has grown as the agency has acquired more and more evidence indicating that Iran had such a program prior to 2003 and probably still has an ongoing effort of some kind. In February

2010, the IAEA declared that they had extensive evidence of "past or current undisclosed activities" by the Iranian military to develop a nuclear warhead, and that the activities continued past 2004—an important point since the U.S. intelligence community declared in 2007 that it believed the Iranians had discontinued their weaponization program in 2003. The IAEA further stated that they had uncovered evidence that Iran was exploring ways of detonating nuclear weapons, and designing warheads to fit on top of a missile.[31] By September 2011, the IAEA announced that it was "increasingly concerned" about credible evidence provided by "many member states," which it felt was "extensive and comprehensive," indicating that Iran was continuing to work on developing a nuclear warhead for a missile and other aspects of weaponization.[32] The agency indicated that it possessed several Iranian documents that showed that the Iranian military was involved with Iran's nuclear program, an alarming development.[33]

The November 2011 IAEA report on Iran included an extensive annex that described the IAEA's information on Iran's weaponization efforts, as well as the facilities Iran had built for this purpose.[34] At that time, the IAEA stated that "[t]he information which serves as the basis for the Agency's analysis and concerns, as identified in the Annex, is assessed by the Agency to be, overall, credible. The information comes from a wide variety of independent sources, including from a number of Member States, from the Agency's own efforts and from information provided by Iran itself. It is consistent in terms of technical content, individuals and organizations involved, and time frames." It went on to assert that Iran had acquired information and documentation regarding the development and testing of nuclear weapons—which the report noted had no possible application to civilian uses.[35]

The Warning: Similarities and Differences with Iraq

Perhaps this all sounds familiar. It may seem like déjà vu all over again, to quote Yogi Berra. Didn't we make the same claims about Iraq having an aggressive nuclear (and biological and chemical) weapons program? And weren't we (including, painfully, this author) completely wrong about Iraq's WMD programs? So, then, why should we believe any of these claims about Iran?

Good questions, and questions we need to keep asking given the Iraq experience. We did get the Iraq WMD problem wrong—the United States' intelligence community, and the intelligence agencies of Britain, France, Germany, Israel, Iran, and many others. Nor can we blame it all on an overzealous and reckless Bush 43 administration. It was the U.S. intelligence community that had this wrong and the Bushies just ran with it (while adding exaggerations or worse about Iraqi connections to al-Qa'ida).[36] And that history should make us wary of being overly confident about what we think we know about the Iranian program. There are some discomforting similarities.

In particular, the public has not seen any "smoking gun" evidence of an Iranian weaponization program. That is the key to the whole crisis. Iran acknowledges it is enriching uranium but claims that it is doing so for energy and medical purposes. The United States, the IAEA, the Europeans, Israelis, and others all say that this claim is just a cover for a weaponization program. But those same entities also believed that Iraq was concealing WMD programs, too (although their estimates about what Iraq was concealing varied widely). As was the case with Iraq, the IAEA and all of these governments are telling the public, "Trust us, our information is rock solid." Which is also what we heard (this author included) prior to the invasion of Iraq.

Nevertheless, we need to recognize that there are a number of important differences from the Iraq case. First, in 2002 Iran was caught red-handed enriching uranium and separating plutonium at clandestine facilities that it had concealed from the IAEA in violation of its NPT obligations. In Iraq after 1991, the IAEA could never find a covert program that would have allowed Saddam to manufacture the fissile material for nuclear weapons. Since 2002, Iran has tried to build at least one additional covert enrichment facility (the Fordow plant at Qom), only to have it discovered in 2009. So we can be certain that Iran has an industrial-scale program that would allow them to manufacture the fissile material for nuclear weapons, that it does not need this capability for civilian uses, and that it keeps trying to hide these efforts. None of that was true for Iraq.

In the case of Iraq after 1991, the international community kept sending UN and IAEA inspectors to sites where Iraq was purportedly working on WMD. When they eventually got into those sites, they found nothing. The Iranians have blocked inspectors from seeing the sites where they have allegedly conducted weaponization work. In one case, the Iranians allowed the inspectors in—but only after they had bulldozed the entire facility, replaced much of the topsoil, and turned it into a park. Not even Saddam had thought of that.[37]

It is also worth comparing the current Iranian and post-1991 Iraqi situations within the wider context of the history of nuclear proliferation. Specifically, there has never been a country that attempted to conceal a peaceful nuclear program. Lots of countries have *overt* peaceful nuclear programs. North Korea, Libya, and Iraq before 1991 all had covert enrichment programs (at least they were covert at first) like Iran's, but these *were* weapons programs, not civilian programs. Similarly, Israel and Pakistan pursued what they claimed to be civilian nuclear programs but are widely alleged to have been covers for secret weapons programs (and were recognized as such early on).[38] Moreover, it is worth noting that after 1991, Iraq had neither a covert enrichment program nor a covert weaponization program—at least not by 2003. When Iraq had a covert enrichment effort it was because it was pursuing a nuclear weapon. When it decided to forgo that prospect (to put it off to a later point, according to the definitive postwar study), it did not retain a covert enrichment program.[39] Iran's efforts to conceal an enrichment program are historically only consistent with other efforts to conceal a *weapons* program.

Last, it is important to remember that what Saddam did that confused the intelligence communities of the world was so bizarre and foolish that it bordered on irrational. Saddam got rid of his nuclear program at some point in the 1990s, retaining only some plans, the knowledge in the heads of his scientists, and a few buried parts to aid a reconstitution effort at some point in the future after he had succeeded in having the last of the faltering UN sanctions lifted or nullified. He hoped that if the IAEA and UN inspectors could not find any pieces of a nuclear (or wider WMD) program, the UN would have to lift the sanctions. However, he also wanted his own people and, secondarily, the Iranians, to believe that he had retained an extensive, secret program so that neither would feel confident attacking him. Of course, foreign intelligence agencies picked up on his efforts to propagate the latter and assumed that it was proof that he was lying about the former.[40] Before the invasion of Iraq, only a tiny number of people either inside or outside Iraq believed that Saddam had eliminated all of his WMD assets.[41] Even those Americans who argued against an invasion did so overwhelmingly in the belief that Saddam had reconstituted his WMD programs, but that he could be deterred and contained even with these capabilities.

Saddam's behavior was close to madness. This is not how nation-states behave, which is why no one imagined that this was what Saddam was doing—not even the handful of people who believed before the invasion of Iraq that Saddam did *not* have a WMD program. Although we have seen Iran behave in ways that make little sense to outsiders (because they were driven by domestic political considerations that went unrecognized by outsiders), we have never seen them do something as incredible as Saddam's WMD gambit. And why would Iran *want* to follow Saddam's approach given that it resulted in the invasion of Iraq, Saddam's fall from power, and his execution at the hands of his own people?

These specific differences with the case of Iraq after 1991, the similarities with Iraq pre-1991 (as well as Libya and North Korea), and the evidence of Iran's efforts at weaponization all point in the direction that Iran is pursuing a nuclear weapons capability and that we are not making the same mistake we made with Iraq in 2003. But confidence, even high confidence, is not the same as certainty. The post-1991 Iraq example should be another important cause for humility and caution as we feel our way toward a new Iran policy.

Status Report

Right now, and for some time to come, Iran's nuclear program appears to be focused on giving Iran the ability to build nuclear weapons. Whether the regime has made the decision to go ahead and field one or more weapons, however, is a matter of debate. Iran's approach has been a clever, but obvious, one. The Nuclear Non-Proliferation Treaty states that nations may acquire peaceful nuclear technologies, but not nuclear weapons. Iran has been trying to use this ambiguity to cover its nuclear weapons–making project—as Iraq, North Korea, Libya, Syria, and others have before it. Prior to the 2002 revelation of its fissile material fabrication plants at Natanz (uranium enrichment) and Arak (plutonium extraction), Iran appears to have had an active nuclear weapons research program. In 2003, with the entire nuclear program under international scrutiny and facing the threat of sanctions or even invasion, Iran ratcheted back (or possibly discontinued) its covert weaponization program while declaring its enrichment activities. Since the enrichment activities were sanctioned by the terms of the NPT, Iran may have decided to continue to pursue that track (even in defiance of the legally binding UN Security Council resolutions) until it got far enough along with both its stockpile of enriched uranium and operational centrifuges to be in a position to withdraw from or just ignore the NPT. If this is what Iran has been doing, it makes a great deal of sense. Since Iran needs time to build its sort-of-justifiable enrichment capacity anyway, there is no reason not to focus on that while leaving the impossible-to-justify weaponization program to catch up later.

Because Iran did come clean about its enrichment activities, to the best of our knowledge, this is one important area of Iranian behavior about which we know a good deal. We know about two sites where Iran is enriching uranium. First is the large, well-defended underground facility at Natanz. It houses more than 14,000 operational centrifuges as of mid-2013 and enriches uranium to both 3.5 percent purity (low-enriched uranium, or LEU) and 19.75 percent purity (sometimes referred to as medium-enriched uranium, or MEU).[42] Natanz can accommodate as many as 50,000 centrifuges. Then there is the smaller, but even better protected, facility outside Qom, called Fordow. Fordow has roughly 2,800 operational centrifuges, and while it has enriched uranium to 3.5 percent purity, it appears to be concentrating mostly on MEU production. In addition, the IAEA reported in early 2013 that Iran is now making progress on its plutonium separation plant at Arak. Tehran has notified the IAEA that it plans to start operating Arak in early 2014, which will create an entirely new supply of fissile material.[43]

By August 2012, Iran had enriched 6,876 kilograms of U-235 to 3.5 percent purity. Theoretically, it would take about 1,300 kilograms of LEU to make the fuel for a nuclear weapon, although it requires considerable additional enrichment to boost low-enriched uranium to the 90 percent purity (highly enriched uranium, or HEU) needed for a bomb.[44] In theory, Iran had enough LEU for five nuclear weapons. By that same point in time, Iran had enriched 189.4 kilograms of uranium to 19.75 percent purity. It typically requires anywhere from 125 to 210 kilograms of MEU for a bomb, and while it requires some additional enrichment to get to 90 percent, it takes much less than that required for LEU. Iran probably still does not have enough MEU to manufacture a bomb—although if it wanted to do so, it could supplement its MEU by further enriching LEU.[45] The generalizations about how much of each purity of uranium is required for a bomb are variable based on a wide range of factors, and the time required to further enrich the uranium to the HEU needed for a weapon varies even more based on the numbers of centrifuges, the quality of those centrifuges, the starting purity of the uranium feedstock, and several other factors.

Given how much uranium Iran has enriched and the levels of purity it has attained, experts on the Iranian nuclear program are increasingly concerned about Iran's efforts to develop a new generation of more advanced centrifuges based on the more sophisticated Pakistani P-2. Iran has installed some of its advanced IR-2s and IR-4s at both Natanz and Fordow and notified the IAEA in January 2013 that it would begin to operate some of the IR-2s.[46] This decision will accelerate Iran's ability to enrich uranium, something that will increase just as significantly when they get their IR-3 and IR-4 models working.

It is possible that Iran has constructed—or is in the process of building—additional enrichment sites or additional weaponization research and testing facilities. Certainly, between Natanz, Arak, and Fordow, Iran has demonstrated both an interest in and an ability to build large, sophisticated nuclear facilities and to keep them secret for at least some period of time. Experts from various Western governments and the IAEA believe it is unlikely that they have missed large, covert Iranian enrichment facilities. However, it is worth remembering that in 1991, the United States intelligence community was certain that Iraq had only two nuclear facilities and that neither of these was far along in developing the capability to enrich uranium, only to find out after the Persian Gulf War that Iraq had nineteen *other* nuclear facilities—fourteen of them large and important— that the United States did not even know existed. Baghdad was much closer to being able to build a workable bomb than anyone realized.[47]

Western intelligence communities and the IAEA are much better equipped today than they were then, and they have learned many lessons from the Iraq experience, but we should not rule out the possibility that we have missed one or more secret Iranian nuclear facilities. We ought to keep in mind the statements of Ahmadinejad and others from 2009 that Iran would build multiple, alternative enrichment sites in other mountains elsewhere in Iran. It might be bluster, or it might be a clue. In August 2010, Iran notified the IAEA of its intent to start construction at one new site that it identified as one of the ten that Ahmadinejad mentioned, suggesting that his statement was not merely bluster.[48] And if Iran does have other enrichment facilities, not only would that change how quickly Iran could produce enough HEU for a bomb, but it would also change how soon we might realize it.

THE WEAPONIZATION DEBATE. In November 2007, the U.S. National Intelligence Council—the senior analytic body of the U.S. intelligence community—issued a National Intelligence Estimate on Iran's nuclear program. Most NIEs are boring, and I say that as someone who has both helped draft them when I worked at CIA, and read them when I worked for the National Security Council. This one was a bombshell. The opening sentence of the NIE's key judgments stated: "We judge with high confidence that in fall 2003, Tehran halted its nuclear weapons program; we also assess with moderate-to-high confidence that Tehran at a minimum is keeping open the option to develop nuclear weapons." It went on to say, "We assess with high confidence that until fall 2003, Iranian military entities were working under government direction to develop nuclear weapons." And then, "We assess with moderate confidence Tehran had not restarted its nuclear weapons program as of mid-2007, but we do not know whether it currently intends to develop nuclear weapons."[49]

In other words, in the early fall of 2007, U.S. intelligence had acquired information that convinced the entire U.S. intelligence community that Iran had had a program to build a nuclear weapon (and that the uranium enrichment and plutonium separation programs were intended to produce the fissile material for that weapon). But that same information also indicated that the Iranians had shut down that piece (the weaponization part) of the nuclear program in 2003, although the uranium enrichment and plutonium separation projects continued to move forward as they were more easily justified under the terms of the NPT. Moreover, the American intelligence community also concluded, with somewhat less confidence, that the Iranians had not restarted the weaponization program by late 2007. At that time and since, the intelligence agencies of various other countries (including Israel, Britain, France, and Germany) have said that they agree that Iran had a weaponization program—and that the uranium and plutonium programs were married to it—but disagreed with the United States about just what, if anything, had been stopped in 2003. In the words of Britain's MI6 chief, "The Iranians are determinedly going down a path to master all aspects of nuclear weapons; all the technologies they need." [50]

The first thing to take from this incident is that it constitutes another piece of evidence that Iran's nuclear program is about weapons, not energy. At least some portion of the evidence that the United States (and our allies) used to reach these conclusions has been turned over to the IAEA and is part of the reason that the agency's reports on Iran have been ever more willing to assert that Iran is either not fully disclosing or simply lying about its weaponization program. It is why the IAEA keeps demanding that Iran prove that it does not have a weapons program and admit to what it had been doing in the past. No one outside the U.S. government (and the IAEA and other foreign governments) has seen that evidence, so we have no way of judging its credibility. And it is important to remember that when Colin Powell reviewed the intelligence on Iraq's WMD arsenal in 2003, just before his famous session at the UN, he found that the intelligence was a lot less compelling than the analysts and intelligence community leadership had been claiming it was. [51] Consequently, we should not take the intelligence community's word for it—and as someone who, like Secretary Powell, was assured by the intelligence community that Saddam had reconstituted his WMD but had not tried as hard as Powell to verify their judgments, I am wary of doing so again. Nevertheless, it is an important data point that there does seem to be much agreement on this matter even after the traumatic Iraq experience. [52]

So much for the area of agreement. Ever since the NIE, there has been considerable debate among various Western intelligence services over the status of Iran's weaponization program. Contrary to the American position, several European and Israeli intelligence services contend that Iran did not shut down its weaponization program in 2003. [53] As best we can glean from the unclassified reporting, there is widespread agreement among the American, European, and Israeli intelligence services that Iran retained some kind of a clandestine nuclear weaponization program under the same man who had been running it before 2003: Mohsen

Fakhrizadeh-Mahabadi. The program is more dispersed and more secret than it had been before 2003. It is also smaller than it had been before 2003, although just how small seems to be the primary area of disagreement between the Americans on one side and the Europeans and Israelis on the other. My interpretation of the disagreement, based on what has surfaced in the media, is that the Americans believe that the program is small enough that it can no longer be considered a serious weaponization program, whereas the Europeans and Israelis believe that it still represents a significant effort to build a functional weapon. Although the unclassified reporting provides no specific details about the discrepancies, they seem to focus on differing estimates of the numbers of personnel involved, the amount of money devoted to the program, the priority the program is assigned by the regime, and the progress it is making.[54]

For its part, the IAEA agrees that Iran has resumed at least some work on weaponization under Fakhrizadeh. In its November 2011 report, the IAEA laid out its understanding and concerns about Iran's weaponization program in an extensive annex. This section of the report provided detailed claims that Iran had performed work on every aspect of the design, engineering, and even testing of a nuclear device, as well as considerable work on the design of a nuclear warhead for a ballistic missile.[55] The annex also contained a discussion of the evidence supporting these claims and concerns, which included more than a thousand pages of documentation, information from ten other nations, and information discovered by the IAEA itself. As a result, the IAEA concluded that it found the information provided in its annex to be "overall credible."[56] However, the IAEA report does not indicate whether the agency concurs with the American assessment of the Iranian weaponization program or the European/Israeli assessment.

TIME LINES. Despite the rancorous debate over the extent to which Iran is working on the weaponization piece, most of the estimates about when Iran will cross various thresholds are consistent. In particular, there is a consensus that Iran has crossed certain key thresholds already. It has acquired adequate know-how, centrifuges, and enriched uranium to be able to manufacture at least one (and probably more like three to five) nuclear weapons if Tehran chose to do so. Most Western governments estimate that if Iran were willing to break out of the NPT and use its existing array of centrifuges to enrich its existing stockpiles of LEU and MEU, it would probably take Iran less than a year (and possibly only a few months) to have enough HEU for one nuclear weapon. The more Iran can use MEU rather than LEU, and the more it can rely on more advanced centrifuges, the faster it will be able to produce enough fissile material for a weapon.

Although our knowledge of Iran's weaponization efforts is far more limited than our understanding of its enrichment activities, Western governments believe that it would take Iran at least a year to manufacture a crude nuclear device to receive the HEU it has manufactured.[57] In March 2013, both President Obama and Israeli prime minister Benjamin Netanyahu publicly agreed that Iran would require roughly a year to build a nuclear weapon, from the time of a decision to do so.[58] Nevertheless, a report by the respected researchers of the Institute for Science and International Security noted that "[i]f Iran were to attempt to make a nuclear weapon, it would likely face new engineering challenges, despite work it may have done in the past. Iran would thus need many additional months to manufacture a nuclear device suitable for underground testing and even longer to make a reliable warhead for a ballistic missile."[59] In other words, it would take Iran at least a year to build a crude nuclear weapon deliverable by truck, large aircraft, or ship. Making one usable in a missile warhead would take considerably longer. By way of comparison, seven years after North Korea first detonated a nuclear weapon most experts doubted that it had nuclear warheads for its missiles, and North Korea's nuclear and missile programs are both far more robust than Iran's.[60]

Of course, as Iran adds new quantities of both LEU and MEU, and as it masters its more advanced centrifuges, these time lines will change. In late 2012, French foreign minister Laurent Fabius announced that Paris expected that by mid-2013, Iran would have so refined its ability to manufacture the needed HEU that it would have a breakout capability—

although he omitted any reference to whether France also believed that the Iranian weaponization program was far enough along to keep pace. Most estimates suggest that it is not.[61]

The Goal of the Iranian Program— A Weapon or a Capability?

Iran's adherence to the NPT precludes it from building or fielding nuclear weapons. So far Iran has not been willing to withdraw from the NPT, probably out of fear of an even harsher international backlash (including the possibility of military strikes). The NPT grants every nation the right to all aspects of nuclear energy and development, except a weapon itself. Its framers did not recognize that this loophole would allow states to traverse most of the path needed to manufacture nuclear weapons, and get so close as to be a few months—or theoretically less—from possible weaponization. A nation on the brink of a weapon could decide to withdraw from the NPT and race the last few months or even weeks to assemble one or more weapons to present the world with a fait accompli. Such a capability would enable Iran to assemble one or more working nuclear weapons faster than most of the world would react, and possibly faster than the United States or Israel could even react militarily. This condition is what is referred to as a "breakout" capability.

As the above discussion explained, Iran has already achieved something of a nuclear "breakout" capability. The long pole in the tent is whether Iran has a working device in which to put the fissile material and detonate it. We do not know, but most of the world's intelligence agencies seem to think that even if Tehran were to make an all-out effort to acquire it, Iran is at least one year away and probably more—perhaps as many as three and could only produce a crude device that would be difficult to deliver quickly or reliably.

The goal of the current Iranian program appears to be intended to narrow that window to a true breakout capacity, one that would allow Iran to field one or more workable nuclear weapons before the rest of the world could act to stop it. Since UN inspectors travel to Iran every two months, it may be that Iran is looking for a breakout capability of a couple of months, or even a few weeks (if that is possible), so that as soon as the UN inspectors have left after one of their bimonthly visits, the Iranians could start assembling their weapon or weapons and have them ready before the inspectors returned. Because of the complexity of these weapons, that seems unlikely. However, Iran might be able to get most of the way toward having a workable nuclear weapon by the time the inspectors returned and alerted the world to Iran's actions.

What isn't clear is whether the achievement of such a short breakout window is meant to be the stopping point of Iran's nuclear labors or a milestone along the way to the deployment of a full-scale arsenal. Both are possible. Both are consistent with Iran's behavior so far.

HOLDING ON A BREAKOUT CAPABILITY. There is considerable evidence to suggest that, at least for now, all that Iran is looking for is a breakout capability. At times, Iran has demonstrated a willingness to negotiate over its nuclear program, which would suggest that the Iranians are not hell-bent on getting nuclear weapons regardless of the cost. In recent years, the Iranian people have suffered under the harsh sanctions imposed both by the UN and by the West. It seems logical to assume that they might fear additional sanctions if they crossed the forbidden threshold of weaponization. So far, China, India, Russia, and a number of other countries have only participated partially in the sanctions imposed on Iran. However, they have all indicated that they do not want to see Iran acquire a nuclear arsenal. Iran's leadership—particularly Khamene'i—may fear that if they were to take that final step, they might push these countries to embrace more comprehensive sanctions against Iran. Former Iranian nuclear negotiator Seyed Hossein Mousavian has written that Tehran recognizes this possibility and is afraid of it. In his words, "Iran recognizes that by becoming a nuclear weapons state, it will compel Russia and China to join the United States and implement devastating sanctions that would paralyze the Iranian economy." [62] For this reason, stopping at a breakout capability—especially one with a narrow window—might appeal to Tehran as the Goldilocks solution: close enough to having a bomb that they could assemble one with speed, but still on the right side of the NPT and therefore able to deflect the pressure for more severe sanctions.[63]

Moreover, Iran has deliberately refrained from pursuing a nuclear weapon as quickly as possible. Many feared that once Iran had accumulated enough LEU for one bomb's worth, they would immediately begin enriching it to bomb grade to be able to break out. They have never done so. Instead, beginning in 2012, Iran has regularly converted some of its MEU to plates for the Tehran Research Reactor (which make them difficult to enrich for bombs), ensuring that it has less than a bomb's worth of MEU in country.[64] This pattern is consistent with establishing a breakout capability, not breaking out and racing for an arsenal itself.[65] Israel's former chief of military intelligence, Amos Yadlin, and Israeli nuclear expert Yoel Guzansky have called attention to this important pattern, noting that "Iran is not advancing toward the bomb at as rapid a pace as it could. It appears to realize that such progress would bring with it negative strategic repercussions."[66] The chief of staff of the Israel Defense Forces, Lieutenant General Benny Gantz, has even said in public that he believes Iran plans to stop with a breakout capability and will not weaponize.[67]

Any number of Iranian officials, including the hardest of the hardliners, have made public statements in which they have said that they are not seeking nuclear weapons. On June 4, 2006, Khamene'i explained, "We do not need a nuclear bomb. We do not have any objectives or aspirations for which we will need to use a nuclear bomb. We consider using nuclear weapons against Islamic rules. We have announced this openly. We think imposing the costs of building and maintaining nuclear weapons on our nation is unnecessary."[68] And in February 2012: "The Iranian nation has never sought and will never seek nuclear weapons. . . . Iran does not seek nuclear weapons since the Islamic Republic of Iran regards the possession of nuclear weapons as a great sin, in terms of thought, theory and religious edict, and also believes that holding such weapons is useless, costly and dangerous."[69] Even President Ahmadinejad made the point in December 2009: "We do not want to make a bomb. . . . Our policy is transparent. If we wanted to make a bomb we would be brave enough to say so. When we say that we are not making one, we are not. We do not believe in it."[70]

Although no Westerner has seen it, Khamene'i reportedly issued a fatwa in 2003 that the production, stockpiling, and use of nuclear weapons are all forbidden under Islamic law—and therefore that Iran will never acquire them. In 2012, Iranian foreign minister Ali Akbar Salehi penned an op-ed in the *Washington Post* in which he argued that Khamene'i's fatwa "proved" that Iran could not be pursuing nuclear weapons.[71] In early 2013, the Iranian Ministry of Foreign Affairs restated its claims that the fatwa exists and that, for Iran, it is binding.[72] In 2005, the Iranians told the IAEA that "[t]he Leader of the Islamic Republic of Iran, Ayatollah Ali Khamenei has issued the fatwa that the production, stockpiling, and use of nuclear weapons are forbidden under Islam and that the Islamic Republic of Iran shall never acquire these weapons. . . . The leadership of Iran has pledged at the highest level that Iran will remain a non-nuclear-weapon state party to the NPT and has placed the entire scope of its nuclear activities under IAEA safeguards and Additional Protocol, in addition to undertaking voluntary transparency measures with the agency that have even gone beyond the requirements of the agency's safeguard system."[73] Of course, the last part of this statement is less than truthful since Iran has not honored the terms of its Safeguards Agreement nor has it implemented the Additional Protocol. Indeed, some have cited the Shi'i concept of taqiyyah (dissembling to avoid danger) as one reason to suspect that the fatwa is a weak reed.

Of greater importance, the Iranian government has ignored or reversed other fatwas when reasons of state made them inconvenient. In an assessment of this issue, two highly knowledgeable scholars of Iran, Michael Eisenstadt and Mehdi Khalaji, warned that "it is the principle of *maslahat* (the interest of the regime) that guides the formulation of Iranian policy. Before he died, Ayatollah Khomeini ruled that the Islamic

Republic could destroy a mosque or suspend the observance of the tenets of Islam if its interests so dictated. And the constitution of the Islamic Republic invests the Supreme Leader with absolute authority to determine the interest of the regime. He can therefore cancel laws or override decisions by the regime's various deliberative bodies, including the Majlis (parliament), the Guardian Council, and the Expediency Council."[74] After Khomeini's fatwa in 1989 condoning the killing of author Salman Rushdie, Iranian officials went to great lengths to explain to Western diplomats and media that the fatwa was not legally binding on them.

Although we did not know it at the time, Khomeini himself apparently had issued a similar fatwa banning the development and use of weapons of mass destruction, including nuclear weapons, only to reverse it and order Iran to develop these weapons when Saddam began using chemical warfare agents on Iranian troops in the Iran-Iraq War.[75] Indeed, there are reports that, despite Khomeini's publicly published fatwa renouncing nuclear weapons as "unislamic," in April 1984 Khamene'i (then president of Iran) told senior Iranian political and security officials that a nuclear deterrent was the only way to secure the "very essence of the Islamic Revolution from the schemes of its enemies, especially the United States and Israel." He reportedly went on to say that a nuclear arsenal would serve Iran as a "deterrent in the hands of God's soldiers."[76] In February 1987, Khamene'i reportedly told Iran's nuclear scientists that Iran had to make a "tireless effort" to obtain "atomic energy . . . now," so as to "let our enemies know that we can defend ourselves."[77] The next year, then–speaker of parliament Hashemi Rafsanjani gave a speech in which he proclaimed, "With regard to chemical, bacteriological, and radiological weapons, it was made very clear during the war that these weapons are very decisive. . . . We should fully equip ourselves both in the offensive and defensive use of chemical, bacteriological and radiological weapons."[78] We might ask why Iran ever had a weaponization program at all if Khomeini's and Khamene'i's fatwas prohibited the development of nuclear weapons? While we have no smoking gun and the Iraq example should make us cautious, the evidence seems strong that Iran had a program to design, test, and build a nuclear weapon in the past, and may still be pursuing that end today. In the most comprehensive and balanced history yet written of Iran's nuclear program, journalist David Patrikarakos concluded of Iran's nuclear program in the 1980s that, "[t]aken together, Iran's considerable security concerns, the reported statements of regime officials and, most damningly, the scope and nature of its undeclared activities render the claim that all enrichment-related efforts were solely civil in intent, with no thought of the military applications, improbable to a degree that borders on the impossible."[79] If this is the case, it would appear to counter the fatwas' prohibition against the "production" of nuclear weapons.

There is a strong case that Iran may only be seeking a breakout capability and not an arsenal. The supposed fatwas may be part of that body of evidence, but they do not seem like the most compelling element of it.

GOING ALL IN FOR A BOMB. The alternative position, that Iran will not be satisfied with only a breakout capability, but will break out of the NPT to field a nuclear arsenal once it is able to do so, has its proponents as well. First, they note that the Iranians feel that they have a compelling strategic need for a nuclear deterrent, having turned most of their neighbors into enemies, while also demonizing the United States and Israel. Since they face American military forces in the Persian Gulf and parts of Central Asia, and are within range of an Israeli strike, Iran's leaders might well see the need for a nuclear deterrent. The Iranian regime watched as Iraq and Libya tried to acquire nuclear weapons, but before either could detonate a bomb, they were attacked by the United States and their governments overthrown. In contrast, both Pakistan and North Korea were able to acquire nuclear weapons. Their governments remain in power.

Second, it is not clear that Iran would pay a higher price, at least in some ways, for fielding an arsenal than it already is paying for trying to acquire the latent capability to do so. As I discuss later, the West is running out of sanctions to impose on Iran. Some Iranians argue that once North Korea and Pakistan acquired nuclear weapons, the West had to ease its sanctions and provide them with greater assistance to deter them from reckless behavior and prevent their collapse. Although this reading misrepresents the actual history of those two states, some Iranians appear to interpret it that way.[80] Moreover, China and Russia have consistently opposed sanctions on North Korea and Pakistan (for geostrategic reasons) and so again, Iran may see little danger that they would increase sanctions on Iran if Tehran fielded an arsenal.

The Iranians complain of a double standard, arguing that no one reacted to Israel's and Pakistan's acquisitions of nuclear capabilities as they have to Iran's nuclear program. This interpretation misrepresents the actual history since the United States discouraged both countries from traveling the nuclear path, including imposing sanctions on Pakistan.[81] Ayatollah Mohammad Taqi Mesbah-Yazdi, one of the most hardline of Iran's senior clergymen, wrote a book in 2005 called *The Islamic Revolution: A Surge in Political Changes in History*, in which he argued, "The most advanced weapons must be produced inside our country even if our enemies don't like it. There is no reason that they have the right to produce a special type of weapons, while other countries are deprived of it." He went on to write that Iran must acquire the "deterrent weapons" needed to stand up to its enemies. "From Islam's point of view, Muslims must make efforts to benefit from the most sophisticated military equipment and get specific weapons out of the monopoly of powerful countries."[82]

Ayatollah Mesbah-Yazdi's writings are not the only statement by a senior Iranian official arguing the case for a nuclear arsenal. For instance, the conservative newspaper *Kayhan*, which often reflects the views of the Supreme Leader, called on Iran to acquire the "knowledge and ability to make nuclear weapons that are necessary in preparation for the next phase of the battlefield."[83] Still, such pronouncements are outnumbered by those of senior Iranian officials arguing that Iran is only interested in nuclear energy and has no interest in nuclear weapons.

Finally, there is probably some degree of both bureaucratic inertia and political pressure pushing Iran toward an arsenal. Its nuclear program has been ongoing for at least twenty-five years, and some important members of the Iranian leadership—particularly within the Revolutionary Guard—support it. What's more, Iran has endured a considerable amount of pain and suffering to sustain it. All of those elements probably add pressure to see the program through to an ultimate conclusion, the acquisition of weapons themselves. In April 2013, after yet another round of fruitless talks between Iran and the P-5+1, Fereydoun Abbasi-Davani, the head of Iran's Atomic Energy Organization, announced that Iran might have to enrich uranium to 45 or even 56 percent purity for use in nuclear-powered ships or subs. While still not adequate for a bomb, uranium of this purity could be quickly and easily enriched to weapons-grade. This may represent nothing more than Iranian negotiating tactics, but it also may signal an Iranian intent to move further toward full weaponization.[84]

THE LAST MYSTERY. Assuming that Iran's nuclear program is a military one, there is at least one other possibility regarding their ultimate goal: they may not know themselves. At present, their current activities will give them the capability to break out of the NPT and manufacture nuclear weapons—likely in the next few years. Khamene'i may not have decided whether he will exercise that option, wait for a more propitious moment, or never exercise it at all.[85] That seems to be the view of the U.S. intelligence community. In early 2012, Director of National Intelligence James Clapper said of the Iranians, "They are certainly moving on that path, but we don't believe that they have actually made the decision to go ahead with a nuclear weapon."[86] Shahram Chubin also suspects that Iran has not yet made up its mind: "Anticipating Iran's objectives is problematic as rhetoric is not tightly correlated with behavior. In all likelihood, the Iranians themselves do not know whether to build nuclear weapons or stop at the threshold."[87]

Certainly there is no reason that would compel them to make that decision now. It is a decision that can be postponed. From my own experience, having served twice at the White House on the National Security Council staff under President Clinton, and having watched the Bush 41 administration make policy from my perch at CIA, I have observed that policymakers don't make hard decisions before it is necessary to do so (and sometimes not till well after they should). If a hard decision can be deferred, it will be. At a later date, the decision may be easier, the right choice may be more obvious, or the issue might be overtaken by other events. And Khamene'i's history throughout his rule as Supreme Leader is that he is not a man who likes to make hard decisions. He delays, dithers, and then makes half-decisions because he lacks the courage or the confidence to do otherwise. It seems likely that Khamene'i hasn't made a decision about whether to stop with a breakout capability or go the final distance and deploy nuclear weapons themselves. He probably won't until he has no choice but to do so. As always when we ask questions about Iran's thinking on issues of great import, the answer is usually "I don't know" or "it depends." Except when it's both.

3

The Threat of a Nuclear Iran

ne of the worst mistakes we make when we think about Iran is to assume that the problem we face is its nuclear program. However, it is not Iran's possession of nuclear weapons per se that creates a threat to American interests in the Middle East. The United States faced a wide range of threats from Iran when its nuclear program was moribund. Those problems have not changed or abated and may not even if Iran can be persuaded to give up its nuclear ambitions.

If Iran were a peaceful, secure, and satisfied country—one that did not support terrorism, subvert American allies, try to overturn the regional status quo, and inflict harm on the United States in a multiplicity of ways—its nuclear program would likely not concern us at all. We don't fret about what the French will do with their nuclear arsenal, or the British, or the Indians, or even the Russians for that matter. We worry about Iran acquiring that capability because Tehran means us harm, and acts on that intention. It is that intention and those acts that are the threat, not the nuclear program in isolation. Iran's acquisition of a nuclear weapons capability may exacerbate that threat, but it is not the threat itself.

Nevertheless, we have become fixated on the Iranian nuclear program as if it were the entirety of the threat. That has badly distorted our approach to Iran over the past decade or more. Successive American administrations have refrained from acting in response to other harmful Iranian behavior—like encouraging and abetting the killing of American personnel in Iraq and Afghanistan, trying to kill the Saudi ambassador to the United States, oppressing the Iranian people, supporting the Syrian government's bloody crackdowns, and supporting terrorist attacks in Afghanistan, Iraq, Yemen, and possibly Bahrain[1]—so as not to jeopardize a possible deal on the nuclear issue.[2] This tendency makes it all the more imperative to understand the real threat of a nuclear Iran.

It may not be obvious, but at this moment, the Iranian nuclear program is actually a *benefit* to the United States. Tehran's determination to acquire a nuclear weapons capability has so far been helpful to the United States and harmful to Iran. Iran and the United States have been adversaries since 1979. However, at no time since then has Iran been so isolated, so internally divided, so crushed by sanctions, and so weak. As a result of its stubborn determination to continue down the nuclear path, Iran has limited its ability to influence the geopolitics of the Middle East, which was probably one of its paramount objectives for trying to acquire a nuclear capability in the first place. Iran is also in greater danger of being attacked, either by the United States or Israel, than at almost any time since the revolution (with the hostage crisis and the Tanker War being two possible exceptions). Obviously, there is a widespread fear that if Iran were to acquire a nuclear capability all of this would turn around and Iran would become stronger and more dangerous than ever before. But at present and until it acquires that capability, Tehran's pursuit of it is having exactly the opposite effect.

All of this should emphasize that our problem with Iran is *not* its simple acquisition of nuclear weapons. The problem is what the Iranian regime might do when they have them, and how other countries might react under those circumstances.

Red Herrings

Before considering what Iran might do with a nuclear weapons capability, it is important to consider what they almost certainly will *not* do. Nuclear weapons evoke an understandable sense of fear. It often snowballs into panic. Add the opaque workings and often unexpected behavior of the Iranian regime and it is easy to take counsel of one's worst fears when pondering a world with a nuclear Iran. As a result, nuclear weapons have caused people to focus on worst-case scenarios, particularly with Iran.

Such high-impact, low-probability scenarios have typically proven to be wasteful and even dangerous as drivers of policy, especially in the nuclear era. Throughout the late Cold War, the United States and the Soviet Union wrung their hands and spent billions and billions of dollars (or rubles) over the possibility that the other would launch a disarming first strike when neither side ever had the intention of doing so. Looking back on the Cold War, scholars and practitioners now recognize that the fear of a "bolt from the blue" was an enormous waste of time and money, and distorted superpower relations for no good reason because the likelihood was virtually nonexistent.[3]

SURPRISE ATTACK. Although it is the scenario that the Israeli leadership warns about most loudly, the least likely scenario is that Iran would acquire nuclear weapons and use them immediately against Israel. The same goes for Saudi Arabia, Turkey, and any other neighbor or adversary of Iran. The Iranian leadership understands that Israel could devastate Iran on its own. Tehran also knows that if Iran were to use a nuclear weapon against any American ally in the region, it could face the full fury of the last superpower. The only potential exception to this rule is Pakistan, which also has its own nuclear arsenal.

Since the dawn of the nuclear era, politicians, statesmen, generals, and people everywhere have recognized that nuclear weapons are unique because their destructive power is so awesome that only a truly irrational or utterly foolish leader could misunderstand the risks of nuclear retaliation.[4] There is nothing to indicate that Iran's leaders do not understand this reality, and everything to indicate that they do. The Iranian leadership can be accused of many irrationalities, but suicidal tendencies is not one of them. Nor have the Iranians shown themselves to be inadvertently suicidal, like Saddam Husayn. The Iranians have miscalculated from time to time (a topic I explore later), but even when they have miscalculated, it has been on a more reduced scale than Saddam's colossal miscalculations—such as his invasion of Iran, invasion of Kuwait, his decision to fight the U.S.-led coalition for Kuwait, his bid to kill former president George H. W. Bush, his attempt to re-invade Kuwait in 1994, and his ultimately fatal insistence that the United States would not invade Iraq in 2003, to take only the best-known examples.[5]

Iranian leaders are aggressive, anti-American, and murderous, but whenever threatened with severe retaliation, they have pulled back. After the Iranian terrorist attack in June 1996 against the Khobar Towers housing complex in Saudi Arabia, which killed nineteen U.S. servicemen and injured 372 others, Tehran realized that it had infuriated the United States to the point that Washington was considering military retaliation. The Iranians pulled in their horns and moderated their behavior to avoid getting walloped by an American military they knew could have caused massive damage to their country and their regime.[6] Similarly, they have sought to avoid horrific physical damage, the most famous example of which was Khomeini's decision to end the Iran-Iraq War after a combination of Iraqi battlefield victories, U.S. naval intervention, and Iraqi missile attacks on Iranian cities left Iran militarily prostrate and without any hope of victory.[7]

Nor is it the case, as some postulate, that the Iranian leadership has a millenarian vision that demands that the Islamic Republic take apocalyptic action to prepare for the return of the Mahdi—the Shi'i equivalent of the Messiah. Whatever Iranian leaders may believe, there is nothing they have ever done that comports with this notion, whereas much that they have done runs against it. Of greatest importance, Iranian foreign policy has been guided by a ruthless combination of pragmatic strategy and Byzantine domestic politics. While that makes Iran problematic for the United States and difficult to read, nothing about its patterns of behavior give any reason to believe that the Iranians would sacrifice millions of their countrymen in pursuit of a mystical vision. Iran with nuclear weapons is going to be difficult enough; the notion that they would use nuclear weapons unprovoked against the United States, Israel, or other U.S. allies in the region is not among those difficulties.

NUCLEAR TERRORISM. For much the same reasons, it is equally unlikely that Iran would give nuclear weapons (or nuclear material) to terrorist groups. The rationale is simple, straightforward, and compelling: Iran has a long history of support for terrorism, and a long history of having its involvement with these terrorist groups (and specific terrorist attacks) uncovered. From Beirut to Berlin, Delhi to Dhahran, wherever Iran has engineered a terror attack, its role has been discovered, often quickly. While Tehran has too frequently avoided punishment when it has been caught, the Iranians seem to recognize that if the terrorist attack involved weapons of mass destruction, the targeted country (or its inevitable American ally) probably would not feel so constrained.

Iran has supported terrorism and unconventional warfare since the earliest days of the revolution. It has possessed chemical warfare agents since the late 1980s.[8] It has a large and active pharmaceutical industry with samples of all known toxic agents that it could have used to manufacture biological warfare weapons, and the CIA believes that "Tehran probably maintained an offensive BW [Biological Warfare] program."[9] Iran has also possessed radioactive materials that could be used in radiological weapons ("dirty bombs") since at least 2008. However, it has never sought to mix its support for terrorist groups and its possession of WMD. Had it wanted to do so, Iran could easily have passed chemical or biological agents or radioactive material to Hizballah or another terrorist group tied to Iran to use on a possible target—Israel or Saddam's Iraq in particular. Yet Tehran never has. And for good reason.

Iran would likely face crushing retaliation for any terrorist use of WMD manufactured by Iran, but the Iranians would also have to trust the terrorists to use it as they intended. That's the problem with terrorists: they are not fully under your control. Once you have given them their orders, money, explosives, and the like, it is difficult to know what they will do next. They might attack the target you intended, or they might not. They might do nothing at all, or they might hit a completely different target—one that you might not have wanted them to. During the Persian Gulf War, a long list of Middle Eastern terrorist groups journeyed to Baghdad to receive cash and weapons from Saddam to launch terrorist attacks on the United States. None of them ever did.[10] On the other hand, a lot of Saudis gave money to al-Qa'ida, but they did not tell Osama bin Laden to hit the World Trade Center—and many were probably unhappy when he did.

It is easy to understand why Iran has never risked its own safety by giving WMD to terrorist groups, and it seems even less likely that it would do so with a nuclear weapon. Especially early on, when Iran may have only a few weapons, why would it hand one to a terrorist group? If Iran's leaders ever felt the need to have a nuclear device delivered by covert action, their own Quds force and Intelligence Services would be a far better vehicle than unpredictable and uncontrollable terrorists.

Paul Pillar, the former national intelligence officer for the Near East and South Asia, has pointed out that, "No regime in the history of the nuclear age has ever been known to transfer nuclear material to a nonstate group."[11] That list includes Iraq, which relied on WMD throughout the Iran-Iraq War, and Libya, which was a notorious state sponsor of terrorism under Muammar Qadhafi. It also now includes North Korea—a regime so opaque, so unpredictable, and so bizarre as to make the Iranians seem bland and transparent by comparison. Seen from the perspective of a nuclear state itself, as opposed to the perspective of fearful rivals, the notion of giving nuclear weapons to terrorists makes no sense. The risks of horrific retaliation overwhelm any possible benefit from successfully getting away with it. That's why no one has given nukes to terrorists and it's why the Iranians have never given WMD to terrorists.

A Nuclear Shield

The one aspect of Iran's aspirations that we can be sure of is that it would want a nuclear weapons capability, if not a full-blown arsenal, to defend itself.[12]

There is no question that the Iranian leadership is paranoid, xenophobic, conspiratorial. and oblivious to how others read their own actions, all of which has helped the Islamic Republic become internationally unpopular.[13] However, as the old cliché has it, even paranoids have enemies. Iran has been a predominantly Shi'i nation since the Safavids conquered Persia in 1501. Until the creation of a (Shi'a-dominated) proto-democracy in Iraq after Saddam's fall in 2003, Iran was the only majority Shi'i country ruled by a Shi'i elite. More than 90 percent of Iranians are Shi'a, but 90 percent of Muslims worldwide are Sunni. As a result, for more than five hundred years, Iran has borne the brunt of Sunni persecution of Shi'ism, which many Sunnis treat as a form of apostasy. Indeed, al-Qa'ida and other violent Sunni extremists hate the Shi'a—and want to kill them—far more than they hate Christians and Jews. As problems between Sunnis and Shi'a have escalated in recent years in Iraq, Lebanon, Bahrain, Syria, Pakistan, Yemen, and Saudi Arabia, the Sunnis have tended to blame Iran for the problems.

Piled on top of Iran's religious persecution has been its history of foreign intervention. For roughly two centuries, Iran has been attacked and even invaded by Western powers. Throughout the nineteenth and early twentieth centuries, Iran was one of many lands fought over by Russia and Great Britain as part of their "Great Game." By the turn of the twentieth century, the two great European empires dominated or owned much of the key governmental and economic institutions in the country then still called Persia. During World War I, Persia became a battleground for

British, Russian, and Turkish armies, and was devastated by the fighting. In World War II, Iran was invaded by Soviet and British armies, and the Allies jointly occupied and administered Iran, including the Americans after Pearl Harbor. Great Britain relied on Iranian oil and the Allies used Iran's road and rail network to transport more than one-third of all of the Lend-Lease aid provided by the United States to the Soviet Union. After the war, both London and Moscow tried to maintain their joint occupation, only to have the Truman administration force them out. Even still, the Brits made one last bid, in 1952, when they tried to mount a military intervention to topple the popular anti-British prime minister, Mohammad Mosaddeq, only to have U.S. secretary of state Dean Acheson and President Harry Truman forbid them from doing so.[14]

During the period of American ascendancy throughout the Cold War, Washington never invaded Iran—and never interfered in Iranian affairs to the extent that most Iranians believe—but neither was the United States benign. In 1953, the Eisenhower administration helped engineer Mosaddeq's fall and the reinstatement of Mohammad Reza Pahlavi as the Shah of Iran.[15] As the Shah's regime was crumbling under the blows of the Islamic Revolution in early 1979, the Carter administration dispatched General Robert E. Huyser to Tehran to try to convince the Iranian military to mount a counterrevolution. (Huyser concluded it was impossible within days of arriving.)[16] The United States has had a desultory covert action program against Iran since the 1990s, although that project garnered little by way of resources or attention for most of its history.[17] Numerous press accounts suggest that that program has been reinvigorated in recent years as the Bush 43 and Obama administrations have sought to employ cyberwarfare against Iran's nuclear program.[18] During the Iran-Iraq War, Iran was infuriated that neither the United States nor any other country made any effort to stop Iraq from employing massive numbers of chemical warfare munitions against Iran. This history could only have reinforced Iran's determination to acquire any and all weapons to defend itself, since Tehran felt it could not count on anyone else's help.[19]

Of course, what a great many Iranians, and the current regime's leadership, fail to recognize is that it is Tehran's own hostile actions that have stoked American anger at Iran, fueling the threat of American intervention that the Iranians argue they are trying to prevent. From the U.S. Embassy hostage crisis of 1979–81 to the Beirut attacks of 1983–85 to the Tanker War of 1987–88 to the Lebanese hostage crises of the 1980s and '90s to the Khobar Towers attack in 1996, down through the long history of Iranian-backed attacks on Americans in Iraq and Afghanistan in the 2000s, and right up to the stillborn plot to kill the Saudi ambassador to the United States in 2011, Iran has mounted direct attacks on Americans. In most of these cases, there was no hostile act by the United States against Iran preceding it. Instead, the attacks seem to have been triggered by Iranian exaggerations or misperceptions of U.S. actions and intentions. Yet this long list of incidents (among others) has fired up American animosity toward Iran, and, on several occasions, raised the specter of a U.S. military operation against Iran.

Whether real or imagined, the threat from the United States is dangerous for Iran. Although the Iranians claim a willingness and ability to fight the United States and win, their capacity to do so is slight. Iran could inflict some considerable pain on American forces, especially if the United States ever decided to invade the country and overthrow the regime, but it has no hope of defeating a massive campaign by the U.S. armed forces. Given Iran's fear of American conventional military power, it is not hard to imagine that Tehran would want a nuclear deterrent as the only possible way to defend itself against Washington's military power. Indeed, some Iranians now explicitly say that they want nuclear weapons so that they never again have to fear American retaliation.[20]

In recent years, Iranian fears of two other powers—Israel and Pakistan—have also increased. Tehran may desire nuclear weapons to deter them as well. For most of its existence, the Islamic Republic hated Israel but saw little reason to fear an Israeli attack. Iran's pursuit of a nuclear weapons capability, however, has perversely drawn them into a security dilemma with Israel. Today, an attack by Israel is now a real fear, and so Iran can add that to its list of reasons for wanting to acquire a nuclear deterrent.[21] Likewise, Iran has rarely concerned itself with Pakistan. However, Islamabad's nuclear tests in 1998 clearly rattled the Iranian leadership, with numerous Iranian newspapers depicting the event as the advent of a "Sunni Bomb."[22] Moreover, Iran has increasingly come into conflict with Pakistan over the drug smuggling and terrorist operations being conducted by the Baluch population that spans their common border.

Enabling Aggression?

At some level, we can understand why Iran would want a nuclear deterrent. Even taking into account only those times when foreign powers *did* invade or interfere in Iran's internal affairs and setting aside those Iran has imagined, exaggerated, or brought upon itself, its history might make a nuclear shield desirable. We may even theorize that Iran's acquisition of nuclear weapons could be positive because it would create a balance of nuclear power between Israel and Iran, America and Iran, Pakistan and Iran, and so on. Alternatively, we might hope that once Iran acquires nuclear weapons it will feel safe, and therefore will not need to act against its neighbors, the United States, and other countries. This case has been argued by Professor Kenneth Waltz, one of the great figures of academic international relations theory. Waltz also believed that nations that have acquired nuclear weapons become more restrained and less aggressive.[23] In his words, "With nuclear weapons, it's been proven without exception that whoever gets nuclear weapons behaves with caution and moderation."[24]

Although this book is not the place for a full rebuttal of Waltz's simplistic claims, it is worth making a few points before returning to the specifics of Iran.[25] First, Waltz made numerous historical assertions that were at best disputable if not incorrect. For example, while a strong argument can be made that Israel has shown restraint on a number of important occasions since it is rumored to have acquired a nuclear arsenal in the 1960s, this statement is relative and Israel has still acted aggressively on numerous occasions since then.[26] During the 1973 October War, Israel opted not to preempt the opening Arab attack, and in 1991 Israel refrained from retaliating against Iraq for launching forty-two modified Scud missiles at Israel. Of course, both of these (and many other examples of Israeli restraint) were primarily a response to American pressure. However, Israel's sense that it could fall back on its nuclear capability if all else failed probably did play a role as well.[27] Yet Israel has conducted major military operations at least nine times since then and more limited strikes on countless occasions; hardly a history of "restraint."[28]

North Korea was already prone to rash attacks on the South before it acquired nuclear weapons in 2006–2009. Nevertheless, its shelling of South Korean positions in November 2010 ("one of the heaviest attacks on its neighbor since the Korean War ended in 1953"), its sinking of a South Korean warship in March 2010, and the nuclear crisis it initiated with Seoul and Washington in 2013 do not speak to more cautious behavior.[29] At most, one could argue that Pyongyang has been no more aggressive after acquiring nuclear weapons than it was before getting them.

Another example that contradicts Waltz's optimism, one of far greater relevance to Iran, is Pakistan. Waltz asserted that Pakistan became more restrained and less bellicose after it tested its nuclear weapons in 1998.[30] History demonstrates the opposite. The Pakistanis were not necessarily cautious before they acquired nuclear weapons—their role in both the 1965 and 1971 Indo-Pakistani wars testifies to that. However, since acquiring nuclear weapons, Islamabad's behavior has become outright reckless. Pakistan acquired nuclear weapons for defensive purposes—to balance the Indian nuclear arsenal and deter an Indian attack on Pakistan, conventional or nuclear. Once Islamabad had done so, and had proven to the world that it had them in 1998, however, its perception of its strategic situation changed. The Pakistanis concluded that their nuclear shield was so effective that they were safe from the threat of Indian conventional or nuclear use under any circumstances. India would never risk Pakistani nuclear retaliation or escalation from conventional to nuclear conflict. Consequently, the Pakistanis concluded that their nuclear parity with

India opened up the unconventional warfare spectrum to them, with no danger that India would respond to Pakistani covert action. Accordingly, Pakistan sent several thousand intelligence agents into Kashmir to mount sabotage operations, assassinations, and other disruptive attacks. Then, in 1999, Pakistani paramilitary units infiltrated Kashmir and ultimately occupied the Kargil region on the Indian side of the Line of Control. This encroachment enraged New Delhi, which responded with a major military operation to retake the lost terrain and a two-month conflict that resulted in about one thousand killed on both sides. This clash provoked a wider crisis between the two sides that brought them dangerously close to a nuclear exchange.[31] Indeed, even after a nuclear war over Kargil was averted, Pakistan has continued to wage unconventional attacks on India, most notably planning and supporting the horrific, coordinated attacks by Pakistani terrorists in Mumbai that killed 164 people and wounded another 308 in 2008. This event nearly provoked an Indian conventional attack on Pakistan, which was only averted by the intercession of the United States and other great powers.[32]

Then there's China. In 1964, China tested its first atomic bomb. That same year, Chairman Mao Zedong demanded that the Soviet Union return land that he claimed the Russians had stolen from China decades, if not centuries, earlier. Both sides began building up military forces along their border, and the rhetoric on both sides heated up. Many feared war between them. In 1969, Mao launched several attacks by Chinese troops against Soviet forces along the Sino-Soviet border, probably intended both to convince Moscow not to attack and to galvanize domestic support for the regime amid the chaos of Mao's "Cultural Revolution." According to Colin Kahl, an exceptionally able former defense official, "Mao was probably confident that China's recently acquired nuclear capabilities would limit the resulting conflict."[33] Indeed, in August of that year, after some of the largest and most dangerous battles between Chinese and Russian forces, the Soviet government felt out the Nixon administration on how the United States would react to a preemptive Soviet strike on the Chinese nuclear arsenal.[34] Ultimately, Soviet conventional and nuclear superiority convinced Mao that he had to back down, but for many months, expert observers, including Chinese government officials, feared a major war between the Soviet Union and the People's Republic of China.[35]

Another example is Iran's western neighbor. Postwar tapes of Saddam Husayn's conversations with his inner circle reveal that he too saw the possession of a nuclear arsenal as enabling aggression, and a key element of his desire to get them.[36] As two experts on the captured tapes and documents from Saddam's regime concluded, "Although Saddam did believe that a nuclear capability would provide protection against attack by enemies such as Israel and Iran, the theme he returned to again and again . . . was essentially offensive and coercive in nature . . . his attraction to nuclear weapons . . . revolved around fundamentally revisionist objectives."[37] In one conversation, Saddam explained that he needed a nuclear weapon so that Iraq and Syria (and possibly other Arab states) could go to war against Israel. He argued that an Iraqi nuclear arsenal would deter Israel from using its own, and this would allow Iraqi and Syrian forces to wear down Israel in a yearlong war of attrition that Saddam expected to win at the cost of fifty thousand Arab casualties.[38] There is nothing radical about fearing that Tehran would see a nuclear arsenal as useful not just to deter an attack on Iran, but to enable aggression by Iran.

The greatest fear conjured by a nuclear Iran stems from the danger that Tehran will feel safe and secure. But the fear is that that sense of security will not engender greater restraint as Professor Waltz believed. It will convince Iran's leaders that they can pursue their goals of overturning the regional status quo, overthrowing unfriendly governments, and assisting violent extremist groups without fear that the United States, Israel, or anyone else would dare to stop them.[39]

Nuclear Blackmail?

Since the dawn of the nuclear era, states have worried that nuclear-armed adversaries would attempt to coerce them into doing things that they never would have done otherwise or face atomic annihilation. In his classic work on deterrence and compellence from 1966, *Arms and Influence*, Thomas Schelling theorized that countries armed with nuclear weapons might coerce other states—possibly even including other states possessing nuclear weapons.[40]

The empirical evidence has tended in the opposite direction. Cold War studies concluded that in practice it was hard to find instances where countries acted purely and unambiguously based on fear of nuclear threats.[41] There have been occasions when a state with nuclear weapons compelled another to do something, but it was rarely clear that the nuclear trump card was the key to that outcome. In 1946, Harry Truman convinced Joseph Stalin to withdraw Soviet troops from northern Iran by ostentatiously alerting five American divisions in Europe for immediate deployment to Iran. How much was Stalin's decision to withdraw governed by fear of the American nuclear arsenal (for which he had no match at that time) and how much by fear of a conventional war with the United States? We do not know, but the Soviets did not begin to withdraw until after Truman alerted those divisions.[42] President Eisenhower obliquely threatened to introduce nuclear weapons into the Korean War in 1953 if China did not agree to end the conflict, and the Chinese did agree to do so. How much was it Ike's threat, and how much sheer exhaustion from the stalemated fighting? Again, it is impossible to know, but most historians seem to think that the former made it palatable for Beijing to accept the latter.[43] Throughout the Cold War, Finland tempered its foreign policy so as not to offend the neighboring Soviet Union, but Finland did so even before Moscow acquired nuclear weapons. It was fear of a Red Army invasion, not nuclear annihilation, that shaped Helsinki's course.[44]

In contrast, we can point to other cases where a nuclear power attempted to coerce a non-nuclear state to do something and failed. One need look no further than the subject of this book for one example. The United States (and Britain, France, and Israel) have all been trying to compel Iran to halt its nuclear program—and Israel has been making explicit military threats as part of this effort—since at least 2002. All have failed. The list of other examples of nuclear-armed states failing to coerce non-nuclear states short of war (and in some cases, failing even then) goes on and on: Russia failed to compel Yugoslavia to abandon its pursuit of an independent foreign policy in the 1960s, China failed to compel Vietnam to halt its invasion of Cambodia in the 1970s, Britain failed to compel Argentina to withdraw from the Falklands in the 1980s, the United States failed to compel Saddam Husayn to withdraw from Kuwait in the 1990s, and Washington also failed to compel Iran to stop supporting violent extremist groups killing Americans in Iraq and Afghanistan in the 2000s. After India tested a nuclear weapon in 1998, Indian national security advisor Shivshankar Menon tried to justify having done so by claiming that on at least three occasions before the nuclear test, New Delhi had been subjected to blackmail threats by other nuclear powers—all of which India ignored, he boasted.[45]

Thus, while this problem would seem like an obvious corollary to the danger that Iran would see a nuclear weapons capability as enabling aggression at lower levels of warfare, the historical record demonstrates that the risk of nuclear blackmail is slight.[46] Unfortunately, much of the region does not see it that way. Officials and elites from Qatar, Kuwait, the United Arab Emirates, Bahrain, Jordan, and even Saudi Arabia fear that if Iran acquires a nuclear arsenal, it will use it to force far-reaching concessions. As one Gulf official put it, "What happens after Iran gets a nuclear bomb? The next day they will tell the king of Bahrain to hand over power to the [Shi'a-dominated] opposition. They will tell Qatar to send the American Air Force home. And they will tell King Abdallah [of Saudi Arabia], 'This is how much oil you may pump and this is what the price of oil will now be.'"[47] Such fears are common across the region, especially from Arab officials and elites.[48]

Unfortunately, such perceptions can take on a certain reality, especially in the Middle East. The fear that Iran will be in a position to coerce neighboring states once it acquires a nuclear weapons capability cannot be dismissed by the United States as unfounded. History indicates that were Iran ever to try nuclear blackmail, it would probably fail. The Iranians will be hard-pressed to make good on any threat to employ a nuclear weapon if the target country refuses, as doing so would rally the international community against them.

Nevertheless, Iran's neighbors might decide to take unhelpful, even dangerous, actions themselves to try to preclude the possibility that Iran could engage in nuclear blackmail against them. Some might decide to accede to Iranian wishes on a whole variety of issues to placate Tehran (a phenomenon known as "bandwagoning"). Other regional states may try to balance against a nuclear Iran, and in so doing might take provocative or even dangerous actions that could embroil them or other countries— such as the United States—in unintended crises with a nuclear Iran. Some of these countries may be so fearful of what they perceive as the potential for Iran to coerce them with nuclear weapons that they may decide to acquire a nuclear arsenal of their own.

The Iranian Nuclear Threat and the Arab Spring

The internal upheavals that began in 2011 across the Arab world have affected every aspect of Middle Eastern politics. The threat from Iran is no exception. The events of this Arab Awakening, or "Arab Spring," are likely to produce two contradictory trends related to the threat from a nuclear Iran.

The Arab Spring has engendered tremendous instability that Iran has tried to exploit, making its acquisition of a nuclear weapons capability even more frightening to the states of the region. Since the Second World War, the Middle East has rarely been described as "tranquil." It is perpetually on the brink of chaos. Yet the tectonic shifts since 2011 have made the Middle East's past appear serene by comparison. In many ways, nothing could be better for Iran. The Iranians have done what they could to ratchet up the unrest and topple conservative, anti-Iranian (and to some extent, pro-American) regimes in hopes of reshuffling the regional balance.[49] Whether cheering from the sidelines in Egypt and Libya, or providing substantive assistance to oppositionists in places such as Yemen and Bahrain, the Iranians consistently have been on the side of greater turmoil.[50] To the extent that a nuclear Iran is even more inclined to support terrorism, subversion, civil wars, and insurgencies than in the past, the Arab Spring will create far more opportunities for doing so.

However, over the longer term, the political transformations that began in 2011 could have an important palliative effect on this same problem. If these changes produce more stable, legitimate, and pluralistic Arab political systems, such states are likely to be less sensitive to Iranian mischief-making and less vulnerable to Tehran overall. The threat from Tehran is the threat of subversion, not the threat of conventional attack. Legitimate new democracies should be far less susceptible to this method of attack because they tend to have fewer cracks for Iran to exploit than illegitimate and repressive autocracies. Consequently, the political turmoil of the Arab Spring could make the danger from a nuclear Iran worse in the short term, but over the longer term could dampen Iran's threat to the region.

Weighing Our Fears

The world will not end the day after Iran detonates a nuclear warhead, or acquires the wherewithal to break out of the NPT. There is little reason to indulge our worst fears when it comes to the Iranian nuclear threat. There is no reason to believe that Iran will use nuclear weapons unprovoked when it gets them, or that they will turn them over to terrorists.

Since Hiroshima, people have worried that a country would behave in a reckless fashion after it acquired nuclear weapons. Mao's China was the first, understandably given Mao's inexplicable and self-destructive behavior. Yet China did not go off on an atomic binge after it crossed the nuclear threshold in 1964. North Korea was another. For years, experts, politicians, and pundits all feared that North Korea would use nuclear weapons after it acquired them. The North was prone to aggressive behavior, at times so bizarre as to lead many to suspect Pyongyang's collective sanity—like trying to kill the president of South Korea, and hijacking or blowing up South Korean airliners.[51] Indeed, if there was one country that everyone feared would use nuclear weapons if it acquired them, far more than Iran, it was North Korea. North Korea probably acquired a nuclear device in the 1990s, tested one in 2006, and in 2009 announced that it had nuclear weapons. And yet, the world has not ended. Nor has Pyongyang used these weapons despite frequent claims that it would. If North Korea can defy these apocalyptic fears, we should have greater confidence that Iran will, too.

That said, it would be Pollyannaish to believe that Iran would behave better—more restrained, less aggressive—than it does now. Contrary to Professor Waltz's claims, the pattern of states that have acquired nuclear weapons is that their behavior does not change once they cross that threshold. The United States, Russia, China, India, Britain, France, and North Korea behaved pretty much the same before they developed nuclear weapons as they did after, no better and no worse. Israel may have become marginally less aggressive after it acquired a nuclear capability, but that shift came at the same time as a number of other important shifts such as the Arabs' realization after the Six-Day War that they could not destroy Israel by conventional military means. Those other factors may better explain Israel's modestly greater restraint. Pakistan, in contrast, became significantly more aggressive and reckless after it acquired nuclear weapons.

This pattern suggests that Iran's international actions are unlikely to improve after it crosses the nuclear threshold. For more than thirty years, Iran has backed a vast array of terrorists, separatists, insurgents, nihilists, and revolutionaries. It has rarely missed a chance to inflict harm on the United States and our allies in the region, and when it has, it typically passed up the opportunity only for fear of suffering much worse from an American response, a caution that might well be removed if Iran believes that a nuclear deterrent has rendered it immune.

Whether Iran's motives have been defensive or offensive is irrelevant. Experts on Iran argue over this question incessantly, but what will matter with a nuclear Iran is *how* they behave, not why. Whether Iran is lashing out in response to perceived threats from the United States, or in pursuit of an ideological agenda or hegemonic aspirations, all that matters is the act itself. If they behave as they have in the past, as seems most likely, that will be a source of considerable problems. If they keep supporting all manner of violent extremists, waging unconventional warfare, attempting to destabilize regional governments, and otherwise trying to overturn the regional status quo, the United States and its allies will have to react. And our reactions will provoke crises, retaliation, and conflict regardless of Tehran's motives.

4

Proliferation

nuclear Iran would pose an additional threat to American interests: the threat of further nuclear proliferation. A great many of Iran's neighbors fear that once Iran acquires nuclear weapons it will pursue an aggressive foreign policy. Consequently, if or when Tehran crosses the nuclear threshold, other Middle Eastern states may seek nuclear weapons of their own to deter an Iranian attack, covert or overt. Those outside the region considering whether to acquire nuclear weapons might even draw the lesson from the Iranian case that the penalties for developing a nuclear weapon would be less than they feared.

Since the Second World War, the United States has had an interest in limiting the number of countries with nuclear arsenals because proliferation increases the number of potentially dangerous states with unquestionably dangerous weapons. However, we have been famously inconsistent in applying that principle. The United States has been willing to accept a half dozen or more countries—including Britain, France, and

India—acquiring nuclear weapons because Washington did not see them as dangerous. In contrast, the United States actually tried to dissuade Israel from going down the nuclear path.[1] One of the strongest justifications for toppling Saddam Husayn's regime was that he was a dangerous, aggressive, and hard-to-deter leader, and was (mistakenly) believed to be close to acquiring nuclear weapons. Moreover, because others saw him as dangerous, Saddam's acquisition of nuclear weapons would have been a major spur to further proliferation.

Saudi Arabia

The country most likely to follow Iran down the nuclear rabbit hole is Saudi Arabia.[2] Since before the Iranian Revolution, Riyadh has been a rival of Tehran. Since then, and since the fall of Saddam Husayn, the Saudis have seen themselves as Iran's principal opponent. Saudi Arabia is the leader of the Arab world, particularly as it confronts Persian Iran. As the home of Mecca and Medina, Saudi Arabia is also the champion of the Sunni world against Iran, the great Shi'i power. Of equal importance, the Saudi royal family, the Al Sa'ud, are (with some notable exceptions) fearful of change—especially violent change—worrying that it will destroy their enviable existence. The behavior of the Saudis stands in contrast to Iran's determination to undermine or overthrow the status quo. Across the region and beyond, the Saudis back one group while the Iranians back its rival, regardless of the venue: Lebanon, Iraq, Syria, Yemen, the Palestinian territories, Afghanistan, Bahrain, and points beyond.

The Saudis may exaggerate Iran's capability to hurt them, but they are not necessarily wrong about Tehran's malign intent. The Iranians have tried to overthrow the Al Sa'ud before. In 1981, 1982, 1986, and most notably in 1987, Iran sent agents to the Hajj in Mecca to start riots meant to provoke an all-out revolution in the Kingdom. The 1987 incident resulted in the deaths of more than four hundred people, including eighty-five Saudi police.[3] In 1987, in the midst of the Iran-Iraq War, the Iranians attempted to mount a major naval operation to destroy Saudi oil facilities in the Gulf, which was only aborted by the unexpected intervention of the U.S. Navy.[4] Tehran created a Saudi version of Hizballah in the 1990s, which it used to attack the Khobar Towers housing complex in Dhahran—an attack that killed nineteen American military personnel and injured 372 others. In 2011, as noted earlier, Tehran apparently tried to kill the Saudi ambassador to Washington.

Iranian subversive efforts are frightening to the Saudis because Shi'a constitute about 10–15 percent of the Saudi population. Saudi Sunnis practice a fundamentalist version of Islam that has little sympathy for Shi'ism—typically branding the Shi'a as heretics. Consequently, the Saudi Shi'i community is the target of both persecution and prejudice. This persecution has made Saudi Arabia's Shi'i population prone to protest and revolt, and receptive to Iranian support. Worse still for Riyadh, the Saudi Shi'i population is overwhelmingly concentrated in the Kingdom's Eastern Province (ash-Sharqiyya, literally "the east" in Arabic), where Saudi oil production is concentrated. The Shi'i have an outsized presence in Saudi Aramco, the world-class organization that runs the Kingdom's gigantic oil industry. In 2012, a computer virus infected thirty thousand Aramco computers. The Saudis are convinced that the virus was made in Iran and introduced into the Aramco system by a Shi'i employee. The damage was limited, but it terrified the Saudis—and the global oil market, reliant as it is on the Kingdom's exports.[5]

The Saudis also seem to have a straightforward way to acquire nuclear weaponry. Throughout the 1970s and '80s, Riyadh bankrolled the Pakistani nuclear program and Saudi financing was critical to Islamabad's success. No one believes that the Saudis did that selflessly.[6] When I worked as a Persian Gulf military analyst for the CIA, we used to say informally that somewhere in the basement of Pakistan's Kahuta nuclear plant there is a nuclear weapon that has stenciled on its side, PROPERTY OF THE KINGDOM OF SAUDI ARABIA. There have been periodic reports of a nuclear agreement between Pakistan and Saudi Arabia, most notably in 2003.[7] Whether that is true or not, whether the Saudis have some claim on specific Pakistani nuclear weapons, is known only to the highest levels of the Pakistani and Saudi governments. However, there should be no question that the Kingdom's support for the Pakistani program gives Riyadh some claim on Pakistan. The Saudis may be able to take delivery of a weapon long promised by the Pakistanis. They might be able to buy one, providing Islamabad with needed capital in return for one or more weapons.[8] Given Saudi oil wealth, Riyadh might even be able to buy a bomb elsewhere, such as North Korea, if the Pakistanis demur.

Consequently, Saudi Arabia is the most likely candidate to acquire nuclear weapons if Iran does.[9] In private, Saudi officials have repeatedly warned American officials and former officials (including this author) that if Iran crosses the nuclear threshold, Saudi Arabia will follow—and nothing will stop them.[10] They will not live in a world where Iran has a nuclear weapon and they do not. Prince Turki al-Faisal, the former Saudi intelligence chief, has gone so far as to repeat that warning in public.[11] In 2011, Turki announced, "It is in our interest that Iran does not develop a nuclear weapon, for its doing so would compel Saudi Arabia, whose foreign relations are now so fully measured and well assessed, to pursue policies that could lead to untold and possibly dramatic consequences."[12]

That sounds ominous, and the risk of Saudi proliferation is real. But there are still a lot of "buts." First, it is not entirely clear what Iran's crossing the "nuclear threshold" means, whether the Saudis would know it, and at what point they would act. Because the Iranians may be willing to halt their nuclear program once they have achieved a breakout capability, it may not be clear to outsiders for some time—perhaps years—exactly where the Iranian program stands. If Iran is willing to stop short of fielding an arsenal, the Saudis may feel less compelled to match them. Indeed, Saudi Arabia's response may be the most compelling reason for Iran to stop short of crossing that threshold, potentially far more persuasive than additional international sanctions in restraining Iran.

Riyadh is also a signatory to the NPT, and it has taken its commitment (indeed, all of its treaty obligations) more seriously than the Iranians. Although Israel has become far more comfortable with the Saudis in recent decades, Jerusalem has never forgotten Saudi support and even participation in the various Arab-Israeli wars. Moreover, the Israelis fear that someday the House of Sa'ud may fall and any accumulated weapons will end up in the hands of far more radical successors or violent factions in an Arabian civil war. In addition to Israel's influence in Washington, American policymakers themselves have long opposed Saudi acquisition of a nuclear capability. In the 1980s, when the Kingdom acquired nuclear-capable intermediate-range ballistic missiles from China, the U.S. government weighed in heavily with Riyadh to ensure that no nuclear warheads would accompany the missiles.[13]

The Saudis are often more subtle and creative than others give them credit for. They may not take the obvious path and buy a nuclear weapon itself. There are many ways that they could create ambiguity and make Iran (and others) wonder whether they had acquired a nuclear capability without declaring that the Kingdom had joined the nuclear club. Riyadh could build a nuclear plant of its own and begin to enrich uranium, perhaps even hiring large numbers of Pakistanis and other foreigners to do so quickly, in the same manner as the Iranians have. A favorite scenario of Israeli intelligence is that one day after Iran crosses the nuclear threshold, satellite imagery of Saudi Arabia would reveal the presence of a half dozen nuclear-capable Pakistani F-16s at a Saudi air base. Pakistan has long contributed military support, equipment, and even whole formations to Saudi defense, so a Pakistani air presence would not be extraordinary. Yet everyone would wonder whether the F-16s had brought nuclear weapons with them and the Saudis could simply ignore the question. Neither the Iranians nor anyone else would know, but Tehran would have to calculate that Riyadh had in effect acquired a nuclear weapon. Yet there would be no proof that the Kingdom had done so and therefore no particular basis to impose sanctions or otherwise punish the Saudis.

The United Arab Emirates

Only slightly less likely to proliferate than the Saudis are the Emiratis. Although the Iranians have never tried to overthrow the UAE government (to our knowledge), the depth of fear and hatred in Abu Dhabi for the Islamic regime in Tehran is no less than in Riyadh. In 1971, Iran seized three small but strategically located islands from the UAE located in the midst of the shipping channel through the vital Strait of Hormuz. This has been a source of enmity ever since. Moreover, the UAE leadership shares the Saudi preference for the status quo and has seen Iran's efforts to stir up upheaval across the region as the greatest threat to their own interests.

To demonstrate their concern about Iran's nuclear program, the UAE has done something clever, but also potentially ominous. In 2008, the UAE announced it was developing its own nuclear industry to support a civilian nuclear energy program.[14] There is good reason for the Emiratis to pursue nuclear energy: the less that the UAE consumes its own oil production in powering its own economy, the more it will be able to export its finite hydrocarbon resources. However, the UAE has chosen to develop its own nuclear program within all of the guidelines of the NPT. Abu Dhabi's point in doing so has been to make clear that it is possible to develop a civilian nuclear program in conformity with the NPT as a way of highlighting the falsity of Iran's claims.

Of course, the UAE's program may serve another rationale. Although the Emiratis take care never to say so in public, in private they make clear that their program is not just a foil, but a warning to Iran.[15] If Abu Dhabi ever wanted, it could use its civilian program as the foundation for a nuclear weapons program, and Emirati officials will sometimes confirm in private that they want the Iranians to believe that if Tehran crossed that nuclear threshold, so too would the UAE.

Yet the UAE's procession down this path is also not a certainty, even if the Iranians do weaponize. Like Saudi Arabia, the UAE has not acquired nuclear weapons, even though its strategic circumstances have created powerful incentives for them to do so for a decade or more. The same set of counterpressures that operate on the Saudis affect the UAE, and perhaps to an even greater degree. The UAE is smaller than Saudi Arabia, its oil production is much less than that of the Saudis, and its income is more tied to international finance than the Kingdom's, all of which makes it more difficult for Abu Dhabi to defy the international community than it is for Riyadh.

The Emiratis have another consideration, and that is Saudi Arabia itself. The dirty little secret of the Gulf region is that all of their governments are suspicious of one another. All have grievances, irredentist claims, and long-standing grudges against one another. And all of the small Gulf emirates have some fear of their massive Saudi neighbor, just as they rely on Riyadh as their leader and principal voice on the world stage. Riyadh and Abu Dhabi have been working in lockstep in recent years, but the Emiratis must still worry that the Saudis will not want to see them acquire a nuclear weapon of their own. Riyadh's perspective may well be that if any Gulf state gets a nuclear capability to balance Iran's, it should be Saudi Arabia itself, and not its "little brothers" in the Gulf Cooperation Council (GCC). That may be the greatest constraint on the UAE: Abu Dhabi might be willing to ignore international protests, even sanctions (which it could assume would be much weaker than those imposed on Iran, because no one fears the UAE). But it probably will not be willing to defy a demand by Riyadh to cease and desist, because the Saudis have the capacity and potentially the willingness to take action in the UAE.

Egypt

Egypt, another country often mentioned as a potential proliferant should Iran cross the nuclear threshold, is probably the least likely of the candidates to follow Iran down the proliferation path.[16] Egypt had an extensive nuclear development program of its own in the 1970s. It first delved into the nuclear realm in 1955, when Cairo inaugurated a civilian atomic energy program. At that time, the Egyptian military leadership suggested that Egypt begin research into nuclear weapons, but President Gamal 'Abd al-Nasser turned them down.[17] Six years later, Nasser changed his mind. On December 21, 1960, Israeli prime minister David Ben-Gurion confirmed that Israel was building a nuclear reactor at Dimona. In response, Nasser ordered a full-blown Egyptian effort to develop nuclear weapons. He insisted that Egypt would "secure atomic weapons at any cost."[18]

From 1961 to 1967, Egypt tried to make good on Nasser's pledge. Cairo tried purchasing them from the Soviets, in 1964 and again in 1965, but was rebuffed on both occasions.[19] Simultaneously, the focus of Egypt's indigenous nuclear program shifted from civilian power to weapons. Egypt began negotiations to augment its nuclear facilities to pursue a weapons capability. Cairo signed agreements with Yugoslavia, China, France, and India, and also negotiated with the Soviets, West Germans, and British for nuclear-related research and manufacturing capabilities.[20]

Yet Egypt never acquired a nuclear weapon. After the 1973 October War, President Anwar as-Sadat discontinued the program. He did so because the effort was a drain on Egypt's economy, it became unnecessary strategically when peace with Israel became a real alternative, and because Sadat felt that a good relationship with the United States—with all of the economic, political, and military aid it promised—was more important. The Americans insisted as a condition for improved relations that Egypt abandon its nuclear aspirations.[21]

This history casts an important shadow on the notion that Iran's acquisition of nuclear weapons would prompt Egypt to follow. Israel is Egypt's neighbor. It smashed Egyptian armies repeatedly between 1948 and 1973. Losses to Israel resulted in the overthrow of King Farouk's government in 1952, and threatened Nasser's regime in 1956 and again in 1967. Nasser feared the same in 1969, during the War of Attrition. These threats prompted Egypt to try to acquire a nuclear arsenal in the first place.

If this compelling strategic and political threat was not sufficient to cause Egypt to acquire nuclear weapons—even after so much time, effort, and money spent trying to do so—it seems unlikely that Egypt would do so in response to an Iranian nuclear capability. Iran is much farther away. Unlike Israel, it poses no threat to Egyptian territory, only a minor threat to the safety of Egyptian citizens, and not much more of one to the Egyptian government. Today and for the foreseeable future, Egypt's own internal economic, social, and political problems are likely to prove a far more compelling priority for the new Egyptian government than an abstract threat from Iran. Since coming to power in 2012, Egypt's new president, Muhammad Morsi, has exchanged visits with his Iranian counterpart and his spokesmen have been talking about warming relations. This statecraft hardly suggests that the new Egypt sees Iran as a threat.

Former Egyptian autocrat Husni Mubarak believed Iran was one of his greatest foes. He saw Iran's hand in every unfortunate event to befall Egypt, including the failed assassination attempt against him in Addis Ababa in 1995. There were few greater foes of Iran among the Arabs than Mubarak, and he joined any effort that promised to hamstring the Islamic Republic. During Mubarak's rule over Egypt, Iran's nuclear program accelerated—enough to galvanize the Saudis, Emiratis, and other Arab states to action. And Mubarak openly admitted he was uncomfortable with Iran's nuclear pursuit, warning in a 2009 interview that "[a] nuclear armed Iran with hegemonic ambitions is the greatest threat to Arab nations today." [22] Despite that, Mubarak saw no need to bring back Egypt's nuclear program to try to match Tehran. If Mubarak did not feel the need for a nuclear weapon to defend against Iran, it is hard to imagine that his successors would, at least in the near term. One Israeli assessment posits that Egypt would be more likely to redouble its demands for a Nuclear-Weapons Free Zone in the Middle East than to try to obtain nukes of its own in the event Iran goes nuclear. [23]

Over time, this position may change. If Iran's acquisition of a nuclear capability results in nuclear dominoes falling across the region, and several more Middle Eastern states acquire nuclear weapons, Egypt may begin to feel otherwise. Egypt's desire to lead the Arab world could make Cairo feel that it must acquire nukes to command the prestige to play that role. Indeed, if the Saudis have a nuclear arsenal, the Egyptians may feel that they have to have one just to match the Al Sa'ud. Likewise, if a new, stable Egyptian state emerges from the postrevolutionary rubble, Cairo may feel that it can afford to do so and, in a more nuclearized Middle

East, that there will be fewer penalties for doing so. Even in this case, however, it is important to note that Egypt would be trying to acquire a nuclear capability to match its Arab brothers more than to confront its Persian rival.

Turkey

Perhaps the most complicated case for proliferation arising from Iranian acquisition of nukes is Turkey.[24] If it seems more likely than not that Saudi Arabia would try to acquire a nuclear capability of some kind, and that Egypt would probably refrain, Turkey could go either way.

Turkey has an important rivalry with Iran. There is a quip, usually attributed to the late Egyptian diplomat Tahseen Bashir, that in all the Middle East there are only three nations—Egypt, Iran, and Turkey—and all of the rest are mere "tribes with flags." Just as Egypt seeks to be the leader of the Arab world, so too does Turkey see itself as one of the great powers of the region, as does Iran. This perception is especially keen after Turkey's reemergence on the Middle Eastern scene under Prime Minister Recep Tayyip Erdogan. Erdogan's foreign policy is often described as "neo-Ottoman," reflecting the conscious desire on Ankara's part to play a leading role across the Middle East. Just as Iran seeks to dominate southwest Asia, so too does Turkey. And like Egypt, there is reason to suspect that if Iran were to acquire nuclear weapons, Turkey would desire to do the same if only to match Tehran's newfound status.[25]

Turkey's sense of threat from Iran goes beyond this abstract contest for leadership. Turkey shares a border with Iran—as well as an unhappy Kurdish population that would prefer to be independent. Yet Iran has at times supported Kurdish PKK terrorists against Ankara.[26] Moreover, although Turkey's official ideology is secularism, it is a Sunni nation with a Sunni Islamist government. The rising tide of Sunni-Shi'a animosity also affects Iranian-Turkish relations, and shapes specific differences on policy matters. In Syria, Turkey backs the Sunni opposition while Iran just as staunchly backs the Shi'i/Alawi regime. Turkey sees the civil war in Syria as a critical threat to its national security, and Iran's support for the regime infuriates Turkey. But Iran is just as enraged by what it sees as Turkey's efforts to extirpate Iran's last ally, Asad's Alawi regime. In Iraq, Turkey backs Mas'ud Barzani's Kurdistan Democratic Party and sees itself as a protector of Iraq's Sunni Arab community. Iran, of course, is the patron saint of all of Iraq's Shi'i groups and the two compete both directly and by proxy there. In almost every arena of conflict, Turkey lines up on one side and Iran on the other. As a result, Iran's potential acquisition of nuclear weapons does concern Turkey.[27]

However, Turkey also faces a series of countervailing pressures. First is the state of Turkey's economy. Turkey's reemergence as a critical regional and even global power rests on the foundation of its economic revival. That revival in turn has been a product of internal Turkish reforms, engineered by the Erdogan government, that made possible enhanced trade with the Middle East, with Europe, with the United States, and with the Far East. This economic revival is intertwined with critical political reforms. Ankara cannot afford to jeopardize these trade ties for fear that it will undo both Turkey's economic progress and political amity. Pursuing nuclear weapons could do just that.

Although under Erdogan Turkey has tried to be neither East nor West, neither wholly of Europe nor wholly of the Middle East, but something beyond and above both, its ties to Europe and the wider West remain of great importance. The European Union is Turkey's number-one import and export partner, with total trade amounting to €120 billion in 2011. Turkish trade with the EU constituted 42 percent of all Turkish trade in 2010, and the United States added another 5.4 percent. Nothing else comes close in terms of importance to the Turkish economy. By comparison, Iran accounted for only 3.6 percent of Turkish trade that same year.[28] The cornerstone of Turkish security remains its membership in the North Atlantic Treaty Organization (NATO) alliance, which further ties Ankara to Europe and the United States. From Iraq to Syria to the Balkans to the Caucasus, Ankara has tried to address its foreign policy and security needs through the mechanisms of NATO and the Western alliance.

Turkey will be sensitive to Western and international reactions when it considers a nuclear arsenal, if Iran obtains one.[29] Ankara will have to weigh how important it is for Turkey to stand toe-to-toe with a nuclear-armed Iran, or to avoid jeopardizing its crucial security and economic ties to the West. Moreover, those same ties will likely make it easier for Turkey to abjure the nuclear path. As a NATO member, Turkey can be confident that it has the full support of the United States and Europe if there is any threat to Turkey's security. Rather than acquire a nuclear deterrent of its own, Ankara can decide that it already is defended by a nuclear arsenal—America's (and France's and Britain's, for that matter)—an arsenal far more intimidating to Iran than anything that Turkey might ever build. That, and all of the other benefits that Turkey receives from its NATO membership, are likely to make it an asset that Ankara will be loath to discard.

A comprehensive study of Turkey's nuclear policy by the Turkish think tank the Centre for Economics and Foreign Policy Studies (or EDAM) in 2011 concluded that Turkey was unlikely to develop nuclear weapons of its own in response to Iran's moves. In their words:

A Turkish decision to proliferate would seriously complicate its international standing, undermine its economic resurgence and seriously damage relations with the United States and its other NATO allies. Moreover, any Turkish move towards weaponization would draw a harsh rebuke from the United States and would likely be met by an American proposal to strengthen security guarantees, as well as the threat of sanctions if Turkey were to continue its weapons efforts. Given Turkey's non-nuclear history and its long-standing reliance on the NATO security guarantee, it is hard to imagine a scenario where Turkey would simply cast aside its long-standing non-nuclear policy in favor of an independent weapons capability. As a whole, Turkish actions and statements suggest that Ankara will remain committed to the NATO security guarantee, while developing indigenous capabilities to increase its intelligence, surveillance and information management capabilities.[30]

The Impact of the Arab Spring

Just as the events of the Arab Spring have the potential to exacerbate the impact of a nuclear Iran on the instability of the region, so too is there an important interaction between nuclear proliferation and the tumultuous changes that began in 2011. The internal transformations racking the Arab world are likely to dampen proliferation concerns in the short term, but could turn around and amplify them later as stable new Arab states emerge from the chaos.

The events of the Arab Spring were not about foreign policy and international security, and are not likely to be about those issues for some time to come. The revolts sweeping the region since 2011 (2009 in the case of Iran) originated in the economic, political, and social stagnation of the Muslim Middle East.[31] All of their governments—the new and the old— are focused on addressing those problems in ways that they never had before. Where the ancien régimes were overthrown, their successors are trying to pull together new, workable alternative systems. If they succeed, they will have to confront the residual economic and social dilemmas. Foreign policy issues, even on matters where their publics care passionately, like the Israeli-Palestinian dispute—have figured low as priorities. That is likely to remain so for some time to come.[32]

The surviving autocracies, largely monarchies, have continued to pay much greater attention to foreign affairs, particularly the threat from Iran and the Sunni-Shi'a split, which reinforces the greater likelihood that they (in the form of Saudi Arabia and perhaps the UAE) might choose to acquire a nuclear capability to match Iran. Yet even they are being forced to pay far more attention to their internal political, economic, and social dynamics than in the past. Especially for troubled monarchies such as Jordan and Bahrain, but also for the Saudis, who have the same set of internal challenges, the survivors have less time, energy, and resources to put into foreign policy because they have to devote so much more to domestic matters.

Domestic demands should dampen the ardor of these states to make a major investment in nuclear weapons, at least until their internal problems have been addressed. However, this same dynamic could produce a different set of outcomes over the longer term. One particular aspect of the Arab Spring that could make proliferation a greater problem over time is the emergence of Arab public opinion as a driving force in Arab politics. The Arab autocracies were never quite as inured to popular sentiment as often claimed, and they would take action in response to public pressures (or prejudice) on foreign policy matters to avoid antagonizing their populations unnecessarily, given their much greater interest in preserving public quiescence on domestic matters. A good example of this tendency was the increasing Arab discomfort with the U.S. sanctions and air strikes on Iraq in the late 1990s, a tendency driven by a combination of Saddam's bribes and popular distaste—principally the latter in the Gulf states, which were immune to Saddam's payoffs.

The political upheavals in the Arab world since 2011 have made public opinion a critical factor in Arab foreign policy moving forward. The new democracies will be far more sensitive to public attitudes. Even the remaining autocracies (and the new illiberal democracies that may emerge instead of true democracies in places such as Iraq or even Egypt) will likely be more deferential to popular sentiment for fear of triggering a revolt against themselves. Now that everyone knows that Arab publics will not remain passive forever, all of the governments will have to work much harder to keep them from rising up again.

Arab public opinion is not necessarily more anti-Iranian than that of their elites, and in some ways, it is less so. All public opinion, however, tends to be fickle. It is also susceptible to the siren song of demagogues. As time passes, the leaders of the various Arab states may find it harder to cope with the internal problems that gave rise to the revolutions in the first place, and some of those leaders may choose to try to divert rising popular unhappiness to an external scapegoat. While Israel and the United States are both potential (and traditional) candidates for that role, so too are Iran and Shi'ism. And if Iran becomes the scapegoat of choice, some of these leaders may decide to push for a nuclear capability—or suggest that one is needed—to confront the scapegoat. (Of course, the same could be true if Israel is the preferred distraction, as it has been in the past.) Indeed, some might even see in North Korea's nuclear history a hope that pursuing nuclear weapons could secure additional economic aid that would help with domestic problems.

The effects of the Arab Spring relate to nuclear proliferation—and the Iranian nuclear issue—in one other potentially unhappy way. As we have seen in the Middle East and as is the case with most revolutions, for many years after the fall of its old regime, a country may be consumed by instability and frequent changes of government. If such states still manage to acquire nuclear weapons their instability will be a cause for alarm, raising the fear that their nuclear arms might fall into the hands of terrorists. Saudi Arabia is the state most experts and policymakers fear will experience revolutionary instability, and it is not out of the question that it would do so after acquiring a nuclear capability of some kind in response to Iran's acquisition of the same. A revolution or civil war in Saudi Arabia would be bad enough because of the potentially catastrophic impact this would have on the global energy market. The addition of nuclear weapons to that mix could make that scenario the worst of all possible worlds.

Proliferation Beyond the Region

America's interest in nonproliferation in the Middle East also has a component that transcends our narrow interests in the region. The United States has always feared a more general threat to global security from the proliferation of weapons of mass destruction (WMD), a fear based on two different concerns. The first of these is that the more states that have WMD, the greater the likelihood that such weapons will fall into the hands of terrorists (or other dangerous individuals) or be used accidentally. This fear is statistical: the more countries with a nuclear arsenal, the greater the probability that one or more will fail to safeguard them properly, the greater the probability that one or more will choose to sell a weapon or give one to terrorists, and the greater the probability that political instability (and even governmental collapse) will lead to "the worst weapons" falling into the hands of "the worst people," as President George W. Bush warned. Now that North Korea and Pakistan have nuclear weapons, and Iran is making considerable progress in the same direction, these fears are not idle.

The other fear relates to the tendency of nuclear proliferation to cause more nuclear proliferation. In a number of cases, one country's possession of nuclear weapons has convinced another to do the same. America's acquisition of the first nuclear weapons caused the Soviets to develop their own. To deter both superpowers, China decided to acquire its own nuclear arsenal. Fearing the Chinese, the Indians concluded that they too had to have a nuclear weapon, which in turn propelled the Pakistanis down the same path. The more Middle Eastern states acquire nuclear weapons, the more likely that others, inside the region and out, may feel the need to do the same.

Historically, the greatest incentive for countries to refrain from acquiring nuclear weapons has been the threat of sanctions and other forms of punishment. Since 1945, a number of countries have started down the path of acquiring nuclear weapons but ultimately chose not do so. Egypt, Sweden, Switzerland, Australia, Italy, Japan, South Korea, Taiwan, Brazil, and Argentina all discontinued nuclear programs before they had acquired a weapon. In every case an important element in their decision to do so was the potential price they believed they would pay in terms of international opprobrium, if not formal sanctions.[33]

Consequently, the more that countries are able to acquire nuclear weapons (or other WMD) without incurring heavy penalties for doing so, the more that it could convince others that it would be worth it for them to do so as well. Already, Israel, India, and even Pakistan are widely seen as having crossed the nuclear weapons threshold without paying much of a price.[34] Moreover, the more states that have successfully proliferated in the face of international pressure not to do so, the less international pressure that can be expected to be applied against the next state to try, potentially eroding the entire nonproliferation regime over time.

In contrast, there are three well-known cases in which a would-be proliferator paid a terrible price. Saddam's Iraq was invaded to prevent it from acquiring nuclear weapons. Qadhafi's Libya faced harsh sanctions to compel it to give up its nuclear and other WMD programs and then, after it did so, the regime was overthrown with help from the United States and its allies. North Korea succeeded in acquiring nuclear weapons, but only because it cut itself off from the rest of the world and suffered terrible privations for doing so. These three examples have cooled the ardor of many other states that might otherwise have wanted nuclear weapons.

Given this three-versus-three lineup, Iran looks like the rubber match. Yet, more than just being the final game in a best-of-seven series, the outcome with Iran is important because of the unusual public commitment that all the great powers have made to this crisis. Although their preferred tactics vary, all of the great powers have stated that Iran should not be allowed to acquire a nuclear weapons capability. In January 2012, China's then-premier Wen Jiabao stated that the Chinese government "adamantly opposes Iran developing and possessing nuclear weapons."[35] The following month, Russian president Vladimir Putin stated, "We're not interested in Iran becoming a nuclear power.... It would lead to greater risks to international stability."[36] It is also why both Beijing and Moscow have voted for six UN Security Council resolutions demanding that Iran halt its program.

In light of this unusual consensus among the great powers that Iran cannot be allowed to acquire nuclear weapons, if Tehran were nonetheless able to do so, it could send an unhelpful signal to other would-be proliferators. If the world is not willing to stop Iran—whose acquisition of nuclear weapons has been universally condemned—who is going to stop Japan? Or South Korea? Or Brazil? Or Argentina? Those countries could all assume that they would face far less international opposition than Iran as they are seen as so much less threatening than Iran. Consequently, supporters of nuclear nonproliferation fear that if Iran defies the international community and acquires a nuclear weapon, it could represent a very serious blow to nonproliferation efforts more generally. Some even fear that it could spell the end of the NPT as a tangible restraint on nuclear proliferation.

Part II

Prevention

5

Setting the Scene

There is no reason to believe that Iran's development of a nuclear capability would mean the start of Armageddon. Nevertheless, it would be a problem for the United States and a threat to the Middle East. It would be a situation best avoided whether Tehran is content to stop with a breakout capacity or seeks a full-blown arsenal. For that reason, it's important now to turn to the options left to the United States and our allies to try to prevent that unhappy situation and try to assess whether the costs of doing so outweigh the risks of not doing so.

The Last Options

Even at this late stage, it is worth considering policies that seem to hold some prospect of preventing Iran from acquiring a nuclear weapons capability. There are four worth exploring: a revised version of the current carrot-and-stick strategy (referred to by the Obama administration as its

"Dual Track" policy); a plan for regime change to try to topple the current ruling leadership before it acquires a nuclear capability; an Israeli military strike on key Iranian nuclear facilities; or an American military operation to keep Iran from acquiring nuclear weapons.

It is important to recognize that the first three proposed courses of actions are not "final" or "complete" options. Their ultimate success or failure lies outside American control. For these three policies, ultimate success would only be possible if the Iranian government (even a new Iranian government, in the case of the regime change scenario) agreed to end its pursuit of a nuclear weapons capability. In every case, the Iranians might simply soldier on toward a nuclear weapon or a narrow breakout window.

Only the fourth course, an American military campaign, constitutes a final option because even if the United States started with limited measures, it could escalate to a full-scale invasion and occupation of Iran. In that case, whatever else it might accomplish and might cost, Iran's nuclear ambitions would end for the foreseeable future, just as our invasion of Iraq ended Saddam's dream of a nuclear arsenal once and for all, even if at a much higher price than anyone signed up to pay. In that sense, only an American invasion of Iran constitutes a true alternative to containment. The other three are gambits that might succeed in accomplishing our goal, but also carry the risk of failure. And if they fail, they will still leave the United States with the choice between war and containment.

None of these four policy options are dumb ideas. None of them is craven. All have merits and advantages. All have been proposed and advanced by smart, experienced, patriotic, and insightful men and women. Ultimately, however, I fear that none of them will succeed at an acceptable cost. Two of them—a revised Dual Track approach and some aspects of regime change—have enough promise to try. They are both worth trying *regardless of their likelihood*. The other two possible options—an Israeli strike or an American military effort—I see as entailing more risks and costs than the likelihood of success merits. The rest of this part of the book will examine each of these four options, before turning to a fuller discussion of what the alternative to prevention, containment, would entail.

The Shadow of the Future

When it comes to choosing among our options toward Iran, one of the most important and least acknowledged factors to understand is that where you start shapes where you end up, and where you are willing to end up shapes both how far you are willing to go and, to a great extent, where you start. This is the case for two reasons. First, everyone must make certain assumptions to fill in the many gaps in our knowledge of Iran. These assumptions will determine whether you prefer the costs and risks of a war with Iran or the costs and risks of containing a nuclear Iran if all else fails. Second, what you are ultimately willing to accept, in terms of war or containment, also goes a long way to determining how far you are willing to go in exploring alternatives to war as a means of preventing Iran from acquiring a nuclear capability.

To understand these phenomena a bit better, it seems best to start with the second point, that when all else fails, whether you prefer containment or war shapes what you are willing to do and willing to try before the United States gets to that point.

Think of it this way. If you are ultimately willing to live with a nuclear Iran, believing it possible to do so and that the costs and risks of containment are "better" than the costs and risks of a war with Iran, why not make the effort to try to convince the Iranians to give up their nuclear program peacefully? The worst that could happen would be that Iran uses the negotiations as a ploy to buy time to complete their work on nuclear weapons. However, if you are willing to contain a nuclear Iran, that end-state is something that you are already willing to accept. It may not be an ideal outcome, but it is not unacceptable to those willing to opt for containment. On the other hand, if the carrot-and-stick approach works—if it convinces the Iranians to slow down their program, stick with a break-out capability, or accept more intrusive inspections (or a variety of other limits), any and all of this would create a situation better than the status quo. And since those willing to contain a nuclear Iran must also ultimately be ready to accept the status quo, any improvement is a victory. Moreover, if the carrot-and-stick approach could convince Iran to give up its nuclear program altogether, then that is the jackpot, and there is no reason not to give that option every chance to succeed since you are already willing to accept even the worst-case scenario if it fails.

The same logic largely holds for regime change. If you are willing to contain Iran, even a nuclear Iran, and prefer that course to a war with Iran, why not try regime change? The time it could take to work or prove that it has failed (one of the greatest problems with this option) is irrelevant. Since you were always willing to contain even a nuclear Iran, if Iran acquired a nuclear capability before regime change worked or demonstrated that it had failed, it doesn't matter. Of course, there are still reasons why it would be best to topple the regime before it crossed the nuclear threshold, such as avoiding the messy question of what happens to any nuclear weapons in the midst of a revolution or palace coup and preventing the current regime from gaining any value from its nuclear arsenal before it is overthrown. However, a willingness to contain *this* regime with nuclear weapons presupposes a willingness to take the actions necessary to prevent it from taking advantage of them for as long as necessary. Similarly, the containment scenario assumes that there will be a political transition in Iran at some point (and probably a messy one), and therefore the problems of such a transition cannot be reasons to eschew regime change.

The exact opposite is the case if you are unwilling to contain a nuclear Iran and are willing to go to war to prevent it. If that is the case, you will want to ensure a successful military campaign to prevent Iran from acquiring either a nuclear arsenal or the ability to field one. Once Iran has a nuclear weapon, it is unimaginable that the United States, let alone Israel, would attack it, except in dire circumstances. Consequently, the United States could not afford to wait too long to attack, lest Iran exercise its breakout option.

Thus, if you prefer war to containment when all else fails, you can try both the carrot-and-stick and regime change policies for a little while, but not for very long. Not so long that Iran may have a narrow enough break-out window to field a weapon before the United States can do whatever is necessary to end the program. The amount of time the United States would need for a successful military campaign is variable, however, as it rests on whether we can achieve our objectives with only an air campaign or if it becomes necessary to follow up with a ground invasion.

Likewise, if war is the preferred *ultima ratio,* the United States will need a good casus belli to generate as much domestic political and international support for going to war with Iran as possible and avoid repeating our post-Iraq-invasion isolation. The most obvious way to do both would be to put a good deal on the table for Iran as an ultimatum: Either Tehran accepts the offer or—instead of imposing still more sanctions— the United States will attack.[1] And the ultimatum would need a time limit to prevent Iran from dithering, giving half answers, accepting then rejecting the deal, accepting parts of it, or anything else short of a full "yes." The worst thing for someone who prefers war to containment is for Iran to be able to drag out negotiations, all the while making progress toward a nuclear bomb. So this too means that those who prefer war can only give a revamped carrot-and-stick a short time to succeed before they have to shift to the military option. Since no one really knows how close Iran is to a breakout capability, for those willing to go to war, how much time they can afford for diplomacy is also unknown.

If you are willing to accept all the costs and risks of a war with Iran, for the same reason, you cannot accept anything except a very good deal with Iran. For those willing to accept war as the last resort, the worst nightmare is a weak or partial agreement that allows the Iranians either to keep a narrow breakout window or to cheat and so narrow the window (or even develop a weapon itself) in secret. If that happens, Iran could surprise the world with a nuclear weapon before the United States could go to war to prevent it. In other words, a bad deal with Iran could leave the United States and its allies with no choice but to contain Iran. If you are willing to accept containment, that's fine; if you prefer war to containment, it's a disaster.

GOOD DEALS AND BAD DEALS. The objective of all the alternative policies to force or containment is to convince Iran to agree to a negotiated settlement of the nuclear impasse. As always, no one, probably including most of the Iranian leadership, knows just what the Iranians would be willing to accept in a nuclear deal. However, if we compare Iran's rhetorical declarations and the West's demands, it is possible to imagine a deal between the two sides in which Iran gets the multilateral sanctions lifted and what would amount to a rudimentary breakout capability—limited enrichment and possession of LEU that would theoretically enable Tehran to assemble a nuclear weapon in six to twelve months—in return for Iran agreeing to forgo the possibility of achieving a rapid breakout capability and accepting intrusive UN inspections to assure the international community that it is not cheating on the agreement. Such a deal seems to fall into the narrow area of overlap between the two sides' declared positions.

Whether you are willing to accept war or containment will determine whether you see such a deal as miraculous or disastrous. If you are willing to contain Iran, this deal looks great because almost any agreement that imposes real constraints on the Iranian nuclear program is worthwhile. Right now, Iran is moving smartly down the path toward a nuclear arsenal. It already has acquired the theoretical capacity to develop nuclear weapons, although it would probably require at least a year before it could field one from a decision to do so. With each passing day, the amount of time that Iran would require to build a nuclear weapon diminishes, and at some point in the next few years, Tehran will probably be at a point where it could build a bomb in just a few months from a decision to do so. That is the baseline, the starting point for containment. Consequently, any time that the United States can buy, any limits on the Iranian program, any additional monitoring and inspections, any additional pressure on Iran—any improvement over the status quo—is worth it because it leaves the situation with Iran better off than it otherwise might be. Therefore, any halfway-decent deal produced by the carrot-and-stick approach is going to make containment easier, stronger, and less risky than it would be without such a deal.

From the opposite perspective, if you prefer to go to war, you will likely see this deal as enabling Iran to retain an unacceptable, even if longer-term, breakout capability. The mere fact that a deal had been struck—a deal potentially easy for Iran to honor—would also be dissuasive because it would make it far more difficult to build either domestic or international support for war, since the Iranians will be seen as behaving reasonably, honoring international agreements, and demonstrating the "peaceful" intent of their nuclear ambitions. Such a deal would make it even harder to build support for military action than was the case before the 2003 invasion of Iraq, when Saddam's allies claimed that he was "mostly" complying with the UN resolutions and therefore military action was premature. Moreover, many who favor war with Iran over containment tend to believe that Iran will find ways to cheat on any agreement. For that reason, too, they tend to be willing to accept only deals with Iran that altogether eliminate Iran's breakout window by prohibiting all enrichment activities. That it seems even less likely that Iran could be convinced to agree to such terms is not meaningful for this group, since they are willing to go to war, and may be looking for the justification to do so.

The Shadow of the Past

When it comes to Iran, the discomfiting truth is that we just don't have the kind of information that we would like to figure out how best to handle the Islamic Republic and its nuclear program. We don't know what Tehran's aim is for its nuclear program: whether it is meant to build nuclear weapons, achieve a breakout capability, or even remain peaceful—implausible though that may be. Nor can we be certain how the Iranian regime will behave after they acquire whatever status they seek. Perhaps

Professor Waltz was right, and Iran will become more restrained. Perhaps the Iran experts are wrong and the Iranians will prove to be insane millenarians who will launch nuclear weapons at Israel and Saudi Arabia the moment they have them. If either of these extreme visions were accurate, it would argue for extreme approaches to Iran—doing nothing in the case of the former and doing anything to prevent the latter. Moreover, there are vast uncertainties about how others will behave. Will the Saudis, Turks, and Egyptians seek to acquire nuclear arsenals of their own, or can they be dissuaded from doing so? How will Hizballah, Hamas, and other radical, Iranian-backed groups react? What will the Israelis do? And will the interaction of their various actions bolster the security of the region or suck it into even more violent disorder?[2]

Since we cannot know the answers to any of these huge questions, the best that we can do is make informed guesses about them. However, we need to recognize that the assumptions we make will inevitably dictate the policy (or policies) we prefer, because different policies only make sense based on specific assumptions. This is why the debate over Iran policy is often so vitriolic and unproductive: the various sides see the fundamental issues so differently that it is hard for them to find any common ground. It is challenging to discuss how best to make a policy work when people hold fundamentally opposite views about the basic assumptions underpinning the policy. At best, the debate becomes about the assumptions themselves—which is useful and honest, but ultimately inconclusive since none of us can actually prove which assumptions are correct.

Thus, the more you believe that Iran is likely to use its nuclear weapons unprovoked or to give them to terrorists, the more inclined you should be to use force against Iran. That should be obvious. If you believe that Iran is going to start nuking people, then going to war to prevent Tehran from getting the weapons in the first place is not just the best relative course of action, it is an absolute necessity to save the world from the horrors of nuclear conflict. On the other hand, if you agree with Waltz that a nuclear Iran will probably behave in a more restrained and prudent manner, then you probably see no need to try a revamped carrot-and-stick approach, let alone explore the possibility of accelerating regime change to try to keep the Islamic Republic from acquiring a nuclear capability. In fact, if you think that a nuclear Iran will be more restrained than it currently is, why do anything at all? Pursuing any of the policy options to prevent Iran from acquiring a nuclear capability will be costly in myriad ways. If you think it unnecessary because you believe that Iran will be pacified by its acquisition of a nuclear arsenal, why pay the price—any price?

A similarly important and ambiguous set of assumptions concerns how any of these policies would work. The more you believe that inspections in Iran would follow the North Korea model—in which the inspectors were constrained, they saw little, and there was even less desire on the part of the great powers to punish Pyongyang for its transgressions—the less faith you are likely to have in any agreement with Iran. The extent to which you believe that a new inspections regime in Iran could more closely resemble the Iraqi model of intrusive, effective inspections coupled with a willingness on the part of the international community to act against misbehavior, the more likely that you will feel comfortable reaching the kind of deal with the Iranians that they just might be willing to accept.

The best that any of us can do is to simply be explicit about our assumptions and the evidence and methodologies we have used to arrive at them. I have given you my own answers to these questions in the preceding chapters, along with the evidence I have used to reach these conclusions. However, as you read the chapters that follow, you ought to be asking yourself how much you agree with me—and if you don't, in what ways your own views differ. The more that you disagree with my assumptions, the more you will likely disagree with my policy preferences because, in the case of Iran, it is your assumptions that determine your preferences.

Why Not Engagement Alone?

There is one last issue that needs to be addressed before plunging into a discussion of each of the four proposed strategies for preventing Iran from acquiring a nuclear weapons capability. That is why there is not a fifth option: pure engagement.[3] In Ray Takeyh's words, a policy of pure engagement rests on the assumption that "Iran's nuclear ambition stems from a desire to craft a viable deterrence capability against a range of evolving threats, particularly from the United States. Instead of relying on threats of sanctions, a more effective way to convince Iran to suspend the critical components of its nuclear infrastructure is to find ways to diminish its strategic anxieties. Should Washington dispense with its hostilities, assure Iran that its interests will be taken into account as it plots the future of the Persian Gulf, and relax its economic prohibitions, then the case of nuclear proponents within the clerical state would be significantly weakened."[4]

Between 2002 and 2009, a number of people, particularly on the left, advocated a policy of pure engagement with Iran—that is, the carrot without any threat of the stick. This group included many of the most accomplished and empathetic scholars of Iran.[5] Their arguments were cogent, based on a reasonable interpretation of the evidence and, at that time, mostly untested. If I were writing this book prior to June 2009, I would have included pure engagement as a fifth option. But since then, too much has happened for engagement alone to remain a plausible approach.

The historical record always suggested that a policy of pure engagement was unlikely to succeed. In their compelling synthesis of the theoretical and historical records of engagement as a strategy, Richard Haass and Meghan O'Sullivan concluded that "[e]ngagement works best in pursuit of modest goals and often falters in pursuit of ambitious ones."[6] Changing Tehran's behavior on an issue of such importance as its nuclear program falls far into the ambitious category, suggesting that engagement alone was not practical. Similarly, Haass and O'Sullivan found that historically, "to be most effective, incentives offered in engagement strategies almost always need to be accompanied by credible penalties."[7] In their words, the "honey" of engagement had to be combined with the "vinegar" of penalties such as sanctions to have a realistic chance of success.[8] Indeed, the German scholar Johannes Reissner concluded that Europe's effort to pursue what in effect amounted to an engagement-only approach to Iran in the 1990s, called the "critical dialogue," failed because it included no threat of retribution, no stick to accompany the carrot. As he wrote, the case of Europe's engagement with Iran in the 1990s "argues that sanctions should not be excluded from any engagement strategy, and, if endorsed, their role should be explicitly stated in policy pronouncements."[9]

Indeed, these theoretical and historical objections to an engagement-only approach to Iran point to other problems. The fundamental assumption of this approach is that Iran's objectionable behavior is predicated on its perception of threat from the United States *and* that if the United States were to take actions that reduced Tehran's perception of threat, the Iranian leadership would diminish or cease that objectionable behavior. The first part of that sentence—that Iran's behavior is a defensive reaction to an American threat—is unknowable, and may vary from Iranian to Iranian. Some Iranian leaders, perhaps all, may be motivated by what they see as a defensive stance toward what they see as a pervasive American threat. We don't know, either for any given individual or for the leadership as a collective.

The second half of that sentence—that the United States can take actions that would reduce Iran's sense of that threat and that this diplomacy could in turn produce "better" Iranian behavior—is demonstrably false. Since the 1979 revolution, there have been a number of occasions when the United States and its allies either reached out to Iran to improve relations or made little or no effort to harm/threaten Iran, and Iran did *not* diminish its threatening behavior. In several of those cases, the Iranians acted in a *more* threatening and aggressive fashion toward the United States and its allies. A quick summary of these instances include:

- 1979: The Carter administration, having reconciled itself to the Iranian Revolution, attempted to develop a nonconfrontational relationship with the new regime. It had not imposed any sanctions on Iran and had given up its flirtation with the idea of supporting a counterrevolution by the Iranian military (which the Iranians did not know about at the time). In response, Iranian students seized the U.S. Embassy and Khomeini endorsed this diplomatic outrage, launching the "hostage crisis."[10]

- 1982–89: Israel was trying hard to rebuild the close, if clandestine, relationship it had had with Iran under the Shah. It was covertly selling arms to Iran, which Iran desperately needed to fight Iraq at a time when no one else would sell it weapons. Nevertheless, when Israel invaded Lebanon—a move that did not threaten Iran in any way—Tehran responded by dispatching roughly one thousand Revolutionary Guards to the Bekaa Valley to arm, train, advise, and otherwise aid Lebanese forces fighting Israel. Iran would later go further to help organize and mount suicide bomber attacks against Israeli (and later American and French) diplomats and military forces in Lebanon.[11] Again, none of these personnel, even the soldiers, posed any kind of threat to Iran itself.

- 2001–2012. From 2001 to 2005, the George W. Bush administration (Bush 43) largely tried to ignore Iran. Although his administration indulged in some unhelpful hostile rhetoric on a few occasions, it had also engaged in tacit cooperation with Iran over Afghanistan. Of greatest importance, the United States had made it clear to Iran that its invasions of Afghanistan and Iraq were not intended to threaten Iran, and the United States took no actions in either Iraq or Afghanistan that were harmful to Iran. Our toppling of the Taliban and Saddam, and our efforts to build democracies in both nations (which would ensure Shi'a predominance in Iraq), benefited Iran. Iran explicitly assisted U.S. efforts in Afghanistan and implicitly assisted them early on in Iraq. However, in both places Iran later began to support attacks on U.S. troops unprovoked. Especially in Iraq, Iran mounted a vast program of providing weapons, money, training, advice, and even operational planning to help indigenous groups kill American soldiers to try to drive the U.S. military out. This campaign preceded the new U.S. and UN sanctions on Iran related to its nuclear program, which did not begin until 2006. Nor did this campaign abate during the Obama administration's year-long effort to engage Iran in 2009, during which time no new sanctions were imposed on Iran.

Clearly it is not American behavior that generates Iran's objectionable actions. It is either the Iranian leadership's pathological perceptions of the United States or its own aggressive ambitions, neither of which appears to be affected by less threatening American behavior. There is no reason to believe that unilaterally moderating American actions toward Iran will produce a similar change from Tehran.

Contrary to the central logic of the engagement-only approach, the only times that Iran has signaled a willingness to repair relations with the United States have come when it felt most threatened by American actions.

- In 1995, when the United States was imposing, for the first time, comprehensive economic sanctions on Iran—and would go on to impose the first secondary sanctions on foreign firms doing significant business with the Iranian oil industry—President Rafsanjani signed a deal with the U.S. firm Conoco to develop a pair of Iranian offshore oilfields.[12] This bid was important for Rafsanjani (albeit, not necessarily for the rest of the Iranian regime) to improve relations. It came at a moment when the United States was ratcheting up pressure on Iran.[13]
- In 1997–2000, Iran's reformist president, Mohammad Khatami, made a sustained effort to begin a real rapprochement with the United States. Ultimately, Khatami failed because Iran's conservative establishment (led by Ayatollah Khamene'i himself) opposed him. Although Khatami's election reflected popular Iranian unhappiness with many aspects of the clerical regime's rule, one aspect of that unhappiness was displeasure with the deepening antagonism between Iran and the United States, which had resulted in comprehensive economic sanctions on Iran by the Clinton administration in 1995–97. This economic

displeasure was one reason that Khatami made such a determined effort to repair relations with the United States.[14]

- Briefly in 2003, the Iranians made a conciliatory gesture to the United States. In May a message was delivered via the Swiss Embassy purporting to be a "road map" of how Iran and the United States might reconcile. Although the provenance and importance of this gesture remain contested, it appears to have been—at the very least—an Iranian gambit to convince the United States not to invade Iran after the invasions of Afghanistan and Iraq. There is no question that the Iranian leadership feared that the United States would attack Iran next, and this anxiety prompted Tehran to agree to the most far-reaching concessions on its nuclear program that it ever made: suspending enrichment and signing the Additional Protocol of the NPT.[15] The May 2003 message to the United States was part of that effort, but it may also have been a bid by more moderate elements of the Iranian regime to try to start a wider rapprochement between the two countries (although this is far from proven).[16] In the words of the principal Iranian author of this missive, Ambassador to France Sadegh Kharrazi, "In 2003 there was a wall of mistrust between Iran and the U.S. and they could attack us at any moment. Therefore, the government accepted my suggestion and sent a conciliatory letter to the U.S. administration."[17] Likewise, Hamid Reza Taraghi, another important Iranian hardliner, has explained that "[a]fter 9/11 and its consequences, we were very worried and a group of the [Iranian Parliamentary] Deputies met with the Supreme leader and explained the root of their fear. We reached the conclusion that Iran was facing a real threat and we could be occupied as it happened in 1941. . . . We asked the Leader to be more moderate toward the U.S. He accepted our view and through the government and other officials, wisely and successfully managed that dangerous time."[18]

In 1995 and again in 1997–2000, the personality and policies of the Iranian presidents also played an important role in their efforts to reach out to the United States. Still, it seems more than coincidental that they made such far-reaching bids at a time when Iran had suddenly come under much greater American pressure. It is not necessarily that threatening American behavior is more likely to produce Iranian concessions, although this claim is consistent with the evidence. It is simply that, as a matter of evidence, Iran did not make its greatest concessions at times when the United States was trying to diminish its pressure and threats on Iran. Quite the contrary.

There are at least four other good reasons to set aside any consideration of pure engagement of Iran without sanctions. First, there is evidence that the sanctions have sparked a debate among the Iranian leadership, with more pragmatic figures arguing for making some concessions in return for a lifting of the sanctions. This debate is what the sanctions were intended to produce, and constitutes some evidence that they are having the desired effect. Second, whether they convince the Iranians to negotiate or not, the sanctions are critical to making clear to Iranians and other would-be proliferators that defying the international community comes at a price. Third, even if the sanctions do not cause Tehran to change its behavior, they are critical as a foundation to contain a nuclear Iran in the future.

The last reason that, wrong or right, it is not worthwhile to consider this option is that the sanctions on Iran are a reality. They are not going to be repealed short of a deal with Iran on its nuclear program. The U.S. Congress, the U.S. president, the European Union, and the UN Security Council will not do so. Period. Even if there were still reason to believe that engagement without sanctions, or penalties of any kind, might work better, it is not realistic to posit that as an option. We might as well argue that the best way to handle Iran's nuclear program would be to have never assisted in Mosaddeq's overthrow, but that too is a reality that cannot be undone merely by wishing it were so.

6

Bigger Carrots, Bigger Sticks

The obvious place to start to assess the options to prevent Iran from acquiring a nuclear weapons capability is with the policy in place. The United States settled on a carrot-and-stick strategy toward Iran after toying with others. None offered the same payoff of convincing Tehran to forgo its nuclear program at a reasonable cost to the United States with minimal risks. It is the "Goldilocks" solution: it fits just right for most Americans. It fits so well that it is hard to imagine that there was a time when its few advocates (including this author) were excoriated by both the left and the right. Many assume that it has been our policy all along.

The problem with this policy option, therefore, is not that it does not fit, but that it may not work. This idea may seem bizarre given how well the policy seems to be working. After all, as the Obama administration rightly argues, the United States has built an unprecedented international coalition of states all cooperating—to a greater or lesser extent—with this approach. That has led to unprecedented international and multilateral sanctions on Iran, which in turn has created unprecedented economic problems for the Islamic Republic. However, just because the policy has successfully attained these intermediate goals does not mean that it will succeed in achieving its ultimate objective.

As isolated and besieged as Iran may be, there is real reason to doubt that its government will make meaningful compromises on its nuclear program despite the painful impact of the sanctions. So far, Tehran has resisted, and while even some Iranian hardliners are suggesting at least a tactical retreat, the Supreme Leader has insisted that Iran will never give in. He believes the United States is only interested in the overthrow of his regime.[1] In his own words after talks with the IAEA collapsed in February 2012, "With God's help, and without paying attention to propaganda, Iran's nuclear course should continue firmly and seriously. Pressures, sanctions and assassinations will bear no fruit. No obstacles can stop Iran's nuclear work."[2]

Despite all of the tactical successes that the carrot-and-stick strategy has racked up so far, the realization of its strategic goal remains out of reach. Many people are beginning to ask what else the United States could do, and whether it is time to shift to more extreme measures, such as the use of force.

But before we conclude that the patient is dead, it is worth asking whether he can be resuscitated and reinvigorated. The carrot-and-stick strategy is perfectly tailored to America's needs when it comes to Iran. We should be loath to abandon it. That has been the conclusion of the Obama administration, and their initial response at the start of their second term was to ask if they could pursue the same policy but do it better, by doing it bigger: a renewed offer of engagement, a more enticing deal on Iran's nuclear program, and the threat of even harsher punishments if Iran remains recalcitrant. Once again, this policy is not stupid. Politically, it makes good sense, and from a strategic perspective, it would be ideal if Washington could pull it off. The only question is whether we can.[3]

The Theory of the Case

The carrot-and-stick approach, or what the Obama administration has called its "Dual Track" policy to Iran, relies on the debate within Iran over the relative importance of its nuclear program compared to the country's economic and political well-being.[4] On the one side of this debate are Iran's moderates, including figures such as former presidents 'Ali Akbar Rafsanjani and Khatami, and now President Rowhani; and on the other, radical hardliners such as Guardian Council head Mohammad Jannati and the leadership of the Revolutionary Guard. The moderates have argued that while it would be great for Iran to have a nuclear deterrent, the country's highest priority is its decrepit economy. They argue that the only way for the regime to maintain its control over the country is to rebuild its legitimacy, which in turn will require demonstrating to the Iranian people that they can deliver prosperity and good governance. Not surprisingly, the moderates have indicated a willingness to compromise on the nuclear program so as to rebuild Iran's ties to the global economy. For their part, the more ideologically minded hardliners have downplayed the importance of the economy and instead emphasized Iran's role as regional hegemon, spreading the Islamic Revolution, and their deep-seated fear that the United States is seeking to overturn the regime—all of which, in their minds, argue for the continuation of the nuclear program and even the acquisition of a nuclear deterrent.[5]

Poised at the fulcrum of this debate is the Supreme Leader, Ali Khamene'i. Khamene'i is unquestionably the deciding vote. The key assumption of this policy, and it is nothing but an unproven although not unreasonable assumption, is that even though Khamene'i has shown sympathy for the hardline position, he is capable of being swayed to side with the moderates. Thus, the idea is to design a comprehensive incentive structure that will convince Khamene'i and his closest advisors that Iran would be better off agreeing to compromise on the nuclear program. It is a strategy intended to help bolster the arguments of Tehran's moderates against those of its hardliners by reinforcing the formers' argument that

Iran will enjoy huge benefits for agreeing to compromise, and will suffer excessive harm by refusing.

The practical aspects of the strategy are meant to offer Iran a series of attractive rewards if it agrees to compromise and impose an ever more stringent string of punishments on Iran if it resists—hence a "carrot-and-stick" strategy. The "sticks" portion of the policy are well understood: they are the sanctions that have been imposed unilaterally by the United States, multilaterally by the West, and internationally by the UN Security Council since 2003. These sanctions have prohibited arms sales to Iran, severed its ties to the international financial system, choked off aid and foreign investment, and curtailed its oil exports and thus its government revenues. The "carrots" piece of the strategy is both less understood and less practiced. In theory, the carrots could have included not just the lifting of the sanctions, but economic assistance, an end to Iran's international isolation, and mechanisms to address Iran's legitimate security concerns. They could also include a comprehensive rapprochement with the United States.

Dual Track So Far

The carrot-and-stick approach became the guiding principle of America's Iran policy during the George W. Bush administration, albeit grudgingly. At first, the Bush administration did not have a defined Iran policy. In current American politics, it is often the case that one side or the other will dismiss its rivals' approach to an issue by claiming that they "don't have a policy." That is rarely the case, and what the partisans typically mean is that they don't like their rivals' policy on a given issue. However, in the early years of the Bush 43 administration, for Iran this lack of a policy was literally true. The administration was divided between its neoconservative wing, which wanted to overthrow the Iranian regime—either militarily as they had done with the Taliban and Saddam Husayn, or by an aggressive covert action campaign—and its realist wing, which had no interest in taking on another challenge beyond Afghanistan and

Iraq. Moreover, none of these courses of action seemed simple, easy, or even plausible given the complexities of Iranian politics. Consequently, they relegated Iran to the "too hard box."

Not surprisingly, the Bush administration's early moves toward Iran were often contradictory. They accepted covert Iranian help against the Taliban and al-Qa'ida after the 9/11 attacks, but then President Bush named Iran as part of the infamous "Axis of Evil" in his 2002 State of the Union address. Many of his neoconservative underlings even mused indiscreetly about bringing regime change to Tehran after Kabul and Baghdad.

Only after the surprising progress of Iran's nuclear program was revealed in 2002–2004 did Washington adopt a deliberate approach to Tehran. When it did, it chose a version of the carrot-and-stick, albeit one much heavier on the stick than the carrot, in keeping with the administration's conservative proclivities. Nevertheless, the U.S. officials charged with implementing the administration's policy of diplomatic pressure on Iran played a weak hand well. Despite the constraints placed on them—particularly their inability to offer significant positive incentives to Iran or to other key international actors to secure their cooperation—they devised novel financial sanctions that caused real pain in Tehran and convinced reluctant foreign governments to apply ever greater pressure, including six UN Security Council resolutions enacted under Chapter VII of the UN Charter.

OBAMA TAKES OVER. When the Obama administration took office in January 2009, they too adopted a carrot-and-stick approach, but they did so readily, even eagerly. In unsurprising contrast with their predecessors, the new administration initially favored the carrots over the sticks.

It seems that engagement was President Obama's preferred approach toward Iran. He raised the idea during the election campaign, and his Democratic and Republican rivals alike lambasted him for it.[6] When Obama took office, he embraced engagement as the principal focus of his Iran policy, although he also made clear that his policy was one of carrot-and-stick and that he would turn to sanctions and other forms of punishment if Tehran proved uninterested in his offers of engagement. He spoke of establishing direct discussions with the Iranian government, stressed that he wanted a relationship of mutual respect, and offered to renounce any efforts to overturn the Iranian regime.[7] He wrote two private letters to Khamene'i offering a sincere effort at reconciliation and indicating he had no goal to overthrow the Iranian government.[8] He offered to open an American interests section (a small diplomatic mission, much smaller than a full embassy and without an ambassador) in Tehran as a tangible sign of the administration's determination to repair relations with Iran. He offered conciliatory gestures to Tehran, including calling the regime by its preferred name—something no American president had done before—and broadcast them on all channels, in public and in private, and through a wide variety of interlocutors.[9] As late as the fall and winter of 2012, Washington was still sending private messages to Iran that it wanted direct talks to try to resolve the nuclear impasse and begin a process of more general reconciliation.[10] After Obama's reelection in November 2012, Washington again reached out to Tehran and offered to resume the nuclear talks.[11]

There are those who argue that the Obama administration's effort at engagement was only a brief, halfhearted flirtation. My friend Trita Parsi has disparaged Obama's approach to engagement with Iran as "a single roll of the dice."[12] While I respect Trita's erudition, I disagree with his characterization of the administration's thinking and its conduct.[13] My own experience of their approach was that they were sincere in their desire to secure a rapprochement with Iran and sustained this effort for at least a year before refocusing on sanctions. I saw this determination time and again in my own conversations and arguments with senior Obama administration officials, certainly throughout 2009, but well after then, too.

In fact, during the second half of 2009, after Iran's disputed presidential election in June, the birth of the Green Movement and its brutal suppression by the regime in the summer of that year and on into the fall, the Obama administration was noticeably (even reprehensibly) quiet about Tehran's gross violations of human rights. As many commentators observed, the administration barely condemned the events there, and was criticized by conservative Americans, liberal Europeans, human rights groups, and Iranian opposition figures for its silence. This reticence was not accidental but deliberate. As senior administration officials explained, they believed that they had to convince the Iranian regime that the United States was not trying to overthrow them if they were going to get Iran to accept the offer of engagement and agree to a deal on the nuclear program. They said that they felt bad for Iranian oppositionists being killed, tortured, and imprisoned by the regime, but they were not going to make a bunch of "empty statements" condemning the human rights abuses and so jeopardize engagement and a deal on the nuclear issue.[14] As Karim Sadjadpour and others have pointed out, Iranians recognized this American choice, too; many in the Iranian opposition were "concerned that the U.S. has focused far too much on the nuclear issue and far too little about their plight."[15] The administration was so intent on securing a nuclear deal that they were willing to condone the regime's brutality to get it.

In the spring of 2010 I traveled to Beijing to meet with a range of Chinese officials to discuss Iran. What I found most striking about these conversations was that, unprompted, many of the officials I met with volunteered that they felt that the Obama administration had "done everything that Iran needed if it wanted a rapprochement" with the United States.[16] Several of them pointed out that, given China's own history of having engaged in the difficult process of rapprochement with the United States in the 1960s and '70s, they knew what a genuine change looked like and what each side needed to make it work. They believed that the Obama administration was sincere and had done what was necessary if Iran were interested. They indicated then that if Iran were not willing to accept the American offer, Beijing would take this recalcitrance as a sign that Iran was not sincere and so China would join the West in imposing heavy sanctions on Iran through the UN Security Council. Less than two months later, Beijing made good on that threat, stunning the Iranians by voting in favor of UNSC Resolution 1929, which banned all weapons sales to Tehran and enabled the financial and oil sanctions on Iran that have proven so crippling to the Iranian economy. It had been assumed that Beijing would continue to oppose sanctions on Iran on principle, because China has extensive trade with Iran and because the Chinese government feared giving the United States a precedent to go to war with Iran as it had done with Iraq. China's decision to support Resolution 1929 demonstrated which party the Chinese felt was trying to resolve the impasse, and which was not.[17]

FROM ENGAGEMENT TO SANCTIONS. In late 2009, the Obama administration all but gave up on its initial bid at reconciliation with Tehran. It remains official U.S. policy that Washington will begin direct talks with Tehran aimed at resolving the nuclear impasse and, in the longer run, restoring good relations between Iran and America. Obama administration officials continue to indicate that this preference is real. But the events of the fall of 2009 convinced American officials that neither a resolution nor a rapprochement was likely, at least not in the short term, and not until Tehran became convinced that its stubbornness would prove costly.

In October of that year, representatives of the P-5+1 countries (the five permanent members of the UN Security council—the United States, Britain, France, Russia, and China—along with Germany) met with Iranian officials first in Geneva and then later in Vienna. The P-5+1 proposed a confidence-building agreement in which Iran would agree to ship out 80 percent of its stockpile of LEU. In return Iran would receive processed uranium in the form needed to produce medical isotopes by the Tehran Research Reactor (TRR). At that time, Iran was claiming that it needed the LEU to fabricate new plates to refuel the TRR, while the rest of the world feared that Iran would take its stockpile of LEU (which was approaching the amount needed for a single nuclear weapon) and begin enriching it to bomb-grade purity for use in a weapon. Thus, the deal would allay international concerns and meet Iran's ostensible desire to refuel the TRR. In Vienna, the Iranian representative, Saeed Jalili, agreed. But when he reported back to Tehran, his superiors quashed the deal. The TRR proposal appeared to the international community to be a "no-brainer." If Iran was just interested in civilian uses, why not ship out the LEU in return for fuel for the TRR, which would be difficult to enrich to bomb grade? Tehran's refusal convinced Washington and its international partners that Iran was not looking for civilian uses.[18]

The Iranians claimed, both at the time and since, that they turned down the TRR deal because they did not trust the international community to make good on its pledge to provide Iran with the uranium assemblies for the TRR. In the past, both Germany and France have reneged on nuclear agreements with Iran for diplomatic and security reasons, so Iran does have reason to fear depending on the West for its nuclear needs. Others have opined that Iran's refusal said less about the intentions of its nuclear program and more about the Supreme Leader's paranoid obsession with the United States, to the extent that any deal that the United States favors must, ipso facto, be bad for Iran—even if he may not be able to see how it would be.[19] Along these lines, in the summer of 2010, after the passage of Resolution 1929, Khamene'i dismissed a deal with the United States by declaring, "The change of behavior they want—and which they don't always emphasize—is in fact a negation of our identity. . . . Ours is a fundamental antagonism."[20] Indeed, Iran later accepted a very similar proposal worked out by Brazilian president Luiz Inácio Lula da Silva and Turkish prime minister Recep Tayyip Erdogan, but the West rejected that deal, both because by then Iran's stockpile of LEU had grown to the point that the amount to be shipped out represented barely half of the Iranian stock, and because the P-5+1 concluded that this was merely a desperate bid by Iran to avoid the impending blow of UNSC Resolution 1929, the most powerful sanctions resolution measure imposed on Iran, and a direct response to Iran's intransigence both in refusing Obama's offers of reconciliation and the TRR deal.[21]

In response, the administration shifted its energy, attention, and diplomatic efforts to the sanctions track. Here they excelled. In large part because so many countries around the world were convinced by the sincerity of their peaceful overtures to Tehran, the administration found widespread support for adopting harsh new sanctions on Iran. Moreover, the administration proved deft in its approaches to countries such as China, Russia, India, and Japan, all of which had voiced their opposition to Iran's nuclear program in the past but had done little about it—at least in part because they did not trust the intentions of the Bush 43 administration. Likewise, Obama's diplomats convinced the Saudis and other Gulf Arabs to use their economic clout in support of the case for sanctions against Iran in ways that no other administration had ever been able to do.[22] As a result, by the summer of 2012, Washington could boast of having put together an unprecedented coalition of states determined to put pressure on Iran, which in turn produced unprecedented levels of international sanctions on the Islamic Republic.

It was a remarkable diplomatic performance. Of course, Washington did not do it all on its own. It had help from a number of other countries, including France, Britain, Germany, Canada, the UAE, Saudi Arabia, Denmark, and Israel, to name the most active. Three of these deserve fuller mention. For decades, the United States and the Kingdom of Saudi Arabia have shared a close strategic relationship, agreeing on nearly everything—at least everything big—under the Middle Eastern sky. However, it has been a constant frustration of American diplomats that the Saudis rarely do anything to advance our common strategic purposes. Typically, Washington and Riyadh agree on what needs to be done, and then the Saudis leave it to the United States to do it. It was a constant source of frustration throughout the 1990s, whether the matter was Iran or Iraq or forging an Arab-Israeli peace. Not so this time around. This time the Saudis came through big. They went to the Chinese and guaranteed Beijing that they (and the Kuwaitis and Emiratis) would see to all of China's oil needs if the Chinese joined the sanctions on Iran—a major source of Chinese oil.[23] It proved to be a key piece of the international diplomatic effort against Iran.

The second diplomatic key was Israel. Since 2002 the Israelis have been panicked about the Iranian nuclear program. Every few months Jerusalem, particularly in the figure of Prime Minister Benjamin Netanyahu, has gone on a media rampage, decrying the Iranian nuclear program as the four horsemen of the apocalypse rolled into one. The Israelis, and Netanyahu in particular, have been reproached for "crying wolf" over the Iranian nuclear program by many, and accused of worse by some. Many Americans, Europeans, and others find Israel's endless warnings annoying, frustrating, even maddening. Even some of the most perspicacious now blame Israel itself for the problems, accusing Jerusalem of having engineered and "distorted" American policy on Iran. But had it not been for the Israelis' beating the Iran drum, the world—and probably the United States—would have forgotten about the Iranian nuclear program long ago. Most countries did not care, and for much of the past ten years, the United States wanted to focus its attention on other matters, whether that was Iraq under Bush 43 or domestic priorities under Obama. Moreover, much of the willingness of European and East Asian nations to take unprecedented steps and impose unprecedented sanctions on Iran was driven by their fear that if the Israelis did not see other countries doing everything they could to stop Iran's program peacefully, then Jerusalem would try to do it militarily and the result would be a catastrophic war across the Middle East. Had it not been for the Israelis' repeatedly sounding the alarm, enraging though that may have been, the Iranians probably would have crossed the nuclear threshold long ago.

As important as the Israelis were in rousing many European states to action, there was one that moved on its own and played a critical role by doing so: France. Since the 1960s, France has insisted on pursuing an independent foreign policy, even withdrawing its military forces from the common NATO framework at the height of the Cold War. In so doing, Paris became the darling of the Third World and the bête noire of Foggy Bottom. I am not going to defend French foreign policy for those long decades (the French drove me to madness with their coddling of Saddam Husayn when I worked in the U.S. government). However, in spite of that—or perhaps because of it—no one has played a more helpful role on

Iran than France. Early on, the French government under Jacques Chirac, but continuing through the administrations of Nicolas Sarkozy and François Hollande, applied a principled nonproliferation stance to Iran's nuclear program. Paris decided that Iran could not be allowed to have nuclear weapons or even the latent capability to make them and there could be no exceptions to this position. Since then, France has been the staunchest member of the anti-Iranian coalition, taking the hardest line in negotiations. It has been France, not Britain, that has demanded that Washington not "go wobbly" on the Iranians. Moreover, the French have proven themselves creative, flexible, and adroit in their diplomacy. By consistently taking much harder-line positions than those of the United States, they have been invaluable in allowing Washington to look moderate on Iran. In many ways, France has been spending all of the diplomatic capital it saved up from five-plus decades of thumbing its nose at the United States, and the United States and many other countries have been the beneficiaries. For numerous governments, the fact that France has been taking a harder line on Iran than the Americans has brought them around to the view that it must be right to follow Washington's more reasonable lead. It is hard to know just how many countries lined up with the West because of French exertions and Paris's principled stance, but it was no small number.

THE SANCTIONS. As a result of all of this diplomatic energy to make Tehran pay a price for its noncompliance with the binding resolutions of the UN Security Council, a range of powerful sanctions now hobbles Iran. While a complete list would require more space to enumerate than it would be worth, even a summary of these restrictions is daunting:

- The UN Security Council has banned the supply of all materials and technology related to ballistic missiles, nuclear energy, or nuclear weapons to Iran. It has banned the export of all major weapons systems (tanks, warplanes, helicopters, artillery pieces) to Iran. It has frozen the assets of key individuals associated with Iran's nuclear program and prohibited their travel abroad. It has banned all financial ties or the provision of financial services to a list of Iranian entities involved in Iran's nuclear program, including Iran's Central Bank and other major financial institutions. As a specified element of the ban on financial transactions, it has prohibited insurance companies from providing insurance or reinsurance to Iranian ships—another major hindrance to Iranian oil exports. It has frozen the assets and prohibited all interaction with a number of designated Iranian entities associated with its nuclear program.

- For the United States, a number of laws and executive orders dating back to the Bush 43, Clinton, and earlier administrations bans virtually all U.S. economic interactions with Iran. Americans may only export food, medicine, and a short list of other humanitarian goods to Iran. In effect, all imports from Iran, all financial transactions, all services, and all investments in Iran are prohibited.[24]

- Another series of U.S. laws and executive orders imposes secondary sanctions on third parties conducting business with Iran related to the Iranian hydrocarbons industry or its financial sector, buying Iranian petroleum products, providing sensitive technologies, transferring currency to Iran in payment for Iranian goods, or conducting financial transactions with Iran related to entities involved with Iran's nuclear program (and, in some cases, terrorism and human rights violations). Several of these regulations impose penalties on foreign entities that have commercial contact with designated Iranian individuals and entities connected to the Iranian nuclear program, support for terrorism, or human rights violations.[25]

- The European Union (EU) has imposed an embargo on Iranian oil purchases, frozen the assets of Iran's Central Bank, and restricted its trade and the provision of financial services, insurance and reinsurance, and technology to Iran.[26]

- Canada, Australia, Japan, South Korea, India, Switzerland, and other countries have adopted a range of lesser sanctions in addition to those imposed by the UN.

- The Society for Worldwide Interbank Financial Telecommunication (SWIFT), the international financial transaction web, has disconnected all of Iran's major banks—including its Central Bank—from its network, further attenuating Iran's financial ties to the global economy.[27]

THE MISSING CARROT. As skillfully as the Obama administration has engineered the imposition of crippling sanctions on Iran, its handling of the Dual Track approach has not been flawless. While I disagree with many of the administration's critics on the left about Washington's sincerity or determination to pursue engagement with Tehran, I agree that what has been offered to the Iranians has been sorely lacking.

The administration's thinking appears to have been that it would offer Iran a genuine process of reconciliation, and as part of that process Iran would agree to give up or curb significantly its nuclear program. Meanwhile, the United States would dismantle its sanctions apparatus and the result would be normal economic and diplomatic relations between America and Iran that would, in and of themselves, be highly beneficial to Iran. Later, after the administration shifted to the sanctions track, the principal carrot became the lifting of sanctions—or even just the promise that no new sanctions would be imposed. In other words, the "carrot" was that we would stop beating them with the stick.

Since we don't know why Iran has not responded either to Obama's effort at engagement or to the impact of the sanctions, we cannot know for certain whether the absence of meaningful carrots beyond the offer of engagement was part of the problem. But there is reason to believe that it might have been. The Iranian economist Bijan Khajehpour warns that most Iranians believe that the sanctions are entirely punitive because they do not see any carrots—any incentives to change their behavior. He warns that this plays into the regime's narrative that the West just wants to hold Iran back.[28] For his part, because Khamene'i fears and loathes the United States—and has repeatedly said that he sees engagement with the United States not as a benefit to Iran, but as a subversive ploy intended to undermine the Islamic Revolution—offering him specific incentives tied to specific Iranian actions on the nuclear track might have worked better. For instance, Khamene'i might have been more comfortable agreeing to a specific limit on the Iranian program, such as halting enrichment beyond 5 percent, in return for a similarly specific offer from the other side, such as an international agreement to subsidize the construction of nuclear power plants in Iran.

We cannot know if a more concrete, tit-for-tat approach to compromise would have succeeded where the nebulous offer of "engagement" failed, but it could not have hurt and there is evidence to suggest that it might have worked. After Iran rejected the 2009 TRR deal in Vienna, Tehran floated a number of compromise positions that posed a more sequenced process in which Iran would receive incremental returns for making equivalent concessions, rather than the original proposal, which would have required Iran to ship all of the LEU up front. Thus, as well as the Obama administration has managed the carrot-and-stick, or Dual Track, policy so far, there is still room for improvement. A revised policy, especially one that featured more discrete and tangible benefits for Iran in response to specific concessions, might do better the next time.

The Impact of Sanctions

Since engagement did not succeed and few other carrots were on offer, the ultimate verdict on the first four years of the Obama administration's Iran policy must rest on the impact of the sanctions on Iran. The evidence that sanctions are having a pronounced impact is extensive.[29] As early as December 2010, Iran decided to cut the subsidies on fuel prices they provided the Iranian people, in part to deal with the economic pressure from the first rounds of sanctions. The decision caused prices to quadruple overnight. Iranians protested in the streets, forcing the regime to deploy its Law Enforcement Forces to keep order.[30] The EU prohibition on purchasing Iranian oil—coupled with American and European efforts to convince China, India, Japan, South Korea, and other countries to reduce their own imports of Iranian oil—have had an even more profound effect. Together, these efforts more than halved Iranian oil exports, falling from 2.3 million barrels per day on average in 2011, to just 1.1 million barrels per day on average in 2012.[31] By early 2013, these cuts were costing Tehran $4–8 billion per month in lost oil revenues.[32] By the fall of 2012, Iran's currency, the rial, had plunged to 35,000 to the dollar—a 300 percent drop from December 2011.[33] In that same period, unemployment ballooned by 36 percent and prices rose 87–112 percent.[34] By September 2012, inflation had reached 50 percent, and Iranians feared the situation would worsen. "Everyone from the butcher to the industrialist will say that beneath the surface they are months from economic collapse," one Iranian told a *Time* magazine journalist at that time. Another confessed that while she believed that Iran should have nuclear weapons, it was not worth the hardships caused by the sanctions.[35] Crime, corruption, and smuggling are about the only things thriving in Iran.[36]

Iran's economic difficulties produced a renewed debate among its leadership. Moderates and pragmatists, banished from the center of power but still with access to media outlets, renewed their calls to negotiate with the West over the nuclear program to get the sanctions lifted.[37] Likewise, during the late summer of 2012, Iran converted some of its 19.75 percent enriched uranium to assemblies for the Tehran Research Reactor (making it difficult to use the same uranium for a weapon), which many in the West saw as an Iranian gesture of goodwill.[38]

Of far greater interest, however, were signs that even some of the regime's core supporters, the hardline elements, were beginning to entertain the notion that Tehran should make some compromises to ease the sanctions burden. In December 2012, Khamene'i's principal mouthpiece, the newspaper *Kayhan,* published a remarkable article titled "Worn-out Revolutionaries and the Conspiracy of the Poisoned Chalice." The title alludes to Khomeini's speech at the end of the Iran-Iraq War in which he said that he would accept a cease-fire with Iraq even though it was more bitter to him than drinking a cup of poison. In the hardline version of history, it was Rafsanjani and other moderates who pushed Khomeini to do so. In this case, the *Kayhan* piece admitted that there were numerous voices agitating for compromise with the West, although it mocked them as the "regretful, worn-out" revolutionaries, who have "always adopted a pragmatic, tolerant strategy and mild-mannered approach which is in pursuit of amicable relations with the enemies of the revolution."[39] Days later, Iran's foreign minister, Ali Akbar Salehi, also stated that both Iran and the international community "have reached a conclusion that they must exit the current stalemate."[40] These comments struck many outside observers as signs that key elements within the regime were now advocating a settlement of the nuclear issue to get the sanctions lifted.

However, as always in Iran, nothing is that simple. First, it is not clear that the sanctions will cause the Iranian economy to "collapse," whatever that may mean, or even that the stress that they can apply will be enough to force the regime to change. Mohammad Ali Shabani, an Iranian political analyst, summed up the situation as, "If you're talking about collapse, that is not happening."[41] Although inflation is bad, Tehran has so far avoided any balance-of-payments crisis. The loss of Western trading partners has opened the door to Chinese firms, such that Sino-Iranian trade has gone from just $3 billion in 2002 to more than $44 billion in 2011.[42] In February 2013, the *New York Times* reported from Tehran, "The sanctions, while the source of constant complaint and morbid jokes, have not set off price riots or serious opposition to the Iranian government. In fact, the past year has not been all that bad." The *Times* quoted Saeed Ranchian, a Tehran shopkeeper, who observed that given Iran's currency predicament, "you would expect people to buy less. But in Iran, when prices go up, people start buying more, fearing even higher prices . . . [the country's economy] has rules that no one understands."[43]

Even at its current, greatly reduced level of sales, Iran was estimated to have made roughly $45 billion in oil revenues in 2012, still twice what it earned in 2000, and just shy of the $49 billion Iran needed to cover its latest government budget.[44] Historically, Iran has gone long periods without exporting significant oil when it felt it necessary for national purposes. In 1979–81, Iranian oil exports fell by 80 percent as a result of the hostage crisis, the Iranian Revolution, and the Iran-Iraq War, but Tehran did not shift course.[45] Likewise, in 1951–53, when the Iranian government under Mohammad Mosaddeq fought the British over the nationalization of the Anglo-Iranian Oil Company (today's BP), Iran could not export any oil, yet did not change its policy until the government was overthrown.[46] In 2012, when the oil sanctions began to take effect, Iran had at least $70 billion in hard currency reserves and the regime was making money by playing the currency market. In a way that only he could, Iranian president Mahmud Ahmadinejad claimed in October 2012, at the height of the panic over sanctions, that the Iranian people were better off economically than they had been when he came to office.[47] While that claim may be hard to justify, it is certainly the case that many of Tehran's most powerful have not only survived, but in fact have thrived on the sanctions. Indeed, those lobbying the regime about the sanctions are more often pressing it to reform its economic policies than its nuclear policies.[48]

True experts on the Iranian economy have long urged caution about the impact of the sanctions. Bijan Khajehpour notes that even with oil exports having dropped to roughly 1 million barrels per day from sanctions, the per capita income Iran gets from crude is only down to about $750 per year, still above the historical average of the Islamic Republic.[49] Djavad Salehi-Isfahani likewise warns that the structure of the Iranian economy—in which the regime controls nearly all foreign exchange—diminishes the impact of the devaluation of the rial. He notes that the government protects the cost of essential items, which matter most to lower-class Iranians, the principal supporters of the regime. Middle-class Iranians, who rely more on the black market for luxury goods and have savings that are getting diminished (or wiped out), are the ones getting hurt. That is not good for the regime, but neither is it disastrous. As Salehi-Isfahani has put it, "Does all this mean that Iran's economy is on the verge of collapse, as Israel's Finance Minster reportedly said? The answer is no, because most of the economy is shielded from this exchange rate, though not from the ill effects of the sanctions, which will continue to bite for a while. Would it cause sufficient economic pain that would push the Iranian government to make concessions in its nuclear standoff with the West? The answer is not likely. The multiple exchange rate system, as inefficient as it is, will protect the people below the median income, to whom the Ahmadinejad government is most responsive." [50]

My Brookings colleague Suzanne Maloney, one of the finest scholars of Iranian political economy, echoes these warnings in a conclusion worth quoting at some length:

> With $70–100 billion in reserves, a diversified economy, and well-honed capabilities for smuggling, sanctions-busting, and insulating the regime from sanctions, Iran may well be able to ride out this pressure for the short-term and even beyond. The outcome is more likely to be the corrosion of the economy, rather than its outright collapse. Of course, what really matters is the psychological impact—both on the population and on the leadership. Panic is fueling the run on the black market, and if the sense that things are spinning out of control intensifies, all bets are off. And while the economic catastrophe and popular dissatisfaction add urgency for Tehran to find some accommodation on its nuclear ambitions, it seems unlikely that they would produce a dramatic or immediate about-face. The regime has every reason to fear economic pressure and the nascent backlash within society—but the deep mistrust of Washington's intentions and its conviction that its adversaries at home and abroad will exploit any concession as a sign of weakness almost surely outweighs any pragmatic impulses. They know that their repressive instruments are plenty capable of managing the home front. [51]

Perhaps of greatest importance, there is no sign that the Supreme Leader has changed his mind about negotiations with the West. Khamene'i has consistently and publicly indicated that the sanctions will never change his mind about the nuclear program. At the darkest hour, when the rial was collapsing in the fall of 2012, Khamene'i announced that Iran would not change its course. He dismissed the currency slide as the mistakes of Iranian bureaucrats, and told the West that their economic problems were far worse than Iran's: "The West's economy is frozen. You are worse off and you are moving towards collapse and recession. These problems cannot bring the Islamic Republic to its knees."[52] In early 2013 he ruled out direct talks with the United States to end the impasse, saying, "Talks will not solve any problems. . . . You are holding a gun against Iran saying, 'Talks or you'll fire.' The Iranian nation will not be frightened by such threats."[53] Echoing the Supreme Leader's position, President Ahmadinejad warned the West, "You think that by resorting to oil and currency issues, you are able to press the Iranian nation and stop it from its path? You are wrong. Maybe this works like a quick tap on the brakes in driving, but the Iranian nation will find its way quickly and will continue."[54]

In all of the hubbub over the December 2012 *Kayhan* piece, what seems to have been overlooked is that the article's principal point was that the Supreme Leader (as well as *Kayhan*) was uninterested in compromise. It notes that the moderate position has been opposed by "a hardened, uncompromising, combater of Arrogance [i.e., Western/U.S. hegemony] that is demanding perpetual resistance against the West and endurance against the pressure of sanctions. *This is the current backed by the Supreme Leader*" (emphasis added). It argued:

> Sanctions are the subterfuge of the worn out revolutionaries to prevail on society and the Supreme Leader to accept their beliefs. By exaggerating the effects of American and European Union financial and economic sanctions, they constantly emphasize this point that the pressure of the superpowers has reached intolerable levels and they can't be resisted any longer. . . . It seems that the worn out revolutionaries at this sensitive point have the intention with their engineered targeting of the conditions of country and application of pressure from all directions to the Supreme Leader, to force him of his own volition to drink the poisoned chalice and retreat; withdrawing from revolutionary positions and [thus initiate] negotiations with America. . . . They want to inflame and make insecure the political atmosphere by offering incorrect analyses and relating all the problems to foreign sanctions and thereby provoke public emotions, so

that the Leader has no other choice but to submit to their demands for the preservation of the interests of the country and the revolution.[55]

None of this writing reads much like the words of a leader ready to make an about-face. Seyed Hossein Mousavian, a former Iranian ambassador and member of its Supreme National Security Council, explains that Khamene'i's "mind-set is that under threat and pressure, to show flexibility or compromise would be seen as weakness. Therefore under such conditions, he consolidates and hardens his position. This is critical in understanding the position of Iran on nuclear negotiations."[56] Khamene'i and the hardliners have always emphasized Iran's willingness to sacrifice to achieve its paramount goals.[57] Moreover, Iran's hardliners have argued that the experience of both Pakistan and North Korea shows that the West may try to pressure Iran to desist before it has acquired nuclear weapons, but once it crosses the nuclear threshold, the West will be forced to accept reality and lift the sanctions.[58]

Iranian officials can also point to signs that the sanctions are already beginning to erode.[59] In December 2012, South Korea—which had been the first Asian nation to cut Iranian oil purchases—resumed its import of Iranian crude, along with Taiwan. Likewise, Japan offered to cover the insurance for Iranian oil shipments, skirting the EU ban on maritime insurance for Iran.[60] India too is setting up a fund to back local insurers that import Iranian oil.[61] Iran also found creative ways to get around the sanctions to export its oil. During the summer of 2012, Iranian oil exports had dipped to an average of just 400,000 tons per month, but were up to nearly 650,000 tons per month during the fall.[62] During the first quarter of 2013, Iranian fuel oil exports rose a further 12 percent over the last quarter of 2012.[63] Meanwhile, Russia and China have been lukewarm to the idea of further pressure on Iran, and in October 2012, Russian deputy foreign minister Gennady Gatilov stated, "Any additional sanctions against Iran would be perceived by the international community as an instrument for regime change in Tehran."[64] All of this hesitation may help bolster Khamene'i in his beliefs that Iran can withstand the sanctions, and that it must do so, lest it fall to the nefarious plots that he assumes the United States is spinning to subvert the Islamic Republic.

Trying Again—Bigger Carrots

All things considered, it seems unlikely that the status quo will produce the outcome that we desire. Still, the current policy has produced many positive developments for the United States, from the unification of the international community around sanctions to placing enormous pressure on the Iranian regime by means of those sanctions. For that reason, the first possibility we ought to consider in terms of a new Iran policy that can move beyond the status quo is whether it is feasible to take the current policy and enhance it. If it is pursued with more vigor and more resources, will it achieve our goal? Given how far the current policy has already taken us, why not see if we can tweak it in the hope that it can get us the rest of the way to our goal?

As in 2009, when the Obama administration first took office, a revamped carrot-and-stick approach should start with a new offer of reconciliation to the Iranians. The second Obama administration has already done that. This is important because the only way that this policy will succeed is if we can convince the Iranians that we are serious about finding a negotiated solution. The United States will have to persuade Tehran, and specifically Khamene'i, that we will take "yes" for an answer from them. That means that if Iran agrees to make the kinds of extensive concessions on its nuclear program that the United States seeks (and quite likely, similar compromises on terrorism and Iran's other mischief-making in the Middle East), the United States and the wider international community will end their efforts to isolate and punish Iran.

However, it is important to understand that the process of reconciliation and engagement will almost certainly not be enough to convince Tehran to change its behavior. It simply hasn't worked so far: not with Obama, not with Clinton, not with Bush 41, not with Reagan. Every time that the United States has made a good-faith offer of reconciliation with

Iran and promised to lift the extant sanctions, it has failed to move Tehran. The Iranian leadership does not seem to believe that it needs a better relationship with the United States and its allies, and Iranian hardliners fear that such a process would be a cover for America to undermine and overthrow the Islamic regime. In Karim Sadjadpour's words, "For Khamene'i, the carrots *are* the sticks." This is why the Obama administration's offer of engagement had no impact on Tehran, and why a new effort needs to go well beyond it.

If a renewed effort to make this policy work is to succeed where it has failed in the past, it will need to go further than what was tried in the past. That does not mean abandoning the offer of engagement—quite the contrary. The United States should continue to hold out the prospect of a normal, peaceful relationship as our preferred end state. However, Washington will have to go well beyond the vague offer of an eventual rapprochement and put a more attractive and tangible set of benefits for Iran on the table than successive American administrations have so far been willing to do. It will mean offering Iran concrete benefits tied to specific Iranian actions that could be taken in an incremental and reciprocal fashion. We do something that the Iranians want in return for their doing something that we want. The specific incentives would need to be determined through a process of negotiation with both Iran and America's allies. In many cases, they are likely to be complex. However, most will probably fall into four broad categories: nuclear energy and technology, economic inducements, security guarantees, and political incentives.

NUCLEAR ENERGY AND TECHNOLOGY. This set of incentives is complicated. Let's start with the easy part. On the nuclear front, previous offers during the Bush 43 administration included attractive terms to allow Iran to build light-water reactors to generate power and arrangements for Iran to participate in an international program to master enrichment technology. Light-water reactors can be more easily monitored, are harder to convert to military purposes, and spent fuel would be returned by arrangement to the providing country so that it could not be employed for bomb making. Since Iran has insisted that it wants only technology and energy from its nuclear program, Tehran would have to be offered this opportunity regardless of whether its claims are genuine.

What will be far harder for many Americans and other Westerners to accept is that, as part of any negotiated resolution with Iran, *we are going to have to make concessions regarding the Iranian uranium enrichment program.* It is true that there is no good reason why Iran should need this capability. Iran's intent in acquiring it is almost certainly to create a breakout capability, if not to build a nuclear arsenal itself. But given how much the Iranians have invested in their nuclear program, how much progress they have already made, how committed to it they have become, and how much pain they have endured to hang on to it, it is simply not plausible that they will agree to do away with it altogether. Even the Israelis understand this, with former Israeli Defense Intelligence chief Amos Yadlin and Yoel Guzansky acknowledging that, "(in) any possible deal between the international community and Iran, Iran will be granted legitimacy for enriching uranium."[65] No less an Iran hawk than former defense minister and prime minister Ehud Barak has indicated that he is ready to accept ongoing Iranian enrichment and even possession of a small stockpile—but only up to 3.5 percent purity.[66] If we are going to find a negotiated settlement to the current impasse, we are going to have to allow the Iranians to retain certain aspects of their current nuclear program. The key is which aspects.

At this point, we cannot say with certainty that the Iranian hardline leadership is ready to accept any limits on the Iranian nuclear program. A number of Iranian officials have suggested that Tehran would be willing to agree not to enrich any more uranium to 19.75 percent purity (often rounded up to "20 percent"). In October 2012, Foreign Ministry spokesman Ramin Mehmanparast said, "If a guarantee is provided to supply the 20 percent (enriched) fuel for the Tehran Research Reactor, our officials are ready to enter talks about 20 percent enrichment."[67] A day later, Foreign Minister Salehi confirmed this intent, announcing, "If our right to enrichment is recognized, we are prepared to offer an exchange. We would voluntarily limit the extent of our enrichment program, but in return we would need a guaranteed supply of the relevant fuels from abroad."[68]

These statements suggest several things. First, they imply that the Iranians may be willing to accept some limits on their nuclear program, although just because the foreign minister said they are willing to accept limits does not mean that they are. Second, they indicate that Iran may be willing to agree to limits on the purity to which they are allowed to enrich uranium. While that is not meaningless, it is not as generous as it sounds because the number and quality of centrifuges that Iran retains is as important in establishing a breakout capability as the quality of the LEU it retains. That is why any deal with Iran should also include limits on the numbers of centrifuges Iran is allowed to retain, if not the quality of those centrifuges as well.

However, these statements also reinforce Tehran's constant refrain that it will never agree to give up all enrichment, and must be allowed to continue to enrich uranium to lower levels of purity. That being the case, *any negotiated settlement with Iran is going to leave Tehran with some breakout capability*. As long as Iran is left with the capacity to enrich uranium, the right to perform some enrichment activity, and a stockpile of LEU—all of which the Iranians have stated over and over again are the bare minimum that they would accept—then Iran will have a breakout capability. It could be a breakout window as wide as many months, perhaps even a year, but Iran *will* have the capability to manufacture the fissile material for a nuclear weapon. Unfortunately, at this point in time, that is the best we are going to get. If we are not willing to agree to a deal with Iran that leaves them with such a relatively long-term breakout capability, then there is no point pursuing a carrot-and-stick approach, the ultimate goal of which is to conclude just such a deal.

Because any plausible deal with Iran will leave Tehran with some kind of a breakout capability, even a distant one, it must also include provisions for an intrusive inspections and monitoring regime, to detect any covert Iranian efforts to evade the terms of the deal, and provide ample warning if Iran decides to break out.[69] On this score, there is also some reason for optimism. In 2003 Iran agreed to the Additional Protocol of the NPT, which provides for no-notice, surprise inspections and the ability of IAEA inspectors to go anywhere in Iran—roughly akin to what we had in Iraq in the 1990s. Although at the time we thought that the inspections in Iraq were not working, we learned after the 2003 invasion that they had worked. When coupled with harsh sanctions that Saddam was desperate to see lifted, the inspections kept finding enough of Iraq's hidden WMD programs in 1991–95 that they convinced him to give up his programs altogether sometime thereafter. That should give us confidence that the same kind of inspection regime in Iran would be likely to detect any covert nuclear activities there as well—and probably would deter the Iranians from even trying—as long as they too were tied to harsh sanctions.

That may just be the rub. Iran has not implemented the terms of the Additional Protocol even though it has signed it. Therefore, any new deal with Iran must be tied to Tehran's implementation of the Additional Protocol. If it fails to do so, it must face the immediate reimposition of the sanctions. However, the experiences of Iraq and other countries demonstrate that it is difficult to get the UN Security Council to agree to impose harsh sanctions in response to violations. It typically takes a long time, enormous diplomatic lifting, and blatant recalcitrance on the part of the violator. Building on the lessons from Iraq, any deal with Iran should instead leave the existing sanctions in place permanently, but have them suspended temporarily, and subject to renewable suspensions that the Security Council would have to regularly vote to enact. In this way, anytime that the inspectors determined that Iran was violating the terms of the agreement, it would require nothing more than an American (or French or British) veto to bring the sanctions back into effect.

Many Americans and Israelis insist that any nuclear agreement must require Iran to close the Fordow centrifuge enrichment plant, which the Iranians built deep inside a mountain to render it impervious to attack by Israel and possibly the United States as well.[70] We can certainly ask for its closure, but we should not be hopeful. The only reason that we want Fordow closed is that without it, Iran's nuclear program is much more vulnerable to attack by the air forces of the United States, Israel, and others. That is not the kind of rationale that is likely to appeal to most of the peace-loving nations of the world. For their part, the Iranians have invested an enormous amount in Fordow to diminish their vulnerability and are unlikely to give that up. Alaeddin Boroujerdi, the head of the Iranian parliament's national security and foreign policy committee, made the point that "Fordow will never be shut down because . . . our national duty is to be able to defend our nuclear and vital centers against an enemy threat. . . . This suggestion is meant to help the Zionist regime."[71] What's more, unlike with enrichment itself, the West has no legal basis to demand that Fordow be shut down now that it has been declared to the IAEA for regular inspections.

ECONOMIC INDUCEMENTS. Given the depleted state of Iran's economy, economic inducements are likely to be the most straightforward element of a new international overture to Iran. Under the Bush administration, Tehran was offered membership in the World Trade Organization, the lifting of international sanctions, and the resumption of its pre-sanctions trade agreements with Europe and Japan. These inducements were not enough to convince Iran to take the deal. The Obama administration offered only vaguer promises of the same—along with a willingness to sell Iran spare parts for its aged fleet of Boeing airliners. The latter was a laughable incentive.

A last bid to make the carrot-and-stick approach work with Iran will have to include the promise of greater economic rewards. These should include:

- The prospect of loans and other support from international financial institutions such as the International Monetary Fund and the World Bank.

- The lifting of not only international sanctions but unilateral sanctions against Iran as well, particularly the comprehensive unilateral sanctions imposed by the United States.
- A universal settlement of all claims between Iran and the United States (which include monies owed for some Iranian arms purchases, the freezing of assets, and other matters that the Iranians believe constitute a sizable amount of money).
- The provision of positive inducements for expanded international trade and investment in Iran, including trade credits and investment guarantees for foreign firms putting capital into Iran.
- Development assistance for Iranian agriculture, infrastructure, education, energy, and environmental modernization.

In addition, offering to lift the unilateral American sanctions against Iran—which the Bush administration was never willing to offer explicitly because of its attachment to regime change—could have a major impact on Iranian thinking because the average Iranian and the regime's chief economic officials desire it.

SECURITY GUARANTEES. Whatever other purposes it may serve, Tehran's pursuit of a nuclear weapons capability is almost certainly meant to deter attacks against Iran. Consequently, another set of positive incentives that the international community will likely have to offer are guarantees for the security of the country and its regime—two quite different things.

Many Americans have suggested that the United States pledge not to attack Iran or try to overthrow its government, as President John F. Kennedy did for Cuba as part of the resolution of the Cuban Missile Crisis. Such a pledge may or may not be necessary, but Washington should not assume that it will be sufficient. Tehran will likely want more concrete actions by the United States (and other countries) if it is to give up the safety of a potential nuclear arsenal—even a theoretical one. It is critical that the international community, and especially the United States, provide such tangible demonstrations of good faith both because it is unlikely that the Iranian people will be swayed otherwise, and because it can assuage the residual fears of European and Asian publics that the United States is using the diplomatic process to set up a military operation against Iran.

The more difficult challenge will be to diminish the conventional military threat posed to Iran by American forces in the Middle East and the Indian Ocean without sacrificing America's commitments in the region. The United States has vital interests in the Persian Gulf, and Washington intends to maintain significant conventional military forces in the region for the foreseeable future. Given the power of the American military, those forces will always constitute a threat to Iran.

The United States could make unilateral concessions to Tehran related to military deployments, such as agreeing to station no more than one aircraft carrier battle group in the Gulf or Arabian Sea at any time. However, Tehran is unlikely to view this arrangement as much of a concession because of how easy it would be for the United States to break that agreement if it ever chose to do so. The problem is further compounded by Washington's understandable unwillingness not to go much beyond that (assuming it is willing to go even that far) for fear of jeopardizing its ability to respond to problems in the fragile Gulf region. A new security architecture in the Persian Gulf is probably the only realistic way to meet Iran's legitimate security concerns in a manner that would be palatable to the United States and its allies in the region. A Gulf security process could follow the successful Cold War European model by starting with security discussions, building to confidence-building measures, and eventually reaching arms control agreements. Thus the United States ought to be willing to offer the inauguration of just such a process, using the Commission on Security and Cooperation in Europe (CSCE) as a starting point. Such a process would hold out the potential for Iran to secure constraints on the deployment and operation of American military forces in the region in return for their agreement to take on equivalent limitations on their own forces.[72] Interestingly, a senior Iranian diplomat has already suggested the same in a Western newspaper.[73]

POLITICAL ACCEPTANCE. Any agreement encompassing—but hopefully not limited to—Iran's nuclear program would also have to address Iran's regional aspirations as well. A key question will be whether Iranians are ready to be accepted as a legitimate participant in the international politics of the Middle East, but not the dominant state in the region, as many Iranians seem to want. Views on this matter vary in Tehran, but it is unclear what the Iranian leadership would accept. Direct negotiations with Iran should help ascertain whether compromise is possible. Under no circumstances, however, should the United States grant Iran a position of dominance, nor should we leave any ambiguity about what we see as Iran's appropriate role in the region. Our allies in the GCC fear that Washington hopes to resurrect the alliance with a domineering Iran that the Johnson and Nixon administrations tried to use to keep the peace of the Gulf. Helping Iran address legitimate security concerns and allowing it a political role in the region does not mean granting Tehran regional hegemony.

Bigger Sticks

If Iran can be persuaded to make significant compromises on its nuclear program—and its support for terrorism and other anti–status quo activities—by positive inducements alone, that would be fantastic. But the history of the Islamic Republic should make us skeptical. At the very least, we need to be prepared for them to resist the urge, for some time if not permanently. If that is the case, it will be wise to have a well-developed set of new disincentives with which to try to convince the Iranians to change their minds.

The question is really what we still have left to try in the category of sticks. Specifically, what haven't we tried already? And if we haven't tried it already, is it because there were good reasons not to?

COVERT ACTION. I left the CIA almost two decades ago, and I have no idea what those guys are up to now. But I have noticed that the *New York*

Times is overflowing with articles sourced to senior Obama administration officials claiming that the United States has an active covert action program against Iran.[74] In a stunningly unusual event, the head of Britain's external intelligence agency, MI6, Sir John Sawers, took credit for MI6's involvement in a covert action campaign to derail Iran's nuclear weapons work.[75] The *Times* and other media outlets seem convinced that the U.S. government has mounted an aggressive cyberwarfare campaign against Iran that has disrupted Iran's nuclear program by attacking the program's computer networks.[76] The most famous piece of malware that the United States reportedly developed—along with the Israelis—was the Stuxnet virus that played havoc with the operation of Iran's nuclear centrifuges, delaying the Iranian program by as much as two years.[77] The Iranians believe that the second most famous malware to attack their computer networks, the Flame virus, was built in Israel, and one senior Israeli official implicitly confirmed this notion.[78] Since then, Tehran has claimed to have suffered from or defeated other cyberattacks on its nuclear, security, and oil infrastructures.[79] These attacks have been so threatening that Tehran has taken the extreme step of disconnecting several of its main Persian Gulf oil terminals from the Internet to protect them from cyberattack.[80]

Someone is also killing Iranian nuclear scientists, cutting power lines to their nuclear facilities, blowing up their missile bases, and conducting other forms of sabotage.[81] I have no proof, but I have a lot of Israeli friends who seem to be enthusiastic about these attacks. Israeli (and American) journalists seem to be just as certain that Mossad is behind the assassinations and sabotage campaign as their American counterparts are certain that CIA and the National Security Agency are involved in the cyberwar campaign.[82] At least one former senior Israeli official has implied that Israel is part of this effort, and the Iranians have not exactly been quiet in claiming that this campaign is the work of the Israelis with assistance from the United States and Great Britain. For instance, in July 2012, former Israeli national security advisor Uzi Arad responded to a question from the IDF Radio network regarding an attack on Israeli officials in Bulgaria that Israel believed was conducted by Iranian assets, saying, "We are, to a large extent, the initiators. . . . Mainly, we're leading a struggle against Iran. We're not a passive side. And the other side is the defending, deterring, and attacking one."[83] At times, the Iranians have claimed that they had proof of American involvement.[84] The Iranians have also asserted that the Israelis, Americans, and British have been arming and encouraging Kurdish, Baluch, and Arab separatists.[85] The author Mark Perry has interviewed sources who claim to have seen classified U.S. memos that absolved the CIA of any involvement with the Baluch but indicated that Mossad was supporting them.[86]

Even if all of this chatter is only partially true, it strongly suggests that the Western allies have an aggressive covert action campaign going on against Iran. Which raises the question of how much have Western covert actions been responsible for Iran's new willingness to talk about its nuclear program, and how much could they help convince Iran to make real concessions in the future?

We cannot know for certain. The Iranians complain enough about these attacks that we can say that they do not like them. But no Iranian has directly tied covert action attacks—cyber, assassination, sabotage, support to disaffected Iranian ethnic groups—to the need to negotiate with the West. So far, that argument has been reserved for sanctions. This distinction is noteworthy because the covert attacks *are* part of the Iranian conversation. The hardliners lump together the covert action campaign, the sanctions, and Western support for the Green Movement and other democratic oppositionists as elements of the "soft war" they claim the West is waging against Iran to try to topple the Iranian government. They justify making no concessions based on the need to fight back. The moderates and pragmatists ignore this argument and focus on the hardships created by the sanctions to argue that Iran must make some compromises on the nuclear issue.

Several U.S. military officers familiar with the U.S. cyber effort against Iran have all used the same phrase with me: "We are already at war with Iran" in the cyber arena. They have described fending off constant attacks by Iran and implied that the United States has hurt Iran more than they have hurt us.[87] If that is the case, it is just not clear how much more we could ratchet up the pressure on Iran in the cyber world. To the extent that we can do even more damage to Iran in the future through ramped up cyber and covert action attacks, we should be careful. People die from these attacks. Beyond the moral dimensions, we need to recognize that killing people can cause an adversary to overreact, especially when it is an adversary as paranoid and xenophobic as Iran's Islamic regime.[88]

MORE SANCTIONS? In the end, it is the sanctions that got us to the current point. To the extent that it is now possible to imagine that Iran might accept real constraints on its nuclear program, it is because of the sanctions. Especially because of the uncertainties of covert action, if Iran does not respond to renewed offers of engagement and tangible benefits, we will inevitably have to turn to sanctions once again to try to achieve that objective.

There are two ways to think about ratcheting up sanctions on Iran. To borrow phrases from the military, they are either "vertical" or "horizontal" escalation. Vertical escalation of the sanctions would refer to clamping down even harder on Iranian commerce. The problem is that we are already maxed out at this point. Other than exporting humanitarian goods such as food and medicine to Iran, all American commerce with Iran is prohibited. The same is largely true for Europe. Even the French, the hardest of the hard line when it comes to Iran, confess that there isn't much more that Europe can do. The last sanction that they are holding in reserve is to forbid Iran from conducting transactions in euros with non-EU countries, a move that would hurt Iran, but probably not enough to convince them to change their minds. Paris feels the need to have at least one more sanction available in the event that Iran refuses the P-5+1 again, but the French do not seem sanguine that it will make much difference.

That's where horizontal escalation comes in. Horizontal escalation would mean convincing other countries to join the current Western sanctions. Because there is so little left in terms of vertical escalation, any further intensification of sanctions will need to focus on horizontal escalation. To this end, in late 2012, conservative American congressmen began working on what they referred to as "comprehensive commercial sanctions" against Iran. These sanctions would seize or freeze all Iranian assets overseas and prohibit all imports into Iran except for food, medicine, and some communications equipment (to help Iran's pro-democracy opposition). Under this legislation, any country that refused to comply with its terms would be banned from trading with the United States.[89] If this legislation were enacted and enforced, and if other countries complied with it, it would re-create the same draconian, comprehensive sanctions on Iran that the United Nations imposed on Iraq during the 1990s.

CAN THE SANCTIONS WORK? In recent decades, when the United States has levied economic sanctions against countries, we have tended to do so expecting the psychological blow from the mere imposition of these penalties to be enough to cause the targeted state to reverse course. When the United States led the international community in imposing sanctions on Iraq to try to force Saddam Husayn to give up his WMD programs in 1991 after the Persian Gulf War, the resolutions naïvely included a 145-day clock for him to do so.

Sanctions do not work this way in practice. To the extent that Saddam complied with the resolutions (and he did comply with the spirit of the resolutions, although he refused to acknowledge that he had), it seems to have taken him four to five years. Even then he never complied with the letter of the resolutions and intended to violate their spirit as soon as the sanctions were lifted.[90]

With Iran we have once again imposed crippling sanctions in the expectation that the Iranian regime won't want to allow their economy to erode (or perhaps even collapse). We have done so under the assumption that long before that point, Tehran will agree to change its behavior on one of its most important policies to accommodate American (and global) demands. The problem is that, historically, sanctions don't work that way. Richard Haass has proven himself to be both one of the ablest policymakers and most accomplished foreign policy thinkers of the past thirty years, and it is telling that he concluded his own study of the utility of sanctions for American diplomacy by observing that sanctions "are unlikely to achieve desired results if the aims are large or the time is short."[91]

Sanctions have an uneven record in general. Former undersecretary of state for economic affairs Stuart Eizenstat found that "[s]anctions offer a decidedly mixed bag of beneficial and damaging results to policymakers."[92] Academic work on sanctions has largely borne this out.[93] A famous 1990 study of 115 cases of sanctions found that they "worked" only 34 percent of the time.[94] Daniel Drezner has pointed out what he calls the "sanctions paradox," in which sanctions work best when the target country is a democracy and an ally of the sanctioning state.[95] Neither is the case for Iran. Although sanctions rarely succeed on their own in coercing a nation to change its behavior, they can often accomplish other, lesser goals, such as weakening the target state or forcing it to curb its activities. Moreover, sanctions can be helpful in laying the predicate for even harsher measures—typically military—by demonstrating that the targeted state cannot be persuaded by anything short of force. Of course, for the case at hand, sanctions are only *useful* in this last way if we are looking to go to war with Iran. If we aren't, and I am not, this last point does little good.

The work on sanctions most relevant to our current impasse with Iran remains Meghan O'Sullivan's 2002 book, *Shrewd Sanctions,* which looked at four cases of sanctions against Middle Eastern rogue regimes (including Iran) during the 1990s. O'Sullivan, who would go on to senior positions in the Bush 43 administration, including deputy national security advisor for Iraq and Afghanistan during the surge in Iraq, demonstrated that "[s]anctions whose primary aim is to change certain behaviors of a leadership are in some respects the most difficult to fashion."[96] In which case, "[t]he structure of sanctions must be flexible enough to accommodate and encourage gradual changes in the behavior of the target, ideally by allowing restrictions to be lifted or letting them lapse incrementally as the country takes actions desired by the United States. . . . Sanctions used for this purpose must be accompanied by a dialogue between the two countries, preferably in a regular and institutionalized way that allows each side to articulate its expectations and demonstrate the reforms it has undertaken. . . ."[97] That we have none of that with Iran might make us skeptical that our current sanctions will work at all, let alone quickly.

What all of this work demonstrates is that sanctions only rarely cause a *major* shift in the targeted state's behavior. And when they do work, they take years, even decades, to do so. Libya was a charter member of the U.S. terrorism list in 1979 and came under a set of sanctions associated with that list. Between 1986 and 1996, the Reagan, Bush 41, and Clinton administrations shut down all American commerce with Libya and began to press other countries to do the same. By the end of the Clinton administration and the start of the Bush 43 administration, Qadhafi had taken some steps to try to get back into the good graces of the United States: He had closed terrorist training camps, severed Libyan support for radical groups, and was even trying to play peacemaker in Africa. In September 2000, he gave a speech announcing his desire to rejoin the international community. In December 2003, after months of secret negotiations with the United States and Great Britain (and following the rapid American military campaigns against Afghanistan and Iraq), Qadhafi announced that he would abandon all of his WMD programs and permit international inspectors full access to all of his WMD facilities to verify his compliance; he even created a $2.7 billion compensation fund for victims of the Pan Am 103 bombing over Lockerbie, Scotland, in 1988. Libya was ultimately a major success for American policy, but it took decades and may have required the collapse of the Soviet Union (Libya's former superpower patron) and the threat of an American invasion, on top of sanctions, to produce that result.[98] And Libya is tiny compared to Iran: in 2004 it had one-fifteenth of Iran's current population and one-thirteenth of Iran's gross domestic product.

Sanctions can be difficult to sustain over time, something Iran's hard-liners are betting on. A big problem with sanctions is that once Country A has imposed sanctions on Country B, Country A can end up fighting with its allies and trade partners, rather than with Country B. All through the 1990s and 2000s, the United States fought with its European and East Asian trading partners over their commercial relations with Iraq, Iran, Libya, Sudan, North Korea, Cuba, and so on. The fights sometimes became vicious and distracting, and created rifts between the United States and our key allies when we most needed to be working in lockstep.[99] In 2012, the United States imposed sanctions on Chinese, Singaporean, and UAE companies for their relations with Iran, all of which created as many problems for Washington's relations with Beijing, Singapore, and Abu Dhabi as they did for Iran's economy.[100] It is especially problematic with a major oil producer like Iran, where efforts to limit its oil sales can have an impact on the price of oil—and through it the global economy. In October 2011, Khajehpour estimated that the Iran sanctions then imposed had boosted global oil prices by $8 per barrel while oil analyst Bob McNally's estimate in 2012 was a similar $5–10 per barrel.[101]

For the target state, undermining the sanctions is often its principal goal, and it will devote all of its political and economic energy to do so. Just as frequently, maintaining the sanctions is just one of many things to which the states applying the sanctions must attend. For that reason, even bigger and more powerful states may find it hard to sustain tight sanctions around smaller countries over time. Iraq during the 1990s is an obvious example, but the same problem has already begun with Iran. Ironically, it is often Iraqi banks and smugglers who are helping Tehran to bust the financial and oil sanctions.[102] By early 2013, U.S. government officials warned that Iran was finding ways to get around the financial sanctions by using fake financial institutions, informal couriers, and criminal enterprises—all practices that Tehran will doubtless expand.[103]

ARE WE REPEATING THE MISTAKES OF IRAQ? Hopefully, just suggesting that we are following the same course we took with Iraq will sound a cautionary note. The effects of our policy toward Iraq after 1982 have been complicated. There were things that we did that worked out the way that we hoped, and other things that did not. The story of the containment and sanctions against Saddam were part of that complicated history. The combination of sanctions and inspections did convince Saddam, eventually, to give up his WMD programs—although not his aspirations. However, at the same time, the sanctions were a failure because they proved self-defeating.

Obviously, the tragic implosion of Iraq during the 1990s was not all the fault of the sanctions. Saddam Husayn bears at least half of the blame, arguably more. He refused to comply with the UN Security Council resolutions and used the sanctions to create suffering among his own people for his personal benefit—stoking international sympathy for their lifting and to punish disloyal elements of the Iraqi populace. Nevertheless, we cannot blame it all on him, either. The sanctions were overly severe and poorly designed. They helped to gut Iraqi society. They probably caused thousands, and possibly tens or even hundreds of thousands, of deaths.[104] They undermined Iraq's health and educational systems. They concentrated heretofore unheard-of power in the hands of the central government. They further damaged Iraq's oil, transportation, and communications infrastructures, all of which had been battered by a decade of Saddam's wars. They helped to take what had been one of the most progressive and modern societies of the Arab world and set it back by decades. They turned many Iraqis against the United States even as they also hardened many Iraqi hearts against Saddam.[105]

Worse still, as the damage that the sanctions (as manipulated by Saddam) were doing to Iraqi society became ever more apparent, they turned international opinion increasingly against the entire effort to contain Saddam Husayn.[106] In the late 1990s, I served on the staff of the U.S. National Security Council as the director for Persian Gulf affairs. One of my primary responsibilities was holding together the containment of Iraq. What I saw was that as hard as we fought against it, as hard as we tried to convince the world that the sanctions were not responsible for any of the death and suffering in Iraq—that there were provisions for Iraq to import food and medicine, that the Iraqis were exaggerating the extent of the problems, and that Saddam was deliberately depriving his own people to *cause* death from starvation and disease—it did not matter. It wasn't that no one believed us; they generally did. It was that they did not care. The people of the world just wanted the suffering of the Iraqi people to end, and if Saddam would not do the right thing then the United States and the UN had to instead. And so, by the end of the 1990s, the support for sanctions on Iraq, indeed for the containment of Iraq, was evaporating. The sanctions were collapsing, and Saddam was able to smuggle and cheat more and more. Less than ten years after Saddam's invasion of Kuwait, many countries were simply ignoring the sanctions.[107]

Consequently, still another lesson from our unfortunate Iraq experience that we ought to have learned but appear to be in danger of repeating is that if we make the sanctions on Iran too harsh, they are likely to become unsustainable. It is why O'Sullivan and other scholars of sanctions warn, "Sanctions should almost never be allowed to cause any form of extreme deprivation."[108] Although the current Iran sanctions do not ban exports of medicine, the impact of lower import revenues and higher inflation is making it harder for Iranians to get access to medical supplies, including lifesaving medicines.[109] A comprehensive analysis by the International Crisis Group warned, "Arguably, the most negative consequence (of the sanctions) has been to seriously undercut the healthcare system." Medicine has become extremely expensive and there are shortages of specialized drugs for cancer patients, hemophiliacs, diabetics, and people with multiple sclerosis and other serious conditions.[110] Iran may already be setting in motion an effort to take a page from Saddam's playbook and begin to undermine the sanctions against it by portraying them as having an outsize effect on the wider Iranian populace. In response to new EU sanctions in October 2012, the regime referred to them as "inhuman."[111] It was an incongruous note and perhaps a taste of things to come.

Because the sanctions seem to have had such a powerful impact on Iran, there is a strong temptation to just keep doubling down on them, but the evidence suggests that would be a mistake. There comes a point when they do no more good, and can do great harm, both to the people of Iran and to the strategy they are meant to enforce. We are rapidly approaching that point with Iran, if we have not passed it already.

A Final Thought

There is one last aspect of the revised carrot-and-stick policy that is worth mentioning: the name. Many Iranians bristle at the name "carrot-and-stick" because they say it is derived from the metaphor of how one leads a mule. They say that they find this humiliating and offensive.

An old Chinese saying observes that "the beginning of wisdom is to call things by their right names." Our Iran debate desperately wants for such wisdom. For now, in this context, when our nation needs to have an open and honest conversation about which strategy to pursue toward Iran, I think it important to call things by their right names rather than adding to the confusion with euphemisms. And as for Iranian sensibilities . . . well, what I find objectionable is thirty years of Iran killing Americans in Lebanon, Saudi Arabia, Iraq, Afghanistan, and elsewhere. When the Iranian regime stops doing that I would not only be willing to change how we describe our policy, I would be willing to change the policy itself.

7

Regime Change

Whenever a fellow of the Brookings Institution publishes a book, the organization holds a public event where the author presents his or her principal conclusions and recommendations, and another speaker comments on it, often by providing a critical perspective. In 2004, when my book *The Persian Puzzle* was published, I asked Danielle Pletka, the vice president for Foreign and Defense Policy Studies at the American Enterprise Institute, to share the podium with me. To many in Washington, this pairing seemed strange. Dany was the longtime foreign policy aide to Senator Jesse Helms, the late conservative lawmaker from North Carolina, and she and I had been on opposite sides of a variety of issues when we were both in government. The tension between us had gotten so bad that the NSC's office of Legislative Affairs forbade me from even speaking to her. Nevertheless, she and I shared a grudging respect for one another. After we both left government service, I discovered that she was not only bright, practical, and creative, but also willing to take unorthodox positions on issues. I felt she was perfect to critique my ideas at the Brookings event for my book.

I started the program by making the case for a carrot-and-stick approach toward Iran. I laid out my arguments for developing positive incentives to convince Iran to compromise on its nuclear program and other problematic behavior—and for coupling these incentives with disincentives (such as economic sanctions) to be applied if Tehran refused to cooperate. At the time, this approach did not fit either the left's desire to engage Tehran unconditionally or the right's determination to invade. The assembled experts seemed intrigued, but subdued.

Then it was Dany's turn to speak. She started by commending me for a creative approach to a difficult problem and indicated that she thought it might be worth trying. But she was also convinced that it would fail. She believed that Iran's hardliners were too wedded to their nuclear program to give it up, and Iran's reformists were too weak to overrule them. For those reasons, she believed that the policy the United States should adopt toward Iran was one of "regime change"—although not military regime change. She recognized that after Iraq and Afghanistan there was no longer a popular appetite for that. Instead, she felt that the United States should take a principled stand that we would assist Iranians seeking to replace the Islamic Republic with a true democracy, however we could. She recognized that in 2004 (five years before the birth of the Green Movement), what she was advocating had little chance of success, certainly in the short term and possibly even in the long term. But her argument was that, eventually, the Islamic Republic would fall, and whenever that happened—perhaps not for decades—the only policy that would be justifiable to Iranians, to Americans, to history, would be one of principled opposition to an oppressive, authoritarian regime. She concluded by noting that since the United States had never tried to help the millions of Iranians agitating for democracy (and it was clear even in 2004 that many Iranians ardently desired greater democracy), we could not say for certain that there was nothing for us to do. We ought to at least try. At worst, we would fail, but we would fail doing the right thing. And at best we might succeed. If we succeeded we would have done something remarkable for Iranians and Americans alike.

It was a thoughtful argument, and while I felt it was best to try my carrot-and-stick approach first, I never forgot her ideas. Today, they stay with me because with each passing day, I fear that Dany may have been right.

The Cases for Regime Change

There are three rationales for the United States to try to help overturn the government in Tehran. The first is the argument articulated by Danielle Pletka above. By any standard, the Iranian regime is odious. It is oppressive. It is authoritarian. It has shed nearly all of its democratic pretensions and rules in an increasingly autocratic fashion. It employs extra-judicial killing and torture. It incarcerates those it believes pose the slightest threat to the regime—and incarcerates them for lengthy periods in deplorable conditions.[1] It is hated by a great many Iranians (although certainly not by all). The world, the Middle East, and the Iranian people would all be better off if the current Iranian regime were gone. As Dany suggested, we could support regime change because it is what is right.

REGIME CHANGE TO SECURE AMERICA'S REGIONAL INTERESTS. A second reason to support regime change in Iran, also an element of Dany's remarks, is that this Iranian regime may never be willing to have a nonconfrontational relationship with the United States. Forget about a rapprochement—most Americans and American policymakers would be glad just to ignore Iran and have Tehran leave us alone. (Indeed, that has been the overarching motive of most American administrations since Carter, contrary to the conspiracy theories of the Iranian regime.) Unfortunately, since the revolution, the Islamic Republic has never been willing to leave the United States alone. Instead, they have defined themselves as our enemy and sought to undermine and attack our interests and our allies as best they could. It may not be possible for the United States to secure its interests in the Persian Gulf region as long as the current Iranian regime remains, and remains determined to oppose almost anything we do. If this regime refuses to do what would be necessary to meet America's minimal requirements for peaceful coexistence, we should seek its ouster.

This rationale, however, is a bit tougher to use to justify a policy of regime change. Not only do you have to believe that the United States could never find a way to live with this Iranian regime, which not every American does, but this theory requires a reasonable expectation that a successor regime would be more likely to give up Iran's nuclear program. There is no way to be certain, and the evidence is contradictory, but it seems more likely than not that a change of regime *would* produce a government that the United States could abide.

The evidence against this point is that a number of Iranian reformists—including the leaders of the Green Movement in 2009—have supported Iran's nuclear program, and there is limited public polling data that suggest a strong majority of Iranians are committed to the Iranian nuclear program.

All of that is true, but it is not necessarily dispositive. There is other evidence to suggest that a different regime would almost certainly be better inclined toward the United States. The Iranian regime has turned the nuclear program into a bellwether of Iranian patriotism. Anyone who does not support it gets tarred as an agent of the West—which can be lethal in the Islamic Republic, not just politically but literally. No Iranian leader can do any less than declare his or her support for the nuclear program, at least in public. Second, the regime has sold the nuclear program to its people as being about nuclear energy—not about nuclear weapons. They have long denied that there is any weapons component to the program. When Iranian leaders and ordinary citizens declare support for Iran's nuclear program, they are most often declaring it for a civilian energy program, not for a weapons program.[2]

All polling of Iranians is suspect because the regime generally prevents direct public opinion sampling, forcing foreigners to conduct phone polls from outside the country, a technique susceptible to false results. Such polls tend to show exaggerated agreement with the views of the regime as respondents often assume that the regime is listening and fear they will be harmed if they give answers that don't echo the views of the government. With these qualifications in mind, it is noteworthy that a 2010 RAND Corporation poll found that Iranians supported Iran's acquisition of nuclear energy by 87 percent in favor to just 3 percent opposed. In contrast, when asked if Iran should acquire nuclear weapons, the same respondents came out 46 percent opposed and 44 percent in favor. And again, to the extent that these numbers are inaccurate, they probably *overstate* the degree of support for nuclear weapons.[3] Indeed, the RAND pollsters found that that the more comfortable respondents were taking the survey, the more likely they were to *oppose* Iran acquiring nuclear weapons, whereas the more fearful they were about participating in the survey, the less likely they were to voice opposition to Iran's acquisition of nuclear weapons.[4]

In addition, a 2012 Gallup poll found that the number of Iranians who supported Iran's nuclear program for purely civilian purposes had fallen to just 57 percent, probably reflecting the impact of sanctions. The percentage of Iranians supporting Iran's acquisition of nuclear weapons had fallen as well, down to just 40 percent, although, interestingly, the same poll found that the number of Iranians who outright opposed Iran's acquisition of a nuclear weapons capability had also declined to 35 percent—with a big jump in the number of people saying that they just did not know.[5] That seems like a reasonable response to the frustration of the sanctions.

To the extent that Westerners have been able to speak to Iranian reformist leaders privately, especially during Mohammad Khatami's time as president, the reformists have insisted that they understand Western concerns about their nuclear program and have been ready to accommodate our needs.[6] In 2006, Khatami's brother, Mohammad Reza Khatami, told the Italian newspaper *La Repubblica,* "We have written numerous letters to Leader Khamenei to explain that insisting on uranium enrichment is not the country's interest; that in this way we lose all the benefits gained over the past sixteen years; and that the only proper position is suspension of uranium-enriching activities and negotiations with the aim of fostering trust and having international oversight."[7] Along similar lines, the reformists have also consistently indicated a willingness to accept a peace deal between Israel and the Palestinians in a way that the hardliners haven't.[8] President Khatami himself said on several occasions that Iran would not be more Palestinian than the Palestinians, and "We will honor what the Palestinian people accept."[9] His vice president, Massoumeh Ebtekar, went further, declaring herself a supporter of direct talks between Israel and Iran.[10]

All of these admissions should give us confidence that the removal of the current Iranian regime and its replacement with one more reflective of Iranian public opinion would be a positive development for the United States. We can even say that almost any imaginable change of regime in Tehran would benefit the United States, if only because it is hard to imagine a regime *more* anti-American than the one in place today.

REGIME CHANGE AS ANOTHER STICK. There is still one more rationale for pursuing regime change in Iran: doing so may be the best, or even the only, way to persuade the Iranian regime to make concessions on its nuclear program, end its support for terrorism, and stop adding to the chaos of the Middle East. This rationale for seeking regime change stems from the notion that the United States has failed to persuade Tehran to change its ways because we have not been able to hold at risk anything that the Iranian leadership values more than its nuclear program, its support for terrorism, and so on. The theory behind the sanctions on Iran was that the regime would value its economy more than its nuclear program, and would agree to compromise on the latter to have sanctions lifted on the former. Since that has not worked (at least, not yet), it raises the question of whether there is something else that the Iranian regime values more than the country's economic well-being.

The only obvious answer is the regime's control over Iran itself. No government wants to be replaced, and the Islamic Republic has gone to enormous lengths to retain power. The more cynical rationale to support economic sanctions was not the belief that the Islamic leadership valued the Iranian economy more than their nuclear program, but that crippling sanctions would cause such economic duress that it would spark popular agitation against the regime. This unrest would frighten the leadership that it might lose control over the country, and would persuade them to compromise on their nuclear and foreign policy to get the sanctions lifted. Adopting an explicit policy of regime change under this rationale would mean sticking with the same strategy but focusing on a different approach to threatening the regime.

Bad Reasons to Oppose Regime Change

There are a lot of good reasons to oppose a policy of regime change. Before addressing them, however, it is important to deal with two that crop up from time to time that are not good rationales to eschew regime change. Unfortunately, one of them seems to be a guiding principle of the Obama administration.

THE FALSE CHOICE. Somewhere, someone is likely to point out that the rationales for pursuing regime change listed above are in conflict. If our goal is to replace the Islamic Republic either because it is morally right or because the regime is inherently inimical to American interests and so must be removed, this notion is incompatible with the idea of pursuing regime change in Iran as a "stick" to convince Tehran to make meaningful concessions on its nuclear program. If the Iranians ever were to come to us and say, "If you call off your efforts to overthrow our regime, we will agree to give up all enrichment activities," the third rationale for pursuing regime change would argue that the United States should agree. But this agreement would be inimical to the first and second rationales. By their logic, accepting a deal on the nuclear side would be selling out not only the Iranian people but our own interests.

At a theoretical level, this conclusion may be true enough, but it is unlikely to be compelling in practice and therefore not a good reason to eschew regime change. It is the kind of argument that gets academics wrapped around an axle but rarely happens in the real world—and is more easily solved than is typically recognized. And it is not the case that if we cannot untangle this conundrum, we should not pursue regime change at all.

If the United States pursues regime change, there are four possible outcomes:

1. The policy fails. The regime does not collapse and does not feel enough pressure to make any concessions on its nuclear program or anything else. In this case, this dilemma is moot. Since, as I discuss below, this outcome is arguably the most likely, the most likely probability is that this conundrum is irrelevant.

2. The policy succeeds. A rapid overthrow of the regime ensues, and its fall is so swift that the regime does not even offer us a deal on the nuclear program before it collapses. In this case too, this dilemma becomes irrelevant. Unfortunately, this outcome is also the least likely.

3. The policy succeeds more slowly. Pressured and imperiled, the regime refuses to make concessions, seeing them as a poison pill that would speed its demise. This scenario seems to reflect Iran's general approach to concessions. Again, there is no dilemma for the United States to face, since the regime isn't interested in making concessions.

4. The policy succeeds slowly, but the regime decides to compromise—or at least to see what the terms might be. The regime offers to halt their nuclear program in return for Washington ending its regime change efforts.

Only in that last scenario does the United States face this dilemma at all, and that last scenario is not all that likely. Moreover, solving the dilemma is not hard.

If the Iranians make us that offer, we have a choice. We can tell the Iranians that it is too late, that the deal is no longer on the table, and continue the regime change program in the expectation that it will bring down the regime. Alternatively, we can make the deal, end Iran's nuclear weapons program, and try to find other ways to support the aspirations of the Iranian people in a more indirect fashion. The latter is what we did with the Cubans as part of the Cuban Missile Crisis, and with the Soviets at Helsinki in 1975. In the latter case, we agreed not to try to bring down the USSR or its control over Eastern Europe through direct action, but we continued to provide indirect, rhetorical, and other support to Eastern European opposition movements. We also maintained sanctions and other forms of pressure on the Soviet Bloc (as we did with Cuba after the Cuban Missile Crisis).

One can make the case that this tactic would mean "selling out" the Iranian people. There were people who made that argument about the Cubans after 1962 and the Eastern Europeans after the 1975 Helsinki Accords. If we felt that was the case, or more the case with Iran, we could turn down the Iranian offer and continue pursuing regime change. However, many others saw both the resolution of the Cuban Missile Crisis and the Helsinki Accords as critical elements in avoiding World War III that still allowed for the eventual collapse of the Iron Curtain in 1989—although it has still not resulted in the liberation of the Cuban people.

Nevertheless, if this scenario occurred, the United States would simply have a choice. A painful choice perhaps, but a choice. Making such a choice would not undermine our Iran policy. In many ways it would be a great choice to have—far, far better than the choices available today. It would be a choice born of success, not of failure, as we have today.

Moreover, there are many ways to make that choice. One way would be to assess how close to collapse the Iranian regime seemed. That could only be a judgment call and could be wrong. However, the U.S. government must make judgment calls all the time. Indeed, whatever policy we adopt toward Iran will be a judgment call due to the limits on our knowledge about Iran and its intentions. Nevertheless, if we felt that the regime was imperiled, we might decide to press on and rid the world of these meddlesome priests (to paraphrase Henry II). In contrast, if we believed the regime had a strong chance of surviving no matter what we did, we might decide to accept the deal as being in the best interests of the United States and our allies in the region.

MISREADING HISTORY. From the start, the Obama administration has been working under the assumption that the pursuit of regime change and the pursuit of a nuclear deal with Iran are mutually exclusive. They have assumed that if Khamene'i and the hardliners believe that the United States is determined to overthrow them, they will see no reason to strike a deal with Washington—especially a deal that would deprive them of a nuclear arsenal. To senior administration officials, this assumption is just "common sense," logical behavior by Tehran that requires no evidence to take it as valid. Unfortunately, there is no evidence to support this point of view.

The administration could be right. With Iran, anything is possible. But it seems unlikely. First, Iran's record has been that when the regime feels most threatened (as in 1996–98 and 2003), it is most likely to offer concessions. In the wonderful phrase of Karim Sadjadpour, "Iran does not respond to pressure, but it does respond to a *lot* of pressure." Likewise, there is no evidence to suggest that when Iran does not feel threatened it will make concessions. That has simply never happened.

The Obama administration's own first term exemplifies this phenomenon. Washington tried to avoid giving Tehran any reason to believe that the United States was working to overthrow the Islamic Republic, including making only the most tepid and perfunctory statements of support for the Green Movement at a time when most of the world was offering them full-throated cheers and heaping abuse on the regime for its brutal crackdown. Yet this statecraft yielded no willingness to compromise on the part of the Iranians. Instead, during the Obama administration's first term, what did seem to incline Iran at least to talk was the economic threat of sanctions. And a major element of the relative success of the sanctions has been the gap that they have begun to create between the regime and its people. So the administration's belief that the United States should not threaten the Iranian regime's grip on power because doing so would make Tehran less likely to compromise runs contrary to its own rationale for imposing sanctions on Iran: the sanctions are designed to get the Iranian regime to compromise by conjuring that very threat.

This dynamic is not lost on the Iranians, who see it as "common sense" that the sanctions are intended to undermine the regime's grip on power. While everyone else around the world seemed to recognize that throughout Obama's first term Washington tried to avoid giving any indication that it might be interested in regime change in Tehran, the Iranian leadership continued to insist that regime change was America's only goal. Khamene'i has complained endlessly that the United States under the Obama administration has been waging a "soft war" against Iran. intended to foment a popular revolt against the Islamic Republic. Thus there is no point in refraining from pursuing regime change; the Iranians are convinced that is what we are up to anyway, and it has been our relative success in raising that very fear (via the sanctions) that started the Iranian leaders debating their nuclear program in the first place.

For these reasons, I disagree with the administration's assumption that pursuing regime change would hurt the chances that Tehran would agree to concessions. I think the administration has that backward. There is a danger of mirror-imaging when it comes to Iran. Westerners have a bad habit of asking what they would do if they were Iran's leaders, and then assuming the Iranians will do the same. The history of U.S.-Iranian relations has demonstrated that the Iranians do not think like American decision-makers. They hold different assumptions, different goals, different perspectives on the world, and different interpretations of history, all of which lead them to different ideas about what to do and how to do it. It is one of the most important among many reasons that Americans have so often misunderstood Iranian intentions and failed to predict Iranian actions. Of all the reasons not to pursue regime change—and there are a lot—fearing that our greater pursuit of regime change will make Tehran less willing to compromise on its nuclear program should not be among them.

Is Regime Change Possible?

In the abstract, there are at least three good reasons for the United States to pursue regime change toward Iran. Unfortunately, there are also a number of very practical problems to doing so. Ultimately, it could prove difficult, even impossible, to remove the regime in Tehran. It is not even clear if American efforts to help that process along would help or hurt.

In 1953, the United States helped to engineer the fall of Mohammad Mosaddeq, the popular prime minister of Iran. There are a lot of myths surrounding this event. One that need not concern us is the common Iranian misperception that Mosaddeq was a champion of democracy and had been democratically reelected—he wasn't. (He was democratically elected in 1948, but he subverted the 1952 elections in an unconstitutional fashion).[11] What is of importance is the notion that the CIA toppled Mosaddeq with help from Britain's MI6. The CIA and MI6 tried their hardest, and both did play important *supporting* roles in his ouster, but the truth is that Mosaddeq was primarily brought down by his own internal opponents—Khomeini's intellectual forebear, Ayatollah Abol-Ghasem Kashani; monarchists; middle-class liberals; disaffected military officers; and others. At most, the CIA and MI6 galvanized and assisted those forces, but Mosaddeq's internal foes were gunning for him anyway. It seems unlikely he would have lasted long even without the United States and the Brits. My intent here is not to absolve the United States or Great Britain from its role in Mosaddeq's fall, but to point out that on the one occasion when the United States contributed to regime change in Iran, it was primarily an inside job. This history should make us circumspect about our ability to pull it off a second time.[12]

There has only ever been one other occasion when the United States even tried to affect governance in Tehran. In early 1979, as the Shah's regime was collapsing, the Carter administration belatedly decided to try to prevent the loss of its most important ally in the Persian Gulf. In January, as the Shah was packing up to leave, the White House dispatched General Robert "Dutch" Huyser to Tehran to try to convince the Iranian

Armed Forces to step in, restore order, and assist the Shah's last prime minister (and nominal successor), Shapour Bakhtiar, to establish a liberal democracy. Huyser discovered that the situation had long before passed the point of no return. There was not even an attempt at a counterrevolution.[13] The Huyser mission is noteworthy as it too demonstrates the difficulty, even impossibility, of bringing about regime change in Iran without the participation of powerful internal forces.

After 1979, the United States never again tried to overthrow the Iranian regime, despite the paranoid obsessions of the Iranian leadership. The Reagan administration debated the idea of mounting a covert action program to try to destabilize Iran by building an armed opposition within the country, but the idea went nowhere.[14] The CIA felt that there was no credible group within Iran that could become the kernel around which to build an insurgency, and the State Department feared that trying would cause harsh Iranian reactions against moderates at home, and against the United States and its allies abroad.[15]

Reagan wasn't the last president to wish that he could find a way to get rid of the Iranian regime, nor was he the last to conclude that desirable as regime change might be, it wasn't workable. Many Iranians may dislike their government and want a change, but they tend to be proud nationalists, resentful of foreign meddling in their internal affairs. Since the early twentieth century, political figures depicted as tools of foreign powers have tended to lose whatever popular support they may have had, making it hard for outside powers to back indigenous forces for change. Abbas Milani of Stanford University notes, "Anyone who wants American money in Iran is going to be tainted in the eyes of Iranians."[16] Not surprisingly, the State Department has often struggled to spend the money it has allocated to promote democracy.[17] I used to say that when it came to regime change in Iran, the United States had a "Groucho Marx" problem: we should not give money to any Iranian willing to take money from us—only con men and agents of the secret police would be willing to do so and any legitimate oppositionist would never countenance it.

The regime has demonstrated time and again that it is able to thwart any internal threats with ease. In 1999, 2000, 2003, and 2007, there were large-scale student protests in Tehran and other cities against the regime's political and social controls. All were brutally but effectively crushed by the regime's security forces in just days. The 2009 Green revolt was several orders of magnitude larger and more dangerous, but it took only a few weeks for the regime to smash it. When the Greens attempted to reassert themselves in 2011, feeding off the energy of the "Arab Spring," the regime was able to confuse, disperse, and scatter them in days. No significant demonstrations or marches even coalesced.

The regime is skilled at crushing domestic opposition. It identifies potential opposition leaders and imprisons them. It monitors and disrupts social media and controls broadcast and Internet communications. It intimidates major political figures to prevent them from supporting opposition groups. It polices its various military forces through a traditional network of layered intelligence and security services, each one watching all the others. And it ferrets out foreign intelligence operations in Iran. As Suzanne Maloney notes, "The Islamic Republic has survived every calamity short of the plague: war, isolation, instability, terrorist attacks, leadership transition, drought and epic earthquakes."[18]

RISKY BUSINESS. In addition to the hurdles to regime change, there are also some significant dangers involved. The regime will likely fight back, and fight back as hard as it can, against whatever internal opposition exists, particularly any supported by the United States. The regime is also likely to lash out directly against the United States.

Efforts to promote democracy, to work with opposition figures, or to provide assistance to ethnic and religious minorities resisting the central government by force could prompt the regime to crack down harder. That has been the regime's pattern of behavior. When the Iraqi army invaded Iran in 1980, at a time when the Iranian military was in disarray, most of Iran's Revolutionary Guards were in northwest Iran, crushing a separatist revolt by Iran's Kurdish community. It's noteworthy that the regime kept the Guards in Kurdistan until the revolt was put down, even while the Iraqis were advancing unchecked through oil-rich Khuzestan. The more that the United States tries to support internal groups opposed to the regime, the more we may bring down Tehran's wrath upon them. Our efforts to fund democratic activists in Iran during the Bush 43 administration provoked a crackdown on them. Although the amount of money the United States provided amounted to a fraction of what a sustained democracy program would require, the Iranian regime responded ferociously. Iranian intelligence officials grilled Iranian activists about this money, and often used the suspicion that someone was accepting such funds as grounds to arrest and interrogate them.[19] Many Iranians became wary of any activities that could even be linked indirectly to the United States.[20] Fariba Davoodi Mohajer, a women's rights advocate, argued that U.S. support for civil society became "a ready tool for the Iranian government to use against totally independent activists. It's been very counterproductive."[21]

If new American efforts were to take off and a mass movement develop, the clerical regime's response could cause thousands of deaths, far more than those killed in 2009. Its rhetoric and actions against the reform movement in the past indicate that the Iranian leadership sees violence as a legitimate response to peaceful demonstrators. Evidence from previous revolts suggests that military units would fire into crowds, and the regime would not hesitate to carry out mass trials to stay in power.

Such internal brutality creates an ethical question: should the United States try to help Iranians who want to overthrow their government if doing so might provoke widespread killing by the regime? Some may answer that if oppressed people want to run the risk of opposing their oppressors, it should not be for the United States to question their courage. Others may feel that it is unconscionable to encourage people to take actions likely to lead to large-scale killing, especially if the chances of success are low.

The other risk created by this policy is practical and strategic. Tehran's tendency to lash out whenever it has felt that its control over the country is threatened has extended to foreign affairs as well. As best we can tell, the 1996 Khobar Towers blast was an Iranian response to an $18 million increase in the U.S. covert action budget against Iran in 1995. Although that covert action program posed little threat to Tehran at the time (and $18 million was a paltry sum for the United States), the Iranians apparently saw it as a declaration of covert war and may have destroyed the Khobar Towers complex as a way of warning the United States of the consequences of such a campaign.[22] Similarly, Iran's response to the cyberwarfare attacks being launched against it over the past four to five years (and which Tehran believes originated with the United States, Israel, and the United Kingdom) has been to launch corresponding attacks of its own against whatever targets it can: American banks and Saudi oil infrastructure.[23] Finally, Iran has retaliated with assassination attempts, including an attempt to kill the Saudi ambassador to the United States and attacks on Israelis for what it believes to have been Israeli attacks on Iranian nuclear scientists.[24]

If the United States threatened its grip on power with a dedicated campaign, Tehran would likely take several steps. First, it would increase its support for guerrilla and terrorist groups around the region to encourage and enable them to attack America and its allies. Afghanistan would be a likely theater for an Iranian response given Tehran's ties to the Taliban and other anti-American groups. Iran might try to go after U.S. personnel in Iraq as well, but since the withdrawal of American military forces in 2011, these are smaller and less inviting targets. The Iranians might opt to hit U.S. diplomats, military officers, and even private citizens elsewhere in the Middle East and Europe. They might step up their attacks on U.S. allies—Israel, Saudi Arabia, Kuwait, the UAE, and others—as well. They might also encourage groups like Palestinian Islamic Jihad, Hamas, and Hizballah to be more aggressive toward Israel. Tehran almost certainly would continue its cyberattacks on the United States, perhaps even escalating them if there is anything more that they could do in this area that they have not already tried, like shutting down the power or water infrastructures of major American cities. Finally, the Iranians might even decide to mount terrorist attacks against the U.S. homeland, and in the future they may be better prepared for such operations than they were in 2010 with the half-baked Arbabsiar plot.

Reasons to Reconsider

Despite these reasons to be skeptical of a regime change strategy, there are also arguments in its favor. The first and most obvious is that helping indigenous Iranian oppositionists to change the regime in Tehran could be done at a relatively low cost. If a new Iranian regime made improving relations with the United States a priority, regime change might address more than just the nuclear impasse, conceivably resolving all of America's problems with the Islamic Republic.

The most important rationale in favor of supporting regime change, however, is the emergence of a legitimate, indigenous opposition within Iran. Before 2009, the outside world recognized that at least some Iranians were unhappy with their political, social, and economic circumstances. It was not apparent whether this dissatisfaction was confined to a tiny segment of Iran's middle- and upper-class populations. The events of 2009 changed all that. Millions of Iranians poured out into the streets of dozens of Iranian towns and cities, voicing their opposition not just to what they saw as a fraudulent election but to the Islamic Republic itself.

The Green Movement is an imperfect vehicle for regime change. Its failures in 2009 and 2011 have made it seem ineffective to many Iranians. Moreover, the leaders of the Green Movement were inevitably just the most unhappy of the losing candidates from the 2009 election, Mehdi Karrubi and Mir-Hossein Mousavi. Both of these men are former regime officials and more interested in reforming the regime to save it, rather than overthrowing it altogether. They are the leaders the movement rallied around, but not necessarily those that the Iranian people might have chosen if they could have had a wider range to pick from. Still, there remain signs of popular disenchantment with the regime—and difficulties that the regime is experiencing holding down dissent—that suggest that even since 2009, the latent potential for large-scale unrest persists.[25]

We need to be careful. We don't know how many Iranians supported the Greens or would like to see the regime overthrown. However, we know that roughly 70 percent of the country voted for Mohammad Khatami in 1997, and Khatami was the most change-oriented president ever elected in Iran. And we know that he was elected because Iranians *wanted* change. We also know that several million Iranians took to the streets to demand radical political change in 2009. In a country of 75 million, that may not seem like much, but revolutions are inevitably the work of small minorities. In one of the great books on the Iranian Revolution, Charles Kurzman points out that historically most successful revolutions have been conducted by less than 5 percent of a population. The Iranian Revolution of 1978–79 may have been the most popular protest event in history as it encompassed more than 10 percent of Iranians. Consequently, the size of the protests in 2009 accords with historical norms of successful revolutions.[26] The basic ingredients of regime change exist in Iran.

Over the past ten to fifteen years, the Iranian regime has experienced growing problems with restive minority groups in the country. The Arabs in Khuzestan (the far southwest), the Kurds in the northwest, and the Baluch in the southeast have all chafed against their status. All believe that they are the victims of prejudice and official discrimination. Many Kurds seek to secede from Iran altogether. Other groups may, too. The regime has had to fight a terrorist campaign by Arab Iranians, and guerrilla wars waged by the Kurds and Baluch.[27] There may be other ethnic and religious minorities in Iran willing to take action against the regime, as well.

Moreover, the paranoia of the Iranian regime could be an asset as well as an obstacle to a policy of regime change. Because of its obsessive fears with internal opposition, and especially foreign-aided internal opposition, the clerical regime often overreacts to the slightest hint of domestic unrest. This tendency has helped undermine its own popularity, alienate key internal constituencies, and create foes where none existed. It has probably also caused the regime to punish many innocent people who might otherwise have been allies. Tehran's overreactions have earned it opprobrium from foreign powers as well. Its overreaction at Khobar Towers could easily have resulted in a massive American conventional military strike against Iran had it not been for Mohammad Khatami's election in 1997.[28] While America's ability to hurt Iran through covert action may be modest, the Iranian regime's ability to hurt itself by overreacting to threats of covert action is enormous. American efforts to support regime change in Iran may not have to accomplish much more than piquing the paranoia of the regime, and then allowing it to destroy itself.

How?

Because the United States has not seriously tried to bring about regime change in Iran since 1953, the biggest obstacle of all might be figuring out how to go about it. For decades, experts (including this author) have warned that regime change is a terrible idea, and so the United States never pursued it. Moreover, the Iranian regime has had a frighteningly good track record crushing internal revolts and smashing American intelligence programs directed at it.[29] Knowing what to do, even where to start to think about how to overthrow the Iranian regime, is a considerable challenge.[30]

Because doing so has proven so difficult in the past, the United States and its allies would have to explore a range of options to undercut the regime's grip on power, including some that for good reason have been considered verboten for decades. Even just to explore the possibilities created by the emergence of a large, indigenous opposition, the United States is going to have to advance over unknown terrain. Helping Iranians who want to oppose their own regime would require a great deal of scouting, trial and error, and thinking outside of our traditional "box." Because the circumstances in Iran have changed so dramatically since 2009, we ought to be willing to question whether old taboos still apply or if there are new, smarter, better ways to challenge them. The real question is whether each specific operation has a high enough probability of success, a low-enough probability of failure and attendant harm, and a reasonable expectation that even partial success would be useful.

A critical component of any strategy would be to make connections with the Green Movement. There are many opportunities to connect with Iranian activists. Iran today is a land of labor protests and political demonstrations. The challenge is to establish ties, overt or covert, with important trade unions and student organizations with national networks connected by social media outlets. There are many unhappy mullahs in Iran because Khomeini's ideas were considered heretical by most traditional Shi'i clerics and many others feared that bringing religion into politics would only alienate people from religion. Some of them might be induced to condemn the moral shortcomings of the Islamist regime. We have also seen Iranian diplomats and nuclear scientists defect to the West. We could intensify our efforts to convince others to do the same.

Such tactics run counter to long-standing American thinking that providing active support to Iranian opposition groups would do little to advance their efforts and could taint them in the eyes of their countrymen as foreign spies. This assumption may still be valid, but we ought to be willing to test the proposition. American intelligence and diplomatic personnel should make clear that they are open to meeting Iranian opposition figures and open to providing assistance, if the oppositionists themselves are willing to accept it. At an even more basic level, it would be helpful to establish contact with Iranian oppositionists in hope of finding out from them what the United States might do that could be helpful. We have been so cut off from them for so many years that we have little ability to know what we could do that might be advantageous. Moreover, because of the regime's paranoia, it will doubtless inflate every surreptitious conversation into a full-scale covert campaign and overreact, potentially creating new opportunities for American action.

One of the most important things that the United States and its allies could do to put additional pressure on the Iranian regime would be to expand the focus of the international community's ire at Iran from its nuclear program to its abuse of human rights. Leading Iranian dissidents and average citizens who oppose the regime argue that Iran's leaders are sensitive to any criticism of their human rights record because they fear that it delegitimizes them in the eyes of the world and their remaining domestic supporters. Moreover, calling Iran to account for its deplorable human rights abuses is likely to strike a much more responsive note with countries around the world—even those whose human rights records are far from spotless. Many other Third World countries resent the great powers' monopoly over nuclear weapons, but few will condone gross, systematic human rights violations. Indeed, the European left, once apologists for Iran, have now largely turned against it, incensed by the regime's brutal crackdowns, torture, and tales of prison rape.[31]

On human rights, the United States would have powerful and admired allies in the international human rights community. It would mean acting not just in the service of American interests, but for American and universal values. In a powerful December 2012 report, the respected independent organization Human Rights Watch found that the "[Iranian] government's repression has involved a range of serious and intensifying human rights violations that include extra-judicial killings, torture, arbitrary arrest and detention, and widespread infringements of Iranians' rights to freedom of assembly and expression."[32] Indeed, both the EU and Canada have imposed sanctions on Iran purely for its human rights abuses.[33]

One route to help the Iranian opposition—and hurt the regime—is information warfare. The United States has made some tentative forays here, trying to reopen Internet service to Iran in the face of regime's efforts to choke it off, but much more can and should be done. The United States and its allies should actively seek ways to provide accessible, redundant means of communication (both overt and covert) to the Iranian oppositionists. The more that we can enable them to speak freely, the more the Iranian public and the world will be able to hear their message, and the better they can shake the foundations of the regime.

The United States might also provide support, even modest nonlethal aid, to various Iranian ethno-sectarian minorities actively opposing the regime. None of these groups—not the Kurds, the Baluch, the Arabs, or others—is likely to overthrow the regime and there are serious complications involved in supporting each, but they might help turn up the heat. Moreover, since the regime is convinced that the United States is doing this covert work already, there would appear to be little further downside from stoking Tehran's suspicions.

SANCTIONS AND REGIME CHANGE. If the United States adopted a policy of regime change, it would be critical to revamp the sanctions to contribute to this approach and ensure that they do not undermine it. Lawmakers and advocates of sanctions often overlook this point: sanctions can be employed in pursuit of a range of policy goals, including regime change, but they need to be crafted differently to best serve the particular goals. O'Sullivan noted in her study of the use of sanctions that it is possible to advance the goal of regime change via sanctions, but they need to be tailored to that purpose. In particular, she cited the case of sanctions against South Africa in the 1980s and '90s as helping to bring about regime change, but only because they were part of a wider strategy that also imposed other penalties like international isolation on the government while helping to empower a viable, legitimate indigenous opposition.[34]

Thus, if the United States either shifts wholesale to a policy of supporting internal opposition forces or does so as part of a last effort to make a carrot-and-stick strategy work, the overall question of how to employ economic sanctions has to be reconsidered. They need to be targeted to apply selective pressure on Iran over a prolonged period of time. In particular, the United States should begin to shift its sanctions efforts toward prohibiting foreign investment in Iran. American sanctions have already cut investment in Iran's hydrocarbon sector, and this success has proved painful for Tehran. The United States and its allies should look into targeting other sectors, particularly manufacturing and high-tech industries. O'Sullivan's points about South Africa provide a loose analogy, in that a human-rights-based campaign focused on choking off direct foreign investment in South Africa succeeded in forcing the government to dismantle the apartheid system. The "divestment" campaigns, coupled with state and business actions, hurt South Africa's GDP, but never in a way that caused severe, direct harm to the vast majority of South Africans. Instead, what it did was to paint an unmistakable picture for the South African leadership that if they did not change, their country would be reduced to a poor pariah state. That proved intolerable. Given Iranian pretensions to great power status, a similar perspective might have equally helpful effects.

A Qualified Case for Exploring Regime Change

Over the course of my career, both in government and out, I have made arguments against regime change in Iran. I don't regret having done so. For most of that period, the facts at the time warranted these arguments. Regime change seemed unlikely; it seemed likely to produce a nasty backlash from Tehran, and there were other policy options that seemed more likely to succeed and at a more acceptable cost.

These factors have changed, even reversed. Regime change still does seem unlikely to succeed, but the emergence of a legitimate, indigenous, broad-based opposition to the regime—one willing to take to the streets and risk violence against itself—is a dramatic change. For the first time since 1979, regime change seems possible.

There is no question that the Iranian regime will be furious and will fight back, but given where we now are with them, it is not clear what more we would face. The regime believes that we are trying to overthrow it. It is mounting cyberattacks against us (perhaps "counterattacks" would be more accurate) and it is not clear how much more they can do. There are lots more terrorist operations they could conduct against American targets, both in the region, around the world, and in the American homeland, but I suspect that they have refrained from doing so largely out of fear that such terrorism would provoke an American conventional military response—not out of any sense that the United States isn't trying to undermine the regime. And there is good reason for the Iranians to have this fear: on several occasions since 2007, the Brookings Institution has run crisis simulations ("war games") in which Iran mounted terrorist operations more directly against the United States and the consistent American response was to mount a direct military attack against Iran—which often escalated to much larger exchanges that left both sides worse off, but left the Iranian military and nuclear programs devastated.

Third, and perhaps most important of all, our policy options are narrowing precipitously. Pure engagement is no longer an option, if it ever was. The carrot-and-stick is in danger of being proven a failure as well. We are approaching the awful choice between going to war with Iran to prevent it from acquiring a nuclear weapons capability, or containing an Iran that may well possess a nuclear weapons capability—even an arsenal. Given how terrible that final choice is, we should be willing to consider almost any alternative that promises some possibility of avoiding it. And the events of 2009 have made regime change a faint possibility.

This is *not* to suggest that regime change is the answer to America's prayers, and that we should adopt it as our policy toward Iran in place of anything else. The United States ought to explore the possibility of pursuing a policy of regime change by aiding internal Iranian opposition forces. That's it. At present, we should "explore" this option. Because of all its downsides, all its risks and costs, we don't know if this option is feasible and, if it is feasible, whether it is worth those risks and costs.

Danielle Pletka's argument for regime change constitutes a final reason, and it may be the best of all. In the end, there may be nothing we can do to stop Iran from acquiring a nuclear weapons capability—or at least nothing else we can do to avoid the choice between war and containment. If regime change isn't feasible, if trying would only result in lots of dead Iranians and an undermined American position, it would be hard to make even the moral argument that it was the "right" thing to do. But if it is viable, and if there were reason to believe that it would improve the American position, why not do the right thing? Why not live up to our values for a change and help so many Iranians striving for a better life? Why not be who we aspire to be, not who we so often are?

8

The Sword of David

I srael has been contemplating a military operation against the Iranian nuclear program for a very long time. In 1991, after the Persian Gulf War, Jerusalem purchased twenty-five F-15E fighter-bombers from the United States. At the time, these were the premier long-range tactical strike aircraft in the world and those purchased by Israel were designated the F-15I. The *I* stood for "Israel." But whenever I spoke to Israeli Air Force officers, they would all go out of their way to say, "You may think that the *I* stands for 'Israel,' but to us, it stands for 'Iran.'"

In 1997, I spent more than a year outside government, working at a Washington, D.C., think tank. In the office next to me for part of that time was an Israeli fighter pilot spending six months in Washington between assignments. This guy was a legend. He had numerous air-to-air kills in Israel's various wars and was famous for outflying his American counterparts in training drills, including the major "Red Flag" exercises at Nellis Air Force Base, outside Las Vegas. He was just coming off a tour as the commander of one fighter squadron and was slated to take over another, even more prestigious, unit. He did not deny he was spending the six months thinking about how the Israeli Air Force (IAF) would try to destroy Iran's nuclear program if the Israeli leadership gave the order to do so. Before he left to go back to Israel and take over his new command, he and I had lunch. I asked him what he had come up with regarding a strike on Iran. He was blunt: "We can't do it. We don't have the horses. If someone is going to destroy the Iranian nuclear program, it is going to have to be you [the United States]."

And that is why we and the Israelis are where we are. A lot has changed since that conversation, but his conclusion remains valid. Certainly, the Israeli leadership fears that it is. Israeli leaders warn endlessly that they may have to strike Iran. There is a ferocious debate within the Israeli leadership about whether to strike Iran, a discussion that spills over into the public arena on a constant basis. This is entirely uncharacteristic of Israeli behavior. Almost no one—in Israel, in the United States, or anywhere else in the world—had ever heard of the Osirak reactor at Tuwaitha, Iraq, before the Israelis blew it up in 1981. Almost no one knew that there was a nuclear reactor being built at al-Kibar in the Syrian desert before the Israelis destroyed it in 2007. There were no public warnings, no open debate before either of these operations. Israel is not like the United States or other Western democracies in that sense. It does not "give all other alternatives a chance" before using force. Traditionally it does not see force as "the last resort," or at least its thresholds for that standard are much lower than our own. If Israel has a good military option, it takes it. It doesn't warn. It doesn't debate, at least not in public.[1] It strikes—and it typically succeeds when it does so.

The fact that Israel has not struck Iran despite considering, planning, training, and preparing for such an operation since at least 1997—and that it has warned repeatedly of and debated endlessly such a strike—is an important departure from Jerusalem's traditional approach to security issues. This unusual restraint on the part of the Israelis speaks to the many challenges that Israel faces when contemplating an attack on the Iranian nuclear program.

THE FOUR PARADOXES. Israel faces a set of formidable military problems it would have to overcome to have a significant impact on Iran's progress toward a nuclear weapon (problems that were not present for either the Iraqi or Syrian raids). In addition to the military challenges, for an Israeli strike to succeed in its basic aims, Jerusalem will have to unravel four paradoxes:

1. *It will spur Iran to rebuild, and probably to weaponize.* An Israeli strike would be beneficial only if afterward Iran can be convinced not to rebuild its nuclear program or else be prevented from doing so. However, there are few events that would be more likely to convince Tehran to rebuild its program (and even acquire an outright nuclear arsenal) than an Israeli attack.

2. *It will undermine the inspections and sanctions needed to prevent Iran from rebuilding.* Preventing Iran from rebuilding its nuclear program after an Israeli strike requires that the inspections and sanctions on Iran remain in place after the operation. Yet an Israeli strike would be the surest way to undermine the diplomatic foundations of sanctions and inspections.

3. *It requires American support, but could alienate the United States.* Especially because of the first two paradoxes, an Israeli strike would probably fail to achieve its goals without the full support of the United States. However, there are few events more likely to infuriate the U.S. government than an Israeli strike against Iran, especially if it triggers Iranian retaliation against the United States.

4. *It will provoke that which it is meant to prevent.* An Israeli strike would be intended to prevent future attack by a nuclear Iran and its allies such as Hizballah and PIJ—attacks that would most likely come in the form of terrorism, rockets, and conventionally armed missiles. But an Israeli

strike on the Iranian nuclear program would almost certainly provoke Iran and its allies to attack Israel by those very same means.

These four dilemmas, coupled with the technical military hurdles the Israel Defense Forces (IDF) face, create a vexing set of problems for an Israeli strike against the Iranian nuclear program. They demonstrate that Israel does not have a good military option. And that is why it would be better for everyone—Israel, the United States, the rest of the Middle East, the world, maybe even the Iranian people, too—if Israel were *not* to attack Iran.

The Strike: Military Considerations

An Israeli military strike on the Iranian nuclear program would be operationally difficult for the Israelis. As brilliant and daring as the IDF has proven itself to be, it is ultimately a small military with limited capabilities operating under severe geopolitical constraints.

Israel has both ballistic and cruise missiles that, in theory, might be used in an attack against Iran's nuclear sites, but in practice they are likely to be of secondary importance. Israel has four submarines (soon to be joined by a fifth and eventually a sixth) that can fire Popeye Turbo cruise missiles with a 930-mile range. Each sub, however, can only carry about a dozen of the missiles, each of which has a 400-pound warhead—not much compared to the 2,000-pound or 5,000-pound bombs that Israeli aircraft would carry. These limitations make Israel's cruise missiles much more useful to try to take out key Iranian radars, surface-to-air missile (SAM) batteries, and command and control sites. They might also be useful against Iran's less well-defended nuclear facilities, but not for attacking Iran's hardened, underground enrichment sites. Even then, Israel would have difficulty getting all of these short-range subs in position near Iran to launch simultaneously, and might prefer to hold back some or all of their missiles for follow-on strikes or to respond to Iranian retaliatory actions—neither of which would be easy for Israel's fighter-bombers to handle.

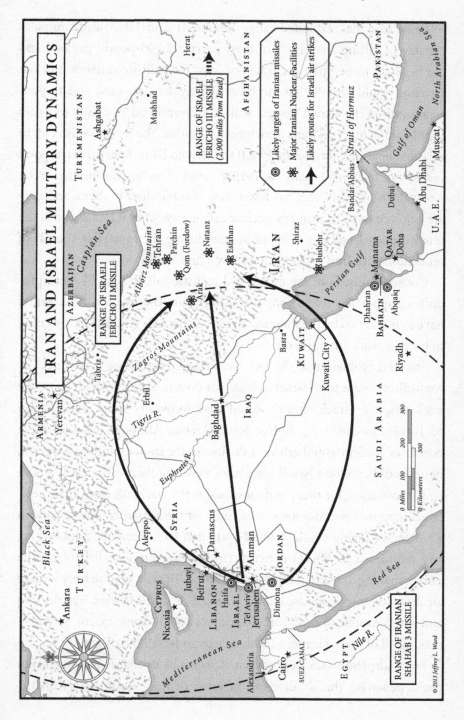

IRAN AND ISRAEL MILITARY DYNAMICS

RANGE OF ISRAELI JERICHO III MISSILE
(2,900 miles from Israel)

◎ Likely targets of Iranian missiles
✳ Major Iranian Nuclear Facilities
➤ Likely routes for Israeli air strikes

RANGE OF ISRAELI JERICHO II MISSILE

RANGE OF IRANIAN SHAHAB 3 MISSILE

Herat

Mashhad

Ashgabat

TURKMENISTAN

AFGHANISTAN

PAKISTAN

North Arabian Sea

Gulf of Oman

Muscat ★

Strait of Hormuz

Bandar Abbas

Dubai

Abu Dhabi

U.A.E.

Caspian Sea

Tehran ✳
Parchin
Qom (Fordow) ✳
Natanz ✳
Esfahan ✳

Alborz Mountains

AZERBAIJAN

Tabriz

Shiraz

IRAN

Bushehr ✳

Persian Gulf

Manama ◎
Doha ◎
QATAR

BAHRAIN ◎
Dhahran ◎
Abqaiq ◎

ARMENIA

Yerevan ★

Arak ✳

Zagros Mountains

Erbil

Tigris R.

Baghdad ★

IRAQ

Basra

Kuwait City

KUWAIT

Riyadh ★

SAUDI ARABIA

0 Miles   100   200   300

0 Kilometers   300

Euphrates R.

TURKEY

Ankara ★

Black Sea

Aleppo

SYRIA

Damascus ★

Amman ★

JORDAN

Red Sea

CYPRUS
Nicosia ★

Jubayl
Beirut
LEBANON
Haifa ◎
ISRAEL
Tel Aviv ◎
Jerusalem ★
Dimona ◎

Mediterranean Sea

Cairo ★
SUEZ CANAL

EGYPT

Nile R.

Alexandria

© 2013 Jeffrey L. Ward

Israel also has extended-range Jericho II and III ballistic missiles capable of hitting Iran. Both of these carry a 2,200-pound payload and are believed to be quite accurate—at least for ballistic missiles. But the Jerichos would actually have to be extremely accurate (and able to penetrate buried, hardened targets with a conventional payload) to cause significant damage to Iran's enrichment facilities. The Jericho II isn't up to this challenge and it is not known if the Jericho III is. Israel also has good reason not to expend many (or perhaps any) of its Jerichos on the strike. Analysts think that Israel has fewer than one hundred of them, and they are believed to be its primary nuclear delivery system.[2] It is also one of the few weapons Israel has to strike at Iran during the inevitable rounds of retaliation with Iran expected to follow a first strike.[3]

Consequently, both the cruise and ballistic missiles are likely to play only a supporting role in any attack on Iran. The main burden would have to be carried by the manned aircraft of the IAF. And the IAF is going to have its work cut out for it.

The first problem that the IAF faces is airspace. There is no direct or semi-direct route from Israel to Iran that does not pass through someone else's airspace. Israeli aircraft would have to overfly some combination of Turkey, Jordan, Iraq, and/or Saudi Arabia. Although none of these countries' leaders would grieve at the loss of the Iranian nuclear program, none would condone Israeli warplanes violating their airspace. It would be a humiliation for them and all would fear a backlash from their anti-Israeli populations. Moreover, as a result of the Syrian civil war, Turkish air defenses facing south (toward Syria *and* Israel) are alert, mobilized, and reinforced by NATO batteries (including American Patriot missile units), making Turkey an inhospitable route. The rest tend to have weaker air defenses, mostly focused in the wrong direction—toward Iran for Iraq and Saudi Arabia, toward Turkey for Syria and, to some extent, Jordan—making all of them far more conducive to an Israeli overflight.

For a surprise attack against Iran, it seems likely that Israeli warplanes could penetrate the air defenses of most of these countries (with the likely exception of Turkey), conduct the attack on Iran, and return to Israel without even being detected. The IAF has demonstrated an ability to evade radar detection by flying at absurdly low altitudes where terrain features mask their planes from enemy radars. More recently, Israel has used a combination of electronic and cyberwarfare to confuse and blind enemy radars.[4] The problem is that once things start blowing up in Iran, these countries will alert their air defenses, making it far harder for Israeli warplanes to mount a repeat strike without having to fight their way through Turkish, Jordanian, Syrian, Iraqi, and/or Saudi air defenses. In addition to the military problem this would create for additional strike waves, it is highly unlikely that Jerusalem would want to pick a fight with another Muslim Middle Eastern state after having attacked Iran. These limitations mean that Israel would realistically get one strike with its air force, unless follow-on rounds of combat escalated to the point where Israel was taking so much damage that it was willing to fight one or more of these other states to get at Iran. The latter is both unlikely and would represent a disastrous outcome for Israel.

The next problem Israel faces is distance. As the crow flies, it is about 965 miles from the relevant Israeli air bases to Qom (where the Fordow facility is located), 985 miles to Natanz, 1,000 miles to Tehran, and about 995 miles to Esfahan. In theory, Israel has 125 strike aircraft capable of reaching targets in Iran. It has 25 of the F-15I Ra'am ("Thunder," the Israeli variant of the F-15E), which have an unrefueled range of about 2,400 miles. It also has 100 F-16I Sufa ("Storm," a Block 52 F-16D with Israeli avionics and conformal fuel tanks), which have a reported unrefueled range of about 1,100 miles.[5] There is no way that Israel's F-16Is can get to Iran and back without being refueled, and that may be the case for the F-15Is as well. While the F-15Is' nominal range would seem adequate to get to Iran and back, reality is more complicated. Because of air defenses and political considerations, the Israeli planes may not be able to fly on a straight line to Iran. Every detour adds miles and burns fuel. Moreover, for significant chunks of these flights, the aircraft would have to fly at low altitude, which burns far more fuel. Plus, there is a trade-off between weight and weapons: the more ordnance you carry, the heavier the plane, the fewer miles you can fly.

Since most or all of these planes cannot make it to Iran and back on their own, they would have to be refueled along the way. Refueling greatly complicates the operation. The best way to refuel would be to use dedicated tanker aircraft, of which Israel has a small number. However, tanker aircraft are both difficult to hide and vulnerable to enemy air defenses. They would likely have to overfly Turkish, Syrian, Jordanian/ Iraqi, or Saudi territory and might have to orbit there for hours, waiting for the strike aircraft to return to fill them up for the return leg. In addition, the refueling requirements of a strike of 125 aircraft to targets more than 950 miles away in Iran might exceed the capacity of Israel's tanker fleet, although there are reports that the IDF has been secretly buying cargo aircraft and converting them to tankers.[6] In spring 2013, the United States and Israel agreed on a new arms deal that will provide Israel with additional tankers, but they are not expected to arrive for a year or more, and even if this solves the problem of numbers, it still does nothing about the problem of tanker vulnerability.[7] Another refueling method the Israelis might employ would be for the strike aircraft to refuel one another in flight (called "buddy" refueling). That eliminates the need to have big, slow, vulnerable tankers flying over hostile airspace, but it would also reduce the number of strike aircraft with the fuel to make it to Iran, shrinking the number of bombs on target. Depending on a variety of technical factors, buddy refueling could cut the size of the actual strike force by 50 or even 75 percent—which could make it impossible for Israel to achieve anything of military value. Another alternative would be for the Israeli warplanes to refuel on the ground. There are no countries on the route that would voluntarily refuel an Israeli strike package, but the IDF might opt to set up a covert, forward refueling point in the desert of Syria, Jordan, Iraq, or Saudi Arabia. While feasible, it would be a risky, complicated addition to the mission.[8]

The problems of airspace and distance mean that, at best, Israel would get one strike during one night, with no more than 125 tactical strike aircraft. Various factors starting with refueling could reduce that number significantly.

Iran's own air defenses probably could not defeat an Israeli strike, but they would make it harder. Iranian radar coverage is incomplete and many of Tehran's radars are old and poorly maintained. Nevertheless, there are enough of them that they would probably force an Israeli strike package to weave its way through one or more of the valleys of the Zagros Mountains and fly low across Iran's central plateau after debouching from the mountain passes to avoid detection. This flight plan would require still more fuel, increasing the likelihood that Israel would have to refuel the strike force more than once.

Both Iran's fighter fleet and its inventory of surface-to-air missiles are unimpressive. Tehran has few modern systems, fewer still procured in the past fifteen years, and none that are properly maintained. It has too few (just 24) of its most capable interceptor, the short-ranged MIG-29, and its dozen or so semi-operational F-14s and Mirage F-1s are obsolete and no match for Israel's modern F-15s and F-16s. Its SAMs are too few, too old, and too limited in capability and range to pose much of a threat to the Israelis. And the competence of Iranian air force and air defense force personnel is no match for the IAF pilots.

Nevertheless, if Iran's air defenses are even modestly alert, they could create additional problems for the Israelis. At the very least, the Israelis would face some tough choices regarding how much effort they would want to take away from bombing the nuclear sites to devote instead to fending off Iran's air defenses. For the Osirak strike in 1981, almost half the planes in the Israeli strike force were dedicated fighter escorts. The IAF may feel that Iran's air force does not merit that much respect, but either way it would be another risk. Similarly, if the Israelis believe that they would need some of their aircraft to act as dedicated SAM suppression, electronic warfare, and jammer aircraft (or merely carry heavy electronic warfare pods for this purpose), that too would limit the number of bomb droppers or the number and size of the bombs. These kinds of trade-offs further demonstrate just how challenging this operation would be and how narrow its margin of possible success.

Then there are Iran's passive defenses. The Iranian nuclear program consists of dozens of different facilities, but the Israelis would almost certainly concentrate on just a few of the most important ones: the Fordow uranium enrichment plant, the Natanz uranium enrichment plant, the Esfahan uranium conversion plant, the Arak heavy-water reactor, the Bushehr reactor, and the Parchin weapons testing facility. In truth, neither Bushehr nor Parchin is likely to be high on Israel's list, as it is no longer clear that these facilities are crucial to Iran's nuclear-weapons-related activities. On the other hand, if Israel can locate wherever Iran is working on weaponization, they might add those sites to their list.

Some of these targets are aboveground and vulnerable to attack, such as Esfahan, meaning that it would not take many bombs to destroy them. Other Iranian facilities are large, bunkered, and underground—such as Natanz and Fordow—and they will be a much bigger problem. Iran's main uranium enrichment plant at Natanz is a large facility—roughly 325,000 square feet with two 80–100,000-square-feet centrifuge halls. It is also well protected. Its chambers are located twenty-five feet belowground, covered by a seventy-two-foot mound of dirt, and further defended by two concrete walls, one of which is eight feet thick.[9] Iran's newer (but smaller) Fordow enrichment facility is even more formidable. It was built inside a mountain near Iran's holy city of Qom, beneath nearly three hundred feet of rock.[10]

Since Natanz and Fordow are Iran's primary known enrichment venues, it is essential for Israel to destroy them in any attack. Israel has 2,000-pound GBU-27 and 5,000-pound GBU-28 "bunker busting" bombs, designed to penetrate earth and reinforced concrete. These bombs could waste the Natanz facility if several dozen of them struck it accurately.[11] However, neither bomb is big enough to give Israel a high probability of destroying the Fordow site. Israel would have to drop scores of them on the same point on the mountain to have even a remote chance of damaging the Fordow facility. By one estimate, if Israel used all 25 of its F-15Is (which are the only Israeli planes that can carry the GBU-28) to attack Fordow with 25 GBU-28s and 50 GBU-27s, and all 75 of those bombs hit precisely the same point in the mountain, there would be some probability that *one* of those bombs would damage the Fordow plant itself. Even then, the extent of the damage would be impossible to predict and might well be negligible.[12] Although both bombs are precision-guided, they still can miss, making the likelihood of this long shot closer to a miracle.

Worse still, even trying such an attack would leave no F-15Is, and therefore none of the heavy GBU-28s, left to hit Natanz. That would force Israel to devote scores of F-16Is with the smaller GBU-27s to attack Natanz, leaving few aircraft to strike other Iranian targets let alone provide air defense and electronic warfare escorts. The Israelis might also try to seal Fordow by destroying its entrances, but this effort might have little to no impact on the centrifuge halls (or the centrifuges themselves) and the entrances could probably be reopened in weeks, if not days.

Moreover, this analysis assumes that Iran has no hidden nuclear facilities. The Iranians have a penchant for building covert nuclear facilities that they have been able to hide from the world for some period of time, usually several years. There are some caveats to that point. The facilities that we know about were all discovered before they became operational, and Israel, the United States, the IAEA, and several European countries are all investing enormous resources into discovering hidden Iranian nuclear facilities. But neither we nor the Israelis can rule out the possibility that Iran may have concealed one or more large, important nuclear facilities. The Iraqis did before 1991. Ahmadinejad warned in 2009 that Iran would build ten more secret mountain enrichment plants like Fordow.

Some have speculated that Israel might employ special forces (SF) troops as part of an attack on Iran.[13] The Israelis are a remarkable bunch. In 1976, they flew a hundred commandos (famously led by Prime Minister Netanyahu's older brother, Yonatan) more than 2,500 miles to rescue one hundred Israeli and Jewish hostages captured by Palestinian terrorists and held at the Entebbe airport in Uganda. They pulled it off with only one fatality, Yoni Netanyahu. That should make us wary of claiming that they won't or can't do something just as remarkable. However, against Iran it would be even harder.

Because of Iran's distance, Israeli troops would have to be flown by large, slow, and vulnerable transport aircraft that would be far more vulnerable than IAF fighter jets to being detected and intercepted by Iranian air defenses. Even if Israel tried to fly the commandos to a location nearby and then use helicopters to fly them to the assault location, the fiasco of Desert One in 1980—in which American SF troops attempted just such an operation to rescue the American hostages in Iran, and failed disastrously—is an important warning of how difficult such a raid would be. In April 2013, Israel agreed to purchase U.S.-made V-22 Osprey tactical transport aircraft, which would be ideal for a commando assault on Fordow or other nuclear facilities, but these planes would also have to be refueled several times for a mission to Iran, and they are not expected to be delivered and operational until 2014 at the earliest, by which point Iran may well have further bolstered its defenses at these sites.[14] Even if Israeli troops made it to one of the Iranian sites, they would have to fight their way in and carry enough explosives to destroy these large complexes. Israel would have to accept the risk of having some, perhaps many, of these troops killed or, worse still, captured by the Iranians. Israel may be the most casualty-sensitive country in the world, routinely releasing hundreds, even thousands of enemy prisoners in return for just one Israeli captive, or the remains of an Israeli soldier. Given that most Israelis are ambivalent about a strike on Iran (see below), it would be even harder for an Israeli prime minister to risk captured Israeli soldiers. On top of all this, a daring commando raid might add little to the damage that the IAF could inflict on its own.

Israeli skill, creativity, and technical competence are high enough that we should not assume that they can't pull it off. If anyone can, it is the IDF. But neither should we assume that it would be easy. It sure won't be. Getting the planes there, getting through Iran's air defenses, destroying the targets, and getting back home are all significant challenges, much more difficult than those Israel faced for the Entebbe, Osirak, Tunis, or al-Kibar operations. It would be the most daring mission the IDF ever attempted. Anthony Cordesman, one of the finest military analysts in the United States, and Abdullah Toukan, the former science advisor to the king of Jordan, ultimately reached a similar assessment: for an Israeli strike, "the number of aircraft required, refueling along the way and getting to the targets without being detected or intercepted would be complex and high risk and would lack any assurances that the overall mission will have a high success rate."[15] It isn't that Israel can't do it, just that it would be very hard to succeed and very easy to fail.

Impact of a Strike

Given the number of variables involved in an Israeli attack on the Iranian nuclear program, solving the equation to determine how much damage such a strike would do is difficult. How many Israeli warplanes will be launched and how many will make it to Iran? Of those, how many will be dedicated to fighter escort or SEAD (suppression of enemy air defenses) roles, and how many will be left to drop bombs? If the IAF maximizes the number of strike aircraft and takes the risk of leaving Iranian air and air defense forces unengaged, how much will those Iranian defenders be able to disrupt the strikes? Will the Israelis try to take out Fordow or leave it alone and concentrate on other key targets? If they do attack Fordow, will they do any damage to it—and what other targets will they have the planes left to strike? How accurate will the strikes be? Will they employ their Jerichos or Popeye Turbos in an opening attack or save them for restrikes and responses to the inevitable Iranian retaliation?

These questions overwhelm any calculus. They require critical assumptions and their interdependence creates highly imprecise estimates. It makes predicting the damage that the Israelis might cause to the Iranian program effectively impossible. That's why the many estimates of the extent to which an Israeli strike on Iran would set back Tehran's nuclear program range from a few months, to a year or two, to as many as three to five years.

Not surprisingly, the U.S. government (which opposes an Israeli strike) and dovish Israelis tend to believe that an Israeli strike would set Iran back by one to two years at most, whereas hawkish Americans and Israelis both contend that it could set the program back by three to five years.[16] Who is right? Who knows?

One way to approach these questions is to ask who is making the predictions. I have a lot of confidence in Tony Cordesman and Abdullah Toukan. Both are known for their ability and integrity. They lay out their analysis in considerable detail in their published reports on this subject so that you can see how they came to their conclusions, and Cordesman in particular has proven to be scrupulously objective in his analysis over the years, acknowledging when he does not know the answer to a question or cannot make a judgment. So I find it noteworthy that their 2012 study concluded that "Israel does not have the capability to carry out preventive strikes that could do more than delay Iran's efforts for a year or two."[17] A number of highly respected former senior Israeli intelligence officers have echoed these comments, with Efraim Halevy concluding that an Israeli strike would only set Iran back a year, and Rafi Eitan insisting that the Iranians would be set back "not even three months."[18]

Another way to approach this question is to ask nuclear physicists and technical experts how much damage an Israeli strike might accomplish. Here the estimates from various nuclear specialists—American, Israeli, European, and others—seem far more consistent, and they cluster around the one-to-two-year end of the spectrum.[19] A senior Israeli official told veteran journalist Karl Vick in 2012 that the experts on Israel's Atomic Energy Commission had concluded that an Israeli strike could only expect to delay the Iranian program by a year at most, and more likely just a few months.[20] Likewise, Dr. Ali Vaez, the director of the Iran Project at the Federation of American Scientists, said in 2012 that an Israeli strike on the Iranian nuclear program "will delay the program for a couple of years, but would galvanize Iran to dash toward the ultimate deterrent."[21] The technical expertise, meticulous work, and objectivity of David Albright, Jacqueline Shire, and Paul Brannan of the highly regarded Institute for Science and International Security is always important to heed.

Their 2008 assessment argued that "an attack on Iran's nuclear program is unlikely to significantly degrade Iran's ability to reconstitute its gas centrifuge program."[22] (And that judgment was rendered even before we knew that Fordow existed.) Albright, Brannan, and Shire noted that Iran has dispersed the plants at which it builds centrifuges, has stockpiled critical equipment and raw materials, and may well have additional centrifuges in reserve, all of which would make reconstitution relatively quick.[23] Moreover, the Iranians have now gone through the entire process once, so they understand how to do it and know how to avoid mistakes. Repeating the process would doubtless be faster.

Official American statements also seem to accord with this time frame, suggesting that this is also the conclusion of the U.S. intelligence community's own nuclear scientists and technical experts. A *New York Times* story cites one of the WikiLeaks cables that provided a readout from a meeting between the French defense minister and then–secretary of defense Robert Gates in February 2010. According to the *Times*, the cable reports that Gates told his French counterpart that an Israeli strike "would only delay Iranian plans by one to three years, while unifying the Iranian people to be forever embittered against the attacker."[24] At my own center's annual Saban Forum in December 2011, then–secretary of defense Leon Panetta was asked about an Israeli strike on Iran. He answered, "At best it might postpone it maybe one, possibly two years."[25] The chairman of the U.S. Joint Chiefs of Staff, General Martin Dempsey, explained in a CNN interview with Fareed Zakaria in 2012 that "I think that Israel has the capability to strike Iran and to delay the production or the capability of Iran to achieve a nuclear weapons status, probably for a couple of years. But some of the targets are probably beyond their reach and, of course, that's what—that's what concerns them."[26]

General Dempsey's remark about targets beyond Israel's reach raises another important factor in assessing the impact of an Israeli strike: Fordow. Israel just may not be able to destroy the Fordow enrichment plant, and if it cannot, that will greatly—perhaps even fatally—compromise the effect of the operation regardless of any other damage the Israelis might do. Fordow has nearly 3,000 centrifuges and has already enriched uranium to 3.5 and 19.75 percent purities. Even if the Israelis destroy Natanz (with its roughly 14,000 centrifuges), if Israel cannot do the same to Fordow, Iranian uranium enrichment would be slowed but not halted. What's more, the Iranians recently installed more advanced IR-2 centrifuges there. Once they can get these machines operational at Fordow, the diminution in Iran's overall production of enriched uranium from the loss of Natanz alone might not be significant at all.

Thus, to significantly set back Iran's nuclear program, Israel has to destroy both Natanz *and* Fordow. However, if the Israelis made an effort against Fordow as part of an air raid, even committing all of their F-15Is against it, they would still have very little chance of destroying it and, in trying, would so diminish the damage that they could inflict on other Iranian targets as to make the raid undesirable. Thus the most likely outcome of an Israeli attack would be that Natanz, Arak, Esfahan, and perhaps one or two other sites would be destroyed or badly damaged, but Fordow and the rest of the program would be left intact. And practically speaking, the existence of an operational centrifuge plant at Fordow negates the utility of an Israeli air strike.

One way around the Fordow problem would be to eliminate Iran's ability to supply the centrifuges there with uranium hexafluoride, the feedstock that the centrifuges use to make enriched uranium. The Iranian plant at Esfahan that produces uranium hexafluoride has the great advantage of being aboveground and relatively unprotected, making it easier to destroy by air strike. But it would be hard to know how much uranium hexafluoride the Iranians would have stockpiled at the time of the attack and harder still to eliminate those stockpiles. In the words of Albright, Brannan, and Shire:

> Iran's uranium conversion facility at Esfahan, which produces the natural uranium gas that is introduced into centrifuges for enrichment, has already produced many years worth of uranium hexafluoride that is under safeguards. Destroying the facility would not eliminate this stockpile, now

over 300 tonnes of uranium hexafluoride, or enough to produce weapon-grade uranium for over 30 nuclear weapons, if it were moved prior to a strike. In any case, an attacker would be hard pressed to destroy all of the uranium hexafluoride at Esfahan, since it is stored in many, relatively small, thick metal canisters designed to withstand sabotage and severe transportation accidents. The bombs or missiles would likely need to hit close to the canisters to ensure their destruction. Yet, the attackers might not know their precise location within Esfahan.[27]

Unless the Israelis somehow destroyed those stockpiles, too, the loss of Esfahan might not have much impact.

Israeli defense minister Ehud Barak once argued that when Fordow became operational Iran would enter a "Zone of Immunity" from attack by Israel.[28] Unfortunately, Fordow became operational in the fall of 2012, meaning that Iran has already entered Barak's "Zone of Immunity." Israel could still strike, but if it can't destroy Fordow, the impact on Iran's nuclear program will be *much* less than it otherwise might.[29]

After the Dust Settles: The First Three Paradoxes

On June 7, 1981, eight Israeli F-16s escorted by six F-15s operating at the extreme edge of their range obliterated Iraq's Osirak (or more properly, "Tammuz") reactor, located at Tuwaitha, in the desert outside Baghdad. The strike has been celebrated ever since. At the time, and until well after the 2003 U.S. invasion of Iraq, it was believed that the Israeli strike crippled Iraq's nuclear program, setting it back so much that Baghdad was unable to develop a nuclear weapon prior to Saddam's 1990 invasion of Kuwait. In that version of history, the Osirak strike was crucial to preventing Saddam from acquiring a nuclear weapon—an event that would have made Operation Desert Storm impossible.

Information that has come to light in the years following Saddam's fall has forced us to revise that story. This evidence indicates that the Osirak strike had a much more mixed impact on Iraq's nuclear program, and ultimately did more to accelerate Saddam's drive for the bomb than it did to impede it. The emerging consensus among scholars who have studied this evidence is that had the Persian Gulf War not put an end to Saddam's nuclear weapons program with massive, repeated air strikes followed by comprehensive inspections, Iraq would have acquired a nuclear weapon by the early to mid-1990s.[30] Iraq's program in the 1980s was desultory and poorly funded. The Israeli attack infuriated and humiliated Saddam, prompting him to invest far more heavily in a new program that pursued several feasible paths to a weapon and put Iraq on the way to acquiring a bomb by the time of Operation Desert Storm.[31] In the words of the most comprehensive and evenhanded assessment of Osirak: "The Israeli attack intensified the Iraqi elite's determination to acquire nuclear weapons and secure sufficient resources to establish and expand the nuclear weapons program over time."[32] This same study found that "[t]he attack on Osirak triggered a well-funded covert program to produce nuclear weapons, which increased the proliferation risk posed by Iraq in the long term," and that ultimately, "the Israeli attack was ineffective."[33]

The critical lesson of Osirak is therefore not that an Israeli air strike could eliminate the Iranian nuclear program. The real lesson is that even a successful air strike, like the Osirak raid—which would be far harder for Israel to replicate against Iran—is unlikely to convince the targeted state to give up on nuclear weapons altogether. It could in fact cause them to redouble their efforts. Moreover, even a successful air campaign requires comprehensive inspections and the threat of sanctions to force compliance with those inspections. In the case of Iraq after 1981, there were neither inspections nor sanctions and so Baghdad rebuilt its program bigger and better. In contrast, after 1991, Iraq was bound by both invasive inspections and crippling sanctions. Those measures ultimately succeeded in preventing Saddam from rebuilding, although it still required a long and painful struggle.

THE FIRST PARADOX. In the ideal scenario, an Israeli strike on the Iranian nuclear program would prove so devastating that Iran would give up on its nuclear dreams. Is that scenario possible? Sure. After all, Iranian politics are complicated and unpredictable. Unfortunately, it is hard to make the case that this is the likely outcome of an Israeli attack. The opposite seems far more likely.

Some have argued that Iran might give up the nuclear ship because a successful Israeli strike would humiliate the regime and might incite popular unrest. If either of these were to prove true, it could trigger a change in the Iranian regime, bringing to power a different group of leaders who would put repairing the economy and ending Iran's isolation high on their list of priorities and rebuilding a nuclear infrastructure low on their list, if it were to appear at all.[34]

It is always important to acknowledge these as possible outcomes because of how hard it is to predict Iranian behavior. However, all run contrary to the history of air campaigns and Iran's history since the 1979 revolution. For instance, it is unlikely that the regime would even admit that an Israeli strike (or an American one, for that matter) had been successful. Because it would be difficult to see the damage to Iran's underground facilities, it would be hard to disprove their claims. Consequently, it is not clear whether anyone would even try to move against the regime in the belief that it had been damaged or humiliated. Even then, the protesters would still face the regime's proven willingness and ability to crush internal unrest, a capability that almost certainly would not be affected by an Israeli strike. Indeed, historically, being bombed does not bring about regime change, and only rarely brings about significant changes in regime behavior—and even then typically requires a range of other factors.[35] Saddam never gave up his nuclear ambitions after the successful Osirak raid, the ineffective Iranian attacks during the Iran-Iraq War, or even the massive bombing campaigns of Operation Desert Storm. Only the combination of comprehensive inspections tied to crippling sanctions did that, and even then it was a temporary, tactical retreat.[36]

It seems more likely that, like Saddam before them, the Iranians would respond to an Israeli strike by rebuilding their nuclear program as fast as possible. The U.S. government understands this problem implicitly.

As General Michael Hayden, George W. Bush's brilliant director of the CIA, put it, "The view among Mr. Bush's top advisers was that a strike (by Israel) would drive them (the Iranians) to do what we were trying to prevent."[37] It is also, by the way, the widespread Israeli expectation. Ephraim Kam, a former Israeli intelligence officer and the deputy director of the Institute for National Security Studies, notes, "The common assumption is that an attack on its facilities would not stop the program, but would at most postpone its completion by several years. This is a realistic assumption. It is likely that the Iranian regime would feel committed to rebuild its nuclear facilities as fast as possible and continue to advance the program while assimilating lessons from the strike, including improving fortifications and dispersing sites."[38]

THE SECOND PARADOX. If an Israeli strike fails to convince Iran not to rebuild its nuclear program, the next best option is for the international community to prevent it from doing so by wielding the same kind of intrusive inspections and harsh sanctions that worked in Iraq. When you speak to Israeli policymakers, military officers, and intelligence analysts, this outcome is their real goal because few believe that there is any likelihood that Iran won't try to rebuild.[39] In the words of Major General Amos Yadlin, "After the Osirak attack and the destruction of the Syrian reactor in 2007, the Iraqi and Syrian nuclear programs were never fully resumed. This could be the outcome in Iran, too, if military action is followed by tough sanctions, stricter international inspections and an embargo on the sale of nuclear components to Tehran."[40] Yadlin may well be right, but the "if" in that statement is a big one.

The good news in the case of Iran is that we already have an intrusive inspections regime coupled with crippling sanctions. The bad news is that an Israeli strike would jeopardize both.

There is a high probability that after an Israeli strike, Iran would withdraw from the NPT.[41] Iranian officials have argued about whether to adhere to the treaty for decades because of the complications it creates for Tehran's nuclear program.[42] In recent years, Tehran has claimed that the

IAEA is furnishing information on the Iranian nuclear program to Israel, Britain, and the United States to help them to attack it.[43] Senior Majles member Javad Jahangirzadeh railed against the NPT and the IAEA in late 2012, claiming that "[IAEA director Yukiya] Amano's repeated trips to Tel Aviv and asking the Israeli officials' views about Iran's nuclear activities indicates that Iran's nuclear information has been disclosed to the Zionist regime (Israel) and other enemies of the Islamic Republic. . . . If the agency's actions lead to Iran cutting cooperation with this international body, all responsibility will be with the IAEA director general."[44] In September 2012, the commander of the Revolutionary Guard, Mohammad Ali Jafari, warned that Iran would withdraw from the NPT if its nuclear program were attacked.[45] Iran's envoy to the IAEA, Ali Asghar Soltanieh, even warned the agency's thirty-five-nation board in November 2012 that if Iran were attacked it might withdraw from the NPT and evict the inspectors.[46] Doing so might not be cost-free for Iran because some countries have argued that states like Iran that violate their obligations should not be allowed to withdraw. However, Tehran would count on international opprobrium against Israel to shield it from any such measures, and may not care at that point, especially having endured so many sanctions already.[47]

If Iran withdraws from the NPT, it means the end of the inspections and potentially of the sanctions, too.[48] The IAEA inspection regime in Iran is entirely derived from Iran's adherence to the NPT. If Iran withdraws from the treaty, the inspections go with it. Likewise, the legal foundation for all of the UN Security Council resolutions against Iran (upon which rest nearly all of the multilateral sanctions on Iran) is its failure to adhere to its obligations under the NPT. If Iran withdraws from the NPT, this decision could compromise the legal basis of the sanctions. Iran and its advocates have challenged the legality of the sanctions, and its withdrawal from the NPT would exacerbate those claims. In practical terms, the West would argue that the sanctions resolutions have standing beyond Iran's violation of its NPT obligations and therefore should be unaffected. The reality is that the Chinese, Russians, and potentially others are likely to be furious at Israel for launching a strike. That anger would be played out both in the UN Security Council and in the court of world opinion. At the very least, it would become much harder for the West to secure new sanctions. Even if the existing sanctions remained on the books, there is a high risk that various states would simply start ignoring them, as happened when international opinion turned against the sanctions on Iraq in the late 1990s.

Iran might go even further, dropping their claimed abstention from nuclear weapons and announcing their determination to pursue an arsenal to ensure that Israel (or anyone else) never attacks it again. Tehran could argue that the Israeli strike demonstrated that Iran's conventional deterrent was inadequate to protect itself, and it had to acquire a nuclear arsenal instead. A great many people would not only sympathize with this sentiment; they would blame Israel for having brought it about. Although many Arab governments would like to see Iran's nuclear program eradicated—even by the Israelis—their people detest any Israeli use of force, especially against fellow Muslims. Thus, much of the Muslim world might follow, as could many other developing countries who see Israel as arrogant, aggressive, and unwilling to make peace with the Palestinians.

THE THIRD PARADOX. The problem with the second paradox is that it is not just the worst-case scenario; it is the most likely outcome of an Israeli strike on Iran's nuclear program. That is why the smartest Israelis place so much emphasis on American support, because they hope that the United States would be able to mitigate or eliminate the second paradox—an Israeli strike can only succeed if the sanctions and inspections remain in place to prevent Iranian rebuilding, but the strike itself is likely to undermine the sanctions and inspections. It is also part of the reason why polls in Israel demonstrate that few Israelis (18–22 percent, depending on the poll) favor an attack on Iran without American support, but far more (43–52 percent) would support one with American backing.[49] In addition to the greater punch that the United States brings, the Israelis in the latter group are betting that the Americans will solve the problem of the second paradox.

Unfortunately, that just brings up another problem. While Israel's faith in the United States is touching, it may also be misplaced. It isn't entirely that the United States won't want to do so—it may. The issue is as much that the United States may not be *able* to. Over the years, I have had the opportunity to participate in numerous crisis simulations ("war games") that attempted to explore the aftermath of an Israeli strike on Iran's nuclear facilities. I have even run four of them at the Saban Center at Brookings since 2009. In every case, the United States' initial reaction to an Israeli strike was the same: Washington refused to "pile on" by conducting follow-on strikes against Iran to finish the job the Israelis started, it offered defensive aid to the Israelis (Patriot batteries and AEGIS cruisers to help Israel shoot down incoming Iranian missiles, information about Iranian actions and the like), and it tried to prevent the unraveling of the sanctions and inspections on Iran. And just as consistently, the United States could not prevent Iran from withdrawing from the NPT and other countries from turning against the sanctions and inspections and blaming Israel for having made the mess in the first place.[50]

There are several scenarios for how the sanctions might break down after an Israeli strike. The most likely would be a repeat of the Iraq experience, where the sanctions remained on the books but fewer and fewer countries adhered to them. America's unilateral sanctions would remain, including our secondary sanctions, which threaten other countries with economic retaliation if they don't abide by our sanctions. These secondary sanctions have been an important element in galvanizing international effort against Iran. However, as was the case with Iraq, it is just not clear how much Washington would be willing to try to apply them in an environment where much of the world has lost interest in sanctioning Iran and enforcement would mean protracted fights with dozens of U.S. allies and trading partners.

Secondary sanctions are forbidden by the terms of the World Trade

Organization, to which the United States is an adherent and enthusiastic proponent. No one has been willing to challenge the United States on our secondary sanctions because most of the other key members of the WTO agree about Iran. However, if that changed as a result of an Israeli attack, they might be willing to do so. Alternatively, they might dare us to apply our own secondary sanctions. These are powerful tools if there are only a few offenders who can be forced to choose between trading with Iran or trading with America—a decision the United States almost always wins. If large numbers of countries are trading with Iran, however, then Washington would face a much more difficult situation. Sanctioning too many countries and cutting our trade with them could hurt the U.S. economy as much as it hurts theirs.

Moreover, the U.S. government, under both Presidents George W. Bush and Barack Obama, have made clear that they oppose an Israeli strike. In 2008, then Israeli prime minister Ehud Olmert reportedly discussed the possibility of an Israeli strike on Iran with President Bush, who apparently told him flat out not to attack.[51] Other reports claim that Israel also requested more powerful bunker-buster bombs, additional refueling aircraft, and the right to overfly Iraq—occupied by U.S. military forces at the time—only to have their requests turned down by the Bush administration.[52] The Bush 43 administration was routinely accused of being overly fond of Israel, a criticism that has never been leveled at the Obama administration. So it is not surprising that they too have given Israel a "red light" whenever the idea of an attack on Iran has been broached.[53] Instead, in the spring of 2012, President Obama promised that if Israel refrained from attacking and the Iranians refused to compromise on their nuclear program, the United States would act instead.[54] Thus if Israel were to attack Iran anyway, it may well find an American government unenthusiastic about helping it secure the diplomatic requirements it needs to nail down any military accomplishments.

This problem is undoubtedly another reason that Israel has not attacked Iran so far. The United States keeps demanding more time to let diplomacy, carrots and sticks, have their effect and Israel keeps agreeing.

The Israelis understand both the military-technical and strategic hurdles their own strike would face, and so would prefer either a negotiated solution or an American attack to their own. But another element of that restraint is that Jerusalem needs to keep accommodating Washington's requests so that if it ever feels compelled to attack Iran on its own, the United States will not be able to say that it hadn't been warned or that Israel had not given the Americans every chance to find a different solution.

Counterattack: The Fourth Paradox

In 2003, I had a long conversation in Tel Aviv with Eli Levite, then one of the brightest stars of the Israel Defense Forces. Talking about an attack on Iran and whether it made sense for Israel to launch one, Eli made clear that he feared that Israel might someday have to, but he foresaw many obstacles to overcome to make a strike worthwhile. Of all the smart things that Eli told me that day, I think that the smartest was this: "What is it that we fear from a nuclear Iran? We're not afraid that they are going to use a nuke on us. They aren't suicidal. They know what we could do to them. What we are afraid of is that the day after Iran gets a nuclear weapon, they turn to Hizballah and Hamas and say, 'We gave you ten thousand rockets, now go ahead and use them against Israel because we [Iran] aren't afraid of them [Israel] anymore.' But if we attack Iran, what is going to happen? They are going to turn to Hizballah and Hamas and say, 'We gave you ten thousand rockets, now go and use them against Israel.' We could be making inevitable exactly what we are trying to prevent."

That is the heart of Israel's fourth paradox.

The principal threat Israel will face from a nuclear Iran is more aggressive terrorism, unconventional warfare, and rocket attacks against Israel by Iran's proxies and allies, and possibly by Iranian intelligence and military services themselves. When you speak to Israeli military and civilian leaders, *that* is their real fear. That Hizballah, Hamas, Palestinian Islamic Jihad (PIJ), the Popular Front for the Liberation of Palestine–General

Command (PFLP-GC), and all of the other groups trying to kill Israelis will be armed, trained, supported, and encouraged to do so to an even greater extent than they already are. The history of the Cold War demonstrated that nuclear powers had to treat one another far more cautiously to avoid escalation than they did non-nuclear states.[55] Pakistan and possibly North Korea have felt less constrained to wage unconventional warfare against their historic foes after they acquired nuclear weapons and Saddam Husayn sought nuclear weapons to enable conventional military operations, specifically against Israel.[56]

If Israel attacks Iran's nuclear program to try to prevent it from acquiring a nuclear weapons capability, Iran will almost certainly retaliate.[57] Iran would be infuriated by an Israeli attack and would doubtless feel the need to make Israel pay a price for its attack if only to convince Israel not to do so again. Whenever Iran has perceived that it has been attacked (even when it actually wasn't), it has responded—from tanker attacks during the Iran-Iraq War, to Khobar Towers, to the more recent assassinations of Israelis in Georgia, India, and Bulgaria in response to Israeli hits on Iranian nuclear scientists. Last, there would be little downside for Iran to go to war with Israel and big potential benefits for it to do so. As long as Iran keeps its retaliation to terrorism and conventional rocket and missile attacks, Israel will have little ability to do more than respond in kind. After having had some of its nuclear sites flattened by an Israeli first strike, the Iranians may feel that they can sustain what are likely to be smaller and weaker Israeli follow-on attacks more easily than the casualty-conscious Israelis can tolerate Iran's blows.

War with Israel after an Israeli first strike has two other advantages for Iran. First, it brings about precisely the regional instability that so many countries feared would follow an Israeli strike and so led them to urge Israel not to attack in the first place, and therefore would likely amplify international opprobrium against Israel. Second, it could rally at least some portion of the Arab and Islamic worlds to Iran's defense (even if only diplomatically and rhetorically) because Iran will have been attacked by the hated Israelis. Even those Muslim countries that hate the Iranians would find it hard to criticize Iran, let alone take action against it. As Ephraim Kam has acknowledged, "There is hardly any doubt that Iran would respond to an attack with the use of force, unlike Iraq's decision in 1981 and Syria's decision in 2007 to refrain from retaliating."[58]

The methods Iran would try to use to retaliate are also straightforward. The Iranian air force lacks the range, refueling capability, and skill to penetrate Israeli air defenses and strike Israeli targets. Thus, if Iran wants to strike Israel directly, it will have to do so with ballistic missiles. The Iranians have several hundred ballistic missiles and some portion of them are believed to be modified Shahab-3s, Ghadr-1s, and Sajjil-2s, which could reach Israel—although some have raised doubts regarding how many of these missiles they have.[59] All of these have small warheads (generally about 1,650 pounds) and poor accuracy, making them useful only for attacks on large, undefended targets—like cities.[60]

Along with ballistic missiles, there are also rockets. Iran has provided tens of thousands, possibly even hundreds of thousands, of rockets of various sizes and ranges to Hizballah, Hamas, PIJ, and other groups, all of whom could attack Israel.[61] Some of these groups, like PIJ, are effectively proxies of Iran and so would undoubtedly participate in any retaliation against Israel. Hamas and Hizballah have close ties to Iran, but are independent and therefore could choose not to attack Israel even if Iran is hit.

This is basically the same list of likely suspects to conduct terror attacks against Israel in retaliation for a strike on Iran. Tehran has its own capabilities in the Revolutionary Guard and its intelligence services that it would undoubtedly employ. PIJ, PFLP-GC, and other groups would mount their own attacks as best they could. Israel does such an effective job policing its own territory that Iran and its allies would undoubtedly look to hit Israeli targets abroad as well. In the past, Iran and its friends have attacked Israeli targets in South America, Europe, Asia, and the Middle East and they could easily expand their activities to Africa and North America. Israeli journalist Ronen Bergman has claimed that Iran and Hizballah have forty sleeper terrorist cells around the world ready to conduct attacks in retaliation for an Israeli strike.[62] He might be right.

Then again, there might be four hundred such cells. Or four. Or four thousand. It is impossible to know. But there is no reason to doubt that Iran and its allies would hit Israelis (or even just Jews) wherever they can to retaliate for an Israeli strike.

The real question is not whether Iran and its allies would retaliate, but how bad the retaliation would be. Ten years ago, there was reason to believe that Iranian retaliation could create severe, even disastrous problems for Israel and the United States. Today the extent and impact of the retaliation is much less clear.[63] In particular, both Hizballah and Hamas may have reasons to show restraint.

Despite its close ties to Iran, there are incentives for Hizballah to hold off in the face of an Israeli attack on Iran. Hizballah continues to claim victory in its 2006 war against Israel, but it has refrained from provoking Israel ever since, suggesting that the Israeli campaign, poorly implemented as it was, inflicted serious damage on Hizballah. Soon after the fighting stopped, Hizballah leader Hassan Nasrallah himself admitted that he had not expected that the kidnapping of two Israeli soldiers would trigger such a fierce Israeli response, and that if he had it to do all over again, he wouldn't. "We did not think, even one percent, that the capture would lead to a war at this time and of this magnitude. . . . You ask me, if I had known on July 11 . . . that the operation would lead to such a war, would I do it? I say no, absolutely not," he said.[64] This admission implies that Hizballah is not looking for a repeat of the beating it took in 2006, especially since it is widely believed that the IDF has studied the mistakes it made and could hurt Hizballah far worse in a repeat performance. In particular, in the 2012 fighting in Gaza, Israel unveiled its new Iron Dome antirocket system, which should mitigate Hizballah's ability to hurt Israel, although there is an ongoing debate about the extent of the system's success.[65] On top of that, Hizballah worries about its ability to hold on to its dominating position in Lebanon now that it has lost Syrian support. This concern might convince the Shi'i Arabs of Hizballah to avoid tying themselves even more closely to Shi'i Persian Iran at a time when the Sunni Arab world has lost a lot of its patience and sympathy for Tehran.

Nevertheless, it seems more likely that Hizballah would retaliate. Its ties to Iran run deep, and they are spiritual, historical, operational, and even familial. So far, the specter of losing Syria has made Hizballah more dependent on Iran, not less. Nasrallah announced in September 2012 that if Israel attacked Iran, Hizballah would join the retaliation against Israel. As he put it, "A decision has been taken to respond and the response will be very great." The Iranians seem to think so, too, as former Iranian IRGC commander Yahya Rahim Safavi said at about the same time, "If, one day, the Israeli regime takes action against us, resistance groups, especially Hezbollah . . . will respond more easily."[66] It would be hard for Hizballah to back away from such an unequivocal commitment even if they wanted to, although they might honor it with less than fulsome effort.

If Hizballah leans toward retaliating for an Israeli strike on Iran, Hamas appears to lean away. Iran's backing of the Shi'i Alawi regime in Damascus has offended Sunni Arabs across the region, and the Sunni Islamists of Hamas have tried to distance themselves from both the Syrians and Iranians. Moreover, Hamas suffered from Israel's Operation Pillar of Defense in November 2012 and its leadership seems wary of picking another fight with the Israelis.[67] If an Israeli-Iranian conflict came to be seen as an Israeli-Muslim conflict, or if Hamas had specific motives related to its own interests, it might well join in. Still, Hamas might wait at least for the early days of an Israeli-Iranian conflict to see how the rest of the Arab world reacted—and detect any shifts that might make it palatable for them to join Iran before doing so.

CAN ISRAEL TAKE IT? A critical element of the argument of those who advocate for an Israeli strike on Iran—either now or at a future moment of "last resort"—is that the Israeli public will be willing to accept the price of Iranian retaliation to stave off the threat of an Iranian nuclear capability, at least for a few more years.

Certainly the Israeli public is long inured to making sacrifices for their personal safety and the security of the state. Prior to Israel's military campaign in Gaza in 2012, Operation Pillar of Defense, it endured 797 rockets fired from Gaza, and another 630 the year before.[68] During the operation, Israelis suffered 1,456 more rocket attacks, which killed five people and injured another 219.[69] During the 1991 Persian Gulf War, Saddam launched forty-two Scud missiles at Israel, killing two people and injuring 230 more.[70] All of these numbers demonstrate a willingness on the part of Israelis to endure the kind of rocket and missile attacks that Iran would be expected to mete out in response to an Israeli strike on Tehran's nuclear facilities. Israelis have routinely faced terrorist attacks, and while they go to extraordinary efforts to protect themselves, they accept that a certain number of deaths is the price to pay for their freedom, even their existence. By one count, 3,721 Israelis have been killed in various terrorist attacks between 1920 and 2012 (from a Jewish population that ranged from about 80,000 in 1920 to about 6 million in 2012).[71] While that may or may not be precise, it gives a sense of the order of magnitude. And over that ninety-three-year period, there were only five years in which no Israeli was killed by an act of terrorism.[72]

Israeli toughness is not the only consideration, however. These kinds of wars impose a high price on Israel's economy, one that could become unbearable in a protracted conflict. An Israeli-Iranian war following an Israeli strike on the Iranian nuclear program could go on for weeks or months, with terrorist attacks even years later.[73] A good example to illustrate these costs is Israel's monthlong war against Hizballah in 2006. During that conflict, Hizballah launched 3,970 missiles and rockets at Israel. Israel suffered 43 civilians and 119 soldiers killed, and 4,262 wounded or traumatized by the attacks. The war cost the government of Israel $1.6 billion, representing 1 percent of GDP. One million Israelis spent the entire conflict living in bomb shelters, while six thousand homes were destroyed or damaged by rocket fire. Ultimately, the economic shutdown of northern Israel (where 630 factories were forced to close), the damage caused by the rocket and missile attacks, and the losses from tourism cost another $5.3 billion (and another 3.3 percent of GDP).[74] All of that from just one month of conflict. Iron Dome (and Israel's Arrow antiballistic missile system) could reduce such costs, but it would not eliminate them. Indeed, in crisis simulations looking at the aftermath of an Israeli strike on Iran, the economic costs of long-term Iranian-Hizballah retaliations loom large, potentially driving Jerusalem to far-reaching and risky measures to try to end it.[75]

Moreover, there is another important consideration for an Israeli government seeking to attack Iran: the Israeli public does not favor it. Even if Iran's retaliation for an Israeli strike proved less than apocalyptic, it could still prove problematic for Jerusalem because the Israeli populace appears less than convinced that an attack on Iran is necessary.

In poll after poll, the Israeli public has shown itself to be lukewarm to an attack on Iran. Most Israelis do not seem to think a strike even necessary. A 2009 poll found that only 21 percent of Israelis believed that Iran would attack them with a nuclear weapon.[76] Three years later, in 2012, a poll by Israel's Institute for National Security Studies asked the same question and found that only 18 percent of Israelis believed that.[77] A joint Israeli-Palestinian survey also conducted in 2012 found only 20 percent of Israelis who feared this.[78] Quite consistently, no more than one in five Israelis fears that Iran would use nuclear weapons against them unprovoked. In a similar vein, a January 2013 survey by the *Times of Israel* concluded that only 12 percent of Israelis saw Iran as the top priority facing the government that would take office after the elections that month, compared to 16 percent who felt that Israel's top priority should be deteriorating relations with the Palestinians, and 43 percent who said economic problems.[79] Indeed, the poor showing of Prime Minister Netanyahu's coalition in the January 2013 elections and the unexpectedly strong performance by centrist parties were largely a function of public interest in addressing Israel's social and economic problems, and their relative deprioritization of the Iran issue.[80] A February 2012 poll by my colleague Shibley Telhami and Israel's Dahaf Institute found that only 22 percent of Israeli Jews supported an attack on Iran regardless of the circumstances, another 43 percent would back it if the attack had

American support, and 32 percent said they opposed it on all grounds.[81] In September 2012, the joint Israeli-Palestinian survey reported that only 18 percent of Israelis supported a strike by Israel alone, 52 percent supported an attack in conjunction with the United States, and 24 percent opposed a strike under all circumstances.[82]

If part of the reason that Israelis are so ambivalent about a strike is that few fear that Iran would use nuclear weapons against them, another part lies in the fear that Israelis evince for what they believe will be a protracted war with Iran and its allies afterward. The joint Israeli-Palestinian poll from September 2012 showed 77 percent of Israelis believed that an Israeli strike on Iran would produce a "major regional war."[83] The Telhami-Dahaf poll from February 2012 found that "a majority of Israelis polled, roughly 51 percent, said the war would last months (29 percent) or years (22 percent), while only 18 percent said it would last days." That same survey found, "Two-thirds of Israelis, meanwhile, believe Hezbollah would most likely join Iran in retaliation against Israel—even if Israel did not strike Hezbollah forces." And in the last piece of the puzzle, the Telhami-Dahaf poll found that only "22 percent of Israelis said a strike would delay Iran's capabilities by more than five years, while . . . 31 percent said it would delay its capabilities by one to five years, 18 percent said it would not make a difference and 11 percent said it would actually accelerate Iran's capabilities."[84] It is hard not to agree with the insightful, left-wing Israel analyst Daniel Levy, who has observed that an "oft-overlooked aspect is the absence of public pressure in Israel for military intervention or of a supposed Iranian threat featuring as a priority issue for Israelis. The pressure to act is top-down, not bottom-up. And to the extent to which there is trepidation among the public, that is a function of fear at the blowback from Israeli military action, rather than fear of Iranian-initiated conflagration."[85]

These findings would not surprise anyone who has visited Israel in recent years. Life is good there. The economy is booming. Israelis have never been safer, thanks in large part, it must be said, to the construction of the two security barriers isolating Gaza and the West Bank from Israel's primary population centers.[86] It's not that Israelis don't have complaints—they are Israelis after all—but they are far more interested and concerned about affordable child care, food prices, and Israel's growing secular-religious divide than about Iran. The *Times of Israel* poll seems accurate when it reports that Israelis see—by wide margins—social, economic, and domestic political questions as far more pressing than the Iranian nuclear threat.[87] The large number of Israeli military and intelligence personnel who oppose an attack on Iran reinforces this sentiment. The veteran reporters Nahum Barnea and Shimon Shiffer wrote in Israel's largest circulation newspaper, *Yedioth Ahronoth*, over the summer of 2012, "There is not a single senior official in the establishment—neither among the [Israel Defense Forces] top brass nor in the security branches, or even the president—who supports an Israeli strike at the moment." Even accepting the usual hyperbole of the Israeli press, their depiction seems more right than wrong.[88] Even Israel's ultra-orthodox and radical right-wing settlers are not pushing for war with Iran, because they fear that regional conflict resulting from an Israeli attack would mean international pressure on Israel to make concessions to the Palestinians.[89]

This public sentiment puts Prime Minister Benjamin Netanyahu out of step with his electorate. In contrast to the Israeli public's desire for him to focus on economic and social problems, Netanyahu told a visiting delegation of U.S. senators the same month as Israel's election, "My priority, if I'm elected for a next term as prime minister, will be first to stop Iran from getting nuclear weapons."[90] He reportedly believes that the United States does not understand Iran and its leadership, at least as he believes they should be understood, saying of the American government, "They know it's [Iran with a nuclear weapons capability] a very bad thing, but they need to understand the convulsive power of militant Islam . . . the cult of death, the ideological zeal."[91] And the prime minister is not entirely alone in his fears. As noted above, about 20 percent of the Israeli populace seems to share his views. The revisionist Israeli historian Benny

Morris writes about an Iranian bomb in apocalyptic terms: "The Iranians are driven by a higher logic. And they will launch their rockets. And, as with the first Holocaust, the international community will do nothing. It will all be over, for Israel, in a few minutes—not like in the 1940s, when the world had five long years in which to wring its hands and do nothing."[92]

In the end, the decision to strike will rest with Israel's prime minister and his or her top advisors and political partners, not with the Israeli public. If the prime minister decides to launch the attack and can convince the cabinet and the IDF to go along with that decision, Israel will attack. However, the views of the Israeli public are not irrelevant to this decision because they will ultimately have to pay the price for any such attack. They will bear the brunt of Iranian retaliation, not the prime minister. The evidence that they do not feel an existential threat from the Iranian nuclear program, that they do not want to attack Iran without the full participation of the United States, and that they believe that Israel has more pressing concerns all suggest that they may be loath to pay those costs.

A FINAL THOUGHT ON THE FOURTH PARADOX. There is a variant on the fourth paradox that should also be considered. The main thrust of this paradox rests on the assumption that the principal threat that a nuclear Iran poses to Israel is greater unconventional aggression— terrorism, rocket, and missile attacks. However, the logic holds even if you believe instead that Iran might be crazy or messianic enough to want to use nuclear weapons against Israel or give them to terrorists to do so, no matter how unlikely this is in reality. If you believe that Iran's leadership might consider nuking Israel unprovoked, there is nothing that is more likely to convince them to do so than an unprovoked Israeli attack on their nuclear facilities. If that is how the Iranians think, then an Israeli strike would undoubtedly convince them to withdraw from the NPT, rebuild their nuclear program in secret, acquire a nuclear weapon as quickly as they could, and then use it on Israel immediately. Or more realistically, if there is anything that *might* convince the Iranian leadership to use a nuclear weapon against Israel or give one to terrorists to do so, it would be an unprovoked Israeli attack on Iran to prevent it from acquiring a nuclear capability. In other words, in the long run, an Israeli strike is likely to hurt more than it helps regardless of your view of Iranian aims and motives.

Would Iran Retaliate Against American Targets?

It is not a foregone conclusion that Iran would respond to an Israeli attack by hitting American targets. The Iranians like to say that the United States and Israel are indistinguishable. Such rhetoric serves their geopolitical purposes.[93] In the real world, Tehran has had little difficulty distinguishing between the two of us. Whenever they have been attacked by the United States (or believed that they were attacked by the United States), they have retaliated against American targets. Israel has never been caught in the cross fire. Likewise, whenever the Iranians have believed that they were being attacked by Israel, they retaliated against Israel and the United States never got hit. Iran believes it is being cyberattacked by the United States and Israel, and believes that the Israelis are killing Iranian nuclear scientists. How have they reacted? With cyberattacks against the United States and Israel, and assassination and terrorist attacks against Israel.

There is one exception to that rule, the failed "Arbabsiar plot" to assassinate Adel al-Jubeir, the Saudi ambassador to the United States. The assassination never took place, and technically the target was not an American, but the U.S. government claims to have irrefutable evidence that the assassination had been authorized, and the intended bomb almost certainly would have killed Americans. Unless the Iranians believe that the United States was complicit in a similar act of terrorism against them, this incident would be one instance where Iran retaliated against an American target in response to Israeli attacks. Then again, it might have been retaliation for our purported cyberattacks. Numerous crisis simulations, including those conducted by my own Saban Center and reportedly by U.S. Central Command's annual "Internal Look" war game in 2012, have suggested that in certain circumstances, Iran either might choose to retaliate against American targets or might accidentally do so because it was unsure of the provenance of an attack.[94]

My own guess is that in most scenarios, the Iranians would be careful not to attack the United States after an Israeli strike.[95] These same war games also reveal that if an Israeli strike failed to cripple the Iranian nuclear program, it could be a godsend for Tehran in many ways. A failed Israeli strike would inflict minimal pain on Iran and create golden opportunities for it to withdraw from the NPT, evict inspectors, undermine sanctions, and become the champion of the Muslim world by fighting Israel at a low level and from a distance. This possible success could be rendered meaningless if the Iranians make the mistake of hitting the United States because the Americans swing a much bigger bat than the Israelis. In these same simulations, the Iranians do well until they do something foolish to the Americans, at which point they start suffering massive damage from U.S. retaliation. It is also why, in the real world, the Iranians have been quite careful about not crossing U.S. red lines for the use of force. Karim Sadjadpour likes to say that the Iranians would have to carefully calibrate their response to an Israeli attack "because if they respond too little they lose face, and if they respond too much they lose their heads."

However, we cannot be certain of that and need to recognize the potential. The Israelis cannot be sure of it, either, and another aspect of the third paradox is that an Israeli strike could strain the U.S.-Israeli relationship if an Israeli strike on Iran resulted in Iranian attacks on American targets. It could even drag the United States into a war it did not want to fight. While some Israelis might rejoice that their own attack forced the United States to do what they had always hoped it would, in the longer run, these events could be disastrous for the "special relationship" between Israel and the United States.

WOULD IRAN TRY TO CLOSE THE STRAIT OF HORMUZ? Iran is unlikely to try to close the Strait of Hormuz in response to an Israeli attack, despite its threats to do so.

The Iranians have threatened to close the Strait of Hormuz in the event of an Israeli or American attack loudly and often. But they make threats all the time and don't follow through on them, frequently after warning that they always make good on their threats. The Iranians have threatened to close the Strait if the United States, United Nations, and European Union passed sanctions against them. They have threatened the Arab states for cooperating with sanctions. They have threatened the Turks for cooperating with sanctions. And they have threatened to halt their own oil sales if the West imposed more sanctions. However, they never made good on any of these threats.[96] In January 2012, when the United States shifted an aircraft carrier out of the Persian Gulf on a routine redeployment, Iranian Revolutionary Guard general Ataollah Salehi warned the United States not to move another carrier back in, saying "Iran advises, recommends and warns them [the U.S.] not to move its carrier back to the previous area in the Gulf because Iran is not used to repeating its warnings and warns just once."[97] The United States has deployed multiple carriers to the Gulf since then and the Iranians seem to have forgotten that they ever made such a threat. In several war games I have run or participated in, various Iran teams felt compelled to at least threaten the Strait in response to an Israeli attack because they felt that they had to do something to show that their rhetoric was not meaningless—and in at least one case, this decision led to unintended escalation to a U.S.-Iran clash. However, most of the Iranian teams, including the most aggressive Iran team I ever observed, have tried hard to avoid taking any action in the Gulf for fear of how the United States would respond.

It is important to understand that Iran's rhetoric about closing the Strait in the event of an Israeli attack serves two useful purposes for Tehran. First, it is meant as a deterrent. The Iranians are not stupid, and they realize that the one thing that the United States and the rest of the world cares about in the Persian Gulf is its oil. Thus they know that a possible disruption of the oil supply terrifies the United States and the entire developed world. So they frequently warn that any attack on them would cause them to cut off Gulf oil flows. Second, threatening to close the Strait is Iran's best method of conducting economic warfare against the United States and the West. Every time that Tehran does so, the price of oil jumps as traders get nervous about oil supplies, and that jump means a higher cost to oil importers (most of the Western nations) and higher revenues for oil exporters (like Iran). Tehran sees the sanctions as a form of economic warfare being waged against them by the United States and its allies. It isn't surprising that they would try to fight fire with fire as best they can.

Still, there are also lots of reasons why the Iranians are unlikely to actually try to close the Strait of Hormuz. They receive 90 percent of their imports by ship through the Persian Gulf, and that loss would throw their already reeling economy into chaos.[98] But the most important reason the Iranians won't try is that they know they can't. If they try, it is a virtual certainty that they will have their navy, air force, air defense forces, coastal defense forces, and possibly whatever is left of their nuclear program obliterated by the U.S. armed forces.

Iranian conventional capabilities in the Gulf are dangerous enough that if they acted with surprise to close the Strait—by secretly beginning to mine it and suddenly launching "swarming" attacks with their small boats, antiship cruise missiles, and aircraft—they probably could do considerable damage to a handful of unprepared American warships, and frighten away other vessels for some period of time.

However, the moment that they did so, the widespread expectation is that the rest of the world would turn to the United States and in effect say, "Do whatever you need to do to reopen the Strait of Hormuz." The United States has privately warned Tehran that if it tries to make good on its threats to close the Strait, the United States will counterattack regardless.[99] And Iran simply does not have the military capacity to resist the full force of the U.S. Navy and Air Force. Iran's air defenses are woefully inadequate to deal with American airpower, which would systematically tear up Iran's air and air defense forces, then its coastal defenses, then sink its navy before moving in to clear away any remaining mines. It would be a relatively big operation, and might take weeks or even a few months to build up the forces and execute the campaign plan, but there is virtually nothing that Iran's conventional forces could do to prevent it.[100] And the Iranians seem well aware of this.

The Iranians would also have to fear that once the United States began a major military operation, we might decide to clear up a few other problems while we were in the neighborhood. We might decide to smash whatever elements of the Iranian nuclear program the Israelis missed. We might even decide to get rid of the root cause of the problem, the Iranian regime. Consequently, while we would have to be on our guard to defend the Strait in the event of an Israeli attack on Iran, the chances that Iran would try anything are low.

The Worst Option

From an American perspective, an Israeli strike is a terrible idea. It would have a low probability of achieving even a short-term benefit and a high probability of creating significant long-term problems. One of the few foreign policy items that the Bush 43 and Obama administrations could agree upon was the need to convince the Israelis not to strike Iran. If anyone is going to attack Iran's nuclear facilities, it should be the United States, not Israel—although my own sentiment is that an American strike would also be problematic except in certain specific circumstances.

Many Americans who favor an Israeli strike say that they do so because at least the Israelis have the guts to do it, whereas the U.S. government doesn't. They would prefer that the United States employed force against Iran, but since the United States won't, an Israeli strike is their next choice. That makes no sense to me. Just because someone is willing to do something difficult does not mean that they are the best person to do that job.

As for those Israelis who favor a strike, their rationale is the fear that Iran will prove irrational once it acquires a nuclear weapon and use it unprovoked against the Jewish state. Setting aside the great weight of historical evidence that this fear is groundless, even then an Israeli conventional attack on Iran would make little sense. Such a strike would be unlikely to halt the Iranian nuclear program. It would be more likely to make the situation worse both by providing Tehran with an excuse to withdraw from the NPT and evict the inspectors and an incentive to further disperse its nuclear program (potentially making it impossible to strike again in the future) and to go ahead and weaponize. Thus, for those Israelis who truly fear that Iran would use nuclear weapons against them unprovoked, the only sensible option would be to strike Iran with nuclear weapons *first* to ensure that the Iranian program was obliterated with little chance it could be rebuilt. After all, if the alternative is that at some point in the next few years Iran will have a nuclear weapon and Israel will not have the ability to stop it, and if you believe that Iran will unquestionably use a nuclear weapon on Israel, then no Israeli could worry about respecting moral and political niceties like the taboo against first use of nuclear weapons. The logic compels Israel to use nuclear weapons as its first move, not its last.

What an awful mess. Israel has played Hamlet for nearly two decades because the Israelis see the same awful choices. They recognize all the problems and paradoxes that they would have to overcome for a conventional military operation to work and they fear that it will not do the job. They know that if it doesn't, then they will be left with the choice of launching a nuclear attack on Iran or living with an Iranian nuclear capability, and they also know that a failed conventional strike might make a nuclear strike impossible.

These conundrums explain why Israel has not struck Iran's nuclear program as it did Iraq's and Syria's even though the Israelis have been debating, planning, training and otherwise preparing for it since the 1990s. It also reflects why the likelihood that Israel will strike Iran is lower than so many think.

Israel might still strike. It might even succeed. People sometimes behave in ways that defy all logic—especially in the Middle East. And against all probabilities, sometimes those things work. But such an outcome is unlikely. It is far more likely that an Israeli attack on Iran would not work out well for Israel, for the United States, or for anyone else.

A Return to Arms

Except under certain specific circumstances, I do not favor the use of force against Iran by the United States as the solution to our problems with Tehran's nuclear ambitions. This chapter will explain why.

However, I do not dismiss this option, either. Although I ultimately do not agree with it, the use of force against Iran is a serious alternative to containment and has a great deal to commend it.

To start with, the United States military is far more powerful than anything Iran could hope to defeat. Since 1991, the U.S. armed forces have engaged in a half-dozen military campaigns that have given them tremendous experience in how to wage modern warfare. They have worked out many of the bugs and learned how to overcome much of the friction that hinders military operations. In contrast, Iran's military is small, weak, technologically backward, and tactically maladroit. Iran is not helpless, and the Iranians could do some damage to American forces—especially if the United States were as cavalier about a war with

Iran as we were about the invasion and occupation of Iraq. But barring some unforeseeable development, there is little doubt that the United States would "win" the military aspects of any conflict with Iran. Wars are unpredictable, but the balance of power between America and Iran lies overwhelmingly in favor of the United States.

The use of force against Iran also offers the prospect of a "complete" solution to the problems of Iran—not just its nuclear program but also its support for terrorism and other efforts to oppose the United States and cause trouble in the Middle East. This is because we could choose to use sufficient force to invade Iran, topple the clerical regime, and help build a new political system in its place. I don't know of a single American in favor of this idea, but the possibility is inherent in the resort to force.

Setting aside the discomforting question of an invasion, using force also holds out the alluring possibility that Washington could act unhindered by other diplomatic constraints, such as the views of allies and adversaries. The need to work within the constraints and preferences of other nations has been a major source of frustration to many Americans. A great many countries do not share our perspective on Iran. The need to rely on diplomacy, even covert action, has forced us to take those views into consideration and to limit our actions. Many Americans fear that these other countries do not understand the threat posed by Iran, and thus their insistence on restraint, on patience, and on accommodation of the Iranians will prove disastrous. For Americans holding such a belief, the military option is the only way for the United States to shed these diplomatic shackles and act to guarantee its own security and the safety of our allies.

The use of force could also enable the United States to pursue an active policy toward Iran, one in which our disproportionate strength promises to allow us to dictate the course of events—"retain the initiative," in military parlance—in most circumstances. Likewise, within the military realm, we will always have what is called "escalation dominance" over Iran, the ability to ratchet up the fight to another level by adding more or different kinds of forces. If Iran seemed to be "winning" any tactical engagement, we could always send reinforcements or hit them in a different area. We would have a good chance of controlling the fight.

Because of America's unmatched military capabilities and the size and scope of our armed forces, there are a range of different military options we might pursue. This chapter looks at the three principal ways in which the United States might employ force against Iran: a blockade, air strikes to destroy its nuclear program, and a full-scale invasion.

The use of American force against Iran might prove to be the answer to all of our problems with Iran, but it also might prove to be a disaster. There are serious costs and risks involved in the use of force, even if the United States employs only limited force, such as an air campaign directed at Iran's nuclear program. We may well have to pay those costs and risks even if we secure all the advantages of force, and we could end up paying all of those costs and risks without getting any of the advantages. That is what concerns me.

Blockade

A naval blockade is one possible military action the United States might employ against Iran. The United States certainly has the capacity to impose a blockade on Iran, but it's just not clear why we would want to do so. A blockade is an act of war that has little likelihood of solving American problems with Iran.

The international, multilateral, and unilateral sanctions are already imposing severe costs on Iran. A blockade might help some, but probably not much. As a result of the sanctions alone, Iran's maritime trade fell by more than 50 percent in 2012, measured by ships calling at Iranian ports.[1] Where there are sanctions there is smuggling, but in the case of Iran, what smuggling there is does not seem to be offering significant relief to the Iranians.[2] Much of the smuggling moves overland across Iran's long, porous borders, and more of it would shift to that route in the event of a naval blockade.[3] As I noted in chapter 6, Iranian oil exports have fallen significantly as a result of the American and European sanctions (from

2.3 million barrels per day on average in 2011, to just 1.1 million barrels per day on average in 2012) and the major impediment to further diminishing Iran's oil exports is not smuggling, but rather the unwillingness of countries such as China and India to adopt the sanctions themselves.[4]

Looking at the imports side of smuggling, the inflated fuel prices caused by the sanctions and Tehran's own bizarre edicts that penalize "imports" to try to build autarkic domestic industries have both undercut smugglers.[5] Iran continues to smuggle prohibited items related to its military and WMD programs, but these are already covered by the Proliferation Security Initiative, an agreement among ninety-eight countries (including the United States, which proposed the idea) that authorizes the states to search all vessels believed to contain prohibited items and seize any contraband.[6] No further blockading authority would be needed to deal with this area of harmful smuggling. Finally, a great deal of what is smuggled into Iran consists of drugs and alcohol. It would be difficult to justify an expensive blockade that could spark diplomatic problems and even firefights to shut down Iran's illicit trade in these goods.[7]

Recent history suggests that when UN sanctions are respected, they do not need military enforcement; when they aren't, military enforcement does little to solve the problem. The Iraq sanctions from the 1990s are a perfect example of this phenomenon. Initially, when the world supported the containment of Saddam, the sanctions were respected by Iraq's trading partners with little need for enforcement. Where they weren't—by Turkey and Jordan, for instance, who demanded special exemptions—or later, when more and more countries began to ignore them, the United States was unable to enforce the sanctions militarily even though the U.S. Navy maintained a blockade of Iraq. The problem was simple: enforcing the sanctions meant picking fights with Iraq's trading partners, not with Iraq, and Iraq's trading partners were America's trading partners, including China, Russia, Egypt, and France. With only a few exceptions, the United States was not going to intercept their ships, planes, and trucks, or even the goods themselves, for fear of creating a diplomatic incident, a trade war, or worse.

One could make the case that a blockade imposed to enforce the current sanctions or harsher, future sanctions would have a useful psychological effect on Tehran. But it is unlikely that a blockade would move Tehran to abandon its nuclear program. Given the kind of hardships Iran has already shrugged off, it seems far-fetched to believe that a blockade—a passive military operation that would remain unseen off Iran's shores—could succeed instead. Still, any use of military power to enforce the sanctions could appear more menacing to the Iranians than relying on sanctions alone. In particular, it might suggest to Tehran that more offensive military action might be forthcoming. In that sense, a blockade could be a temperate shot across Iran's bow.

The utility of such a signal would have to be measured against the potential downside of a blockade. As the blockading state typically prevents the ships (and planes and trucks) of third countries from moving to and from the blockaded country, blockades create severe problems between the blockader and those third parties, even causing wars. American history is replete with examples of the diplomatic complications of blockades. From the War of 1812 (sparked by the British blockade of Napoleonic Europe), to the American Civil War (in which the Union's blockade of the South nearly brought British intervention on the side of the Confederacy), to World War I (when the U-boat blockade was a key element bringing the United States into the war against Germany), Americans have faced unwanted conflicts as a result of blockades.

A blockade of Iran would probably have little impact on the nuclear impasse itself.[8] It would not solve our problems on its own, or even in conjunction with toughened sanctions. It would add little in a material sense to the impact of the sanctions, and any psychological impact could be offset by the problems it might create between the United States and other countries still trying to trade with Iran.

All that said, there are two possible rationales for a blockade. First, as noted, it might send a psychological signal to Iran to get serious about making compromises on its nuclear program and accept a deal with the P-5+1 before the West shifts to more aggressive methods. In that sense, it might be useful as part of a last step to get the Iranians to agree to a negotiated settlement before we face the ultimate choice between war and containment.[9] Alternatively, one could make a cynical case for a blockade that it might provoke Iran to do something foolish that would turn international and domestic opinion so strongly against it that much larger uses of force would become more palatable. Historically, when Western (particularly American) naval forces are in proximity with Iran's Revolutionary Guards, and especially when those Western naval forces take actions that the Iranians see as antithetical to their interests, the Guards have a habit of acting in ways not always authorized by Tehran. Some of these incidents could have escalated quickly had the U.S. government not moved to rein in its military forces. If one were looking to create the context for war with Iran, a blockade might do the trick, although even that is not a guarantee.

Air Strikes

When most people discuss "the American military option" toward Iran, what they mean is air strikes, and specifically air strikes against Iran's nuclear program. Air strikes would be a direct blow to the Iranian nuclear program and could do severe damage, unlike a blockade, which would have little more than symbolic value. Yet they also offer the tantalizing prospect of allowing the United States to eliminate Iran's nuclear facilities—and hopefully knock Iran's nuclear weapons bid back to square one—without the exorbitant costs of a full-scale invasion. Especially in light of America's experiences in Iraq and Afghanistan, that would appear to be a key criterion for any military move against Iran.

The concept behind such an operation is straightforward. Its minimal goal would be to destroy the key facilities of Iran's nuclear and ballistic missile facilities. In that sense it would be a close parallel to the idea of an Israeli strike. However, the specifics of an Israeli air raid and an American air campaign against Iran's nuclear facilities differ markedly in their military, diplomatic, political, and even economic particulars. These dif-

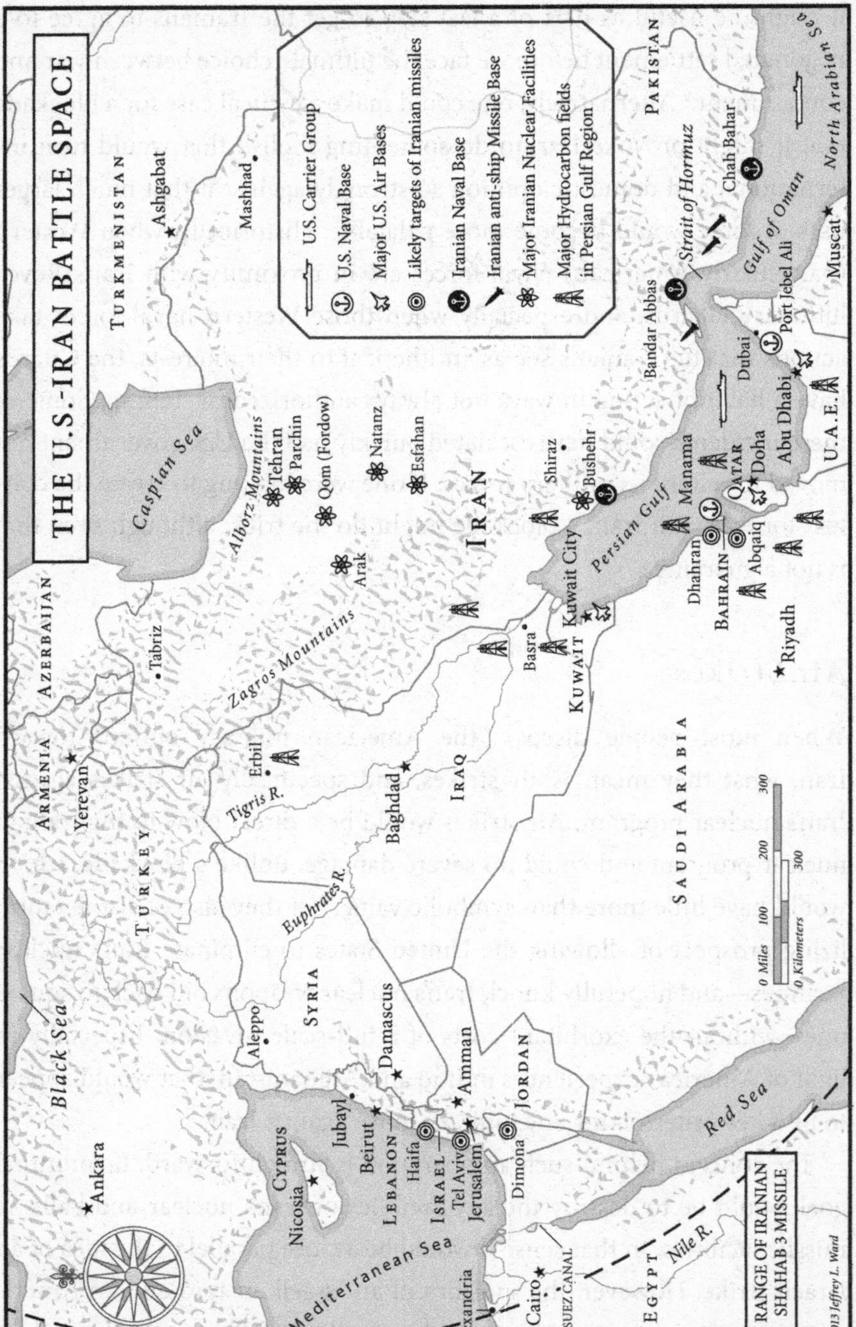
THE U.S.-IRAN BATTLE SPACE
U.S. Carrier Group
U.S. Naval Base
Major U.S. Air Bases
Likely targets of Iranian missiles
Iranian Naval Base
Iranian anti-ship Missile Base
Major Iranian Nuclear Facilities
Major Hydrocarbon fields in Persian Gulf Region
TURKMENISTAN
Ashgabat
Mashhad
PAKISTAN
Strait of Hormuz
Chah Bahar
Gulf of Oman
North Arabian Sea
Muscat
Bandar Abbas
Port Jebel Ali
Dubai
Abu Dhabi
U.A.E.
QATAR
Doha
Manama
BAHRAIN
Abqaiq
Dhahran
Persian Gulf
Bushehr
Shiraz
IRAN
Natanz
Esfahan
Tehran
Parchin
Qom (Fordow)
Arak
Alborz Mountains
Caspian Sea
AZERBAIJAN
Tabriz
Zagros Mountains
Kuwait City
KUWAIT
Basra
Riyadh
SAUDI ARABIA
ARMENIA
Yerevan
Erbil
Tigris R.
Baghdad
IRAQ
TURKEY
Euphrates R.
SYRIA
Aleppo
Damascus
Amman
JORDAN
Black Sea
Ankara
CYPRUS
Nicosia
Jubayl
Beirut
LEBANON
Haifa
ISRAEL
Tel Aviv
Jerusalem
Dimona
Mediterranean Sea
Alexandria
Cairo
SUEZ CANAL
EGYPT
Nile R.
Red Sea
RANGE OF IRANIAN SHAHAB 3 MISSILE
0 Miles 100 200 300
0 Kilometers 300
© 2013 Jeffrey L. Ward

ferences make an American air campaign far more compelling than an Israeli strike.

Compared to what Israel could bring to bear, the United States has more aircraft capable of reaching Iran, our planes would not need to fly through other countries' airspace, and they can carry much bigger and more powerful weapons. The United States can employ huge, long-range bombers such as the B-52, B-1, and B-2 and a vast fleet of refueling tankers, allowing the bombers to launch from bases in the United States itself, if necessary. America's ability to operate from the British island of Diego Garcia in the Indian Ocean, however, provides a far more convenient in-theater base. These big bombers can also carry many more bombs and much bigger bombs than anything in the Israeli arsenal, including the 30,000-pound Massive Ordnance Penetrator, which is the only conventional weapon that may be able to destroy Iran's Fordow enrichment plant. The U.S. Navy still has ten enormous *Nimitz*-class aircraft carriers, each one of which typically deploys with thirty-six to forty-eight F-18 fighter-bombers and twenty-eight support aircraft. Although three carriers are normally on station around the world at any time, in times of crisis, the Navy can surge four or even five if necessary. Another advantage that the United States has over Israel is a vast fleet of unmanned aerial vehicles (UAVs, or "drones") and large numbers of air- and sea-launched cruise missiles. The United States has basing rights at airfields in Kuwait, Qatar, and the UAE—and at times has also been able to use facilities in Saudi Arabia, Bahrain, and Oman. If those states allow American aircraft to use their bases, additional wings of American Air Force fighters and strike planes (F-15s, F-16s, F-22s, F-117s, and someday F-35s) can be added to the lineup for an air campaign against Iran.

As a result, the United States could attack far more sites than the Israelis, with much greater certainty that they would be destroyed. Whereas the Israelis probably could go after no more than about six of Iran's most important nuclear facilities, the United States could attack dozens of other targets: secondary nuclear sites, ballistic missile production plants and bases, leadership targets, even research facilities that support both the nuclear and missile programs.

These forces also give the United States a wide range of options for how to attack Iran. Washington could decide to employ only stealthy forces to effectively eliminate the problem of Iranian air defenses. In such a scenario, the United States would target Iran's aboveground, unfortified nuclear facilities (like the Esfahan uranium conversion plant and its various centrifuge and ballistic missile manufacturing facilities) with scores of air- and sea-launched cruise missiles launched from B-52 bombers and Navy ships in the Persian Gulf and Arabian Sea. The United States might complement this attack by targeting key leadership sites or small facilities located in populated areas with UAV-fired weapons. Iran's large and heavily fortified sites—such as Fordow, Natanz, and Parchin—would be left to B-2 bombers carrying bunker-busting munitions including the MOPs. If necessary, the B-2s could even be escorted by stealthy F-22 fighters. Such an operation would be small, perhaps consisting of no more than several hundred cruise missiles, UAVs, and manned aircraft sorties. Conceivably, it might take place all in one night. However, an attack such as this one might only be able to destroy a dozen or more of Iran's highest-value nuclear and ballistic missile sites, which might not set back Iran's pursuit of a nuclear weapons capability much more than an Israeli strike would.

If a stripped-down operation can't do the job, the United States has almost limitless options to go bigger. Larger campaigns would sacrifice stealth for brawn, but could hit many more targets and have a far greater certainty of destroying them. Larger, more comprehensive air campaigns would likely be structured and sequenced somewhat differently from scaled-down versions. In the first wave of sorties, some strikes might be directed against key Iranian nuclear facilities, especially those containing assets believed to be easy for Iran to move. But this type of campaign would likely focus its initial efforts on destroying Iranian air defenses, including radars, surface-to-air missiles, and fighter aircraft, to establish air supremacy. The initial waves would be followed by attacks against Iranian nuclear facilities, ballistic missile production and storage sites, research centers, and leadership targets. American intelligence and reconnaissance aircraft (and satellites) would monitor the attacks to assess damage while follow-on sorties would restrike targets missed the first time. Some targets, such as Natanz and Fordow, might require repeated strikes to ensure that penetrating munitions could "dig" all the way to the centrifuge halls themselves. Some sorties might be directed—or held in reserve—against Iranian air and naval forces along the Strait of Hormuz to prevent them from attempting to close the Strait in retaliation for the American strikes.

A large air campaign would likely involve thousands of sorties and cruise missile attacks, and could last anywhere from several days to several weeks. By way of comparison, Operation Desert Fox—a three-day air campaign against Iraq in 1998 that sought to destroy thirteen purported Iraqi WMD facilities and nearly fifty "regime-protection" and leadership targets—required 650 manned aircraft sorties and 415 cruise missile strikes.[10] American aircraft and munitions are more capable today than they were then, and we can rely on UAVs to perform some of the missions for which we once had to use manned aircraft, but Iran's air and air defense forces are somewhat more formidable than Iraq's, and the United States might want to destroy more targets than during Desert Fox.

Impact of Air Strikes

An American air campaign is likely to do more damage to the Iranian nuclear program than an Israeli strike. An American air campaign could potentially do *much* more damage to the Iranian nuclear program than an Israeli strike, especially if the United States opted to mount a large, sustained operation involving thousands of missiles and air strikes over days or weeks. Beyond that, predictions get murky. Cordesman and Toukan concluded in their study of an American air campaign against Iran that "[d]epending on the forces allocated and duration of air strikes, it is unlikely that an air campaign alone could alone [sic] terminate Iran's program. The possibility of dispersed facilities complicates any assessment of a potential mission success, making it unclear what the ultimate effect of a strike would be on Iran's nuclear facilities." [11]

As an example of the uncertainties surrounding an American air campaign, the United States believes that the MOP bomb can destroy the Fordow facility, but no one is sure. Repeated strikes on Fordow with MOPs almost certainly would render the facility unusable by collapsing tunnels, sealing entrances, closing off air shafts, and the like. But this would mean hitting the facility with quite a few of these enormous bombs, which can only be carried by the B-2, including restrikes over several days to be certain that the facility was sufficiently damaged. [12] The most cogent pro-air-campaign argument yet presented acknowledged that the MOPs might not be able to destroy Fordow, and recommended striking before it was fully operational. [13]

Then there is the constant problem of secret Iranian facilities. The IAEA and the Western powers are all combing Iran for any sign that Tehran is building secret facilities. This probably makes it less likely that the Iranians are hiding something from us, but we don't know what we don't know. We assume that because we have found several secret Iranian facilities, that means that it is unlikely that the Iranians could hide other facilities from us. Yet in almost every case, it took about three years from the time that Iran began work on a secret site to when we discovered it. Are there sites in Iran that they began one, two, or even three years ago that we simply haven't found yet because they have not reached a stage of completion that we can detect? Are there other sites out there that are near completion or even fully operational that we just never found? Even if we suspect that there aren't, we cannot be certain, and given our history, we should not be. In the 1980s we found several secret nuclear facilities that the Iraqis tried to hide from us and that too made us confident that we knew where all of Iraq's hidden nuclear sites were, only to find out in 1991 that we didn't. Former director of the Central Intelligence Agency Michael Hayden has publicly dismissed the notion of an American (or Israeli) strike on Iran, because he doubts that the United States (or Israel) knows where all the key targets are and he fears that attacking would instead ensure a desperate Iranian push for the bomb.[14]

Another frustrating uncertainty akin to those of an Israeli air strike is over how fast the Iranians could rebuild from scratch. If an American air attack were wholly successful and wiped out the Iranian nuclear program completely, and the Iranians still decided to rebuild, how long would it take them? The United States can wreck Iran's centrifuge halls, mangle the centrifuges themselves, obliterate their power sources, and so on, but we can't remove the knowledge from the heads of their scientists. Most estimates of the degree of Iranian scientific knowledge about enrichment and nuclear weapons indicate that the Iranians have advanced to where they could start from scratch and be back to their current state in somewhere between two and five years, with some willing to go as high as seven. A 2012 report by the Congressional Research Service concluded that Iran could rebuild most of its centrifuge workshops within six months after an attack, after which Iran could start manufacturing replacement centrifuges. The report also warned that neither the United States nor Israel knew for certain where all of Iran's nuclear facilities were located and therefore that it was "unclear what the ultimate effect of a strike would be on the likelihood of Iran acquiring nuclear weapons."[15] Perhaps for the same reasons, former deputy secretary of defense Colin Kahl has warned, "Senior U.S. defense officials have repeatedly stated that an attack on Iran's nuclear facilities would stall Tehran's progress for only a few years."[16]

While it is not impossible for the United States to wipe out Iran's nuclear program completely, especially if Washington were willing to mount a massive, sustained air campaign, it is more likely that even American strikes would not succeed quite to that level. A major American air campaign against Iran would undoubtedly do extensive damage to the Iranian nuclear and ballistic missile programs, but how extensive? If an Israeli strike would be expected to set the Iranian nuclear program back by a year or two, how much longer would an American campaign set it back? Eighteen months? Three years? Five? We do not know.

IMPACT ON IRANIAN POLITICS. Those who oppose air strikes invariably argue that such a campaign would engage Iranian nationalism and latent anti-Americanism and create a "rally 'round the flag effect" that would galvanize the Iranian people to greater support of the regime.[17] For instance, then–secretary of defense Leon Panetta, in his remarks at the Saban Forum in December 2011, said that one likely unintended consequence of a military strike on Iran's nuclear facilities would be that "the regime that is weak now . . . would suddenly be able to reestablish itself, suddenly be able to get support in the region."[18] Those who favor air strikes disagree, insisting that any such impact would be short-lived and would eventually be replaced by deepening popular unhappiness with the regime, because most Iranians would blame the regime for having made the mistakes that provoked the American attack.[19] In what is probably the definitive article promoting an Israeli strike on Iran, the cannily iconoclastic Iran expert Reuel Gerecht has charged, "An Israeli strike now— after the rise of the Green Movement and the crackdown on it—is more likely to shake the regime than would have a massive American attack in 2002, when Tehran's clandestine nuclear program was first revealed. And if anything can jolt the pro-democracy movement forward, contrary to the now passionately accepted conventional wisdom, an Israeli strike against the nuclear sites is it."[20]

This debate is of more than passing importance. It is part of the question of whether Iran would reconstitute its nuclear program after American air strikes. There is too little evidence and too many unknowns to be certain, but here is how I add up the evidence. I see three factors that bear on this question.

The first is the general pattern of air campaigns and their impact on the civilian population of the targeted country. The evidence is overwhelming and compelling: when people are bombed by another country, they do not blame their own government for provoking the bombing—they blame the country doing the bombing. From Spain in the 1930s to Germany and Japan in the 1940s, to Vietnam in the 1970s, to Iraq and Iran in the 1980s, and Iraq and Serbia in the 1990s, this pattern has held.[21] However, there are some important divergent aspects worth noting. In all of these wars, bombing campaigns directed against the civilian population did help cause the populace to tire of the war. Second, the air campaign against Serbia apparently made Slobodan Milosevic concerned that it was turning the Serbian populace against him, and this fear does appear to have been part of his rationale for conceding Bosnia.[22] Third, at least in Iraq, disenchantment with the regime for bringing about the prolonged bombing and sanctions did not bring about any commensurate increase in popularity of the United States. Most Iraqis hated Saddam's policies and the misfortune they had brought on Iraq, but they also blamed the United States for their misery.[23]

With regard to Iran specifically, several points are relevant. Many Iranians are strident nationalists who have had it ingrained in them that foreign interference is the root cause of Iran's problems and therefore that they must resist any and all foreign interference in Iranian affairs. Many Iranian dissidents have shied away from taking money or other support from foreign governments, and Iranian regimes (and even just politicians, dating back to Mosaddeq) try to discredit rivals by branding them as tools of foreign regimes. In addition, the regime easily crushed the Green Movement in 2009—and prevented it from even mounting protests in 2011. This suggests that popular unrest is unlikely to have much impact on the regime regardless of its inspiration, at least unless some dramatic change takes place. At present and for the foreseeable future, there is nothing apparent that will change the regime's determination to hold power by dint of force whenever it is necessary.[24]

Based on all this, it seems most likely that American air strikes will make Iranians angry at the United States, but may not have much impact on their feelings about their own government one way or the other. Those Iranians who support the government will hate the United States even more, and those who dislike their government won't like their government any more, but they probably will like us less. The regime, I suspect, will play up these sentiments to justify whatever it wants to do in the aftermath of an American strike: arrest even more dissidents and political opponents, withdraw from the NPT, demand greater hardships from the Iranian people in the name of combating the United States, and rebuild its nuclear program.

Moreover, based on the historical pattern of air strikes and the history of Iranian nationalism, if this outcome proves wrong, it seems more likely that it will be wrong in the direction of rallying the Iranians to support their government than in the direction of causing Iranians to turn against the regime. It is not that the latter is impossible. Just that the history does not appear to support it as strongly as the other two possibilities. What's more, even in the best case for the United States, in which our air strikes do rouse the Iranian people to try once again to take action against the regime, I suspect that the regime will be able to crush the unrest once again absent direct, large-scale American military intervention on behalf of the revolutionaries.

WOULD IRAN REBUILD ITS NUCLEAR PROGRAM? As with an Israeli strike on Iran, another critical question is whether the Iranians would try to rebuild after. Here as well, there are some differences from the Israeli case. Proponents of an American strike argue that the fact that the United States had attacked Iran would demonstrate that Washington had the capability and the will to do so, and therefore could do it again in the future. They contend that this would probably convince Iran to give up on its nuclear ambitions altogether, lest it face repeated American air campaigns. Others argue that, contrary to my assessment laid out above, American air strikes will cause such deep internal political problems for the Iranian regime that they will be unable or unwilling to rebuild their nuclear program. These are not foolish ideas. They could be correct.

However, I suspect that they are less likely than those scenarios in which Iran does choose to rebuild its nuclear program. Again, I think it more likely that an American air campaign would either bolster or at least would not further exacerbate the Iranian regime's relationship with its people. More than that, I expect that the regime would contain any unrest that followed American air strikes. I see the Iranian hardline leadership, particularly Khamene'i, as convinced that the United States is seeking to overthrow him and the whole Islamic Republic. This suggests that American air strikes would only harden his desire to have nuclear weapons to deter another such attack. Finally, I suspect that the Iranians will believe that they could rebuild their nuclear program as long as they evict the IAEA inspectors and act in greater secrecy, employing even greater dispersal and digging even deeper underground wherever possible.

My view seems to echo those who have some insight into this question.[25] I have already noted former CIA director Michael Hayden's conclusion that American (or Israeli) air strikes would doubtless prompt Tehran to rebuild as quickly as it could.[26] Likewise, Colin Kahl argues, "By demonstrating the vulnerability of a non-nuclear-armed Iran, a U.S. attack would provide ammunition to hard-liners who argue for acquiring a nuclear deterrent."[27] My remarkable colleague Michael O'Hanlon has surveyed the landscape of expert opinion and reached the same conclusion, writing, "Most U.S. (and Israeli) nuclear experts now think that Tehran is so far along with its nuclear program that it would be able to rebuild the entire program in two years. In this light, a successful air campaign would be a Pyrrhic victory—if even that, given the ambiguity surrounding the exact nature and extent of Iran's nuclear facilities."[28] Perhaps the best case for an air campaign so far has been made by former Pentagon aide Matthew Kroenig, yet he too worries that air strikes would only delay the Iranians and would not keep them from reconstituting: "Even if the United States managed to eliminate Iran's nuclear facilities and mitigate the consequences, the effects might not last long. Sure enough, there is no guarantee that an assault would deter Iran from attempting to rebuild its plants; it may even harden Iran's resolve to acquire nuclear technology as a means of retaliating or protecting itself in the future."[29]

Saddam rebuilt (and vastly expanded) his nuclear weapons program after the 1981 Israeli attack on Osirak, and he initially intended to do so again even after the massive destruction of Operation Desert Storm in 1991. In the first years after the Gulf War, he played ridiculous games with the UN inspectors to try to hide those elements of his nuclear program that weren't destroyed by the coalition air campaign. Indeed, the definitive post-invasion assessment ultimately concluded that right up to the bitter end in 2003, Saddam still planned to rebuild his nuclear program whenever he was able to do so.[30] Khamene'i's Iran is not Saddam's Iraq, but Tehran's determination to acquire nuclear weapons (or merely a nuclear weapons capability) and to disregard all manner of sanctions and other hardships to do so appears similar, if not identical.

Recognizing the unknowns, it is still the case that the logic of the circumstances, the historical analogies, and the limited information available all suggest that it is more likely than not that the Iranian regime would try again to build nuclear weapons even after an American air campaign. Of course Khamene'i has every incentive to say so before an attack, but he has indicated that he would continue Iran's nuclear program under all circumstances, declaring in February 2012, "No obstacles can stop Iran's nuclear work." Because of this likelihood, in weighing whether to launch such an air campaign against Iran, the president of the United States would have to assume that the Iranians would reconstitute.

COULD WE USE AN AIR CAMPAIGN TO HELP OVERTHROW THE IRANIAN REGIME? One way to overcome Iran's determination to revive its nuclear program even after an American air attack would be to go after the regime itself. This is especially appealing to those who believe that air strikes might destabilize the Islamic republic. However, there is still the problem that the regime has consistently demonstrated an overwhelming ability to crush domestic opposition movements, even including the massive 2009 Green revolt. To try to square that circle, some have mused about the possibility of using an air campaign to go beyond destroying

Iran's nuclear program and help the Iranian opposition overthrow the regime. Imagine the Green Revolution all over again, but this time with American airpower intervening to smash the regime's security forces and allow the opposition to seize power over a carpet of American bombs. The NATO air effort in support of the Libyan rebels in 2011 is the obvious analogy here, but so too is the U.S. air campaign that allowed Afghanistan's Northern Alliance to evict the Taliban in 2001.

If U.S. air strikes also targeted the regime's security services, internal command and control network, key transportation choke points, leadership targets, all the while providing on-call fire support for Iranian rebels facing regime security forces, there is some probability that Iranian revolutionaries might defeat the regime's security forces and gain power. However, doing so would require a massive air campaign on its own, on top of whatever necessary sorties were needed to destroy the Iranian nuclear sites. By way of comparison, during the six weeks of Operation Desert Storm, the coalition air forces flew 38,000 interdiction sorties to cripple Iraqi forces in the Kuwait Theater of Operations that began with more than 500,000 men.[31] Although those strikes did tremendous damage to Iraqi forces, key units (principally Saddam's Republican Guard) still fought fiercely against the overwhelming coalition ground offensive and still retained the strength to crush both the Kurdish and Shi'i revolts that broke out after the end of Operation Desert Storm.[32] Thus, an air campaign to enable regime change in Iran would have to do better. Nor does Kosovo provide a more hopeful example. In Kosovo, NATO air forces flew 3,400 interdiction sorties over seventy-eight days against roughly 100,000 Serbian troops, and caused much less damage than against Iraq.[33] Those air strikes failed to enable the Kosovo Liberation Army to make any significant headway against Serbian Forces.[34] Finally, in Libya in 2011, NATO flew more than 9,700 interdiction sorties over 203 days that helped Libyan rebels defeat 20,000–40,000 Libyan regime troops and paramilitary forces.[35] NATO's success in Libya was largely a function of the incompetence and apathy of Qadhafi's troops.[36] Every one of those campaigns also required thousands more sorties for air superiority, electronic warfare, suppression of enemy air defense, command and control, reconnaissance, and logistics to support the strike sorties.

Historically, victory in these kinds of campaigns hinges on the commitment of the regime's forces. The more determined they are, the harder it is to defeat them, the more sorties, and the more time it takes to enable opposition ground forces to prevail.[37] From what we have seen of Iran's security forces, there is no reason to believe that they would be unenthusiastic in defense of the regime. Iran's 150,000-strong Revolutionary Guard can call on hundreds of thousands of Basiji militia to bolster their numbers. Iran's regular armed forces, the Artesh, have competed for years to prove that they are just as loyal to the regime as the Guards are. And beyond them, the regime can call on tens of thousands of Law Enforcement Force personnel and thugs from Ansar e-Hizballah—paramilitary groups that it uses to beat up and kill Iranian protesters.[38]

There are many questions to answer to determine how much airpower would be needed to give Iranian rebels a shot at overthrowing the clerical regime: how much of Iran's security services would have to be defeated, how many cities would be involved, would the morale of the Iranian security services crack, and so on. The United States might need anywhere from a few thousand to tens of thousands of sorties and, as in Iraq and Kosovo, even that might not be enough. Cracking the morale of enemy ground forces (let alone destroying them physically) by airpower alone is a very difficult undertaking, requiring repeated applications of force over many days. Never have small doses of airpower broken an enemy army by itself. And incorporating this mission into an air campaign meant to knock out Iran's nuclear program would be adding a massive additional undertaking; one that runs contrary to the whole point of a policy option meant to destroy Iran's nuclear facilities and disengage to *avoid* a wider war with Iran. Trying to use airpower to assist a revolution against the Iranian leadership would produce that wider war. If the United States were looking to overthrow Iran's government by force, it would be better to do the job right by invading with ground forces rather than gamble on airpower alone.

International Reaction to an American Air Campaign

As always when discussing American air campaigns, the military dimensions make the idea seem easy, straightforward, and entirely under our control. But of course, as Carl von Clausewitz warned two centuries ago, that is never the case in war because "everything in war is very simple, but the simplest thing is difficult."[39] Nothing about Iran is easy or straightforward and there are many potential complications to an American air campaign against Iran to eliminate its nuclear sites.

The reaction of other peoples and governments to an American strike could be particularly important and difficult to manage. Although the United States might not face the same degree of international outrage as Israel for attacking Iran's nuclear program, in many scenarios, we would incur considerable ill-will. That would be more problematic for the United States because of our greater reliance on international cooperation, both against Iran and around the world.

INTERNATIONAL LAW. For some people, international law is sacrosanct. They believe that it would be much better to live in a world of laws than an anarchical international order where might often makes right. Or they believe that the United States benefits from the current system of international law, and therefore the U.S. should not undermine it. For others, however, international law is worse than irrelevant: it is something that the powerless use to constrain the powerful. They tend to regard advocates of international law as dangerous dreamers who would hamstring the United States in pursuit of a utopian will-o'-the-wisp. In the case of air strikes against Iran, indeed any military action against Iran, there are reasons why both groups need to pay attention to international law.

The basic problem is that absent an Iranian provocation, it will be hard for the United States to justify using force against Iran. Since the 1990–91 Persian Gulf War, the United States has typically relied on UN Security Council resolutions to justify force. There have been a few exceptions. For

Operation Enduring Freedom, the 2001 campaign against Afghanistan, the United States invoked the right to self-defense under Article 51 of the UN Charter in response to the 9/11 attacks. In Kosovo in 1999, NATO had no legal basis for intervention and some legal scholars branded the war illegal. What mattered, however, was that all of the NATO nations, all of the EU countries, and many other countries ultimately supported the intervention—indeed, then UN secretary-general Kofi Annan asserted that the war was "legitimate" even if the absence of Security Council authorization did not necessarily make it "legal."[40] Interestingly, the United States had a far stronger legal basis for the 2003 invasion of Iraq, resting on the UN Security Council resolutions from 1990–91 authorizing the use of force to ensure Saddam Husayn's compliance with all of the conditions imposed by the UN after the Persian Gulf War. Yet the invasion of Iraq was denounced in many quarters as illegal. Arguably, the problem in this case was the opposite of Annan's remark about Kosovo: whereas that campaign may have been illegal but legitimate, the Iraq War was legal but eventually seen by many as illegitimate.

An attack on Iran could fall on the wrong side of both the Kosovo and Iraq experiences. Since 2006, there have been six UN Security Council resolutions against Iran enacted under Chapter VII of the UN Charter. However, every one of these resolutions has noted that it does not authorize the use of force. This assertion is not accidental: it was demanded by Russia and China (and others) as a condition for their voting in favor of the resolutions. Many Americans oppose the use of force (a topic addressed in greater detail below). Even America's European allies have drawn stark lines between supporting sanctions and supporting military operations.[41] Unless Iran does something stupid that constitutes an unquestionable casus belli, it is unlikely that the Chinese and Russians would allow a new resolution authorizing the use of force to pass the Security Council.

The legacy of the Iraq War is part of the issue and a major impediment to winning over international support for an attack on Iran. Absent an inexcusable Iranian provocation, an American attack would probably look to many like a replay of the Iraq War. The United States and its allies will have been claiming that Iran is developing weapons of mass destruction, specifically nuclear weapons, while the Iranians—like the Iraqis before them—will be denying it. The Iranians will continue to argue that their nuclear program is for peaceful civilian purposes, and despite the evidence against that, many people will believe it. If the United States attacks anyway, justifying the strike by resort to the UN Charter's right to self-defense, many will brand it illegal—and they will be on much firmer ground than those who insisted that the Iraq War was illegal. Some respected American legal scholars have already rendered opinions that such an attack would be unlawful.[42] In one widely cited law review article, Mary Ellen O'Connell and Maria Alevras-Chen declared, "The law governing the use of force is found in the United Nations (UN) Charter, in customary international law, and in the general principles of law. . . . Under these rules, no use of military force can be justified against Iran for carrying out nuclear research."[43]

Some international legal experts have argued that Iran's nuclear facilities are not materially different from those of Japan, and therefore are barred from attack by an IAEA General Conference resolution. Others will dispute whether those resolutions have the force of law, or whether there are material distinctions with Japan's nuclear program.[44] The International Court of Justice has gone so far as to assert that violations of the NPT and even acquisition of nuclear weapons themselves would not, on their own, constitute a violation of the UN Charter or international law justifying the use of force.[45] Of course, Iran's own claims that the UN sanctions are somehow illegal have been repeatedly refuted, but that does not furnish a legal basis for an attack.[46] What is clear is that making a legal case for going to war against Iran would be much, much harder than going to war against Iraq in 2003. In the words of John Bellinger and Jeff Smith, two legal scholars who have both wrestled with these issues as general counsels of the State Department and CIA, respectively, "In the absence of U.N. authorization, many nations, including some of our allies, are likely to believe that a pre-emptive attack (on Iran) would violate international law."[47]

For some Americans, this legal prohibition alone might be enough to oppose an attack on Iran. For others, the issue is more practical. The lack of a clear legal basis will make an operation that is going to be hard enough to pull off politically and diplomatically that much harder. Matt Waxman, who fought the legal trespasses of some of his more zealous colleagues in the Bush 43 administration, worries that in the case of Iran, "Dubious legality makes military action more costly—including in terms of military, political, and diplomatic repercussions, as well as long-term precedent that may be exploited by others—and therefore affects its perceived merits relative to other options."[48]

If the president of the United States ever has to take to the airwaves to announce that we have attacked Iran to prevent it from making any further progress toward a nuclear weapons capability, he or she could have a hard time justifying the legality of an attack. That would make a hard political and diplomatic sell even harder. A September 2012 report signed by thirty-five distinguished former national security officials, generals, and experts on Iran warned that "if the U.S. and/or Israel end up attacking Iran's nuclear program without [an international] mandate, hard-won international support for maintaining sanctions against Iran could be substantially weakened. China and Russia would loudly condemn military actions against Iran, and some European nations might pull back from a sanctions regime after such attacks. Iran would be seen by many around the world, Muslims and non-Muslims alike, as the victim of unjustified American and/or Israeli military action."[49] Thus, even if you don't regard international law as meaningful in and of itself, in the case of military operations against Iran, international law will play a role—and potentially a significant one—in determining international support for America's actions.

As a final point on this topic, there are some smart, well-meaning people who have suggested that the United States might not acknowledge an attack on Iran, just as Israel has never acknowledged its attacks on the Syrian nuclear reactor at al-Kibar, an arms factory in Khartoum, and other sites.[50] This idea is beyond far-fetched. The United States of America isn't the state of Israel. The only time that the United States tried to conduct a massive bombing campaign unacknowledged was Nixon's secret bombing of Cambodia in 1969–70, and that ended badly for all involved. If the United States launches an air campaign against Iran, it is going to become known immediately and the American people are going to demand an explanation—and the president is going to have to give it to them. This attack will not be a drone strike against an al-Qa'ida terrorist isolated in the mountains of Yemen or Pakistan, where the governments have granted the United States permission to conduct such strikes.[51] It will be a major military operation, an act of war against a sovereign government, that will result in Iranian and American casualties, especially as a result of Iranian retaliatory acts. Every American will want to understand why the president thought it necessary, what the U.S. government hopes to achieve, how the U.S. armed forces will try to accomplish these goals, and what to expect in the future. The Congress will (rightly) demand an explanation, if not its blessing. A campaign on this scale is not something any president can ignore or cover up, nor could I imagine that any would want to do so.

BASES. There are several reasons why international support will be important to a U.S. military campaign against Iran. First off, it would be extremely helpful for the United States to be able to use foreign bases near Iran. The United States has Air Force units routinely deployed in Kuwait, Qatar, and the UAE, and has also used facilities in Turkey, Bahrain, Saudi Arabia, and Oman on previous occasions for military operations in the area. The U.S. military would also love to have access to bases in Central Asia and the Caucasus for an air campaign against Iran. Of course, we can only use those bases with the permission of the host governments. Because of the capabilities of U.S. military forces, not being able to use those bases would not be a showstopper: American planes flying from the continental United States, from Diego Garcia, and from carriers in the Gulf and the North Arabian Sea, along with cruise missiles fired from ships at sea, could handle the job alone. However, it would be much more work for them to do so. It might mean limiting the number of targets struck, accepting lesser levels of destruction, or drawing out an air campaign for much longer than would otherwise be necessary.

The problem is that while the GCC, Central Asian, and Caucasus states are America's friends and allies, they have not always allowed the United States to use those bases. In 1996, the Saudis, the Turks, the Jordanians, and the Kuwaitis did not allow the United States to fly aircraft from their bases in response to Saddam's attack on the Kurdish city of Irbil.[52] For Operation Desert Fox in 1998, the problems got worse: Saudi Arabia refused to allow the United States to fly combat aircraft from its bases, impeding the execution of the plan.[53] Similarly, for the 2003 invasion of Iraq, Saudi Arabia refused to allow the United States to fly combat aircraft from its bases, although it did permit support planes to do so.[54] Turkey denied the United States altogether in 2003.[55] And the reaction of Central Asian and Caucasus states is even more unpredictable. Thus, the more international support for an air campaign against Iran, the more likely that the United States will have access to regional bases, easing the planning, operational, and logistical requirements of an attack.

THE DAY AFTER. If an American air campaign lacked widespread international support, it could incur the same post-strike problems as an Israeli military operation. In the worst case, Iran might garner widespread sympathy and be able to withdraw from the NPT and evict the IAEA inspectors without facing any serious consequences. Many countries, potentially including Russia, China, India, Brazil, and other major powers, might condemn the American attack and begin to ignore the UN-imposed sanctions as they did with Iraq in the late 1990s. The ability of the United States to prevent Iran from reconstituting its nuclear program would be diminished, calling into question the utility of the strike in the first place.

Such an outcome is hardly impossible; in fact it may be the most likely course of events given the current state of international sentiment. The Russians continue to insist that there is no basis for an attack on Iran because there is no reason to believe that the Iranian nuclear program has any military component.[56] Russian foreign minister Sergei Lavrov declared in January 2013, "Attempts to prepare and implement strikes on Iranian nuclear facilities and on its infrastructure as a whole are a very, very dangerous idea. We hope these ideas will not come to fruition."[57] In late November 2012, after the IAEA stated that it was becoming worried about a possible military dimension to Iran's nuclear program and published an extensive dossier outlining its concerns, Russian deputy foreign minister Sergei Ryabkov responded, "We, as before, see no signs that there is a military dimension to Iran's nuclear program. No signs."[58] The Chinese have stuck to more realistic concerns about the dangers of war to signal their opposition. Chen Xiaodong, head of the Chinese Foreign Ministry's West Asian and North African affairs division, cautioned in April 2012, "If force is used on Iran, it will certainly incur retaliation, cause an even greater military clash, worsen turmoil in the region, threaten the security of the Strait of Hormuz and other strategic passages, drive up global oil prices and strike a blow at the world economic recovery. . . . There may be 10,000 reasons to go to war but you cannot remedy the terrible consequences of plunging the people into misery and suffering and the collapse of society and the economy caused by the flames of war. . . . The international community has a responsibility to restrain itself from war."[59] Brazil, India, and Turkey also oppose an attack on Iran by either Israel or the United States.[60]

As for America's Arab allies, their views are more complicated. At least in private, many Gulf leaders have urged the United States to attack. The *New York Times* reports that the WikiLeaks cables showed that America's Arab allies privately "clamored for strong action—by someone else," but "they seemed deeply conflicted about how to deal with it—diplomacy, covert action or force."[61] King Abdallah of Saudi Arabia is reportedly a staunch advocate of an American attack on Iran, as is Muhammad bin

Zayed, the crown prince of the UAE and possibly the most intellectually formidable of all of the Arab leaders.[62] Nevertheless, the Gulf leaders demur from openly backing a military operation against Iran.[63] Meanwhile, other Arab leaders have opposed it. In 2007, then Arab League chief Amr Moussa and then IAEA chief Mohamed ElBaradei (both now leading Egyptian politicians) both denounced the idea of an attack on Iran, with ElBaradei calling it "an act of madness."[64] Likewise, in November 2011, Prince Turki al-Faisal, former Saudi intelligence chief and former Saudi ambassador to Washington, said of a military attack on the Iranian nuclear program, "Such an act I think would be foolish and to undertake it I think would be tragic. . . . If anything it will only make the Iranians more determined to produce an atomic bomb. It will rally support for the government among the population, and it will not end the program. It will merely delay it if anything. . . . An attack on Iran I think will have catastrophic consequences . . . the retaliation by Iran will be worldwide."[65] And Qatar's minister of state for foreign affairs, Khalid bin Mohamed al-Attiyah, said an attack on Iran "is not a solution, and tightening the embargo on Iran will make the scenario worse."[66]

The potential for air strikes on Iran to send oil prices soaring is part of the opposition to an American (or Israeli) attack on Iran, and how this plays out in the event of an actual conflict will affect international reaction to the attacker. Ultimately, there is no way to predict what will happen to oil prices. It will depend on how the Iranians retaliate. The more they threaten the Strait of Hormuz and demonstrate a capacity to disrupt tanker traffic, the higher oil prices will climb. One sober analysis from 2012 that seems neither to underplay nor to exaggerate the potential impact on oil prices concluded that a strike on Iran's nuclear program could cause an immediate price increase of about $23 per barrel. This could be expected either to drop to about $11 extra per barrel in the case of a short disruption, or climb to as much as $61 more per barrel in the event of a sustained disruption, depending on how much of international oil reserves were released.[67]

So there is a real prospect that an American air campaign against Iran would encounter widespread international opposition, and this opposition could cripple the sanctions, inspections, and other measures currently hamstringing Iran's nuclear progress, all of which would be crucial after a strike to impede or prevent Iran from rebuilding.

Some have argued that even if the Iranians were to rebuild, the United States could just attack again. This idea strikes me as infeasible and improbable. The only time that the United States has been willing to do something like that was against Iraq in the 1990s, when we repeatedly struck Iraqi targets to enforce compliance with the UN resolutions and no-fly zones. Within a few years (probably by 1996 and unquestionably by 1998), however, the international community had tired of these constant strikes and turned against them. Once that happened, even our most enthusiastic Arab allies found it increasingly difficult to support such operations.

In every other conflict—in Iraq in 1991, in Kosovo in 1999, and again in Iraq in 2003—when air strikes alone could not do the job and the adversary resumed its course, the United States felt it had no choice but to escalate to a ground invasion (one that fortunately proved unnecessary in the end in Bosnia and Kosovo). It is understandable that Washington would act this way. The president of the United States cannot be seen as clinging to ineffectual military operations. If airpower does not eliminate the Iranian nuclear program for all time the first time, the president will face tremendous pressure to escalate to a much greater level of force to get the job done. When the American people are roused to war, they want to see it won as quickly as possible to minimize casualties and other costs, and so that they can go back to peace. Repeatedly going to war with Iran is something that the United States simply cannot sustain.

Securing International Support

The best way to build international support for an air campaign is old-fashioned diplomacy.

The two Bush administrations together furnish us with everything we need to understand how to build diplomatic support for a war with a Middle Eastern state believed to be trying to acquire weapons of mass destruction. The Bush 41 administration did everything right in fashioning a coalition to evict Saddam from Kuwait in 1991. The Bush 43 administration did everything wrong in its rush to topple Saddam from power in 2003. Between what the Bush 41 administration did and what the Bush 43 administration did not do, we have an excellent blueprint for how to secure international support for a war against Iran. The most important lessons include:

1. *Take your time.* Going slow is important to demonstrate that the United States is not rushing to war. The United States does not have forever. It would have to attack before Iran acquired a workable nuclear weapon—not just adequate fissile material, a canard that gets bandied about. However, even the worst-case estimates indicate that the United States has at least one to three years before Iran would be able to do so from a decision to start—a decision that has not been given, as best we can tell. If these estimates are inaccurate or the Iranians stick with a breakout capability, as many expect, Washington will have even more time. Using that time for diplomacy would be vital to demonstrate that the United States had exhausted all the alternatives and given Iran every opportunity to solve the impasse.

2. *Make Iran a great offer.* If the United States is going to convince other countries to support a military operation, it will have to convince them that it was willing to take "yes" for an answer and the Iranian regime wasn't. That would mean putting a deal on the table that the entire international community would see as a great deal for Iran if it were only seeking nuclear energy, and so other countries would also see no reason for Iran not to accept it. Dennis Ross, President Obama's former chief Iran advisor, and Iran expert Patrick Clawson—with whom I agree on almost nothing—have both made this suggestion, and they are right that it is necessary to do so to build international support before the United States could even consider military operations.[68]

3. *Enlist others to help improve the offer and help convince Iran to accept it.* Russia and China, Turkey and Brazil, India and others all need to be a part of the process. The United States should ask them to help fashion the deal, take their advice, and encourage them to speak to the Iranians. Once the deal has been crafted, these same countries need to be encouraged to convince Iran to accept it, and be given the time to do so. They can't take forever, but the time limits would need to be measured in months, not weeks, let alone days. Everyone must believe that the United States gave peace every chance and turned to war only when there was no other choice.

4. *Go all the way.* Any offer to Iran cannot give the Iranians everything they want. However, the United States can and should go much further than it has. The United States needs to give the Iranians what they want related to civilian nuclear power (and throw in some incentives to make it easier to build nuclear power plants), to be ready to accept limited Iranian enrichment, and to prepare to rely on inspections and monitoring to prevent an Iranian breakout.

AN ULTIMATUM, NOT A NEGOTIATION. A critical difference between this approach and what we have done so far is that if the United States decided that it was ready to go to war, it should handle the negotiations with Iran differently from the past. In the talks so far, the United States has assumed that there would be a protracted negotiation between Tehran and the P-5+1, and the United States would be expected to make gradual concessions in return for the same. Consequently, the United States has resisted making any major concessions up front for fear that Tehran would "pocket" them and demand additional compromises during the negotiations. This concern was reasonable, but has proven self-defeating. The United States has been willing to put so little on the table that the Iranians have seen no point even in negotiating seriously. If the United States is ready to go to war with Iran, the talks need to be conducted in a wholly different manner: the offer needs to be an ultimatum, not a bargaining position.

However, for the United States to deliver an ultimatum to Iran that would be accepted as a legitimate casus belli by other countries, that ultimatum will have to pass their muster. The Russians and Chinese in particular will not support a war against Iran if the ultimatum presented to Iran does not appear reasonable to them.

TWO CONUNDRUMS. If four paradoxes would confound an Israeli strike, building the diplomatic support for an American strike faces two conundrums of its own. To gain international support, the United States would have to present Iran with an ultimatum that Russia, China, Brazil, India, and other major countries who oppose war with Iran would see as "acceptable" to Iran. However, at least some of those countries (starting with Russia) so oppose a war with Iran that they will probably declare unacceptable any offer the United States makes in the form of an ultimatum, to try to deny Washington international legitimacy for a strike.

This problem is daunting, but it may not be insurmountable. The United States should be able to work with other countries such as China, India, and Turkey to craft a proposal that should meet Iran's legitimate needs. If Russia continues to object, it could block action in the Security Council, but would not necessarily deny the operation informal international legitimacy. During the conflict in Kosovo, the Russians similarly opposed a war against Serbia so vehemently that they blocked all action in the Security Council, but the United States and its allies handled themselves so well (and Milosevic so badly) that NATO garnered widespread support for the operation even without a UN Security Council resolution.

The second conundrum for the United States is that Iran might accept the terms of an ultimatum, and if they did so, the United States would have to accept it as well and call off the war. An ultimatum to Iran should look something much like the deal proposed in chapter 6, as the ultimate goal of a carrot-and-stick approach: Iran would be allowed to have civilian nuclear power, would be allowed to enrich uranium up to 5 percent purity, would be allowed a limited number of centrifuge plants and centrifuges, and would be allowed to have a small stockpile of LEU, in return for forswearing any enrichment and stockpiles beyond that, and accepting intrusive and comprehensive monitoring and inspections.

As was the case with the carrot-and-stick approach, whether one is willing to accept that deal determines whether this is a problem or not. For someone like me, who is willing to accept containment over war, this situation is win-win: Iran accepts a deal that would curtail its nuclear activities as well as forcing it to accept intrusive inspections *and* the United States does not have to go to war. However, many who favor air strikes do so because they would not accept such a deal. Either they believe that Iran would cheat and get away with it, like North Korea, or they do not want to leave Iran with even a latent, long-term breakout capability. For them, air strikes are preferable to a deal. But the problem is that the only way to get international support that could make air strikes successful comes at the cost of having to accept such a deal if the Iranians will.

I do not see a good way around this second conundrum. If the United States does not offer Iran a reasonable ultimatum, it will not have international support for war. Instead, we will face the same kind of situation as in 2003. Like then, it won't matter much for the opening act, the takedown, but it could prove fatal in the crucial succeeding acts, the follow-through. As has often been our mistake, the United States might win the "war" and lose the "peace," and the latter matters far more than the former.[69]

DOMESTIC SUPPORT. Another challenge for an American president seeking to employ air strikes against the Iranian nuclear program will be generating domestic support here in America. So far, the American people have shown little eagerness for military operations against Iran. President Obama and his political advisors made their perception of American war-weariness a critical theme of the president's 2008 and 2012 electoral campaigns, and one of the few remarks in the president's second inaugural address related to foreign policy was Obama's pronouncement, "A decade of war is now ending."[70]

Polls of the American public have demonstrated a schizophrenic reaction to war with Iran. Polls that ask a simple binary question—some version of "If Iran is close to developing a nuclear weapon, should the United States use force against it?"—have typically shown results that have varied from a strong majority in favor of war to a strong majority opposed. A March 2012 survey conducted by Reuters-IPSOS found that respondents favored a military strike against Iran 56 to 39 percent if Iran were developing nuclear weapons.[71] The Foreign Policy Institute's 2012 National Survey, conducted in September 2012, showed 62 percent of respondents favored military action to prevent Iran from getting nuclear weapons against only 23 percent who opposed it.[72] A Fox News survey from October 2012 concluded that 63 percent of Americans supported the United States taking military action to keep Iran from getting nuclear weapons, and only 27 percent opposed it.[73] In contrast, the 2012 Chicago Council on Global Affairs annual survey found that Americans opposed even a UN-sanctioned attack on Iran by 51 to 45 percent, while 70 percent of respondents opposed a unilateral American attack on Iran's nuclear program.[74] In October 2012, a CBS News/New York Times poll found that only 20 percent of Americans felt that Iran was "a threat to the United States that requires military action now," compared with 55 percent who felt that it could be contained by diplomacy now, and another 16 percent who felt that it was not a threat at all.[75]

However, whenever Americans have been asked to choose among a variety of ways that the United States could respond to Iran nearing the acquisition of a nuclear weapon, only a small minority favor the use of force, while a much larger majority oppose it. Only 17 percent of respondents to a January 2012 survey by the Princeton Survey Research Associates International backed an air campaign against Iran's nuclear sites if sanctions proved inadequate. This number compared to 47 percent who supported increased sanctions and 13 percent who favored more aggressive covert action.[76] Likewise, a February 2012 NBC News/Wall Street Journal poll asked respondents how the United States should respond if Iran's nuclear program got "close to developing a nuclear weapon." Only 21 percent felt that the United States should "take direct military action," compared to 75 percent who opposed direct military action, although some of these favored other courses of action (supporting an Israeli strike, or more diplomatic and economic actions).[77] A CNN/ORC International poll from the same period found that only 17 percent of Americans wanted the United States to use force against Iran to "shut down" its nuclear program, with 60 percent arguing that diplomatic or economic action was the right response, and 22 percent saying no action should be taken at that time.[78]

This mixed bag suggests that while a determined president could mobilize the American people to act against Iran if he were determined to do so, he might find that support fragile. The Bush 41 administration concluded that it was critical to demonstrate strong international support for evicting Saddam's army from Kuwait to build domestic support for the Gulf War. So too might a president need to show the American people that much of the world agreed with us and was ready to help us in a fight with Iran, to gain the kind of domestic political support that he or she would undoubtedly want before launching military operations against Iran. And it is always important to keep in mind that in March 2003 most Americans backed the invasion of Iraq.

Retaliation

It isn't inevitable that Iran would lash out in response to an American air campaign, but no American president should assume that it would not. Iran hasn't always retaliated for American attacks against it. After the destruction of Pan Am Flight 103 in December 1988, many believed that this act of terror was Iranian retaliation for the shooting down of Iran Air Flight 455 by the American cruiser USS *Vincennes* in July of that year. All of the evidence now points to Libya as the culprit, which if true would suggest that Iran never did retaliate for its loss. Nor did Iran retaliate for America's Operation Praying Mantis in 1988, which resulted in the sinking of a number of Iran's major warships. It is possible that Iran would simply choose to play the victim if attacked by the United States, assuming that this gambit would win the clerical regime international sympathy. Iran might decide that withdrawing from the NPT, evicting the inspectors, and rebuilding its nuclear program would be retaliation enough.

Nevertheless, it seems more likely that Iran would fight back as best it could. The Iranians have threatened to hit pretty much everything in the region that the United States might value even a little: American bases, Israel, Turkey, Saudi Arabia, and any other country that provided assistance to the United States for the operation.[79] Khamene'i has repeatedly threatened heavy responses to any American or Israeli attack, and so Tehran might feel compelled to retaliate or else lose any ability to deter subsequent attacks.[80]

The quickest and most direct response that Tehran could employ would be to lob ballistic missiles at U.S. bases, oil facilities, and other high-value targets located in the Gulf states, Israel, or other U.S. allies. Iran probably has several hundred ballistic missiles that could be used for this purpose, but they are inaccurate and unlikely to do much damage unless directed at cities. Nevertheless, this contingency could drive up oil prices and would still require the United States to deploy considerable antiballistic missile defense assets in the region and provide as much warning to U.S. allies as possible.

Because many Iranian leaders would look to emerge from the fighting in as advantageous a strategic position as possible, they might refrain from any direct retaliatory actions. As Kroenig explains, "Tehran would certainly feel like it needed to respond to a U.S. attack, in order to reestablish deterrence and save face domestically. But it would also likely seek to calibrate its actions to avoid starting a conflict that could lead to the destruction of its military or the regime itself."[81] Thus Iran might keep such missile attacks small and limited, and might refrain from targeting sensitive sites such as the Saudi oil fields, because any damage to them might provoke an even greater American response—and in that case, potentially with widespread international support.

Iran would almost certainly seek to convince Hizballah, Hamas, PIJ, or its other proxies and allies in the Levant to attack Israel with rockets, missiles, mortars, and any other weaponry on hand.[82] From Iran's perspective there would be little to lose and much to gain. Because Israel's ability to strike directly at Iran is limited (especially compared to the damage that the United States would have just inflicted on Iran), Tehran might have little to fear. Indeed, Israel's most likely and most powerful responses would be directed against the attackers themselves and the Iranians are probably more than willing to fight to the last Palestinian or Lebanese. However, by attacking Israel, Iran and its allies might be able to stir Arab and Muslim public opinion, possibly even painting the conflict as a new Arab-Israeli or Muslim-Israeli war. That may be a long shot, but given the limited downside for Tehran, why wouldn't they try? Indeed, most Israeli experts expect that they will.[83]

All that said, by far the most likely methods of Iranian retaliation would be covert: cyberwarfare and terrorist attack. Such responses could be immediate and coincident with a U.S. air campaign. Iran is believed to have extensive contingency plans for attacks on American targets, and it might be possible for Tehran to execute some terrorist operations in days and cyberattacks in hours. The U.S. intelligence community took the Arbabsiar case as proof that Iran is now willing to conduct terrorist attacks on American soil and believes that Iran is readying more such attacks to respond to an American military action.[84]

Iranian covert retaliation might also come well after the fact. If Tehran wanted to retaliate in spectacular fashion, especially on American soil, it might take longer to arrange. Major terrorist operations require extensive planning and preparatory work, and they have been especially difficult to execute in the United States ever since the security improvements that followed 9/11. Likewise, Iran might have to develop a more deliberate and complex cyberattack to get past U.S. defenses and cause significant harm to a significant American target or network. At a minimum, the United States would have to take steps to secure and harden U.S. targets against possible Iranian retaliation by cyber or terrorist attack and even then they might not prove fully effective.

Iranian terrorist and cyber attacks might also target America's allies, particularly those Iran might be looking for an excuse to attack anyway. Iran might try to stir up trouble against the governments of U.S. allies in the Gulf, especially Bahrain, Kuwait, and Saudi Arabia, all of whom have large Shi'i populations in which Iranian intelligence services have made significant inroads. Iran has attempted to overthrow all of these governments in the past, and they might be tempted to do so again.[85]

WOULD IRAN ATTACK THE STRAIT OF HORMUZ THIS TIME? It is somewhat more likely that the Iranians would attempt to disrupt traffic in the Strait of Hormuz in response to an American air campaign than an Israeli operation. At an obvious level, the Iranians have threatened to close the Strait in response to an American attack and might feel the need to demonstrate that they meant what they said. In a 2012 crisis simulation we ran at Brookings's Saban Center, the Iran team saw restoring its deterrent as a compelling motive for Tehran and ordered limited mining and harassment of U.S. naval forces in the Strait. In the game, both of these actions got out of hand and provoked the United States to mount a massive military campaign to obliterate Iranian naval and air forces along the Strait of Hormuz littoral.[86] Of course, the Iranians have also threatened to close the Strait if the West imposes new sanctions on Iran, and they have never made good on those threats, suggesting that the actual Iranian leadership may behave more cautiously than our Iran team in the simulation.[87]

Uncertainty is another factor that might push Tehran to move against the Strait of Hormuz. In most cases, if the United States decided to attack Iran's nuclear sites it would go for a bigger, longer campaign to ensure the maximum damage. In these scenarios, the United States would probably begin by building up its air, naval, and ground forces. This buildup, which might be fairly brief, would be followed by an initial wave of strikes against air defenses, key command and control facilities, and some leadership targets, to create a permissive environment for the strikes against the nuclear facilities. This sequence of events is effectively identical to how the United States would mount either a decapitating air strike against the leadership or start a full-scale invasion. Thus the Iranians could not assume that a limited American buildup meant only limited American military objectives.

In addition, because Iran's command and control network is old and imperfect, Tehran might be too confused by the initial American attacks to glean precise information about Washington's intentions. The Iranian leadership may only know that the United States is flying lots of strike sorties against it and is destroying a wide variety of important targets. In either of these circumstances, the regime might decide that it cannot afford to be wrong if it is a U.S. invasion, and might order a defensive closing of the Strait to try to prevent it.

Nevertheless, closing the Strait would hardly be an automatic response for Tehran. Iran's nuclear program is not the regime's highest priority, even if it is high on that list. They value their lives and their control of Iran even more. They also care a great deal about their oil production and export facilities, since those are the lifeblood of the Iranian economy and their own personal wealth. There is also their conventional military power, particularly their ability to threaten the Strait of Hormuz, which effectively constitutes their only economic and strategic leverage over other countries. All of these assets would also be vulnerable to American attack. The Iranians would hopefully recognize that they have even more to lose if they provoke the United States to escalate further, particularly by threatening the world's oil lifeline through the Strait of Hormuz—as long as they can recognize that the United States is discriminating among these target sets.[88]

Moreover, as discussed in the previous chapter, while Iran might be able to close the Strait for a limited period, American air and naval assets should be able to reopen it in a matter of weeks or months.[89] In so doing, the United States would probably cause enormous damage to Iran's air-, sea-, and ground-based military assets in the area. Iran has spent huge sums to build up these forces over the past two decades, and they are far too valuable to Iran as latent threats with which to manipulate the oil market to risk losing them by closing the strait.

If the Iranians did move against the Strait and closed it for some period of time, the damage they could do to the global economy could be significant albeit short-lived. At present, about 17 million barrels per day (bpd) flow through the Strait of Hormuz, amounting to 35 percent of global seaborne traded oil.[90] If that oil cannot be exported through the Strait, there is no way to replace it by producing more elsewhere, as virtually all of the world's spare oil production capacity is located in the Gulf countries.[91] About 2.5 million bpd could be rerouted through pipelines across Saudi Arabia and the UAE, but the 14.5 million bpd that would still be trapped by the closure of the Strait amounts to more than 16 percent of global oil consumption.[92] In theory, the strategic oil reserves of developed nations could make up for the loss of 14.5 million barrels per day, and could do so for about one hundred days.[93] (There are also private stocks of oil held by companies, but these fluctuate markedly. Thus, while they would certainly help, and potentially a lot, it is hard to calculate by how much.) Nevertheless, if strategic reserves cannot be released with efficiency and speed (and releases have typically proven slower than projected), the price of oil could rise significantly. Likewise, if the Strait were closed for more than three to five months, prices would rise as well. Meanwhile, eleven of twelve major American postwar recessions were preceded by a jump in oil prices.[94]

From Air Strikes to Invasion

Many people believe that it would be possible for the United States to mount limited air strikes against the Iranian nuclear program without having to commit to a wider war, or an invasion of Iran. This is one of the most important arguments in favor of air strikes. While I think this is possible, I think it much less likely than its proponents believe. I see a considerable risk, even a likelihood, that it would not be possible to do so.

There are several dynamics at work that make it fairly likely that air strikes against the Iranian nuclear program would be the start of a much larger U.S.-Iranian war, *one that could well push us into an invasion of Iran.* That is a big statement. It means that what seems like a major undertaking by the United States itself—several hundred or several thousand air and missile sorties against Iranian nuclear and air defense sites over the course of days or weeks—could morph into a truly massive American ground invasion of Iran requiring several hundred thousand ground troops occupying the country for years or even decades. Yet wars are always inherently unpredictable and often turn out much worse than their authors intended, especially when the instigators do not prepare for it to go badly.

First, there is the likelihood of Iranian retaliation. We don't know what the Iranians will do, how effective their retaliation will be, or how effective our defenses will prove. The available evidence indicates that they will retaliate, they will want to inflict significant pain, and that they have a reasonable capability to do so—primarily by terrorist and cyberattack. If Iran is able to hit us or our allies hard, there will be significant pressure on the United States to respond, especially if Iran is not content with a few retaliatory shots but continues to wage asymmetric campaigns (terrorism, cyberwarfare, periodic missile and rocket attacks) for weeks, months, even years—all of which it is capable of doing and has threatened to do. Moreover, if any such attacks were to cause major loss of life, or if the Iranians make any move to threaten the Strait of Hormuz, there would be tremendous pressure on the U.S. government to respond with overwhelming force to reopen the Strait, deny Iran the capacity to further threaten the United States or our allies, and convince Tehran to stop attacking us.

Depending on the extent and length of this retaliatory damage, there is a real risk of an escalatory spiral between the two sides that would lead to a much wider war. War games of small-scale crises between Iran and the United States have repeatedly demonstrated how easy escalation is between the two countries, given the hard feelings, deep suspicions, constant misinterpretations, and painful history between them. Similar studies and simulations of a conflict with Iran have also pointed to the difficulty of bringing such a war to an end short of an invasion— something reinforced by America's difficulties convincing Iran to desist during the "Tanker War" of the 1980s.[95]

Second, any American president who commits the United States to war with Iran, even if it starts out with discrete air strikes, will have a difficult time halting operations short of Iran's full capitulation (at least on the nuclear issue), regardless of the success or failure of that air campaign. If the president goes before the nation and explains that the threat of a nuclear Iran to American interests is so grave as to warrant the United States going to war with Iran (unprovoked) by launching hundreds or thousands of air sorties against dozens of Iranian targets, possibly resulting in hundreds or even thousands of deaths, he or she is not going to be in a position to announce a few weeks later that the strikes failed and Americans will just have to learn to live with a nuclear Iran. Nor is the president going to be able to accept a defiant Iran announcing after successful air strikes that it will rebuild its nuclear program and this time will not stop with enrichment but will continue on to field an arsenal. In either circumstance, if the threat were that grave to begin with— grave enough to court retaliation that could result in further American casualties—the American people would demand that we commit more of our fearsome military power to finish the job.

It is conceivable that the air strikes will do the job on their own and will either bring about a regime change or convince the Iranians not to begin rebuilding their nuclear program. It is also possible that Iran will retaliate in a modest fashion so as not to provoke a larger American response, or that Iranian retaliation will be defeated by American countermeasures and whatever pain we suffer will be modest enough to ignore or to respond to with equally limited measures.

However, these more optimistic scenarios appear to be the less likely outcomes. Although the United States is in a far stronger position than Israel would be on either of these scores, it appears more likely that the Iranian regime will not be overthrown and that whatever damage the air strikes may do, it seems probable that the regime will choose to reconstitute rather than give up. Likewise, the Iranians will almost certainly try hard to inflict considerable damage on the United States and will have a good chance of doing so.

No American president could order air strikes without recognizing the likelihood that doing so will end up committing the United States to a wider war with Iran and possibly a ground invasion. More to the point, *it would be irresponsible for a president to order air strikes against Iran without having accepted that doing so may mean committing the United States to an eventual invasion.*

As we should have learned from our painful experiences in Afghanistan, Iraq, and the Balkans, when the United States starts down the path of military action it is extremely difficult for our nation not to walk that road to its very end, whatever that end may be. In all of those cases, the United States tried limited military operations at first, only to find itself forced to commit to larger operations and eventually a major invasion and occupation. In the case of the Balkans, Milosevic's concessions on Kosovo in 1999 ultimately obviated the need for ground invasions and limited the extent of the postwar commitment. However, the United States was reluctantly gearing up for a ground invasion just when Milosevic's capitulations relieved us of the need to actually execute it. The same might happen in Iran, but no responsible president could start down the path of military action assuming it will. And unfortunately, the pathologies of the Iranian regime create the very real likelihood that it will require a much greater military effort, even an invasion and occupation of the country, either to prevent it from reconstituting its nuclear program or to force it to halt its retaliatory attacks against the United States.

It is easy for those who do not sit in the Oval Office to dismiss the prospects of a wider war with Iran or the need for an invasion and occupation of the country growing from "limited" air strikes against Iran's nuclear program. The person who sits there cannot. He must think through what his decision will entail, what it may commit the United

States to accomplish. It would be reckless and irresponsible for him to assume that air strikes would *not* lead us into a situation requiring a greater military effort.

Invasion Iran

Since air strikes against Iran raise the specter of an invasion, unwanted though this would be for virtually every American, it is important to sketch out the basics of such an operation.

MILITARY ASPECTS OF AN INVASION.[96] As with Iraq and Afghanistan, the military requirements for an invasion of Iran could prove deceptive. The invasion itself would be a major military operation, but one well within the capability of American forces. Although Iran's armed forces are roughly twice as large as Saddam's were in 2003 (750,000 to 1 million in the Iranian Armed Forces today, compared to about 400,000–500,000 in Iraq's various military services then) and probably would perform somewhat better than the Iraqis, they are outclassed by the American military. Once in, however, a long-term commitment would be necessary, greatly increasing the likely requirements.

A U.S. invasion force would face two primary military obstacles against Iran: terrain and insurgents. The first of Napoleon's "Military Maxims" was "The frontiers of states are either large rivers, or chains of mountains, or deserts. Of all these obstacles to the march of an army, the most difficult to overcome is the desert; mountains come next, and broad rivers occupy the third place." Iran has few broad rivers, but many mountains and deserts, the hardest types of military terrain. Iran has considerable experience with guerrilla warfare through its long association with Hizballah and the support it provided for the latter's guerrilla wars against Israel in southern Lebanon. After watching the American blitzkrieg to Baghdad in 2003, the Iranians have concluded that the best way to fight the U.S. military would be through a protracted guerrilla war, bleeding American forces as they wend their way through the arduous mountain chains that fence in the Iranian heartland and wearing them down in what Tehran has dubbed a "mosaic defense."[97]

To deal with the terrain and Iran's defensive strategy, an American invasion of Iran would require a variety of forces. First, it would probably involve a significant contingent of Marines (two to four regimental combat teams, or about 15,000–30,000 Marines) to seize a beachhead and then a major port at one of four or five general locations where such a landing could be staged along the Iranian coastline. To get past the mountains, the United States would want large numbers of air mobile forces—the brigades of the 101st Air Assault Division and the 82nd Airborne Division, and possibly the 173rd Airborne Brigade as well. Beyond that, the United States would want at least one, and as many as three, heavy armored divisions for the drive on Tehran itself (depending on the extent to which the Marines and air mobile units are tied down holding the landing area and mountain passes open, as well as providing route security for the massive logistical effort that will be needed to supply the American expedition). A force of four to six divisions amounting to 200,000–250,000 troops may lead the charge, larger than that employed at any time during Operation Iraqi Freedom and much larger than the 55,000 ground troops that took down Saddam's regime in the initial invasion.

Although Washington might secure bases in the Gulf states (and perhaps in some Central Asian countries as well), it seems unlikely that Iraq, Turkey, Pakistan, or Afghanistan would allow us to mount the invasion from their territory. Consequently, an invasion would require a large naval contingent to secure the Persian Gulf and carry the invasion force to the shores of Iran. It is thus unlikely that the United States could launch such an enormous military operation without the Iranian government getting a sense of what was headed its way.

In these circumstances, where the regime's survival would be at stake, the Iranians would have no incentive to show restraint in fighting back any way they could: with terrorist attacks anywhere they could hurt Americans, with rocket and missile attacks across the Persian Gulf, and by trying to close the Strait of Hormuz. Iran has some dangerous air, sea, and missile capabilities, but, as noted earlier, if the U.S. Navy and Air Force brought their full might to bear, they could crush Iran's air and sea defenses in a matter of weeks or months. This effort, however, would require a major commitment of American minesweeping, surface warfare, and air assets. It also would require a cutoff of Persian Gulf oil flows for at least as long as the Iranians contested the waters of the Gulf and the Strait.

As with an air campaign against Iran, the U.S. Air Force and Navy probably could handle the airpower requirements without the use of Saudi, Kuwaiti, Qatari, Emirati, Omani, Turkish, or Central Asian air bases, but it would be much easier with them. Long-range bombers could fly from the continental United States or Diego Garcia (with British permission), but unless the Gulf or Central Asian countries could be persuaded to allow the U.S. Air Force to operate from nearby airfields, the vast majority of American aircraft would have to operate from aircraft carriers. Given the extent to which modern U.S. ground operations rely on air support, three or more carriers might be needed for this campaign, at least until Iranian air bases could be secured and developed to handle U.S. Air Force planes.

Similarly, if the United States were denied access to its many bases in the Persian Gulf region, the Navy would have to bring in everything needed to support the invasion, and U.S. engineers would have to build facilities at Iranian ports to enable them to support a massive force. Indeed, because the expanses of Iran would be much greater than in Iraq (distances from major Iranian ports to Tehran are anywhere from one and a half to three times as great as those from the Kuwaiti border to Baghdad), and because of the much more difficult terrain, the logistical requirements for an invasion of Iran could be considerably more demanding than those for Iraq.

THE OCCUPATION. So much for the takedown. Now to the hard part. In both Iraq and Afghanistan, the United States tried to get rid of the regime and then go home, leaving the country in the hands of a hastily cobbled-together successor government of exiles. In both cases, the effort failed, and the country began to descend into chaos. In both places the Bush 43 administration was forced, against its will, to embark on a long-term occupation and reconstruction of the country.

It is unimaginable that the United States would not find the exact same thing in Iran. Iran is an even bigger oil producer than Iraq. It too occupies a central position in this vital region. Its influence and relationships throughout southwest Asia make it a key actor. If it fell into civil war and chaos, the spillover would infect the entire region. And the occupation of Iran would be a major undertaking.

This will likely prove true even if Washington has learned all the lessons of Iraq and mounts the invasion and occupation of Iran exactly as it should have in Iraq. Iran is a much bigger country than Iraq, with nearly three times the population and roughly four times the landmass. It too has myriad ethno-sectarian divisions and grievances, and a traumatic history of sanctions and authoritarian misrule. Thus the challenges of occupying and building a stable new Iran are likely to be nearly identical to those of Iraq, just bigger.

All low-intensity conflict operations, whether a counterinsurgency campaign or a stability operation like securing post-invasion Iran, require large numbers of security forces, because the sine qua non of success is securing the civilian populace against widespread violence. Scholars and low-intensity conflict experts have found that it takes about 20 security personnel per 1,000 people to secure civilians against insurgencies, militias, and other forms of violence common in postconflict reconstruction.[98] This ratio suggests that an occupation force of 1.4 million troops would be needed for Iran. That ratio is basically the same that succeeded in stabilizing Iraq in the 2007–2008 "surge" (taking into account American troops, security contractors, allied contingents, and the enlarged and improved Iraqi Security Forces).[99]

There is reason to believe that high-quality troops with lavish support assets (like the U.S. military) can get away with less than the canonical figure. But even if the United States, by relying on far superior training, technology, and tactics, could cut that number in half, the remainder still represents the *entire* active-duty component of the U.S. Army and Marine Corps. Even if it were only necessary to maintain such a large force for the first six months, after which the United States could begin drawing down its forces quickly (as experience in the Balkans and even Iraq suggests is possible), such a commitment would still require a massive mobilization of the National Guard and both the Army and Marine Reserves.

Again, assuming a best-case scenario in which the proper application of the lessons learned from Iraq and Afghanistan enables the invasion and occupation of Iran to go more easily, it would still take years to establish a stable, legitimate government with competent, loyal security forces. During that time, the United States would doubtless have to maintain several hundred thousand troops in Iran, even under ideal circumstances of full Iranian cooperation and minimal resistance.

THE COSTS OF AN INVASION. Of course, it would be unwise to assume the best case. The Bush 43 administration's insistence that only the best case was possible in Iraq lies at the root of the concatenation of mistakes that produced the worst case there from 2003 to 2006. Iranians are nationalistic, and while many would welcome the end of the current regime and a better relationship with the United States, the evidence suggests that most would oppose a U.S. invasion. Indeed, the fact that the regime is preparing to wage a guerrilla war against the United States if it invades means we could have a long, hard slog ahead of us there.[100]

The United States lost nearly 4,500 troops securing Iraq, and more than 2,000 in Afghanistan as of early 2013, although it did not have any killed during the earlier occupation of Bosnia. It is impossible to know how many troops we might lose in a similar operation in Iran, but we should not assume it will be as easy as Bosnia, and it could be as costly as Afghanistan or Iraq, or worse. Hundreds or possibly thousands of

American military personnel would die in the invasion itself. Thereafter, casualty levels would depend on both the extent of Iranian resistance and the competence of the American security effort. The remarkable success of American forces in Iraq after 2007 demonstrated that the right numbers of troops employing the right tactics in pursuit of the right strategy can secure a country at much lower cost in blood than inadequate numbers of troops improperly employed. Prior to the surge—and during its heated early months when U.S. troops were fighting to regain control of Iraq's streets—American military deaths were running at seventy to eighty per month. Once that fight had been won, they fell to five to fifteen per month. U.S. casualties during the occupation and reconstruction of Iran could thus vary considerably. Only in the best-case scenario—where the securing of Iran is as smooth as NATO's securing of Bosnia—should policymakers expect minimal casualties. In more plausible but still favorable scenarios, where Iranian resistance approximates Iraqi levels of violence after the surge, the United States should still expect a dozen soldiers and Marines killed each month, on average, for several years. In worst-case scenarios, in which the United States mishandles operations in Iran as badly as it did initially in Iraq, those numbers could run into the hundreds each month, or worse.

Washington would have to expect Tehran to retaliate against American targets outside of Iran, too. In the case of an invasion, the Iranians would have no reason to show restraint and every reason to try to hurt us as much as they possibly could to try to get us to back off. Iran has a more formidable ballistic missile arsenal than Saddam had in 1991 and a far more extensive and capable network to mount terrorist and cyber attacks against the United States and our allies. Whether the Iranians could pull off a catastrophic attack—along the lines of 9/11—would depend on how much time they had to prepare for such an operation, how well developed their contingency plans were at the time, and how well American defenses performed. Iran has one of the most competent terrorist networks in the world, we worry that they have much more powerful cyber-weapons in reserve, and they may actually have some of the WMDs that Saddam did not. Even if such attacks ended with the fall of the regime, since an invasion might take six months or more from the time the first U.S. Navy warships began to clear the Strait of Hormuz to the removal of the clerical regime, the United States would have to prepare to prevent such attacks—and live with the failure to do so—for at least this stretch.

The monetary costs of an invasion of Iran would be incurred principally in the initial invasion, the number of troops needed for occupation multiplied by the length of time they would be needed, added to the financial cost of casualties, and whatever money was directed at Iran for economic assistance and reconstruction. By way of comparison, the Iraq War cost $806 billion over roughly eight and a half years.[101] That strikes me as a good minimum of what we ought to be prepared to pay in Iran given its greater size, even taking into account the lessons we have learned from Iraq and Afghanistan. Most of these costs would be spread out over five to ten years, which would diminish their impact, but they would not be negligible.

In addition to the costs, an invasion also entails running a significant set of risks. A botched reconstruction, like the one in Iraq, could unleash a Pandora's box of problems both inside the country and out. Various Iranian ethnic groups might declare independence, setting off a civil war with the country's Persian majority and creating the risk of drawing in Iran's various neighbors. Iran's oil wealth would be a major driver of both internal conflict and external intervention. Chaos and conflict could jeopardize Iran's oil and gas exports, and would complicate the security problems of Iraq, Afghanistan, and Pakistan.

Extenuating Circumstances

There is one important exception to all of these points about the costs of and risks of the military options. If, for whatever reason, Iran attacks the United States first, the logic behind many of the downsides to air strikes against Iran may be mitigated or even reversed. In these circumstances, bombing Iran would not only become a much more desirable (or at least, much less undesirable) approach; it might even be a "good" option.

There are many possible scenarios for why and how Iran might strike first. In one crisis simulation we ran at Brookings in 2012, we posited that a combination of U.S. cyberattacks and Israeli covert action prompted Tehran to mount terrorist attacks against both an American and an Israeli, and the hit on the American ended up inadvertently killing a large number of American tourists in the Caribbean. Modeled roughly on the Arbabsiar plot, the attack prompted the U.S. team to respond in what it saw as a measured, discreet way—a cruise missile attack against a remote IRGC base where the Revolutionary Guards trained and equipped Taliban fighters to kill Americans in Afghanistan. The American team felt that this was the absolute minimum that they could do in response to such a brazen Iranian terrorist attack. But the Iran team went ballistic—almost literally—and responded far more aggressively than the Americans had expected. Iran made moves in the Strait of Hormuz that convinced the Americans (and much of the rest of the world) that Iran was trying to close the Strait. As the game ended, the debate within the American team was over whether to obliterate all of Iran's naval, air, and missile forces around the Strait of Hormuz, or to obliterate all of those forces *and* take out Iran's nuclear sites as well.[102]

It isn't hard to imagine other circumstances in which American actions, or Iranian perceptions of American actions, could lead Tehran to take actions of their own that the United States and the rest of the world would see as outrageous, unprovoked acts of war. In the 1980s, Iran's misunderstanding of American actions and our role in the Iran-Iraq War led Tehran to attack American forces in both Lebanon and the Gulf. Likewise, in the 1990s, Iranian misperceptions of an aggressive U.S. covert action program against them led them to hit the Khobar Towers complex. The Arbabsiar plot is another example, although it might have been in response to real American actions, not just imagined.

In the event that Iran overplayed its hand, many of the problems attendant on air strikes against its nuclear program might abate or even turn around. First, the American people would be enraged and would demand that the United States strike back, and strike back so hard that Iran would never think about conducting another one. Iran's nuclear sites would be the ideal target for such a response: they are part of an Iranian enterprise that the UN Security Council has demanded Iran halt. They are a threat to the stability of the region, a point echoed by all of the great powers, including all five permanent members of the Security Council. They are a threat to American interests in the region, and those of our regional allies. And they are valuable to the Iranian regime.

So the president could count on strong domestic backing and little international opposition—and possibly strong international support, just as the United States enjoyed tremendous international support after the 9/11 attacks. Many people around the world would see Iran as a dangerous, rogue regime supporting terrorism, and many more would feel that the Iranians had only themselves to blame. Because Iran would be seen as the aggressor, it would be much easier to maintain the sanctions and inspections in place after a strike. It would be much harder for the Iranians to play the victim as cover to withdraw from the NPT. Iran would look even more like a dangerous country that needed to be restrained, contained, and prevented from acquiring a nuclear capability.

Perhaps of greatest importance, it would also be much easier for the American president to refrain from further escalation and so avoid being pulled into an invasion. If Iran attacked us, *that* would be the justification for the attack. The president would not have to convince the American people of the dangers of the Iranian nuclear program. Iran might retaliate, but the United States could also continue to respond against other target sets—Iranian conventional forces around the Strait of Hormuz, Iranian oil facilities, Revolutionary Guards facilities, air force bases—without feeling the need to finish off the regime once and for all. Of course that risk would not be entirely absent. If Iranian retaliation also proved far more painful than expected—if Iranian cyber or terrorist attacks killed large numbers of people in the United States, for instance—then the president might still feel such pressures.

A clear and outrageous Iranian provocation will create the most advantageous circumstances possible for the United States to use force to take out Iran's nuclear program. It might even make this the preferable course of action. But like everything with Iran, it is not without costs and risks. With Iran, the worst is always a possibility.

Part III

Containment

10

The Strategy That Dare Not
Speak Its Name

Containment has become a dirty word in the debate over Iran policy. In Washington, it is denounced as criminal by those on the right, while those on the left insist that they never had any intention of embracing it. In September 2012, the Senate voted 90–1 in favor of a nonbinding "sense of the Senate" resolution that "rejects any United States policy that would rely on efforts to contain a nuclear weapons-capable Iran; and joins the President in ruling out any policy that would rely on containment as an option in response to the Iranian nuclear threat."[1] Not to be outdone, President Obama and his senior lieutenants have insisted over and over again that containment is neither their policy nor their intent. After meeting with Prime Minister Netanyahu in March 2012, President Obama explained, "We will not countenance Iran getting a nuclear weapon. My policy is not containment; my policy is to prevent them from getting a nuclear weapon."[2] Six months later, in his speech to the UN General Assembly in New York, President

Obama warned, "Make no mistake: A nuclear-armed Iran is not a challenge that can be contained . . . that's why the United States will do what we must to prevent Iran from obtaining a nuclear weapon."[3] In his February 2013 State of the Union address, Obama devoted precious little time to foreign policy and only a single sentence on Iran, but it made the same point: "Likewise, the leaders of Iran must recognize that now is the time for a diplomatic solution, because a coalition stands united in demanding that they meet their obligations, and we will do what is necessary to prevent them from getting a nuclear weapon."[4]

Somehow, somewhere along the way, containment became confused with appeasement. Many now assume that it means that the United States would accept Iran's acquisition of nuclear weapons and adjust to Iranian ambitions—in a passive manner. This misunderstanding is a shame. Not only because it is not what a strategy of containment would entail, but also because the United States has always employed a strategy of containment against Iran, we are practicing containment of Iran today, and we will continue to do so for as long as there is a government in Tehran that sees itself as the enemy of the United States.

What Is Containment?

Containment is not appeasement. Quite the contrary. The most basic way to understand a strategy of containment is that it seeks to prevent a hostile nation from causing harm to American interests and allies, by "containing" it within its borders until the structural flaws in its political system bring an end to the regime itself.[5] It means preventing the regime being contained from attacking other countries in any way—militarily, diplomatically, economically, clandestinely, politically, even psychologically—to the greatest extent possible. In the words of a thoughtful essay on the containment of Iran by Karim Sadjadpour and Diane de Gramont, "The goal should be not to contain Iran ad infinitum but to limit its destructive influences while facilitating its transition to a nation that can begin to realize its potential to serve as a constructive force in the world."[6] Or to quote the summary of containment's purpose from an outstanding study by Thomas Donnelly, Danielle Pletka, and Maseh Zarif, containment "should seek to block any Iranian expansion in the Persian Gulf region; to illuminate the problematic nature of the regime's ambitions; to constrain and indeed to induce a retraction of Iranian influence, including Iranian soft power; and to work toward a political transformation, if not a physical transformation, of the Tehran regime."[7]

The United States has adopted a strategy of containment whenever a nation has been hostile and unwilling to have a normal, peaceful relationship with the United States, but the American people were unwilling to bear the costs and risks of a war to eliminate its government or bend it to our will. Containment is what the United States does when it does not want to appease a nation but is also not willing to try to conquer it. It is our traditional "third way."

Although containment is not cost-free, it has allowed the United States to minimize the resources it expends on Iran, and to devote far less than would be needed to overthrow its regime. Iranian assertions to the contrary notwithstanding, the goal of every American administration since Carter has been to pay as little attention to Iran as possible without jeopardizing American interests elsewhere in the Middle East.

Containment is also not the same thing as deterrence. Containment is a strategy and deterrence a tactic often employed as part of that strategy. The two terms are often used synonymously, but containment is much more than mere deterrence, typically encompassing political, economic, diplomatic, and other methods as well, and having both offensive and defensive dimensions. Deterrence is a purely defensive tactic and in this context is limited to the narrow military aim of preventing aggression. During the Cold War, the United States contained the Soviet Union, and one of the ways that we did so was to employ both nuclear and conventional deterrence to keep the Soviets from attacking the U.S. homeland directly or invading Europe, the Middle East, and Japan. Similarly, with Iran since 1979, the United States has employed containment to minimize the Islamic Republic's ability to cause harm abroad, and part of that has been by deterring an Iranian (conventional) attack on U.S. allies in the region.

Understanding Containment

The basic concept of containment is as old as civilization. Thucydides describes how Sparta tried to contain Athenian power after the defeat of Persia in 480–479 BC. For Americans, the intellectual framework for "containing" an unfriendly state derives from George Kennan's work on U.S. policy toward Russia at the beginning of the Cold War. Kennan started from two key assumptions. First, for both ideological and geo-strategic reasons, the Soviet Union would always be an adversary of the United States. Second, because of the unimaginable costs of conquering the Soviet Union, the United States would not seek to eliminate the communist regime by war. Containment, as Kennan proposed it, would be an alternative strategy to prevent Soviet military expansion and political aggrandizement until the Soviet regime collapsed of its own dysfunction-alities. In this sense, it was a defensive effort to prevent Soviet aggression, limit Moscow's ability to gain allies or undermine American allies, and erode the Soviet economy—upon which Soviet military power rested. However, it also contained a crucial "offensive" element as well in that it sought the demise of the communist regime. Containment worked ad-mirably in the Cold War struggle with the Soviet Union, although critics claimed that the strategy was failing from the moment it was unveiled to the moment before it succeeded with the collapse of the USSR in 1991.

Thanks to the success of containment toward Russia, Washington came to see containment as a useful strategy in a host of lesser cases during the Cold War and after. The United States has pursued containment strategies at various times against China, North Korea, Cuba, Libya, Iraq, Nicaragua, Angola, Ethiopia, and Afghanistan, among others. The range of instances in which the United States has employed a strategy of containment also makes clear that it is a highly flexible one, encompassing a wide range of tactics. What's more, those tactics can be employed in a broad range of combinations so that there can be lots of different "flavors" of containment.[8]

At different points during the Cold War, the United States pursued variants of containment toward Russia that emphasized engagement and arms control (Nixon and Carter's policies of détente), or aggressive unconventional or proxy warfare and information operations (under Eisenhower and Reagan). Against Cuba, containment relied on sanctions and information operations, but a lower-key approach to covert action after the Cuban Missile Crisis. At that point, the United States largely ended its support to Cuban insurgents, but fought back whenever Cuban emissaries attempted to stir up trouble in Latin America and Africa. Against Saddam Husayn's Iraq, containment featured draconian international sanctions, overt and covert efforts to topple the regime, and the periodic use of air strikes to prevent Saddam from breaking free. Containment of Nicaragua, in many ways an outgrowth of the containment of Cuba, featured considerable assistance to insurgents attempting to overthrow the regime. In short, the basic theory of containment is typically just the foundation of the strategy, and many different kinds of policies can be developed from it.

Because the American commitment to containment of Iran has been so ambivalent, Washington's application of the strategy has been erratic. At times, America has pursued containment of Iran in a more confrontational manner, and at others Washington has paid little attention to it at all. Some administrations have employed sanctions and other punishments to try to pressure Iran to change its behavior, others have tried offers of rapprochement to change its course.

Although the intensity with which they have been employed over time has varied, the essential elements of America's containment of Iran have remained largely unchanged. These have consisted of:

- *Diplomatic efforts* to isolate Iran and enlist as many countries as possible to help the United States in containing it.

- *Sanctions* to prevent Iran from becoming economically or militarily powerful. These have focused on preventing or dissuading Iran from acquiring ballistic missiles or weapons of mass destruction, particularly nuclear weapons.
- The delineation, either explicitly or implicitly, of *"red lines"* that would trigger the use of force by the United States against Iran if Tehran crossed them.
- The *basing of American military forces in the Persian Gulf* to defend American allies, deter an Iranian attack, and enforce the red lines.
- And on occasion, modest *covert action* to support various groups inside Iran that have opposed the regime politically.

Containing Iran: A Brief History

After the Iranian Revolution and the Carter administration's brief flirtation with counterrevolution, Washington reached out to the new regime and offered to establish normal relations. That policy went up in smoke in November 1979, when a group of Iranian students seized the U.S. Embassy in Tehran, kicking off the 444 days of the hostage ordeal. Carter and his senior aides considered a range of military options in response to the embassy seizure, but settled for a policy of pressuring Iran via economic sanctions and diplomatic isolation. Moreover, in response to the fears of other American allies in the Persian Gulf, the United States began to increase its military assets in the region to deter or defeat an Iranian attempt to spread the revolution by force. In effect, if not original intent, it was a policy of containing Iran—limiting its ability to cause harm beyond its borders and hindering its ability to generate greater power to do so.

Although the Reagan administration took office convinced that everything its predecessor had done had been a mistake, they retained containment as their Iran policy. Despite their aggressive "cowboy" reputation, Reagan's team showed a remarkable reluctance to confront Iran throughout their eight years in office. They were mostly content to continue the buildup of U.S. military forces in the Gulf, and ramp up arms sales to Saudi Arabia and the other GCC states.

In 1982, Iran's battlefield victories in the Iran-Iraq War allowed the Islamic Republic to counter-invade Iraq to try to overthrow Saddam in what Tehran proclaimed would be a march to Mecca or Jerusalem. In response, the Reagan administration "tilted" toward Iraq as a way of preserving containment. Washington began to provide Baghdad with trade credits and critical intelligence on Iranian military moves, while encouraging its European allies to supply weapons to Iraq. Even after Iran helped drive American forces from Lebanon by creating Hizballah and directing it to seize American hostages and launch horrific terrorist attacks on the U.S. Marine barracks and the U.S. Embassy in Beirut, the Reagan administration made no effort to adopt a more aggressive policy toward Iran.

Later the Reagan administration would depart from containment, attempting a rapprochement with Iran through a series of backchannels to Hashemi Rafsanjani, then the Iranian Majles speaker. This effort, part of the wider Iran-Contra scandal, would end in humiliation when Iranian hardliners throttled Rafsanjani's scheme. Thereafter, the Reagan administration reverted to its restrained version of containment. When Iranian forces began attacking Gulf Arab oil tankers in the Persian Gulf in 1986–87, the United States initially shied away from defending them for fear of being dragged into a fight with Iran. When the United States agreed to the reflagging and the deployment of additional U.S. Navy ships to defend the reflagged tankers, American rules of engagement were kept tight and Washington intervened repeatedly to prevent conflict with Tehran. It took ever more aggressive Iranian attacks on American forces to provoke limited American military countermoves—although the disparity in strength was so great that the U.S. Navy still managed to sink half of Iran's major surface warships in a single encounter.

George H. W. Bush took office looking to improve relations with Iran and signaled to Tehran in his inaugural address that "goodwill begets goodwill." Seeing an opportunity, Rafsanjani (by then Iran's president) secured the release of a number of American hostages being held by Lebanese allies of Iran in the hope that this would start a rapprochement. But he proved unable to control other groups—and even parts of his own regime—from taking new hostages and threatening American interests in other ways. Meanwhile, the many other demands on the administration's plate—the fall of communism, the crisis with China over Tiananmen Square, and the Persian Gulf War—forced Bush 41 to rely on a passive version of containment toward Iran. Indeed, Washington was so determined to minimize the amount of energy and resources it committed against Iran so as to maximize its efforts elsewhere that it virtually ignored Iran.

The Clinton administration was the first to publicly embrace the term, announcing a policy of "Dual Containment" of both Iran and Iraq.[9] Clinton and his advisors believed that there was an opportunity to forge a comprehensive peace between Israel and the Arabs, and they wanted to pursue it as hard as they could. They feared that Saddam's Iraq and revolutionary Iran would both seek to undermine an Arab-Israeli peace process. Thus both Iran and Iraq would have to be prevented from killing the peace process, but the United States had to minimize the resources it expended on them so that it could instead focus on the peacemaking itself. That meant containment—Dual Containment.

Iran pushed back hard on Dual Containment, waging an aggressive, asymmetric campaign against the United States and its allies in the Middle East. This campaign, in turn, convinced the Clinton administration to get tougher still, shifting from a more passive version of containment to a much more aggressive one. Goaded by a Congress that had little love for Iran, the administration imposed comprehensive unilateral sanctions against Iran, threatened secondary sanctions against non-American companies doing significant business with the Iranian oil industry, and even modestly rejuvenated the moribund covert action campaign against Iran.[10]

If Clinton's first term saw the most aggressive version of containment ever pursued against Iran to that point, his second term saw a dramatic reversal. In 1997, Iran elected the reformist Mohammed Khatami as president, who reached out to the United States to try to improve relations. The Clinton administration accepted the offer, seeing in Khatami's opening a chance to finally end the long, debilitating enmity between Iran and America. However, once again, Iran's hardliners stepped in and killed the budding reconciliation.

In the wake of Clinton's failed rapprochement, the George W. Bush administration saw little reason to accommodate Iran, but could not agree on a more aggressive policy. Ultimately, they slipped back into containment as well, and initially a laissez-faire version at that. After the September 11, 2001, terrorist attacks, the United States and Iran engaged in extensive cooperation against their mutual adversaries, the Taliban and al-Qa'ida. There is evidence that some in the Iranian regime hoped to turn this tacit cooperation into a wider opening, but it came to naught. Although there was some evidence that the hawks in the administration hoped to pursue regime change in Iran after Afghanistan and Iraq, the disastrous mishandling of the Iraq War put an end to any such notions and the United States settled in to renewed containment instead.

Washington's complacency was shattered in 2002 by the news that Iran was making far greater progress toward acquiring the capability to make nuclear weapons than previously believed. Americans feared that this progress would undermine the containment of Iran and lead to widespread instability, if not outright warfare. In response, first the Bush 43 administration and then the Obama administration attempted to employ a carrot-and-stick approach to convince Tehran to halt its nuclear program. In both instances, the United States and its allies offered Iran (modest) economic and diplomatic inducements to halt the program while threatening to impose new, more stringent sanctions on Tehran if it refused to do so.

Both administrations saw this policy as having two goals. First, the policy was intended to buttress containment. In that sense it was a continuation of America's long-standing effort to prevent Iran from increasing its military power, in this case by acquiring nuclear weapons. However, both administrations also hoped that Iran would be willing to accept the American offer of a negotiated resolution. This was especially true of the Obama administration, which genuinely sought engagement as a path to real reconciliation. They hoped that Iranian pragmatists willing to accept restrictions on the Iranian nuclear program in return for concessions from the West would prevail over hardliners unwilling to give up the nuclear program. Implicit in this gambit was the possibility that a victory by the pragmatists might lead to their ascendance, which in turn might create broader openings for rapprochement. In this way, the carrot-and-stick approach was not only an effort to bolster containment, but also a bid to end it by shifting the composition and the policies of the Iranian regime.

The Persistence of Containment

Looking back on that history, a number of themes emerge. First, containment is not a "one-size-fits-all" policy. Against Iran, the United States has employed both passive and aggressive versions. This flexibility makes it useful to Washington, which has been able to dial up or scale back the pressure on Tehran based on many factors—strategic, political, and otherwise.

Second, although American administrations have typically played up whatever they have added onto the foundation of containment, American policy toward Iran has been quite consistent over the years because it has always been built around containment. The attempted openings to Iran under Reagan, Bush 41, Clinton, and Obama were important efforts to see if there was a way beyond containment, but none ever succeeded in finding it. Likewise, the efforts to pressure or punish Iran under Clinton, Bush 43, and Obama always had the goal of preventing Iran from causing mayhem beyond its borders—keeping it contained.

Looking forward, all of America's options toward Iran except one would require the continuation of containment in one form or another because containment will remain necessary as long as the Iranian regime remains our adversary. The conditional engagement on offer as part of the Obama administration's carrot-and-stick approach would have to start as just a tactic—a way of managing the confrontation, like détente during the Cold War—until Iran stopped pursuing objectives incompatible with our security. Over time, if Iran were to halt activities that threatened American interests, engagement might become a path out of containment to peaceful relations, but that would be a long way off and it would start from the basis of containment. Likewise, sanctions and other forms of pressure might someday cause Iran to make significant compromises on its nuclear program, but again, until Tehran is willing to engage in a real rapprochement with the United States, even that would not eliminate the need to contain an anti-American Iranian regime, although it would ease the costs of doing so. Regime change might someday produce a new Iranian government, one that did not threaten U.S. security or interests, which would then allow us to jettison containment in favor of normal relations. However, until that day, a regime change policy would have to rely on containment to play "defense" until its "offensive" elements brought about a transformation in Tehran. Ultimately, regime change is just a policy that would simply emphasize the "offensive" aspects of containment. Even air strikes, by Israel or the United States, would still require containment to prevent Iran from reconstituting and retaliating afterward. Indeed, air strikes are really a means of *bolstering* containment—not superseding it—by trying to deprive Iran of its nuclear potential.

Ultimately, the only approach that offers a true alternative to containment is an invasion of Iran. Yet that is the policy the United States is least likely to pursue, barring some unforeseen and unlikely Iranian provocation of such magnitude as to rearrange the priorities of the American people. That is what happened on 9/11 and it would doubtless require an Iranian misstep of equivalent proportions to move the American people to accept a commensurate military effort one more time.

The last pattern threading the history of America's containment of Iran is that the United States has almost never wanted to acknowledge that it was practicing containment of Iran. Several U.S. administrations went to great pains to describe their policy toward Iran as something other than containment because the strategy is typically seen as too weak by the right and too strong by the left. The right dislikes it because it often feels purely defensive and only indirectly exerts pressure to halt Iran's nuclear program, let alone bring about the end of the regime altogether. The left dislikes it because it requires frequent confrontation and the occasional threat of conflict with Iran. The only time that an American administration honestly described its policy as containment, under Clinton, critics from the left and the right shelled it. The Obama administration has denied that it is relying on containment, even a little bit. It may be a fiction, but unfortunately, in American politics today, it is a necessary fiction. Given how badly mischaracterized containment has become, acknowledging that American policy toward Iran involves any element of containment—let alone that the administration recognizes that containment will likely have to remain the basis for U.S. policy toward Iran in the future—would cause a political firestorm.

But that's not the only reason that no U.S. administration, and certainly not the Obama administration, is likely to acknowledge that containment is its policy. The other is that embracing containment might signal to Iran, to Israel, and to other American allies that the United States no longer cares about Iran's pursuit of a nuclear weapons capability. That this reading would be a severe misrepresentation of containment would be immaterial if that were what the Iranians and our allies believed. That could be disastrous for our efforts to convince Iran to make compromises on its nuclear program and to keep Israel from launching a military operation that could cause more problems than it solves.

In the future, it seems likely that the Obama administration and its successors will continue to pursue one or another version of containment but will insist on calling it "pressure" or "conditional engagement," or something else like that. It would be better if we could call our Iran policy by its right name, but that seems unlikely.

Containment and America's Regional Allies

Many Americans seem exasperated with our allies in the Middle East, but I can only find sympathy for them. None of them—not even Israel—has the ability to deal with Iran's nuclear threat alone. Short of employing nuclear weapons of its own against Iran, which is a nonstarter except if its national existence is threatened, Israel could damage but not eliminate Iran's nuclear program. The Turks, Iraqis, Saudis, and other Gulf states have even fewer options. Only the United States could eliminate that threat altogether, and if the United States opts to rely on deterrence and containment, our Middle Eastern allies have no choice but to support that strategy.

An American decision to adopt containment is a decision made by the United States for the West as a whole. If we choose containment, our allies must choose it, too. It seems only fair in that if we choose war it is we, the American people, who will be expected to absorb most of the costs and risks. The Iranians would doubtless attack Israel and the GCC states in the event of a U.S.-led war, but they would come after the United States, too, and we would have to pay in blood and treasure to do whatever was necessary to bring the fight to a successful resolution, including perhaps invading and occupying Iran.

However, it is also why we as Americans need to sympathize with the endless warnings coming from Israel in particular about the dangers of a nuclear Iran. The Gulf states have echoed these warnings, but they have preferred to do so in private. Thus it has been Israeli voices that have been the mainstays urging immediate action and predicting dire consequences if action is not forthcoming. There is no question that this can be tiresome. However, it is important to recognize that Israel's threats and warnings have been useful and even necessary.

Without unremitting Israeli (and GCC) threats, the world would have forgotten about the Iranian nuclear program long ago. There is good reason to believe that the Iranians would have nuclear weapons already. In 2002, and for several years thereafter, the world did not want to be bothered by Iran's nuclear program. The Europeans, led by the French, British, and Germans, did some important things, but even they were not considering the kind of sanctions that have since been enacted. The United States, preoccupied by al-Qa'ida, Afghanistan, and Iraq at that time, wanted even less to do with Iran. As for the rest of the world, no one outside the Middle East could rouse themselves to worry about Iranian nuclear weapons—especially after it was revealed that the warnings of Saddam's WMD had been wildly incorrect. On numerous occasions since, had the Israelis not threatened to go to war, it would have been virtually impossible for those few countries working to do something about the Iranian program to secure international support for sanctions. Diplomats from Scandinavian, Mediterranean, Latin American, and East Asian states have all admitted—often grudgingly—over the years that had it not been for the constant Israeli threats to go to war, their governments would never have supported this economic sanction or that diplomatic initiative. In that sense, though we may find these repeated warnings irksome, we should recognize that they were necessary to keep the great powers and the wider international community as focused on Iran as they have been since 2002.

THE REALITY AND HYPERBOLE OF EXISTENTIAL THREATS. Although the United States should remain sympathetic to the plight of its regional allies, we cannot allow their fears to overwhelm our interests and experience. Some Israelis in public and some Gulf Arabs in private can hit hysterical heights of panic when it comes to the "existential threat" they face from a nuclear Iran. They see this fear as requiring that anything and everything possible be done to prevent it.

Is a nuclear Iran an "existential" threat to Israel and the GCC states? Technically speaking, yes. Given the small size of the populations of Israel and the GCC states and their heavy concentration in just a few cities, once Iran has an arsenal of five to ten weapons that it can deliver against any of those countries, it will have a theoretical capability to wipe out anywhere from 20 to 90 percent of their populations. That sounds terrifying, and it should.

Yet the reality is far more mundane. Since the advent of the nuclear era, a great many countries have lived, and even thrived, under an existential threat. For forty years, the United States feared a Soviet nuclear attack that would have incinerated our nation. People built bomb shelters in their backyards. Schoolchildren were taught to "duck and cover" under their desks. Buildings in cities across the country boasted signs designating them as fallout shelters. Yet, the country survived. In fact, we did quite well. We still live with such an existential threat: Russia retains about 2,500 nuclear weapons that could end our existence.

The Western European nations shared this threat during the Cold War, perhaps even more than we did, because the thousands of tactical nuclear weapons deployed on either side of the Iron Curtain made a local nuclear exchange somewhat more likely than a homeland exchange between superpowers. Yet under that shadow Western Europe developed into one of the most prosperous and peaceful lands history has ever known. Japan, South Korea, Taiwan, Hong Kong, Singapore, and the other Asian "tigers" faced (and still face) existential threats from both Russia and China, but their economic performance and cultural development outstripped that of even Europe and the United States. The existential threat of nuclear obliteration did not frighten off investment, cause mass emigration, or distort domestic policies (although it monopolized foreign policies).

India has been locked in a vicious struggle with Pakistan since the violent birth of the two nations in 1947. Since then, they have fought four wars and experienced any number of crises. Although most Indians want to see an end to the conflict and have Pakistan leave them alone, much of Pakistan's elite remains obsessed with India—scheming to get back all of Kashmir, seeing Indian plots behind every problem in Pakistan, fearing Indian attack, and launching repeated attacks against India for various convoluted reasons. Pakistan is overrun with terrorists and violent extremists, its economy and social systems are in shambles, and it is waging guerrilla wars in Afghanistan and Kashmir. Many analysts fear that the state is on the brink of collapse.[11] Pakistan also possesses something on the order of one hundred nuclear weapons aimed at India and has continued to attack India and provoke nuclear crises with New Delhi even after it crossed the nuclear threshold sometime between 1985 and 1990.[12] If Pakistan launched those hundred nuclear weapons at India's fifty to one hundred largest urban areas, tens of millions of people would die, and India would effectively cease to exist as a functional nation. India has every reason to fear a Pakistani launch either stemming from escalation out of a crisis or as a result of the implosion of the tenuous Pakistani state, yet India has survived. And it too has thrived, posting phenomenal rates of economic growth and achieving something of a high-tech miracle.

North Korea first obtained nuclear weapons in the 1990s, although it did not test until 2006. Today it is believed to have as many as ten nuclear weapons. If it launched those weapons at Japan or South Korea's largest cities, they would kill tens of millions of people and would cripple both nations. The "Hermit Kingdom" is a land so bizarre, so belligerent, so impenetrable, and so unpredictable that it makes Iran look like Canada by comparison. North Korea hurls all manner of threats at South Korea. During the spring 2013 crisis, Pyongyang repeatedly and luridly threatened to launch nuclear weapons at South Korea and the United States.[13] Earlier that year, a North Korean diplomat publicly threatened the South with "final destruction," at the United Nations Conference on Disarmament, of all places.[14] In 2012, the official North Korean army Supreme Command issued a statement announcing to South Korea that it was about to "reduce all the rat-like groups [the government of South Korea] and the bases for provocations to ashes in three or four minutes, (or) in much shorter time, by unprecedented peculiar means and methods of our own style."[15] In 2011, the North Korean military released an official statement threatening to turn South Korea's Blue House—their equivalent of the White House—into a "sea of fire" if South Korean forces ever fired a single shot into North Korea's territory.[16]

Israelis and Gulf Arabs sometimes respond that they are much smaller and therefore more vulnerable to nuclear obliteration than India and even South Korea (at least in population). But when it comes to nuclear weapons and existential threats, size does not matter. Pakistan has the ability to do to India what a nuclear Iran would have the ability to do to Israel. North Korea has the ability to do to South Korea what a nuclear Iran would have the ability to do to Saudi Arabia. And both Pakistan and North Korea have fought far more and threatened far more than Iran has toward either Israel or the GCC states.

I am painfully and personally aware of the tragic history of the Jewish people and the many perils the state of Israel has had to endure. I have written extensively on the military history of the Middle East. I am a great proponent of the U.S.-Israel strategic relationship and have defended it, in print and out loud, and have been viciously attacked for doing so, both in public and behind my back.[17] I do not dismiss the fears of the Israeli people or the real security needs of their state. Yet that does not mean that Israel is somehow different from every other nation and that those experiences somehow should not apply to issues related to Israeli security—especially when they also entail enormous import for the security of the United States and other countries. Polls of Israeli public opinion show a huge majority of Israelis who do *not* share this exaggerated fear that Iran's acquisition of nuclear weapons means their own annihilation. With nuclear weapons, the risk is always there, but we have to separate the risk from the reality.

To counteract the hysteria with a bit of understatement, it is unquestionable that Iran's acquisition of a nuclear capability would be a major adjustment for Israel and the Gulf states. It would cause a number of significant problems and threats. And technically, it would constitute an existential threat to all of them, just as the Soviet Union constituted an existential threat to the United States, Europe, and East Asia. Just as Pakistan constitutes an existential threat to India. Just as North Korea constitutes an existential threat to South Korea and Japan—the only country on earth to experience the horrors of atomic attack. Every nation that lives under the existential threat of nuclear annihilation must work to ensure that that threat is never realized, and there are no guarantees in this world that they never will be. Containing a nuclear threat always entails some element of risk, and it must be pursued assiduously to reduce that risk to an infinitesimal, irreducible minimum. But we should not exaggerate that risk out of all proportion.

The word *existential* is frightening, but there is no reason it should take over our lives or the lives of any other nation. Many generations have lived, loved, and prospered under the distant specter of a nuclear threat. Few of them suffered for it, and most never noticed it at all. We should not—we cannot—ignore the dangers of a nuclear Iran or the challenges of containing it, but we must distinguish the real threats from the exaggerated.

11

Deterrence and
Extended Deterrence

If the United States is to contain Iran even after it develops a nuclear capability, possibly even a full-blown arsenal, it will have to lean on deterrence.[1] And not just deterrence, but the related concept of extended deterrence.[2] If deterrence means convincing Iran not to attack the United States, extended deterrence means convincing Iran not to attack our allies.

Both deterrence and extended deterrence are age-old concepts, common in strategic writings going back thousands of years. They frequently succeed, but they can also fail—and when they fail they fail in an ugly fashion, with wars and conquests. During the Cold War, with its specter of nuclear annihilation, these subjects were practiced as a high art. As early as 1946, the brilliant Yale strategist Bernard Brodie recognized the simple yet compelling logic of nuclear deterrence. That because the destructive power of nuclear weapons is so enormous, it is impossible for anyone who is not irrational to understand what would happen to him and his society if he were subject to a nuclear attack.[3] And because it only took an attack by a small number of nuclear weapons, perhaps no more than one, it was unlikely that either side in a nuclear exchange would not suffer unacceptable damage, and it was therefore unlikely that either side would take any action that might result in such a nuclear exchange. Thus, as Brodie would summarize later, what distinguished nuclear deterrence from conventional deterrence was that it was intolerable that deterrence should fail for either side in a nuclear balance, as it was unmistakable what would happen to them both.[4] This logic was the origin of what came to be called "mutual assured destruction" (MAD), the foundation of Cold War strategic thought.

Since the Second World War and the birth of the nuclear era, the logic of nuclear deterrence and extended deterrence has been put to the test a number of times. Remarkably, the two have a perfect track record so far. The reasons that nuclear deterrence has been so successful—rooted in the simple and compelling concepts first articulated by Brodie—are well understood. Many intelligent people have argued that they are foolproof, and that we should rely on them without any second thoughts.[5]

Still, there have been several dozen instances in which nuclear deterrence or extended deterrence has been challenged since 1945. The lessons are more complicated than a simple affirmation of the power of deterrence. None has resulted in a nuclear exchange, or even a single nuclear explosion. None has ended with a nuclear power being conquered, nor even one of their allies conquered despite an explicit threat of nuclear retaliation. But some have come too close for comfort. The Berlin crisis. The Cuban Missile Crisis. The 1973 Arab-Israeli War. The Sino-Soviet clashes of the 1960s. The Kargil War of 1999. We just don't know how close or how far any of these events was from triggering a nuclear war, but these and several others should make us cautious about assuming that nuclear deterrence cannot fail. As powerful as the logic of Brodie's absolute weapon has proven, humans have an extraordinary capacity to err.

Rationality and Deterrence

At a bare minimum, nuclear deterrence requires that your adversary is rational.

At least some Americans, Israelis, and others argue that Iran's leadership fails even this most basic criterion. Bret Stephens of the *Wall Street Journal*, whose work I admire even when I disagree with it, has written, "To suggest that there is some universal standard of 'pragmatism' or 'rationality' where Iran and the rest of the world can find common ground is a basic (if depressingly common) intellectual error."[6] Stephens's evidence of Iranian irrationality is their ideology, their willingness to pick fights with stronger powers, their willingness to endure tremendous suffering in pursuit of their goals, and their support for terrorism. Despite my respect for him, I find Stephens unpersuasive here.

Let's take each of Stephens's concerns in reverse order, starting with the notion that Iranian support for terrorism constitutes a basis to doubt their rationality. As Richard L. Kugler, a wise old former RAND analyst, put it,

> As a general rule, historical experience shows that even nation-states with extremist ideologies tend to value their interests and survival enough to act prudently when faced with credible guarantees that they will be frustrated in pursuing their goals and/or punished severely if they commit aggression or otherwise behave in menacing ways. . . . Although the future is uncertain, Iran's fundamentalist Islamic ideology is not prone to committing national suicide, and thus far its government has demonstrated a capacity to calculate carefully in ways suggesting that while its policies are self-interested, they are often guided by rational perceptions of costs and benefits. Making selective use of suicide bombers to target Israel entails limited risks and costs—only the suicide bombers lose their lives, not the people directing them. Exposing the entire country of Iran, including its leaders, to U.S. nuclear retaliation is a quite different, less attractive proposition.[7]

Indeed, Iranian behavior overwhelmingly demonstrates ruthlessness and pragmatism, not irrationality. Iran's support for terrorism, even suicide terrorism, does not make it irrational. In many ways, it speaks to a cunning rationality. As Kugler notes, suicide terrorism may be irrational for the suicide bomber, but for the state or group controlling him, it is an effective form of attack against a powerful adversary. As David Menashri, the dean of Israel's Iran experts, has argued, nothing could be more pragmatic, or more ruthless, than Iran's support for regional terrorists and other violent extremists because it allows them to strike at their enemies where they, the Iranians, are strong and their enemies weak, and to minimize the danger of escalation.[8]

Iran's willingness to endure severe costs is at times extreme, but hardly insane. Throughout history a great many countries have refused to bow down to the will of another and endured extreme hardships for their defiance. In many cases, we laud those examples as heroic. Perhaps a more rational nation than Churchill's Britain would have made peace with Hitler's Germany in 1940 rather than withstand the Blitz, the U-boat blockade, and other horrors, yet we are all grateful that they did, and we remember it as their "finest hour." We don't agree with the Iranian narratives that justify these extreme sacrifices—and not all Iranians do, either—but that does not make them irrational. Sending tens of thousands of young Iranians into battle with nothing but a Koran and a prayer, only to be slaughtered by Iraqi artillery and machine guns, may seem horrific and wasteful, but was it irrational? Was British leadership irrational to send tens of thousands of young men to die from German artillery and machine guns at the Somme and Passchendaele? How about the hundreds of thousands of Russians whom Stalin sent into battle without weapons during the Second World War? Such conduct may be obscene, but it is all too rational from the perspective of the leadership.

Similarly, smaller nations have stood up to larger nations time and again throughout history. Just as often, they were lionized by some and demonized by others for doing so, based on whose side one was on. The American people have a great fondness for the state of Israel, which defied a coalition of much larger Arab states for at least twenty-five years (and eventually won). In 1948, the odds were much worse for Israel against the Arabs than they have ever been for the Islamic Republic against the United States. Again, we object to Iran's characterization of the conflict and their perceptions of our motives (and even our actions), but that is hardly a novelty in history or a reason to dispute their rationality.

It is Iran's ideology that is hardest for Westerners, particularly Americans, to come to terms with. And while we may find Iran's hardline ideology bizarre, wrongheaded, even incongruent with the facts, that does not make it irrational any more than say, communism—about which the same things could and were said. Iranian leaders start with different assumptions and beliefs about the world from those of the West. This ideology is foreign to our way of thinking, but it is nonetheless consistent with their own reading of their history. The fact that we do not agree with their interpretation of history does not make them irrational either. Enmity toward the United States, Israel, and the conservative states of the Middle East is a core element of Tehran's assumptions and beliefs, but the Iranians aren't the only ones who make such assumptions or act in an aggressive manner based upon them. And many other states that share some of Iran's assumptions, including their sentiments about the United States—such as North Korea, Cuba, Qadhafi's Libya, even the late Chávez's Venezuela—have also demonstrated a clear respect for the logic of deterrence.

Stephens is right to point out that the Iranians are driven by different motives than we are, but that is not proof that Iran's leaders are irrational or immune to the logic of nuclear deterrence. And there is nothing in the Iranian behaviors he cites that is inconsistent with deterrence logic—albeit of an aggressive type. That aggression makes Iran's leaders harder to deter than others, but by no means impossible.

This last point is a critical one, because it gets at a larger truth about deterrence and extended deterrence: rationality is a necessary but not sufficient condition for a successful containment regime. What else is needed on the part of the targeted nation is not just rational decision-making, but prudent decision-making.

Are They Prudent?

One of the worst mistakes that Americans indulge in foreign policy-making is the cardinal sin of "mirror imaging": assuming that leaders of foreign countries share American values, assumptions, and assessments of history, and therefore will behave like Americans would in their position. It is the age-old fallacy of "putting yourself in the other guy's shoes." This practice has gotten our nation into trouble on too many occasions to count. As Keith Payne and Paul Bracken have both warned, the danger of mirror-imaging is even greater in what they have called "the Second Nuclear Age," the post–Cold War world in which the number of nuclear powers is growing, and these countries are not motivated to act in accordance with Cold War dynamics.[9] A country like North Korea is different from the United States or the Soviet Union (or France or Britain) in terms of its goals, how it makes policy, and the position it occupies in the geostrategic order. All of that could lead it to handle its nuclear arsenal in ways fundamentally different from how the United States and USSR did during the Cold War.

These caveats should warn us against the easy assumption that because nuclear deterrence worked for the United States and the Soviet Union, it will work with Iran. Nevertheless, what we have seen from the Iranian leadership during the era of the Islamic Republic is that their behavior is aggressive, anti-American, anti–status quo, anti-Semitic, duplicitous, and murderous, but it is not irrational, and overall, it is not imprudent. It is sometimes risk-tolerant, but never reckless. Moreover, merely being risk-tolerant does not necessarily make one a threat to the international order. George W. Bush was highly risk-tolerant after the 9/11 attacks. For its part, Iran frequently tries to figure out where American red lines lie and then to come right up to the edge of those lines. Sometimes, the Iranians miscalculate and cross the line—as they arguably did at Khobar

Towers in 1996. And while that example is important to keep in mind, it is equally important to note that Iran pulled back afterward when it realized that it had crossed a line and was in danger of facing an American conventional military response. Similarly, we have seen that Iran is willing to absorb considerable damage in the pursuit of its goals, but again it is not insensitive to damage: even Khomeini (who was far more reckless, risk-tolerant, and damage-acceptant than Khamene'i has shown himself to be) brought the Iran-Iraq War to a close in 1988 when it became clear that Iran's military was in ruins and its civilian population was under threat from Saddam's missiles. Khamene'i has forced the Iranian people to endure the pain of the sanctions, but unpleasant as they may be, they do not match the hardships of the Iran-Iraq War.

There are a number of other useful examples of Iranian rationality and prudent deterrence behavior. Throughout the 1987–88 Tanker War in the Persian Gulf, Iranian naval vessels had strict rules of engagement intended to allow them to harass American vessels without provoking a conflict—in line with Tehran's belief that the United States was an enemy and an ally of Iraq, but one too powerful to take on openly.[10] After the U.S. Navy's Operation Praying Mantis resulted in the sinking of half of Iran's major surface combatants, Tehran halted all of its naval attacks in the Gulf for nearly a month so as not to give Washington any excuse for further combat operations, and then resumed them in a more cautious manner.[11] During Operation Desert Storm, while the United States had more than 500,000 military personnel, nearly 2,000 combat aircraft, and six carrier battle groups deployed to the Gulf to obliterate Saddam's military, the Iranians made no effort even to harass U.S. forces, including American warplanes that occasionally violated Iranian airspace. Tehran only issued a perfunctory protest when a U.S. fighter-bomber attacked what turned out to be an Iranian patrol boat in the northern Gulf.[12] Even after segments of Iraq's Shi'a population revolted against Saddam in the wake of the Persian Gulf War, Iran did not send its own personnel in to assist the revolt, for fear of crossing the United States.[13] Similarly, in 2003, during the U.S. buildup and invasion of Iraq, the Iranians made no move that might have triggered an American reprisal. Afterward, when they feared that the United States would turn on them next, Tehran suspended its nuclear program to avoid giving Washington cause.[14] All of this speaks to not just rational, but prudent, behavior on Tehran's part.

EXCEPTIONS. There are at least two important outliers to this pattern of behavior. As I described earlier, in March 2007, during the occupation of Iraq, Iranian Revolutionary Guards seized fifteen British sailors and marines from Iraqi waters in the Shatt al-Arab. This action went well beyond the widespread Iranian clandestine support for Iraqi terrorists, insurgents, and militias looking to kill Americans. It was an overt act of international piracy, if not terrorism or war. Because the British were part of the U.S.-led coalition, the United States could have retaliated against Iran on behalf of the larger coalition. There is ample evidence in this case that the problem was reckless freelancing on the part of a mid-ranking Iranian naval commander, not the deliberate intention of the Iranian regime itself.[15] Consequently, this incident cannot count against Tehran as an imprudent act. However, it raises the specter that the Iranian regime is not in full control of its own military—a different kind of problem related to nuclear weapons.

Then there is the Arbabsiar terrorist case, which I have mentioned several times already. In this incident, Iran plotted to kill the Saudi ambassador to the United States by blowing up a popular Georgetown restaurant. Had that attack come off as planned (and apparently ordered) it might have moved the United States to respond with force. There are several possible explanations for what happened—none of them good for the United States, but all of them problematic in different ways. The first is that the Iranians were reckless and cavalier. That is certainly possible.

A second possibility is that the Iranians calculated America's red line correctly. Given President Obama's constant rhetoric about getting America out of wars in the Middle East, his precipitous withdrawal of U.S. troops from Iraq, his impending drawdown in Afghanistan, and his reluctance to commit U.S. forces elsewhere in the Middle East, the Iranians may have concluded that, even in the event of a terrorist attack on American soil, the Obama administration would not respond with force and would instead retaliate in some other way—more sanctions or another cyberattack. It is worth pointing out that even after the plot was revealed, the Obama administration made no move to retaliate against Iran for it, certainly not one of which the public is aware. In contrast, President Clinton launched cruise missiles against the headquarters of Iraq's intelligence service for Saddam's stillborn effort to assassinate President George H. W. Bush and the emir of Kuwait in 1993. Likewise, it is hard to imagine that President George W. Bush would have refrained from retaliatory military action if the Arbabsiar plot had been uncovered on his watch. Hence, this incident may say less about Iran's willingness to risk crossing American red lines and more about where the Iranians believe those red lines lie under Obama—and that they may be right in their assessment.

The third possibility is that contrary to our understanding of how the Iranian regime plans and approves terrorist attacks, this operation was not approved by Khamene'i and was effectively a "rogue" operation by the Revolutionary Guards. If that is what happened, then as with the seizure of the British sailors and marines in 2007, it sets off alarms about whether there might be similar freelancing if Iran acquires nuclear weapons. Would more aggressive and less prudent Revolutionary Guard figures have access to Iran's nuclear weapons? Might they set one off on their own? Or give one to terrorists? These are important questions. Ultimately, as with so many things Iranian, we just don't know the answers.

Nevertheless, the evidence we have indicates that such scenarios are unlikely. First, Iran has supported terrorist groups of all stripes since 1979 and it has possessed chemical and biological warfare agents since about 1989 (and radioactive material for at least the last decade), and we have never seen these two aspects of Iranian security policy combined—on purpose or by rogue freelancers. Whether that indicates that no Revolutionary Guard ever considered doing so, or that the security measures Iran has in place to guard its WMD are so strong that they have prevented it, we don't know. But empirically, the system has worked. It indicates that Iran has a greater degree of prudence and caution where WMD is concerned, and that should be reassuring.

In other countries with similar problems, such as Pakistan—which has both nuclear weapons and a powerful intelligence service that seems to have considerable ability to freelance—there has never been a problem related to the nukes. The government makes extraordinary efforts to ensure that its nuclear weapons will only be used when the regime wants to do so deliberately. Senior American officials and intelligence officers under successive administrations have testified that they have great confidence in Pakistan's security for its nuclear weapons.[16] This assurance should not be surprising since it has been true of every state that has acquired nuclear weapons, with the sole exception of the United States, which treated its nuclear arsenal in ways so cavalier that any other country would have been horrified.[17]

It is not surprising that these views regarding Iran's ultimate rationality and relative prudence are shared by others who favor containment and deterrence of Iran, including many who believe that it would be much easier to contain and deter a nuclear Iran than I do.[18] What is more noteworthy is that this view appears to be the dominant position of my colleagues among the Iran experts.[19] As Karim Sadjadpour put it with his usual flair, "Iran is a rational actor in the sense that staying in power is paramount. The regime is homicidal but it is not suicidal."[20]

It is also a view held by many Israelis, and people close to the Israelis.[21] In April 2012, Israel's armed forces chief of staff, Lieutenant General Benny Gantz, told the Israeli newspaper *Haaretz*, "I think the Iranian leadership is composed of very rational people."[22] His predecessor, Lieutenant General Gabi Ashkenazi, told the Israeli Knesset, "The Iranian regime is radical, but it's not irrational."[23] In the words of Israeli strategic analyst Yair Evron, "In view of Israel's widely assumed large nuclear arsenal and numerous delivery vehicles, including various protected platforms that form a second strike capability, it appears highly improbable that even a fanatic leadership would choose [to attack Israel]. The dangers are enormous, not only to Iran as a country but first and foremost to the regime itself. No regime, even if endowed with the most extreme ideology, chooses to commit suicide."[24] And most striking of all is that it is a view held by many of the most savvy advocates of air strikes as well.[25] For example, Matthew Kroenig states categorically, "To be sure, a nuclear-armed Iran would not intentionally launch a suicidal nuclear war."[26]

Keeping Things in Perspective

Is there a chance that Iran's leadership would prove irrational or wildly reckless once it acquired nuclear weapons? Sure. There is always a chance, especially given the Iranian regime's various pathologies—its opacity, its Byzantine mechanics. The evidence we have, however, suggests that it is extremely unlikely. We have a huge amount of evidence, both general and specific, that indicates that the Iranian leadership is rational and not reckless, despite the fact that it is aggressive, murderous, paranoid, and operates according to a set of assumptions and goals that few outside of Tehran share. In contrast, we have almost no evidence to indicate the contrary, and those actions that appear at first blush to contradict it are probably exceptions proving the rule rather than undermining it.

One of the most important lessons of the Cold War was that incessantly worrying about low-probability, high-impact cases was a mistake.[27] The United States and Soviet Union wasted obscene amounts of money, energy, manpower, and brainpower preparing for the proverbial "bolt from the blue," which subsequent histories showed neither side's leadership ever seriously contemplated. Looking back on that era, Paul Bracken concluded, "At no time in the cold war did either side seriously consider a calculated nuclear strike on the other."[28] Moreover, by obsessing about it, we may have created crises unnecessarily and made other situations far more dangerous than they needed to be. In 1983, the Soviets misread a U.S. military exercise called ABLE ARCHER 83 as preparations for a surprise attack on the USSR.[29] The Russians panicked, causing a crisis in

Moscow that, in the words of then-KGB officer Oleg Gordievsky, brought the world to the brink of nuclear annihilation: "The KGB concluded that American forces had been placed on alert—and might even have begun the countdown to war. . . . [The world] had, without realizing it, come frighteningly close [to a nuclear exchange]—certainly closer than at any time since the Cuban missile crisis of 1962."[30]

In this sense, I am arguing against what author Ron Suskind called the "1 percent doctrine" of the Bush 43 administration.[31] This idea, most associated with Vice President Dick Cheney, posits that after the 9/11 attacks, the United States had to protect itself by doing whatever was necessary to eliminate threats with even a "1 percent" likelihood. Both Suskind and Cheney himself suggested that this calculus was a critical motivation in the administration's decision to invade Iraq and oust Saddam Husayn. In his memoirs, Cheney recalls reading an op-ed by former Bush 41 national security advisor Brent Scowcroft that opposed an invasion of Iraq, "As I read Brent's piece, I found myself thinking that it reflected a pre-9/11 mind-set, the worldview of a time before we had seen the devastation that terrorists armed with hijacked airplanes could cause. We had to do everything possible to be sure that they never got their hands on weapons that could kill millions."[32] Of course, Saddam never gave weapons of mass destruction—not chemical, biological, or radiological weapons—to terrorists, nor do we have any indication in the material recovered since the fall of Baghdad that he ever had any intention of doing so.

All of this history should serve as both a reassurance and a warning. To start, the likelihood that Iran would use nuclear weapons unprovoked or give them to terrorists is extremely low. Probably a lot less than a 1 percent probability, even if the likelihood is not zero. It would be a terrible mistake to make policy based on such a remote possibility. Doing so would lead us to make major exertions, bear huge costs, and run significant risks to blot out a minor risk, while creating a host of new but avoidable problems. Such an excessive focus on what is the least likely risk will distract us from dealing with a number of other, much more likely, and still dangerous problems that Iran's acquisition of nuclear weapons would create. I ultimately believe that containment, with its inherent reliance on deterrence, is a better course for the United States to pursue than war, but it is hardly a perfect policy. Nevertheless, we should not obscure its real problems by becoming obsessed with nightmare scenarios unlikely ever to occur.

12

The Problems of Containment

The problems inherent in containment, and particularly containment of a nuclear Iran, fall into six broad categories, representing critical factors that will change once Iran crosses the nuclear threshold—factors that the United States would have to deal with to make containment work. These are:

- **Increased Iranian support for terrorists, insurgents, militias, and other groups attempting to subvert U.S. allies in the region.** The real threat from a nuclear Iran is not that it would launch nuclear weapons or give them to terrorists, but that it would see its nuclear shield as allowing it to pursue its traditional, anti–status quo foreign policy in an even more aggressive fashion.
- **Crisis management.** Because Iran is unlikely to become restrained in its goals or behavior after it crosses the nuclear threshold, there will be crises—with Israel, with Saudi Arabia and other regional states, and quite possibly with the United States. Crises between nuclear powers

are far more dangerous and complex. The greatest risk of Iran's acquisition of a nuclear weapons capability is the potential for a crisis to get out of hand.

- **Perceptions of American reliability, especially as it pertains to the threats of nuclear blackmail and co-optation.** Given how much the United States has invested in preventing Iran from acquiring a nuclear weapons capability, if Tehran does so, it will affect many people's thinking about America's commitment to the region and Iran's new power. Some states in the region may fear that Iran will act against them and the United States will not prevent it. Some may even try to preempt this scenario by accommodating Iranian demands in ways that they otherwise would not.

- **Proliferation.** Other countries will become even more determined to resist Iranian power and pressure, and some may choose to acquire nuclear arsenals of their own to do so.

- **The cost of containment.** If the United States is to address the other four issues listed above, it will require time, energy, and other resources to do so.

- **The long term.** The possession of nuclear weapons isn't necessarily forever, but it can last a long time. If Iran crosses the nuclear threshold, containment needs to work not just for the next three or five years, but until there is real regime change in Tehran. Succession may bring to power worse leaders than Khamene'i and the regime might end in chaos, running the risk that Iran's nuclear capabilities could fall into the wrong hands.

All of these represent real issues, albeit of varying magnitude, that a containment regime would have to address. As with air strikes and every other policy option, the question will remain whether the costs and risks of containment are more bearable than those of the other options.

The Prospects for Extended Deterrence

As difficult as containing a nuclear Iran will be, there are also reasons for optimism. Containing a nuclear Iran will be several orders of magnitude less challenging than containing the former Soviet Union, something the United States accomplished for forty-five years. Iran has only a fraction of the size, populace, and resources of the USSR. It is unlikely that its nuclear forces would ever compare to the tens of thousands of sophisticated nuclear weapons mounted on Russian land- and submarine-based ballistic and cruise missiles, bombers, artillery shells, torpedoes, and rockets. Iran's scientific base is nothing to scoff at, but it cannot rival the innovative capacity of the former Soviet Union's massive technological complex.

One of the most important ways that a nuclear Iran would differ from the Soviet threat is in the realm of conventional military power. Throughout the Cold War, Soviet ground forces and Frontal Aviation represented the most powerful conventional force on the Eurasian landmass. This conventional might gave Moscow enormous capacity to project power beyond the Iron Curtain. For most of the post–World War II era, NATO worried that its conventional forces would be unable to hold back a Soviet assault for more than a week or two before the Red Army overran most of Western Europe or NATO was forced to resort to nuclear weapons to stop it.

This threat gave rise to one of the worst dilemmas of the Cold War, the core problem of American extended deterrence in Europe. Since NATO's conventional air-ground strength was likely to prove insufficient to defend Western Europe against a Soviet invasion, the United States had to be willing to employ nuclear weapons to halt it, but once nuclear weapons were introduced into an all-out war between NATO and the Warsaw Pact, it would have been very difficult to control escalation. During the Cold War, this dilemma was often framed as whether the U.S. government would be willing to "trade Boston for Bonn." Was the U.S. government willing to risk the obliteration of American cities to prevent the conquest of West European cities? This question posed a huge problem because it was irrational for any American president to do so. As a result, the United States and NATO resorted to all kinds of convoluted and even dangerous steps to try to convince the Soviets either that we would do so even though it was irrational, or that we would not be able to avoid doing so. President Nixon acted in ways that he hoped would make the Soviets believe he was an unpredictable "madman" who might do something just that irrational. Other presidents deployed tactical nuclear weapons to various NATO countries under weak security conditions so that the Russians would have to calculate that in the event of a war, the countries themselves would be able to get access to the weapons and fire them in their own defense—a rational decision for *them* to make.

Today, some who favor air strikes against Iran's nuclear program have argued the United States would face the same problem with a nuclear Iran—and that it would be worse this time around. They argue that if it was hard to convince the Soviets that the United States would be willing to risk the destruction of American cities to save the cities of Europe, it would be almost impossible to convince the Iranians that the United States would risk American cities to defend those of the Arab oil emirates for whom Americans feel little love and often outright animosity.[1]

Although this would seem to be a compelling problem at first glance, in actuality it is not an issue at all. The problem during the Cold War was the inability of NATO conventional forces to prevent the Red Army from conquering Western Europe. No one believed that the Russians intended to just nuke Bonn. We feared that they wanted to conquer it and had the ability to do so. The extended deterrence dilemma had nothing to do with Soviet nuclear strikes against European cities. It was about whether the United States would countenance escalation to nuclear strikes to prevent conventional conquest.

At present and as far out into the future as we can discern, this problem does not apply to Iran. Iran's conventional forces are not hapless, but they cannot be compared to those of the Cold War USSR, let alone the present-day U.S. Armed Forces. Iran has an extremely limited ability to project power beyond its borders. If pitted against its regional rivals,

Iran could probably mount some punishing ground incursions into Iraq, it might be able to seize and hold chunks of Iraqi or Afghan territory, it could probably cut traffic through the Strait of Hormuz for some period of time, and it would have some ability to mount small amphibious incursions across the Persian Gulf—possibly even seizing Bahrain if it had the advantage of strategic surprise. But that represents the upper limit of Iran's power projection capabilities, and even that is an artificial assessment since it leaves out American military forces. When American military forces are added to the equation—and it need only be those forces that the United States maintains in the region on a routine basis—Iran's ability to threaten its neighbors, particularly the Persian Gulf states, evaporates.

American air and naval power *already in the Gulf* so dwarfs Iran's capabilities that it is not credible to argue that Iran could threaten any of the cities of the GCC countries with conventional conquest. There is zero reason to believe that the United States would have to face the dilemma of whether to trade Dallas for Doha or Dubayy. Iran has no capacity to threaten to conquer Doha or Dubayy—or Manama or Dhahran—as long as the U.S. Navy and Air Force remain in the Gulf at or near present force levels. The situation is the reverse of that which created the dilemma of extended deterrence during the Cold War. The dilemma would be Tehran's to ask whether it would be willing to risk losing Esfahan to prevent the United States or Israel from clearing Hizballah out of its strongholds in the Bekaa Valley in Lebanon, should either ever decide to do so.

Dealing with Iranian Subversion and Unconventional Warfare

If conventional attack is not a problem with a nuclear Iran, there are other issues. The most obvious among them is the threat that so many fear: the threat that a nuclear Iran will believe that no other power—including the United States—would dare retaliate against it, and so it would increase its support to terrorists, insurgents, militias, would-be revolutionaries, and other subversive elements throughout the Middle East and South and Central Asia. This is the real threat both now and in the future, if Tehran acquires a nuclear arsenal. Indeed, in the latter case, it could be a much greater threat.[2] In a sobering essay on the problems of containment, Eric Edelman, Andrew Krepinevich, and Evan Braden Montgomery warned, "The Iranian actions that are easiest to deter, namely, a deliberate conventional or nuclear attack, are the least likely forms of Iranian aggression, whereas Iran's most likely form of aggression, in particular support for terrorism and subversion, are the most difficult to deter."[3]

It would not be the first time that nuclear powers have supported subversive efforts. Throughout the Cold War, the United States tried a variety of methods to convince the people of Eastern Europe to rise up against their Soviet masters. Washington also supported a range of insurgencies against the Soviets and their allies, from the Nicaraguan Contras to the Afghan mujahideen. Likewise, the Soviets supported communist movements across the Western and Third Worlds, funneled money to peace activists and antinuclear groups, and aided insurgents and terrorists from the Viet Cong to the Palestine Liberation Organization. Yet no one ever threatened nuclear war over any of these efforts because it was patently absurd to imagine risking nuclear devastation over covert campaigns that did not threaten the grip of either government and mostly harmed their allies and proxies.

Then there is India and Pakistan. Unlike either the Soviets or the Americans, the Pakistanis support terrorists and insurgents who have caused significant damage to the Indian people and the Indian government and are trying to wrest disputed territory away from Indian control. The result has been dangerous crises in 1999, 2001–2002, and 2008, where the threat of escalation to nuclear war was very much on the table and in the air.[4] The difference, of course, was that Pakistan's subversive terrorist activities were seen as posing a threat to India itself, whereas during the Cold War, neither the USSR nor the United States was able to do so—until arguably, the Soviet collapse, although in that case, American involvement was tenuous and indirect.

The Cold War does not always furnish perfect lessons for understanding an Iran with nuclear weapons. Actions that did not threaten to escalate when inflicted by Soviets and Americans on one another may do just that when it is Iran and Israel or Iran and Saudi Arabia. Taken together, these examples suggest that if Saudi Arabia were to acquire nuclear weapons to match an Iranian arsenal, the Saudis might act with greater restraint if Iran attempted to destabilize Bahrain by stirring up its Shi'a population than it would if Iran tried to stir up the Shi'a of the Kingdom's own Eastern Province. Riyadh might see the latter as a threat to the stability or territorial integrity of Saudi Arabia, no less dangerous than an Iranian invasion of Dhahran, and the Saudis might react as if it were.

Even if Iranian efforts to subvert and attack American allies in the region do not produce nuclear crises, these efforts alone would still represent a threat to American interests and the interests of our allies, although the extent of the threat would vary. The Middle East is already dangerous and unstable, and Iran already adds too much to these problems even if it is rarely the main culprit. If Tehran were emboldened to undermine Middle Eastern governments, aid violent extremist groups, and otherwise stoke the endemic mayhem of the region, it would only make a bad situation worse. Some regional governments might be pushed to the breaking point or beyond, provoking new revolutions, civil wars, failed states, and insurgencies. Looking around at the situation of Syria, Libya, Egypt, Iraq, Yemen, Bahrain, and others, we should not want their circumstances to get any worse, nor should we want to see Jordan, Morocco, let alone Saudi Arabia or the UAE, experience similar levels of conflict and instability. Consequently, while an Iranian nuclear capability would not necessarily enhance Iran's ability to subvert regional governments and aid violent extremists directly, a nuclear Iran may increase its support for these kinds of activities. And such increased support could produce nuclear crises with the United States or other nuclear rivals.

Unfortunately, there is no magic solution to the problem of Iranian efforts to destabilize U.S. allies, but neither has the problem proven insurmountable. The United States and its allies have been trying to deal with it since 1979, with mixed but mostly positive results. Iran has not been able to overthrow any of the other governments of the region despite its efforts to do so, and Iran cannot be held solely responsible for any of the terrorist groups, insurgencies, civil wars, or even popular unrest that Tehran supports. All stem principally from the deep economic, political, and social problems of the states of the region, and the Iranians have merely tried to exacerbate these problems as best they could. But Iran has found ways to enflame problems across the region, and at times, these problems have boiled over into more serious crises for the United States and its allies. Israel's wars against Hizballah and Hamas, various crises in Bahrain, the Iraqi civil war, and even Yemen's most recent internal conflict have all been aggravated by Iranian support.

PLAYING DEFENSE. Many of Iran's gains in recent years have had less to do with their skill than with our mistakes. The best way to keep the Iranians from gaining a foothold in other countries of the region and stoking unrest is to eliminate the causes of the unrest in the first place. The more unhappy the populace, the more willing they are to listen to Iran and its agents in the region. The happier they are, the more likely they will be to tell Iran and its allies to get lost.

A critical element of containing Iran in the future will be addressing the messes in the region as best we can. It is another reason for the United States to help those Arab states that have already undergone major political upheavals—Egypt, Tunisia, Yemen, Libya, and Iraq—to build viable governments able to secure their territory, get their economies moving, and provide basic services for their entire populations. Likewise, it will mean pressing those Arab states that have not undergone a major transition to embrace and actually implement meaningful long-term reforms to address the popular demands for political, economic, and social change that have swept the Arab world since 2011. It will also mean doing what we can to prevent new failed states, new civil wars, and new insurgencies. The more chaotic these places are, the more Iran will be able to exploit that chaos.[5]

The unfortunate paradox is that the fear of Iranian subversion growing all across the Arab world is liable to make the remaining Arab dictators and monarchs *less* willing to embark on new reforms, for fear that doing so will cause the kind of dislocation and unrest that Iran typically tries to exploit. This ambivalence will be yet another challenge for the United States and its allies, and just as in the 1990s, when we tried to help Israel, Jordan, Syria, and the Palestinians take risks for peace, so in the future must we try to help the Arab regimes take risks for reform.[6]

Of course, this is easier said than done.[7] The needs of the emerging Arab democracies are huge and the determination of the Arab monarchies to resist further change is deep. Some, like the kings of Morocco and Jordan, have made modest efforts, if only because they feared that to do otherwise would push them off the same cliff from which Mubarak, Ben Ali, and Saleh all tumbled. Others, such as King Abdallah of Saudi Arabia, recognized the potential for revolution long before, and so, in the Saudi case, the king began his own gradual shift in favor of reform in a way that has so far immunized the Kingdom from the unrest elsewhere sweeping the region. Yet it is just not clear that even Abdallah's reforms are moving quickly enough. The Saudis are hard-pressed to move any faster and they are facing an imminent transition in leadership that could derail Abdallah's gradual reforms.

The obvious alternative to a process of reform is a greater emphasis on counterinsurgency techniques to augment the already formidable counterterrorism capabilities of many of the regional security services. Since 9/11, both the United States and the governments of the region have invested a tremendous amount in counterterrorism, principally to combat the threat of al-Qa'ida and like-minded terrorist groups. There is still more that could be done. The United States could organize a more coordinated effort to neutralize Iranian-backed terrorist groups. In the past, this was difficult for the Arab states because many of the most important groups that Iran supported were also the principal opponents of Israel. One of the great benefits of the Arab Spring and the civil war in Syria, however, has been that most of these groups have been forced to choose sides: the Sunni fundamentalists of Hamas have distanced themselves from Iran, whereas Shi'i Hizballah has not and has lost considerable support among the majority Sunni Arab population as a result. An effort to coordinate opposition against Iranian-backed terrorist groups would not have to make Hamas a principal target (and if the Arab states could be persuaded to join, it would put additional pressure on Hamas to cut its ties to Tehran altogether). The Sunni Arab states would probably have little compunction about targeting Hizballah and other Shi'i groups much closer to Iran, like Asaib ahl al-Haq and Kataib Hizballah in Iraq.

The Iranians also like to support militias and insurgencies, which—because they are bigger and can often control territory—tend to be far more dangerous to regional governments than terrorist groups. Although counterterrorism and counterinsurgency operations have a great deal in common, they also have important differences, ones that regional militaries often flub when they confront an insurgency or militia because they tend to fall back on inappropriate counterterrorism practices. In contrast, after a decade of honing (or relearning) its low-intensity conflict (LIC) skills in Iraq and Afghanistan, the United States Armed Forces now have unparalleled experience in these operations, which they could pass on to other Arab states to buck up their ability to combat an Iranian-backed insurgency should they face one.

Now, there is a catch. The regional governments take the training, techniques, and weaponry we provide them to deal with terrorists, insurgents, and militias but they often use them against their own legitimate, internal opposition. This problem is significant in its own right, but equally so in the context of trying to strengthen the ability of regional governments to resist Iranian subversion, because employing repression against legitimate internal opposition groups will simply make the anger and frustration of the populace worse, creating just the kinds of political and social divisions upon which Iran preys. Consequently, the U.S. government should only embark on such a program to bolster region-wide LIC capabilities and coordinate inter-state counterinsurgency campaigns if these programs are tied to tangible progress on political, economic, and social reforms in the participating states—a practice with which we have had some important successes in Latin America.

GOING ON THE OFFENSIVE. In the parlance of deterrence theory developed during the Cold War, the steps above constitute what is called "deterrence by denial." This idea means convincing an adversary not to take an action because it is bound to fail to achieve its goal. Another approach is "deterrence by punishment," in which an adversary is convinced to desist by inflicting pain on it in a variety of other ways. In the case of the Iranians, we need to play defense to prevent them from making gains where they are strongest—in subverting regional governments and destabilizing the region. Given how low-cost it is for the Iranians to support terrorist and insurgent groups, we should not expect that the defensive measures treated above are going to be enough to convince them to stop or even diminish their efforts.

This is where the flexibility of a containment strategy is an asset. The United States can and should also choose from a wide variety of methods to impose costs or inflict pain on Iran depending on the circumstances. There are tactics that the United States and its allies could employ on a sustained basis to make Iran feel pain for its overall support of various subversive, terrorist, insurgent, and other violent groups. The most obvious example of this is economic sanctions. Although the current panoply of sanctions might need to be revised to make them sustainable over the long term, it would be helpful if not crucial to carry them over from the carrot-and-stick strategy to a longer-term containment regime, including to ensure that Iran continues to pay a price for supporting terrorists, insurgents, and other violent extremists.

There are also discrete actions that the United States could take in response to specific Iranian moves. Conditional arms sales to American allies in the region is a good example. One question we will have to try to answer in the context of containment is how we could help deter various Iranian-backed terrorists from attacking Israel more aggressively after Iran has acquired a nuclear capability and feels safe from retaliation. One way to do so could be to make clear to Tehran that the United States would be willing to sell additional weapons to Israel and the GCC states that would be discomfiting for Iran. Contrary to popular opinion, there are weapons systems that the United States has never sold Israel, and does not plan to in the future—such as the F-22 Raptor stealth air superiority fighter. The Israelis also want more bunker-buster bombs, aerial refueling tankers, and intelligence collection platforms to enable offensive operations against Iran. Similarly, the United States could sell the GCC states and other regional allies additional arms that Iran would find threatening.

In addition, Washington could launch specific covert actions, including both cyber operations and support to Iranian opposition groups, in response to specific Iranian moves. Especially to the extent that the United States is able to maintain its edge over Iran in cyberwarfare, covert action responses could prove a useful tool with which to combat the unconventional threat from a nuclear Iran. So far, at least as the press reports it, the United States appears to be employing cyberattacks to hinder Iran's nuclear program and convince Tehran to agree to compromise on that program. In future circumstances where a deal is no longer in the offing—and Iran may even possess a nuclear arsenal—these same cyber weapons can be employed to different ends. Although, under a policy of containment, the United States ought to be considering means of effecting regime change in Tehran at all times, Washington's willingness to act on those impulses may vary over time based on both Iranian behavior and the likelihood of success. On the former point, the regime is highly sensitive to any external (particularly American) support to its many dissidents. Whenever Iran began to stoke regional instability or mounted a particularly dangerous effort to subvert an American ally, the United States could respond with its own clandestine efforts: cyber blows and increased support to Iranian opposition groups, thus striking at Tehran's worst fears.

Crisis Management

The most dangerous problem that the United States and the world would face in attempting to contain a nuclear Iran is crisis management.[8] In their superb study of the challenges of containing a nuclear Iran, Tom Donnelly, Danielle Pletka, and Maseh Zarif make the point that Iran has pursued a nuclear weapons capability in the face of international opposition that is both broad and deep, indicating a willingness on Tehran's part to run risks to advance its more expansive goals, even if the regime's leaders are not irrational, millenarian, or suicidal.[9] Similarly, Iran's likely willingness to increase its support to terrorists, insurgents, militias, and other violent extremists will undoubtedly provoke the countries they are targeted against. Thus, if a nuclear Iran remains both aggressive and risk-tolerant, as seems most likely, crises are sure to follow. What's more, there is a high probability that some (perhaps most) of these crises will involve other nuclear states, or states allied with other nuclear powers, like the United States.

After the Cuban Missile Crisis, President Kennedy famously estimated that the chances of that crisis escalating to a nuclear war were somewhere between one in three and even odds. His national security advisor, McGeorge Bundy, felt that they were more remote—more like 1 in 100.[10] We will never know what the true odds were, but post–Cold War revelations that the Soviets had deployed tactical nuclear weapons to Cuba and that the Politburo considered delegating launch authority to the local military commander in the event of an American attack—which most of the American National Security Council favored—suggest that Kennedy may have been somewhat closer to the mark than Bundy.[11]

The Cuban Missile Crisis may be the closest that the world has ever come to a nuclear exchange, but it is not the only moment when the danger lurked: the Berlin crisis of 1961, the Sino-Soviet clashes of 1969, the October War of 1973, the Kargil War of 1999 all qualify as moments when the world came uncomfortably close to nuclear war. If Iran acquires a nuclear capability, there will almost certainly be crises with Iran and these will be the moments of great anxiety.

The example of the October War of 1973 is also important because it suggests that although Iran's behavior would be an important determinant of the frequency and severity of crises after Tehran crosses the nuclear threshold, it will not be the only variable in play. On October 6, 1973, Egypt and Syria launched a surprise attack on Israel that stunned the Israelis. Nevertheless, the Israel Defense Forces (IDF) regained its balance and counterattacked, quickly routing both Arab armies. With their armed forces on the brink of disaster, the Arabs called on the USSR to secure a UN cease-fire that would halt the Israeli counteroffensives before they lost even more. When Israel and its American ally ignored Moscow's demands, the Soviets responded by alerting a half dozen airborne divisions for immediate deployment to the Middle East. The White House was itself surprised by this move and by the implication that the Russians were going to intervene in the conflict. In response, President Nixon alerted U.S. nuclear forces to warn the Russians against sending in their troops. Neither the United States nor the USSR had sought the 1973 nuclear crisis, nor was it caused by the designs of either. At worst, both had done nothing to restrain the offensive actions of their allies. Both superpowers were passive, and their intentions effectively benign, at least toward each other, yet they found themselves enmeshed in a frightening nuclear crisis.

The events of October 1973 caution that in a world where Iran has nuclear weapons, crises can occur even if neither side is looking for a fight. The history warns that even if Tehran becomes more defensive after acquiring nuclear weapons, even if it were to give up its hegemonic aspirations, forswear Khomeini's ideology, disband the Quds force, and ban its "death to America" rhetoric, it is still possible that it would end up in nuclear crises from miscalculation or uncontrollable events simply because of the dynamics of a nuclear balance.

And crises with a nuclear Iran are likely to be particularly problematic. Of greatest importance, the experience of various earlier crises demonstrate that three factors are critical to ensuring a nuclear crisis does not escalate to a nuclear war. First is the ability of the two sides to communicate. Second is that each side possesses a good understanding of the other's assumptions, goals, fears, decision-making procedures, and worldview. Third is the ability of both sides to "read" each other's signals so that when one side makes a gesture toward the other, the recipient interprets it as the sender intended.

The problem is that throughout the history of relations between the United States and the Islamic Republic, none of these factors has ever been present and it will be hard to engineer them in the future. Washington and Tehran have no ability to communicate directly. We have employed a variety of interlocutors over the years but no channel has proven reliable. Despite American offers to take steps that could improve communications—such as opening an interests section in Tehran and establishing rules for American and Iranian ships to interact in the Persian Gulf—the Iranians have refused to participate in any direct communications channels. As for the second problem, the frequency with which Iran and America have misread each other is staggering, reflecting the opacity of the Iranian system, both sides' constant mirror-imaging of the other, and our mutual tendency to ascribe the worst motives to each other. Similarly, whenever one side has attempted to signal to the other, the "miss" rate on such messages has not necessarily been high because the two sides tend to be blunt with each other to minimize misunderstanding. Yet misinterpretations still occur with a disconcerting frequency. There is no question, for instance, that Washington misread the import of the 1995 Conoco deal and possibly the 2003 Iranian note.

This is a troubling pattern, and the United States will have to take the lead to try to correct it. Establishing some kind of "hotline" as we did with the Soviets and even the North Koreans would be helpful, but doing so seems problematic given the Iranian regime's paranoia when it comes to direct contact with the U.S. government. Greater dialogue, academic and cultural exchanges, even military-to-military talks would all be positive steps toward building understanding on both sides. A regional security forum at which Americans, Iranians, and all of the major regional states would gather to discuss both general and immediate concerns would be similarly helpful.[12]

The U.S.-Iranian dimension may be the least important aspect of this problem. It is at least as likely that Israel, Saudi Arabia, Turkey, Pakistan, and other states will find themselves in a crisis with Iran—one in which the United States may or may not then become involved. In these cases, the risks are both worse and better than crises involving the United States more directly.

Such regional crises could be much worse because these countries would be far more vulnerable to whatever damage a nuclear Iran could inflict than the United States. The U.S. homeland is largely out of range (at least of Iranian nukes delivered by missile) and the American nuclear arsenal is so massive that we could probably be more relaxed about the prospect that Iran would even try to attack us directly. In contrast, Hashemi Rafsanjani famously warned the Israelis in 2002 that a single nuclear detonation would devastate virtually their entire population, and other regional states would not be much better off.[13] However, it is also the case that these states have typically had more success getting their messages across to the Iranians. Even the Israelis have found back channels to Iran. Nevertheless, in the context of a nuclear crisis, whatever arrangements these countries have employed for exchanging signals with Tehran might prove inadequate; signals may need to be more complex, and the time and space needed to comprehend them may be unavailable. Consequently, it would be important to try to establish more reliable communications and interpersonal exchanges to mitigate these problems.[14]

But these problems will inevitably persist. They are dangers inherent in crises, and particularly so with nuclear weapons. It is the flip side of Brodie's comforting logic about nuclear weapons being the "absolute weapon." Because their destructive power is so enormous, the vast majority of the time a country with nuclear weapons can feel secure that no one, even another nuclear-armed state, would dare to attack it. It simply makes no sense to do so. However, when one country takes actions that lead another to believe that that country may be contemplating just such a strike, no matter how far-fetched, those same factors can reverse themselves abruptly. The second country may overcompensate to prevent an attack. And it is those overcompensating reactions that can start a crisis. Again, Brodie's basic logic is so powerful that no nuclear crisis has ever spiraled out of control, but a number of countries have felt the tug of these centrifugal forces. Given the Iranian regime's innate paranoia, difficulty comprehending the actions of the rest of the world, and tendency to ignore the impact of its own actions on others, Tehran seems more likely than most to experience these problems. While we should do everything we can to apply the lessons of the Cold War regarding how to mitigate this dangerous tendency, it is unlikely that we will be able to eliminate it altogether as long as the Islamic Republic rules Iran.

THE DANGERS OF AN IMMATURE ARSENAL. Because a nuclear war has never been waged (thankfully), we have little real evidence to understand what it would be like. In the absence of that hard data, during the Cold War, both the United States and the Soviet Union employed extensive and creative academic exercises as surrogates to try to understand these considerations. Extensive theoretical exercises, war-gaming, and game theory produced ideas about nuclear war that became enshrined in superpower force structure and strategic thinking.

One of these is the danger posed by nascent nuclear arsenals. When a country first acquires nuclear weapons, it is likely to have only a small number. These weapons are often stored in relatively vulnerable structures, command and control is usually immature and brittle, and there is unlikely to be either the procedures or the physical capacity to conduct sophisticated operations under conditions of enemy attack. As a result, the nuclear force of a new nuclear power is often vulnerable to attack by an adversary—using either nuclear weapons or powerful and sophisticated conventional weapons.

These circumstances can produce a "use it or lose it," or "first strike," danger.[15] Imagine a situation in which Israel and Iran become embroiled in a high-stakes crisis at a time when Iran has just a handful of nuclear weapons stored in only moderately hardened facilities known to the Israelis. Israel would calculate that if it attacked the Iranian nuclear arsenal first, it would have a good chance of 1) destroying the arsenal altogether, 2) crippling its command and control so that the Iranians were unable to launch, and/or 3) degrading the Iranian force so that any Iranian retaliatory strike would almost certainly be far less dangerous to Israel than if Iran were given the time and opportunity to launch on its own terms. This set of assumptions could create pressure on the Israeli leadership (which has a strategic doctrine emphasizing preemptive and preventive attack to minimize damage to Israel) to launch just such a strike, raising the likelihood that the crisis would descend into war and the potential use of nuclear weapons. Moreover, the Iranians would fear that Israel would launch just such a preemptive strike. This foreknowledge would, in turn, pressure Iran to launch an attack on Israel before the Israelis could preempt them. One side's vulnerability could push both countries into a war that neither wanted.

Traditionally, the "right" answer to this problem is for the new nuclear state to make its nuclear forces more difficult to destroy. This generally consists of hardening its nuclear sites to withstand attack, making nuclear forces mobile (by putting missiles on trucks, trains, or submarines) and dispersing them at the first sign of a crisis, and by having enough nuclear weapons that no adversary could reasonably expect that it would be able to destroy all of them (including by a combination of offensive preemptive strikes and ballistic missile defenses). This practice is typically what is meant by a "secure second-strike" capability: a nuclear force that is likely to have enough forces to survive an enemy's first strike, retain cohesiveness and control, and still inflict horrific damage on the other side. Once both sides achieve that capability, MAD is secure, and the dangers of the first-strike dynamic disappear.

At the simplest level, the United States might want a nuclear Iran to develop a secure second-strike capability to get past the dangerous dynamic of its inevitable early vulnerability to a first strike. In terms of regional crisis dynamics, that would be preferable, but the issue is more complicated than that.

The vulnerability of a nascent Iranian nuclear force could exacerbate crises with other regional states whose own capabilities might be greater than Iran's in the early years of an Iranian nuclear arsenal. However, in a crisis with the United States itself, Iran's vulnerability would be an enormous advantage for Washington, one we should be loath to surrender. Until Iran acquires ballistic missiles with intercontinental ranges that can quickly deliver nuclear warheads against American targets, Iran's ability to employ its nuclear arsenal against the United States will be *very* limited. Iran would have to strike at regional targets that the United States values—bases in the region, possibly our allies—or it would have to find covert means of delivering a nuclear weapon to the United States (secreted on board a cargo ship, for instance), which would be difficult to pull off and could take weeks if it works at all.

American conventional and nuclear capabilities are so enormous that we would have a good chance of effectively disarming the Iranians. For some period of time even after Iran crosses the nuclear threshold, the United States will be able to do enormous damage to Iran—including only to Iran's nuclear forces if we choose—and the Iranians may have little or no ability to do significant damage to us in return. In Cold War parlance, that would give the United States "escalation dominance."

In theory, such a situation could prompt the weaker state to attack first, again to exploit what capacity it has to cause damage while it can. However, in practice, escalation dominance has not produced that dangerous dynamic, but instead has prompted the opposite: the weaker state backs down, while the stronger state feels more secure and therefore does not need to act precipitously. Throughout the 1940s, 1950s, and even the early 1960s, the United States possessed a (diminishing) escalation dominance over the Soviets. As a result, in the 1946 Iran, 1948 Berlin, 1950 Korean, 1956 Suez, 1961 Berlin, and 1962 Cuban crises, the Russians knew that they were in no position to provoke a war with the United States, and Washington knew that Moscow knew it. This is not to imply that those crises were not dangerous. By the early 1950s the Russians could theoretically nuke at least a few American cities, and that was far too many for America's leaders. But these crises were less dangerous than they might have been because both sides recognized the enormous American advantages and the Russians were careful not to push too hard as a result.[16] One of the reasons that Khrushchev wanted to put nuclear missiles in Cuba was to redress this imbalance.[17] However, because the longer-range missiles on Cuba were not operational at the time of the crisis, the United States still held a significant advantage, which was partly responsible for the Soviet retreat—and one reason why it was so important for Kennedy and his advisors to resolve the crisis before all of the Soviet missiles on Cuba were operational.[18] In short, escalation dominance has proven to be a valuable advantage that the United States should retain for as long as possible, despite the near-sacred value attached to secure second-strike capabilities and MAD.

This history also suggests another point worth making. Although in theory, the "use it or lose it" dynamic exists, and in some historical circumstances one side or the other in a nuclear dyad contemplated a first strike against a rival, in practice it never happened. There were a few occasions when one country contemplated a nuclear first strike against a rival: some Americans advocated doing so to Russia early in the Cold War, and both the United States and USSR contemplated strikes against the Chinese nuclear program to obliterate it in its infancy. However, there is little evidence that anyone suggested pursuing this course of action during a crisis. Likewise, on both the American and Soviet sides, no one ever proposed launching a surprise first strike against the other to disarm it. The United States never discussed a preemptive strike against the Soviet Union during any of our crises, nor did the Soviets ever seriously consider launching first to preempt an American surprise attack.[19]

This history reinforces Bracken and Payne's warnings against assuming that our conduct during the Cold War should always serve as a model for our conduct with other, smaller nuclear powers. In the case of a nuclear Iran, we can afford to act differently and should do so because of the huge advantages we will thereby accrue. In particular, the United States should do everything it can to maintain its escalation dominance over Iran. This determination could require developing a somewhat more versatile nuclear force than we possess. Right now, the United States has a lot of powerful, survivable, and accurate weapons. We also have a remarkably powerful and versatile conventional military. That gives us a wide range of options for how we might attack an Iranian nuclear arsenal. In the future, if Iran tries to diminish this advantage of ours, we may want to try to preserve it by acquiring nuclear forces with a wider range of capabilities, including focused blast, earth-penetrating, enhanced radiation, low-yield, hyper-accurate, or other features, to give us a much wider range of options to go after Iran's nuclear forces no matter how they are configured and deployed.[20]

There are several other improvements to our military capabilities that we ought to implement to enhance our ability to resolve nuclear crises with Iran peacefully and in our favor. First, it will be critical to continue to develop and deploy ballistic missile defenses in the Middle East to try to ensure that any Iranian missile attack—whether degraded by an American first strike or not—would have a reasonable prospect of being stopped by these defenses. Second, while the United States possesses a conventional arsenal of unmatched capabilities, those capabilities need to continue to improve to ensure that we have a wide range of options against Iran, and so that the Iranians must fear that we could mount disarming, or devastatingly punishing operations without even resorting to our nuclear arsenal. In an insightful piece on dealing with a nuclear Iran, former NSC director Kori Schake proposed that rather than threatening Iran with nuclear obliteration, the United States should threaten to target their leadership as we did to Iraq in 1991 and as we have done to al-Qa'ida and its various affiliates since 9/11.[21] Such a strategy could be terrifying to Iran's leaders, and it represents the kind of options that the United States should be developing to maximize our leverage over even a nuclear Iran. As part of this, the

United States needs to continue to build massive intelligence, surveillance, and reconnaissance capabilities that we could deploy against Iran to give us an accurate intelligence picture in short order.

The more sophisticated our conventional and nuclear forces, the more usable they are, the longer we will be able to target Iran's nuclear forces with a reasonable expectation that we could do tremendous damage to them and they would probably do little to us. And what must be borne in mind is that what matters is the *Iranian* calculus, not our own. What made the Soviets more pliable during the 1940s, 1950s, and early 1960s was that they believed we had escalation dominance and that we might use it. The fact that we had no intention of using it and did not even consider doing so was irrelevant. As always, what matters in deterrence is the calculations of the deterred.

The second injunction that the history indicates is the importance of the United States inserting itself into any nuclear crisis involving Iran. Again, this logic seems counterintuitive, especially from the perspective of the Cold War, a key lesson of which seemed to be that a country should try to avoid nuclear crises whenever possible. But one reason for such involvement is that it has historically proven useful to have an influential third party intercede to defuse a crisis, especially a nuclear crisis. For instance, a key element in defusing the nuclear crisis between India and Pakistan arising from the Kargil War of 1999 was the intervention of external parties, particularly the United States.[22]

The more important point here is that a nuclear crisis between a nuclear Saudi Arabia or Israel or Turkey and a nuclear Iran is likely to be far more dangerous than a nuclear crisis between the United States and a nuclear Iran, at least until Iran develops the capacity to hit the U.S. homeland with nuclear weapons and probably even after that point. With the Saudis, Israelis, or Turks, there might well be use-it-or-lose-it pressures. With the United States, there is no such dynamic; there is only escalation dominance—especially if the United States does continue to modernize its nuclear arsenal, deploys ballistic missile defenses, and keeps improving its conventional attack capabilities.

The different dynamics of a U.S.-Iranian nuclear balance—different both from the later U.S.-Soviet balance and from a hypothetical Iran-Israel/Saudi/Turkey nuclear balance—reverse the logic that emerged as gospel from the late Cold War. It might be helpful to think about it this way: we may not be willing to risk the destruction of Tel Aviv or the Saudi oil fields to an Iranian nuclear strike, but the Iranians would have to worry that we would. The evidence suggests that they would and that their decisions would be affected by that fear. Because Iran will not be able to effectively target our cities but we can threaten theirs, Tehran has to calculate that it has far more to lose than we do in a U.S.-Iranian nuclear exchange. Consequently, the best thing that the United States could do both to keep the peace and protect its allies would be to immediately insert itself into any nuclear crisis with the Iranians, "taking over" for any of our regional allies, because doing so would actually be the best way to ensure that the crisis does not escalate and ends with Iran securing the fewest gains.

FIRST IMPRESSIONS. As Paul Bracken explains, "The first nuclear crisis could take on transcendent importance for the same reason the 1948 Berlin crisis did in the first nuclear age. Norms of what is and is not permissible without causing major escalation will be determined. The first crisis could set a pattern for a long time to come."[23] Indeed, one of the most important and dangerous aspects of nuclear deterrence is the learning curve. States new to nuclear dynamics make mistakes that states with more experience do not, which is why the early Cold War was more dangerous and pockmarked with nuclear crises than the later Cold War. The more that the United States and USSR learned about nuclear dynamics and each other, and the more that we worked out rules for how to conduct ourselves, the fewer problems we had.[24]

It is possible that Israel, or Saudi Arabia, Pakistan, or Turkey would handle the first crisis or crises with a nuclear Iran well and not only avoid both war and surrender, but do so in ways that establish a modus vivendi that would minimize further crises and diminish the risk of escalation.

But given the wisdom that the United States garnered from our experiences with the Soviet Union, it could only be better for all involved if Washington took a leading role, both in defusing the crisis at hand and using it to help the two sides establish a code of conduct that would ameliorate their tensions moving forward.

RED LINES. During the intellectual madness of the Cold War, the simple concept of drawing "lines in the sand" became translated into the notion of "red lines." A red line is simply one country telling a rival not to take a particular action because doing so would mean war. Establishing red lines with a nuclear Iran is a critical element of crisis management. Red lines can help prevent a crisis by making clear to Iran what actions it might take that would provoke one, in hope that the Iranians would not take that action. And, of course, it would be important for the Iranians to clarify their own red lines, as it would for Iran's various regional rivals to do the same. It is not that bright red lines will prevent all problems, but they can help eliminate misperceptions and miscalculations that can produce unintended crises.[25]

Immediately before the North Korean attack on the South in 1950, Secretary of State Acheson famously defined America's defense perimeter in the Pacific as excluding Korea, which may have led the Soviets to believe that an attack on South Korea would not cross America's red line.[26] However, when the North attacked, Washington decided that South Korea was a vital interest and so we joined the Korean War on their behalf. A better defined red line might have precluded that conflict altogether.

Thus the purpose of laying down red lines to Iran is to make clear to Tehran what actions on its part would trigger an American military response, conventional or nuclear. It is not just that our Cold War experiences demonstrated that clear red lines are indispensable; it is also that any discussion of red lines forces a discussion of other issues related to American goals, priorities, and capabilities that would be equally useful, even essential. When confronting a nuclear-armed adversary, the United

States should only threaten the use of force when we mean it. Thus defining red lines can provoke a useful debate about America's true interests in an issue.

In the past, Washington assumed that Iran recognized that any Iranian attack on the U.S. homeland—including by terrorism—would trigger an American response, including the potential use of force, and possibly on a massive scale depending on the nature of the Iranian attack. The Arbabsiar case calls into question the sanctity of that red line. Tehran may be under the impression that this is no longer a red line, or that what constitutes "crossing" it has changed. Regardless of what policy the United States adopts toward Iran in the future, right now the Obama administration needs to demarcate this red line clearly.

Perhaps the most obvious red line the United States should lay down is that any Iranian use of conventional or nuclear force beyond its own borders will be met by whatever means the United States requires to defeat it. The United States cannot allow Iran to employ force or the threat of force against its neighbors, and Tehran needs to understand that Washington will prevent it from doing so using all means at our disposal, potentially including nuclear weapons.

A second issue that would require the articulation of a red line is the possibility of Iranian transfer of nuclear material or nuclear weapons to a third party, particularly one of the many terrorist groups Tehran supports. Such a transfer would be unlikely because the red line is implicit, but the lesson of history is to never assume.

Another important threat that the United States and its allies may face from a nuclear Iran is that Tehran may believe that its nuclear shield will protect it from *all* retaliation by the United States (both conventional and nuclear) as long as it does not cross the red lines related to its use of force or transfer of nuclear material. This may create the impression in Iranian minds that the unconventional realm—subversion, non-nuclear terrorism, insurgencies, and the like—are all fair game. Tehran might calculate that the United States would never respond with nuclear weapons for a non-nuclear terrorist attack or insurgency. The Iranians might further assume that the United States would not even retaliate with conventional forces because of the risk of escalation to a nuclear exchange, and that therefore they could be more aggressive in employing asymmetric forms of warfare. To deter or at least diminish Iran's pursuit of unconventional wars against the United States and its allies, Washington might want to convey to Tehran that asymmetric warfare on its part will be met by disproportionate asymmetric responses on our part—by supporting insurgent and separatist groups inside Iran, undermining Iran's currency, or mounting relentless cyberattacks against Tehran.

Will these red lines work? It is hard to know for certain, but the evidence suggests reasons for optimism.[27] Since 1979, but especially since Khomeini's death in 1989, the Iranians have avoided American, Israeli, Turkish, and even most Saudi red lines, as best Tehran understood them. The occasions when Iran appears to have crossed them stand out because they were the exceptions to the rule. The most salient examples of Iran crossing American red lines—the Arbabsiar plot and the seizure of British sailors and marines in the Shatt al-Arab—are better explained not as instances in which Iran crossed American red lines, but as one instance when Iran may have believed that the red line lay elsewhere and another where a lower-level official freelanced. Again, these incidents are troubling in their own right, but they seem more likely to constitute exceptions proving the rule than disproving it.

There is still one more problem with red lines: they have to be "mutually" agreeable. The United States could announce that one of its red lines is that Iran can no longer support any terrorist groups. The Iranians might simply say, "No." The United States would then have to decide whether to try to enforce the red line by going to war with Iran when it continued to support various terrorist groups. Having refrained from going to war with Iran over its support for terrorism in the past, including during periods when Iran was far more involved in attacks on Americans (during our interventions in Lebanon in the 1980s and Iraq in the 2000s, for instance), the U.S. government is not likely to consider, or the American people to support, a war with Iran today absent an egregious Iranian provocation. This aspect of red lines has prompted Tom Pickering, perhaps the most accomplished American diplomat of his generation, to observe that many red lines often prove to be "pink lines" in practice.

What is important to take from this is that U.S. red lines need to be enforceable. Iran needs to believe that we can enforce them. And from time to time the Iranians may test them, including by lower-level commanders freelancing. If we fail to enforce those red lines, they are going to blur or disappear altogether. Whenever those red lines are tested, we are going to have to decide whether to push back, recognizing that to do so could mean triggering a crisis that could escalate to war, but that not to do so would weaken the red line, either ceding the matter to the Iranians or creating exactly the kind of ambiguity that can produce crises from misperception—the avoidance of which is the point of establishing firm, clear red lines. With a country as problematic as Iran, red lines can help, but they are not a perfect solution to the problems. Nothing ever is, and the persistence of these problems, to whatever extent, constitutes part of the unavoidable risks and costs of containing a nuclear Iran.

THIRD-PARTY RED LINES. Because of Israel's own capability to do enormous damage to Iran, Jerusalem will need to put forth red lines of its own. Although they lack the capability to do real damage to Iran, both because they might acquire that capability in the future and because of their potential ability to call on the United States for nuclear and conventional military backing, the Gulf states may want to do the same.

The most obvious red line Israel is likely to lay down for Iran is that any direct use of force by Iran against Israel would trigger a military response by Israel. Because the Israeli leadership believes that deterrence is best reinforced by responding with disproportionate force, they likely would convey to Iran that any direct attack on Israel or its citizens will be met by a much stronger Israeli response.

Similarly, it seems likely that Israel would *not* draw a red line prohibiting attack by Iranian proxies against Israel—or against direct Iranian attack on Israeli proxies. Throughout the Cold War, U.S. and Soviet proxies fought one another, as well as the actual forces of the other superpower, without engendering a forceful response. Iranian proxies (Hizballah, Palestinian Islamic Jihad) have attacked Israel and Israelis without provoking Israeli military retaliation against Iran for decades. And for its part, Israel may be providing support to Iranian opposition forces in Khuzestan, Kurdistan, and Baluchistan, but this alleged assistance has not triggered an Iranian attack on Israel. It seems unlikely that Israel would try to lay down a red line on this matter for fear that it would prove unenforceable and would compromise Israel's deterrent credibility.

Beyond these rather clear decisions, there are several big "unknowns," actions that Israel might choose to try to forbid Iran from taking by threatening a military response. However, in every case there is considerable ambiguity and uncertainty that would make it difficult for Israel to know for certain what had happened, let alone prove it to the rest of the world. And this complexity might convince Jerusalem not to make them red lines for Tehran.

A low-probability but high-impact concern for Israel would be the possibility that Iran might transfer nuclear technology, radioactive material, or even nuclear weapons themselves to one or more of its terrorist allies. As unlikely as it may be, Israel would probably want to ensure that Iran understands that this is a red line for Jerusalem rather than leaving any possible doubt in Tehran's mind. The specifics of such a red line are unclear. Many Israeli policymakers might prefer to warn Tehran that just the transfer of nuclear-related materials to a terrorist group would trigger a direct Israeli attack on Iran, in hope of convincing Tehran not to even think about doing so. Since Israel might not know about any transfers, and because any information they got could be deeply suspect, Israeli decision-makers could be loath to act on it, especially if "acting" on it meant launching a nuclear strike on Iran.

The alternative would be to lay down a different red line, namely that any use of nuclear material or weapons against the state of Israel by any nonstate actor will be met with a massive Israeli response *against Iran*. For some Israelis, this red line will be inadequate because it only punishes Iran after the fact. However, it would eliminate most of the intelligence problems associated with threatening a nuclear response to a mere transfer. Again, Iran has never provided any of its terrorist allies or proxies with chemical or biological agents, almost certainly because Tehran feared that any country attacked by those agents would retaliate massively *against Iran* regardless of what it could or could not prove in a court of law.

As for the GCC states, they would doubtless seek to lay down red lines against any Iranian attack on them—nuclear, conventional, or by subversion. It is the last that will prove the most problematic for the reasons described above. The GCC states will see Iranians behind every palm tree and have often blamed Iran unfairly for internal problems. Moreover, unless or until the GCC states develop nuclear or conventional military capabilities of their own, they will be reliant on the United States to enforce any warnings to Iran, and therefore the red lines themselves will have to be negotiated with Washington.

Reputation, Co-optation, and Proliferation

For at least a decade, the United States has been insistent that Iran's acquisition of nuclear weapons would be "unacceptable" and that we would "prevent" Iran from acquiring this capability. This overblown rhetoric has served a purpose, but if Iran ever does deploy a nuclear arsenal it will come back to haunt us. Other countries will question American resolve and that doubt could creep into other corners of their thinking about the United States. If the United States was unwilling to back up this claim, could it be relied on to back up other claims? "Imagine what Khamenei and the Revolutionary Guard Corps will think of the Americans, and especially the Israelis, if, after announcing repeatedly that an Iranian nuclear weapon is 'unacceptable,' they permit it?" asks Reuel Gerecht.[28] Gerecht leans hard right on this issue, but he is an intelligent and experienced observer of Iran. He is also not alone. Other experts and policy-makers on the right worry about the same issue.[29]

The jury is out regarding the importance of reputation in international politics. Some scholars believe that past behavior does affect the calculus of other states.[30] Others argue that this consideration is minor because leaders tend to focus far more on the interests of a state and its capability to defend those interests in the matter at hand.[31]

Historical examples can be cited in both directions. America's withdrawals from Lebanon and Vietnam played an important role in Saddam Husayn's thinking about how to handle the United States before and during the 1990–91 Persian Gulf War. Based on this, he famously told U.S. ambassador April Glaspie, "Yours is a society which cannot accept 10,000 dead in one battle," a week before launching his invasion of Kuwait.[32] Turning to more typical decision-makers, the Kennedy administration worried that to do nothing in response to the Soviet deployment of nuclear missiles to Cuba would cause Moscow to see Washington as irresolute and so the Russians might come to doubt the U.S. commitment to Berlin. For his part, Khrushchev apparently did see Kennedy as naïve and weak at their summit in Vienna in June 1961, prompting the shift to nuclear brinksmanship that produced both the 1961 Berlin and 1962 Cuban Missile crises.[33] In contrast, the Soviets reportedly believed that the American withdrawal from Vietnam in 1973 would make Washington more bellicose and willing to back up our deterrent commitments, not less, which successive American administrations had feared. Moreover, in those instances when a country has contemplated attacking another, even when reputational considerations have played into those deliberations, they have often been outweighed by the balance of power and other more tangible matters.[34]

How would a tarnished American reputation actually affect the dynamics of the Middle East in the event Iran acquired a nuclear arsenal? If the Iranians believed that the United States had been proven to be a paper tiger by its failure to prevent them from acquiring a nuclear weapon, they might be further emboldened to press ahead with acts of subversion and unconventional warfare. Similarly, like Khrushchev, they might opt to employ a more aggressive form of brinksmanship that would lead to more nuclear crises. While this would be dangerous, it is hard to know just how dangerous it would be. At least some nuclear crises will be inevitable if Iran acquires nuclear weapons, and what is unknowable is how many more nuclear crises we would face as a result of an Iranian perception of weak American resolve.

There is nothing innately different about a nuclear crisis motivated in part by an Iranian perception of our reputation. As the Kennedy administration learned during the Cuban Missile Crisis, prior reputational considerations will not necessarily keep us from prevailing in a nuclear crisis. Moreover, once that crisis is resolved, its outcome creates a new reputation, superseding any prior considerations. For instance, Saddam was not the only Middle Easterner who took America's retreats from Vietnam and Lebanon as proof of American diffidence, even cowardice. However, after Desert Storm, there was no one in the Middle East who believed that. Thus, even if the Iranians did pick a fight with the United States in part because they believed that our unwillingness to prevent them from crossing the nuclear threshold revealed us to be weak and cowardly, staring them down in that crisis would become the dominant reputational consideration coming out of it.

Beyond the ambiguous and potentially temporary role it might play in both encouraging Iranian unconventional aggressiveness and triggering nuclear crises, the greatest potential impact of any American reputation for weakness stemming from a failure to prevent Iran's acquisition of a nuclear arsenal would be on the alignment and behavior of America's allies in the region. If America's regional allies saw this failure as a sign that America was weak and unwilling to stand up to Iran on their behalf, one course of action open to them would be to cozy up to Tehran, accommodate its wishes, even appease it. Alternatively, they could decide to find other ways to resist Iran on their own, without American support. The former behavior is what scholars call "bandwagoning" or "co-optation," and the latter is called "balancing."[35] Both are potentially dangerous, albeit in different ways, and both constitute further challenges of containment.

BANDWAGONING, BALANCING, AND BLACKMAIL. Bandwagoning behavior by weak states is meant to avoid conquest or other forms of punishment by more powerful states. It is ultimately a response to implicit or explicit blackmail by the more powerful state. However, pure "nuclear blackmail" is a nonstarter. The historical evidence of it is both meager and ambiguous at best. More to the point, no country has ever told another, "Give up such-and-such piece of your territory or else we will nuke you," and gotten away with it. In theory, Tehran could call up Riyadh and tell the Saudis that if they did not transfer control of the Kingdom's heavily Shi'a, oil-rich Eastern Province to Iran then Riyadh would be vaporized. In the real world, the United States would step in and back the Iranians off. Only an utterly craven United States would act otherwise.

A more realistic concern would be the problem of Finlandization, the impalpable accommodation of regional actors to Tehran's wishes. Barry Rubin, the director of Israel's Begin-Sadat Center, fears that many of the Gulf states would "subtly" bandwagon with Iran, accepting American security guarantees but acting in ways to ensure that they do not cross Iran on any major issues.[36] Obviously, this would not apply to Israel—because it can stand on its own military power—and probably not to Turkey, either, which can always rely on its NATO membership. However, the GCC states would not necessarily have either to fall back on.

Nevertheless, we should not assume that even a widespread presumption that the United States will not back them in a showdown with Iran would produce bandwagoning. It is at least equally likely that the GCC states would look for ways to balance against a nuclear Iran even without reliable American support. Historically, balancing has been the consistent preference of countries around the world, over bandwagoning. Over the past two centuries, the GCC states have consistently opted for balancing rather than bandwagoning behavior, allying with Britain against Iraq and Saudi Arabia, allying with the United States (and Iraq) against revolutionary Iran, allying with the United States against Saddam's Iraq, and finally allying with the United States against a resurgent Iran. As the noted Arabist Marc Lynch pointed out at the height of the Arab Spring in 2011:

> There is little sign of any regional bandwagoning with Iran today among either regimes or newly empowered publics. Indeed, Iran's push for a nuclear weapon and regional influence has alarmed the regimes of the Gulf. Arab regimes have chosen to balance against Iran rather than join it in a challenge to U.S. policy, and are deeply fearful of Iranian power. They have moved closer to the United States and to Israel out of fear of Iranian power, and have been increasingly active in their efforts against Iran. They have also intensified their military relations with the United States, including massive arms purchases and military cooperation. These leaders fear that American engagement with Iran will come at their expense, and are as worried about abandonment as they are to exposure to Iranian retaliation.[37]

The Saudi and UAE threats to acquire nuclear weapons of their own are the ultimate form of balancing behavior. Neither country is suggesting that it is ready to acquiesce to what they fear would be a domineering nuclear Iran. Quite the contrary: They are insistent that they plan to resist it however they can, including by matching Iran's nuclear capability with their own if need be. That is what balancing is, and it is the exact opposite of bandwagoning.

It is logically impossible to fear that in response to an Iranian nuclear capability, the GCC states will both proliferate (balance) and Finlandize (bandwagon). They will do one or the other, not both. Nor is it likely that some would do one and others the opposite: when it comes to matters of such importance, the GCC acts as one, with Saudi Arabia leading the way. Nor is it clear that it would matter much even if the GCC states split on this. If Saudi Arabia decides to balance against Iran—something Kuwait, Bahrain, and the UAE will axiomatically adopt—does it matter if Qatar or Oman decides to take a more accommodating line with Iran?

In theory, it is possible that the GCC might try a mild form of accommodation with Iran first, as a way of buying time to build nukes of their own, but in practice this is not credible. Historically, states that decide to balance against a threat by acquiring a nuclear arsenal of their own make clear their determination to balance right from the start. For good reason, history has never seen a state feign accommodation with an overbearing nuclear neighbor only to turn against it when the country had acquired a nuclear weapon. That is the stuff of pulp fiction.

By the same token, it would also be a mistake to assume that the GCC states will balance against Iran and dismiss the danger of proliferation. Given historical proclivities as well as past GCC behavior, it is far more likely that they will balance against a nuclear Iran rather than bandwagon with it. But this also means that they will be sorely tempted to acquire nuclear weapons of their own to ensure that they can do so without any external assistance, just as they have threatened repeatedly. In the end, they may choose not to, but the inclination to balance is going to push them hard in that direction and it will require a major effort on the part of the United States to convince them not to, if it is possible at all.

Thus it is probably the case that balancing is not just the higher probability but the greater danger for the Gulf region, especially if the United States proves feckless in the face of a nuclear Iran. In that case, not only will GCC incentives to acquire nuclear weapons of their own soar, but they would probably try to *aggressively* balance against Iran to ensure that Iran understands that if it tries anything with the GCC, it is going to have a fight on its hands. Tehran may see such a reaction as either threatening or just arrogant, and it may try to subvert the GCC governments and stir up internal unrest against them in response. Inevitably, this would provoke the GCC to do the same to the Iranians, and at some point this war of subversion could boil over into one or more crises that they would have difficulty resolving on their own. Consequently, if the United States is not willing to back up the Gulf oil monarchies against Iran, the endemic instability of the region is likely to reemerge either in the form of bandwagoning that produces Iranian domination or, far more likely, in aggressive balancing and possible proliferation that leads to renewed conflict.

There is a reasonable answer to this problem: responsible but assertive American involvement. It is not impossible for the United States to convince the GCC countries to avoid the perils of both accommodation and proliferation. The former should be relatively easy because of their natural preference and the massive American conventional and nuclear superiority over Iran. The latter will be more difficult. The key is that the GCC states will have to be reassured early and perhaps often that they can count on the United States in these significantly altered circumstances. That in turn will require constant American involvement in the region, especially when there is a challenge from Iran, and assurance that the United States can and will prevent Iran from realizing any gains from its nuclear arsenal.

Additional Reassurances— or Unnecessary Encumbrances?

Drawing on America's experiences from the Cold War, other experts have proposed additional steps that the United States might take to mollify the risks of both bandwagoning and balancing in response to a nuclear Iran. I see these measures as strategically unnecessary and even counterproductive; nevertheless they are important to address because they may ultimately prove to be diplomatically essential.

INCREASED CONVENTIONAL FORCES IN THE REGION. A number of the advocates of air strikes argue that because the United States maintained a large conventional force in Europe during the Cold War as part of our effort to contain and deter the USSR, we would have to do the same to contain and deter the Iranians.[38] They fear that the United States would have to engage in a massive force buildup in the Gulf. Militarily and strategically, there is no reason for us to do so.

The problem during the Cold War was that the Soviets fielded a massive conventional military and the United States and NATO struggled to match it to avoid an overreliance on nuclear deterrence. During the Eisenhower administration, the United States relied on nuclear deterrence, and so we kept a relatively weak conventional force in Europe—and did so to save money. Under Kennedy, the United States and NATO decided that it would be better to create at least some possibility of defeating a Soviet invasion with conventional forces so that we did not have to ignite a nuclear holocaust to "save" Europe. From that point on, the United States built up much larger conventional forces in Europe (and northeast Asia), but it was because we were facing the enormous conventional might of the Red Army.

With Iran, the problem is absent. The current level of American forces is more than adequate to handle any Iranian conventional move against the GCC states. Typically, United States forces in the Gulf include an aircraft carrier battle group (often with a second nearby in the Arabian Sea, Indian Ocean, or Mediterranean); about a dozen other surface ships (including several minesweepers); two to three Air Force combat squadrons in Kuwait, Qatar, and the UAE; and the equipment for two full-strength Army brigades and a Marine combat regiment.[39] This force amounts to about forty thousand American soldiers, sailors, airmen, and Marines in the region on a routine basis, although the vast majority of these are administrative, headquarters, and other support personnel.[40] In a crisis, the United States can fly in the troops to man the ground force equipment in a matter of days, along with Air Force bombers and tankers to Diego Garcia and additional fighter-bombers to the Gulf states. Even if the GCC militaries proved so hapless that they added no combat capability of their own, this level of force would be more than adequate to crush any Iranian conventional attack on any of the GCC states. There simply is no military need to augment these forces.

What's more, doing so could be counterproductive. Right now, the GCC states are very comfortable with the current American force level in the region. Although American troops are not terribly welcome in much of the Middle East, the smaller Gulf states recognize the strategic need for them and have tolerated them at current, relatively low levels. Through-out nearly a decade of popular unrest in Bahrain, including major riots in 2011, none of that animosity has been directed at American forces there despite the presence of the headquarters of the U.S. Fifth Fleet and its five thousand personnel. There have been no attacks on American troops or facilities. That speaks to how comfortable the Gulf populations have become with current U.S. force levels. In the past, however, when U.S. forces were deployed in Saudi Arabia and at much greater force levels (for example, during the Persian Gulf War and the occupation of Iraq), there were problems, and GCC governments took greater heat both from the anti-American elements of their own societies and from other Arab populations. One of Osama bin Laden's principal grievances against the Al Sa'ud was that they had invited infidel soldiers into the Kingdom. In short, increasing American forces in the region is unnecessary and could create problems for the host governments.

TACTICAL NUCLEAR WEAPONS. A second possibility to further reas-sure America's regional allies if Iran joins the nuclear club would be to preposition U.S. tactical nuclear forces in the Gulf. Again, this is a notion that advocates of air strikes have raised based on the Cold War experi-ence. Once again, however, the logic that drove the United States to go this route during the Cold War does not apply to Iran. There were two different strategic rationales underlying the deployment of tactical nu-clear weapons to Europe and East Asia then. Early on, both sides believed that tactical nuclear weapons were needed to "win" the conventional battle for Europe. In those early years, nuclear weapons were seen as little more than big conventional weapons, and both NATO and the Warsaw Pact integrated tactical nuclear weapons into their conventional force structures as a matter of routine.

Over time, however, both sides came to realize that nuclear weapons were categorically different from conventional forces, but that left NATO with the fundamental dilemma of Cold War extended deterrence: the Soviets had overwhelming conventional superiority, but it was not rational for the United States to "trade Boston for Bonn." Moreover, there was a fear that if one side could dominate the battlefield with tactical nuclear weapons, the other would have no choice but to escalate to strategic homeland exchanges—launching ICBMs against each other's home cities—which would be unacceptable to everyone. Consequently, the United States might have been forced to accept the loss of Europe instead. In addition, by retaining large numbers of tactical nuclear weapons in Europe (many with the range to strike Russian cities), the Americans forced the Soviets to worry that even if the American president did not want to escalate to strategic homeland attacks, either the troops on the ground (many of whose families were with them overseas and therefore vulnerable to Soviet armies) or the Europeans themselves would get control of the tactical nuclear forces and launch them at the Russian homeland. All of this might sound like madness (or MADness), and it was, but it was how we won the Cold War.

In the Persian Gulf, however, all of this is unnecessary. Unlike in Europe, the United States retains both conventional and strategic nuclear superiority over Iran and should be able to do so for the foreseeable future. This obviates any strategic or military need for tactical nuclear weapons. There is just no conceivable scenario in which the United States would need tactical nuclear weapons to do something that we could not do with our conventional forces or, at worst, with our strategic nuclear forces. Moreover, tactical nuclear weapons become a target for antinuclear activists wherever they have been deployed. In the Gulf, these forces would create unnecessary headaches both for Washington and the host nations.

BUILDING UP REGIONAL MILITARIES. Some commentators have suggested that deterring and containing Iran will require a major augmentation of the armed forces of the Gulf states, Turkey, and Israel, in turn requiring huge new arms sales to the region. This is a bit more complicated than whether to add more conventional forces or tactical nuclear weapons to the region.

The GCC countries still have considerable room for improvement when it comes to their military capabilities, although they have made some important changes and acquisitions in the past decade or so. They have better integrated their air and air defense forces under American auspices, and are now doing the same for their ballistic missile defenses. At bottom, however, it is the U.S. military presence in the region and specifically in their own countries that provides their most important assurance against Iranian attack. The United States has major military bases in Kuwait, Bahrain, the UAE, and Qatar, as well as access to facilities in Saudi Arabia and Oman. As long as those bases are there, any Iranian attack on Kuwait, Bahrain, the UAE, or Qatar would engage the United States directly, as it would threaten the security of those troops. There are no longer American combat forces in Saudi Arabia, but no one doubts that United States forces would rush to Saudi Arabia's defense were they ever attacked by Iran.

It may well be that Iran's acquisition of a nuclear arsenal would result in further, massive arms sales to the GCC states. These sales would not be a *burden* on the United States, nor would Washington have to impose such sales on unwilling Gulf allies. The U.S. government tries to convince all kinds of countries, and the GCC states in particular, to buy American weapons. Helping American companies sell their wares is something that the U.S. government does all the time, whether it is American cars, corn, computers, or jet fighters. And it is particularly helpful with weapons, because foreign arms sales help drive down the costs when the U.S. military wants to buy those same weapons. Yet in the case of the GCC states, the real impetus does not come from the United States trying to force them to improve their military capabilities by buying our weapons. Exactly the opposite: The GCC states spend lavishly on American weapons to ensure the U.S. commitment to their defense.

That is why the Saudis, Emiratis, Kuwaitis, and Qataris spend tens of billions of dollars on American weapons: not because they really expect to use the weapons themselves, but because these purchases constitute a contribution to the American economy, to the American military-industrial complex, and to every American administration to ensure that we will defend them if they are ever threatened. That's also why these countries buy weapons from France, Britain, and occasionally from Russia. They have even started to eye Chinese kit as well. Having different kinds of equipment from many countries creates logistical nightmares, so efficiency and effectiveness would argue for the opposite. While some have suggested that the Gulf states do it to diversify their sources, the truth is that they are rewarding the United States and its allies (and the other great powers) for having defended them in the past and to ensure that we will continue to do so in the future. The GCC states might go on another arms-buying spree after Iran acquires nuclear weapons, but it will most likely be driven not by an American effort to reassure the Gulf states, but by the Gulf states' desire to guarantee our commitment to their defense.

That said, there are some military systems that the United States would want the GCC to have. In particular, the GCC states need to continue to modernize and integrate their air, air defense, and ballistic missile defense forces to allow them to repel (or help the United States repel) any Iranian attack. The stronger these capabilities are, the less vulnerable the GCC states are, which in turn strengthens America's military advantages over Iran. It is equally important for their own peace of mind and to demonstrate to their domestic constituencies that they are contributing to their own defense—a source of pride for many Gulf populations.

Turkey would fall into a similar situation. Turkey's conventional forces are already more formidable than those of the GCC, and it has the added advantage of the forbidding mountains on its borders with Iran. But Turkey's greatest advantage, its ultimate trump card, is its membership in NATO. Any Iranian attack on Turkey is automatically an attack on the United States and Western Europe, making it highly unlikely Iran would ever attack Turkey. America's real incentive to build up Turkey's military capabilities lies in the potential to involve Turkey more closely in the defense of the Gulf states.[41] Because of Turkey's own relative strength and its NATO membership, involving it more in the defense of the Gulf could be helpful in reassuring the Gulf states. That it is a (Sunni) Muslim state might also make it more palatable. Thus, if Washington could find ways to bring Ankara into Gulf security matters in a constructive way, it might be worthwhile to help Turkey build up the power-projection capabilities to do so.

Finally, there is Israel. Israel does not need American help to defend itself against Iran. It has its own strategic deterrent, the most powerful conventional forces in the region, some of the most formidable ballistic missile defenses anywhere, and it is even building a secure second-strike capability by acquiring a half dozen conventional submarines that can fire nuclear-capable long-range cruise missiles.[42] Of course, Israel does face a broader range of threats—particularly rockets, missiles, and terrorist attacks from Iranian allies (like Hizballah) and proxies (like PIJ). Yet here as well, Israeli conventional air and ground forces, now complemented by the Iron Dome anti-tactical rocket system, as well as Patriot, David's Sling, and Arrow antiballistic missile systems, give Jerusalem everything it would need to deal with these threats. As Israel needs more sophisticated versions of these capabilities to deal with new generations of threats, it will develop them itself or buy them from the United States, as it has for many decades. Instead, what Jerusalem will want from the United States will be increased funding for its armed forces and increased access to American technology to enable it to maintain its current range of advantages over Iran and its partners. That's not nothing, and it could mean a fairly significant increase in aid to Israel, but neither is it a wholesale departure from past U.S. practice or likely to break the bank.

DEFENSE TREATIES. Although the record of formal defense treaties is somewhat mixed, on balance, the history of the Cold War suggests that having a regional military alliance of some kind that includes the United States would be helpful to contain a nuclear Iran. There are several reasons:

- The existence of the NATO and Southeast Asia Treaty Organization (SEATO) treaties provided a legal basis for the deployment of American forces during the Cold War that mitigated the domestic political costs of American unpopularity for the regional states. At various times the United States was unpopular with European publics, but the sanctity of the NATO treaty eliminated any move to evict U.S. forces. In the Gulf, American forces are well tolerated by the GCC states, but if that were to change in the future, having stronger legal cover could be helpful.
- The NATO and SEATO treaties prevented the USSR from creating political rifts between the United States and its regional allies that could have eliminated the American presence from Soviet borders.
- NATO and SEATO provided the countries of Western Europe and East Asia with an excuse, a set of incentives, and political cover to work together and on one another's behalf in ways that might have been difficult otherwise. The core mutual interests expressed in these two treaties bound the states of Western Europe and East Asia together in ways that a series of bilateral treaties with the United States never would have. Especially in the case of the Persian Gulf, where the GCC has often had difficulty practicing cooperative defense planning, such a multilateral treaty could be quite useful.

Of course, the region has already had one such treaty, the 1955 Baghdad Pact/Central Treaty Organization (CENTO), which failed and is largely seen as a symbol of the foolishness of trying to extend such treaty arrangements to the Middle East. While the failure of CENTO should stand as a warning, it should also be remembered that the region is very different from what it was then. The conditions that destroyed CENTO are no longer present.[43] Other impediments remain, however, and thus while desirable, it is far from clear that a new treaty pact for the region is feasible.

It is also not clear that such measures would be necessary for American allies in the Middle East, at least for the specific reasons that they were seen as necessary for Europe and Japan. Turkey is a member of

NATO, so it needs nothing more by way of treaty arrangements with the United States. Israel, Bahrain, and Kuwait (and Jordan and Egypt) are "Major Non-NATO Allies" of the United States, which gives them preferable access to American equipment and other benefits but does not entail any formal defense commitment. Nevertheless, there are American forces already based in most of the GCC states. Given that the United States threatened to employ its nuclear forces to prevent the Soviet Union from intervening against Israel in the 1973 October War, fought Iranian warships to defend Kuwaiti oil tankers in 1987–88, deployed 250,000 troops to defend Saudi Arabia from Iraqi attack in 1990, sent American antiballistic missile batteries to defend Israel against Iraqi missile attack in 1991, committed more than 500,000 troops to liberate Kuwait that same year, and deployed 35,000 troops to Kuwait to prevent another Iraqi invasion in 1994, one could argue that the United States has established a good track record demonstrating that it will defend these countries however it has to do so. Certainly the Iranians do not seem to be under any illusions that the United States won't defend them. In Chubin's words, "As long as there is a sizeable U.S. presence in the Arabian peninsula, any such threats would inevitably involve the United States and its deterrent. The extension of a formal nuclear guarantee to the GCC states beyond this would appear excessive and certainly premature."[44]

THE GREAT UNKNOWNS. Deterrence is an exercise in political psychology. It is about convincing one's adversary not to try something, because it will fail or will result in greater pain than any gain it might produce. Extended deterrence is even more complicated, a bank-shot version of the same. It involves not only deterring a potential aggressor, but convincing the possible target state that they do not have to fear the aggressor. As one perceptive scholarly work on extended deterrence put it, reassurance is "in the eye of the beholder."[45] The only way that the United States can prevent the GCC states from bandwagoning with Iran, or (more likely) from balancing against Tehran in aggressive ways that could start wars or by acquiring nuclear arsenals of their own, is to convince these states that they can count on the United States to protect them no matter what.

Although the United States will be far better positioned to do so for the GCC states (and Israel and Turkey and others) against a nuclear Iran than we were for Western Europe and Japan in the face of the Soviet threat, there are no guarantees. Former British defense minister Dennis Healey once famously observed that it often takes more to reassure allies than it does to deter an adversary.[46] We cannot know what it will take to reassure our Gulf allies. All of the points above *should* be enough. Yet they may not.

Perhaps just at first, to get them over that shock or to reassure their publics that nothing has particularly changed and they are not now threatened in a way that they previously weren't, the United States may have to do a number of things that have no particular military value but are critical to psychological reassurance. In 1991, during the Persian Gulf War, Saddam began firing modified Scud missiles at Israel. The missiles were militarily irrelevant and ended up causing few casualties, but their psychological (and economic) impact on the Israeli people was far-reaching. General Norman Schwarzkopf, the commander of coalition forces, planned to do almost nothing to try to stop the launches because they were militarily irrelevant. But the Israeli government put tremendous pressure on President Bush to stop them. Ultimately, Schwarzkopf had to divert more than a thousand aircraft sorties and even insert special operations forces into western Iraq to try to stop the Scud launches—which they effectively did, even though we never destroyed a single Scud launcher. Schwarzkopf was right that the Scud attacks on Israel were militarily irrelevant, yet he was foolish to insist that therefore they could be ignored.

In similar fashion, there is no military or strategic reason that the United States would need to deploy more conventional forces or tactical nuclear forces to the region, try to build up GCC military capabilities to match Iran's, or even sign mutual defense pacts with any of the countries of the region to better deter a nuclear Iran. Yet the United States may be compelled to do so anyway, or at least forced to consider it, because of the fears of our allies in the region and the need to reassure them. A better way to reassure them would be to convince them that the forces we have in place are more than adequate to block any Iranian conventional move, that our nuclear forces so outmatch Iran's that we have escalation dominance over them, that the presence of American forces in many of those countries and our history of defending them demonstrates our commitments to their security, and therefore, only if Iran's leaders were truly insane would they believe that it would be worthwhile to try to attack America's regional allies.

Hopefully, all of that would be enough. But it may not be. If not, the United States would be advised to look into one or more of these steps. Building up the GCC militaries and increasing our own conventional forces in the region would be the preferable ways to help reassure skittish regional populations, because these represent mere augmentations of existing conditions. Signing defense pacts, let alone deploying tactical nuclear weapons, would mean introducing new dynamics into the region that could have unexpected consequences. Moreover, an increasingly isolationist Congress might reject the treaties, and international opinion (including Arab public opinion) would probably reject the tactical nuclear weapons.

The Costs of Containment

Containment would not be a cost-free policy, although its costs are nowhere near as significant as its risks. One of the attractive aspects of containment is that it would be comparatively low-cost, which is an important selling point for at least some of its supporters. Many of containment's detractors have argued that its costs could be high in terms of financial costs, opportunity costs, and political costs, but I find these arguments to be overstated.

BUILDING UP AMERICAN CONVENTIONAL MILITARY FORCES IN THE GULF. American conventional forces in the region, especially when considered alongside the forces that the United States can move there quickly, are more than adequate to defeat any Iranian conventional move against the GCC. Neither Israel nor Turkey needs American assistance to deal with a conventional threat from Iran. Our starting assumption should be that our forces in the region will not have to be augmented. There is absolutely no military reason that they need to be.

To reassure our regional allies, the United States may feel the need to augment its forces in the Gulf anyway. This gesture would be purely psychological, so there is no reason that it would need to be big. A third combat air wing, a third Army brigade set, or some additional surface naval vessels—all played up through a public diplomacy campaign that stressed the superiority of American forces over Iran's military—should be more than enough to check this box. Moreover, although the actual numbers are kept under tight wraps, the GCC countries pay much of the costs for the American forces stationed in the region. The United States still pays for salaries, benefits, training, and all of the other normal costs for the personnel and their equipment, but the host countries pay for the bases, their upkeep, and for part or all of the provisions. Consequently, it is sometimes cheaper to have these units based in the GCC than on bases in the United States.

It is a canard to posit that defending the Persian Gulf requires us to sustain forces we would not otherwise have, and therefore imposes an unnecessary cost. The assets the United States maintains in the Gulf region are a fraction of our overall force structure. There is no reason to believe that if the Persian Gulf did not exist we would not have all of these forces in our order of battle and so might save the cost of maintaining them.[47] The United States Navy has ten aircraft carriers and there is nothing to suggest that if there were no requirement to defend the Persian Gulf, the United States would have fewer. The desire to have ten carriers stems principally from a desire to maintain a certain overall force structure for use in an emergency anywhere in the globe, rather than from a strict calculation of the needs of securing different regions. The Air Force keeps five of its fifty-seven wings in the Gulf, but only two of these are combat wings and each typically has only a single squadron on hand. The Army and Marines don't have any formations permanently based in the Gulf, just equipment sets, which cost far, far less than fully manned formations. It is true that the Navy maintains at least one carrier in the Gulf region at all times, but having ten carriers allows the United States to have three on station at all times, and it is important for the readiness of those carriers as well as the security of the United States that we maintain carriers deployed on station at all times. As Henry Kissinger once famously remarked, at the start of any crisis the first question he invariably asked the NSC staff was, "where are the carriers."[48] Given that the United States is going to have three carriers on station at all times for the foreseeable future, is there another region somewhere in the world that would benefit from having a carrier on station more than the Persian Gulf? Typically, the other two carriers are in East Asia, the Indian Ocean, or the Mediterranean. Do we desperately need a carrier in the Caribbean? The South Pacific? Even absent the threat of a nuclear Iran, chances are that we would want one of those carriers in or near the Persian Gulf.

Along these same lines, it is important to recognize that there just aren't opportunity costs involved in keeping so modest a force in the Gulf region on a regular basis. That remains true even if the United States decided to augment our forces there slightly to reassure nervous GCC populations. There is no other part of the world being deprived of American military power because of the needs of the Gulf. That statement was not true back when the United States had 160,000 troops in Iraq and another 20,000–30,000 elsewhere in the Gulf. To the extent that another part of the globe is being deprived of military force because of the needs of an ongoing war, that war is in Afghanistan—not part of the Gulf and not a country that the United States would be expected to defend against an Iranian attack. With the war in Afghanistan winding down, even that requirement is disappearing. The bottom line is that our forces in the Gulf are more than adequate to deter or defeat any Iranian conventional move but are not anywhere near big enough as a proportion of the overall American force structure to impinge on the needs of other theaters, nor is it likely that we would disband those forces if there were no requirement to defend the Gulf.

Finally, it is important not to overstate the political problems our forces cause for the Gulf states. At times, the presence of American forces has caused domestic unhappiness in some Arab countries. We should not be blasé about this problem. It does exist. But at present levels, the forces we have in place are not creating any problems. Even if we have to augment the current force structure modestly to reassure our regional allies, there is no reason to believe that that increase would upset the status quo. That could change, and the United States should be leery of engaging in a massive force buildup in the region or positioning troops in countries where the public seems poised to reject them, but there is nothing about Iran's acquisition of a nuclear arsenal that suggests that either of those changes would be necessary.

In short, we should set aside the fear that a nuclear Iran would require a massive and costly American conventional buildup in the Gulf, and that this would draw desperately needed forces away from other, more important theaters. Exactly the opposite is the case: we have more than enough forces in the Gulf, those forces are small and quite cheap, the Gulf region is fragile enough and important enough that we would likely maintain similar-size forces in place regardless of Iran's nuclear program, these U.S. forces are not creating problems for the countries hosting them, and they are not keeping us from deploying forces we would like to in other parts of the world.

A GCC MILITARY BUILDUP. As with a conventional American military buildup in the Gulf, a military buildup by the GCC would be unnecessary, and in this case it would probably *benefit* the United States economically since the GCC states would probably be buying from American companies.

One concern with such sales is always that it could compromise Israel's qualitative edge over the Arabs. Maintaining Israel's qualitative edge over the Arab states, its ability to fight and win a war against any combination of Arab adversaries, is important to Israel and important to U.S. interests. Washington has formally committed itself to maintaining this edge as part of its wider commitment to the security of the state of Israel.[49]

If the GCC states were to build up their military strength, the United States would focus them on defensive systems: antiballistic missile, anti-aircraft, anti-mining, and anti-amphibious assault capabilities. There would be no need for them to acquire power-projection capabilities (which would be most dangerous to Israel) to deal with the threats from a nuclear Iran. The United States has an excellent track record of de-conflicting GCC defense requirements with the need to preserve Israel's qualitative military edge. Despite decades of American arms sales to the Arab states, Israeli forces hold a greater advantage over the Arab militaries today than they have at any time in their history.[50]

THE REAL MILITARY COSTS. Nevertheless, there may be real military costs associated with containment. The first of these is the possible need for revamped American nuclear forces and the certain requirement to continue to expand ballistic missile defenses. The best way for the United States to reassure its regional allies and maintain both deterrence and effective extended deterrence of Iran will be to retain escalation dominance. At some point in the future, that could require a more so-phisticated and flexible nuclear force than we currently possess. It is yet another paradox of this problem, but it is a commonplace in the world of nuclear strategy that the best way to ensure that we do not have to engage in a nuclear war with Iran is to ensure that we are ready to win it—and win it in a meaningful sense, or at least in a sense that the Iranians will recognize.

This need for more sophisticated nuclear capabilities, not a massive conventional military buildup in the Gulf, could be the principal military cost of going with containment to the extent that there is one.

Several qualifiers are in order. First, the United States is already in the process of deploying an array of ballistic missile defenses in the United States and the Middle East to protect these areas from an Iranian missile attack. The cost of these systems has already been included in U.S. defense spending projections and so they would not constitute an additional cost of containment.[51] Perhaps the only missing piece is a ground-based mid-course defense system for the Middle East similar to that being built for the continental United States and proposed for Europe—both of which are intended to defend those regions from attack by Iranian medium-range ballistic missiles (MRBMs) and future ICBMs. Adding a ground-based mid-course defense system to the defenses already being built for the Middle East would cost something on the order of $9–14 billion over a period of twenty years.[52] Even then, it is likely that the Gulf states could be expected to pay much of these costs if we jointly agreed to deploy it.

Second, developing the offensive capability to threaten Iran's nuclear forces with sophisticated nuclear forces could be helpful, but it isn't necessarily critical to contain a nuclear Iran. American nuclear forces already possess considerable flexibility, accuracy, and numbers such that we have escalation dominance and will possess it for as long as can be imagined. The United States also possesses a range of highly capable and flexible conventional capabilities that could be expected to do the job, in some ways better than nuclear forces and in other ways not quite as effectively. Developing more flexible nuclear forces would enhance America's overall superiority. Moreover, there is an argument to be made that the United States should undertake such a modernization of its nuclear forces for reasons beyond Iran, having much more to do with China, North Korea, and other threats.[53] Thus the cost of such a modernization program cannot be laid entirely at the doorstep of containing a nuclear Iran. Nevertheless, it is a potential cost. And the more certain that the United States wants to be that containment will succeed, the more that Washington seeks to minimize the risks of containment, the more important it would be to pay these costs.

Another cost associated with containment would be a further increase in the intelligence network to monitor Iranian activities. Nuclear platforms such as ballistic and cruise missiles tend to be relatively small and frequently mobile, and they often do not have much of a "signature" for intelligence collectors to pick up on, necessitating a greater system to detect and track them than bigger, more obvious targets like air bases and armored divisions. The United States would want extensive coverage of large swaths of Iran, with the ability to read out information in real time if necessary—especially if the United States hopes to preserve the option of striking Iran's nuclear forces to knock them out before they could be used. That surveillance will require lots of satellite coverage, lots of drones, lots of signals interception collectors, lots of computers to process the information, and lots of analysts to make sense of it.

That said, since 2002 (and arguably for many years before that) the United States has been building up its capabilities to collect on Iran, the Iranian Armed Forces, and the Iranian nuclear program.[54] It is not clear how much more would have to be done to build on the already extensive intelligence collection architecture now in place, but without access to the classified figures we should not assume it would be cheap.

Another military-related cost of containment would be the potential need to increase U.S. aid to Israel. Since the 1970s, Israel has been one of the top recipients of American aid every year, and it has frequently been the single largest recipient.[55] From 2013 to 2018, Israel is set to receive more than $3.1 billion annually in American aid, although 74 percent of that money must be spent buying American weapons and equipment so that the aid is seen by many as a subsidy to American industry as well.[56] The United States has already provided extensive financial and technological assistance to Israel for the kinds of systems that Jerusalem would want for dealing with the increased threat environment that it would face from a nuclear Iran, but it seems unimaginable that Israel would not look for additional help in these areas.[57]

THE OIL PREMIUM. If Iran acquires a nuclear arsenal, the Middle East will be a more tense and dangerous place. There is little reason to believe that Iran will become more restrained and good reason to fear that it will become less so.

Terrorist attacks, nuclear crises, and general instability are exactly the kind of stuff that spooks the international oil market.[58] Oil is highly responsive to geopolitical problems, especially in the Persian Gulf, both because of its structural instability and the enormous quantities of oil it still produces. As of 2013, roughly 20 percent of all of the world's oil exports passed through the Strait of Hormuz on a daily basis. There is little spare oil production capacity in the world, which simply heightens the jitters of the international oil market. Worse still, the majority of that spare production is concentrated in the Gulf states, overwhelmingly in Saudi Arabia.[59]

Anything that seems to threaten that flow—whether it might affect production or export—has an impact on the price of oil. It is what energy analysts call the "risk premium" of oil. The greater the risk of a disruption, the more it drives up the price of oil. That fear, and the price increase it causes, can persist (albeit at reduced levels) for years or decades. As long as people fear that there might be a significant loss in production or exports, the price will stay higher than it otherwise might. And if there is an actual cut in supply, the price will spike, at least until the supply is restored or it becomes clear that the cut is not as bad as originally feared.

It is hard to imagine that Iran's acquisition of a nuclear arsenal will *not* affect the price of oil. Unless Iran unexpectedly becomes entirely peaceful, people will rightly fear both more frequent problems in the region and the potential for those problems to get worse than they have been in the past. Especially early on, when there will be the greatest uncertainty about how the geopolitics will all play out, the oil traders (who tend to exaggerate risks in the face of uncertainty for various reasons) will assume it and the price of oil will rise accordingly.

Unfortunately, we do not have good estimates of how much a nuclear Iran might add to the existing oil risk premium or what kind of price spikes we might expect. Little work has been done on this question, and what has been done has some big problems associated with it (for those interested, see the lengthy endnote for this sentence).[60] In truth it is hard to make accurate predictions regarding the impact on oil prices, as they depend on when Iran crosses the nuclear threshold and general geopolitics at that time. A vast range of global political, economic, and security factors, ranging from the state of the Chinese economy to the political situation in Saudi Arabia to the status of the U.S. defense budget, will all affect the dynamics of that future oil market in addition to how Iran behaves, potentially creating significant deviations from any straight-line estimate of current conditions.

Nevertheless, history can provide some benchmarks. In January 2012, when the Iranians warned the United States not to return an aircraft carrier to the Persian Gulf, oil prices briefly jumped by $5–$10 (5–10 percent) per barrel.[61] The 2006 Lebanon War caused a $4 or about 3.5 percent increase in the price of oil.[62] Bigger wars in the Persian Gulf itself have had a considerably greater impact on oil prices: the Persian Gulf War of 1990–91 caused oil prices to jump by 93 percent for several weeks. However, the oil market only saw a 28 percent increase in the price of crude in response to the 2003 invasion of Iraq, which was coupled with a major strike in Venezuela. The Venezuelan strike accounted for an equal amount of oil taken off the market as the invasion. Consequently it is probably more accurate to say that the invasion of Iraq produced a 14–15 percent increase in the price of oil.[63] The decline in the severity of the price shocks over time are a product of any number of factors related to global economic performance and the changing structure of the global energy market, but they also reflect both the market learning from previous crises and the deliberate efforts of various governments to address oil market jitters. Most oil analysts seem to believe that the general instability of the Middle East has already added a risk premium of anywhere from $5–$25 to the price of a barrel of crude.[64]

If all that a nuclear Iran's behavior produces is more events like Israel's 2006 war with Hizballah, there will be an impact, but it won't be meaningful—and could be drowned out by a thousand other factors influencing the oil market. Even if this increase became a more or less permanent oil risk premium, it would have a negligible impact on the U.S. economy. On the other hand, if a nuclear Iran means larger wars—or a persistent fear of a larger war—this could have a considerably greater impact on oil prices. Most likely this would be on the scale of the impact of the 2003 invasion of Iraq (so about 15 percent), which would be painful but not catastrophic. However, if the fear of such wars caused the oil risk premium to climb instead to the level of the impact of the 1990–91 Persian Gulf War (a doubling of oil prices in essence) and remain there in perpetuity, this jump would have a pronounced economic impact, including a statistically significant impact on growth, inflation, unemployment, and other measures of economic performance. It seems unlikely that oil prices would climb to this extent, but it is not out of the question and that is among the risks of containment.[65]

There is also the improbable but not impossible likelihood that a crisis with a nuclear Iran gets out of hand and produces a war that results in a significant disruption of oil exports from the Persian Gulf. In that case, all bets are off. Because of the world oil market's dependence on Persian Gulf oil (which will remain for decades to come, regardless of how much oil the United States itself produces), such a disruption could cause catastrophic damage to the global and U.S. economies, including a major recession. By way of comparison, the 1973 Arab oil embargo resulted from a reduction of just 2.75 percent of global oil production. The 1979 Iranian Revolution pulled 5.68 percent of global production off the market.[66] Yet these relatively mild oil price shocks were responsible for the worst recessions in U.S. history between the Great Depression and the 2008 recession.[67] Saudi Arabia accounts for about 10 percent of annual oil production alone, while all of the oil that flows through the Strait of Hormuz constitutes almost 20 percent of global consumption.

As difficult as it is to come up with even rough estimates of how a nuclear Iran could affect the price of oil, these various points concerning the risks related to oil should make us recognize several critical issues. First, Iran's acquisition of a nuclear arsenal is more problematic for the United States than, say, North Korea's extant nuclear arsenal, not because the Iranians are more likely to use nuclear weapons or even because they are more likely to take greater and more frequent risks than the North

Koreans, but because there is the potential for Iranian actions to affect the price of oil, which in turn affects the U.S. economy and that of every other country on earth.

Second, economic considerations reinforce the importance of the first crises with Iran after it crosses the nuclear threshold because the oil traders will take their cues from those events. An Iran with nuclear weapons will mean the introduction of a significant unknown into the calculus of the international oil market. At least initially, that market is likely to react (or overreact) to any development related to Iran that might affect oil flows. The outcome of those early events will become important in conditioning the market's behavior over time. If the oil market sees the United States intervene in crises with a nuclear Iran, sees those crises resolved without any impact on actual oil flows, and sees those crises as having diminished Iran's ability or willingness to cause problems in the future, over time the market will adjust. Future crises will cause less of a price spike and overall, the oil risk premium will decline.

The opposite is also true: if oil traders do not see the United States defusing crises and preventing Iran from creating greater problems, if there are disruptions of the oil supply, and if the crises end with Iran emboldened and other countries fearful—even destabilized—let alone if the crises lead to wars, the oil markets will become more volatile. Traders will fear that every next crisis will be worse than the last, leading to more frequent and much higher price spikes. An oscillating oil market would be terrible for the U.S. and global economies.

Prudence would counsel that the United States, the GCC states, and other major oil consumers take actions now to diminish the impact of a potential nuclear Iran on oil prices. As any number of astute analysts have pointed out, even if we do not want to contain a nuclear Iran, there is a high risk that we still will have to do so anyway.[68] And there are a number of things that we could do. Several respected oil experts, including Gal Luft of the Institute for the Analysis of Global Security and Robert McNally of the Rapidan Group, have argued for expanding the capacity to move oil by pipeline across the Arabian Peninsula (and so avoid the Strait of Hormuz).[69] McNally has advocated a number of other smart, sensible steps, including increasing the size of strategic petroleum reserves held by governments; increasing commercial stockpiles of oil, especially outside of the Gulf countries themselves; and creating a crisis coordinating entity that would include both China and the United States and could develop strategy to handle any such disruptions.[70] Indeed, because China shares our interest in the stability of Persian Gulf oil exports, making Beijing a partner on this matter could prove invaluable should such a crisis ever occur.[71]

Iran over the Long Term: Succession and Regime Collapse

Another problem with nuclear weapons is that they have no expiration date. Countries that develop nuclear weapons tend to hang on to them. The situation is not hopeless: four countries have given up nuclear weapons after they acquired them. Given that there are only nine countries today believed to have nuclear weapons, that's not a terrible ratio. However, all four of the countries that did give up a nuclear arsenal (South Africa, Belarus, Ukraine, and Kazakhstan) did so only after a revolutionary change in the nature of their governments.

If Iran acquires nuclear weapons, it is likely to have them for some time, at least until the fall of the regime. That should give us an added incentive to try to speed the end of the regime if it does acquire nuclear weapons, but it gives us a lot to think about, and worry over, until then.

SUCCESSION. If Iran acquires nuclear weapons, it will likely possess them under Khamene'i's successor as Supreme Leader and the de facto autocrat of Iran. We have no clue who might succeed Khamene'i, and in truth the Iranians don't, either. There are many possible candidates. Some of them are partisans of one camp or another, others grand old men of the revolution or noncontroversial nonentities. Although perhaps unlikely, it is not impossible that the Iranians might even decide not to decide and instead appoint a council to wield the powers of the Rahbar.

The recent spectacle of former president Ahmadinejad brawling with the Larijani brothers (who head the judiciary and legislature) makes for jaw-dropping political theater, and may have been every bit as ferocious (perhaps even more so because it *is* personal) as the battles in the days when Khatami's reformists squared off against the regime establishment. These deep rifts within the hardline ranks could produce a stalemate and the decision to go with a noncontroversial arrangement that would not threaten any of the hardline factions.

Such a successor would still probably lean hardline, and would be influenced by the Revolutionary Guard and other powerful hardline-controlled institutions, like the Guardian Council. However, chances are they would behave like Khamene'i, especially Khamene'i early in his career, and would work to preserve the status quo, avoid making big decisions, and eschew dramatic moves for smaller, safer, incremental changes. If Khamene'i died before Iran acquired a nuclear weapon or even decided to go ahead and weaponize, there is a reasonable chance that such a successor would stick with the status quo and would sit on a breakout capability rather than taking the dramatic step to deploy an arsenal. If Iran already possessed an arsenal, or Khamene'i had taken the fateful step of ordering weaponization before his death, such successors would still probably behave in a prudent, cautious manner and would try to avoid moments of high drama.

Although it may seem less likely, it is not impossible that a partisan from one camp or another will win out and take power after Khamene'i. At this moment in history, it seems highly likely that if one of Iran's competing factions were to win outright and pick one of its favorite sons for the Supreme Leader's position, it is likely to be Iran's hardliners—or more specifically, one of the hardline factions. If that is the case, we could get a very aggressive Iranian leader who would order full speed ahead for weaponization, if Khamene'i has not crossed that Rubicon, and who might order greatly stepped-up support for subversion, terrorism, and unconventional warfare if he has. Such a leader might be more likely to take risks, like Khrushchev if not like Saddam, and these risks could produce more and worse crises.[72]

In that less likely but far from impossible scenario, there would still be steps the United States could take to influence Iranian behavior, but not a whole lot. In particular, the United States and its allies would have to find ways to try to educate this new kind of Iranian leader regarding the dangers of aggressive behavior in the nuclear world. We would need to find ways to communicate with him, perhaps in moments less fraught than the Cuban Missile Crisis or the Kargil War. We would also have to find ways to make clear to him our determination to defend our allies in the region and vouchsafe our red lines, perhaps by deploying some additional conventional forces to the Gulf or signing new defense pacts. It is not impossible: Khrushchev himself learned from his mistakes, although the Politburo still decided to remove him because of his foolish risk-taking. In Iran, we may not be so lucky, and if that is the case, we may have few other options than to prepare for the inevitable crises as best we can, do everything we can to ensure that those crises turn out as we hope, and push for regime change as best we are able. This too is one of the risks of containment.

WHEN THE DOG CATCHES THE CAR. What happens when the Islamic Republic does fall? Fall it will, someday, and hopefully soon. We may desire it to happen, but we may not be ready for it when it does.

The structural flaws of the Islamic Republic are deep and pronounced, and while the regime could continue to creak along for several more decades like Cuba and North Korea, it could also collapse within the next few years. As a result of 2009, both the internal purges within the ranks of the regime and the open splits that have now emerged between the regime and large chunks of the Iranian populace, the Islamic Republic has been delegitimized and is starting to hollow out.

If the Islamic Republic possesses a nuclear arsenal at the time of its demise, things could get ugly. Ideally, the end of the regime would come at the hands of a new, popular government and would take place with minimal violence, like the "color" revolutions of Eastern Europe. It's worth pointing out that there are lots of cases of nasty autocracies being replaced by more liberal (even democratic) successors without much violence—from Milosevic to Ceauşescu to Pinochet, from post-Franco Spain to post-Machel Mozambique to post–Chun Doo-Hwan South Korea. We can now add Ben Ali and Mubarak to the long list of autocrats who stepped down after limited bloodshed. That a smooth, peaceful transition to a new government is quite possible, perhaps even probable, should be a cause for optimism. As noted above, a number of new governments have given up nuclear arsenals acquired by their autocratic predecessors. Moreover, there is every reason to expect that a new Iranian government would want a better relationship with the United States, the West, and the international community—and would be willing to compromise on its nuclear program to get it.

Nevertheless, there is no guarantee that Iran would undergo such a smooth transition. It could go terribly wrong. The regime could collapse without an obvious successor. Various ethnic groups and parts of the country might declare independence or make bids for power. Different political leaders might try to mobilize support for themselves, which could turn into street battles. Indeed, there is some potential for the country to dissolve into anarchy and chaos altogether, like contemporary Somalia, or Afghanistan after the Soviet withdrawal in 1989. Iran does have a strong political culture, important institutions of civil society, and a nationalist tradition stretching back millennia, all of which will provide some security against outright collapse, but the worst case is still possible.

In that event, what will become of Iran's nuclear weapons?[73] Will they be used by the dying embers of the regime in a last-ditch effort to stave off defeat? If so, would they be launched at internal foes or external ones—like Israel—in a desperate bid to rally the populace around a common, external enemy? Will they find their way into the hands of terrorists, perhaps even transferred by the shreds of the Revolutionary Guard in the hope that they can at least gain some revenge against the Israelis, the Americans, the Saudis, or whoever else they might blame for the fall of their regime? Will they be captured by various internal factions and warring militias to be used in an internal struggle for control of Iran?

It all may sound far-fetched, and it probably is very low probability. But when the regime falls, these scenarios will become significant concerns. And there won't be a whole lot that the United States can do about it. We have the exact same fears about the demise of Pakistan and North Korea. Pakistan is already something of a failing state, gripped by terrorism and factionalism. Many worry that it could fall soon, and with al-Qa'ida, Lashkar-e Taiba, the Taliban, and a potpourri of other vicious terrorist groups already infesting the country, there is real reason to fear that its fall will spread nuclear weapons to the worst groups imaginable.[74] The U.S. military reportedly has plans to descend on Pakistan as it collapses and whisk away its nukes, but no one is confident that such an operation would work, and certainly not that it would get every one of Pakistan's purported one hundred nuclear weapons.[75] North Korea is surreal, a starving "hermit kingdom" with numberless artillery tubes and a nuclear arsenal. It could implode tomorrow or last forever and no one would ever be able to say why, and this uncertainty also must make us wonder what would happen to their nuclear weapons when the end comes. Would we even know when it is falling, to be able to try to go in and secure its nukes? Could we be sure that the regime would not launch them as its final act, for reasons that none of us could fathom? Thus, Iran might be in good company, but it is a bad lot. And that too is a risk of containment.

13

Making Containment Work

Many Americans think containment is a defensive strategy. That is understandable, but incorrect. Although one aspect of containment's purpose is the defensive aim of preventing the target country from expanding its power beyond its borders, the other is the offensive one of seeing a change of regime in the target country at some point in time. Even within the defensive piece of containment strategy, however, there can and should be offensive tactics. None of the many containment strategies that the United States has employed since the Second World War has been wholly defensive, although some have been more so than others.

The archetypal American containment experience was, of course, the forty-six-year containment of the Soviet Union. This was the challenge for which George Kennan formulated the strategy, and many others, most notably Dean Acheson, Paul Nitze, Henry Kissinger, and Ronald Reagan, added important features. Nevertheless, as the great historian of the Cold War John Lewis Gaddis details in his seminal work *Strategies of Containment*, at various points during the Cold War the United States employed different variations on the general theme of containment, some of which were more defensive in nature and others more offensive.

During the 1970s era of détente, American policy was more focused on shoring up the defensive aspects of containment, whereas during the 1980s (partly in response to the tenor of American strategy in the prior decade) the United States focused more on the offensive aspects of containment. On the defensive side, the tactics consisted of nuclear deterrence itself, the conventional military preparations to block a Soviet invasion of either Europe or northeast Asia, information operations and covert programs to prevent the Soviets from subverting key Western countries, and the widespread effort to shore up governments friendly to the West (some of them unsavory) throughout the Third World. The offensive side of the containment of the USSR featured information operations to boost Eastern European unhappiness with the Soviet empire, economic sanctions to hinder Soviet growth and technological development, diplomatic moves to increase the number of threats that the USSR faced, and a widespread effort to undermine Soviet allies and client states in the Third World through both military and nonmilitary means.

America's containment campaigns against other countries featured some applications of the basic strategy that were more defensive in nature, and others more offensive. Our containment strategies toward North Korea after 1953 and Cuba after 1962 were more defense-oriented even than our approach to the Soviet Union itself. We put comprehensive sanctions in place against both, isolated them diplomatically as best we could, pushed back hard on Cuba's allies in Latin America, and ensured that North Korea could not overrun the South, but otherwise left them alone. In contrast, America's containment of the Sandinistas' Nicaragua and Saddam's Iraq entailed enormous pressure on both regimes. Against Nicaragua, the United States supported an insurgency effectively and overtly and considered direct military moves like mining its harbors. Against Iraq, the United States imposed comprehensive economic sanctions, an aggressive covert action program to overthrow Saddam, backed various opposition groups waging irregular wars against his regime, and mounted periodic air campaigns, rising to strikes on a near-daily basis after 1998. Indeed, America's containment of Iraq was far, far more aggressive than any other containment regime. It was one containment regime where the emphasis was much more on speeding the collapse of the regime than it was on preventing the regime from expanding its power beyond its borders—although the United States expended considerable energy and resources doing that as well. Our containment of Libya, Syria, Vietnam for several decades after 1975, and China in the 1950s and '60s fell somewhere between these extremes.

So too has America's containment of Iran oscillated between a more defensive and a more offensive focus. In truth, Washington tended to take its lead from Tehran in this matter. Since the Iranian Revolution, U.S. policymakers have mostly regarded Iran as an unnecessary headache and have tried to have as little to do with it as they could. That was why the Reagan administration was so reticent to get into a fight with the Iranian military in the Persian Gulf, why Clinton explicitly chose to contain Iran passively compared to its aggressive containment of Iraq, and why Bush 43 went after Iraq and Afghanistan but could barely formulate a policy toward Iran. Iran has often been put in the "too hard" category of American foreign policy. In so doing, we have ceded the initiative to the Iranians.

If the United States continues to pursue containment toward a future nuclear Iran, we will have to continue to employ both offensive and defensive aspects of containment, and at times may need to focus more on the offensive aspects and other times concentrate primarily on its defensive features. However, what must change is our tendency to cede the initiative to the Iranians and react to their behavior. This is important because a nuclear Iran will present greater threats and challenges to the region than in the past, and the United States will need to regularly gauge whether it is better for our own interests and those of our allies to take a more defensive or a more offensive posture toward Iran. Some of that will be based on opportunities—opportunities to push for regime change as well as opportunities to shore up various defenses. Yet another part should be designed to shape Iran's behavior as best we can to help minimize the inherent problems of containment: the potential for expanded Iranian subversion and irregular warfare, the potential for more crises with Iran, and the potential for proliferation in particular.

Figure 1: The Dangers of a Nuclearizing Iran

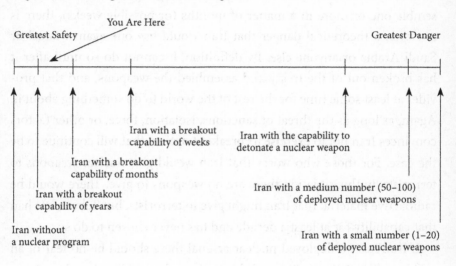

Breakout Capability Versus Arsenal

There are many reasons for Washington to continuously reassess and recalibrate the offensive and defensive aspects of its containment of Iran. However, one of the most important is the need to dissuade Iran from fielding an actual nuclear arsenal even after it achieves the capability to do so quickly. In the end, containment might mean containing a nuclear Iran, even one with an actual nuclear arsenal. While that may prove necessary, it would be undesirable. It would be far safer and easier instead to contain Iran if it were limited to a theoretical breakout capability, even a relatively narrow one. The difference in the dangers posed by an Iran with a breakout capacity of even a month or two and an Iran with a deployed nuclear arsenal is greater than the difference between Iran without a breakout capability at all and Iran with a breakout capacity.[1] It is also another reason why containment cannot become mere appeasement—allowing Iran to build and do whatever it wants as long as it does not employ nuclear weapons.

If Iran has only a breakout capability, all of the problems of containment discussed in the previous chapter vanish. Think about it: As long as Iran does not have actual weapons and only a potential ability to assemble one or more in a matter of months (or possibly weeks), there is not even a theoretical danger that Iran would use one against Israel or Saudi Arabia or anyone else. By definition, it cannot do so until after it has broken out of the treaty and assembled the weapons, and that provides at least some time for the rest of the world to do something about it. Again, as long as the threat of sanctions, isolation, force, or other factors convinces Iran not to exercise its breakout option, that will continue to be the case. For those who worry that Iran would give nuclear weapons to terrorists, in this situation there are no weapons to give. There would be radioactive material that Iran might give to terrorists, but Tehran has had that capability for at least a decade and has never chosen to do so.

If Iran has no deployed nuclear arsenal there should be no fear of an accidental launch or accidental detonation of one. Likewise, there is no danger of a bureaucratic or operational mistake—or someone exceeding orders or authority—during a nuclear alert in the midst of a nuclear crisis. Indeed, if Iran has never tested an actual weapon, it would probably be far more wary of getting into any situation in which it might feel the need to use one quickly for fear that the design will prove faulty.

If Iran did not have the capacity to threaten with its nuclear arsenal—either directly or as the ultimate force behind its unconventional warfare operations—there would be even less reason to fear other Middle Eastern states bandwagoning with it. As we have seen with Japan, South Korea, and Taiwan, all of whom have breakout capabilities, a theoretical capacity to build a nuclear arsenal does not endow countries with the kind of awe, fear, and prestige that sway people's thinking. Likewise, India's standing before 1998 suggests that even a demonstrated capability to produce and detonate a nuclear weapon does not bring anything like the same political-psychological benefits as possession of an actual arsenal.

The proliferation problem declines precipitously if Iran can be convinced not to weaponize. First, if Iran has only a theoretical capability and not a deployed arsenal, other countries will feel much less of a need to have their own arsenal. To the extent that they feel those pressures, they might only look to develop a theoretical capability. Japan's development of a theoretical breakout capability did not goad anyone to do the same—although China's actual arsenal spurred India's program and India's did the same for Pakistan (which got help from China). Moreover, the fact that Iran will have chosen not to cross that last threshold will help reinforce the disincentives that have kept other countries from doing so. If a regime as callous and willing to accept costs as Iran chose not to pay such a price, then why should other countries who value the prosperity of their citizens far more?

If Iran were to stick with a breakout capability rather than fielding an actual arsenal, it would also tell us some important things about Tehran's thinking. It would indicate that Iran's goal was only to acquire the capability to deter attack on Iran itself, since that is all that such a breakout capability is good for. Yes, anyone can devise convoluted scenarios whereby the Iranians do things and sequence events in ways that allow them to surprise everyone with a weapon at the right moment, but in the real world such schemes are bureaucratically, operationally, and technically implausible. We would not know if that had always been Tehran's aim, or they were convinced to fall back to such a minimal deterrent option by the pressure they faced, but we could assume that at that time, a minimal deterrent for homeland defense was all they wanted.

Whatever Iranian intentions were when they first set out down the nuclear path, if they stop with a breakout capability it also suggests that something stopped them—sanctions, international isolation, the threat of a military strike, or something else. We would not know which, but we could assume that it was one or some combination of them. Even if Iran had never wanted anything other than the capability to defend itself against attack, there would be no reason to stop with a breakout capability if there were no cost to proceeding to an actual arsenal. Taiwan, South Korea, Argentina, and other countries that have stopped with what amounts to a breakout capability all did so because of the price to be paid by going further. If Iran were not concerned about that price, why stop? This would demonstrate that the Iranian regime actually was sensitive to some degree of external resistance, which should give us confidence that Tehran would only move to full weaponization if they had reason to believe that the externally imposed cost no longer applied, or if the regime had a newly compelling reason to weaponize that suddenly made it willing to absorb that cost in a way that it wasn't in the past.

CRISIS MANAGEMENT AND A NONWEAPONIZED IRAN. The problem of crisis management also becomes far, far easier if Iran has only a theoretical breakout capacity rather than a deployed arsenal. In any situation where Iran is not the instigator of the problem and it has not specifically chosen beforehand to use the crisis to transition from a breakout capability to an actual arsenal, its latent nuclear capability becomes irrelevant. As it would take Iran weeks or months to assemble a nuclear weapon, that capability would not be germane to the crisis at hand. Iran would not be able to threaten anyone with its nuclear forces because it won't have any. It can't even threaten uncontrollable escalation because it would not be able to escalate to the nuclear level. The dangerous and perplexing problems of nuclear crisis management would not be present. Which also means that both before and after crises, the two sides would not have to go through the expensive and destabilizing rigmarole of preparing for a potential nuclear crisis, with all of its attendant risks, complexities, and dangers. The dangers of nuclear crisis management would not have to drive strategy, force structure, arms purchases, doctrine, operating procedures, or decision-making because the crises wouldn't be nuclear. That would be an enormously beneficial state of affairs.

Many of the dangerous scenarios that we all fear if Iran possesses a nuclear arsenal become a lot less hair-raising if Iran has only a potential capability to field an arsenal. Imagine if Israel and Hizballah start going at it. Iran cannot step in and raise the specter of escalation to a nuclear exchange to force Israel to back down, because Iran would not have nuclear weapons. At most, Iran could threaten to break out of the NPT and deploy an arsenal at some point in the near future after the crisis had passed. This might be enough to get Israel to back down, but not because Israel would fear uncontrollable escalation. Nor is it reasonable to believe that the Israelis would fear that Iran would assemble a weapon months later and use it against them. There would no longer be a "heat of the moment" problem and cooler heads would have plenty of time to prevail. Ultimately, the only reason that Israel might choose to back down would be if it did not want Iran to weaponize. That kind of pressure might still not be great from Israel's perspective or our own, but it is vastly better than having actual nuclear crises.

Even if Iran had come to the decision that it wanted to go ahead and weaponize, and was now willing to endure whatever costs had brought it up short in the past, it would be difficult for Tehran to somehow use it as part of a crisis. The IAEA inspects Iran's facilities every six to eight weeks, so Iran's breakout window would have to be under six weeks for it to gain any possibility of surprising a rival with a deployed nuclear arsenal. In theory, Iran might wait till after an IAEA inspection, then begin to break out and weaponize, and simultaneously begin an offensive action. That sounds scary, and if this were a movie, it would happen just like that. But in the real world, it is difficult to make such exquisite timing work out. Iran would be taking a big risk that its nuclear activities would not be discovered by other countries as it secretly enriched and assembled its weapon(s). It would be running a second risk that the weapon would be ready and functional in time to stave off the failure of whatever offensive operation it was mounting.

Stepping outside the realm of theory to look instead at the actual history is equally optimistic. Prior to the 1998 Pakistani and Indian nuclear tests, there were no nuclear crises between them. India had the capability to deploy and employ nuclear weapons after 1974 and it had no IAEA inspectors present, since it was not a signatory to the NPT. Thus its status was several steps beyond an NPT "breakout capability." Likewise, Pakistan probably acquired nuclear weapons at some point in the late 1980s, and it too was not a signatory to the NPT, although it had never tested before 1998.[2] So by the late 1980s or early 1990s, both sides had nuclear weapons, but because Pakistan had not tested and neither side acknowledged its capability, there were no nuclear crises between them. After they both tested and acknowledged their deployed arsenals, crises followed in rapid succession: the Kargil War of 1999, the 2001–2002 Kashmir crisis, the 2008 Mumbai bombing crisis, and smaller incidents in 2011 and 2013. Without deployed, acknowledged nuclear arsenals on both sides, the dangerous dynamics of nuclear crises are not engaged, and that makes for fewer crises and less dangerous crises when they occasionally occur.

THE NEED FOR A DEAL. There should be no doubt that it would be much better for all concerned—including the Iranians, for that matter—if Iran were to halt its progress short of deploying an actual nuclear arsenal. In the words of Shahram Chubin, "In the event that Iran remains with a virtual capability, its influence and potential for exploiting the capability, will remain as it is, limited, creating a source of anxiety for the GCC and strategic concern for Israel but not fundamentally changing the strategic picture."[3] It would be better still if Iran not only refrained from weaponizing, but agreed to an enhanced monitoring and inspections regime that could give every other country in the world much greater confidence that Iran was not secretly moving ahead with weaponization. The likelihood that the world would find out if Iran tried to break out would increase, as would the likelihood that Iran would be caught secretly trying to narrow its breakout window further.

Interestingly, there seems to be a meeting of the minds on this between the United States and Iran. President Obama has carefully indicated that his red line for Iran is weaponization: in his speeches and other public statements, the president says that he will prevent Iran from developing *a weapon*—not a narrow breakout capability, which is where Prime Minister Netanyahu keeps trying to set the collective red line. At the UN in 2012, President Obama said, "[T]he United States will do what we must to prevent Iran from obtaining a nuclear weapon."⁴ In the 2013 State of the Union address he said, "we will do what is necessary to prevent [Iran] from getting a nuclear weapon."⁵ He and his senior staff have been very clear about that.

Meanwhile, Supreme Leader Khamene'i keeps intoning that Iran will never acquire nuclear weapons themselves—endlessly repeating that he has issued a fatwa declaring that nuclear weapons are against Islam and Iran will not develop them. He could be lying, but the Iranians don't like getting caught in lies and bristle when they are accused of it. Moreover, Khamene'i seems to feel that his public statements are as much, if not more, for the consumption of the Iranian people as they are for outsiders, and so to go ahead and weaponize would be to lie to his own people. I am not saying that this is impossible—he also insists that Iran's elections are fair and free—only that Khamene'i seems loath to put himself in a position where he can be caught lying to his people. That, in turn, suggests that he may genuinely mean he intends to achieve a breakout capability and then stop at that point.

Obama and Khamene'i's seeming convergence on this point creates the prospect that the two sides might be able to reach an agreement that would give Iran the right to enrich, allow it a small stockpile of LEU and limited numbers of centrifuges, the right to manufacture fuel for its civilian reactors, and a lifting of the sanctions, in return for a renewed Iranian commitment not to weaponize, an agreement not to enrich beyond these terms, and acceptance of a highly intrusive and comprehensive monitoring and inspections program—one that went somewhat beyond even the Additional Protocol of the NPT. As always, there is no proof that either the United States or the Iranians would actually accept such a deal, and both sides have numerous obstacles that could prevent one even if it were the case that both sides were willing to accept such a compromise. Nevertheless, there is enough evidence to suggest that such a deal is possible to make it worth trying. Especially because it would be so much better than the alternatives. Whatever it would require from the Iranians, on our part, it is going to mean that our political leaders will have to show the courage to tell the American people that this deal may be the best we can do, and that it is in our interest to take it rather than demanding a perfection that we can never attain unless we are willing to pay the costs of another major war.

WHAT IF IRAN WON'T TAKE THE DEAL? Of course, Iran may not take the deal even if we offer it, and we may never offer it. If there is no deal, then the difference between containing an Iran that possesses only a breakout capacity and one with a deployed arsenal should mean placing a premium on actions we can take to convince Iran not to take the final step and weaponize.

One thing that the United States could do in the absence of a deal with Iran to try to convince the Iranian leadership not to weaponize would be to threaten air strikes if they do. That is certainly what President Obama seems to be implying in his various statements. It may also be necessary to keep that threat alive, since it does seem to be the case that the Iranians fear an American military attack and might believe we could hit them before they could have a usable nuclear weapon with which to deter us. For that reason, it was a mistake for so many other senior administration officials to have been so dismissive of the idea early in Obama's first term.

However, the United States may have neither the international nor domestic political support for a war with Iran under those circumstances. Threatening Iran with air strikes if they appear to be weaponizing (let alone if they don't accept such a deal) would almost certainly constitute an unacceptable ultimatum to the Chinese and Russians. Beijing and Moscow would probably do everything they could to undermine such a move—and then try to block us as best they could if we went ahead with it anyway. After the experience of Iraq, I am skeptical that we would have support for a war to prevent Iran from weaponizing based solely on intelligence, no matter how many countries agreed on the evidence.

Moreover, the Iranians probably would not announce they were weaponizing, but would instead move to assemble one or more devices in secret, perhaps withdrawing from the NPT first, and then confront us with a full-blown arsenal later. Nor do I think that Iran's withdrawal from the NPT will be enough of a rallying point to secure the kind of support we would need, especially if they withdraw under the pretext that the IAEA is providing intelligence to the United States, Israel, and the West—which it effectively is—and if Tehran swears that it won't weaponize. We may not even have domestic political support for a war under those circumstances, given the country's general war-weariness, along with the fear that Iran would retaliate with terrorist attacks here in the U.S. homeland and would rebuild its nuclear program even after an air campaign.

There are two other tactics the United States should pursue instead to convince Iran not to move from a breakout capability to a full-fledged arsenal. The first of these would be to threaten to expand the economic sanctions on Iran horizontally, by bringing China, Russia, and India more on board. None of these countries likes the idea of the United States going to war with Iran, but all of them have repeatedly stated that they would find it unacceptable for Iran to acquire nuclear weapons. All of them have backed up those statements by voting for far-reaching sanctions against Iran. At present, they are resisting many of the more stringent unilateral and multilateral sanctions imposed on Iran by the United States and Europe, because they dislike sanctions in principle and want to see if those already imposed will be adequate. However, if they believed that in the event that Iran decided to weaponize the only alternatives were America going to war or their joining the sanctions, there is reason to believe that they would sign up for the sanctions.

Thus, the United States should press Moscow, Beijing, Delhi, and other like-minded governments now to declare that they would join the Western multilateral sanctions against Iran if Iran begins to weaponize. There may well be doubt and wrangling over what constitutes sufficient evidence if the situation ever were to arise, but chances are it would constitute a powerful deterrent to keep Iran from ever moving down that path.

In 2010, the Iranians were shocked when China and Russia voted in favor of the harsh sanctions contained in UNSC Resolution 1929, and Tehran seems loath to repeat that unpleasant experience.

The second tactic the United States should employ to dissuade Iran from weaponizing is the threat of regime change. Tehran needs to fear that if it moves from a theoretical breakout capability to a deployed arsenal, the United States and (hopefully) our allies will make an all-out effort to bring down the Islamic Republic however we can. There are many ways that we could try to do so. We could arm anyone who hates the Iranian regime and wants to attack them. We could wage relentless cyberattacks against the regime. We could sabotage their infrastructure, jam their communications, and bombard their people with information. We could oppose Iran in every international forum simply for being Iran. None of this activity may succeed in bringing down the regime, at least not in the short term. However, it would be a painful and terrifying experience for the regime, all the more so because Tehran would doubtless magnify the extent of our efforts—and our successes. And it would be threatening the one thing that we know that this regime cares about most, more than its nuclear program and certainly more than its economy: its control over the Iranian nation.

I suspect that if the Iranians believed that a move to weaponization would trigger Chinese, Russian, and Indian adherence to the Western economic sanctions and an all-out take-no-prisoners effort at regime change on the part of the United States and its allies, they would likely choose to stick with a breakout capability. I suspect that they already fear that this would be the response if they moved to weaponize, and that this fear is an important reason they are broadcasting so loudly that they don't intend to do so.

Sanctions and Containment

One of the trickiest pieces of American strategy toward Iran over the long term will be sanctions. The current sanctions on Iran were intended to cause tremendous short-term pressure to try to convince the regime to compromise on its nuclear program. If that does not work, we will find ourselves in a difficult position. The United States and the Europeans have few remaining sanctions options left to turn up the heat on Iran. Of equal importance, having gone so far up the sanctions ladder, we have reached a point we probably cannot sustain over the long term, yet it would be handing Iran a major psychological victory to climb down unilaterally. Indeed, if we had the chance to do it all over again, I think it would have been far better to have ramped up the sanctions on Iran in a slower and more deliberate fashion, and to have left more of them in reserve.

The erosion or collapse of sanctions would be disastrous for any American policy toward Iran, and containment would be no exception. Sanctions have been a prominent element in virtually every American containment policy since the Second World War, and they could be of further value with Iran, if only to keep Tehran from building up its military strength and limit the economic assets it has available to support its subversive activities; to make it pay a price for its support to terrorists and insurgencies; to keep it on the defensive; and to demonstrate to other countries that proliferation is not worth the price they would have to pay. Thus losing sanctions would be a double blow for containment: a psychological victory for Iran, and the loss of useful tools that would make it much easier to contain Iran, even a nuclear Iran, well into the future.

Moreover, containment does not require the comprehensive, draconian sanctions currently in place, especially since they are likely to become a liability because they are unsustainable. Describing the effective use of sanctions in the containment of Yugoslavia, Meghan O'Sullivan concluded that "[a] sanctions regime whose aim is the containment of a government or country need not have all the bells and whistles of a behavior change approach."[6] Looking just at the needs of the containment of Iran, the appropriate sanctions could and probably would be much leaner. In essence, the sanctions needs of a containment strategy boil down to:

- The ban on military sales to Iran, to keep its conventional and nuclear forces weak and small;
- The ban on high-technology sales to Iran, both to hinder its indigenous military development and cause stagnation in its economic base;
- Restrictions on the travel of Iranian personnel abroad, preferably accompanied by similar constraints on Iranian airlines, to hinder the ability of Iranian intelligence personnel to wage asymmetric warfare;
- Limiting foreign investment in Iran, especially in the Iranian hydrocarbon sector to limit the resources available to the regime.

Either as part of a shift to containment or as a result of circumstances beyond our control, we may find it necessary to redefine the sanctions, preserving these critical elements while giving up on others of lesser value or those that could be more difficult to maintain over the long term. We tried to do the same in Iraq with an idea that was eventually known as "smart sanctions," preserving the bans on weapons and dual-use technology while giving up on the purely civilian sanctions. Unfortunately, we waited so long—until the sanctions were already hemorrhaging—that we had no leverage anymore. By then our offers to lift civilian sanctions were laughable because most countries were already ignoring them. And so the bid for smart sanctions failed.

With Iran, we should learn that lesson and move toward such revisions early on, while we still have concessions to make that are meaningful. Ideally, we would lift sanctions only conditionally, with the caveat that they would be reimposed on Iran if it undertook more egregious actions like withdrawing from the NPT, weaponizing, or increasing its support for terrorists, insurgents, and other violent extremists. Inevitably, Tehran would claim as a major victory any reform of sanctions that included even the temporary or conditional suspension of some of the sanctions. That will be painful, but it may be necessary to reforge the sanctions so that they are sustainable for years, if not decades. If we don't, we could hand Iran a much bigger victory.

The last point that flows from this discussion is that it would be a mistake to try to impose any more major sanctions on Iran. There is a movement among some American groups to slap a comprehensive trade ban on Iran (forbidding even the sale of humanitarian goods such as food and medicine) and then applying secondary sanctions against any other country unwilling to abide by our terms. Doing so would make the Iran sanctions not just the equal of the ill-considered Iraq sanctions; it would make them even harsher. If the current sanctions prove inadequate to persuade Iran to give up its nuclear program, it seems unlikely that choking off food and medicine would change their minds. And doing so would make it a certainty that we would be unable to hold these sanctions together for very long. The incentives for smuggling will be too great, the hardships imposed on the Iranian people (and manipulated by the regime) will be too dramatic, and the effort the United States will have to maintain will be too taxing. Chances are that turning the screw that tight will strip its threads and cause the sanctions to lose their grip. The sanctions regime could collapse around us, and we would not have them either for short-term pressure or for long-term containment.

Human Rights and Containment

Pressing Iran on its egregious human rights record should be part of any regime change agenda that the United States pursues against Iran, but that should not be the sum total of our concern with human rights as part of a new strategy for Iran. It should also be part of any containment strategy as well. We should learn from the history of the Cold War that our championing of human rights mattered. It may not have brought down the Soviet empire, but it told the captive peoples of Eastern Europe that they were not forgotten. That gave them hope, and that hope gave them the will to resist. It all seemed for naught for decades, until Lech Walesa and Solidarity tore down the whole Iron Curtain and the Eastern Europeans were able to tell us how much it had mattered to them.[7]

We should not hold human rights hostage to other considerations. We must recognize that championing human rights pays off over the long term. It allows us to connect with the people themselves and what they care about most, so that when the odious regime is gone, the people will remember that we worked on their behalf to make their lives better. For that reason, it is important to resist the temptation to look the other way at human rights violations when the regime dangles something enticing before us. The Obama administration made a terrible mistake when it whispered meek words of sympathy for the Green Revolution rather than giving it full-throated support.

Whenever possible, we should hew to a consistent line on human rights, arguing for them regardless of whatever else is happening. The championing of human rights is a long-term good—in our relationship with the rest of the world as much as with the Iranian people. It will pay off in myriad ways. The United States is not a perfect nation, and we have committed human rights violations of our own. That should not stop us from calling out the Iranians (or others) for their (far worse) human rights abuses. One does not have to be without sin to castigate someone else for being a rapist or a murderer.

Last, we need to recognize how harmful calling Tehran to account for its misdeeds is to the Islamic Republic. It robs the regime of the legitimacy that they crave and suspect that they have lost. It takes from them any moral superiority. The Islamic Republic is obsessed with concepts of justice, arguing against actions by the United States, the EU, and the UN on the grounds that they are somehow unjust to Iran. Pointing up the hypocrisy of other countries' actions is often their favorite means of mounting an implicit defense of their own behavior. Undercutting these claims is a great blow to their own prestige. Moreover, it is a powerful method of shaming other countries into holding Iran accountable for its repugnant behavior. We do the Iranian people and our own diplomacy a great disservice when we fail to make human rights an issue. Over time, it could prove to be among the most powerful weapons we might wield against the Islamic Republic, and it has the added virtues of being both popular and right.

Israel and Containing a Nuclear Iran

Working with our Israeli allies will be one of America's greatest challenges should we choose to contain Iran, but it is not a lost cause. The Israelis uniformly would prefer never to see Iran acquire a nuclear arsenal. Who can blame them? If it comes to pass, inevitably, some Israelis will be more fearful than others, and it could be problematic if the Israeli prime minister is one of them. Moreover, as Dima Adamsky has discussed in an interesting essay on the subject:

> First and foremost, the Israeli government would have to wrestle with the image of Iran that it has constructed. For years, Israeli leaders have appealed to popular fears by cultivating the specter of a second Holocaust in which Iranian President Mahmoud Ahmadinejad is equated with Hitler and the United States is equated with Neville Chamberlain's United Kingdom. The Iranian leadership has consistently been presented as fanatical and irrational. If Iran crosses the nuclear threshold, the Israeli government will likely seek to assure its population that Israel possesses effective countermeasures and that a stable MAD regime is feasible. However, to make this explanation convincing, the Israeli establishment will have to spell out that Iran is a rational strategic player that can be deterred. Such a message would be confusing and disorienting for Israelis because it contradicts everything that the Israeli government has been preaching to itself, its citizens, and the world for decades.[8]

However, there is no reason to believe that Israel can't live with a nuclear Iran or that it won't. There are small, undercover groups within the Israeli government who have been tasked with thinking and planning for just such an eventuality. They are working through how Israel could best deter Iran and what Israel would need to give itself the greatest likelihood of success.[9] Israel has quietly been putting in place everything that it would need to maximize the likelihood that it could deter a nuclear Iran. It has one of the most aggressive and comprehensive ballistic missile defense programs in the world, exceeding even America's on a per capita basis. Between the Arrow II and III, David's Sling, the American-made Patriot, and its own Iron Dome, Jerusalem has the most extensive missile/rocket defense complex in the world. It has acquired Dolphin subs from Germany, which can launch long-range Popeye Turbo cruise missiles able to carry a nuclear warhead, and therefore give Israel a secure second-strike capability. On top of all that, the IAF (which will eventually receive as many as seventy-five of the newest American F-35 stealth strike aircraft) has a limited conventional capability to try to attack and suppress Iranian missile launches.[10] Yet Israel's comfort level with an American policy of containment of Iran is likely to be determined principally by two things: their confidence in their own deterrent, and the aggressiveness and involvement of the United States.

AN ISRAELI SECOND-STRIKE CAPABILITY. For more than a decade Israel has been developing long-range cruise missiles capable of carrying nuclear weapons that can be launched from submarines—and acquiring the submarines to launch them. This is the nucleus of an Israeli second-strike capability. Israel may ask the United States for additional help in the form of newer or better cruise missiles (or the technology to build them), more subs, more survivable long-range strike aircraft (like the F-22), or even more robust ballistic missile defenses to hinder Iran's ability to destroy Israel's own nuclear assets with a preemptive strike of its own. Just because the Israelis have made great progress in all of these areas does not mean that they will feel that it is enough.[11]

AN AGGRESSIVE AMERICAN POLICY TOWARD IRAN. Many Israeli military, intelligence, and political leaders fear that Iran's acquisition of a nuclear capability will signal the start of a wide-ranging, multi-front unconventional war against Israel by Iran, one waged by Iran's various allies and proxies. Although these same Israeli leaders are determined to fight that battle and never give up, they will also be looking for considerable assistance from anywhere they can get it, but particularly from the United States. They will want money, weaponry, and technology to help with that fight, but more than that, they will look for the United States to aid them in waging these battles wherever possible. They will likely push American leaders to be confrontational with Iran to keep it weak, constrained, and "on its heels." They will encourage the United States to take action against Iran's various proxies and allies, possibly even including Hizballah in Lebanon. The more that the United States is pushing back on Iran, the less of the burden Israel will feel it needs to shoulder. Israeli leaders may also try to involve the United States in its own "counteroffensive" operations, like supporting Iranian Kurds, Baluch, and Arabs against the regime.

As a corollary to this point, it would probably be the case that the more aggressive the United States is in fighting back against Iran's various allies and proxies, the more likely that even the most hawkish Israelis will feel either that they don't need to do so themselves, or else that doing so would be counterproductive, as it could hinder the ability of the United States to garner support for this fight from the Arab states. Even the ultra-hawkish Yitzhak Shamir was convinced not to take direct action against Iraq in response to Saddam's Scud missile attacks on Israel in 1991 because the Bush administration made the case that there was nothing Israel could do that the United States was not already doing, and Israeli participation could create real problems for the United States with its Arab allies.

From Détente to Confrontation with Iran

Taken as a whole, these various issues underline the overarching notion that the containment of Iran cannot be rigid. It should not be a one-size-fits-all policy, let alone a one-time-fits-all policy. There are a wide variety of issues that containment has to address and a wide variety of tools available to do so. The challenge will be in sensing when to shift from one variant of containment to another and when to employ the different tools at our disposal.

Iran is not the Soviet Union. It lacks Russia's strength, its resources, its size, its empire, and so containment of Iran can afford to be more aggressive than the containment of the USSR should we choose to make it so. Because we are so much stronger than the Islamic Republic, a willingness to invest in the offensive components could pay off in accelerating the regime's demise and making it more pliable in the meantime. Nevertheless, we should never lose sight of the problems of containing a nuclear Iran and never fall into believing that we can do so easily. There is a minimum of time, energy, and resources that we will have to devote to making containment work with Iran. We cannot specify it beforehand, but we should err on the side of caution until we can know for sure just where the threshold lies.

Inevitably, taking a more aggressive or a more passive approach to containment at any given time will mean making trade-offs. The more aggressive we are, the more time, energy, and resources it will require us to devote to Iran. That is likely to be the case, in part, because the more assertive we are, the more that Iran is likely to lash out in response. Consequently, there may be times when we choose to throttle back on the more offensive elements of containment because other problems require American attention. However, we also need to recognize that at other times, containment may only be viable if we are willing to make a considerable investment in it. Sometimes, saving containment might even require a very assertive approach, either to push back on dangerous challenges from Iran or to reassure skittish allies. Containment cannot become a purely passive approach. If it does, it will wither. The real question we will constantly have to ask ourselves regarding containment of Iran is how much we are willing to invest in it.

In all of these considerations, the key will be to focus ruthlessly on what is most important, the key problems of containment, without getting distracted by lesser concerns or impossible aspirations. What stands out among the goals of containment are preventing Iran from weaponizing, reassuring Israel and keeping the rest of the Middle East from acquiring nuclear arsenals of their own. If we can address these issues, containment will be significantly easier than if we can't. This argues for offering Iran a less confrontational approach to containment if they don't weaponize and warning them that we would adopt a no-holds-barred version if they did. For the most part, reassuring Israel and convincing the Gulf states not to proliferate will both require a more assertive, more offensively minded approach to Iran at least early on, to convince our allies that they do not need to stray into the dangerous terrain of trying to balance a nuclear Iran on their own.

The USSR lasted for roughly seventy years. The Islamic Republic has already had more than thirty. It seems hard to imagine that it will hang on for as long as the Soviet Union. Yet it might. North Korea is much smaller and more self-destructive than the Soviets ever were and yet their regime is approaching seventy years, too. The United States can also do far more to try to hasten the political transformation of Iran than it could with the USSR or than it has wanted to try with North Korea. Yet we might end up containing a nuclear Iran for several decades. There is no reason that this cannot be done. But it will not be easy and it may not be cheap. And of greatest importance, we are going to have to constantly recalibrate our pursuit of containment to fit both our interests and developments in Iran, taking advantage of opportunities when they present themselves, trying to shape Iran's behavior where we can, and reacting to Iranian moves as needed. In that sense, I agree with the proponents of containment that there is no reason to believe that it cannot work—and good reason to believe that it can—with Iran. However, I also agree with the critics of containment that its success is not assured, nor will it come easily.

Conclusion

CHOOSING THE LEAST BAD OPTION

I f the previous thirteen chapters have demonstrated anything, it is that there are no good options left when it comes to dealing with Iran and its pursuit of a nuclear capability. That is not to say there aren't options that are relatively better and worse, just none that are good in an absolute sense. There are none that are low cost, low risk with a high probability of success. Our choices are awful, but choose we must.

It should also be self-evident why there remains a broad consensus that the United States should try to make a revised carrot-and-stick policy work. It is unquestionably the best of our bad choices. The Obama administration is right to pursue it, and to pursue it for as long as it offers any prospect of hope. There are three related aspects of the administration's approach that are particularly important to consider moving forward.

The administration is correct to focus on weaponization as the key red line for Iran's nuclear program—the step that we have to try to prevent if we can—and not the achievement of a narrow breakout capability.

Iran already has a breakout capability. Moreover, any deal secured by the carrot-and-stick approach will leave Iran with some kind of a breakout capability, and it is hard to affix a specific time span to what a certain set of capabilities would translate into in terms of a breakout window. The difference between even a narrow breakout window of just a month or two and Iran's possession of a deployed nuclear arsenal is huge. In short, the administration is correct to not let perfect become the enemy of good enough, because if we demand perfection, we will probably get nothing at all.

Building off the previous point, the administration is right that there is no reason to impose false time constraints on the negotiations. The real deal-breaker would be Iranian weaponization. Short of that, there is no reason not to keep negotiating, and to keep pushing Iran to make compromises by dint of sanctions and other forms of pressure. This does not mean that we should hold off on imposing these forms of pressure on Iran indefinitely. There is no reason we cannot tell the Iranians that they have until a specific date to accept the terms of an offer or they will be subject to additional penalties. Just that the real decision point for the United States is when we see Iran moving to weaponize, and we should not create false, artificial deadlines based on the fear that Iran is about to pass some other milestone related to a breakout window rather than to weaponization.

The Israelis have tried to create such artificial deadlines as a way of holding the world's feet to the fire. Jerusalem's rationale is entirely understandable, it has worked so far, and it was probably necessary for them to do so. But we should note that at least a half dozen such Israeli red lines have passed by without an Israeli attack, and therefore we should not short-circuit the process and give up what would be the best feasible outcome because of a false deadline created principally to galvanize international action. Israel's ability to cause meaningful damage to the Iranian nuclear program has now diminished to the point where it should not be a driving consideration in our approach to Iran. Again, the administration has been right to maintain that if anyone were going to bomb Iran, it should be the United States, and we have a lot more time than the Israelis do. Because of our much greater capabilities, we have until Iran begins to weaponize. We do not need to act before then, if we choose to act in this fashion at all.

For my part, I will also say that I fully agree with the administration's focus on securing a deal with Iran that would cap its nuclear progress short of weaponization and enable extensive, intrusive inspections to ensure that Tehran complies—and ensure that we would know it if they don't. I do not believe that it is necessary to roll back Iran's nuclear progress to eliminate any breakout capability, nor do I believe that such a standard is possible any longer. The Iranians have made it clear that they will not agree to a deal that does not allow them some enrichment capability; therefore we should focus on getting a deal that gives us the greatest confidence that Iran would not weaponize rather than trying to make it physically impossible for them to do so. As our experience with Iraq should teach us, the former is all we need and holding out for the latter will likely prove self-defeating.

However, by the same token, I think it a mistake for the administration to disdain even to examine and test a program of regime change for Iran, in particular by trying to find ways to help the Iranian opposition. I say this in full expectation that regime change probably will not work in Iran. However, if the carrot-and-stick approach fails to secure an acceptable halt to the Iranian program and Tehran proceeds toward weaponization, we should want to try almost anything else that might work—that might let us avoid the ultimate choice between war or containment. Even if regime change is a low probability, and I grant that it is, trying a low-probability approach is worth it if there is any chance that it might head off the need to accept either war or containment.

What's more, I believe that the administration has misread the impact of a regime change strategy on the Iranian regime. The historical evidence we have available, limited as it is, suggests that applying additional pressure in the form of regime change is likely to make Tehran more willing to compromise rather than less. Even then, it may not be enough to convince Tehran to agree to a deal. If that is the case, then as Danielle Pletka pointed out all those years ago, all that will matter is whether we supported the legitimate aspirations of the Iranian people, a great many of whom have demanded a different government. Given the numbers and the dedication of those who revolted against the regime in 2009, we cannot say that there is no longer a large, legitimate domestic opposition to the regime. Our values and experience both argue that we should support them as best we can. And if doing so also helps us achieve a solution to the nuclear impasse before we must make the awful choice between war and containment, so much the better.

Judging the Final Choice

Yet a renewed effort to secure a deal and whatever we might do to help the Iranian opposition may all fail in the end. And that end may not be far away at this point. If that is the case, we will face the last choice, the choice between war and containment. Having worked through each of these approaches separately, it is now time to compare them and reach some kind of a conclusion.

I am going to lay out my logic and I am going to do so writing in the first person. My reason for presenting this analysis in this fashion is to emphasize that this analysis derives from my assumptions, my assessments, and my preferences. They are why I prefer containment over war in the majority of circumstances. It is also meant to underscore what should be obvious: that a different person with different assumptions and preferences might assess the balance very differently. My hope is less to persuade you that I am right and more to persuade you that every American, certainly every American concerned about this critical foreign policy issue, needs to weigh the costs and risks as they are, not as we would like them to be. And that we have to weigh all of them, not just the ones we like, although every American will weight each of the factors differently based on his or her idiosyncratic views and preferences. In the end, if you decide instead that war is the least bad option, so be it. As long as we all recognize all of the risks and costs and prepare for them accordingly.

Air Strikes Versus Containment

So let's get started. I am going to begin by looking at the pros, cons, and other factors of pursuing U.S. (*not* Israeli) air strikes against the Iranian nuclear program before I do the same for containment, and then will explain how I see them interacting. Please note that in the lists of advantages and disadvantages I have drawn up, what matters is not the quantity of the pros and cons but their quality. One really big advantage could outweigh many smaller and/or less likely disadvantages.

THE ADVANTAGES OF AIR STRIKES. I see seven potential advantages to air strikes. I have highlighted those I believe most salient in **bold italic**.

- Air strikes play to our greatest advantage—our enormous conventional military superiority over Iran.
- *U.S. air strikes would probably set the Iranian nuclear program back somewhere between two and ten years.* Lower figures are probably more likely given Iran's demonstrated ability to build new nuclear facilities from scratch and the fact that even extensive air strikes could not eliminate Iran's understanding of the enrichment process. There is some risk that air strikes would set back the Iranian program by less than two years—either because our strikes are not as effective as expected, the Iranians have hidden sites we do not know about at the time of the attack, or they receive considerable foreign assistance in rebuilding after an attack.
- There is a possibility that Iran would never rebuild after successful air strikes or that they would not be able to rebuild because other events would prevent them from doing so. While this seems less likely than

the prospect that Tehran would rebuild, it is certainly possible. The regime might fear getting struck again and might decide that the game is just not worth the candle. After the Israeli air strike against the Syrian nuclear facility at al-Kibar in 2007, the onset of the Arab Spring in 2011 meant that the Asad regime never acquired the nuclear weapon it desired. (Of course, in that case the evidence is overwhelming that it was the Arab Spring, not the al-Kibar strike, that precluded the Asad regime's acquisition of a nuclear weapon. Syria was not even close to having a nuclear weapon in 2007 and even had Israel not struck the facility, it would not have been able to produce a nuclear weapon before the Arab Spring plunged the country into civil war in 2011.)

- There is some possibility that air strikes would exacerbate popular unhappiness with the regime, conceivably even enough to lead to the downfall of the regime—or merely to convince them not to rebuild for fear that another American strike might be cause for another popular revolt. The former seems highly unlikely, the latter just unlikely.

- *Air strikes would be comparatively low cost.* Depending on how many days or weeks we had to run them, they probably would cost only tens of billions of dollars—comparatively cheap, especially if the air campaign actually solves the problem. However, they would doubtless cause the oil market to spike. The duration of the spike could vary considerably depending on how Iran responds and how able the United States and its allies are to deal with Iranian retaliation.

- Iran might be so afraid of further America strikes that it would not retaliate at all or its efforts to retaliate would be too weak to overcome our defenses. The former strikes me as highly unlikely, whereas the latter is much harder to gauge but certainly quite possible.

- If air strikes succeed, they will do so quickly, allowing the United States to turn to other problems.

THE DISADVANTAGES OF AIR STRIKES. I see eleven potential disadvantages to air strikes. I have again highlighted those I believe most salient in *bold italic*.

- *It is more likely that the Iranians would rebuild their nuclear program than not.* In the event that they rebuild, they would most likely withdraw from the NPT and banish the inspectors to be able to rebuild unfettered and without the IAEA reporting on their efforts to the world. They might even announce their intent to deploy actual weapons to prevent another American strike. A determination to rebuild is both far more in line with this regime's past behavior and rhetoric, and is more consistent with the limited historical evidence. The Iraqis rebuilt their nuclear program (or tried to do so) after the successful Israeli air strike in 1981 and the partially successful American air campaign in 1991. Syria does not seem to have tried to rebuild the al-Kibar facility after the 2007 Israeli air strike, but the unclassified evidence is paltry; we do not know if Damascus had started to reconstitute elsewhere, or what might have happened had the Arab Spring not intervened in 2011.

- *It is far more likely that Iran would retaliate than not.* Moreover, the available evidence strongly indicates that they would try to retaliate here in the United States itself with both cyber and terrorist attacks. How much damage they would inflict would depend on how good our homeland and cyber defenses are compared to how good their attacks would be. The Iranians might retaliate over the course of months or years, during which time they could improve on their tactics if early attacks failed. The Arbabsiar plot suggested that their capability to mount terrorist attacks in the United States was negligible in 2010, but according to press reports, the U.S. intelligence community believes that Iran has been working hard to expand it. In addition, Iranian retaliation could further drive up the price of oil, potentially keeping it high for many months.

- *It is highly likely that Iran would retaliate against Israel and probably the GCC states.* There is a reasonable probability that Hizballah would participate in such retaliation, and a significantly lower probability that Hamas would join as well. Again, depending on the balance between Israeli/American/GCC defenses and Iranian/Hizballah/PIJ offensive capabilities at the time that the air strikes were launched (and for potentially a long period of time afterward), *the damage from such retaliation could range from the utterly inconsequential (a few rocket attacks and a few tourists killed) to the truly catastrophic (crippling the Israeli economy for weeks or months and cutting Gulf oil production).* The Iranians might also ramp up their efforts to subvert American Arab allies, although this would unfold over a much longer period of time.

- Iran might try to close the Strait of Hormuz. This seems unlikely as long as the Iranians can tell that the air strikes are not the start of an invasion or a decapitation campaign, but it is not impossible.

- *As a result either of highly damaging Iranian retaliation or an Iranian decision to rebuild its nuclear program, the United States could be forced to invade and occupy Iran—or live with a nuclear Iran that will be hostile, intent on revenge, and in possession of nuclear weapons.*

- Air strikes might fail. Either because we are not aware of all of Iran's nuclear facilities, Iranian defenses prove tougher than we expect, our own forces experience unexpected problems, or some combination of all of the above, we may do much less damage than we expect. I think this probability low, but not zero.

- It is more likely that air strikes would either stoke Iranian nationalism and rally people around the regime, or turn them against the United States, than it is that they would cause the people to turn more against the regime. Historically, that is just how air campaigns work.

- Air strikes would totally consume our attention in the run-up, the execution, and for some time thereafter. If we were forced to invade, that would consume far more of our attention (and resources) for far longer than either the air strikes on their own or possibly even containment.

- Even if the air strikes are highly successful, except in the unlikely circumstances in which the regime opts not to rebuild its nuclear program (and it is very clear to the outside world that this is their decision) or is overthrown by the Iranian people as a result of them, air strikes would leave the United States still relying on containment—albeit containment of a non-nuclear Iran.

- *If the air strikes are unsuccessful*—meaning either that they failed to set back the Iranian program by much or that Tehran announced afterward its determination to rebuild and build weapons—and the United States opts not to invade, *we would be forced back onto a policy of containing a nuclear Iran anyway.* Moreover, it would be containing a much more dangerous nuclear Iran, one that would almost certainly be implacably hostile, bent on revenge, and uninterested in any agreements with the United States. It could also mean containing a nuclear Iran *without the invaluable help of the NPT and the IAEA inspectors to constrain Iran.*

- Air strikes would likely deepen anti-American sentiment in the Muslim world, although it would be unlikely that this would have any concrete, near-term effects.

THE ADVANTAGES OF CONTAINMENT. I see seven potential advantages from containment.

- *It would have a much lower risk of involving the United States in a war with Iran than air strikes* (where the risk is 100 percent since attacking Iran with air strikes *is* going to war). Under containment, crises could get out of hand and result in a war, so the probability is not zero. However, one of the goals of containment would be to try to avoid a war and there are numerous steps the United States could take to try to minimize the probability of inadvertent escalation.

- *It would have a much lower risk of involving the United States in an invasion and occupation of Iran along the lines of what the United States mounted in Iraq and Afghanistan.* It is hard to the point of impossibility to imagine circumstances in which the United States would invade a nuclear Iran. At most, we might feel compelled to mount limited incursions to secure Iranian nuclear weapons in the event the regime were to collapse and we became concerned about the status of its nuclear weapons. That could be difficult and ugly, but would be nothing like an invasion and occupation.

- It holds out the prospects for a negotiated resolution to our problems with Iran at a later date. Détente is a distinct possibility under containment and it is not inconceivable that by pursuing this course rather than going to war, we could eventually work out confidence-building measures and even arms control agreements with Iran that would diminish or eliminate many of the problems of containment. It might even set us on the road to an eventual rapprochement with Iran.

- It seems more likely that containment would exacerbate the divisions between the Iranian regime and so many of its people than would air strikes. Again, air strikes appear to have a higher probability of helping the Iranian regime to hold power than undermining their control because of the visceral reaction that accompanies any act of war against a people. In contrast, the constant pressure and isolation of the international community against Iran has undeniably contributed to the regime's unpopularity. It is impossible to know how much foreign pressure was responsible for this popular disillusionment compared to factors wholly internal to Iran, but they unquestionably had a positive impact. Thus, the more likely *negative* impact of air strikes has to be compared to the more likely *positive* impact of continued containment.

- It would probably garner international sympathy, especially in the short term. At least for some period of time—varying based in large part on how well we handle ourselves—we could count on a fair degree of international support for our containment efforts. The key would be to invest that support in building a durable containment regime, one that can last for the long term.

- It would probably require less attention and resources concentrated on Iran than even successful air strikes, at least in the short term. Successful air strikes would mean a high expenditure of both attention and resources for some period of weeks or months, diminishing markedly over the long term. In contrast, containment would mean lesser commitments throughout but paid out regularly for potentially much longer. Then again, unsuccessful air strikes would likely mean both large outlays in the short term and significant commitments over the long term, too.

- It could result in increased arms sales to the GCC.

THE DISADVANTAGES OF CONTAINMENT. I see nine potential disadvantages from containment.

- Iran will continue to try to subvert the governments of American regional allies; it will back terrorist groups, insurgencies, militias, and other violent extremists. There is a strong probability that it will do so even more than it has in the past, although its ability to do so successfully and the likelihood that this support will produce the outcomes Iran seeks will be determined by a range of factors beyond its control.
- *Deterrence may fail. The combination of Iran's likely aggressive behavior and the potential for the GCC states or Israel to respond in equally assertive fashion will probably spark crises. Either as a result of deliberate action or inadvertent escalation, one or more of these crises could lead to a war, and potentially even the use of nuclear weapons by one side or both.*
- *It is highly likely that the GCC states will seek to balance a nuclear Iran rather than bandwagon with it.* That could help produce crises with Iran. *It could also produce nuclear proliferation, particularly on the part of Saudi Arabia,* but potentially by the UAE as well. Proliferation by Turkey and Egypt seem far less likely, but not impossible.
- There are a number of increased costs attendant on containment, although most are modest: possibly modernizing our strategic nuclear forces, adding a mid-course missile defense system to the Middle East's defenses, possibly augmenting slightly our conventional forces in the region, and probably increasing military aid to Israel, but the costs pale

in comparison to the potential costs of a war with Iran, especially an invasion and occupation.

- *The price of oil would almost certainly be affected by fears related to a nuclear Iran. However, that impact could range from marginal to disastrous.* The actual impact is likely to be determined heavily by how early crises with a nuclear Iran work out—whether the United States involves itself early, whether the crisis results in a war, whether it results in any actual cuts to oil production or exports, and whether Iran is seen as having been emboldened by the outcome or chastened by it.

- Iran will continue to attack the United States with cyber weapons and possibly some forms of terrorism at least for as long as we continue to do similar things to them. Again, they might be so emboldened by their acquisition of nuclear weapons that they might try to increase the severity of these attacks and/or continue to pursue them even if we desist. Nevertheless, there is no reason to believe that, even if Iran adopted this pattern of behavior early on, the United States could not mitigate the impact and convince them to modify or discontinue it by our own actions—as we have done at various points in the past.

- Iran's acquisition of nuclear weapons could convince other countries outside the Middle East that the NPT has lost its bite, the norm against nuclear proliferation is breaking down, and therefore that they would suffer less if they pursued a nuclear capability. Of course, Iran has already suffered for its pursuit of such a capability in defiance of the international community to an extent greater than almost any other country (except North Korea) would tolerate, which would be an important check on this problem.

- It is most likely that Supreme Leader Khamene'i will be replaced by another weak figure unlikely to deviate significantly from Iran's current course (or possibly by a committee that would probably do the same). However, *there is a lesser probability that a more dangerous man might take his place, one far more aggressive and reckless*—Saddam Husayn in a turban. Such a leader would be more likely to provoke crises with the United States, the GCC, Israel, and other American allies. He might also be far more difficult to deter than Khamene'i, which would call into question the central premise of containment.

- At some point, the Islamic Republic is likely to pass from history. *There is a risk that this will occur with a bang, rather than a whimper—the state will fracture and collapse. If that happens, there is also a risk that elements of its nuclear arsenal could be used or transferred to some of Tehran's vicious terrorist friends.* While this is certainly a real concern, it is worth noting that historically a nuclear state has never fractured and collapsed into chaos; the Soviet Union fractured, but it never collapsed into chaos and the issue of "loose nukes" from the USSR was handled without tragedy, albeit not without some drama.

Head-to-Head

This brief comparison should reinforce the ultimate point that both of the options, air strikes and containment, are pretty rotten. For both paired lists, the disadvantages outweigh the advantages. There should be little doubt that if we have other options, like the carrot-and-stick or even regime change, we ought to try them rather than going with either of these two.

In addition, I hope you recognize how ultimately subjective so many of these statements are, and how hard it is to ascribe any real precision to their likelihood. There are simply too many unknowns at work here to be able to say much with real confidence. The best we can do, as I have tried throughout this book, is to lay out the evidence from Iranian and international history relevant to each of these issues, the deductive logic behind each, and how other, similar states have behaved in similar circumstances. That is not terrible, and it is certainly the best we are going to be able to do, but is a far cry from certainty.

Now let me explain how I get to where I get to.

AIR STRIKES. My starting point is a simple one. I have a great deal of concern about air strikes. I am an old military analyst, and this operation rubs me the wrong way. I am certainly no shrinking violet. I am no pacifist. I believe that force can advance our national interests and should be employed when necessary. I supported a war against Saddam, albeit not the one that the Bush 43 administration waged. I was among the first to argue that the United States had to shift to a true counterinsurgency strategy in Iraq, and supported the "surge" there when the Bush administration finally came around to this realization.[1] I am also a firm believer that airpower can do some remarkable things, including on its own. I supported the U.S. strategy in Operation Enduring Freedom against Afghanistan—and said so in print. I also supported Operation Desert Fox, and said so in print. In fact, I wanted it to go on longer and go after more of Saddam's security apparatus. Nevertheless, I get very nervous when people start telling me that a limited air campaign can solve all of our problems. That is something that has been promised repeatedly throughout history and has almost never proven close to being true.

Still, my thinking about air strikes has changed over the years. I once saw a great many risks inherent in the air strike option that have since faded. The American effort to secure and rebuild Iraq was probably the biggest of those. At one time, it was too important and too vulnerable to Iranian retaliation to risk. Today, for good or ill, it is gone and therefore cannot be a reason to oppose an air campaign. Similarly, although I am hardly 100 percent confident that we know where all of Iran's nuclear sites are, I have a lot more confidence than I did ten years ago. The intelligence services of the United States and other countries have been going over Iran with a fine-tooth comb and the discoveries of Natanz, Arak, and Fordow suggest that they have learned something from their past mistakes. I may not be 100 percent confident, but I am more comfortable than I once was.

Yet each time I work through the air strikes option, I cannot get it to work out right. As you have read, I am concerned that air strikes will prove to be nothing more than a prelude to invasion, as they were in Iraq and almost were in Kosovo. I note that even Matt Kroenig, a passionate advocate of air strikes, shares my fears, writing, "In the midst of such spiraling violence, neither side may see a clear path out of the battle, resulting in a long-lasting, devastating war, whose impact may critically damage the United States' standing in the Muslim world." I find I concur with the way that Tom Donnelly, Dany Pletka, and Maseh Zarif, three people normally found on the rightward side of the political aisle, put it in their analysis of the problems of containment: "We agree that escalated confrontation with Iran—and there is undeniably, a low-level war already being waged by Iranian operatives or proxies in Iraq, Afghanistan, and elsewhere—would throw an already volatile region into chaos, perhaps spread and involve other great powers, and place a heavy burden on over-stretched American forces and finances. The costs of war are all too obvious and painfully familiar."[2]

I fear that Iranian retaliation will prove more than we are willing to bear or that Iran will choose to reconstitute its nuclear program—and will do so as a weapons program, without the constraints of the NPT. Both seem like quite high likelihoods based on past Iranian practice, Iranian public and private statements, and the behavior of other, similar regimes under similar circumstances. If either proves to be the case, let alone both, I think it will be difficult for the president to avoid shifting to an invasion. I was there, in the room in 1999 when the Clinton NSC reached the conclusion that the NATO air campaign was not accomplishing its mission and therefore the United States would have to invade Kosovo if Milosevic did not back down before the ground force was deployed and ready. It was a grim moment.

If the United States attacked Iran to destroy its nuclear sites and the Iranians retaliated in ways we found too painful to bear, or they stood up from the rubble, brushed off the dust, and vowed to rebuild and this time to get a bomb—the fatwa be damned—I do not believe the president, any president, could just stop. The president would have to defend the American people and the American homeland against attack, retaliatory or otherwise. Likewise, if the president commits the nation to war to defend against what he will have to say is a grave threat to our vital national interests, he is going to have to finish the job with ground troops if air strikes alone fail to get it done.

CONTAINMENT. As with air strikes, I start with the history. My reading of history is that nuclear deterrence works. Certainly, it has never failed—at least not yet. I am persuaded that the logic of nuclear deterrence is so simple and dramatic that it is compelling and the vast majority of people will be swayed by it. However, I do not think that nuclear deterrence is easy, perfect, or self-sustaining. While I have no idea just how close the world came to a nuclear war during the Cuban Missile Crisis or the Kargil War, I don't particularly like taking any steps in that direction.

Similarly, my reading of the history of the containment of Iran is that it has worked quite well. Amid our fourth decade of containment, Iran is weak, isolated, internally divided, and externally embattled. It stirs trouble in the region as best it can, but it is no threat to the territorial integrity of any other country and its unconventional warfare campaigns have tended to be lethal nuisances far more than they have contributed to meaningful shifts in the balance of power—or even threatened the leadership of key states. Although they keep trying and someday might succeed, Iran has never overthrown the government of an American ally. Likewise, it has exacerbated a lot of regional conflicts but never caused one. In short, my reading of the history is that both nuclear deterrence and containment of Iran are powerful concepts that have proven themselves reliable over time.

Nevertheless, I recognize the dangers of both, and am concerned about how Iran's acquisition of nuclear weapons could change the dynamics that produced both of those historical patterns of success: nuclear deterrence and containment of Iran. The problems that loom largest to me are the potential for nuclear crises, especially in the early years after Iran acquires a nuclear weapon but has not yet learned the rules of the nuclear road; the potential for proliferation, particularly by Saudi Arabia and perhaps the UAE; the potential for the oil market to go haywire; and the potential for Khamene'i's successor to prove more dangerous than he is. In general, I am concerned about each of these problems, but I suspect that each is not catastrophic to begin with and could be significantly mitigated by American action.

Crisis management is my greatest concern about containing a nuclear Iran. I am far more concerned about the potential for crises to escalate than I am about the impact of more aggressive Iranian unconventional warfare. I expect that a nuclear Iran would become more aggressive in its support for terrorism, insurgents, and other subversive groups, and I believe that will further destabilize the Middle East. But given the accomplishments of Iranian unconventional warfare to date, I do not see an expansion of that effort as a compelling argument in favor of going to war with Iran instead. That is especially so since it seems highly likely that an American air campaign would cause the Iranians to do exactly the same thing, perhaps with even greater zeal and less restraint, since they will have just been attacked. In contrast, if the United States were relying on containment, Iranian subversive efforts would take place under a rubric of red lines and a desire to poke at us without provoking us. In fact, unless Iran finds a way to overthrow a foreign government in a way it never has in the past, the worst that is likely to happen from this would be that Iran's efforts would provoke a nuclear crisis. That would certainly be dangerous, but what would make it dangerous was the fact that it was a nuclear crisis, not the Iranian subversive activities. So that just brings me back to my concern about nuclear crises.

Crises, especially nuclear crises, suffer from a variety of inherent problems related to time, uncertainty, communications, all of which are going to be worse with the Iranians simply because of the nature of their system and their perceptions of the United States. However, as I have also described in the preceding pages, there are important mitigating factors. The first is that the logic of nuclear deterrence is incredibly powerful, and I have seen nothing in Iran's behavior under Khamene'i, or even Khomeini for that matter, that makes me feel that they will not understand it as well. I feel quite comfortable about that judgment. I wish that I could be certain, but that is never possible and the small residual doubt cannot be allowed to be determinative. We could not be certain that nuclear deterrence would work with the Soviet Union, China, Pakistan, or North Korea either, yet it has worked in every case so far.

The second important mitigating factor is that America's possession of escalation dominance over Iran is an extremely powerful force to ensure that nuclear crises with Iran do not get out of hand, and that they end to our advantage. Once we are involved in a crisis, there is no level of warfare at which Iran can defeat the United States The smartest thing they could do would be to back down, de-escalate, and try to go back to fighting at the unconventional level where they may have an advantage over us—although even that is no longer certain after Iraq, Afghanistan, the war on terror, and the Arab Spring. At any other level of warfare, we will do infinitely greater damage to them than they can do to us. There is always the potential for catastrophic miscalculation, but in every nuclear crisis in the past, regardless of the participants—including India and Pakistan—the moment that their nuclear arsenals were engaged, all sides suddenly began to demonstrate enormous care and caution, and a willingness to tolerate humiliating defeat rather than face annihilation. That includes risk-tolerant and casualty-tolerant leaders like Khrushchev, Stalin, and Pakistan's generals. Iran's leaders would thus have to be categorically different kinds of people to act differently—again, they would have to be as different as Saddam Husayn, who was willing to gamble on the ruin of his regime and his own death on numerous occasions from 1980 until his final miscalculation in 2003. There is nothing about the behavior of Iran's leaders that looks to me like they belong in that narrow category.

The Saudis also worry me. My experience of the Saudis is that they don't bluff lightly, unlike some of our other Middle Eastern allies. I take them at their word when they say that they plan to get a bomb of their own if the Iranians do. Nevertheless, I suspect that when it comes down to it, doing so will prove harder for the Saudis than it might seem now. First, I am skeptical that the Iranians will weaponize, at least for some time, because they fear Russia, China, and India joining the sanctions;

they fear the United States mounting an all-out regime change campaign against them; and they may even fear an American or Israeli military response. In the ambiguous circumstances in which Iran abstains from weaponizing, would the Saudis go for a bomb? To the rest of the world, it will look like international pressure is working with Iran—and then the Saudis come along and wreck it by getting a bomb of their own? Maybe. There is also the question of whether the Pakistanis will actually give it to them if they ask for it, no matter how much Riyadh may have contributed to Islamabad's bomb-making program. The Pakistanis have actually been remarkably careful with their nuclear arsenal, and they may fear that if they are caught giving a bomb to someone, they will come under severe international sanctions that they simply cannot tolerate—and from which neither the Americans nor the Chinese will save them. The Saudis, too, may still calculate that it is more useful for them to have a strong defense relationship with the United States than to go out on their own, acquire a small nuclear arsenal, and perhaps sour the long strategic relationship with the United States that has been the cornerstone of their security since the Second World War.

Then there is the issue of Khamene'i's successor. First, I suspect that for their own reasons the Iranians are not going to pick a crackpot to succeed him. Next, in a post-Khamene'i era, my guess is that the Supreme Leader will be more constrained even than he is now. This is the nature of bureaucratic autocracies: they dislike strong leaders who want to push for particular visions. Left to choose their own leaders, they tend toward safe choices—nonentities, consensus builders, and committees. Just looking at the current Iranian political scene, it strikes me as difficult for one of the real firebrands to get himself named Supreme Leader. Even if one of them could, I think it highly unlikely that they would be even as bad as Khomeini, who still abided by deterrence logic and respected the overwhelming strength of the United States even if he fought it however he could. So to the extent that I worry about Khamene'i's successor, it is not as much as I worry about the risks and concerns of a war.

Finally, there is the issue of oil. I am certainly very concerned about the potential for the price of oil to swing wildly as a result of a range of factors related to Iran's acquisition of nuclear weapons. However, I am struck by how dependent this problem is on American behavior. That's why I wanted to come to this last. Oil prices do not operate in a vacuum. They are determined by traders trying to predict outcomes—traders who can panic, but who also learn. And it is what they learn that is likely to have the greatest impact, because the overall risk premium (the long-term increase in the price of oil) is likely to prove far more important than spikes resulting from individual crises. The global economy can overcome virtually any single spike, but a series of spikes resulting in ever-worsening long-term volatility would be devastating.

However, what is so important about the oil issue is what is so important to so many aspects of containment: the American role. In speaking to oil experts and reading their work for decades—and then specifically about this issue for this book—what stands out is how much they believe that American behavior is likely to prove decisive. The more that the United States is seen involving itself early and actively in problems related to Iran's acquisition of a nuclear weapon and to threats in the region more generally, the more reassured they will be. Similarly, the more that regional crises are resolved quickly and without escalation, the more that the oil markets will be reassured, and that too will be much more likely if the United States intervenes quickly and decisively. Finally, if regional crises end with Iran chastened rather than emboldened, that too will calm the oil markets and that too is far more likely if the United States gets involved than if it doesn't.

That is an important point to me because it echoes the conclusions of so many other points about containment: that it is far more likely to prove successful if the United States is an active participant rather than a passive bystander. Crisis management, proliferation, the potential over-reactions of our own allies, and oil price volatility are all likely to prove highly sensitive to the American role. The more that the United States acts as the "guardian of the Gulf," stepping in to crises between Iran and other states, reassuring its allies, facing down the Iranians whenever it is necessary, mediating conflicts whenever it is possible, the more that all of these problems will be ameliorated. Thus, another advantage I see in containment is that its success is likely to depend heavily on how the United States acts—because if we act, there is good reason to believe that containment can succeed.

However, the alternative is also true. That the less we act, the more likely that containment will fail. The more that we leave crises to the states of the region to work out themselves, the greater the likelihood that they will end badly. The more that we stay in the background, the more that our regional allies will feel the need to deter or push back on Iran themselves, and that will not only provoke more such crises: it will push them to seek nuclear weapons to be on a par with Iran when they do so. And the more that oil traders see these kinds of problems cropping up and not seeing the United States doing anything about them, the more frightened they will become, the more that the price of oil will rise, and the easier for small incidents to produce very big swings in the price of oil. The price of oil is the ultimate "public good" and the United States remains the only country capable of providing that public good. If the oil markets see the United States walking away from that role, they will panic and that will be very bad for business—everybody's business.

I also contrast this with air strikes in another way. Again, what this analysis of containment reveals is how much the potential success or failure rests on how the United States acts, which I find reassuring. With air strikes, the ultimate outcome depends on how Iran acts: how they choose to retaliate, whether they choose to reconstitute their nuclear program, when they agree to stop fighting. Those will be their decisions to make and we will have relatively little ability to influence them. Yet this could be the difference between success and failure, between a relatively brief air campaign and an invasion and occupation. And that troubles me.

The Rule and the Exceptions

Thus, when I compare the costs and risks of air strikes to the costs and risks of containment, I ultimately judge that I am more comfortable paying the costs and running the risks associated with containment than I am those associated with air strikes, or more properly, war. I do not say that lightly.

What's more, I think it important to add four brief caveats to this conclusion. First, I am much more comfortable espousing containment if it is pursued by a United States that is militarily and diplomatically involved in the region, not aloof and disconnected. The Obama administration has been trying to remove itself from Middle Eastern disputes wherever and however it can. The Middle East is not better off for it, and I fear that we will pay a price for it as well. Likewise, many of the most ardent—and most intelligent and knowledgeable—proponents of containment do so in the name of a policy of "restraint" that would similarly see the United States less active and engaged in the problems of the Middle East. That approach strikes me as being particularly dangerous as part of the containment of a nuclear Iran. It is not that it is bound to fail, only that it will be much harder for it to succeed. Far better for the United States to play an active role and boost the odds of containment's success along with it. After all, one of the greatest problems with containment is that if it fails it potentially could fail catastrophically.

Second, to return to one of the themes of the last chapter, all of this underscores just how much better it would be if Iran could be kept from weaponizing, even if that means allowing them a narrow breakout window. All of the problems of containment—crisis management, proliferation, oil prices, and so on—are ameliorated if not eliminated if Iran is kept from weaponizing.

Third, although I generally oppose the idea of going to war with Iran and prefer to contain Iran, even a nuclear Iran, if left with only the choice between these two, I believe it would be a huge mistake to let the Iranians believe that the United States has ruled out the military option. It is one thing for some former government official at a Washington think tank to say that we should not go to war; it is something else entirely for the sitting president or secretary of defense to say it—or even imply it. We do not know just how much Iran's own restraint with regard to its nuclear program stemmed from a fear that the United States might attack, but it was almost certainly part of their thinking. I suspect that Iran would prefer not to be attacked by Israel, but I think it is frightened of being attacked by America, and I think that fear has had a salutary effect on their behavior, including helping to convince them that they shouldn't weaponize, or at least should not weaponize yet.

Last, I want to return to one point I made in discussing American military options: the calculus for war changes if Tehran takes some foolish action that would justify an attack on Iran in the eyes of the American people and international public opinion. So many of the problems of air strikes relate to the difficulty we may have generating political and diplomatic support, coupled with the difficulty of bringing such a war to a close short of an invasion. However, if the Iranians attack us first, then we would be well within our rights to respond by crushing their nuclear program and then walking away. If they wanted to retaliate themselves, there would be plenty more target sets we could hit that would make such a conflict increasingly painful for Tehran. The key differences would be that the military operation would not have to be justified by the grave threat posed by Iranian nuclear weapons to America's vital interests, and international and domestic opinion would be with us. In these circumstances, bombing Iran's nuclear sites, and perhaps buying ourselves anywhere from two to ten years, would not just be acceptable, it might well be the best option of all.

Stop the Madness

I have been reading books, articles, memos, and policy papers making the case for one or another way of handling the Iranian nuclear program for at least a decade and a half. In researching this book I have gone back over many of these pieces—and read many that I hadn't earlier. One of the most dispiriting aspects of this survey has been to see how much hysteria has come to surround this issue. Many of the brightest, most experienced, most able of our nation's thinkers and policymakers are guilty of this practice. On both left and right, advocates of one position or another have employed some of the most outrageous, unrealistic, even ridiculous forms of argumentation. Both sides consistently present only the worst case for the course of action favored by the other, and only the best possible case for their own preferred policy.

On the left, many smart, well-intentioned people put forth preposterous claims about what will happen if the United States bombs Iran, to persuade the undecided of the virtues of containment. This includes the argument that the "Arab street" or even "the entire Muslim world" will rise up against the United States if we strike Iran. No, they won't. It's not just that people have been making this prediction repeatedly for several decades about any number of other American actions and been proven wrong every time. It's also that most Arabs, and a whole lot of Muslims, are ambivalent at best about Iran and its nuclear program. They won't like an American (let alone an Israeli) air campaign, some might use it as an excuse to vent their anger about other issues, but most will have their own problems to worry about.

For some on the right, the preferred course of argumentation seems to be to try to discredit containment by holding it to ridiculous standards. The most obvious of these is the insistence that we can only trust containment if we are 100 percent certain that Iran's leaders are not messianic or insane. Of course, we can never be 100 percent certain of any human enterprise and so it is absurd to establish that as the standard for anything. We can't be 100 percent certain that air strikes against Iran would not cause the end of the world, either. The evidence we have strongly indicates that Iran's leaders are not messianic or insane, and there simply is no good evidence that they are. That is as good as it gets for mere mortals, and more than adequate for countless policy decisions of similar import in the past.

Another example of this ploy is that some who oppose containment and favor air strikes have argued that for containment to be considered successful, it would have to prevent Iran from transferring nuclear technology to other countries. It's hard to know what "success" would mean in this case, but if it means that we have to bomb Iran unless we can be certain that they won't give another country blueprints for a centrifuge, then this criteria is hard to take seriously. After all, Pakistan's A. Q. Khan network transferred all manner of plans and nuclear equipment to a variety of countries, including Libya, North Korea, and Iran. It's tough to think of countries we would have less wanted to receive nuclear technology than these three. Yet we did not bomb Pakistan. In fact, they are now one of the largest recipients of American aid. North Korea then turned around and transferred nuclear technology to Asad's Syria (one of the other countries we really did not want to receive such assistance), and still we have not bombed North Korea, either. Thus, this cannot be a reasonable standard for the "success" or "failure" of containment, and it certainly cannot be a basis for mounting air strikes against Iran.

Still another alarming issue raised by those who oppose containment is the possibility of an accident involving Iranian nuclear weapons—an accidental detonation or even an accidental launch. However, there is no reason to suspect that Iran will be any more careless with its nuclear weapons than Pakistan, India, North Korea, or someday a nuclear Brazil or Argentina will be. These countries have actually demonstrated great care with their nuclear forces. In truth, to the best of our knowledge, the country that has behaved most cavalierly with its nuclear forces and had the most accidents with them has been the United States. For periods of the Cold War, we had bombers in the air loaded with nuclear weapons on a regular basis—and at least once, a bomber accidentally dropped four nuclear bombs on Spain (fortunately, they did not set off a nuclear explosion). No other nuclear power has ever behaved so carelessly.[3]

Thus, while there is certainly some validity to this fear, it is a problem with nuclear proliferation, not necessarily with Iran. The more countries with nuclear weapons, then simply by the law of averages, the greater the likelihood that there will be an accident. But that is hardly a justification for attacking Iran. If that is our standard, why didn't we attack North Korea when it crossed the nuclear threshold? Or Pakistan? Or India? Or Israel? Similarly, should we attack Brazil if someday it decides to acquire nuclear weapons? Or South Korea? In other words, this is a reasonable concern and an issue that should be addressed, but it is not a valid criterion for attacking Iran to prevent it from acquiring a nuclear weapon.

I will not speculate on the motives behind this unnecessary and unfortunate hysteria from both sides around the Iranian nuclear issue. I do not know whether these reflect a sense that in today's polarized world this is what it takes to persuade a broader audience of one's preferred position, or a genuine—but genuinely irrational—fear of the consequences of the other side's position. It probably varies from person to person and in many cases may reflect some mix of the two. Whatever the motives, it needs to stop. The experts need to stop indulging in this unhelpful behavior, but more than that, the public needs to recognize it for the hysteria that it is.

The Iranian nuclear issue is hard enough as it is without such exaggeration. Adding to it simply turns what is already a difficult conversation into a useless screaming match.

As I have noted earlier, the world will not end the day after Iran acquires nuclear weapons. It did not end when Russia got them. Or when Mao's China, or Pakistan, or North Korea got them, either. The world will be more difficult and there will be real and dangerous risks, but the apocalypse is low on that list. It is highly unlikely that Iran will use nuclear weapons unprovoked or give them to terrorists. I say that as an American, but as a reminder, polls have consistently demonstrated that four out of every five Israelis believe the same.

By the same token, a war with Iran is not going to cause the fall of the United States of America. It will not bankrupt the country. It will not result in massive loss of American life on the scale of the Civil War or World War II. It will not mean the end of Western civilization. It will not drag the United States into a vast war with the Islamic world. It will not cause the Arab street to "rise up" against the United States, or Israel.

Yet to listen to the two sides, this would appear to be the choice we have before us.

So I want to put in a plea that we set aside the hysteria—the not-inconceivable but exceptionally unlikely claims bandied about by partisans of both sides to play on our worst fears. In the realm of policy, there is always uncertainty. When nuclear weapons are involved, that uncertainty can quickly turn to fear. Yet despite that lingering uncertainty, the only responsible thing we can do is to make decisions based on what is likely, not on the possibilities that fear can conjure. If we learn nothing else from the Cold War, it should be that allowing highly unlikely but catastrophically bad scenarios to drive our planning, spending, and decision-making was ruinously wasteful and dangerously distorted policy in ways that made us all less safe rather than more.

If You Can't Be with the One You Love . . .

Few countries have practiced strategies of containment and deterrence as deliberately, as skillfully, and as successfully as the United States. Historically, a great many cases of containment when practiced by other countries have ended in war. Think of the French efforts to contain Germany after 1870: the outcome was the two world wars. Not successful by anyone's standards, but certainly not for France. British efforts to contain France itself under Louis XIV and Napoleon succeeded, but produced war after war (which may have been unavoidable in the pre-nuclear era). Britain did an admirable job containing Russia in the eighteenth century (what they referred to as "the Great Game"), but it isn't clear just how necessary it was for them to do so. Of all the containment regimes the United States practiced during the twentieth century—against the USSR, China, North Korea after 1953, Cuba, Vietnam after 1975, Iran, Nicaragua, Libya, and Iraq—only the last resulted in a war. Every other containment strategy succeeded in preventing war, the conquest of additional territory, and any other meaningful increase in the power of the target state. Most of the states on that list are now our friends and staunch trading partners, in no small part because of the success of containment. It seems we are good at containment.

Yet we hate it. We hate it because it is ambiguous—a situation that is not war, but not peace, either. We hate it because it is protracted, leaving us in this state of limbo for decades in most cases. We hate it because it is not tough enough for conservatives and not compassionate enough for liberals. We hate it because it seems passive—even though most of the containment strategies we employed were actually pretty aggressive—and we are a people who admire action. We hate it because it gets monotonous, even though that is often the measure of its success. Perhaps it is related to why so few Americans enjoy soccer? Any sport in which a draw is something to be celebrated turns us off. Maybe any strategy that promises only perpetual draws, or just 1–0 victories, can't win our hearts, either.

In the case of containing a nuclear Iran, there are reasons to be concerned about containment. It entails some not insignificant costs and some real risks. But there are also real reasons to be concerned about air strikes, both whether they will work and what they will get us into. Because of the unpredictability of conflict, going to war always means opening Pandora's box. Sometimes we may be ready for what flies out. Sometimes we may prevent anything truly bad from escaping. But there are too many instances throughout history of war releasing furies that were never imagined. And with Iran our uncertainties are greater than almost anywhere else, except maybe North Korea. Making allowances for the uncertainty that pervades Iran must be a critical element of our decisions about how to deal with it.

We need also to remember the lessons of Iraq. With Iraq we felt just as certain about Saddam's WMD activities, perhaps even more so than we are today about Iran. Almost no one believed that Saddam had not reconstituted his WMD programs, at least to some extent, and those who did were castigated as deranged. And yet, we were wrong. Terribly wrong.

And that should make us more humble and more careful when contemplating our actions toward Iran.

We can all wish that we had better options. That some perfect strategy will appear before us and save us from the choices we have left. The time for that is long past. We can only choose the best from among the detritus.

Let us hope that we can persuade Iran to negotiate a halt to its nuclear program. Nothing would be better, even if it will be far from perfect. If that fails, let us try to help the people of Iran to change their circumstances and in so doing, change ours.

If all else fails we will face the fork in the road between war and containment. Neither is a good path. Neither may get us to our destination.

Yet choose we must. Unless circumstances change dramatically, I will choose the path of containment. It feels better, safer to me. If our nation chooses the path of war, may we walk it with greater care than in our last few forays and in the full understanding of its costs and risks. Perhaps the outcome will be better, but at least we will not have to say we did not know.

Acknowledgments

The more books I write, the more I value the help I receive in writing them. This book was yet another step on that road. I have a lot of thank-yous to offer, but little way to express the full measure of my gratitude.

I will start by saying that, as always, in writing this book I have stood on the shoulders of giants. Shaul Bakhash once again lent me his prodigious knowledge of Iran, his endless good sense, and his patience wading through an early draft of this book and helping me to turn it into something easier on both the eyes and the facts. My dear friend Ray Takeyh did the same, helpfully pointing out where both my facts and my opinions were wrong, and occasionally offering up some of the gems of wisdom that only he can dig up about the Islamic Republic. The remarkable Karim Sadjadpour was another who slogged through the manuscript and by his labors made it far better than it was. I never cease to envy Karim both his insights into Iran and his wonderful turns of phrase, a number of which I have used in the preceding pages. I am especially grateful to another friend, Reuel Gerecht, who also reviewed the manuscript. Reuel is not only an astute observer of Iran; he is a committed advocate of bombing. In some ways, his points were most useful of all in seeing the weaknesses in my own arguments about how best to deal with Iran. Finally, Cliff Kupchan somehow found time to go over the section of the book on containment with a fine-tooth comb. Cliff is another expert whose scholarship and policy sense I have always admired, and his lengthy comments only reinforced my respect. He saved me from a number of pitfalls and I am very thankful to him for doing so.

Turning from the Iran experts to the strategic experts, I am grateful for the help of three other people who gave me more good comments and criticisms than I had any right to expect. Here I need to start with Richard K. Betts and Michael E. O'Hanlon. Dick Betts is rightly a giant in the field of security studies. His expertise, his experience, and his knowledge of the scholarly and policy debates over containment, deterrence, the Cold War, and the entire panoply of security issues were extraordinarily helpful—as were his occasionally biting comments about the early manuscript. Michael O'Hanlon is one of the finest men I know and one of the best things about Washington, D.C. I am deeply grateful to him for correcting me, calling me out, and pushing me on a range of topics, large and small, in this book. I have always been grateful to Mike for his friendship, but now I can add to that his hard work and terrific observations about this book. Matt Kroenig, a smart young scholar who has made the best case for war with Iran I have yet seen, was generous enough to review the sections on an Israeli and American strike on Iran and made any number of great points that made me stop and think about what I really believed and why.

Then there is Garrett Mitchell, the perspicacious author of "The Mitchell Report." Whenever I write a book I like to give it to someone I consider a smart, knowledgeable "non-expert" on the subject. Someone with enough familiarity to know if I am making sense, without being so steeped in the subject as to lose sight of what the majority of readers would be looking for. I hit the jackpot with Garry Mitchell, who generously agreed to serve in that role for this book, but undoubtedly did not realize just how generous he was being when he agreed to it. If this book makes any sense at all, it is thanks to his voluminous comments on everything from typos to the central argument and structure of the book. I could not have asked for more helpful criticism and I cannot imagine how I can repay him for it.

Several of my colleagues at the Saban Center took the time to read part or all of the manuscript and they also have my sincere thanks. First among them is Dan Byman, my alter ego. Dan went over the various containment chapters, along with the conclusions, to help me nail down this important but difficult section of the argument. As always, Dan was terrific, pointing out both what he thought I was doing right and what I was doing wrong—without any of Reuel's glee or Dick's exasperation. I cannot imagine writing a book without Dan to help me think it through and I only hope that I never have to try. Bruce Riedel and Mike Doran also have my gratitude for offering a number of important critiques based on their own areas of expertise, and for making sure I stayed on the right track throughout. Another colleague I would like to thank is Natan Sachs, a terrific young scholar whom I am proud to claim as my last hire when I was director of the Saban Center. Natan went over the chapter on an Israeli strike, lending me his knowledge of Israeli politics and security to make sure that I did not say anything too ridiculous about the subject—and fortunately catching several potential gaffes.

Many other friends and colleagues helped along the way. Bob McNally, Gal Luft, Raad Alkadiri, and the team at PIRA Energy all helped me to get a handle on the energy markets and their relationship to the many different issues touching upon America's Iran policy. My remarkable friend Tim Naftali stepped in with some critical points on the history of the Cuban Missile Crisis and Khrushchev's thinking about nuclear weapons. Jonathan Pollack, my colleague at Brookings, carried me through the thickets of Chinese security and North Korean foreign policy at several key junctures. Likewise, my old friend Daryl Press threw me a lifeline on various nuclear force structure issues, a topic on which he has been doing a lot of innovative thinking recently.

Much of the most important material in this book is the product of hours upon hours of interviews with some of the smartest and most well-versed people involved in this issue. Unfortunately, nearly all are government (or former government) officials from the United States, Israel, Iraq, Turkey, Saudi Arabia, the UAE, Qatar, France, Great Britain, China, Iran, and other countries who agreed to discuss this delicate matter with me on different occasions over the years. Because of the sensitivities involved, very few felt comfortable being quoted by name. Most were unwilling to be acknowledged in any way, but they have my genuine thanks nonetheless. Their thoughts were critical to helping me understand the many different perspectives that make up the puzzle of the Iranian nuclear impasse.

I have also been blessed with some wonderful benefactors. As always, first and foremost comes Haim Saban, the founder of the Saban Center at Brookings. When I began work on this book I was the director of the Saban Center, although I stepped down in 2012, in part to concentrate more fully on its writing. Both while I was director and since, Haim has been nothing but a pleasure. I am deeply grateful to him and to his wife, Cheryl, not just for their generosity but for their friendship over the years—and for allowing me to step down so that I could concentrate on this book! My gratitude is increased by the fact that I doubt Haim is going to like the conclusions I reach in this book. But I know that he wouldn't have it any other way and no one could ask for more from a patron.

While I am thanking those who have supported me, I would like to add my gratitude to those who supported me with my supporters: Sadie Jonath, Elisa Glazer, and Peggy Knudson, of the Brookings Foreign Policy Development office. They have thankless but essential tasks and I hope that they know how much I appreciated all of their hard work on my behalf. Especially Sadie, with whom I have been through so many donor wars that I am amazed we are not both shell-shocked. She just keeps smiling and keeps going, and I have always cherished her for both.

This will be the last book that I write with the help of my longtime research assistant, Iren Sargsyan. As always, I am enormously appreciative of her Herculean labors on my behalf, both on this book and for so many other projects during the years she has been with me. Iren has outgrown this role and I cannot wait to see her blossom professionally in the years ahead. But she will always have my gratitude for the time she gave me, and I will miss her. She will always be the standard against which her successors will be measured.

I also wanted to offer a word of thanks to Christal Shrader, formerly my assistant as director of the Saban Center and now the center's office manager. All organizations are imperfect, even Brookings. What makes their imperfections bearable are certain special people. Christal Shrader is one of those. I was blessed to have had her help when I served as director. She is so smart, so able, so professional but also so caring, so thoughtful, and so considerate that she made what was an extremely difficult situation—as I tried simultaneously to write this book and run the Saban Center—more than bearable. I always knew that Christal would handle whatever came at us. I always knew that she would do it better than I needed it (or often than I could have imagined it). I knew she always had my back. And she always did it with grace and kindness and humor, even through times of great sadness of her own. I could not have asked for more from a colleague or a friend. Christal has more than my gratitude; she has my affection and my admiration.

This book is the first that I wrote with Simon & Schuster, but the third with Jon Karp, now the president and publisher of the Simon & Schuster Group. In my home, on the holidays, we always say a special prayer of thanks for Jon. Anything I know about writing and publishing books is courtesy of Jon and I have been thrilled to be working with him again. As always, Jon was incredibly good to me, and this time one of the best things he did for me was to pair me with Ben Loehnen as an editor. In this day it is rare to find an editor willing to take the time to really work over a book to make it better. I find this disheartening because I like having my work edited by a good editor. Ben has been the answer to my prayers. He hacked apart the manuscript, chopped off all kinds of unnecessary pieces, and put it back together, paragraph by paragraph, better than it was before. It was such a pleasure to read how he had reworked my text. That is a rare compliment, and the highest I can pay to any editor. But Ben deserves it, along with my deepest thanks.

In addition to Jon and Ben, there are a number of other folks at Simon & Schuster I would like to thank for their work and assistance. Brit Hvide took care of everything I needed, and did so cheerily and efficiently. Thanks to Marie Kent and Leah Johanson for their wonderful publicity and marketing efforts, to Lisa Erwin, Lisa Healy, and Ruth Lee-Mui for overseeing the production managing, production editing, and design, and to Tom Pitoniak for his expert copyediting.

I also wanted to express my thanks to Dave and Lydia (who must remain last-nameless) of the CIA's publications review board, who shepherded the manuscript through both the CIA and NSC bureaucracies to have it cleared for publication. As part of my obligations to both of my former employers, I am required to note that all statements of fact, opinion, or analysis expressed herein are those of the author and do not reflect the official positions or views of the CIA or any other U.S. government agency. Nothing in the contents should be construed as asserting or implying U.S. government authentication of information or agency endorsement of the author's views. This material has been reviewed by the CIA to prevent the disclosure of classified information.

In penultimate place, I wanted to say just a word about Barry Posen and Steve Van Evera, the two men to whom this book is dedicated. Barry and Steve were my professors and mentors in the Security Studies Program at the Massachusetts Institute of Technology, the chairman and second chair of my doctoral thesis committee, respectively. They are also remarkable thinkers, two of the finest analytic minds I have ever known. Few people have ever taught me more, and they did so at a time when I really did not think I had that much left to learn. Although I see them too infrequently, there is not a day that goes by that I do not remember their wisdom and benefit from it. I could not be more grateful to them for the time and attention they lavished on me.

Last, but never least, comes my family. In particular, my amazing wife, Andrea, and my adorable son, Aidan. They are the lights of my life. My reasons for waking up in the morning and what I give thanks for every night before I go to sleep. As always, this book was a burden they carried as well. I am so grateful to them for their love, support, and tolerance. I could not do it without them.

Notes

Introduction: Coming to the Crossroads

1. For those looking for a history of the U.S.-Iran relationship, I will recommend three books. First, there is my own book, *The Persian Puzzle: The Conflict Between Iran and America* (New York: Random House, 2004), which tries to present a balanced perspective on the U.S.-Iran relationship up through 2004. Ali Ansari's *Confronting Iran: The Failure of American Foreign Policy and the Next Great Crisis in the Middle East* (Cambridge, Mass.: Basic Books, 2006), tells the same story from an Iranian perspective. Finally, the most recent book on the subject is David Crist's *The Twilight War: The Secret History of America's Thirty-Year Conflict with Iran* (New York: Penguin Press, 2012). Crist's book tends to focus on the military rather than the political and economic aspects of the relationship, and is largely presented from the American perspective, but it is well done and brings the story up to 2012.

2. Herman Kahn, *Thinking About the Unthinkable* (New York: Horizon Press, 1962).

Chapter 1. Iran from the Inside Out

1. Hooman Majd, *The Ayatollah's Democracy: An Iranian Challenge* (New York: Norton, 2010), p. 45.

2. John L. Esposito, ed., "Taqiyah," *Oxford Dictionary of Islam* (Oxford: Oxford University Press, 2003).

3. Shahram Chubin, "Extended Deterrence and Iran," *Strategic Insights* 8, No. 5 (December 2009).

4. For two superb books that delve deeply into the impact of Persian culture on Iranian foreign politics, see Graham E. Fuller, *"The Center of the Universe": The Geopolitics of Iran* (Boulder, Colo.: Westview, 1991); and Nikki R. Keddie and Rudi Matthee, eds., *Iran and the Surrounding World: Interactions in Culture and Cultural Politics* (Seattle: University of Washington Press, 2002).

5. Rouhollah K. Ramazani, "Iran's Foreign Policy: Contending Orientations," in Rouhollah K. Ramazani, ed., *Iran's Revolution: The Search for Consensus* (Bloomington: Indiana University Press, 1990), p. 59.

6. Among other sources, see Geneive Abdo, "Iran's Internal Struggles," in Patrick Clawson and Henry Sokolski, eds., *Checking Iran's Nuclear Ambitions* (Carlisle, Pa.: U.S. Army War College, 2004), pp. 39–60; Wilfried Buchta, *Who Rules Iran? The Structure of Power in the Islamic Republic* (Washington, D.C.: Washington Institute for Near East Policy, 2000); Hossein S. Seifzadeh, "The Landscape of Factional Politics and Its Future in Iran," *Middle East Journal* 57, No. 1 (Winter 2003): 57–75.

7. On the political influence of the Revolutionary Guard, see Ali Alfoneh, "The Revolutionary Guards' Role in Iranian Politics," *Middle East Quarterly* 15, No. 4 (Fall 2008): 3–14; Emanuele Ottolenghi, *The Pasdaran: Inside Iran's Islamic Revolutionary Guard Corps* (Washington, D.C.: Foundation for the Defense of Democracies, 2011); Kenneth Katzman, *The Warriors of Islam: Iran's Revolutionary Guard* (Boulder, Colo.: Westview, 1993); Frederic Wehrey, Jerrold D. Green, Brian Nichiporuk, Alireza Nader, Lydia Hansell, Rasool Nafisi, and S. R. Bohandy, "The Rise of the Pasdaran: Assessing the Domestic Roles of Iran's Islamic Revolutionary Guards Corps," RAND Corporation, 2009, available at http://www.rand.org/pubs/mono graphs/2008/RAND_MG821.pdf.

8. Karim Sadjadpour, "Reading Khamenei: The World View of Iran's Most Powerful Leader," Carnegie Endowment for International Peace, 2008, esp. pp. 4–8, 14–21.

9. Of course, since 2010 increasingly severe international and multilateral sanctions have crippled the Iranian economy, inflicting real hardship on the Iranian people—albeit not to the same extent as the suffering of the Iran-Iraq War.

10. For the most recent and insightful accounts of Iran's decision-making to end the Iran-Iraq War, see James G. Blight, Janet M. Lang, Hussein Banai, Malcolm Byrne, and John Tirman, *Becoming Enemies: U.S.-Iran Relations and the Iran-Iraq War, 1979–1988* (Lanham, Md.: Rowman & Littlefield,

2012), pp. 195–226; and Ray Takeyh, *Guardians of the Revolution: Iran and the World in the Age of the Ayatollahs* (Oxford: Oxford University Press, 2009), pp. 101–107.

11. Karim Sadjadpour, "The Nuclear Players," *Journal of International Affairs* 60, No. 2 (Spring/Summer 2007): 127.

12. Takeyh, *Guardians of the Revolution*, pp. 240–41.

13. Ottolenghi, *The Pasdaran*, pp. 15–27; Wehrey et al., "The Rise of the Pasdaran," esp. pp. 8–18, 35–43, 81–88.

14. Sadjadpour, "Reading Khamenei," p. 9.

15. See for instance, Ali Akbar Dareini, "Iran President Backs Down in Political Clashes," Associated Press, November 2, 2012.

16. Ali M. Ansari, "Iran Under Ahmadinejad," in Amin Tarzi, ed., *The Iranian Puzzle Piece* (Quantico, Va.: Marine Corps University Press, 2009), p. 13.

17. Sadjadpour, "Reading Khamenei," pp. 11–12; Sadjadpour, "The Nuclear Players," esp. p. 126.

18. Mohsen Milani, "Tehran's Take: Understanding Iran's U.S. Policy," *Foreign Affairs* 88, No. 4 (July/August 2009): 48–49.

19. Sadjadpour, "Reading Khamenei," p. 14.

20. Sadjadpour, "Reading Khamenei," pp. 17–19, 22–24; Sadjadpour, "The Nuclear Players," p. 126.

21. Takeyh, *Guardians of the Revolution*, p. 162.

22. Sadjadpour, "Reading Khamenei," p. 20. See also Takeyh, *Guardians of the Revolution*, pp. 164–65.

23. Shahram Chubin, "Iran's Strategic Environment and Nuclear Weapons," in *Iran's Nuclear Weapons Options: Issues and Analysis*, ed. Geoffrey Kemp (Washington, D.C.: Nixon Center, 2001).

24. For those interested, an English translation of Khomeini's Testament can be found at http://www.imam-khomeini.com/web1/english/showitem.aspx ?cid=1341&h=13&f=14&pid=1430.

25. On the 1996 coup plot, see "Bahrain Coup Suspects Say They Trained in Iran," *New York Times*, June 6, 1996; "Bahrain Holds 44 It Says Are Tied to Pro-Iran Plot," *New York Times*, June 5, 1996; and Richard A. Clarke, *Against All Enemies: Inside America's War on Terror* (New York: Free Press, 2004), p. 112. On annexing Bahrain, see Saud al-Zahed and Eila Jazaeri, "Iran's Khamenei-Run Newspaper Calls for Bahrain Annexation After GCC Union Talks," *Al-Arabiyya*, May 16, 2012.

26. David Menashri, "Iran's Regional Policy: Between Radicalism and Pragmatism," *Journal of International Affairs* 60, No. 2 (Spring/Summer 2007): 155–56.

27. David Crist, *The Twilight War: The Secret History of America's Thirty-Year Conflict with Iran* (New York: Penguin Press, 2012), pp. 514–15.

28. Douglas Jehl, "For Death of Its Diplomats, Iran Vows Blood for Blood," *New York Times*, September 12, 1998.

29. The composition and powers of this council are described in Article 111 of the Iranian constitution. An English translation is available at http://www.iranonline.com/iran/iran-info/government/constitution-8.html.

30. For a superb discussion of the mechanics and politics of succession in Iran, including the potential for a leadership council to retain power rather than an individual successor, see Alireza Nader, David E. Thaler, and S. R. Bohandy, *The Next Supreme Leader: Succession in the Islamic Republic of Iran* (Santa Monica, Calif.: RAND, 2011), esp. pp. 73–76.

31. For a superb account of the 2009 presidential elections and the dramatic events that followed, see Majd, *The Ayatollah's Democracy*, pp. 3–66.

32. For scholarly reports making the case that the 2009 election results were fraudulent, see for instance Ali Ansari, Daniel Berman, and Thomas Rintoul, "Preliminary Analysis of the Voting Figures in Iran's 2009 Presidential Elections," Chatham House, June 21, 2009, available at http://www.chathamhouse.org/sites/default/files/public/Research/Middle%20East/iranelection0609.pdf; Walter R. Mebane, Jr., "A Note on the Presidential Election in Iran, June 2009," University of Michigan, June 29, 2009, available at http://www-personal.umich.edu/~wmebane/note18jun2009.pdf.

33. Casey L. Addis, "Iran's 2009 Presidential Elections," R40653, Congressional Research Service, June 22, 2009, pp. 7–8; Robert Tait, Ian Black, and Mark Tran, "Iran Protests: Fifth Day of Unrest as Regime Cracks Down on Critics," *Guardian*, June 17, 2009; Robert F. Worth, "A Struggle for the Legacy of the Iranian Revolution," *New York Times*, June 20, 2009.

34. Ansari, "Iran Under Ahmadinejad," pp. 12–14.

35. Numbers of killed during the Green Revolution is hotly disputed. A figure of about one hundred seems to be the consensus, but the sources for this figure are unclear. See "Iran Election: Faces of the Dead and Detained," *Guardian*, January 28, 2010, available at http://www.guardian.co.uk/world/interactive/2009/jun/29/iran-election-dead-detained.

36. See for instance, Ali Ansari, "The Revolution Will Be Mercantilized," *National Interest*, No. 105 (January/February 2010); Abbas Milani, "Iran: A Coup in Three Steps," *Forbes*, June 15, 2009, available at http://www.forbes.com/2009/06/15/iran-elections-khamenei-mousavi-ahmadinejad-opinions-contributors-milani.html; Karim Sadjadpour, "Epilogue: The 2009 Iranian Presidential Election and its Implications," in Tarzi, ed., *The Iranian Puzzle Piece*, pp. 84–86.

37. Emanuele Ottolenghi, *The Pasdaran: Inside Iran's Islamic Revolutionary Guard Corps* (Washington, D.C.: Foundation for the Defense of Democracies, 2011), pp. 37–39.

38. Ottolenghi, *The Pasdaran*, p. 29.

39. Ray Takeyh, "Iran's Missing Moderates," *International Herald Tribune*, March 18, 2012.

40. Karim Sadjadpour, correspondence with the author, April 2013.

41. On the divisions among even Iran's current, uniformly hardline leadership see Ali Akbar Dareini and Brian Murphy, "Ahmadinejad Rivals Rack Up Parliament Wins in Iran," Associated Press, March 3, 2012; Yeganeh Torbati, "Iran's Khamenei Warns of Government Divisions After Rial Plunge," Reuters, October 10, 2012; Thomas Erdbrink, "Iran's Political Infighting Erupts in Full View," *New York Times*, October 22, 2012; "Iran's Ahmadinejad Denied Visit to Evin Prison," Reuters, October 23, 2012.

42. For a cogent argument that Iran's foreign policy is principally defensive, see Milani, "Tehran's Take," pp. 46–62.

43. On this see, Geneive Abdo, "Iran's Internal Struggles," in Patrick Clawson and Henry Sokolski, eds., *Checking Iran's Nuclear Ambitions* (Carlisle, Pa.: U.S. Army War College, 2004), pp. 57–60.

44. Quoted in Amir Taheri, *The Persian Night: Iran under the Khomeinist Revolution* (New York: Encounter Books, 2009), p. 189.

45. "Iran's Struggle with America Should Continue," Reuters, November 13, 2009, www.reuters.com/article/2009/11/13/us-iran-usa-cleric-idUSTRE5AC 21I20091113.

46. Charlie Savage and Scott Shane, "U.S. Accuses Iranians of Plotting to Kill Saudi Envoy," *New York Times*, October 11, 2011; Crist, *The Twilight War*, pp. 562–66.

47. Office of Public Affairs, "Two Men Charged in Alleged Plot to Assassinate Saudi Arabian Ambassador to the United States," United States Department of Justice, October 11, 2011, available at http://www.justice.gov/opa/pr/2011/October/11-ag-1339.html.

48. Benjamin Weiser, "Man Pleads Guilty in Plot to Murder a Saudi Envoy," *New York Times*, October 17, 2012.

49. On the Mykonos trial, see Roya Hakakian, *Assassins of the Turquoise Palace* (New York: Grove Press, 2011).

50. See David E. Sanger, "America's Deadly Dynamics with Iran," *New York Times*, November 5, 2011. Most speculation focuses on Israel as having been behind those killings. While not impossible, it seems unlikely that the United States would have participated because of the extreme American aversion to assassination after the firestorm of the 1970s, in which CIA

involvement in a number of assassination plots was revealed, senior CIA officials were interrogated and embarrassed, new congressional oversight tools were established, and a sacrosanct executive order was issued prohibiting CIA participation in assassination. Since then, the CIA (as well as the U.S. military) has, to the best of anyone's knowledge, steered well clear of traditional assassinations.

51. On the Tanker War, see, Crist, *The Twilight War*, pp. 235–379; Kenneth M. Pollack, *The Persian Puzzle: The Conflict Between Iran and America* (New York: Random House, 2004), pp. 217–33; Steven R. Ward, *Immortal: A Military History of Iran and Its Armed Forces* (Washington, D.C.: Georgetown University Press, 2009), pp. 279–96.

52. Crist, *The Twilight War*, pp. 511–37; Mohsen Milani, "Iran's Ties to the Taliban," Iran Primer, United States Institute of Peace, August 10, 2011, available at http://iranprimer.usip.org/blog/2011/aug/10/iran's-ties-taliban; Khwaja Basir Ahmad, "Alleged Spies Say Iran's Revolutionary Guards Trained Them," Pahjwok Afghan News, May 7, 2012, available at http://www.pajhwok.com/en/2012/05/07/alleged-spies-say-iran's-revolutionary-guards-trained-them; Aamer Madhani, "Experts Discuss Iran-Taliban Relationship," *USA Today*, July 22, 2010.

53. For a superb encapsulation of how Iran dealt with the first year of the Arab Spring, see Suzanne Maloney, "Iran: The Bogeyman," in Kenneth M. Pollack and Daniel L. Byman, eds., *The Arab Awakening: America and the Transformation of the Middle East* (Washington, D.C.: Brookings Institution Press, 2011), pp. 258–67.

54. David Ignatius, "The 'Day After' in Syria," *Washington Post*, July 25, 2012.

55. For instance, see "Egypt's Top Cleric Voices Sunnis' Worries of Iran," Associated Press, February 5, 2013.

56. Lolita C. Baldor, "U.S. Blaming Iran for Persian Gulf Cyberattacks," Associated Press, October 12, 2012; Dan De Luce, "Cyber War on Iran Has Only Just Begun," Agence France-Presse, July 13, 2012; Siobhan Gorman and Julian E. Barnes, "Iran Blamed for Cyberattacks," *Wall Street Journal*, October 13–14, 2012.

57. Joel Greenberg and Simon Denyer, "Israel Blames Iran for India and Georgia Bombing Attempts; Tehran Denies Role," *Washington Post*, February 13, 2012; Nicholas Kulish and Eric Schmitt, "Hezbollah Is Blamed for Attack on Israeli Tourists in Bulgaria," *New York Times*, July 19, 2012.

58. For a good summary of Iranian support to various terrorist groups, see Kenneth Katzman, "Iran: U.S. Concerns and Policy Responses," Congressional Research Service, RL32048, September 5, 2012, pp. 43–65.

59. For an excellent discussion of the anti-Semitism and anti-Zionism among

Iran's current leadership, see Reuel Marc Gerecht, "Should Israel Bomb Iran? Better Safe Than Sorry," *Weekly Standard* 15, No. 42 (July 26, 2010).

60. Dalia Dassa Kaye, Alireza Nader, and Parisa Roshan, *Israel and Iran: A Dangerous Rivalry* (Santa Monica, Calif.: RAND, 2011), pp. 57–77; Takeyh, *Guardians of the Revolution*, pp. 20–21, 62–69.

61. For a lovely and informative vignette of this community, see Majd, *The Ayatollah's Democracy*, pp. 212–53.

62. Mark J. Gasiorowski, *U.S. Foreign Policy and the Shah: Building a Client State in Iran* (Ithaca, N.Y.: Cornell University Press, 1991), pp. 120–24.

63. Trita Parsi, *Treacherous Alliance: The Secret Dealings of Israel, Iran, and the United States* (New Haven, Conn.: Yale University Press, 2007), p. 145; Ray Takeyh, *Hidden Iran: Paradox and Power in the Islamic Republic* (New York: Times Books, 2006), p. 141.

64. Shahram Chubin, *Whither Iran? Reform, Domestic Politics, and National Security* (Oxford: Oxford University Press, 2002), p. 73.

65. Gawdat Baghat, "Nuclear Proliferation: The Islamic Republic of Iran," *Iranian Studies* 39, No. 3 (2006): 307–27; Kaye, Nader, and Roshan, *Israel and Iran*, pp. 65–70.

66. "65 Suspects Arrested on Charges of Blast in Southeast Iran," Fars News Agency, February 16, 2007; M. K. Bhadrakumar, "Foreign Devils in the Iranian Mountains," *Asia Times*, February 24, 2007, available at http://www.atimes.com/atimes/Middle_East/IB24Ak$1.html; "Iran: Many Die in Zahedan Mosque Bombing," BBC, May 28, 2009, available at http://news.bbc.co.uk/2/hi/middle_east/8072795.stm; William Lowther and Colin Freeman, "U.S. Funds Terror Groups to Sow Chaos in Iran," *Telegraph*, February 25, 2007; Mark Perry, "False Flag," *Foreign Policy*, January 13, 2012, available at http://www.foreignpolicy.com/articles/2012/01/13/false_flag?page=0,0. It is worth noting that the United States has denied any involvement in these attacks. In 2010, the U.S. government designated the Baluch extremist group Jundallah a terrorist organization, thereby making it a crime for any U.S. government personnel to provide material support to them.

Chapter 2. The Iranian Nuclear Program

1. David Patrikarakos, *Nuclear Iran: The Birth of an Atomic State* (London: Tauris, 2012), pp. 14–82. See also Chris Quillen, "Iranian Nuclear Weapons Policy: Past, Present, and Possible Future," *Middle East Review of International Affairs* 6, No. 2 (June 2002): 17; Ray Takeyh, *Guardians of the Revolution: Iran and the World in the Age of the Ayatollahs* (Oxford: Oxford University Press, 2009), pp. 242–43; Steven R. Ward, *Immortal: A Military*

History of Iran and Its Armed Forces (Washington, D.C.: Georgetown University Press, 2009), pp. 319–20.

2. Patrikarakos, Nuclear Iran, pp. 50–54.

3. Ibid., pp. 102–130; Takeyh, Guardians of the Revolution, p. 243.

4. George Jahn, "Iran Says It Will Speed Up Nuclear Program," Associated Press, January 31, 2013, http://www.google.com/hostednews/ap/article/AL eqM5jPHLK4rK7Md1f42qK3DZwSHvQM_A?docId=82f8ffeeab294344bc 57c3df6f719acc.

5. David Albright and Christina Walrond, "Iran's Gas Centrifuge Program: Taking Stock," Institute for Science and International Security, February 11, 2010, available at http://isis-online.org/isis-reports/detail/irans -gas-centrifuge-program-taking-stock/. Richard P. Cronin, Alan Kronstadt, and Sharon Squassoni, "Pakistan's Nuclear Proliferation Activities and the Recommendations of the 9/11 Commission: U.S. Policy Constraints and Options," RL32745, Congressional Research Service, January 25, 2005, p. 11.

6. Kenneth M. Pollack, The Persian Puzzle: The Conflict Between Iran and America (New York: Random House, 2004), p. 318.

7. Patrikarakos, Nuclear Iran, pp. 141–43.

8. Pollack, Persian Puzzle, p. 362; Ward, Immortal, p. 320.

9. One superb recent study has concluded that Iran could have purchased the same fuel abroad for 10 percent of the cost of manufacturing it domestically—and that does not include the cost of sanctions, lost investment, and other penalties Iran has suffered that dwarf the simple cost comparison. See Ali Vaez and Karim Sadjadpour, "Iran's Nuclear Odyssey: Costs and Risks," Carnegie Endowment for International Peace, April 2013, esp. pp. 13–17.

10. Seth Carus, "Iran and Weapons of Mass Destruction," pre-publication copy prepared for the American Jewish Committee Annual Meeting, May 3, 2000, pp. 2–4; Gary Milhollin, "The Mullahs and the Bomb," New York Times, October 23, 2003; "Nuclear Weapons—2004 Developments," Glo balSecurity.org, available at http://www.globalsecurity.org/wmd/world/ iran/nuke2004.htm, accessed on August 5, 2004; "Nuclear Weapons—2003 Developments," GlobalSecurity.org, available at http://www.globalsecurity .org/wmd/world/iran/nuke2003.htm, accessed on August 5, 2004; "Nuclear Weapons—2002 Developments," http://www.globalsecurity.org/wmd/world/ iran/nuke2002.htm.

11. In 2005, Iran took out a full-page ad in the New York Times to explain its version of the nuclear standoff and this should be seen as the most authoritative statement of Iranian claims about its nuclear program. See

"An Unnecessary Crisis—Setting the Record Straight About Iran's Nuclear Program," *New York Times*, November 18, 2005, p. A11.

12. Simon Shercliff, "The Iranian Nuclear Issue," in Amin Tarzi, ed., *The Iranian Puzzle Piece* (Quantico, Va.: Marine Corps University Press, 2009), pp. 50–51; Stuart Winer, "Iran Admits It Deceived the West over Nuclear Program," *Times of Israel*, September 20, 2012.

13. As part of signing on to the NPT, countries must have a Safeguard Agreement with the IAEA that describes procedures for handling nuclear materials, notification of changes in the countries' nuclear program, and other basic functions. It is unclear whether violation of the Safeguard Agreement constitutes a violation of the NPT itself, another problem with the NPT.

14. International Atomic Energy Agency, Report by the Director General, "Implementation of the NPT Safeguards Agreement in the Islamic Republic of Iran," GOV/2003/40, June 6, 2003. Also see Joby Warrick and Glenn Kessler, "Iran's Nuclear Program Speeds Ahead," *Washington Post*, March 10, 2003, p. A1. Note that Warrick and Kessler claim that the Natanz facility was designed to house 5,000 centrifuges while the actual IAEA report says 50,000. See IAEA, "Implementation of the NPT Safeguards Agreement in the Islamic Republic of Iran," p. 6.

15. "Iran Signs Additional Protocol," International Atomic Energy Agency, December 18, 2003, available at http://www.iaea.org/newscenter/news/2003/iranap20031218.html.

16. IAEA, "Implementation of the NPT Safeguards Agreement in the Islamic Republic of Iran: Resolution Adopted by the Board on 18 June 2004"; "Iran's Continuing Pursuit of Weapons of Mass Destruction: Testimony by Under Secretary of State for Arms Control and International Security John R. Bolton," House International Relations Committee, Subcommittee on the Middle East and Central Asia, June 24, 2004; Karl Vick, "Another Nuclear Program Found in Iran," *Washington Post*, February 24, 2004, p. A1.

17. For a fuller account of how Iran's claims belie the economic realities of its nuclear program, see Vaez and Sadjadpour, "Iran's Nuclear Odyssey."

18. Ibid., p. 17.

19. See "Tensions Grow over Iran's Nuclear Goals," *PBS NewsHour*, September 27, 2004, available at http://www.pbs.org/newshour/bb/middle_east/july-dec04/iran_9-27.html.

20. Shercliff, "The Iranian Nuclear Issue," pp. 50–51.

21. Patrikarakos, *Nuclear Iran*, pp. 166–68.

22. David Patrikarakos reaches the same conclusion. See ibid., p. 169.

23. For the details of how much more cost-effective it would be for Iran to pur-

sue natural gas rather than nuclear power, see Vaez and Sadjadpour, "Iran's Nuclear Odyssey," pp. 17–21.

24. Author's conversation with senior British officials, Washington, D.C., April 2004.

25. David Albright, Paul Brannan, Andrea Stricker, and Christina Walrond, "Natanz Enrichment Site: Boondoggle or Part of an Atomic Bomb Production Complex?" Institute for Science and International Security, September 21, 2011, available at http://isis-online.org/isis-reports/detail/ natanz-enrichment-site-boondoggle-or-part-of-an-atomic-bomb-production -comp/.

26. Ali Akbar Dareini, "Iran Plans Enrichment Sites in Defiance of UN," Associated Press, November 29, 2009; Thomas Erdbrink, "Ahmadinejad Vows Dramatic Expansion of Iran's Nuclear Program," Washington Post, November 30, 2009.

27. See also David Crist, The Twilight War: The Secret History of America's Thirty-Year Conflict with Iran (New York: Penguin Press, 2012), p. 491.

28. See National Intelligence Council, "Iran: Nuclear Intentions and Capabilities," National Intelligence Estimate, November 2007, p. 5. The text of the declassified version of the key judgments can be found at http://graphics8 .nytimes.com/packages/pdf/international/20071203_release.pdf.

29. Commercial satellite imagery and expert analysis can be found at David Albright and Robert Avagyan, "Suspected Clean-Up Activity Continues at Parchin Military Complex: Considerable Dirt Movement Near Suspect Building," Institute for Science and International Security, June 20, 2012, available at http://isis-online.org/isis-reports/detail/parchin/. On the IAEA efforts to get Iran to discuss its suspected weaponization, see International Atomic Energy Agency Board of Governors, "Implementation of the NPT Safeguards Agreement and Relevant Provisions of Security Council Resolutions in the Islamic Republic of Iran," August 30, 2012, available at http:// www.iaea.org/Publications/Documents/Board/2012/gov2012-37.pdf, p. 3; Kenneth Katzman, "Iran: U.S. Concerns and Policy Responses," Congressional Research Service, RL32048, September 5, 2012, p. 28.

30. "UN Fails in Attempt to Restart Iran Nuke Probe," Associated Press, January 18, 2013.

31. David E. Sanger and William J. Broad, "Inspectors Say Iran Worked on Warhead," New York Times, February 19, 2010, p. A13.

32. George Jahn, "UN: Credible Evidence Iran Working on Nuke Weapons," Associated Press, September 2, 2011.

33. One of these documents has since made its way into the public domain. See George Jahn, "Graph Suggests Iran Working on Bomb," Associated

Press, November 27, 2012, available at http://news.yahoo.com/ap-exclusive -graph-suggests-iran-working-bomb-161109665.html.

34. Kenneth Katzman, "Iran: U.S. Concerns and Policy Responses," Congressional Research Service, RL32048, September 5, 2012, p. 28.

35. International Atomic Energy Agency Board of Governors, "Implementation of the NPT Safeguards Agreement and Relevant Provisions of Security Council Resolutions in the Islamic Republic of Iran," November 8, 2011, Report Gov/2011/65, available at http://www.iaea.org/Publications/Docu ments/Board/2011/gov2011-65.pdf, p. 8.

36. That the WMD fiasco was foremost an intelligence failure and the role of the Bush 43 administration in that disaster, see Central Intelligence Agency, "Misreading Intentions: Iraq's Reaction to Inspections Created Picture of Deception," Iraq WMD Retrospective Series, January 5, 2006, declassified and released June 5, 2012; Robert Jervis, *Why Intelligence Fails: Lessons from the Iranian Revolution and the Iraq War* (Ithaca, N.Y.: Cornell University Press, 2010); Kenneth M. Pollack, "Spies, Lies, and Weapons: What Went Wrong," *Atlantic Monthly*, January/February 2004, pp. 78–92; Senate Select Committee on Intelligence, "Report on the U.S. Intelligence Community's Prewar Intelligence Assessments on Iraq," July 7, 2004, available at http://web.mit.edu/simsong/www/iraqreport2-textunder.pdf.

37. This is the Lavizan-Shian site. On that site, and Iran's efforts to conceal whatever it had been doing there, see Institute for Science and International Security, "Iran: Nuclear Sites: Lavisan-Shian," available at http:// www.isisnucleariran.org/sites/detail/lavisan-shian/.

38. According to declassified documents, the U.S. intelligence community believed by *at least* 1974 that Israel possessed a nuclear arsenal. See the declassified text of the Special National Intelligence Estimate (SNIE), "Prospects for Further Proliferation of Nuclear Weapons," September 4, 1974, available at http://www.gwu.edu/%7Ensarchiv/NSAEBB/NSAEBB181/sa08 .pdf, downloaded on January 16, 2008. The relevant page is the first page of the SNIE, which was also declassified as page 6 of "Memorandum from Atherton and Kratzer to Mr. Sisco, 'Response to Congressional Questions on Israel's Nuclear Capabilities,'" October 15, 1975, Secret, RG 59, Records of Joseph Sisco, Box 40, Israeli Nuclear Capability 1975, available at http:// www.gwu.edu/~nsarchiv/NSAEBB/NSAEBB189/IN-30.pdf, downloaded on October 21, 2007. The third paragraph of the SNIE begins with the sentence: "We believe that Israel already has produced nuclear weapons." This was the estimate's key judgment regarding the Israelis' nuclear arsenal. In addition, another declassified document ("Parker T. Hart to Secretary Dean Rusk, 'Issues to be Considered in Connection with Negotiations with

Israel for F-4 Phantom Aircraft,' " October 15, 1968, Top Secret/Nodis Sensitive, SN 67–69, Def 12-5 Isr, available at http://www.gwu.edu/~nsarchiv/NSAEBB/NSAEBB189/IN-02.pdf, downloaded October 21, 2007) states that as early as October 1968, the State Department had concluded that "[a]ll evidence suggests that present Israeli policy is to maintain its nuclear option and to proceed with a program to reduce to a minimum the lead time required to exercise that option."

39. This report is the so-called Duelfer Report, named for Charles Duelfer, the head of the Iraq Survey Group, the official project to determine what had happened to Saddam's WMD programs between 1991 and 2003. It is more properly titled "The DCI Special Advisor Report on Iraq's WMD." The entire report is available from the CIA website at https://www.cia.gov/library/reports/general-reports-1/iraq_wmd_2004/index.html.

40. Pollack, "Spies, Lies and Weapons," pp. 78–92. Also see "The DCI Special Advisor Report on Iraq's WMD," vol. 1, 2004, available at http://www.foia.cia.gov/duelfer/Iraqs_WMD_Vol1.pdf.

41. For one of the only works to make this argument before the invasion, see the extensive interview of Scott Ritter in William Rivers Pitt with Scott Ritter, *War on Iraq: What Team Bush Doesn't Want you to Know* (New York: Context Books, 2002).

42. David E. Sanger and William J. Broad, "Iran Is Seen as Advancing Nuclear Bid," *New York Times*, May 22, 2013; Anthony H. Cordesman and Abdullah Toukan, "Analyzing the Impact of Preventive Strikes Against Iran's Nuclear Facilities," Center for Strategic and International Studies, September 2012, available at http://csis.org/files/publication/120906_Iran_US_Preventive_Strikes.pdf, p. 14.

43. Frederik Dahl, "Iran Appears to Advance in Construction of Arak Nuclear Plant," Reuters, February 22, 2013.

44. As a practical matter, nations have consistently found that to manufacture the first bomb requires twice as much LEU to produce the needed quantity of HEU because of various forms of wastage and inefficiency. See Mark Fitzpatrick, "Assessing Iran's Nuclear Program Without Exaggeration or Complacency," International Institute for Strategic Studies, October 3, 2011, available online at http://www.armscontrol.org/files/Iran_Brief_10_2011_Mark_Fitzpatrick.pdf, p. 2.

45. International Atomic Energy Agency Board of Governors, "Implementation of the NPT Safeguards Agreement and Relevant Provisions of Security Council Resolutions in the Islamic Republic of Iran," August 30, 2012, available at http://www.iaea.org/Publications/Documents/Board/2012/gov2012-37.pdf, pp. 3–4; Kenneth Katzman, "Iran: U.S. Concerns and Policy

Responses," Congressional Research Service, RL32048, September 5, 2012, p. 30.

46. Jahn, "Iran Says It Will Speed Up Nuclear Program"; Ali Akbar Dareini, "Iran: Advanced Enrichment Centrifuges Installed," Associated Press, February 13, 2013; George Jahn, "Diplomats: Iran Starts Upgrade of Nuclear Site," Associated Press, February 20, 2013.

47. Thomas A. Keaney and Eliot A. Cohen, *The Gulf War Air Power Survey: Summary Report* (Washington, D.C.: U.S. Government Printing Office, 1993), pp. 78–79. Also see Garry B. Dillon, "The IAEA in Iraq: Past Activities and Findings," *IAEA Bulletin* 44, No. 2 (2002), available at http://www.iaea.org/Publications/Magazines/Bulletin/Bull442/44201251316.pdf.

48. International Atomic Energy Agency Board of Governors, "Implementation of the NPT Safeguards Agreement and Relevant Provisions of Security Council Resolutions in the Islamic Republic of Iran," November 8, 2011, Report Gov/2011/65, available at http://www.iaea.org/Publications/Documents/Board/2011/gov2011-65.pdf, Annex p. 3, footnote 19.

49. See National Intelligence Council, "Iran: Nuclear Intentions and Capabilities," National Intelligence Estimate, November 2007, p. 5. The key judgments of the NIE were released to the public almost immediately after the classified version was distributed internally. The full text of the published declassified version of the key judgments can be found at http://graphics8.nytimes.com/packages/pdf/international/20071203_release.pdf.

50. Christopher Hope, "MI6 Chief Sir John Sawers: 'We Foiled Iranian Nuclear Weapons Bid,'" *Telegraph*, July 12, 2012.

51. Bob Woodward, *Plan of Attack* (New York: Simon & Schuster, 2004), pp. 296–306.

52. For insightful accounts of the intelligence failure over Iraq's WMD, see Central Intelligence Agency, "Misreading Intentions"; Jervis, *Why Intelligence Fails*; Senate Select Committee on Intelligence, "Report on the U.S. Intelligence Community's Prewar Intelligence Assessments on Iraq."

53. On non-U.S. assessments of Iran's weaponization program, see Barak Ravid, "Israel Seeks Input on U.S. Iran Report," *Haaretz*, July 25, 2008; Barak Ravid, "Sources: UN Watchdog Hiding Evidence on Iran Nuclear Program," *Haaretz*, August 19, 2009; "European Leaders Considering Iran Sanctions, French Foreign Minister Says," Associated Press, September 16, 2007; Bruno Schirra, "Germany's Spies Refuted the 2007 NIE Report," *Wall Street Journal Europe*, July 20, 2009.

54. IAEA, "Implementation of the NPT Safeguards Agreement," November 8, 2011, Annex pp. 4–12; Avi Issacharoff, "Report: Iran Scientist in Charge of Nuclear Weapons Program Resumes His Work," Reuters, Au-

gust 30, 2012; Jeffrey Lewis, "The Ayatollah's Pregnant Pause," Foreign Policy.Com, August 15, 2012, available at http://www.foreignpolicy.com/articles/2012/08/15/the_ayatollahs_pregnant_pause.

55. IAEA, "Implementation of the NPT Safeguards Agreement," November 8, 2011, Annex pp. 4–12.

56. Ibid., Annex p. 4.

57. Scott Pelley, "The Defense Secretary: Leon Panetta," *60 Minutes,* January 29, 2012, transcript and video available at http://www.cbsnews.com/8301 -18560_162-57367997/the-defense-secretary-an-interview-with-leon-pane tta/?tag=currentVideoInfo;videoMetaInfo; Maseh Zarif, "Current State of the Iranian Nuclear Program," AEI Critical Threats Project, October 2012.

58. Michael D. Shear and David E. Sanger, "Iran Nuclear Weapon to Take Year or More, Obama Says," *New York Times,* March 15, 2012; "Iran Would Need Around a Year to Build Atomic Bomb: Israel," Reuters, March 22, 2013.

59. William C. Witt, Christina Walrond, David Albright, and Houston Wood, "Iran's Evolving Breakout Potential," Institute for Science and International Security, October 8, 2012, available at http://www.isisnucleariran.org/assets/pdf/Irans_Evolving_Breakout_Potential_8October2012.pdf, p. 3.

60. "Experts: North Korea Might Have Know-how to Fire Nuclear-Tipped Missile at South Korea, Japan," *Washington Post,* April 6, 2013.

61. "France: Iran Seems on Track for Nukes by Mid-2013," Associated Press, October 21, 2012.

62. Seyed Hossein Mousavian, "Ten Reasons Iran Doesn't Want the Bomb," National Interest online, December 4, 2012, available at http://nationalin terest.org/commentary/ten-reasons-iran-doesnt-want-the-bomb-7802.

63. For a longer discussion of this issue, see Amos Yadlin and Yoel Guzansky, "Iran on the Threshold," *Strategic Assessment* 15, No. 1 (April 2012): 7–14.

64. Yeganeh Torbati, "Iran Says It Is Converting Uranium, Easing Bomb Fears," Reuters, February, 13, 2013.

65. Michael Makovsky and Blaise Misztal, "Iran's Shrewd Move," *Weekly Standard,* February 22, 2013.

66. Yadlin and Guzansky, "Iran on the Threshold," p. 8.

67. Amos Harel, "IDF Chief to Haaretz: I Do Not Believe Iran Will Decide to Develop Nuclear Weapons," *Haaretz,* April 25, 2012.

68. "Iranian TV: Ayatollah Khamene'i Speaks on Khomeyni's Death Anniversary," Islamic Republic of Iran News Network Television (IRINN), Sunday, June 4, 2006.

69. Office of the Supreme Leader Sayyid Ali Khamenei, "Iran to Break Authority of Powers That Rely on Nukes," February 22, 2012, available at http://www.leader.ir/langs/en/index.php?p=contentShow&id=9183.

70. Barry Parker, "Stop Threats If You Want a Nuclear Deal, Ahmadinejad Tells West," Agence France-Presse, December 18, 2009.

71. Ali Akbar Salehi, "Iran: We Do Not Want Nuclear Weapons," *Washington Post*, April 12, 2012.

72. Ali Akbar Dareini, "Iran: Khamenei's Ban on Nuclear Weapons Binding," Associated Press, January 15, 2013.

73. "Iran Issues Statement at IAEA Board of Governors Meeting," IRNA, August 10, 2005.

74. Michael Eisenstadt and Mehdi Khalaji, "Forget the Fatwa," *National Interest* online, March 13, 2013, available at http://nationalinterest.org/commen tary/forget-the-fatwa-8220.

75. "Iran's Nuclear Theology: Bombs and Truth: Muslim Theological Objections to Nuclear Weapons—Real and Imagined," *Economist*, May 19, 2012; Patrikarakos, *Nuclear Iran*, pp. 117–30.

76. Patrikarakos, *Nuclear Iran*, pp. 120–21.

77. Quoted in ibid, p. 121.

78. Quoted in ibid., p. 130.

79. Ibid., p. 126.

80. Patrikarakos, *Nuclear Iran*, pp. 283–85.

81. Warren Bass, *Support Any Friend: Kennedy's Middle East and the Making of the U.S.-Israel Alliance* (Oxford: Oxford University Press, 2003); Avner Cohen, *Israel and the Bomb* (New York: Columbia University Press, 1998), pp. 99–174; Mordechai Gazit, "The Genesis of the US-Israeli Military-Strategic Relationship and the Dimona Issue," *Journal of Contemporary History* 35, No. 3 (July 2000): 413–22.

82. Ali Akbar Dareini, "Iran Cleric Wants 'Special Weapons' to Deter Enemy," Associated Press, June 14, 2010.

83. Ray Takeyh, "Introduction: What Do We Know," in Robert D. Blackwill, ed., *Iran: The Nuclear Challenge* (New York: Council on Foreign Relations, 2012), p. 9.

84. "Iran May Need Highly-Enriched Uranium in Future, Official Says," Reuters, April 17, 2013.

85. On the internal politics of Iran's nuclear decision-making, see Karim Sadjadpour, "The Nuclear Players," *Journal of International Affairs* 60, No. 2 (Spring/Summer 2007): 125–27.

86. See the Statement by Director of National Intelligence James Clapper in James Risen and Mark Mazetti, "U.S. Agencies See No Move by Iran to Build a Bomb," *New York Times*, February 24, 2012.

87. Shahram Chubin, "Extended Deterrence and Iran," *Strategic Insights* 8, No. 5 (December 2009).

Chapter 3. The Threat of a Nuclear Iran

1. "Iran Summons Bahrain Envoy over 'Terror' Cell Claim," Agence France-Presse, November 22, 2011.

2. The United States did consider retaliating against Iran for its role in the killing of Americans in Iraq, including during the Obama administration. See Elisabeth Bumiller, "Panetta Says Iranian Arms in Iraq Are a 'Concern,'" New York Times, July 10, 2011; Phil Stewart, "U.S. May Act Unilaterally vs. Iran-Armed Militias," Reuters, July 11, 2011.

3. Paul Bracken, The Second Nuclear Age: Strategy, Danger, and the New Power Politics (New York: Times Books, 2012), p. 77.

4. This foundational concept of nuclear deterrence was first articulated in Bernard Brodie, The Absolute Weapon: Atomic Power and World Order (New York: Harcourt, Brace, 1946).

5. On the extent of Saddam's reckless (and inadvertently suicidal) decision-making as we have now come to understand it from documents and interviews secured after the 2003 invasion, see for instance Amatzia Baram, "Deterrence Lessons from Iraq," Foreign Affairs 91, No. 4 (July/August 2012): 76–85; Kevin M. Woods, James Lacey, and Williamson R. Murray, "Saddam's Delusions: The View from the Inside," Foreign Affairs 85, No. 3 (May/June 2006); Kevin M. Woods et al., The Iraqi Perspectives Report (Annapolis, Md.: Naval Institute Press, 2006).

6. In particular, see the grand jury indictment against thirteen members of Saudi Hizballah filed by the U.S. government in Alexandria, Virginia, available at http://news.findlaw.com/cnn/docs/khobar/khobarindict61901 .pdf, accessed July 26, 2004. The 9/11 Commission also found that the evidence of Iran behind the Khobar Towers bombing was "strong." See Report of the 9/11 Commission: Final Report of the National Commission on Terrorist Attacks Upon the United States (Washington, D.C.: U.S. Government Printing Office, 2004), p. 60. In addition, see the now-declassified memorandum "Iranian Response on al-Khobar," September 15, 1999, written by this author while the director for Persian Gulf affairs at the National Security Council, available from the National Security Archive at http://www.gwu.edu/~nsarchiv/NSAEBB/NSAEBB318/doc01.pdf. Also see Daniel Byman, Deadly Connections: States That Sponsor Terrorism (Cambridge, U.K.: Cambridge University Press, 2005), pp. 79–110, esp. p. 85; Richard Clarke, Against All Enemies: Inside America's War on Terror (New York: Free Press, 2004), pp. 112–31; David Crist, The Twilight War: The Secret History of America's Thirty-Year Conflict with Iran (New York: Penguin Press, 2012), pp. 402–413; Timothy Naftali, Blindspot: The Secret History of American Counterterrorism (New York: Basic Books, 2005), pp. 248–51,

260–61; Kenneth M. Pollack, *The Persian Puzzle: The Conflict Between Iran and America* (New York: Random House, 2004), pp. 280–302; Steven R. Ward, *Immortal: A Military History of Iran and Its Armed Forces* (Washington, D.C.: Georgetown University Press, 2009), p. 322.

7. James G. Blight, Janet M. Lang, Hussein Banai, Malcolm Byrne, and John Tirman, *Becoming Enemies: U.S.-Iran Relations and the Iran-Iraq War, 1979-1988* (Lanham, Md.: Rowman & Littlefield, 2012), pp. 195–226; Pollack, *The Persian Puzzle*, pp. 223–35; Ward, *Immortal*, pp. 279–98.

8. "Unclassified Report to Congress on the Acquisition of Technology Relating to Weapons of Mass Destruction and Advanced Conventional Munitions, 1 January Through 30 June 2003," Central Intelligence Agency, available at https://www.cia.gov/library/reports/archived-reports-1/jan_jun2003.pdf, p. 3.

9. Ibid.

10. Paul Pillar, *Terrorism and U.S. Foreign Policy* (Washington, D.C.: Brookings Institution Press, 2001), p. 57.

11. Paul Pillar, "We Can Live with a Nuclear Iran," *Washington Monthly*, March/April 2012, available at http://www.washingtonmonthly.com/magazine/marchapril_2012/features/we_can_live_with_a_nuclear_iran035772.php.

12. On this, see also Ward, *Immortal*, pp. 318–19.

13. Although there is a wealth of excellent work on the drivers of Iranian foreign policy, on this point in particular see Graham E. Fuller, *"The Center of the Universe": The Geopolitics of Iran* (Boulder, Colo.: Westview, 1991); Karim Sadjadpour, "Reading Khamenei: The World View of Iran's Most Powerful Leader," Carnegie Endowment for International Peace, 2008; Ray Takeyh, *Guardians of the Revolution: Iran and the World in the Age of the Ayatollahs* (Oxford: Oxford University Press, 2009).

14. Pollack, *The Persian Puzzle*, pp. 13–71.

15. Mark J. Gasiorowski and Malcolm Byrne, eds., *Mohammad Mosaddeq and the 1953 Coup in Iran* (Syracuse, N.Y.: Syracuse University Press, 2004), esp. pp. 227–80; Stephen Kinzer, *All the Shah's Men: An American Coup and the Roots of Middle East Terror* (Hoboken, N.J.: Wiley, 2003); Pollack, *The Persian Puzzle*, pp. 40–71.

16. Pollack, *The Persian Puzzle*, pp. 147–48.

17. Clarke, *Against All Enemies*, pp. 103–105; Pollack, *The Persian Puzzle*, pp. 273–75.

18. See David E. Sanger, *Confront and Conceal: Obama's Secret Wars and Surprising Use of American Power* (New York: Crown, 2012).

19. Blight et al., *Becoming Enemies*, pp. 98–123.

20. International Crisis Group, "Dealing with Iran's Nuclear Program," October 27, 2003, pp. 11–15; Ray Takeyh, "Iranian Options: Pragmatic Mullas and America's Interests," *National Interest*, Fall 2003, pp. 49–56; Ray Takeyh, "Iran's Nuclear Calculations," *World Policy Journal*, Summer 2003, pp. 21–26.

21. Dalia Dassa Kaye, Alireza Nader, and Parisa Roshan, *Israel and Iran: A Dangerous Rivalry* (Santa Monica, Calif.: RAND, 2011), pp. 57–77.

22. Takeyh, *Hidden Iran*, p. 144; Ward, *Immortal*, p. 320.

23. Kenneth N. Waltz, "Why Iran Should Get the Bomb," *Foreign Affairs* 91, No. 4 (July/August 2012).

24. Scott Sagan, Kenneth Waltz, and Richard K. Betts, "A Nuclear Iran: Promoting Stability or Courting Disaster?" *Journal of International Affairs* 60, No. 2 (Spring/Summer 2007): 137.

25. For others who have provided more fulsome rebuttals of Waltz's arguments, see Colin Kahl, "One Step Too Far," *Foreign Affairs* 91, No. 5 (September/October 2012): 157–61; Emily Landau, "When Neorealism Meets the Middle East: Iran's Pursuit of Nuclear Weapons in (Regional) Context," *Strategic Assessment* 15. No. 3 (October 2012): 27–38; and the various responses of Scott Sagan in his extended debate with Waltz in Sagan, Waltz, and Betts. "A Nuclear Iran: Promoting Stability or Courting Disaster?" and Scott D. Sagan and Kenneth N. Waltz, *The Spread of Nuclear Weapons: A Debate Renewed*, 2nd ed. (New York: Norton, 2002).

26. Avner Cohen, the great historian of the Israeli nuclear program, believes that Israel first acquired nuclear weapons in 1966. See Avner Cohen, *Israel and the Bomb* (New York: Columbia University Press, 1998), pp. 99–174. According to declassified documents, the U.S. intelligence community believed that Israel possessed a nuclear arsenal by *at least* 1974. On this, see Special National Intelligence Estimate (SNIE), "Prospects for Further Proliferation of Nuclear Weapons," September 4, 1974, available at http://www.gwu.edu/%7Ensarchiv/NSAEBB/NSAEBB181/sa08.pdf, downloaded January 16, 2008.

27. Warren Bass, *Support Any Friend: Kennedy's Middle East and the Making of the U.S.-Israel Alliance* (Oxford: Oxford University Press, 2003); Abraham Ben-Tzvi, *Decade of Transition: Eisenhower, Kennedy, and the Origins of the American-Israeli Alliance* (New York: Columbia University Press, 1998); Mordechai Gazit, "The Genesis of the US-Israeli Military-Strategic Relationship and the Dimona Issue," *Journal of Contemporary History* 35, No. 3 (July 2000): 413–22; Lipson, "American Support for Israel: History, Sources, Limits," pp. 129–42; Douglas Little, "The Making of a Special Relationship: The United States and Israel, 1957–68," *International Journal of*

Middle East Studies 25, No. 4 (November 1993): 563–85; Kenneth Organski, *The $36 Billion Bargain: Strategy and Politics in U.S. Assistance to Israel* (New York: Columbia University Press, 1990); Kenneth M. Pollack, *A Path Out of the Desert: A Grand Strategy for America in the Middle East* (New York: Random House, 2008), pp. 34–40; Steven L. Spiegel, *The Other Arab-Israel Conflict: Making America's Middle East Policy from Truman to Reagan* (Chicago: University of Chicago Press, 1985).

28. The nine major military operations since then that I am counting here are the Six-Day War, the War of Attrition, the October War, Operation Litani in 1978, the Israeli Invasion of Lebanon, Operation Accountability in 1993, Operation Grapes of Wrath in 1996, the 2006 Lebanon War, and Operation Cast Lead in 2009.

29. Jack Kim and Lee Jae-Won, "North Korea Shells South in Fiercest Attack in Decades," Reuters, November 23, 2010; " 'North Korean Torpedo' Sank South's Navy Ship—Report," BBC, May 20, 2010, available at http://www.bbc.co.uk/news/10129703.

30. Waltz, "Why Iran Should Get the Bomb," p. 4.

31. P. R. Chari, "Nuclear Restraint, Nuclear Risk Reduction, and the Security-Insecurity Paradox in South Asia," in Michael Krepon and Chris Gagne, eds., *The Stability-Instability Paradox: Nuclear Weapons and Brinksmanship in South Asia* (Washington, D.C.: Stimson Center, 2001); S. Paul Kapur, "Ten Years of Instability in a Nuclear South Asia," *International Security*, No. 33 (Fall 2008): 72; Benjamin S. Lambeth, *Airpower at 18,000': The Indian Air Force in the Kargil War* (Washington, D.C.: Carnegie Endowment for International Peace, 2012), pp. 7, 39; Bruce O. Riedel, *Deadly Embrace: Pakistan, America, and the Future of the Global Jihad* (Washington, D.C.: Brookings Institution Press, 2011), pp. 45–47, 115–16. Lambeth notes that Pakistan's thinking was not necessarily incorrect as the Indian Army and Air Force handcuffed themselves in a wide variety of ways that hurt their retaking of the captured terrain, because India's political and military leadership were terrified of the potential for escalation with Pakistan. See Lambeth, *Airpower at 18,000'*, pp. 12–13, 17, 25–26.

32. Riedel, *Deadly Embrace*, pp. 114–17; Eric Schmitt, Somni Sengupta, and Jane Perlez, "U.S. and India See Link to Militants in Pakistan," *New York Times*, December 2, 2008.

33. Colin Kahl, "One Step Too Far," *Foreign Affairs* 91, No. 5 (September/October 2012): 159.

34. See the declassified document, U.S. State Department Memorandum of Conversation, "US Reaction to Soviet Destruction of CPR [Chinese People's Republic] Nuclear Capability; Significance of Latest Sino-Soviet

Border Clash, etc.," August 18, 1969, Secret/Sensitive, National Archives, SN 67–69, Def 12 Chicom, available at http://www.gwu.edu/~nsarchiv/NSAEBB/NSAEBB49/sino.sov.10.pdf.

35. See the declassified document, State Department cable 143440 to U.S. Consulate Hong Kong, August 25, 1969, Secret, Exdis, National Archives, SN 67–69, Pol Chicom-US, available at http://www.gwu.edu/~nsarchiv/NSAEBB/NSAEBB49/sino.sov.13.pdf.

36. Amatzia Baram, "Deterrence Lessons from Iraq," *Foreign Affairs* 91, No. 4 (July/August 2012): 80.

37. Hal Brands and David Palkki, "Saddam, Israel and the Bomb: Nuclear Alarmism Justified?" *International Security* 36, No. 1 (Summer 2011): 136.

38. Kevin M. Woods, David D. Palkki, and Mark E. Stout, eds., *The Saddam Tapes: The Inner Workings of a Tyrant's Regime 1978–2001* (Cambridge, U.K.: Cambridge University Press, 2011), pp. 222–24.

39. See for instance, Michael Eisenstadt, "Living with a Nuclear Iran?" *Survival* 41, No. 3 (Autumn 1999): 124–48; Colin H. Kahl, Melissa G. Dalton, and Matthew Irvine, "Risk and Rivalry: Iran, Israel and the Bomb," Center for a New American Security, June 2012, pp. 19–23; Clifton Sherrill, "Why Iran Wants the Bomb and What It Means for U.S. Policy," *Nonproliferation Review* 19, No. 1 (March 2012): 40.

40. Thomas C. Schelling, *Arms and Influence* (New Haven, Conn.: Yale University Press, 1966).

41. For scholarly work on this point, see Richard K. Betts, *Nuclear Blackmail and Nuclear Balance* (Washington, D.C.: Brookings Institution Press, 1987); Robert Jervis, Richard Ned Lebow, and Janice Gross Stein, *Psychology and Deterrence* (Baltimore: Johns Hopkins University Press, 1985).

42. On the 1946 Iran crisis, see James A. Bill, *The Eagle and the Lion: The Tragedy of American-Iranian Relations* (New Haven, Conn.: Yale University Press, 1988), pp. 31–35; Pollack, *The Persian Puzzle*, pp. 44–48; Natalia I. Yegorova, "The 'Iran Crisis' of 1945–46: A View from the Russian Archives," Cold War International History Project, Working Paper No. 15, Washington, D.C., May 1996.

43. Edward Friedman, "Nuclear Blackmail and the end of the Korean War," *Modern China* 1, No. 1 (January 1975): 75–91. For historical assessments of the Chinese decision to agree to an armistice in 1953, see Clay Blair, *The Forgotten War: America in Korea 1950–53*, 2nd ed. (Annapolis, Md.: Naval Institute Press, 2003), pp. 859–976, esp. 771–972; T. R. Fehrenbach, *This Kind of War: A Study in Unpreparedness* (New York: Macmillan, 1963), pp. 641–50; Max Hastings, *The Korean War* (New York: Simon & Schuster,

1987), pp. 317–20; Edwin Hoyt, *The Day the Chinese Attacked: Korea, 1950* (New York: McGraw-Hill, 1990), p. 216.

44. For an excellent discussion of Finland's experience and motivations, see the declassified CIA study, "'Finlandization' in Action: Helsinki's Experience with Moscow," Central Intelligence Agency, August 1972, available at http://www.foia.cia.gov/CPE/ESAU/esau-55.pdf.

45. See "India Subjected to Nuclear Blackmail Before 1998 Pokhran Tests: NSA Shivshankar Menon," *Times of India*, August 21, 2012. Of course, Menon's boast begs the question of why India needed a nuclear arsenal if these attempts to coerce it had failed when it *didn't* have one.

46. For additional scholarly work making this point, see Betts, *Nuclear Blackmail and Nuclear Balance*; Jervis, Lebow, and Stein, *Psychology and Deterrence*.

47. Author's interview with senior Arab government official, September 2011.

48. Arab publics often have a more complex view of the Iranian nuclear arsenal, simultaneously fearing it and evincing some degree of support for it because it is something that both Israel and the United States oppose. For instance, in his 2010 and 2011 polls of Arab public opinion, Shibley Telhami found that a majority of Arabs saw Iran's acquisition of nuclear weapons as being a negative development for the region, but nonetheless, similar-sized majorities believed that Iran should not be stopped from pursuing its nuclear program. See Shibley Telhami, "The 2011 Annual Arab Public Opinion Survey," Brookings Institution, November 21, 2011, available at http://www.brookings.edu/~/media/research/files/reports/2011/11/21%20arab%20public%20opinion%20telhami/1121_arab_ public _opinion.pdf.

49. See Maloney, "Iran," in Pollack et al., *The Arab Awakening*, pp. 258–67.

50. With the obvious exception that proves the rule, Syria, where the unrest has threatened Iran's sole remaining ally in the region.

51. For a good overview of North Korea's various aggressive actions since the Korean War, see Dick K. Nanto, "North Korea: Chronology of Provocations, 1950–2003," Congressional Research Service, RL30004, March 18, 2003.

Chapter 4. Proliferation

1. Warren Bass, *Support Any Friend: Kennedy's Middle East and the Making of the U.S.-Israel Alliance* (Oxford: Oxford University Press, 2003); Avner Cohen, *Israel and the Bomb* (New York: Columbia University Press, 1998), pp. 99–174; Mordechai Gazit, "The Genesis of the US-Israeli Military-

Strategic Relationship and the Dimona Issue," *Journal of Contemporary History* 35, No. 3 (July 2000): 413–22.

2. For an even stronger assessment of the disincentives Saudi Arabia would face to acquiring nuclear weapons, see Colin H. Kahl, Melissa G. Dalton, and Matthew Irvine, "Atomic Kingdom: If Iran Builds the Bomb, Will Saudi Arabia Be Next?" Center for a New American Security, February 2013, esp. pp. 32–34, 39.

3. On all of these incidents, see Martin Kramer, "Khomeini's Messengers in Mecca," in Martin Kramer, *Arab Awakening and Islamic Revival* (New Brunswick, N.J.: Transaction, 1996), pp. 161–87.

4. David Crist, *The Twilight War: The Secret History of America's Thirty-Year Conflict with Iran* (New York: Penguin Press, 2012), pp. 300–310.

5. Lolita C. Baldor, "US Blaming Iran for Persian Gulf Cyberattacks," Associated Press, October 12, 2012; Siobhan Gorman and Julian Barnes, "Iran Blamed for Cyberattacks," *Wall Street Journal*, October 13–14, 2012, p. A1; Thom Shanker and David E. Sanger, "U.S. Suspects Iran Was Behind Wave of Cyberattacks," *New York Times*, October 13, 2012.

6. On the Saudi-Pakistani relationship, see Yoel Guzansky, "Saudi Arabia's Nuclear Options," in Emily B. Landau and Anat Kurz, eds., *Arms Control Dilemmas: Focus on the Middle East* (Tel Aviv: Institute for National Security Studies, 2012), pp. 75–82.

7. Arnaud de Borchgrave, "Pakistan, Saudi Arabia in Secret Nuke Pact: Islamabad Trades Weapons Technology for Oil," *Washington Times*, October 22, 2003.

8. On Saudi-Pakistani nuclear cooperation, see Bruce O. Riedel, "Saudi Arabia: Nervously Watching Pakistan," Brookings Institution, January 28, 2008, available at http://www.brookings.edu/research/opinions/2008/01/28 -saudi-arabia-riedel.

9. For a concurring Israeli assessment, see Amos Yadlin and Avner Golov, "A Nuclear Iran: The Spur to a Regional Arms Race?" *Strategic Assessment* 15, No. 3 (October 2012): 7–12.

10. Former White House and State Department official Dennis Ross has publicly confirmed that King Abdallah told him this bluntly in private. See Chemi Shalev, "Dennis Ross: Saudi King Vowed to Obtain Nuclear Bomb After Iran," *Haaretz*, May 30, 2012.

11. "Prince Hints Saudi Arabia May Join Nuclear Arms Race," *New York Times*, December 6, 2011.

12. Jay Solomon, "Saudi Suggests 'Squeezing' Iran over Nuclear Ambitions," *Wall Street Journal*, June 22, 2011.

13. Guzansky, "Saudi Arabia's Nuclear Options," pp. 77–79, 83–85.

14. On the UAE nuclear program, see Christopher M. Blanchard and Paul K. Kerr, "The United Arab Emirates' Nuclear Program and Proposed U.S. Nuclear Cooperation," Congressional Research Service, R40344, December 20, 2010, available at http://www.fas.org/sgp/crs/nuke/R40344.pdf.

15. For instance, see Blanchard and Kerr, "The United Arab Emirates' Nuclear Program," pp. 13–15.

16. For a concurring Israeli assessment, see Yadlin and Golov, "A Nuclear Iran: The Spur to a Regional Arms Race?," esp. p. 21.

17. Jim Walsh, "In the Shadow of Dimona: Egypt's Nuclear Choices, 1954–1981," Draft Manuscript, November 1996, p. 2.

18. Ibid., p. 1.

19. Ibid., p. 2.

20. "Egypt Unveils Nasser's Secret Nuclear Weapons Programme," Deutsche Presse-Agentur, July 24, 1995; Jim Walsh, "A History of Egyptian Nuclear Efforts, 1954–1992," Draft Manuscript, November 1996, pp. 5–9.

21. Walsh, "In the Shadow of Dimona," p. 4; Walsh, "A History of Egyptian Nuclear Efforts," pp. 18–20; Jim Walsh, "The Riddle of the Sphinx: Egypt's Failure to Balance the Israeli Nuclear Threat," *Breakthroughs* (Journal of the Defense and Arms Control Studies Program, MIT), Vol. 3, No. 1 (Spring 1994), p. 13.

22. The Israel Project, "Fact Sheet: Arab Leaders Voice Concerns About Iran and Its Nuclear Program," 2009, available at http://www.theisraelproject.org/site/pp.aspx?c=hsJPK0PIJpH&b=2070505&printmode=1.

23. Keinan Ben-Ezra, "The Iranian Nuclear Program: An Egyptian Perspective," in Landau and Kurz, eds., *Arms Control Dilemmas*, pp. 61–69.

24. On Turkey and nuclear weapons, see Sinan Ulgen, ed., *The Turkish Model for Transition to Nuclear Power* (Istanbul: Centre for Economics and Foreign Policy Studies [EDAM], 2011), esp. pp. 138–77.

25. For a good summary, see Gallia Lindenstrauss, "Towards Turkey's Own Bomb? Not Yet," in Landau and Kurz, eds., *Arms Control Dilemmas*, pp. 91–99.

26. Henri J. Barkey and Graham E. Fuller, *Turkey's Kurdish Question* (Lanham, Md.: Rowman & Littlefield, 1998), p. xii.

27. Aaron Stein, "Understanding Turkey's Position on the Iranian Nuclear Program," WMD Junction, January 12, 2012, available at http://wmdjunction.com/120112_turkey_iran_nuclear.htm.

28. "Turkey—Trade Statistics," European Council, March 2012, available at http://trade.ec.europa.eu/doclib/docs/2006/september/tradoc_113456.pdf.

29. For a concurring Israeli assessment, see Lindenstrauss, "Towards Turkey's Own Bomb? Not Yet," p. 99.

30. Sinan Ulgen, "The Security Dimension of Turkey's Nuclear Program: Nuclear Diplomacy and Non Proliferation Policies," in Ulgen, ed., *The Turkish Model for Transition to Nuclear Power*, p. 140.

31. On these problems, and their relationship to political instability, revolution, civil war, insurgency, and terrorism, see Kenneth M. Pollack, *A Path Out of the Desert: A Grand Strategy for America in the Middle East* (New York: Random House, 2008), esp. pp. 67–120.

32. On the impact of the Arab Spring so far, see Kenneth M. Pollack and Daniel L. Byman et al., *The Arab Awakening: America and the Transformation of the Middle East* (Washington, D.C.: Brookings Institution Press, 2011).

33. Mitchell Reiss, *Bridled Ambitions: Why Countries Constrain Their Nuclear Capabilities* (Washington, D.C.: Woodrow Wilson Center Press, 1995); T. V. Paul, *Power Versus Prudence: Why Nations Forgo Nuclear Weapons* (Montreal: McGill-Queen's University Press, 2000); Ariel Levite, "Never Say Never Again: Nuclear Reversal Revisited," *International Security* 2, No. 3 (Winter 2002–2003): 59–88; and Kurt M. Campbell, Robert J. Einhorn, and Mitchell B. Reiss, eds., *The Nuclear Tipping Point: Why States Reconsider Their Nuclear Choices* (Washington, D.C.: Brookings Institution Press, 2004); James Walsh, "Bombs Unbuilt: Power, Ideas, and Institutions in International Politics" (Ph.D. diss., Massachusetts Institute of Technology, June 2001).

34. I have purposely excluded North Korea from this list. While the North Koreans did proliferate against the will of the international community, they paid an outrageous price for doing so. Three million North Koreans starved to death and many others live in abject poverty in part because Pyongyang refused to give up its nuclear program. No other nation on earth would be willing to make such a sacrifice, and so the North Korean case reinforces the disincentives for proliferation.

35. Michael Wines, "China Leader Warns Iran Not to Make Nuclear Arms," *New York Times*, January 20, 2012.

36. Stepan Kravchenko, "Putin Says Iran Developing Nuclear Capability Would Risk Global Stability," *Bloomberg News*, February 24, 2012.

Chapter 5. Setting the Scene

1. Former senior Obama administration official Dennis Ross has outlined both the logic of this position and the deal he believes that the United States should offer Iran as just such an ultimatum. See Dennis Ross, "Calling Iran's Bluff: It's Time to Offer Tehran a Civilian Nuclear Program," *New Republic*, June 15, 2012.

2. Paul Bracken has a fascinating and illuminating discussion of this issue

in his newest book. See Paul Bracken, *The Second Nuclear Age: Strategy, Danger, and the New Power Politics* (New York: Times Books, 2012), pp. 127–61.

3. For a description of a pure engagement approach to Iran and how it would work, see Kenneth M. Pollack et al., *Which Path to Persia? Options for a New American Strategy Toward Iran* (Washington, D.C.: Brookings Institution Press, 2009), pp. 57–81.

4. Ray Takeyh, *Hidden Iran: Paradox and Power in the Islamic Republic* (New York: Times Books, 2006), p. 223.

5. For instance, see Nathan Gonzalez, *Engaging Iran: The Rise of a Middle East Powerhouse and America's Strategic Choice* (Westport, Conn.: Praeger, 2007); Suzanne Maloney and Ray Takeyh, "Pathway to Coexistence: A New U.S. Policy Toward Iran," in Richard N. Haass and Martin Indyk, eds., *Restoring the Balance: A Middle East Strategy for the Next President* (Washington, D.C.: Brookings Institution Press, 2008), pp. 59–92; Vali Nasr and Ray Takeyh, "The Costs of Containing Iran: Washington's Misguided New Policy," *Foreign Affairs* 87, No. 1 (January/February 2008); Trita Parsi, *Treacherous Alliance: The Secret Dealings of Israel, Iran, and the United States* (New Haven, Conn.: Yale University Press, 2007); Trita Parsi, "The Price of Not Talking to Iran," *World Policy Journal*, Winter 2006; Barbara Slavin, *Bitter Friends, Bosom Enemies: Iran, the U.S., and the Twisted Path to Confrontation* (New York: St. Martin's Press, 2007); Barbara Slavin, "Engagement," in Jon Alterman, ed., "Gulf Kaleidoscope: Reflections on the Iranian Challenge," Center for Strategic and International Studies, May 2012, pp. 11–21; Takeyh, *Hidden Iran*, pp. 217–26; Ray Takeyh, "Time for Détente with Iran," *Foreign Affairs* 86, No. 2 (March/April 2007).

6. Richard N. Haass and Meghan L. O'Sullivan, eds., *Honey and Vinegar: Incentives, Sanctions, and Foreign Policy* (Washington, D.C.: Brookings Institution Press, 2000), p. 167.

7. Ibid., p. 174. This quote is actually one of the subheadings of their concluding, summary chapter, representing one of their key findings.

8. Ibid., p. 175.

9. Johannes Reissner, "Europe and Iran: Critical Dialogue," in Haass and O'Sullivan, eds., *Honey and Vinegar*, p. 46.

10. James A. Bill, *The Eagle and the Lion: The Tragedy of American-Iranian Relations* (New Haven, Conn.: Yale University Press, 1988), pp. 276–93.

11. Crist, *The Twilight War*, pp. 106–174; Pollack, *The Persian Puzzle*, pp. 198–205.

12. Senator Alfonse D'Amato introduced the initial sanctions legislation in January 1995. The Iranians announced that Conoco would be awarded

the contract for two offshore oilfields in March 1995. Pollack, *The Persian Puzzle*, pp. 271–72.

13. Ibid.

14. Ibid., pp. 303–342.

15. See David Patrikarakos, *Nuclear Iran: The Birth of an Atomic State* (London: Tauris, 2012), pp. 181, 185–86, 188–91, 193–201.

16. For various perspectives on the May 2003 Iranian message and its import, see David Crist, *The Twilight War: The Secret History of America's Thirty-Year Conflict with Iran* (New York: Penguin Press, 2012), pp. 476–81; Steven J. Rosen, "Did Iran Offer a 'Grand Bargain' in 2003?" *American Thinker*, November 16, 2008, available at http://www.americanthinker .com/2008/11/did_iran_offer_a_grand_bargain.html; Michael J. Rubin, "The Guldimann Memorandum: The Iranian 'Roadmap' Wasn't a Roadmap and Wasn't Iranian," *Weekly Standard*, October 22, 2007; Slavin, *Bitter Friends, Bosom Enemies*, pp. 200–205; Ray Takeyh, *Guardians of the Revolution: Iran and the World in the Age of the Ayatollahs* (Oxford: Oxford University Press, 2009), pp. 217–18.

17. Asr Iran and Raja News, February 20, 2007, http://www.asriran.com/view .php?id=12170, translated and cited in Hassan Daioleslam, "Iran's 2003 Grand Bargain Offer: Secrets, Lies, and Manipulation," In Search of Truth website, June 25, 2008, available at http://english.iranianlobby.com/page1 .php?id=10&bakhsh=ARTICLES.

18. Emrooz news website from the "Goftegoo" radio station, broadcast on January 31, 2007, translated and cited in Daioleslam, "Iran's 2003 Grand Bargain Offer."

Chapter 6. Bigger Carrots, Bigger Sticks

1. See for instance, Karim Sadjadpour, "The Nuclear Players," *Journal of International Affairs* 60, No. 2 (Spring/Summer 2007): 126.

2. Fredrik Dahl and Parisa Hafezi, "Iran Defiant as UN Nuclear Talks Fail," *Reuters*, February 22, 2012.

3. For a thoughtful analysis both of the general difficulty of making "coercive diplomacy" work, and making it work with Iran in particular, see Robert Jervis, "Getting to Yes with Iran: The Challenges of Coercive Diplomacy," *Foreign Affairs* 92, No. 1 (January/February 2012): 105–115. Jervis is one of the wisest and most sensible scholars of political science writing today and his work on a range of topics relevant to our current problems with Iran is well worth reading.

4. With complete immodesty, but after a thorough review of the literature, I would direct the reader looking for a fuller exposition of the concept

of the Dual Track or carrot-and-stick approach for Iran to my own book *The Persian Puzzle*, which was one of the first to propose this strategy. See Kenneth M. Pollack, *The Persian Puzzle: The Conflict Between Iran and America* (New York: Random House, 2004), pp. 400–424. For a more neutral presentation of the same basic points, see Kenneth M. Pollack et al., *Which Path to Persia? Options for a New American Strategy Toward Iran* (Washington, D.C.: Brookings Institution Press, 2009), pp. 31–56.

5. Sadjadpour, "The Nuclear Players," esp. pp. 126–27.

6. Michael R. Gordon and Jeff Zeleny, "Obama Envisions New Iran Approach," *New York Times*, November 2, 2007.

7. Brian Knowlton, "In Interview, Obama Talks of 'New Approach' to Iran," *New York Times*, January 11, 2009.

8. Karim Sadjadpour, "Interview: Engagement with Iran: An Assessment of Options," *Middle East Progress*, December 8, 2009.

9. Thomas Erdbrink and Glenn Kessler, "Obama Message to Iran," *Washington Post*, March 21, 2009; Eli Bardenstein, "When Iran Said 'No' to Obama," *Maariv*, October 28, 2012, translated by Sandy Bloom, Al-Monitor, October 28, 2012.

10. Bardenstein, "When Iran Said 'No' to Obama."

11. David E. Sanger and James Risen, "Iran's Slowing of Enrichment Efforts May Show It Wants a Deal, Analysts Say," *New York Times*, December 27, 2012.

12. See Trita Parsi, *A Single Roll of the Dice: Obama's Diplomacy with Iran* (New Haven, Conn.: Yale University Press, 2012).

13. For other ardent proponents of engagement with Iran agreeing that the Obama administration had sincerely tried to do so, see, inter alia, Suzanne Maloney, "Progress of the Obama Administration's Policy Toward Iran," Testimony Before the House Subcommittee on National Security, Homeland Defense and Foreign Operations, Committee on Oversight and Government Reform, November 15, 2011; Barbara Slavin, "Post-9/11 Rebuffs Set U.S.-Iran Relations on Downward Spiral," InterPress News Service, September 7, 2011, available at http://www.ipsnews.net/2011/09/post -9-11-rebuffs-set-us-iran-relations-on-downward-spiral/.

14. These were the exact words used by a senior administration official to me in a conversation in July 2009, but these sentiments were echoed by a range of other Obama administration officials around the same time.

15. Karim Sadjadpour, "The Iranian Regime Is Now More Vulnerable than Ever Before," *Qantara*, November 13, 2009, translated into English and available at http://www.carnegieendowment.org/2009/11/13/iranian-regime-is -now-more-vulnerable-than-ever-before/6a2.

16. Again, these were the words of one senior Chinese foreign ministry official, but the sentiment was repeated by a number of others. Author's interviews, Beijing, April 2010.

17. For a concurring view, see Karim Sadjadpour, "Interview: Running a Marathon, Not a Sprint," *Der Spiegel*, February 17, 2010.

18. On the TRR deal, see Mark Fitzpatrick, "Iran: The Fragile Promise of the Fuel-Swap Plan," *Survival* 52, no. 3 (June/July 2010): 67–94; Paul K. Kerr, "Iran's Nuclear Program: Status," RL34544, Congressional Research Service, October 17, 2012, pp. 7–9.

19. Bernard Gwertzman, "Nuclear Quagmire with Iran: Interview with George Perkovich," Council on Foreign Relations, November 23, 2009, available at http://www.cfr.org/iran/nuclear-quagmire-iran/p20831; Karim Sadjadpour, "Interview: Engagement with Iran: An Assessment of Options," *Middle East Progress*, December 8, 2009.

20. "Remarks by Supreme Leader Ali Khamenei," Islamic Republic News Agency, August 20, 2010.

21. Kerr, "Iran's Nuclear Program," pp. 8–9.

22. Arshad Mohammed, Justyna Pawlak, and Warren Strobel, "Special Report: Inside the West's Economic War with Iran," Reuters, December 28, 2012.

23. David D. Kirkpatrick, "Chinese Visit to Saudi Arabia Touches on Oil and Politics," *New York Times*, January 15, 2012; Mark Landler and Clifford Krauss, "Gulf Nations Aid U.S. Push to Choke Off Iran Oil Sales," *New York Times*, January 12, 2012.

24. U.S. sanctions on Iran are summarized in Office of Foreign Assets Control, "Iran: What You Need to Know About U.S. Economic Sanctions," U.S. Department of the Treasury, available at http://www.treasury.gov/resource-center/sanctions/Programs/Documents/iran.pdf.

25. The U.S. Department of State maintains a website with useful summaries of these various sanctions at http://www.state.gov/e/eb/tfs/spi/iran/fs/index.htm.

26. James Kanter and Thomas Erdbrink, "With New Sanctions, European Union Tightens Screws on Iran over Nuclear Work," *New York Times*, October 15, 2012; Justyna Pawlak, "EU Sanctions Target Iran Oil, Gas, Tanker Companies," Reuters, October 16, 2012.

27. Rick Gladstone and Stephen Castle, "Global Network Expels as Many as 30 of Iran's Banks in Move to Isolate Its Economy," *New York Times*, March 15, 2012.

28. Public remarks by Bijan Khajepour, Washington, D.C., Stimson Center–Heinrich Böll Foundation event, March 4, 2013.

29. Initially, much of the impact from sanctions was principally a result of the

regime's mismanaged reactions to them. See "Spider Web: The Making and Unmaking of Iran Sanctions," Middle East Report No. 138, International Crisis Group, February 25, 2013, pp. 24–26, 30.

30. Nasser Karimi and Brian Murphy, "Iran Forces on Alert as Economic 'Surgery' Begins," Associated Press, December 19, 2010.

31. Mohammad Ali Shabani, "Iran Survives Sanctions, Girds for Further Economic War," Al-Monitor, December 20, 2012.

32. Thomas Erdbrink and David E. Sanger, "U.S. Increases Pressure of Economic War on Tehran," *New York Times*, February 6, 2013.

33. Djavad Salehi-Isfahani, "Understanding the Rial's Freefall," Lobelog, October 4, 2012, available at http://www.lobelog.com/understanding-the-rials-freefall/; Yeganeh Torbati, "Iran's Khamenei Warns of Government Divisions After Rial Plunge," Reuters, October 10, 2012.

34. "Spider Web," International Crisis Group, p. 26.

35. Jay Newton-Small, "One Nation Under Sanctions," *Time*, September 24, 2013, p. 42.

36. "Spider Web," International Crisis Group, pp. 37–38.

37. Farideh Farhi, "Iran Debates Direct Talks with the US," Lobelog, December 11, 2012, available at http://www.lobelog.com/iran-debates-direct-talks-with-the-us/.

38. "Iran Pulls Back from Nuclear Bomb Goal: Israeli Defense Minister," Reuters, October 30, 2012; David E. Sanger and James Risen, "Iran's Slowing of Enrichment Efforts May Show It Wants a Deal, Analysts Say," *New York Times*, December 27, 2012.

39. Ruholamin Saeidi, "Worn-out Revolutionaries and the Conspiracy of the Poisoned Chalice," *Kayhan*, December 8, 2012, translated by Eskander Saeghi-Boroujerdi, Iran Pulse of Al-Monitor, December 10, 2012, available at http://iranpulse.al-monitor.com/index.php/2012/12/973/Kayhan-article-indicates-discontent-with-supreme-leaders-course-across-the-political-spectrum/.

40. Yeganeh Torbati, "Iran Says It, World Powers Must End Nuclear Stalemate," Reuters, December 17, 2012.

41. Andrew Torchia, "Analysis: Iran Economy Far from Collapse as Sanctions Tighten," Reuters, February, 20, 2013.

42. "Spider Web," International Crisis Group, p. 31.

43. Erdbrink and Sanger, "U.S. Increases Pressure of Economic War on Tehran."

44. Shabani, "Iran Survives Sanctions, Girds for Further Economic War."

45. Shaul Bakhash, *The Reign of the Ayatollahs: Iran and the Islamic Revolution*, rev. ed. (New York: Basic Books, 1990), p. 230; CIA, *World Factbook*

(Washington, D.C: U.S. Government Printing Office, 1989); Michael M. J. Fischer, *Iran: From Religious Dispute to Revolution* (Madison: University of Wisconsin Press, 1980), p. 224.

46. Patrick Clawson, "Adjustment to a Foreign Exchange Shock: Iran, 1951–1953," *International Journal of Middle East Studies* 19, No. 1 (February 1987): 1–22.

47. David E. Sanger, "Iran Offers Plan, Dismissed By U.S., on Nuclear Crisis," *New York Times*, October 4, 2012.

48. "Spider Web," International Crisis Group, p. ii.

49. "The Impact of Sanctions on Iran, the US, and the Global Economy," National Iranian American Council Policy Briefing, October 4, 2011, podcast available at http://www.linktv.org/programs/the-impact-of-sanctions-on-iran.

50. Djavad Salehi-Isfahani, "Understanding the Rial's Freefall," Lobelog, October 4, 2012, available at http://www.lobelog.com/understanding-the-rials-freefall/.

51. Suzanne Maloney, correspondence with the author, October 2012. Printed with Dr. Maloney's permission.

52. Yeganeh Torbati, "Iran's Khamenei Warns of Government Divisions After Rial Plunge," Reuters, October 10, 2012.

53. Nasser Karimi, "Iran's Supreme Leader Rejects Direct Talks with US," Associated Press, February 7, 2013.

54. Nasser Karimi, "Ahmadinejad Says Western Sanctions Won't Stop Iran," Associated Press, December 18, 2012.

55. Saeidi, "Worn-out Revolutionaries and the Conspiracy of the Poisoned Chalice."

56. Scott Peterson, "Inside the Mind of Iran's Khamenei," *Christian Science Monitor*, December 4, 2012.

57. Ray Takeyh, *Guardians of the Revolution: Iran and the World in the Age of the Ayatollahs* (Oxford: Oxford University Press, 2009), pp. 240–41.

58. Ray Takeyh, *Hidden Iran: Paradox and Power in the Islamic Republic* (New York: Times Books, 2006), p. 150.

59. Ibid., pp. 40–42.

60. Shabani, "Iran Survives Sanctions, Girds for Further Economic War."

61. Nidhi Verma, "India Plans Reinsurance Fund to Cover Refiners Using Iranian Oil," Reuters, March 24, 2013.

62. Humeyra Pamuk and Emma Farge, "Iran Sidesteps Sanctions to Export Its Fuel Oil," Reuters, December 20, 2012.

63. Luke Pachymuthu, "Iran's Q1 Fuel Oil Exports Rise More Than 12 Pct over Q4—Sources," Reuters, April 10, 2013.

64. Ali Akbar Dareini, "Ahmadinejad: Iran Won't Retreat from Nuclear Path," Associated Press, October 9, 2011.

65. Amos Yadlin and Yoel Guzansky, "Iran on the Threshold," *Strategic Assessment* 15, No. 1 (April 2012): 12.

66. Barak Ravid, "Israel Inches Closer to Compromise on Iran Uranium Enrichment, Officials Say," *Haaretz*, May 21, 2012.

67. Yeganeh Torbati, "Iran Could Halt 20 Percent Uranium Enrichment If Given Fuel: Officials," Reuters, October 13, 2012.

68. Ibid.

69. For a concurring, Israeli assessment and emphasis on this point, see Yadlin and Guzansky, "Iran on the Threshold," pp. 8–10.

70. Ibid., p. 12.

71. Yeganeh Torbati, "Iran Will Never Shut Down Fordow Enrichment Plant: MP," Reuters, February 17, 2013.

72. For a fuller discussion of these ideas, see Kenneth M. Pollack, "Security in the Persian Gulf: New Frameworks for the 21st Century," Middle East Memo No. 24, Saban Center for Middle East Policy, Brookings Institution, June 2012, available at http://www.brookings.edu/~/media/research/files/papers/2012/6/middle%20east%20pollack/middle%20east%20pollack.pdf; Kenneth M. Pollack, "Securing the Gulf," *Foreign Affairs* 82, No. 4 (July/August 2003): 2–16. Also see Joseph McMillan, "The United States and a Gulf Security Architecture: Policy Considerations," *Strategic Insights* 3, No. 3 (March 2004); James A. Russell, "Searching for a Post-Saddam Regional Security Architecture," *Middle East Review of International Affairs (MERIA)* 7, No. 1 (March 2003).

73. M. Javad Zarif, "A Neighbor's Vision of a New Iraq," *New York Times*, May 10, 2003.

74. The *Times'* reportage is summarized in David E. Sanger, *Confront and Conceal: Obama's Secret Wars and Surprising Use of American Power* (New York: Crown, 2012), pp. 188–225. In addition, see David E. Sanger, "America's Deadly Dynamics with Iran," *New York Times*, November 5, 2011.

75. Christopher Hope, "MI6 Chief Sir John Sawers: 'We Foiled Iranian Nuclear Weapons Bid,'" *Telegraph*, July 12, 2012.

76. Sanger, *Confront and Conceal*; David E. Sanger, "Obama Order Sped Up Wave of Cyberattacks Against Iran," *New York Times*, June 1, 2012.

77. Sanger, *Confront and Conceal*, pp. 197–203.

78. When asked about the Flame virus, Israel's vice prime minister and strategic affairs minister, Moshe Yaalon, told Israeli Army Radio, "Anyone who sees the Iranian threat as a significant threat—it's reasonable that he will

take various steps, including these, to harm it." Thomas Erdbrink, "Iran Confirms Attack by Virus That Collects Information," *New York Times*, May 29, 2012.

79. Thomas Erdbrink, "Facing Cyberattack, Iranian Officials Disconnect Some Oil Terminals from Internet," *New York Times*, April 23, 2012; Rick Gladstone, "Iran Suggests Attacks on Computer Systems Came from the U.S. and Israel," *New York Times*, December 25, 2012; "Iran Says Defeats Cyber Attacks on Industrial Sites," Reuters, December 25, 2012.

80. Erdbrink, "Facing Cyberattack, Iranian Officials Disconnect Some Oil Terminals from Internet."

81. See, for instance, Crist, *The Twilight War*, pp. 552–53; Eli Lake, "Who Is Sabotaging Iran's Nukes?" *Daily Beast*, September 19, 2012.

82. See for instance, Ronen Bergman, "Will Israel Attack Iran?" *New York Times Magazine*, January 25, 2012; Dan Raviv and Yossi Melman, *Spies Against Armageddon: Inside Israel's Secret Wars* (Sea Cliff, N.Y.: Levant Books, 2012), pp. 312–25.

83. Anshel Pfeffer, "The Bulgaria Attack: Hard Truths from Israel's Former National Security Chief," Haaretz, July 19, 2012.

84. "Iran Sends Rare Letter to U.S. over Killed Scientist," Reuters, January 15, 2012.

85. M. K. Bhadrakumar, "Foreign Devils in the Iranian Mountains," *Asia Times*, February 24, 2007; Frances Harrison, "Iranians Fear of the 'Little Devil,'" BBC News, June 21, 2007, available at http://news.bbc.co.uk/2/hi/programmes/from_our_own_correspondent/6222876.stm; "Iran: Many Die in Zahedan Mosque Bombing," BBC News, May 28, 2009, available at http://news.bbc.co.uk/2/hi/middle_east/8072795.stm; Chris Zambelis, "Balochi Nationalists Intensify Violent Rebellion in Iran," *Terrorism Monitor* 7, No. 3, Jamestown Foundation, February 9, 2009.

86. Mark Perry, "False Flag," *Foreign Policy*, January 13, 2012, available at http://www.foreignpolicy.com/articles/2012/01/13/false_flag?page=0,0.

87. Various Iranian cyberattacks on the United States have also been documented in the press. See, for instance, Lolita C. Baldor, "U.S. Blaming Iran for Persian Gulf Cyberattacks," Associated Press, October 12, 2012; Dan De Luce, "Cyber War on Iran Has Only Just Begun," Agence France-Presse, July 13, 2012; Siobhan Gorman and Julian Barnes, "Iran Blamed for Cyberattacks," *Wall Street Journal*, October 13–14, 2012, p. A1; Nicole Perlroth, "In Cyberattack on Saudi Firm, U.S. Sees Iran Firing Back," *New York Times*, October 27, 2012.

88. On the risks of escalation from the covert and cyber battles with Iran,

see David Ignatius, "Lessons from an Iranian War Game," *Washington Post*, September 20, 2012; Kenneth M. Pollack, "A Series of Unfortunate Events: A Crisis Simulation of a U.S.-Iranian Confrontation," Middle East Memo No. 26, Saban Center for Middle East Policy, Brookings Institution, October 2012, available at http://www.brookings.edu/~/media/research/files/papers/2012/11/us%20iran%20crisis%20simulation%20pollack/us%20iran%20crisis%20simulation%20pollack%20paper.pdf; Kenneth M. Pollack, "Are We Sliding Toward War with Iran?" *New Republic*, January 18, 2012, available at http://www.tnr.com/article/world/99741/war-iran-america#.

89. Bradley Klapper, "Senators Mull Tougher Iran Sanctions," Associated Press, November 9, 2012.

90. See the conclusions of the so-called Duelfer Report, the independent inquiry into Saddam's WMD programs after the fall of Baghdad, *Comprehensive Report of the Special Adviser to the DCI on Iraqi WMD*, December 20, 2004, available at https://www.cia.gov/library/reports/general-reports-1/iraq_wmd_2004/Comp_Report_Key_Findings.pdf.

91. Richard N. Haass, *Economic Sanctions and American Diplomacy* (New York: Council on Foreign Relations, 1998), p. 197.

92. Stuart E. Eizenstat, "Do Economic Sanctions Work? Lessons from ILSA and Other U.S. Sanctions Regimes," Atlantic Council, Occasional Paper, February 2004, p. vii.

93. The classic work on this topic remains David A. Baldwin, *Economic Statecraft* (Princeton, N.J.: Princeton University Press, 1985), esp. the section on trade policy, pp. 206–289.

94. Gary Clyde Hufbauer, Jeffrey J. Schott, and Kimberly Ann Elliott, *Economic Sanctions Reconsidered*, 2nd ed. (Washington, D.C.: Institute for International Economics, 1990), p. 93.

95. Daniel W. Drezner, *The Sanctions Paradox: Economic Statecraft and International Relations* (Cambridge, U.K.: Cambridge University Press, 1999), esp. p. 308.

96. Meghan L. O'Sullivan, *Shrewd Sanctions: Statecraft and State Sponsors of Terrorism* (Washington, D.C.: Brookings Institution Press, 2002), p. 288.

97. Ibid.

98. Eizenstat, "Do Economic Sanctions Work?" pp. 9–12; Richard N. Haass and Meghan L. O'Sullivan, eds., *Honey and Vinegar: Incentives, Sanctions, and Foreign Policy* (Washington, D.C.: Brookings Institution, 2000), pp. 189–91; O'Sullivan, *Shrewd Sanctions*, pp. 173–230.

99. For a concurring view from the man responsible for imposing sanctions during the 1990s, see Eizenstat, "Do Economic Sanctions Work?," pp. 8–9.

100. "China Knocks US Sanctions on State-Run Firm over Iran," Agence France-Presse, January 15, 2012.

101. See Helia Ighani, "Video: Analysts Say New Sanctions Bill Would Increase Gas Prices, Unlikely to Change Iran's Behavior," October 13, 2011, available at http://www.niacouncil.org/site/News2?page=NewsArticle&id=7648; Robert McNally, "Energy Brief: Managing Oil Market Disruption in a Confrontation with Iran," Council on Foreign Relations, January 2012, p. 1.

102. James Risen and Duraid Adnan, "U.S. Says Iraqis Are Helping Iran to Skirt Sanctions," New York Times, April 18, 2012.

103. Rick Gladstone, "Iran Finding Some Ways to Evade Sanctions, Treasury Department Says," New York Times, January 10, 2013.

104. The question of Iraqi deaths from casualties has been an issue of controversy for nearly twenty years. Unfortunately, the matter remains in dispute even long after the fall of Saddam. See, for instance, J. Blacker, M. Ali, and G. Jones, "A Response to Criticism of Our Estimates of Under-5 Mortality in Iraq, 1980–98," Population Studies 61 (2007): 7–13; Michael Spagat, "Truth and Death in Iraq Under Sanctions," Significance 7, No. 3 (September 2010): 116–20; Michael Spagat, "The Iraq Sanctions Myth," Pacific Standard, April 26, 2013. In particular, Spagat cites several post-invasion surveys as strongly disputing the claim that 400,000–500,000 Iraqi children died as a result of the sanctions. His evidence, relying on three post-invasion surveys, suggests that only thousands or a few tens of thousands may have died from the sanctions.

105. On the humanitarian impact of the Iraq sanctions, see Central Organization for Statistics and Information Technology and Kurdistan Regional Statistics Office, Iraq Multiple Indicator Cluster Survey 2006, Final Report (Baghdad: Central Organization for Statistics and Information Technology, 2007); Richard Garfield, Morbidity and Mortality Among Iraqi Children from 1990 to 1998: Assessing the Impact of Economic Sanctions (Goshen, Ind.: Institute for International Peace Studies, University of Notre Dame, 1999); Sarah Graham-Brown, "War and Sanctions: Cost to Society and Toll on Development," in John Calabrese, ed., The Future of Iraq (Washington, D.C.: Middle East Institute, 1997), pp. 31–42; Sarah Graham-Brown, Sanctioning Saddam: The Politics of Intervention in Iraq (London: Tauris, 1999); Youssef Ibrahim, "Iraq Is Near Economic Ruin," New York Times, October 25, 1994; O'Sullivan, Shrewd Sanctions, pp. 105–167; Kenneth M. Pollack, The Threatening Storm: The Case for Invading Iraq (New York: Random House, 2002), pp. 125–40; David Rieff, "Were Sanctions Right?" New York Times Magazine, July 27, 2003; Spagat, "Truth and Death in Iraq Under Sanctions," pp. 116–20.

106. See O'Sullivan, *Shrewd Sanctions*, pp. 105–167, 310–11; Pollack, *The Threatening Storm*, pp. 71–108.

107. On the collapse of sanctions and containment, see in particular the report of the Independent Inquiry Committee into the United Nations Oil-for-Food Programme, "Manipulation of the Oil-for-Food Programme by the Iraqi Regime" (colloquially known as the "Volcker Committee Report"), United Nations, October 27, 2005, available at http://www.iic-offp.org/documents/IIC%20Final%20Report%2027Oct2005.pdf. Also see, O'Sullivan, *Shrewd Sanctions*, pp. 114–22, 130–36; and Pollack, *The Threatening Storm*, pp. 85–108.

108. O'Sullivan, *Shrewd Sanctions*, p. 311.

109. Nasser Karimi, "Iran's Medical Crisis Deepens as Economy Sputters," Associated Press, January 8, 2013; "Spider Web," International Crisis Group, pp. ii, 35–36.

110. "Spider Web," International Crisis Group, p. 34.

111. "Iran: New EU Sanctions 'Inhuman' but Won't Force Nuclear Concessions," Associated Press, October 16, 2012.

Chapter 7. Regime Change

1. On the abuses of the Iranian regime, see "Iran," *World Report 2012*, Human Rights Watch, available at http://www.hrw.org/sites/default/files/iran_2012.pdf. For more intimate accounts, see Maziar Bahari with Aimee Molloy, *Then They Came for Me: A Family's Story of Love, Captivity, and Survival* (New York: Random House, 2011); Haleh Esfandiari, *My Prison, My Home: One Woman's Story of Captivity in Iran* (New York: Harper-Collins, 2009); Roxanna Saberi, *Between Two Worlds: My Life and Captivity in Iran* (New York: HarperCollins, 2010).

2. David Crist, *The Twilight War: The Secret History of America's Thirty-Year Conflict with Iran* (New York: Penguin Press, 2012), pp. 490–91.

3. Sara Beth Elson and Alireza Nader, "What Do Iranians Think? A Survey of Attitudes on the United States, the Nuclear Program and the Economy," RAND Corporation, 2011, pp. 11–13.

4. Ibid., p. 13.

5. Jay Loschky and Anita Pugliese, "Iranians Split, 40% to 35%, on Nuclear Military Power," Gallup, February 15, 2012, available at http://www.gallup.com/poll/152633/Iranians-Split-Nuclear-Military-Power.aspx.

6. Pollack, *The Persian Puzzle*, p. 318. See also, Ray Takeyh, *Hidden Iran: Paradox and Power in the Islamic Republic* (New York: Times Books, 2006), pp. 152–53.

7. "Interview with Muhammad Reza Khatami," *La Repubblica*, March 4, 2006.

8. Takeyh, *Hidden Iran*, pp. 208–211.

9. Quoted in ibid., p. 211.

10. "Israeli Paper Publishes Interview with Vice President Ebtekar," BBC Summary of World Broadcasts, February 3, 1998.

11. Ervand Abrahamian, *Iran: Between Two Revolutions* (Princeton, N.J.: Princeton University Press, 1982), p. 269; Fakhreddin Azimi, "Unseating Mosaddeq: The Configuration and Role of Domestic Forces," in Mark J. Gasiorowski and Malcolm Byrne, eds., *Mohammad Mosaddeq and the Coup of 1953 in Iran* (Syracuse, N.Y.: Syracuse University Press, 2004), pp. 51–52; Elton L. Daniel, *The History of Iran* (Westport, Conn.: Greenwood Press, 2001), p. 151; Stephen Kinzer, *All the Shah's Men: An American Coup and the Roots of Middle East Terror* (Hoboken, N.J.: Wiley, 2003), pp. 136–37.

12. Azimi, "Unseating Mosaddeq," pp. 30–31, 78–82; James A. Bill, *The Eagle and the Lion: The Tragedy of American-Iranian Relations* (New Haven, Conn.: Yale University Press, 1988), pp. 90–91; Daniel, *The History of Iran*, pp. 153–154; Mark J. Gasiorowski, "The 1953 Coup d'Etat in Iran," in Gasiorowski and Byrne, eds., *Mohammad Mosaddeq and the Coup of 1953 in Iran*, pp. 248–66; Mark J. Gasiorowski, *U.S. Foreign Policy and the Shah: Building a Client State in Iran* (Ithaca, N.Y.: Cornell University Press, 1991), pp. 72–73; Richard Helms, *A Look over My Shoulder: A Life in the Central Intelligence Agency* (New York: Random House, 2003), pp. 182–87; Kinzer, *All the Shah's Men*, pp. 162–63.

13. Said Arjomand, *The Turban for the Crown: The Islamic Revolution in Iran* (New York: Oxford University Press, 1988), pp. 131–32; Bill, *The Eagle and the Lion*, pp. 253–56; Zbigniew Brzezinski, *Power and Principle: Memoirs of the National Security Adviser, 1977–1981*, rev. ed. (New York: Farrar, Straus & Giroux, 1985), pp. 382–93; General Robert E. Huyser, *Mission to Tehran* (New York: Harper & Row, 1986), esp. pp. 18, 275–90; Charles Kurzman, *The Unthinkable Revolution in Iran* (Cambridge, Mass.: Harvard University Press, 2004), pp. 160–61; Barry Rubin, *Paved with Good Intentions: The American Experience and Iran* (New York: Penguin, 1981), pp. 226–27; Gary Sick, *All Fall Down: America's Fateful Encounter with Iran* (London: Tauris, 1985), pp. 138–87; Sepehr Zabih, "Iran's Policy Toward the Persian Gulf," *International Journal of Middle East Studies* 7, No. 3 (July 1976): 43–54, 93–111.

14. Crist, *The Twilight War*, pp. 69–71.

15. Ibid., p. 71.

16. As quoted in Tom Barry, "Iran Freedom and Regime Change Politics," *New York Times*, May 19, 2006, available at http://rightweb.irc-online.org/rw/3277.html.

17. Negar Azimi, "Hard Realities of Soft Power," *New York Times*, June 24, 2007.

18. Suzanne Maloney, "Fear and Loathing in Tehran," *National Interest*, No. 91 (September/October 2007).

19. Robin Wright, "On Guard over U.S. Funds, Pro-Democracy Program Leads Tehran to Scrutinize Activists," *Washington Post*, April 28, 2007.

20. Azimi, "Hard Realities."

21. Wright, "On Guard over U.S. Funds."

22. The best unclassified sources at present are Daniel Byman, *Deadly Connections: States That Sponsor Terrorism* (Cambridge, U.K.: Cambridge University Press, 2005), pp. 79–110, esp. p. 85; Richard Clarke, *Against All Enemies: Inside America's War on Terror* (New York: Free Press, 2004), pp. 112–31; Timothy Naftali, *Blindspot: The Secret History of American Counterterrorism* (New York: Basic Books, 2005), pp. 248–51, 260–61; and the grand jury indictment against thirteen members of Saudi Hizballah filed by the U.S. government in Alexandria, Virginia. The indictment in particular provides an excellent overview of the operational elements of the attack, and is available at http://news.findlaw.com/cnn/docs/khobar/khobarindict61901.pdf, accessed July 26, 2004. The 9/11 Commission also found that the evidence of Iran behind the Khobar Towers bombing was "strong." See *Report of the 9/11 Commission: Final Report of the National Commission on Terrorist Attacks upon the United States* (Washington, D.C.: U.S. Government Printing Office, 2004), p. 60. Also see Pollack, *The Persian Puzzle*, pp. 282–84.

23. Lolita C. Baldor, "U.S. Blaming Iran for Persian Gulf Cyberattacks," Associated Press, October 12, 2012; Dan De Luce, "Cyber War on Iran Has Only Just Begun," Agence France-Presse, July 13, 2012; Siobhan Gorman and Julian Barnes, "Iran Blamed for Cyberattacks," *Wall Street Journal*, October 13–14, 2012, p. A1; Nicole Perlroth, "In Cyberattack on Saudi Firm, U.S. Sees Iran Firing Back," *New York Times*, October 27, 2012; David E. Sanger and Eric Schmitt, "Rise Is Seen in Cyberattacks Targeting U.S. Infrastructure," *New York Times*, July 26, 2012.

24. Charlie Savage and Scott Shane, "U.S. Accuses Iranians of Plotting to Kill Saudi Envoy," *New York Times*, October 11, 2011; Crist, *The Twilight War*, pp. 562–66; Benjamin Weiser, "Man Pleads Guilty in Plot to Murder a Saudi Envoy," *New York Times*, October 17, 2012.

25. For instance, see Jamsheed K. Choksy, "Are the Mullahs Losing Their Grip?" *World Affairs* 175, No. 1 (May/June 2012): 17–24.

26. Charles Kurzman, *The Unthinkable Revolution in Iran* (Cambridge, Mass.: Harvard University Press, 2004), pp. 121–22.

27. See for instance, Crist, *The Twilight War*, p. 552; Nazila Fathi, "Relatives of Kurds Executed in Iran Are Denied the Remains, and 2 Are Arrested," *New York Times*, May 11, 2010; Michael Rubin, "Domestic Threats to Iranian Stability: Khuzistan and Baluchistan," *Middle East Forum*, November 13, 2005, available at http://www.meforum.org/788/domestic-threats-to-iranian-stability-khuzistan.

28. See Crist, *The Twilight War*, pp., 404–415; Pollack, *The Persian Puzzle*, pp. 282–86, 298–302.

29. See Crist, *The Twilight War*, pp. 82–83, 372–79, 556.

30. Much of the following section draws heavily from Kenneth M. Pollack and Ray Takeyh, "Doubling Down on Tehran," *Washington Quarterly* 34, No. 4 (Fall 2011): 7–21.

31. Peter James Spielmann, "UN Report Finds Iran's Crackdown Expanding," *Associated Press*, October 11, 2012.

32. "Why They Left: Stories of Iranian Activists in Exile," *Human Rights Watch*, December 13, 2012, available at http://www.hrw.org/sites/default/files/reports/iran1212webwcover_0_0.pdf, p. 1.

33. "EU Expands Sanctions Against Iran," *Associated Press*, October 11, 2011.

34. Meghan L. O'Sullivan, *Shrewd Sanctions: Statecraft and State Sponsors of Terrorism* (Washington, D.C.: Brookings Institution Press, 2002), pp. 291–92.

Chapter 8. The Sword of David

1. Amy Tiebel, "Israel Plunged into Unprecedented Debate About War," *Associated Press*, August 14, 2012.

2. On U.S. government and intelligence sources confirming Israel's possession of nuclear weapons, see the sources in chapter 2, note 32.

3. "Jericho 1/2/3," MissileThreat.com, available at http://missilethreat.com/missiles/jericho-123/.

4. David A. Fulghum, "Why Syria's Air Defenses Failed to Detect Israelis," *Aviation Week* blog, October 3, 2007, available at http://www.aviationweek.com/Blogs.aspx?plckBlogId=Blog:27ec4a53-dcc8-42d0-bd3a-01329aef79a7&plckcontroller=blog&plckscript=blogscript&plckelementid=blogdest&plckblogpage=blogviewpost&plckpostid=blog%253A27ec4a53-dcc8-42d0-bd3a-01329aef79a7post%253A2710d024-5eda-416c-b117-ae6d649146cd; David A. Fulghum, "Israel Used Electronic Attack in Air Strike Against Syrian Mystery Target," *Aviation Week & Space Technology*, October 8, 2007; Eli Lake, "Israel's Secret Iran Attack Plan: Electronic Warfare," *Daily Beast*, November 16, 2011, available at http://www.thedailybeast.com/articles/2011/11/16/israel-s-secret-iran-attack-plan-electronic-warfare.html.

5. "F-16I Sufa (Storm)," Global Security, available at http://www.global security.org/military/world/israel/f-16i.htm, downloaded January 18, 2013; "Israel's Security Chiefs Welcome Arrival of New F-16I Jets," *Haaretz*, February 19, 2004.

6. Anshel Pfeffer, "Israel Could Strike Iran's Nuclear Facilities, but It Won't Be Easy," *Haaretz*, February 20, 2012. For a good summary of the refueling problem, see Anthony H. Cordesman and Abdullah Toukan, "Study on a Possible Israeli Strike on Iran's Nuclear Development Facilities," Center for Strategic and International Studies, March 14, 2009, available at http://csis .org/files/media/csis/pubs/090316_israelistrikeiran.pdf, pp. 70–71.

7. David Alexander, "U.S. Nears $10 Billion Arms Deal with Israel, Saudi Arabia, UAE," Reuters, April 19, 2013.

8. There are occasional rumors that Israel has secured permission to have its aircraft refuel at Azerbaijani bases, but this arrangement seems unlikely. Azerbaijan is in the wrong place, so Israeli aircraft would have to covertly fly to Azerbaijan (across Turkey, Armenia, Russia, and/or Georgia) and then strike Iranian targets. This plan would not necessarily mitigate Israel's problems. It is also unlikely that the Azerbaijani government would have any interest due to the problems it would create for its internal politics and its foreign policy. See Thomas Grove, "Insight: Azerbaijan Eyes Aiding Israel Against Iran," Reuters, September 30, 2012; Lada Evgrashina and Margarita Antidze, "Israel Denies It Has Access to Azerbaijan Air Bases," Reuters, April 23, 2012.

9. "Natanz (Kashan)," GlobalSecurity.org, available at http://www.globalsecu rity.org/wmd/world/iran/natanz-fep.htm, downloaded January 18, 2013; Whitney Raas and Austin Long, "Osiraq Redux: Assessing Israeli Capabilities to Destroy Iranian Nuclear Facilities," *International Security* 31, No. 4 (Spring 2007): 18.

10. Todd Lindeman and Bill Webster, "Hardened Targets," *Washington Post*, March 1, 2012.

11. Raas and Long, "Osirak Redux?" pp. 18–20.

12. "Attacking Iran: Up in the Air," *Economist*, February 25, 2012, available at http://middleeast.about.com/gi/o.htm?zi=1/XJ&zTi=1&sdn=middleeast& cdn=newsissues&tm=20&f=00&tt=2&bt=0&bts=0&zu=http%3A//www .economist.com/node/21548228.

13. Mark Perry, "The Entebbe Option," *Foreign Policy* online, September 27, 2012, available at http://www.foreignpolicy.com/articles/2012/09/27/the _entebbe_option.

14. David Alexander, "U.S. Nears $10 Billion Arms Deal with Israel, Saudi Arabia, UAE," Reuters, April 19, 2013.

15. Anthony H. Cordesman and Abdullah Toukan, "Analyzing the Impact of Preventive Strikes Against Iran's Nuclear Facilities," Center for Strategic and International Studies, September 10, 2012, available at http://csis.org/files/publication/120906_Iran_US_Preventive_Strikes.pdf, p. 81.

16. Ephraim Kam, "An Attack on Iran: The Morning After," *Strategic Assessment* 15, No. 1 (April 2012): 20; "Ex-Mossad Chief: Ahmadinejad Is Israel's Greatest Gift," *Haaretz*, August 20, 2008.

17. Cordesman and Toukan, "Analyzing the Impact of Preventive Strikes Against Iran's Nuclear Facilities," p. 7.

18. For Halevy, see "Ex-Mossad Chief: Ahmadinejad Is Israel's Greatest Gift"; for Eitan, see Ronen Bergman, "Will Israel Attack Iran?" *New York Times Magazine*, January 25, 2012.

19. Amos Harel, "Israeli Strike Would Only Delay Iran's Nuclear Program by Two Years," *Haaretz*, August 3, 2012; Stephen Heintz, William Luers, William Miller, Thomas Pickering, Jim Walsh, Frank Wisner, et al., "Weighing Benefits and Costs of Military Action Against Iran," Iran Project, September 2012, p. 31.

20. Karl Vick, "Can Israel Stop Iran's Nuke Effort?" *Time*, February 6, 2012.

21. Brian Fung, "The Case for Letting Iran (Almost) Build a Bomb," *Atlantic*, February 29, 2012.

22. David Albright, Paul Brannan, and Jacqueline Shire, "Can Military Strikes Destroy Iran's Gas Centrifuge Program? Probably Not," Institute for Science and International Security, August 7, 2008, p. 7.

23. Ibid., p. 1.

24. David E. Sanger, James Glanz, and Jo Becker, "Around the World, Distress Over Iran," *New York Times*, November 28, 2010. For a similar statement by Secretary Gates, see Paul Richter, "Gates Warns Against Israeli Strike on Iran's Nuclear Facilities," *Los Angeles Times*, April 16, 2009.

25. "Remarks by Secretary of Defense Leon E. Panetta at the Saban Center," December 2, 2011, transcript available at http://www.defense.gov/transcripts/transcript.aspx?transcriptid=4937.

26. "Interview with General Martin Dempsey," *Fareed Zakaria GPS*, CNN, February 19, 2012, transcript available at http://transcripts.cnn.com/TRANSCRIPTS/1202/19/fzgps.01.html.

27. Albright, Brannan, and Shire, "Can Military Strikes Destroy Iran's Gas Centrifuge Program?" p. 3.

28. "Interview with Ehud Barak," *Fareed Zakaria GPS*, CNN, November 20, 2011, transcript available at http://transcripts.cnn.com/TRANSCRIPTS/1111/20/fzgps.01.html; Joel Greenburg, "Barak Says Time Running Out for Action Against Iran's Nuclear Program," *Washington Post*,

February 2, 2012. See also Amos Yadlin, "Israel's Last Chance to Strike Iran," *New York Times*, February 29, 2012.

29. Press reports have even begun to claim that since Fordow became operational in the fall of 2012, Israel has been forced to scrap plans for an air strike altogether. "Report: Israel Forced to Change Iran Strike Tactics," *Jerusalem Post* online, November 11, 2012, available at http://www.jpost .com/IranianThreat/News/Article.aspx?id=291295.

30. Bennett Ramberg, "Looking Back: Osirak and Its Lessons for Iran Policy," *Arms Control Today* 42, No. 4 (May 2012): 40. See also Richard K. Betts, "The Osirak Fallacy," *National Interest*, No. 83 (Spring 2006): 22; Dan Reiter, "Preventive Attacks Against Nuclear Programs and the 'Success' at Osiraq," *Nonproliferation Review* 12, No. 2 (July 2005): 355–71.

31. Ramberg, "Looking Back," pp. 40–42.

32. Malfrid Braut-Hegghammer, "Revisiting Osirak: Preventive Attacks and Nuclear Proliferation Risks," *International Security* 36, No. 1 (Summer 2011): 130.

33. Ibid., pp. 129 and 102.

34. Elliott Abrams, "The Grounds for an Israeli Attack," *World Affairs* 175, No. 1 (May/June 2012): 26–27.

35. Ivo H. Daalder and Michael E. O'Hanlon, *Winning Ugly: NATO's War to Save Kosovo* (Washington, D.C.: Brookings Institution Press, 2000), pp. 4–5; Stephen T. Hosmer, *Why Milosevic Decided to Settle When He Did* (Santa Monica, Calif.: RAND, 2001); Robert Pape, *Bombing to Win: Air Power and Coercion in War* (Ithaca, N.Y.: Cornell University Press, 1996).

36. Braut-Hegghammer, "Revisiting Osirak"; "The DCI Special Advisor Report on Iraq's WMD," CIA, 2004, https://www.cia.gov/library/reports/general -reports-1/iraq_wmd_2004/index.html; Hal Brands and David Palkki, "Saddam, Israel, and the Bomb: Nuclear Alarmism Justified?," *International Security* 36, No. 1 (Summer 2011): 133–66.

37. William J. Broad, "How to Help Iran Build a Bomb," *New York Times*, September 28, 2012.

38. Ephraim Kam, "An Attack on Iran: The Morning After," *Strategic Assessment* 15, No. 1 (April 2012): 18.

39. My assessment is based on decades of conversations with senior Israeli officials (serving and retired) on this subject. However, they also typically make the point in print whenever they write about these matters. See for instance, Kam, "An Attack on Iran," pp. 16–19; and Amos Yadlin, "Israel's Last Chance to Strike Iran," *New York Times*, February 29, 2012.

40. Yadlin, "Israel's Last Chance to Strike Iran."

41. Kam, "An Attack on Iran," p. 18.

42. As one example, see Louis Charbonneau, "Iran Slams Anti–Nuclear Weapons Treaty as Discriminatory," Reuters, November 5, 2012.

43. Yeganeh Torbati, "Iran Accuses IAEA of Passing Nuclear Secrets to Israel," Reuters, September 23, 2012.

44. Ibid.

45. "Iran Guard Commander: 'Nothing Will Remain' of Israel if It Attacks," Associated Press, September 16, 2012; ibid.

46. "Any Attack on Iran May Lead Iran to Withdrawal from NPT: Envoy," Reuters, November 30, 2012.

47. On the case for penalizing countries that withdraw from the NPT if they violate their Safeguards agreement, see George Bunn and John Rhinelander, "The Right to Withdraw from the NPT: Article X Is Not Unconditional," *Disarmament Diplomacy,* No. 79 (April/May 2005), available at http://www.acronym.org.uk/dd/dd79/79gbjr.htm.

48. See also William Maclean, "Iran Raid Likely to Drag in U.S. and Hurt Global Economy," Reuters, February 5, 2012.

49. See for instance, "Joint Israeli Palestinian Poll, September 2012," Palestinian Center for Policy and Survey Research, September 20, 2012, available at http://www.pcpsr.org/survey/polls/2012/p45ejoint.html; Shibley Telhami, "Do Israelis Support a Strike on Iran?" *Politico,* February 28, 2012.

50. For those interested, reports on some of these war games can be found at Dan Ephron, "If Israel Attacks Iran . . . ," *Newsweek,* October 15, 2012, pp. 40–45, available online at http://www.thedailybeast.com/news week/2012/10/07/newsweek-s-iran-war-game.html; Kenneth M. Pollack, "Osiraq Redux: A Crisis Simulation of an Israeli Strike on the Iranian Nuclear Program," Middle East Memo No. 15, Saban Center for Middle East Policy, Brookings Institution, February 2010, available at http://www.brookings.edu/~/media/research/files/reports/2010/2/iran%20israel%20strike%20pollack/02_iran_israel_strike_pollack.pdf; David Sanger, "Imagining an Israeli Strike on Iran," *New York Times,* March 27, 2010.

51. "President George W Bush 'Turned Down Israeli Request to Bomb Iran,'" Reuters, September 25, 2008.

52. David E. Sanger, "U.S. Rejected Aid for Israeli Raid on Iranian Nuclear Site," *New York Times,* January 10, 2009.

53. Alexander Bolton, "Israeli Strike on Iran Would Pose Risk for US Economy, Obama Reelection Bid," *The Hill,* February 23, 2012; Anshel Pfeffer, "After Pushing Israel from Iran Strike, Obama Is Suddenly OK with Netanyahu," *Haaretz* online, September 4, 2012, available at http://www.haaretz.com/blogs/the-axis/after-pushing-israel-from-iran-strike-obama-is-suddenly-ok-with-netanyahu-1.462772.

54. Jeffrey Heller and Matt Spetalnick, "Obama, Netanyahu Give No Sign of Narrowing Gap on Iran," Reuters, March 5, 2012; Mark Landler, "Obama Presses Netanyahu to Resist Strikes on Iran," *New York Times*, March 5, 2012.

55. Paul Bracken, *The Second Nuclear Age: Strategy, Danger, and the New Power Politics* (New York: Times Books, 2012), esp. pp. 22–58.

56. On Pakistan, see P. R. Chari, "Nuclear Restraint, Nuclear Risk Reduction, and the Security-Insecurity Paradox in South Asia," in Michael Krepon and Chris Gagne, eds., *The Stability-Instability Paradox: Nuclear Weapons and Brinksmanship in South Asia* (Washington, D.C.: Stimson Center, 2001); S. Paul Kapur, "Ten Years of Instability in a Nuclear South Asia," *International Security*, No. 33 (Fall 2008): 72; Benjamin S. Lambeth, *Airpower at 18,000': The Indian Air Force in the Kargil War* (Washington, D.C.: Carnegie Endowment for International Peace, 2012), pp. 7, 39; Bruce O. Riedel, *Deadly Embrace: Pakistan, America and the Future of the Global Jihad* (Washington, D.C.: Brookings Institution Press, 2011), pp. 45–47, 115–16. On North Korea, see Jack Kim and Lee Jae-Won, "North Korea Shells South in Fiercest Attack in Decades," Reuters, November 23, 2010; "'North Korean Torpedo' Sank South's Navy Ship—Report," BBC, May 20, 2010, available at http://www.bbc.co.uk/news/10129703. On Iraq, see Amatzia Baram, "Deterrence Lessons from Iraq," *Foreign Affairs* 91, No. 4 (July/August 2012); "Saddam, Israel, and the Bomb: Nuclear Alarmism Justified?" pp. 133–166; Kevin M. Woods, David D. Palkki, and Mark E. Stout, eds., *The Saddam Tapes: The Inner Workings of a Tyrant's Regime 1978–2001* (Cambridge, U.K.: Cambridge University Press, 2011), pp. 222–224.

57. For a parallel assessment by two first-rate Middle East military analysts, see Eisenstadt and Knights, "Beyond Worst-Case Analysis," pp. 3–4.

58. Kam, "An Attack on Iran: The Morning After," p. 18.

59. See René Rieger and Markus Schiller, "Pre-Emptive Strike Against Iran: Prelude to an Avoidable Disaster?" *Middle East Policy* 19, No. 4 (Winter 2012): 128–30.

60. Tehran also reportedly purchased nineteen Nodong/Taepodong missiles from North Korea that could hit Israel (although they may have been bought to eventually carry nuclear warheads, in which case Iran probably would not want to expend them in a conventional attack). William J. Broad, James Glanz, and David E. Sanger, "Iran Fortifies Its Arsenal with the Aid of North Korea," *New York Times*, November 28, 2010.

61. Bergman, "Will Israel Attack Iran?"

62. Ibid.

63. For a fuller explication of the argument that Iranian retaliation for an Is-

raeli strike might be less than often imagined, see Michael Eisenstadt and Michael Knights, "Beyond Worst-Case Analysis: Iran's Likely Responses to an Israeli Preventive Strike," Policy Notes No. 11, Washington Institute for Near East Policy, June 2012.

64. Rory McCarthy, "Hizbullah Leader: We Regret the Two Kidnappings That Led to War with Israel," *Guardian*, August 27, 2006.

65. William J. Broad, "Weapons Experts Raise Doubts About Israel's Antimissile System," *New York Times*, March 20, 2013; Reuven Pedatzur, "How Many Missiles Has Iron Dome Really Intercepted?" *Haaretz*, March 9, 2013; Yiftah S. Shapir, "Iron Dome: The Queen of Battle," in Shlomo Brom, ed., "In the Aftermath of Operation Pillar of Defense: The Gaza Strip, November 2012," Memorandum 124, Institute for National Strategic Studies, Israel, December 2012, pp. 39–48.

66. "Iran: Hezbollah Will Defend Us 'Easily' Against Israeli Attack," Reuters, September 14, 2012.

67. Yoram Schweitzer, "Are Changes Expected in Israel-Gaza Relations?" in Brom, "In the Aftermath of Operation Pillar of Defense," ibid., pp. 79–82.

68. "Rocket Attacks on Israel from Gaza," Israel Defense Forces website, November 20, 2012, available at http://www.idfblog.com/facts-figures/rocket-attacks-toward-israel/.

69. Uriel Heilman, "Operation Pillar of Defense: Lessons Learned," JTA, November 21, 2012.

70. Steve Fetter, George N. Lewis, and Lisbeth Gronlund, "Why Were Casualties So Low?" *Nature* 361 (January 28, 1993): 294.

71. "Terrorism Against Israel: Number of Fatalities," Jewish Virtual Library, available at http://www.jewishvirtuallibrary.org/jsource/Peace/osloterr.html; "Jewish Historic Demography," Jewish Timeline, available at http://www.odyeda.com/JewishTimelineEn/jewish-historic-demography/.

72. Ibid.

73. Kam, "An Attack on Iran," p. 20; Eisenstadt and Knights, "Beyond Worst-Case Analysis," p. 7.

74. Julian Borger, "Lebanon War Cost Israel $1.6 Billion," *Guardian*, August 15, 2006; "The Hezbollah-Israel Conflict: By the Numbers," Israel Project, available at http://www.theisraelproject.org/site/c.hsJPK0PIJpH/b.2904297/k.131A/The_HezbollahIsrael_Conflict_By_the_Numbers.htm, downloaded January 20, 2013.

75. See for instance, Pollack, "Osiraq Redux?"

76. "Poll: Most Israelis Could Live with a Nuclear Iran," Reuters, June 14, 2009.

77. Christa Case Bryant, "Israelis Shrug at Netanyahu's Urgent Warnings on Iran," *Christian Science Monitor*, September 25, 2012.

78. "Joint Israeli Palestinian Poll, September 2012," Palestinian Center for Policy and Survey Research, September 20, 2012, available at http://www.pcpsr.org/survey/polls/2012/p45ejoint.html.

79. Crispian Balmer, "Netanyahu Conundrum Faces Iranian Riddle," Reuters, January 14, 2013.

80. Jodi Rudoren, "Tepid Vote for Netanyahu in Israel Is Seen as Rebuke," *New York Times*, January 23, 2012; Isabel Kershner, "Charismatic Leader Helps Israel Turn Toward the Center," *New York Times*, January 23, 2012.

81. Telhami, "Do Israelis Support a Strike on Iran?"

82. "Joint Israeli Palestinian Poll, September 2012."

83. Ibid.

84. Telhami, "Do Israelis Support a Strike on Iran?"

85. Daniel Levy, "Netanyahu Won't Attack Iran (Probably)," ForeignPolicy.com, March 2, 2012, available at http://www.foreignpolicy.com/articles/2012/03/02/netanyahu_won_t_attack_iran.

86. Daniel L. Byman, *A High Price: The Triumphs and Failures of Israeli Counterterrorism* (New York: Oxford University Press, 2011), pp. 324–34.

87. See also Bryant, "Israelis Shrug at Netanyahu's Urgent Warnings on Iran."

88. "Netanyahu, Barak Mulling Fall Strike on Iran," Ynet News, August 10, 2012, available at http://www.ynetnews.com/articles/0,7340,L-4266973,00.html.

89. Levy, "Netanyahu Won't Attack Iran (Probably)."

90. Balmer, "Netanyahu Conundrum Faces Iranian Riddle."

91. Ibid.

92. Quoted in David Remnick, "Blood and Sand," *New Yorker*, May 5, 2008, p. 76.

93. See for instance, Ali Akbar Dareini, "Iran Threatens Attacks on US Bases in Event of War," Associated Press, September 24, 2012.

94. Mark Mazzetti and Thom Shanker, "U.S. War Game Sees Perils of Israeli Strike Against Iran," *New York Times*, March 19, 2012.

95. My friend Elliott Abrams, with whom I have some sharp disagreements regarding the utility of an Israeli strike, seems to agree with me on this specific point. See Elliott Abrams, "The Grounds for an Israeli Attack," *World Affairs* 175, No. 1 (May/June 2012): 29. Here he notes that Iran is fully capable of distinguishing between an American attack and an Israeli attack and of responding only against the party that attacked it. For another concurring assessment, see Eisenstadt and Knights, "Beyond Worst-Case Analysis," p. 3.

96. Daniel Fineran and Amena Bakr, "Iran Says May Stop Oil Sales If Sanctions Tighten," Reuters, October 23, 2012; Ramin Mostafavi, "Iran Threat-

ens to Stop Gulf Oil If Sanctions Widened," Reuters, December 28, 2011; Ramin Mostafavi, "Iran Warns of Consequences if Arabs Back Oil Sanctions," Reuters, January 16, 2012; Brian Murphy and Nasser Karimi, "Iran Revives Gulf Threats After EU Sanctions," Associated Press, January 24, 2012; Robin Pomeroy, "Iran Tells Turkey: Change Tack or Face Trouble," Reuters, October 8, 2011; David E. Sanger and Annie Lowrey, "Iran Threatens to Block Oil Shipments, as U.S. Prepares Sanctions," *New York Times,* December 27, 2011; Yeganeh Torbati, "Iran Threatens Israel; New EU Sanctions Take Force," Reuters, July 1, 2012.

97. Geoff Dyer, Monavar Khalaj, James Blitz, and Jack Farchy, "U.S. Dismisses Iranian Threats Over Carrier," *Financial Times,* January 4, 2012.

98. Eisenstadt and Knights, "Beyond Worst-Case Analysis," p. 6.

99. Elisabeth Bumiller, Eric Schmitt, and Thom Shanker, "U.S. Sends Top Iranian Leader a Warning on Strait Threat," *New York Times,* January 12, 2012; Sanger and Lowrey, "Iran Threatens to Block Oil Shipments, as U.S. Prepares Sanctions."

100. For concurring assessments, see Anthony H. Cordesman, "Iran, Oil, and the Strait of Hormuz," Center for Strategic and International Studies, March 26, 2007; Caitlin Talmadge, "Closing Time: Assessing the Iranian Threat to the Strait of Hormuz," *International Security* 33, No. 1 (Summer 2008): 82–117.

Chapter 9. A Return to Arms

1. Jonathan Saul, "Western Sanctions Swamp Iran's Seaborne Trade," *Daily Star,* October 13, 2012.

2. See for instance, Amir Latif, "Iranian Petrol a Hot Commodity in Pakistan," PakTribune, December 12, 2012, available at http://paktribune.com/articles/Iranian-petrol-a-hot-commodity-in-Pakistan-162821.html.

3. Thomas Seibert, "Fuel Smugglers Run a 'Pipeline of Mules,'" *National,* June 8, 2009; "Gas Oil Smuggling from Iran to Turkey, Pakistan on Rise," AzerNews, November 26, 2012, available at http://www.azernews.az/oil_and_gas/46696.html.

4. Mohammad Ali Shabani, "Iran Survives Sanctions, Girds for Further Economic War," Al-Monitor, December 20, 2012.

5. Ladane Nasseri and Yeganeh Salehi, "Iran's Smugglers Feel the Squeeze," *BloombergBusinessweek,* August 2, 2012.

6. Ken Dilanian, "Illegal Exports to Iran on the Rise, Say U.S. Officials," *Los Angeles Times,* November 17, 2012.

7. See "Iran Black Markets," Havoscope: Black Market Information, updated periodically, available at http://www.havocscope.com/tag/iran/.

8. For a similar assessment by a superb military analyst, see Michael E. O'Hanlon, "Deterrence," in Jon B. Alterman, "Gulf Kaleidoscope: Reflections on the Iranian Challenge," Center for Strategic and International Studies, May 2012, pp. 41–43.

9. Robert McNally, "Time to Tighten the Noose on Iran," *Financial Times*, June 27, 2012.

10. William Arkin, "The Difference Was in the Details," *Washington Post*, January 17, 1999.

11. Anthony H. Cordesman and Abdullah Toukan, "Analyzing the Impact of Preventive Strikes Against Iran's Nuclear Facilities," Center for Strategic and International Studies, September 2012, available at http://csis.org/files/publication/120906_Iran_US_Preventive_Strikes.pdf, p. 19.

12. Joby Warrick, "Iran's Underground Nuclear Sites Not Immune to U.S. Bunker-Busters, Experts Say," *Washington Post*, February 29, 2012.

13. Matthew Kroenig, "Time to Attack Iran," *Foreign Affairs* 91, No. 1 (January/February 2012): 80.

14. Summary of remarks by Michael Hayden, Center for the National Interest, Washington, D.C., January 19, 2012, available at http://cftni.org/Hayden%20_1.19.12.pdf, p. 1.

15. "Impact of Military Strike on Iran's Nuclear Facilities 'Unclear,' Says U.S. Report," *Haaretz*, March 28, 2012. See also Viola Gienger and Tony Capaccio, "Iran Could Recover from Attack on Its Nuclear Sites Within Six Months, Says U.S. Report," Bloomberg, March 28, 2012.

16. Colin H. Kahl, "Not Time to Attack Iran," *Foreign Affairs* 91, No. 2 (March/April 2012): 170.

17. See, for instance, Henri J. Barkey and Uri Dadush, "Why No U.S. President Will Bomb Iran," *National Interest*, January 27, 2010; O'Hanlon, "Deterrence," p. 41; René Rieger and Markus Schiller, "Pre-Emptive Strike Against Iran: Prelude to an Avoidable Disaster?" *Middle East Policy* 19, No. 4 (Winter 2012): 133.

18. "Remarks by Secretary of Defense Leon E. Panetta at the Saban Center," U.S. Department of Defense, December 2, 2011, available at http://www.defense.gov/transcripts/transcript.aspx?transcriptid=4937.

19. For instance, see Elliott Abrams, "The Grounds for an Israeli Attack," *World Affairs* 175, No. 1 (May/June 2012): 26–27.

20. Reuel Marc Gerecht, "Should Israel Bomb Iran? Better Safe than Sorry," *Weekly Standard* 15, No. 42 (July 26, 2010).

21. Robert Pape, *Bombing to Win: Air Power and Coercion in War* (Ithaca, N.Y.: Cornell University Press, 1996).

22. Ivo H. Daalder and Michael E. O'Hanlon, *Winning Ugly: NATO's War to*

Save Kosovo (Washington, D.C.: Brookings Institution Press, 2000), pp. 4–5; Stephen T. Hosmer, *Why Milosevic Decided to Settle When He Did* (Santa Monica, Calif.: RAND, 2001).

23. For a firsthand account depicting both the terror of Saddam and the mixed Iraqi emotions about the United States by an Iraqi diarist, see Nuha al-Radi, *Baghdad Diaries* (London: Saqi Books, 1998). Among the postwar accounts of Iraq, the two that best captured—and most eloquently presented—the complicated feelings of Iraqis are George S. Packer, *The Assassins' Gate: America in Iraq* (New York: Farrar, Straus & Giroux, 2005), esp. pp. 148–295; and Anthony Shadid, *Night Draws Near: Iraq's People in the Shadow of America's War* (New York: Henry Holt, 2005).

24. For a concurring assessment by a bright young scholar who favors an air campaign against Iran, see Kroenig, "Time to Attack Iran," p. 85.

25. William J. Broad, "How to Help Iran Build a Bomb," *New York Times*, September 28, 2012; Cordesman and Toukan, "Analyzing the Impact of Preventive Strikes Against Iran's Nuclear Facilities," p. 19; Stephen Heintz, William Luers, William Miller, Thomas Pickering, Jim Walsh, Frank Wisner, et al., "Weighing Benefits and Costs of Military Action Against Iran," Iran Project, September 2012, pp. 38–39.

26. Summary of remarks by Michael Hayden, Center for the National Interest, Washington, D.C., January 19, 2012, available at http://cftni.org/Hayden%20_1.19.12.pdf, p. 1.

27. Kahl, "Not Time to Attack Iran," p. 171.

28. O'Hanlon, "Deterrence," p. 41.

29. Kroenig, "Time to Attack Iran," p. 84.

30. "The DCI Special Advisor Report on Iraq's WMD," vol. 1, 2004. In particular, see the section on "Regime Strategic Intent," available at https://www.cia.gov/library/reports/general-reports-1/iraq_wmd_2004/chap1.html.

31. Eliot A. Cohen, general editor, *The Gulf War Air Power Survey, Volume V, Part I: Statistical Compendium* (Washington, D.C.: U.S. Government Printing Office, 1993), p. 233.

32. Kenneth M. Pollack, *The Threatening Storm: The Case for Invading Iraq* (New York: Random House, 2002), pp. 314–20.

33. Department of Defense, *Report to Congress: Kosovo/Operation Allied Force After Action Report* (Washington, D.C.: U.S. Department of Defense, 2000), p. 86.

34. Pollack, *The Threatening Storm*, pp. 314–20.

35. "Fact Sheet: Operation UNIFIED PROTECTOR Final Mission Stats," North Atlantic Treaty Organization, November 2, 2011; Simon Rogers, "Nato Operations in Libya: Data Journalism Breaks Down Which Country

Does What," *Guardian*, October 31, 2011, available at http://www.guard
ian.co.uk/news/datablog/2011/may/22/nato-libya-data-journalism-opera
tions-country. In addition, the daily breakdown of sorties is available as
a link to this article at https://docs.google.com/spreadsheet/ccc?key=0Aq
-FnOoJcl-ndG9KUHFFNDgyNENWRW5TTUl6QnFDcXc&authkey=CPe
KjPMB&hl=en_US&authkey=CPeKjPMB#gid=1.

36. On Libyan military performance under Qadhafi, see Kenneth M. Pollack,
Arabs at War: Military Effectiveness, 1948–1991 (Lincoln: University of Nebraska Press, 2002), pp. 358–424.

37. Pollack, *The Threatening Storm*, pp. 293–334.

38. On Iran's armed forces, their capabilities, loyalties, and reliability, see
Emanuele Ottolenghi, *The Pasdaran: Inside Iran's Islamic Revolutionary
Guard Corps* (Washington, D.C.: Foundation for the Defense of Democra-
cies, 2011); Steven R. Ward, *Immortal: A Military History of Iran and Its
Armed Forces* (Washington, D.C.: Georgetown University Press, 2009), pp.
211–326; Frederic Wehrey, Jerrold D. Green, Brian Nichiporuk, Alireza
Nader, Lydia Hansell, Rasool Nafisi, and S. R. Bohandy, "The Rise of the
Pasdaran: Assessing the Domestic Roles of Iran's Islamic Revolutionary
Guards Corps," RAND Corporation, 2009, available at http://www.rand
.org/pubs/monographs/2008/RAND_MG821.pdf.

39. Carl von Clausewitz, *On War*, edited and translated by Michael Howard
and Peter Paret (Princeton, N.J.: Princeton University Press, 1976), p. 119.

40. Mark Devenport, "Kofi Annan's Delicate Balancing Act," BBC, April 13,
1999, available at http://news.bbc.co.uk/2/hi/special_report/1999/03/99/
kosovo_strikes/318104.stm; Albert Legault, "NATO Intervention in Kosovo: The Legal Context," *Canadian Military Journal* 1, No. 1 (Spring
2000): 63–66.

41. For instance, see "Britain Says Opposed to Strike on Iran 'at This Moment,'" Reuters, October 26, 2012.

42. See, for instance, Dan Joyner, "Can the U.S. or Israel Lawfully Attack Iran's
Nuclear Facilities," Arms Control Law online, August 13, 2012, available
at http://armscontrollaw.com/2012/08/07/can-the-u-s-or-israel-lawfully
-attack-irans-nuclear-facilities/; Mary Ellen O'Connell and Maria Alevras-
Chen, "The Ban on the Bomb—and Bombing: Iran, the U.S., and the
International Law of Self-Defense," *Syracuse Law Review*, No. 57, No. 497
(2006–2007).

43. O'Connell and Alevras-Chen, "The Ban on the Bomb—and Bombing,"
p. 498.

44. Joyner, "Can the U.S. or Israel Lawfully Attack Iran's Nuclear Facilities."

45. Suzanne Maloney, "Thinking the Unthinkable: The Gulf States and the

Prospect of a Nuclear Iran," Middle East Memo No. 27, Saban Center for Middle East Policy, Brookings Institution, January 2013, p. 9.

46. My colleague Suzanne Maloney does an excellent job addressing these issues in ibid., pp. 7–9.

47. Jeffrey H. Smith and John B. Bellinger III, "Providing a Legal Basis to Attack Iran," *Washington Post*, September 27, 2012.

48. Matthew Waxman, "What the Cuban Missile Crisis Teaches Us About Iran," CNN.com, October 25, 2012.

49. Heintz, Luers, Miller, Pickering, Walsh, Wisner, et al., "Weighing Benefits and Costs of Military Action Against Iran," p. 37.

50. Ben Hubbard, "Israeli Jets Bomb Military Target in Syria," Associated Press, January 30, 2013.

51. Charlie Savage, "Top U.S. Security Official Says 'Rigorous Standards' Are Used for Drone Strikes," *New York Times*, April 30, 2012; Charlie Savage, "A Not-Quite Confirmation of a Memo Approving Killing," *New York Times*, March 8, 2012; Jane Perlez, "Pakistan Rehearses Its Two-Step on Airstrikes," *New York Times*, April 15, 2009.

52. Pollack, *The Threatening Storm*, p. 83.

53. Mark J. Conversino, "Operation DESERT FOX: Effectiveness with Unintended Effects," *Air and Space Power Journal*, July 13, 2005, available at http://www.airpower.au.af.mil/airchronicles/cc/conversino.html.

54. Williamson Murray and Robert H. Scales Jr., *The Iraq War: A Military History* (Cambridge, Mass.: Belknap Press of Harvard University Press, 2003), pp. 73–74.

55. Bob Woodward, *Plan of Attack* (New York: Simon & Schuster, 2004), pp. 324–25.

56. See, for instance, "Russia and China Warn America Against Iran Strike as Tensions Rise Ahead of Damning Atomic Agency Report," *Daily Mail* online, November 8, 2011, available at http://www.dailymail.co.uk/news/article-2058579/Russia-China-warn-America-Iran-nuclear-strike-tensions-rise.html#axzz2JrwoWhh6.

57. Gabriela Baczynska and Steve Gutterman, "Russia Warns Israel, West Against Attack on Iran," Reuters, January 23, 2013.

58. "Russia Says 'No Signs' of Nuclear Weapons Development in Iran: Interfax," al-Arabiya, November 27, 2012.

59. "China Steps Up Pressure to Prevent Any Attack on Iran," Reuters, April 6, 2012.

60. "Attack on Iran 'Would be Disaster,' Must Talk: Turkey," Reuters, February 5, 2012; "Brazilian President Warns Against Military Aggression Against Iran," FARS News Agency, October 4, 2012, available at http://english

.farsnews.com/newstext.php?nn=9107110372; Dipanjan Roy Chaudhury, "Attack on Iran Will Hit India's Interests, Says S. M. Krishna," India Today, May 9, 2012, available at http://indiatoday.intoday.in/story/attack-on-iran -will-hit-interests-of-india-s.m.-krishna/1/187961.html.

61. David E. Sanger, James Glanz, and Jo Becker, "Around the World, Distress Over Iran," *New York Times*, November 28, 2010.

62. Ibid.

63. Author's interviews with Gulf leaders, 2010–2012. See also ibid.

64. Mark Heinrich and Karin Strohecker, "IAEA Urges Iran Compromise to Avert Conflict," Reuters, June 14, 2007; "Arab States Against Military Action on Iran," iranmania.com, June 18, 2007.

65. "Saudi Prince Warns Against Any Attack on Iran," Reuters, November 15, 2011.

66. "Attack on Iran 'Would be Disaster,' Must Talk: Turkey."

67. Robert McNally, "Energy Brief: Managing Oil Market Disruption in a Confrontation with Iran," Council on Foreign Relations, January 2012, pp. 4–5.

68. Dennis Ross, "Calling Iran's Bluff: It's Time to Offer Tehran a Civilian Nuclear Program," *New Republic*, June 15, 2012; Patrick Clawson, "Obama: Offer Iran a Generous Deal," *Atlantic* online, January 16, 2013, available at http://www.theatlantic.com/international/archive/2013/01/obama-offer -iran-a-generous-deal/267210/.

69. For an outstanding treatment of this tendency in American history, see Gideon Rose, *How Wars End: Why We Always Fight the Last Battle* (New York: Simon & Schuster, 2010).

70. "Transcript: President Obama 2013 Inaugural Address," *Washington Post*, January 21, 2013, available at http://www.washingtonpost.com/blogs/ wonkblog/wp/2013/01/21/transcript-president-obama-2013-inaugural -address/.

71. Jeff Mason, "Most Americans Would Back U.S. Strike over Iran Nuclear Weapon: Poll," Reuters, March 13, 2012.

72. "FPI National Survey: Foreign Policy Matters in 2012," Foreign Policy Institute, September 27, 2012, available at http://www.foreignpolicyi.org/ content/fpi-national-survey-foreign-policy-matters-2012-1.

73. Fox News Poll, October 2012, retrieved February 5, 2013, from the iPOLL Databank, Roper Center for Public Opinion Research, University of Connecticut, available at http://www.ropercenter.uconn.edu/data_access/ipoll/ ipoll.html.

74. Dina Smeltz, "Foreign Policy in the New Millennium: Results of the 2012 Chicago Council Survey of American Public Opinion and U.S. Foreign Policy," Chicago Council on Global Affairs, September 2012, p. 29.

75. CBS News/*New York Times* poll, October 2012, retrieved February 5, 2013 from the iPOLL Databank, Roper Center for Public Opinion Research, University of Connecticut, available at http://www.ropercenter.uconn.edu/data_access/ipoll/ipoll.html.

76. Matthew Cooper, "Voters Favor Obama Ideas but Keystone, Too," *National Journal*, January 31, 2012, available at http://www.nationaljournal.com/daily/voters-favor-obama-ideas-but-keystone-too-20120130.

77. Eli Clifton, "NBC/WSJ Poll: Americans Prefer Diplomacy over Military Action to Prevent Iran from Acquiring Nukes," ThinkProgress.com, March 5, 2012. The original poll can be found at http://online.wsj.com/documents/wsjnbcpoll-03052012.pdf.

78. "CNN Poll: Americans Favor Diplomacy Against Iran," CNN.com, February 15, 2012, available at http://politicalticker.blogs.cnn.com/2012/02/15/cnn-poll-americans-favor-diplomacy-against-iran/.

79. Ali Akbar Dareini, "Iran Threatens to Hit Turkey If US, Israel Attack," Associated Press, November 26, 2011; Ali Akbar Dareini, "Iran Threatens Attacks on US Bases in Event of War," Associated Press, September 24, 2012; Lee Ferran, "Iran: We Can Hit US Bases in 'Minutes,'" ABC News, July 6, 2012; Marcus George, "Iran Threatens to Target U.S. Bases If Attacked," Reuters, June 3, 2012; "Iran Vows 'Proportionate' Response to Any Strike," Agence France-Presse, June 2, 2012; Parisa Hafezi and Mitra Amiri, "Iran's Khamenei Warns U.S., Israel on Atom Site Attacks," Reuters, November 10, 2011; Parisa Hafezi, "Iran Threatens to Hit Any Country Used to Attack Its Soil," Reuters, February 5, 2012.

80. Hafezi and Amiri, "Iran's Khamenei Warns U.S., Israel on Atom Site Attacks"; "Iran's Leader: War Would Be Detrimental to U.S.," CNN.com, February 3, 2012, available at http://www.cnn.com/2012/02/03/world/meast/iran-warning/index.html.

81. Kroenig, "Time to Attack Iran."

82. For a concurring assessment by an outstanding analyst, see Kahl, "Not Time to Attack Iran," p. 170.

83. See for instance, Ephraim Kam, "An Attack on Iran: The Morning After," *Strategic Assessment* 15, No. 1 (April 2012): 24.

84. Greg Miller, "Iran, Perceiving Threat from the West, Willing to Attack on U.S. Soil, U.S. Intelligence Report Finds," *Washington Post*, January 31, 2012.

85. For a concurring view, see Rieger and Schiller, "Pre-Emptive Strike Against Iran: Prelude to an Avoidable Disaster?," p. 134.

86. Kenneth M. Pollack, "A Series of Unfortunate Events: A Crisis Simulation of a U.S.-Iranian Confrontation," Middle East Memo No. 26, Saban Center

for Middle East Policy at the Brookings Institution, October 2012, available at http://www.brookings.edu/~/media/research/files/papers/2012/11/us%20iran%20crisis%20simulation%20pollack/us%20iran%20crisis%20simulation%20pollack%20paper.pdf.

87. Rick Gladstone, "Noise Level Rises over Iran Threat to Close Strait of Hormuz," *New York Times*, December 28, 2011; Ramin Mostafavi, "Iran Threatens to Stop Gulf Oil If Sanctions Widened," Reuters, December 28, 2011; Brian Murphy and Nasser Karimi, "Iran Revives Gulf Threats After EU Sanctions," Associated Press, January 24, 2012; David E. Sanger and Annie Lowrey, "Iran Threatens to Block Oil Shipments, as U.S. Prepares Sanctions," *New York Times*, December 27, 2011.

88. Kroenig argues that the United States should try to convey to Iran during a strike that the U.S. is purposely refraining from hitting these targets to make the point clear to Tehran. I tend to doubt that they will believe anything we tell them in the midst of an attack on their nuclear sites. See Kroenig, "Time to Attack Iran," p. 83.

89. Again, for concurring assessments, see Anthony H. Cordesman, "Iran, Oil, and the Strait of Hormuz," Center for Strategic and International Studies, March 26, 2007; Caitlin Talmadge, "Closing Time: Assessing the Iranian Threat to the Strait of Hormuz," *International Security* 33, No. 1 (Summer 2008): 82–117.

90. McNally, "Energy Brief: Managing Oil Market Disruption in a Confrontation with Iran," p. 1.

91. Ibid.

92. Ibid., p. 7.

93. Ibid, pp. 5–7; the International Energy Agency tracks global reserves of oil and its regularly updated figures can be found at http://www.iea.org/netimports.asp.

94. Alan Greenspan, "Monetary Policy and the Economic Outlook," Testimony Before the Joint Economic Committee, U.S. Congress, April 17, 2002, Federal Reserve Board, available at http://www.federalreserve.gov/BoardDocs/Testimony/2002/20020417/default.htm; Hillard G. Huntington, "The Economic Consequences of Higher Crude Oil Prices," Final Report, EMF SR 9, prepared for the U.S. Department of Energy, October 3, 2005, p. 24; Jad Muawad, "Rising Demand for Oil Provokes New Energy Crisis," *New York Times*, November 9, 2007; Keith Sill, "The Macroeconomics of Oil Shocks," *Business Review*, Q1 (2007): 21, 26.

95. On the potential problem of war termination with Iran, former national coordinator for counterterrorism Dick Clarke describes how the U.S. government discussed these expected dynamics when the Clinton administra-

tion was considering a military attack on Iran in response to the Khobar Towers bombing in 1996. See Richard A. Clarke, *Against All Enemies: Inside America's War on Terror* (New York: Free Press, 2004), pp. 112–21; on American frustrations with Iran over the Tanker War, see David Crist, *The Twilight War: The Secret History of America's Thirty-Year Conflict with Iran* (New York: Penguin Press, 2012), pp. 256–379.

96. This section draws heavily on passages I cowrote with Michael O'Hanlon in Kenneth Pollack, Suzanne Maloney, Daniel Byman, Michael O'Hanlon, Martin Indyk, and Bruce Riedel, *Which Path to Persia? Options for a New Strategy Towards Iran* (Washington, D.C.: Brookings Institution Press, 2009).

97. Steven R Ward, *Immortal: A Military History of Iran and Its Armed Forces* (Washington, D.C.: Georgetown University Press, 2009), pp. 323–24.

98. Bruce Hoffman, "Insurgency and Counterinsurgency in Iraq," RAND Corporation, June 2004; Kalev I. Sepp, "Best Practices in Counterinsurgency," *Military Review* 85, no. 3 (May/June 2005): 9; James T. Quinlivan, "The Burden of Victory: The Painful Arithmetic of Stability Operations," *RAND Review*, Summer 2003, available at http://www.rand.org/publications/randreview/issues/summer2003/burden.html. Also, James T. Quinlivan, "Force Requirements in Stability Operations," *Parameters* (Winter 1995): 56–69.

99. Iraq had a population of 27 million in 2007–2008, thus the canonical ratio would call for a force of 540,000 security personnel. If the three provinces of the Kurdistan Regional Government are excluded (they were secure and therefore did not require extensive Coalition assistance), this arithmetic produces a population of 23 million, requiring about 460,000 security personnel. During that time, the United States maintained 163,000 troops, another 50,000–100,000 security contractors, about 11,000 allied troops and 200,000–300,000 ISF personnel for a total of 425,000–575,000 security personnel. Although U.S. troops working with small numbers of competent and reliable Iraqi security forces were able to secure large swaths of the population within six to twelve months of the start of the Surge, the change in U.S. strategy and tactics, the end of the Battle of Baghdad, and the onset of the Anbar Awakening (all of which occurred in late 2006 and early 2007), they were not able to secure the entire country, and most of southern Iraq—with nearly 40 percent of Iraq's population—lay beyond their control. Only when the total of U.S. and competent Iraqi troops exceeded 450,000–500,000 in early 2008 were these forces able to expand their control to the south without jeopardizing the gains made in the cen-

ter and west. Figures from the "Iraq Index," Brookings Institution, available at http://www.brookings.edu/about/centers/saban/iraq-index.
100. Ward, *Immortal*, pp. 323–24.
101. Amy Belasco, "The Cost of Iraq, Afghanistan, and Other Global War on Terror Operations Since 9/11," RL33110, Congressional Research Service, March 29, 2011, p. 1.
102. Pollack, "A Series of Unfortunate Events."

Chapter 10. The Strategy That Dare Not Speak Its Name

1. The text of Senate Joint Resolution 41 can be found at http://www.gpo.gov/fdsys/pkg/BILLS-112sjres41es/pdf/BILLS-112sjres41es.pdf.
2. "Press Conference by the President," Office of the Press Secretary, White House, March 6, 2012, available at http://www.whitehouse.gov/the-press -office/2012/03/06/press-conference-president.
3. "President Obama's 2012 Address to U.N. General Assembly (Full Text)," *Washington Post*, September 25, 2012.
4. "State of the Union 2013: President Obama's address to Congress (Transcript)," *Washington Post*, February 12, 2013.
5. This simple distillation of the concept ultimately derives from George Kennan's famous "Long Telegram" and his "Mr. X" article in *Foreign Affairs*. For the latter, see George Kennan (writing as "X"), "The Sources of Soviet Conduct," *Foreign Affairs* 25, No. 4 (July 1947). For later expansions on this basic conception, see for instance, John Lewis Gaddis, *Strategies of Containment: A Critical Appraisal of American National Security Policy During the Cold War*, revised and expanded ed. (New York: Oxford University Press, 2005); John Lewis Gaddis, *We Now Know: Rethinking Cold War History* (New York: Oxford University Press, 1998); John Lewis Gaddis, *The Long Peace: Inquiries into the History of the Cold War* (New York: Oxford University Press, 1989); Raymond Garthoff, *Détente and Confrontation: American-Soviet Relations from Nixon to Reagan*, rev. ed. (Washington, D.C.: Brookings Institution Press, 1994); Charles Gati, ed., *Caging the Bear: Containment and the Cold War* (Indianapolis: Bobbs-Merrill, 1974); Michael J. Hogan, *The End of the Cold War: Its Meaning and Implications* (New York: Cambridge University Press, 1992); Walter LaFeber, *America, Russia and the Cold War 1945–2007*, 10th ed. (New York: McGraw-Hill, 2006).
6. Karim Sadjadpour and Diane de Gramont, "Reading Kennan in Tehran," *Foreign Affairs* 90, No. 2 (March/April 2011).
7. Thomas Donnelly, Danielle Pletka, and Maseh Zarif, "Containing and Deterring a Nuclear Iran: Questions for Strategy, Requirements for Military

Forces," American Enterprise Institute, December 2011, http://www.for eignpolicy.com/files/fp_uploaded_documents/111205_AEI%20Iran%20 report%20text%20final%20Dec%206%202011.pdf, p. 10. Let me reiterate that this study is superb. It is insightful, balanced, nuanced, erudite, and constructive. It is well worth reading for those interested in delving deeper into the topic of containment and particularly its challenges.

8. On this topic, the definitive work remains Gaddis, *Strategies of Containment*.

9. On Dual Containment of Iran, for the definitive statement by the Clinton administration, see Martin Indyk, "The Clinton Administration's Approach to the Middle East," Keynote Address at the Washington Institute for Near East Policy's Soref Symposium, May 18, 1993. See also Martin Indyk, *Innocent Abroad: An Intimate Account of American Peace Diplomacy in the Middle East* (New York: Simon & Schuster, 2009), pp. 149–66; Kenneth M. Pollack, *The Persian Puzzle: The Conflict Between Iran and America* (New York: Random House, 2004), pp. 259–65.

10. Richard A. Clarke, *Against All Enemies; Inside America's War on Terror* (New York: Free Press, 2004), pp. 103–104; Pollack, *The Persian Puzzle*, pp. 270–75; James Risen, "Gingrich Wants Funds for Covert Action Against Iran," *Los Angeles Times*, December 10, 1995, p. 1; David Rogers, "Gingrich Wants Funds Set Aside for Iran Action," *Wall Street Journal*, October 27, 1995, p. 1.

11. On contemporary Pakistan, its internal dysfunctions and obsession with India, see Stephen P. Cohen, *The Idea of Pakistan* (Washington, D.C.: Brookings Institution Press, 2006); Stephen P. Cohen et al., *The Future of Pakistan* (Washington, D.C.: Brookings Institution, 2006); Pamela Constable, *Playing with Fire: Pakistan at War with Itself* (New York: Random House, 2011); Ahmed Rashid, *Pakistan on the Brink: The Future of America, Pakistan, and Afghanistan* (New York: Viking, 2012); Riedel, *Deadly Embrace*.

12. Paul K. Kerr and Mary Beth Nikitin, "Pakistan's Nuclear Weapons: Proliferation and Security Issues," RL34248, Congressional Research Service, February 13, 2013, p. 4; Robert S. Norris and Hans M. Kristensen, "Global Nuclear Weapons Inventories, 1945–2010," *Bulletin of the Atomic Scientists* 66, No. 4 (July/August 2010): 78; Karen DeYoung, "New Estimates Put Pakistan's Nuclear Arsenal at More than 100," *Washington Post*, January 31, 2011; David E. Sanger and Eric Schmitt, "Pakistani Nuclear Arms Pose Challenge to U.S. Policy," *New York Times*, January 31, 2011.

13. David E. Sanger and Choe Sang-Hun, "North Korea Issues Blunt New Threat to United States," *New York Times*, January 24, 2013.

14. Tom Miles, "North Korea Threatens South with 'Final Destruction,'" Reuters, February 19, 2013.
15. "North Korea Threatens to Reduce South Korea's Government 'to Ashes,'" NBC News online, April 23, 2012, available at http://worldnews.nbc news.com/_news/2012/04/23/11346567-north-korea-threatens-to-reduce -south-koreas-government-to-ashes?lite.
16. "N. Korea Threatens S. Korean Leader's Office over Drills," Associated Press, November 24, 2011.
17. For those interested, see my defense of Israel as one of America's most important interests in the Middle East, in Pollack, *A Path Out of the Desert: A Grand Strategy for America in the Middle East* (New York: Random House, 2008), pp. 24–49. And for an example of the scurrilous attacks against me motivated by my commitment to the U.S.-Israel relationship, see Max Rodenbeck's front-page review of that book in the *New York Times* Sunday book review: Max Rodenbeck, "War and Peace," *New York Times Book Review*, August 22, 2008, p. 1.

Chapter 11. Deterrence and Extended Deterrence

1. The list of publications related to deterrence theory is too long to present comprehensively. The classics of the field (most of which retain relevance to questions of deterrence as part of a wider strategy of containment) include Bernard Brodie, *Strategy in the Missile Age* (Santa Monica, Calif.: RAND Corporation, 1958); Lawrence Freedman, *Deterrence* (New York: Wiley, 2004); Lawrence Freedman, *The Evolution of Nuclear Strategy*, 3rd ed. (New York: Palgrave Macmillan, 2003); Alexander George and Richard Smoke, *Deterrence in American Foreign Policy: Theory and Practice* (New York: Columbia University Press 1974); Robert Jervis, *Perception and Misperception in International Politics* (Princeton, N.J.: Princeton University Press, 1976), pp. 58–111; Herman Kahn, *Thinking About the Unthinkable* (New York: Horizon Press, 1962); Patrick Morgan, *Deterrence: A Conceptual Analysis* (Beverly Hills, Calif.: Sage, 1977); Patrick Morgan, *Deterrence Now* (New York: Cambridge University Press, 2003); Thomas Schelling, *The Strategy of Conflict* (Cambridge, Mass.: Harvard University Press, 1960); John Steinbruner, "Beyond Rational Deterrence: The Struggle for New Conceptions," *World Politics* 28 (January 1976): 223–45; Albert Wohlstetter, "The Delicate Balance of Terror," P-1472, RAND Corporation, Santa Monica, Calif., November 1958.
2. For some of the more important works on extended deterrence, see Paul K. Huth, *Extended Deterrence and the Prevention of War* (New Haven, Conn.: Yale University Press, 1988); Paul Huth and Bruce Russett, "What Makes

Deterrence Work? Cases from 1900 to 1980," *World Politics* 36 (July 1984); Robert Jervis, "Deterrence Theory Revisited," *World Politics* 31, No. 2 (January 1979): 289–324; Robert Jervis, Richard Ned Lebow, and Janice Gross Stein, *Psychology and Deterrence* (Baltimore: Johns Hopkins University Press, 1989); Richard Ned Lebow and Janice Gross Stein, "Rational Deterrence Theory: I Think, Therefore I Deter," *World Politics* 41(1989): 208–24; Kathleen MacInnis, "Extended Deterrence: The U.S. Credibility Gap in the Middle East," *Washington Quarterly* 28, No. 3 (Summer 2005): 169–86; Thomas Schelling, *Arms and Influence* (New Haven, Conn.: Yale University Press, 1966); Glenn H. Snyder, *Deterrence and Defense: Toward a Theory of National Security* (Princeton, N.J.: Princeton University Press, 1961); Kenneth Watman and Dean Wilkening, with John Arquila and Brian Nichiporuk, "U.S. Regional Deterrence Strategies," MR490, RAND Corporation, 1995; Dean Wilkening and Kenneth Watman, "Nuclear Deterrence in a Regional Context," MR 500, RAND Corporation, 1995.

3. Bernard Brodie, ed., *The Absolute Weapon: Atomic Power and World Order* (New York: Harcourt Brace, 1946).

4. Bernard Brodie, "The Development of Nuclear Strategy," *International Security* 2, No. 4 (Spring 1978): 66.

5. Kenneth N. Waltz, "The Spread of Nuclear Weapons: More May Be Better," Adelphi Paper No. 171 (London: International Institute for Strategic Studies, 1981); Scott D. Sagan and Kenneth N. Waltz, *The Spread of Nuclear Weapons: A Debate Renewed*, 2nd ed. (New York: Norton, 2002).

6. Bret Stephens, "Iran Cannot be Contained," *Commentary* 130, No. 1 (July/August 2010): 61–70.

7. Richard L. Kugler, "An Extended Deterrence Regime to Counter Iranian Nuclear Weapons: Issues and Options," Defense and Technology Paper No. 67, Center for Technology and National Security Policy, National Defense University, September 2009, p. 22.

8. David Menashri, "Iran's Regional Policy: Between Radicalism and Pragmatism," *Journal of International Affairs* 60, No. 2 (Spring/Summer 2007): 159–64.

9. Paul Bracken, *The Second Nuclear Age: Strategy, Danger, and the New Power Politics* (New York: Times Books, 2012); Keith B. Payne, *Deterrence in the Second Nuclear Age* (Lexington: University Press of Kentucky, 1996); Keith B. Payne, *The Fallacies of Cold War Deterrence and a New Direction* (Lexington: University Press of Kentucky, 2001).

10. David Crist, *The Twilight War: The Secret History of America's Thirty-Year Conflict with Iran* (New York: Penguin Press, 2012), pp. 343–44.

11. Ibid., p. 356.

12. Ibid., p. 386.

13. David Menashri, "Iran's Regional Policy: Between Radicalism and Pragmatism," *Journal of International Affairs* 60, No. 2 (Spring/Summer 2007): 156.

14. David Patrikarakos, *Nuclear Iran: The Birth of an Atomic State* (London: Tauris, 2012), pp. 181, 185–86, 188–91, 193–201. Also see Asr Iran and Raja News, February 20, 2007, http://www.asriran.com/view.php?id= 12170, translated and cited in Hassan Daioleslam, "Iran's 2003 Grand Bargain Offer: Secrets, Lies, and Manipulation," In Search of Truth website, June 25, 2008, available at http://english.iranianlobby.com/page1 .php?id=10&bakhsh=ARTICLES.

15. Crist, *The Twilight War*, pp. 514–15.

16. See the remarkable list of statements by senior American officials affirming Washington's confidence in Pakistani nuclear security procedures in Paul K. Kerr and Mary Beth Nikitin, "Pakistan's Nuclear Weapons: Proliferation and Security Issues," RL34248, Congressional Research Service, February 13, 2013, pp. 15–17.

17. For instance, throughout the Cold War, the United States deployed tactical nuclear weapons to various NATO countries like Germany and Turkey with only the flimsiest security, making it highly likely and incredibly easy for the local government to have seized control of the weapons and launched them had they wanted to do so. Indeed, some in a position to know have argued that this was done purposefully by the United States so that the Soviets would have to fear that if they invaded Western Europe the NATO countries themselves would have been able to launch nuclear weapons at Russia regardless of what Washington wanted to do. This helped to avoid the dilemma of extended deterrence (would an American president use nuclear weapons to defend Germany or Greece when doing so would likely result in the incineration of New York or Chicago?) but constituted a phenomenally reckless approach to the security of nuclear weapons. No other country has ever behaved so irresponsibly with nuclear weapons. See Bracken, *The Second Nuclear Age*, pp. 62–63.

18. See, for instance, Roger Cohen, "Contain and Constrain Iran," *New York Times*, November 14, 2011; Bill Keller, "Nuclear Mullahs," *New York Times*, September 9, 2012; James M. Lindsay and Ray Takeyh, "Lindsay and Takeyh Reply," *Foreign Affairs* 89, No. 4 (July/August 2010): 168; Will Marshall, "Yes, We can Contain Iran," ForeignPolicy.com, March 16, 2012, available at http://www.foreignpolicy.com/articles/2012/03/16/yes _we_can_contain_iran; Paul Pillar, "We Can Live with a Nuclear Iran," *Washington Monthly*, March/April 2012, available at http://www.wash ingtonmonthly.com/magazine/marchapril_2012/features/we_can_live

_with_a_nuclear_ira035772.php; Barry R. Posen, "We Can Live with a Nuclear Iran," *New York Times*, February 27, 2006; Fareed Zakaria, "Zakaria: Iran Is a 'Rational Actor,' " CNN.com, March 8, 2012, available at http://globalpublicsquare.blogs.cnn.com/2012/03/08/zakaria-iran-is-a-rational-actor/.

19. See for instance, Shahram Chubin, "Extended Deterrence and Iran," *Strategic Insights* 8, No. 5 (December 2009); Shireen T. Hunter, *Iran after Khomeini* (New York: Praeger, 1992); Suzanne Maloney, "Thinking the Unthinkable: The Gulf States and the Prospect of a Nuclear Iran," Middle East Memo No. 27, Saban Center for Middle East Policy, Brookings Institution, January 2013, pp. 10–12; David Menashri, *Post-Revolutionary Politics in Iran: Religion, Society, and Power* (London: Frank Cass, 2001), esp. chapters 7 and 8; Menashri, "Iran's Regional Policy," p. 155; Ray Takeyh, *Hidden Iran: Paradox and Power in the Islamic Republic* (New York: Times Books, 2006), esp. pp. 140–41; Frederic Wehrey, David E. Thale, Nora Bensahel, Kim Cragin, Jerrold D. Green, Dalia Dassa Kaye, Nadia Oweidat, and Jennifer Li, *Dangerous but Not Omnipotent: Exploring the Reach and Limitations of Iranian Power in the Middle East* (Santa Monica, Calif.: RAND, 2009), pp. 83, 157.

20. Karim Sadjadpour, "Iran Is 'Years Away' from a Nuclear Weapon," interview on MSNBC, available at http://carnegie-mec.org/publications/?fa=47464.

21. See, for example, Louis René Beres and General (USAF, ret.) John T. Chain, "Israel and Iran at the Eleventh Hour," Oxford University Press blog, February 23, 2012, available at http://blog.oup.com/2012/02/israel-iran-nuclear/; "Ex-Mossad Chief: Iran Rational; Don't Attack Now," interview with Meir Dagan for CBS News *60 Minutes*, available at http://www.cbsnews.com/8301-18560_162-57393715/ex-mossad-chief-iran-rational-dont-attack-now/; Yair Evron, "An Israel-Iran Balance of Nuclear Deterrence: Seeds of Instability," in *Israel and a Nuclear Iran: Implications for Arms Control, Deterrence, and Defense*, INSS Memorandum No. 94, July 2008, p. 52; Reuven Pedatzur, "Israel Can Deter Iran," Al-Monitor, translated by Sandy Bloom, October 9, 2012, available at http://m.al-monitor.com/pulse/security/01/10/the-iranian-threat-against-israe.html.

22. Amos Harel, "IDF Chief to Haaretz: I Do Not Believe Iran Will Decide to Develop Nuclear Weapons," *Haaretz*, April 25, 2012.

23. "Ashkenazi: Iran Is Radical, but Not Irrational—It May Still Curb Nukes," *Haaretz*, November 10, 2009.

24. Yair Evron, "An Israel-Iran Balance of Nuclear Deterrence," p. 52.

25. See, for instance, Eric S. Edelman, Andrew F. Krepinevich, and Evan

Braden Montgomery, "The Dangers of a Nuclear Iran," *Foreign Affairs* 90, No. 1 (January/February 2011): 73–74.

26. Matthew Kroenig, "Time to Attack Iran," *Foreign Affairs* 91, No. 1 (January/February 2012): 78.

27. Bracken, *The Second Nuclear Age*, pp. 77, 125–26.

28. Ibid., pp. 125–26.

29. Also see Christopher Andrew and Oleg Gordievsky, *KGB: The Inside Story of Its Foreign Operations from Lenin to Gorbachev* (New York: Harper-Collins, 1991), pp. 583–605; Gordon Brook-Shepherd, *The Storm Birds: The Dramatic Stories of the Top Soviet Spies Who Have Defected Since World War II* (New York: Weidenfeld & Nicolson, 1989), pp. 329–30; Benjamin B. Fischer, "A Cold War Conundrum: The 1983 Soviet War Scare," Center for the Study of Intelligence, Central Intelligence Agency, March 2007, available at https://www.cia.gov/library/center-for-the-study-of-intelligence/csi-publications/books-and-monographs/a-cold-war-conundrum/source.htm #ft12; Geoffrey Smith, *Reagan and Thatcher* (New York: Norton, 1991), pp. 122–23; and Nicholas Bethell, *Spies and Other Secrets: Memoirs from the Second Cold War* (New York: Viking, 1994), p. 191.

30. Andrew and Gordievsky, *KGB*, p. 605.

31. Ron Suskind, *The One Percent Doctrine: Deep Inside America's Pursuit of Its Enemies Since 9/11* (New York: Simon & Schuster, 2006).

32. Dick Cheney with Liz Cheney, *In My Time: A Personal and Political Memoir* (New York: Threshold Editions, 2011), p. 388.

Chapter 12. The Problems of Containment

1. Eric S. Edelman, Andrew F. Krepinevich, and Evan Braden Montgomery, "The Dangers of a Nuclear Iran," *Foreign Affairs* 90, No. 1 (January/February 2011): 75; Bret Stephens, "Iran Cannot be Contained," *Commentary* 130, No. 1 (July/August 2010): 61–70.

2. Karim Sadjadpour and Diane de Gramont, "Reading Kennan in Tehran," *Foreign Affairs* 90, No. 2 (March/April 2011).

3. Edelman, Krepinevich, and Montgomery, "The Dangers of a Nuclear Iran," p. 78.

4. Paul K. Kerr and Mary Beth Nikitin, "Pakistan's Nuclear Weapons: Proliferation and Security Issues," RL34248, Congressional Research Service, February 13, 2013, pp. 15–16; Bruce Riedel, "American Diplomacy and the 1999 Kargil Summit at Blair House," Center for the Advanced Study of India, Policy Paper Series, 2002, available at http://www.ccc.nps.navy.mil/research/kargil/reidel.pdf; Strobe Talbott, *Engaging India: Diplomacy,*

Democracy, and the Bomb (Washington, D.C.: Brookings Institution Press, 2004), pp. 161–62.

5. For more on both the causes of these problems and how best to address them, see Kenneth M. Pollack, *A Path Out of the Desert: A Grand Strategy for America in the Middle East* (New York: Random House, 2008); Kenneth M. Pollack et al., *The Arab Awakening: America and the Transformation of the Middle East* (Washington, D.C.: Brookings Institution Press, 2011). For a concurring opinion, see Sadjadpour and de Gramont, "Reading Kennan in Tehran."

6. Although it is a tall order, the need to combat Iranian support for terrorism, insurgencies, and other subversive efforts would also put a premium on securing a comprehensive peace between Arabs and Israelis to remove that as a source of animosity that Iran regularly exploits. See Yair Evron, "An Israel-Iran Balance of Nuclear Deterrence: Seeds of Instability," in *Israel and a Nuclear Iran: Implications for Arms Control, Deterrence, and Defense*, INSS Memorandum No. 94, July 2008, p. 59.

7. I have written extensively on what needs to be done in the Arab world, how to go about doing it, and the difficulties of doing so. See in particular, Pollack, *A Path Out of the Desert*, esp. pp. 246–329.

8. For other authors agreeing that crisis management—and the associated risk of miscalculation—are the greatest danger stemming from a nuclear Iran, see Shahram Chubin, "Extended Deterrence and Iran," *Strategic Insights* 8, No. 5 (December 2009); Edelman, Krepinevich, and Montgomery, "The Dangers of a Nuclear Iran," pp. 67–69; Evron, "An Israel-Iran Balance of Nuclear Deterrence: Seeds of Instability," p. 60; Richard L. Kugler, "An Extended Deterrence Regime to Counter Iranian Nuclear Weapons: Issues and Options," Defense and Technology Paper No. 67, Center for Technology and National Security Policy, National Defense University, September 2009, p. 14; Barry Rubin, "The Right Kind of Containment," *Foreign Affairs* 89, No. 4 (July/August 2010): 164.

9. Thomas Donnelly, Danielle Pletka, and Maseh Zarif, "Containing and Deterring a Nuclear Iran: Questions for Strategy, Requirements for Military Forces," American Enterprise Institute, December 2011, http://www.foreignpolicy.com/files/fp_uploaded_documents/111205_AEI%20Iran%20report%20text%20final%20Dec%206%202011.pdf, p. 25.

10. Thomas Blanton, "The Annals of Blinksmanship," *Wilson Quarterly* 21, No. 3 (Summer 1997): 93.

11. Graham Allison, "The Cuban Missile Crisis at 50," *Foreign Affairs* 91, No. 4 (July/August 2012): 11; Aleksandr Fursenko and Timothy Naftali,

"One Hell of a Gamble": Khrushchev, Castro and Kennedy 1958–1964 (New York: Norton, 1997), p. 242. In their subsequent book, Fursenko and Naftali write that the Soviets immediately countermanded the authorization for the local commander to employ tactical nuclear weapons and had authorized him to employ only conventional munitions (including nuclear-capable systems). See Aleksandr Fursenko and Timothy Naftali, *Khrushchev's Cold War: The Inside Story of an American Adversary* (New York: Norton, 2006), p. 473.

12. I have discussed this concept of a regional security architecture for the Persian Gulf in greater length in Kenneth M. Pollack, "Securing the Gulf," *Foreign Affairs* 82, No. 4 (July/August 2003): 2–16.

13. Rafsanjani explained, "Israel is much smaller than Iran in land mass, and therefore far more vulnerable to nuclear attack." He went on to point out that a nuclear attack on Israel would obliterate the state, but the Israeli retaliation would only cause "damage" to the much larger Muslim world. *Jerusalem Report*, March 11, 2002.

14. For a concurring Israeli assessment, see Evron, "An Israel-Iran Balance of Nuclear Deterrence," p. 60.

15. On the dangers of the "use or it or lose it" logic if Iran acquires a nuclear capability, see Edelman, Krepinevich, and Montgomery, "The Dangers of a Nuclear Iran," pp. 67–69; James Lindsay and Ray Takeyh, "After Iran Gets the Bomb," *Foreign Affairs* 89, No. 2 (March/April 2010): 39.

16. On these various points, see for instance, Richard K. Betts, "A Nuclear Golden Age: The Balance Before Parity," *International Security* 11, No. 3 (Winter, 1986–1987): 3–32; Fursenko and Naftali, *Khrushchev's Cold War*; Peter J. Roman, *Eisenhower and the Missile Gap* (Ithaca, N.Y.: Cornell University Press, 1995), esp. pp. 66–79; William C. Wohlforth, *The Elusive Balance of Power: Power and Perceptions During the Cold War* (Ithaca, N.Y.: Cornell University Press, 1993), esp. pp. 161–70.

17. Fursenko and Naftali, *"One Hell of a Gamble,"* pp. 170–72, 177–83, esp. p. 182; Fursenko and Naftali, *Khrushchev's Cold War*, pp. 483–86.

18. The Cuban Missile Crisis was infinitely more complex than what I have just noted in these sentences. My point is not to oversimplify the crisis, or even to suggest that one aspect of it was the most important part of it. Instead, it is to note that American escalation dominance was one of a number of important aspects of the crisis—in triggering it, driving decisions, and ultimately resolving it favorably from the American perspective. Therefore, it too illustrates the value of retaining escalation dominance if possible.

19. Bracken treats this history nicely and makes this point explicitly. See

Bracken, *The Second Nuclear Age*, esp. pp. 41, 99, 196–98. Also see the detailed treatment of the Soviet side of all the different crises from 1954 to 1962 in Fursenko and Naftali, *Khrushchev's Cold War*.

20. For fuller explications of these arguments by some truly exceptional strategic thinkers, see Bracken, *The Second Nuclear Age*, pp. 245–70; Keir A. Lieber and Daryl G. Press, "The Rise of U.S. Nuclear Primacy," *Foreign Affairs* 85, No. 2 (March/April 2006):42–54; Keir A. Lieber and Daryl G. Press, "The End of Mad? The Nuclear Dimension of U.S. Primacy," *International Security* 30, No. 4 (Spring 2006): 7–44; Payne, *The Fallacies of Cold War Deterrence*, pp. 97–196.

21. Kori Schake, "Dealing with a Nuclear Iran," *Policy Review*, No. 142 (April/ May 2007).

22. Evron, "An Israel-Iran Balance of Nuclear Deterrence," p. 50.

23. Bracken, *The Second Nuclear Age*, p. 137.

24. Ibid, p. 41.

25. On this entire subject, the best work by far remains the classic, Robert Jervis, *Perception and Misperception in International Politics* (Princeton, N.J.: Princeton University Press, 1976).

26. David S. McLellan, "Dean Acheson and the Korean War," *Political Science Quarterly* 83, No. 1 (March 1968): 16–39.

27. For a smart, pessimistic view, see Edelman, Krepinevich, and Montgomery, "The Dangers of a Nuclear Iran," p. 67.

28. Reuel Marc Gerecht, "Should Israel Bomb Iran? Better Safe than Sorry," *Weekly Standard* 15, No. 42 (July 26, 2010).

29. For other highly regarded, right-wing commentators raising this problem, see Elliott Abrams, "The Grounds for an Israeli Attack," *World Affairs* 175, No. 1 (May/June 2012): 30; Edelman, Krepinevich, and Montgomery, "The Dangers of a Nuclear Iran," p. 76; Rubin, "The Right Kind of Containment," p. 163; Stephens, "Iran Cannot be Contained," pp. 61–70.

30. See for instance, Daniel Byman and Matthew Waxman "Defeating U.S. Coercion," *Survival* 41, No. 2 (Summer 1999): 110–111; Glenn Snyder, "The Security Dilemma in Alliance Politics," *World Politics* 36, No. 4 (July 1984): 461–495; Victor D. Cha, *Alignment Despite Antagonism: The United States-Korea-Japan Security Triangle* (Palo Alto, Calif.: Stanford University Press, 2000), p. 64; Anne E. Sartori, *Deterrence by Diplomacy* (Princeton, N.J.: Princeton University Press, 2005).

31. Jonathan Mercer, *Reputation and International Politics* (Ithaca, N.Y.: Cornell University Press, 1996); Daryl G. Press, *Calculating Credibility: How Leaders Assess Military Threats* (Ithaca, N.Y.: Cornell University Press, 2005).

32. Excerpts from Glaspie's cable to Washington providing a full readout of the meeting (a virtual transcript) are now publicly available. See "U.S. Messages on July 1990 Meeting of Hussein and American Ambassador," *New York Times*, July 13. 1991.

33. On these matters, see Fursenko and Naftali, *"One Hell of a Gamble,"* pp. 128–34, 170–72, 177–83, 227; Fursenko and Naftali, *Khrushchev's Cold War*, pp. 416–21, 483–86; Frederick Kempe, *Berlin 1961* (New York: Penguin, 2011), p. 247.

34. Mercer, *Reputation and International Politics*; Press, *Calculating Credibility*.

35. Stephen M. Walt, *The Origins of Alliances* (Ithaca, N.Y.: Cornell University Press, 1987), esp. pp. 5–29.

36. Rubin, "The Right Kind of Containment," p. 163.

37. Marc Lynch, "Upheaval: U.S. Policy Toward Iran in a Changing Middle East," Center for a New American Security, June 2011, p. 14.

38. Edelman, Krepinevich, and Montgomery, "The Dangers of a Nuclear Iran," pp. 67–68; Kroenig, Matthew, "Time to Attack Iran," *Foreign Affairs* 91, No. 1 (January/February 2012), pp. 78–79.

39. Technically, the United States maintains a presence of "1.7 aircraft carriers" near the Persian Gulf on an annual basis. This means that there is always one carrier in the Gulf itself, in the Arabian Sea, or elsewhere in the northwestern Indian Ocean. In addition, 70 percent of the time, there is a second carrier in the same area. The official figure is quoted in Spencer Ackerman, "Two U.S. Aircraft Carriers Near Iran, with a Third on the Way," Wired.com, January 11, 2012, available at http://www.wired.com/dangerroom/2012/01/iran-aircraft-carriers/.

40. Thom Shanker and Steven Lee Myers, "U.S. Planning Troop Buildup in Gulf After Exit from Iraq," *New York Times*, October 29, 2011.

41. See, for instance, Henri Barkey, "Turkey-Iraq Relations Deteriorate with Accusations of Sectarianism," Al-Monitor, April 30, 2012, available at http://www.al-monitor.com/pulse/originals/2012/al-monitor/turkey-iraq-ties-sour-brover-syr.html; Kenneth M. Pollack, "Reading Machiavelli in Iraq," *National Interest*, No. 122 (November/December 2012): 8–19.

42. Bruce Riedel argues that Israel could benefit from greater American assistance developing a second-strike capability. See Bruce Riedel, "If Israel Attacks," *National Interest*, No. 109 (September/October 2010).

43. The most important conditions that destroyed CENTO were Washington's refusal to become a formal signatory and the 1958 Iraqi revolution. Our organization of such a treaty structure should make repeating the former unlikely, while one of our goals should be to prevent a recurrence of the latter—especially in other Gulf states.

44. Chubin, "Extended Deterrence and Iran."

45. Clark A. Murdock and Jessica M. Yeats, "Exploring the Nuclear Posture Implications of Extended Deterrence and Assurance," Center for Strategic and International Studies, November 2009, p. 11.

46. Dennis Healey, *The Time of My Life* (London: Michael Joseph, 1989), p. 243.

47. For a concurring opinion, see "Should I Stay or Should I Go Now? Assessing U.S. Force Posture in the Persian Gulf," draft chapter for *Crude Calculus: Reexamining the Energy Security Logic of America's Military Presence in the Persian Gulf*, ed. Charles Glaser and Rose Kelanic (Stanford, Calif.: Stanford University Press, forthcoming). For a dissenting opinion, see Michael E. O'Hanlon, "How Much Does the United States Spend Protecting Persian Gulf Oil?" in Carlos Pascual and Jonathan Elkind, eds., *Energy Security: Economics, Politics, Strategies, and Implications* (Washington, D.C.: Brookings Institution Press, 2010), pp. 70–71. O'Hanlon argues that eliminating the Persian Gulf requirement would save the United States roughly $50 billion per year because he believes that the U.S. likely would reduce its force structure if it did not have to worry about the Persian Gulf. While my respect for Mike remains undiminished, I simply disagree. I do not believe the United States would have a single fewer aircraft carriers, Army divisions, or Air Force wings if we no longer had to worry about the Persian Gulf. Since the GCC states pay for the bases and a considerable portion of the upkeep of the forces we deploy there, the only costs we pay are those for transit, hazardous-duty pay and other increased benefits, and the slightly increased maintenance costs for operating in the difficult environment of the Gulf. These costs are negligible—probably less than a few billion dollars per year—in a defense budget of $672 billion for 2013—and even then there are additional offsets to these costs.

48. Admiral James L. Holloway III, *Aircraft Carriers at War* (Annapolis, Md.: Naval Institute Press, 2007), p. xi.

49. For a fuller explication of my take on these matters, see Pollack, *A Path Out of the Desert*, pp. 24–49.

50. For two assessments of the dynamic balance of Arab and Israeli military capabilities across the history of the Arab-Israeli wars, see Anthony H. Cordesman and Abraham R. Wagner, *The Lessons of Modern War*, vol. 1. *The Arab-Israeli Conflicts, 1973–1989* (Boulder, Colo.: Westview, 1990); Kenneth M. Pollack, *Arabs at War: Military Effectiveness, 1948–1991* (Lincoln: University of Nebraska Press, 2002).

51. Thom Shanker, "U.S. and Gulf Allies Pursue a Missile Shield Against Iranian Attack," *New York Times*, August 8, 2012.

52. This amount is the projected cost of the similar system being built to provide coverage of the U.S. homeland against future intercontinental ballistic missiles launched from Iran or North Korea, and which the Congressional Budget Office has suggested could also be built to defend Europe against Iranian ballistic missiles. Making the assumption that a similar system would be required to provide the same coverage of the Middle East, it seems reasonable to assume that the cost would be roughly equivalent. See "Options for Deploying Missile Defenses in Europe," Congressional Budget Office, February 2009, pp. x, 21.

53. For such arguments, see Bracken, *The Second Nuclear Age*, pp. 245–70; Lieber and Press, "The Rise of U.S. Nuclear Primacy," pp. 42–54; Lieber and Press, "The End of Mad?," pp. 7–44; Lieber and Press, "U.S. Nuclear Primacy and the Future of the Chinese Deterrent," *China Security*, No. 5 (Winter 2007): 66–89; Payne, *The Fallacies of Cold War Deterrence*, pp. 97–196. For a contrary perspective, see Michael E. O'Hanlon and Steven Pifer, *The Opportunity: Next Steps in Reducing Nuclear Arms* (Washington, D.C.: Brookings Institution Press, 2012).

54. For hints at the extent to which U.S. intelligence may already be blanketing Iran, see "Iran Acknowledges Espionage at Nuclear Facilities," Associated Press, October 9, 2010; Tabassum Zakaria and Phil Stewart, "Drone Crash Unmasks U.S. Spying Effort in Iran," Reuters, December 10, 2011.

55. Jeremy M. Sharp, "U.S. Foreign Aid to Israel," RL33222, Congressional Research Service, March 12, 2012, p. 30.

56. Herb Keinon, "US Senator Rand Paul Set to Visit Israel," *Jerusalem Post*, January 3, 2013; Sharp, "U.S. Foreign Aid to Israel," pp. 5–6.

57. Sharp, "U.S. Foreign Aid to Israel," pp. 8–15.

58. Charles Robb, Dennis Ross, and Michael Makvosky, "The Economic Cost of a Nuclear Iran," *Wall Street Journal*, December 17, 2012.

59. Interview with Robert McNally, Washington, D.C., February 2013; Office of Technology Assessment, *U.S. Oil Import Vulnerability: The Technical Replacement Capability*, OTA-E-503 (Washington, D.C.: U.S. Government Printing Office, 1991), pp. 12, 39.

60. To date, there has been only one effort to try to predict both the risk premium and potential price spikes stemming from Iran's acquisition of a nuclear capability. This is the report prepared under the auspices of the Bipartisan Policy Center called "The Price of Inaction: An Analysis of Energy and Economic Effects of a Nuclear Iran" (October 10, 2012, available at http://bipartisanpolicy.org/sites/default/files/Iran%20Report.pdf). This report was the product of a group of people consisting of some terrific oil analysts and some equally terrific but quite conservative policy analysts—

without any true experts on Iran or Saudi Arabia. Nearly all of the policy analysts in the group have publicly opposed containment and generally favor air strikes to prevent Iran from acquiring nuclear weapons. The report's conclusions are not credible, and I suspect that they were badly compromised by this "selection bias."

The methodology of the group (described at greatest length at "The Price of Inaction," pp. 37–41) was to devise four scenarios in which a nuclear Iran might take actions that could affect the production/export of oil (five scenarios are presented, but the group inexplicably dropped from their calculus the one scenario that predicted that Iran's acquisition of nuclear weapons might bring *down* the price of oil, further distorting the calculus). The group then assigned probabilities to these scenarios occurring, as well as projections of how much of a disruption each scenario would cause, both in terms of a maximum loss of oil to the international market, and an impact over time that allowed for various forces to compensate and mitigate the loss. These inputs were then plugged into some standard models related to oil price fluctuations.

The problem with the report is that its conclusions are entirely driven by the wholly subjective estimates of the likelihood and extent of the disruptions posited in the various scenarios, all of which are deeply problematic.

The first scenario the group posits is that a nuclear Iran stirs up internal problems in Saudi Arabia, particularly among the Kingdom's Shi'a population, heavily concentrated as they are in the oil-producing regions of eastern Saudi Arabia. This is a reasonable expectation (although it is hardly a certainty, either). But then the group made a series of highly questionable judgments. First, they assume that this "unrest" causes a loss of all Saudi oil exports—all 7.7 million barrels per day (bpd), representing 8 percent of global oil consumption—for six months, slowly recovering from there, but representing an annualized loss of 5.1 million bpd. (The report states explicitly that these export losses are a result of unrest affecting production—in its words, "An uprising there could disrupt production, driving up prices"—and makes no mention of unrest affecting exports in this scenario. "The Price of Inaction," p. 15.) A disruption of this magnitude would be the largest in history, *ever*. By comparison, the Iranian Revolution caused a loss of roughly 4.6 million bpd, amounting to 78 percent of Iranian production and roughly 7 percent of global consumption at the time. Prior to the 2003 invasion, Iraq produced 2.8 million bpd, only to see that fall as a result of its civil war to 1.8 million bpd in 2005 (its lowest level), representing a decrease of 36 percent. Thus, the worst revolution in a Persian Gulf oil producer, and the worst civil war in a Persian Gulf oil producer, still had less of an impact on oil than this scenario posits. Creating such a drastic cut in Saudi production or exports would require a hell of a lot more than "unrest"—it would require a full-scale revolution worse than the Iranian Revolution or a civil war worse than the Iraqi civil war. Yet the group assigned this scenario a probability of occurrence of 40 percent within three years after Iran acquired a nuclear weapon.

I would never suggest that a revolution in Saudi Arabia is inconceivable, especially one derived from the same forces that produced the various revolts in Tunisia, Egypt, Libya, Bahrain, Jordan, and elsewhere during the Arab Spring of 2011. I warned of this possibility even before the Arab spring. (See Pollack, *A Path Out of the Desert*, pp. 133–220.) However, revolutions are rare events in history—especially successful ones—and it would require a "successful" revolution to cause the kind of disruption this scenario posits. In other words, it could not be a large-scale revolt that gets crushed by Saudi security forces, because at no time in history has such a failed revolution caused anything like the kind of oil disruption that this scenario posits. Moreover, as the great historians of revolution—Brinton, Skocpol, Moore, etc.—have repeatedly shown, the vast majority of attempted revolutions are crushed long before they rise above the level of scattered street protests. The Saudis have faced would-be revolutions on at least a half dozen occasions that we know of dating back to 1979 and they have crushed every one of them without the slightest impact on their oil production. Likewise, the only real scenario for a civil war of similar magnitude in the Kingdom would be one sparked by a revolution that successfully challenged the regime's grip on power, as in Libya in 2011 and Syria since 2011. Thus the notion that there is a 40 percent likelihood of a successful Saudi revolution or civil war occurring within three years of Iran crossing the nuclear threshold is completely out of whack with historical norms and the history of Saudi Arabia. Successful revolutions are so rare that even if we accept (as I do) that it is a much more likely possibility in Saudi Arabia at this period of time than it is for most states at most times, the likelihood of a successful revolution is still exceptionally low probability—historically speaking more like 4 percent than 40 percent likelihood, and that would still represent several orders of magnitude higher risk than is the norm for most countries at most times.

However, the report compounds this mistake by then asserting that this successful revolution in Saudi Arabia would be *caused* by Iran's acquisition of a nuclear capability (an even lower probability than the likelihood of a revolution or civil war occurring at all). As rare as successful revolutions are in history, rarer still are those that are caused by the actions of another state. At most, the actions of other states can exacerbate the conditions that produce a revolt (successful or unsuccessful). However, the methodology of the report attributes the problem entirely to the actions of the other state—in this case Iran. It is worth noting that Iran has never caused a successful revolution despite all its long years of trying. So this would be a first.

In other words, the report does not distinguish between a risk premium created by general Saudi internal fragility, which would compose the majority of the premium, and then add on to that an additional increment that would represent the prospect that Iranian action might be the straw that broke the camel's back and triggered the revolt. Instead, it assumes that *all* risk of a Saudi revolt must be attributed to Iranian acquisition of a nuclear weapon. Thus the report takes its horribly inflated probability estimate of a successful Saudi revolt to generate an estimate of the impact of this supposition on the future price of oil *and attributes it entirely to the impact of Iran's acquisition of nuclear weapons.*

As a point of comparison, here is how I might do the math. I might agree that there is a 40 percent chance of *unrest* in Saudi Arabia at any three-year period of the next decade, but by unrest I mean demonstrations, riots, strikes, and the like. In the vast majority of these cases, such unrest would likely have little or no direct impact on Saudi oil production (although it doubtless would still spook the oil market, albeit to a far lesser degree than unrest that actually did have an impact on oil production). Given the Kingdom's significant economic, political, and social problems coupled with the challenge of succession beyond the sons of Ibn Sa'ud, I might put the likelihood of an actual Saudi revolution or civil war during this period at about 4 percent, which as I have already noted, is probably an order of magnitude higher than the historical norm for any given government during any given three-year period of time. I would rate the likelihood that a nuclear Iran would be responsible for causing a revolution or civil war in Iran far, far lower—maybe a 1 percent chance if I were being generous, maybe one one-hundredth of that if I were being more realistic. Iran certainly has some capability to stir trouble in the Kingdom, but there is absolutely no evidence to suggest that they could stir unrest on the scale posited by the report and heaps of evidence to the contrary. Indeed, even if the Iranians really could move Iran's small Shi'a population (about 10–15 percent of the overall population) to open revolt, the most likely scenario would be that the revolt would be crushed swiftly and thoroughly by the majority Sunnis, who dominate the country's highly efficient security services. Consequently, taking all of these probabilities together and then calculating the impact on the price of oil, the risk premium from an Iranian-inspired revolution or civil war in Saudi Arabia producing an unprecedented shutdown of Saudi oil production would be extremely small.

The other three scenarios that the report chose to retain as part of its calculus all have similar problems. And because the report's estimates of both the oil risk premium and potential price spikes created by Iran's acquisition of nuclear weapons depend on the probabilities assigned by the group to these four scenarios occurring (and occurring in the magnitude postulated), I find no reason to accept its estimates of either price.

61. Joby Warrick and Steve Mufson, "Iran Threatens U.S. Ships, Alarms Oil Markets," *Washington Post*, January 3, 2012.
62. Matthew Kroenig and Robert McNally, "Iranian Nukes and Global Oil," *American Interest* 8, No. 4 (March/April 2013): 45.
63. James D. Hamilton, "Historical Oil Shocks," paper prepared for the *Handbook of Major Events in Economic History*, February 1, 2011, available at http://dss.ucsd.edu/~jhamilto/oil_history.pdf, pp. 20, 33.
64. Sharon Epperson, "Oil Risk Premium Rising on Iran Concerns," CNBC .com, February 23, 2012, available at http://www.cnbc.com/id/46487538/Oil_Risk_Premium_Rising_on_Iran_Concerns; Jonathan Ratner, "'Iran Premium' Not Reflected in Oil Prices: Goldman," *Financial Post*, January 11, 2012; Konstantin Rozhnov, "Iran Talks in Early 2013 to Boost Oil Risk Premium, SocGen Says," Bloomberg, December 21, 2012; "How Much Iran Premium in Oil Prices Is Justified?" SoberLook.com, March 18, 2012, available at http://soberlook.com/2012/03/how-much-iran-premium-in-oil-prices.html.
65. Of course, the costs of containment can only be measured relative to the costs of its alternatives, particularly the military option, a task I take up in the concluding chapter of this book. See also, John Allen Gay, "Should We Bomb Iran to Save Money?" *National Interest* online, December 27, 2012, available at http://nationalinterest.org/commentary/should-we-bomb-iran-save-money-7906.
66. Office of Technology Assessment, *U.S. Oil Import Vulnerability: The Technical Replacement Capability*, OTA-E-503 (Washington, D.C.: U.S. Government Printing Office, 1991), pp. 12, 39.
67. George L. Perry, "The War on Terrorism, the World Oil Market, and the U.S. Economy," Brookings Project on Terrorism and American Foreign Policy, Analysis Paper No. 7, Brookings Institution, November 2001, pp. 3–5.
68. For instance, see the conclusions of the superb report by Thomas Don-

nelly, Danielle Pletka, and Maseh Zarif, "Containing and Deterring a Nuclear Iran: Questions for Strategy, Requirements for Military Forces," American Enterprise Institute, December 2011, http://www.foreignpolicy .com/files/fp_uploaded_documents/111205_AEI%20Iran%20report%20 text%20final%20Dec%206%202011.pdf. Although they are careful to omit any direct statement of their preferences, numerous remarks in the report strongly suggest that they would very much prefer not to contain a nuclear Iran if it can be avoided; however, they ultimately conclude that there is a high probability that the United States will find itself doing so regardless.

69. Gal Luft, "Choke Point," ForeignPolicy.com, July 19, 2012; interview with Robert McNally, Washington, D.C., February 2013.

70. McNally interview.

71. For an exploration of the utility of Sino-American cooperation on Persian Gulf and broader Middle Eastern matters, see Jonathan D. Pollack, "China: Unease from Afar," in Kenneth M. Pollack et al., *The Arab Awakening: America and the Transformation of the Middle East* (Washington, D.C.: Brookings Institution Press, 2011), pp. 298–304; Pollack, *A Path Out of the Desert*, pp. 419–430.

72. For a similar concern from a first-rate Israeli strategic thinker, see Evron, "An Israel-Iran Balance of Nuclear Deterrence," p. 54.

73. See also Bracken, *The Second Nuclear Age*, p. 146.

74. Bruce O. Riedel, *Deadly Embrace: Pakistan, America, and the Future of the Global Jihad* (Washington, D.C.: Brookings Institution Press, 2011).

75. Frederick W. Kagan and Michael O'Hanlon, "Pakistan's Collapse, Our Problem," *New York Times*, November 18, 2007; David E. Sanger, "Obama's Worst Pakistan Nightmare," *New York Times*, January 8, 2009; David E. Sanger and Eric Schmitt, "Pakistani Nuclear Arms Pose Challenge to U.S. Policy," *New York Times*, January 31, 2011.

Chapter 13. Making Containment Work

1. For a concurring view, see Shahram Chubin, "Extended Deterrence and Iran," *Strategic Insights* 8, No. 5 (December 2009).

2. Paul K. Kerr and Mary Beth Nikitin, "Pakistan's Nuclear Weapons: Proliferation and Security Issues," RL34248, Congressional Research Service, February 13, 2013, p. 4.

3. Chubin, "Extended Deterrence and Iran."

4. "President Obama's 2012 address to U.N. General Assembly (Full Text)," *Washington Post*, September 25, 2012.

5. "State of the Union 2013: President Obama's address to Congress (Transcript)," *Washington Post*, February 12, 2013.

6. Meghan L. O'Sullivan, *Shrewd Sanctions: Statecraft and State Sponsors of Terrorism* (Washington, D.C.: Brookings Institution Press, 2002), p. 289.

7. Timothy Garton Ash, *The Polish Revolution: Solidarity, 1980–82,* 3rd ed. (New Haven, Conn.: Yale University Press, 2002); Timothy Garton Ash, *The Magic Lantern: The Revolution of '89 Witnessed in Warsaw, Budapest, Berlin, and Prague* (New York: Random House, 1990); Sarah B. Snyder, *Human Rights Activism and the End of the Cold War: A Transnational History of the Helsinki Network* (Cambridge, U.K.: Cambridge University Press, 2011); Daniel C. Thomas, *The Helsinki Effect: International Norms, Human Rights, and the Demise of Communism* (Princeton, N.J.: Princeton University Press, 2001).

8. Dima Adamsky, "The Morning After in Israel," *Foreign Affairs* 90, No. 2 (March/April 2011).

9. "Lieberman Orders 'Day After' Plans for Tackling Nuclear Iran," Reuters, October 25, 2010; author's interviews with various former senior Israeli officials.

10. Haim Malka, "Israel," in Jon B. Alterman, ed., "Gulf Kaleidescope: Reflections on the Iranian Challenge," Center for Strategic and International Studies, May 2012, p. 59.

11. For an argument that the United States should further assist Israel in developing a secure second-strike capability, see Bruce Riedel, "If Israel Attacks," *National Interest*, No. 109 (September/October 2010).

Conclusion: Choosing the Least Bad Option

1. For those interested in my argument for adopting a strategy along the lines of what became the "surge" and the Anbar Awakening, see Kenneth M. Pollack, "Securing Iraq," Testimony Before the Senate Foreign Relations Committee, April 21, 2004; "Saving Iraq," in *The Road Ahead: Middle East Policy in the Bush Administration's Second Term*, ed. Flynt Leverett (Washington, D.C.: Brookings Institution Press, 2005); Kenneth M. Pollack, "Five Ways to Win Back Iraq," *New York Times*, July 1, 2005, p. A19; Kenneth M. Pollack, "Iraq's Security," Testimony Before the Senate Foreign Relations Committee, July 18, 2005; Kenneth M. Pollack, *A Switch in Time: A New Strategy for America in Iraq*, Analysis Paper No. 7, Saban Center for Middle East Policy, Brookings Institution, February 2006; Kenneth M. Pollack, "The Right Way: Seven Steps Toward a Last Chance in Iraq," *Atlantic*, March 2006, pp. 104–111. On my support for the surge itself, see Michael E. O'Hanlon and Kenneth M. Pollack, "A War We Might Just Win," *New York Times*, July 30, 2007.

2. Thomas Donnelly, Danielle Pletka, and Maseh Zarif, "Containing and De-

terring a Nuclear Iran: Questions for Strategy, Requirements for Military Forces," American Enterprise Institute, December 2011, http://www.for eignpolicy.com/files/fp_uploaded_documents/111205_AEI%20Iran%20 report%20text%20final%20Dec%206%202011.pdf, p. 7.

3. For a good overview of the history of U.S. nuclear accidents, see Michael H. Maggelet and James C. Oskins, *Broken Arrow: The Declassified History of U.S. Nuclear Weapons Accidents* (2007), available at LuluPublishing.com.

Selected Bibliography

Abrams, Elliott. "The Grounds for an Israeli Attack." *World Affairs* 175, No. 1 (May/June 2012): 25–30.

Albright, David, Paul Brannan, and Jacqueline Shire. "Can Military Strikes Destroy Iran's Gas Centrifuge Program? Probably Not." Institute for Science and International Security, August 7, 2008.

Alfoneh, Ali. "The Revolutionary Guards' Role in Iranian Politics." *Middle East Quarterly* 15, No. 4 (Fall 2008): 3–14.

Allin, Dana H., and Steven Simon. *The Sixth Crisis: Iran, Israel, America, and the Rumors of War*. New York: Oxford University Press, 2010.

Alterman, Jon B., ed. "Gulf Kaleidoscope: Reflections on the Iranian Challenge." Center for Strategic and International Studies, May 2012.

Anrig, Christian F. "Allied Air Power over Libya." *Air & Space Power Journal* 25, No. 4 (Winter 2011): 89–109.

Ansari, Ali. "The Revolution Will Be Mercantilized." *National Interest*, No. 105 (January/February 2010).

Baghat, Gawdat. "Nuclear Proliferation: The Case of Saudi Arabia." *Middle East Journal* 60, No. 3 (Summer 2006): 421–43.

———. "Nuclear Proliferation: The Islamic Republic of Iran." *Iranian Studies* 39, No. 3 (2006): 307–27.

Bahari, Maziar, with Aimee Molloy. *Then They Came for Me: A Family's Story of Love, Captivity, and Survival*. New York: Random House, 2011.

Bakhash, Shaul. *The Reign of the Ayatollahs: Iran and the Islamic Revolution.* Rev ed. New York: Basic Books, 1990.

Baldwin, David A. *Economic Statecraft.* Princeton, N.J.: Princeton University Press, 1985.

Baram, Amatzia. "Deterrence Lessons from Iraq." *Foreign Affairs* 91, No. 4 (July/August 2012): 76–85.

Barkey, Henri J., and Uri Dadush. "Why No U.S. President Will Bomb Iran." *National Interest*, January 27, 2010.

Barkey, Henri J., and Graham E. Fuller. *Turkey's Kurdish Question.* Lanham, Md.: Rowman & Littlefield, 1998.

Barrie, Douglas. "Libya's Lessons: The Air Campaign." *Survival* 54, No. 6 (December 2012/January 2013): 57–65.

Beres, Louis René, and General (USAF, ret.) John T. Chain. "Israel and Iran at the Eleventh Hour." Oxford University Press blog, February 23, 2012, available at http://blog.oup.com/2012/02/israel-iran-nuclear/.

Bergman, Ronen. "Will Israel Attack Iran?" *New York Times Magazine*, January 25, 2012.

Betts, Richard K. "The Lost Logic of Deterrence: What the Strategy That Won the Cold War Can—and Can't—Do Now." *Foreign Affairs* 92, No. 2 (March/April 2013): 87–99.

———. *Nuclear Blackmail and Nuclear Balance.* Washington, D.C.: Brookings Institution Press, 1987.

———. "The Osirak Fallacy." *National Interest*, No. 83 (Spring 2006): 22–25.

Bill, James A. *The Eagle and the Lion: The Tragedy of American-Iranian Relations.* New Haven, Conn.: Yale University Press, 1988.

Blight, James G., Janet M. Lang, Hussein Banai, Malcolm Byrne, and John Tirman. *Becoming Enemies: U.S.-Iran Relations and the Iran-Iraq War, 1979–1988.* Lanham, Md.: Rowman & Littlefield, 2012.

Bracken, Paul. "If Iran Gets the Bomb." *Wall Street Journal*, November 17–18, 2012, p. C3.

———. *The Second Nuclear Age: Strategy, Danger, and the New Power Politics.* New York: Times Books, 2012.

Braut-Hegghammer, Malfrid. "Revisiting Osirak: Preventive Attacks and Nuclear Proliferation Risks." *International Security* 36, No. 1 (Summer 2011): 101–32.

Brodie, Bernard, ed. *The Absolute Weapon: Atomic Power and World Order.* New York: Harcourt Brace, 1946.

———. "The Development of Nuclear Strategy." *International Security* 2, No. 4 (Spring 1978): 65–83.

Brzezinski, Zbigniew. *Power and Principle: Memoirs of the National Security Adviser, 1977–1981.* Rev ed. New York: Farrar, Straus & Giroux, 1985.

Byman, Daniel L. *Deadly Connections: States That Sponsor Terrorism.* Cambridge, U.K.: Cambridge University Press, 2005.

Campbell, Kurt M., Robert J. Einhorn, and Mitchell B. Reiss, eds. *The Nuclear Tipping Point: Why States Reconsider Their Nuclear Choices.* Washington, D.C.: Brookings Institution Press, 2004.

Cheney, Dick, with Liz Cheney. *In My Time: A Personal and Political Memoir.* New York: Threshold Editions, 2011.

Choksy, Jamsheed K. "Are the Mullahs Losing Their Grip?" *World Affairs* 175, No. 1 (May/June 2012): 17–24.

Chubin, Shahram. "Extended Deterrence and Iran." *Strategic Insights* 8, No. 5 (December 2009).

———. "A Grand Bargain with Iran." *Foreign Affairs* 90, No. 2 (March/April 2011).

———. "Iran's Strategic Environment and Nuclear Weapons." In *Iran's Nuclear Weapons Options: Issues and Analysis*, ed. Geoffrey Kemp (Washington, D.C.: Nixon Center, 2001).

———. *Whither Iran? Reform, Domestic Politics, and National Security.* Oxford: Oxford University Press, 2002.

Clarke, Richard A. *Against All Enemies: Inside America's War on Terror.* New York: Free Press, 2004.

Clawson, Patrick. "Adjustment to a Foreign Exchange Shock: Iran, 1951–1953." *International Journal of Middle East Studies* 19, No. 1 (February 1987): 1–22.

Clawson, Patrick, and Michael Eisenstadt. "Deterring the Ayatollahs: Complications in Applying Cold War Strategy in Iran." Policy Focus No. 72, Washington Institute for Near East Policy, July 2007.

———. "The Last Resort: Consequences of Preventive Military Action Against Iran." Policy Focus No. 84, Washington Institute for Near East Policy, June 2008.

Clawson, Patrick, and Henry Sokolski, eds. *Checking Iran's Nuclear Ambitions.* Carlisle, Pa.: U.S. Army War College, 2004.

Cordesman, Anthony H. "Iran, Oil, and the Strait of Hormuz." Center for Strategic and International Studies, March 26, 2007.

Cordesman, Anthony H., and Abdullah Toukan. "Analyzing the Impact of Preventive Strikes Against Iran's Nuclear Facilities." Center for Strategic and International Studies, September 10, 2012, available at http://csis.org/files/publication/120906_Iran_US_Preventive_Strikes.pdf.

———. "Study on a Possible Israeli Strike on Iran's Nuclear Development Facilities." Center for Strategic and International Studies, March 14, 2009, available at http://csis.org/files/media/csis/pubs/090316_israelistrikeiran.pdf.

Cortright, David, and George A. Lopez, eds. *Economic Sanctions: Panacea or Peacebuilding in a Post–Cold War World?* Boulder, Colo.: Westview Press, 1995.

Crist, David. *The Twilight War: The Secret History of America's Thirty-Year Conflict with Iran.* New York: Penguin Press, 2012.

Dehez, Dustin. "Iran: The Flaws of Containment." Perspectives Paper No. 123, Begin-Sadat Center for Strategic Studies, November 24, 2010.

Dobbins, James, Alireza Nader, Dalia Dassa Kaye, and Frederic Wehrey. *Coping with a Nuclearizing Iran.* Santa Monica, Calif.: RAND, 2011.

Donnelly, Thomas, Danielle Pletka, and Maseh Zarif. "Containing and Deterring a Nuclear Iran: Questions for Strategy, Requirements for Military Forces." American Enterprise Institute, December 2011, available at http://www.foreignpolicy.com/files/fp_uploaded_documents/111205_AEI%20Iran%20report%20text%20final%20Dec%206%202011.pdf.

Drezner, Daniel W. *The Sanctions Paradox: Economic Statecraft and International Relations.* Cambridge, U.K.: Cambridge University Press, 1999.

Edelman, Eric S., Andrew F. Krepinevich, and Evan Braden Montgomery. "The Dangers of a Nuclear Iran." *Foreign Affairs* 90, No. 1 (January/February 2011): 66–81.

——. "Why Obama Should Take Out Iran's Nuclear Program." *Foreign Affairs* online, available at http://www.foreignaffairs.com/articles/136655/eric-s-edelman-andrew-f-krepinevich-jr-and-evan-braden-montgomer/why-obama-should-take-out-irans-nuclear-program.

Ehteshami, Anoushiravan. "Iran's International Posture After the Fall of Baghdad." *Middle East Journal* 58, No. 2 (Spring 2004): 179–94.

Eisenstadt, Michael, and Mehdi Khalaji. "Forget the Fatwa." *National Interest* online, March 13, 2013, available at http://nationalinterest.org/commentary/forget-the-fatwa-8220.

Eisenstadt, Michael, and Michael Knights. "Beyond Worst-Case Analysis: Iran's Likely Responses to an Israeli Preventive Strike." Policy Notes No. 11, Washington Institute for Near East Policy, June 2012.

Eizenstat, Stuart E. "Do Economic Sanctions Work? Lessons from ILSA and Other U.S. Sanctions Regimes." Atlantic Council, Occasional Paper, February 2004.

Esfandiari, Haleh. *My Prison, My Home: One Woman's Story of Captivity in Iran.* New York: HarperCollins, 2009.

Evron, Yair. "An Israel-Iran Balance of Nuclear Deterrence: Seeds of Instability." In *Israel and a Nuclear Iran: Implications for Arms Control, Deterrence, and Defense.* INSS Memorandum No. 94, July 2008, pp. 47–63.

Feldman, Shai, Shlomo Brom, and Shimon Stein. "What to Do About Nuclearizing Iran? The Israeli Debate." Brandeis University, Crown Center for Middle East Studies, Brief No. 59, February 2012.

Fischer, Michael M. J. *Iran: From Religious Dispute to Revolution*. Madison: University of Wisconsin Press, 1980.

Fitzpatrick, Mark. "Iran: The Fragile Promise of the Fuel-Swap Plan." *Survival* 52, No. 3 (June/July 2010): 67–94.

Fuhrmann, Matthew, and Sarah E. Kreps. "Targeting Nuclear Programs in War and Peace." Belfer Center Discussion Paper 2009-11, Harvard Kennedy School, October 2009.

Fuller, Graham E. *"The Center of the Universe": The Geopolitics of Iran*. Boulder, Colo.: Westview, 1991.

Fursenko, Aleksandr, and Timothy Naftali. *Khrushchev's Cold War: The Inside Story of an American Adversary*. New York: Norton, 2006.

———. *"One Hell of a Gamble": Khrushchev, Castro, and Kennedy 1958–1964*. New York: Norton, 1997.

Gaddis, John Lewis. *The Cold War: A New History*. Paperback ed. New York: Penguin, 2005.

———. *Strategies of Containment: A Critical Appraisal of American National Security Policy During the Cold War*. Revised and expanded ed. New York: Oxford University Press, 2005.

Garthoff, Raymond A. *A Journey Through the Cold War: A Memoir of Containment and Coexistence*. Washington, D.C.: Brookings Institution Press, 2001.

Gerecht, Reuel Marc. "Should Israel Bomb Iran? Better Safe Than Sorry." *Weekly Standard* 15, No. 42 (July 26, 2010).

Hamilton, James D. "Historical Oil Shocks." Paper prepared for the *Handbook of Major Events in Economic History*. February 1, 2011, available at http://dss .ucsd.edu/~jhamilto/oil_history.pdf.

Haass, Richard N., ed. *Economic Sanctions and American Diplomacy*. New York: Council on Foreign Relations, 1998.

Haass, Richard N., and Meghan L. O'Sullivan, eds. *Honey and Vinegar: Incentives, Sanctions, and Foreign Policy*. Washington, D.C.: Brookings Institution Press, 2000.

Heintz, Stephen, William Luers, William Miller, Thomas Pickering, Jim Walsh, Frank Wisner, et al. "Weighing Benefits and Costs of Military Action Against Iran." Iran Project, September 2012.

Hunter, Shireen T. *Iran After Khomeini*. New York: Praeger, 1992.

Huth, Paul K. "Extended Deterrence and the Outbreak of War." *American Political Science Review* 82, No. 2 (June 1988).

———. *Extended Deterrence and the Prevention of War*. New Haven, Conn.: Yale University Press, 1988.

Huth, Paul K., and Bruce Russett. "What Makes Deterrence Work? Cases from 1900 to 1980." *World Politics* 36, No. 4 (July 1984): 496–526.

Jervis, Robert. "Getting to Yes with Iran: The Challenges of Coercive Diplomacy." *Foreign Affairs* 92, No. 1 (January/February 2012): 105–15.

———. *Perception and Misperception in International Politics*. Princeton, N.J.: Princeton University Press, 1976.

Jervis, Robert, Richard Ned Lebow, and Janice Gross Stein. *Psychology and Deterrence*. Baltimore: Johns Hopkins University Press, 1985.

Kahl, Colin H. "Not Time to Attack Iran." *Foreign Affairs* 91, No. 2 (March/April 2012): 166–73.

Kahl, Colin H., Melissa G. Dalton, and Matthew Irvine. "Atomic Kingdom: If Iran Builds the Bomb, Will Saudi Arabia be Next?" Center for a New American Security, February 2013.

———. "Risk and Rivalry: Iran, Israel, and the Bomb." Center for a New American Security, June 2012.

Kam, Ephraim. "An Attack on Iran: The Morning After," *Strategic Assessment* 15, No. 1 (April 2012): 15–28.

Katzman, Kenneth. "Iran: U.S. Concerns and Policy Responses." Congressional Research Service, RL32048, September 5, 2012.

———. *The Warriors of Islam: Iran's Revolutionary Guard*. Boulder, Colo.: Westview, 1993.

Kaye, Dalia Dassa, Alireza Nader, and Parisa Roshan. *Israel and Iran: A Dangerous Rivalry*. Santa Monica, Calif.: RAND, 2011.

Kemp, Geoffrey, ed. *Iran's Nuclear Weapons Options: Issues and Analysis*. Washington, D.C.: Nixon Center, 2001.

Kempe, Frederick. *Berlin 1961*. New York: Penguin, 2011.

Kerr, Paul K. "Iran's Nuclear Program: Status." Congressional Research Service, RL34544, October 17, 2012.

Kroenig, Matthew. "Time to Attack Iran." *Foreign Affairs* 91, No. 1 (January/February 2012): 76–87.

Kroenig, Matthew, and Robert McNally. "Iranian Nukes and Global Oil." *American Interest* 8, No. 4 (March/April 2013): 41–47.

Kugler, Richard L. "An Extended Deterrence Regime to Counter Iranian Nuclear Weapons: Issues and Options." Defense and Technology Paper No. 67. Center for Technology and National Security Policy, National Defense University, September 2009.

Kurzman, Charles. *The Unthinkable Revolution in Iran*. Cambridge, Mass.: Harvard University Press, 2004.

Lambeth, Benjamin S. *Airpower at 18,000': The Indian Air Force in the Kargil War*. Washington, D.C.: Carnegie Endowment for International Peace, 2012.

Landau, Emily B., and Anat Kurz, eds. *Arms Control Dilemmas: Focus on the Middle East.* Tel Aviv: Institute for National Security Studies, 2012.

Ledeen, Michael A. *The Iranian Time Bomb: The Mullah Zealots' Quest for Destruction.* New York: Truman Talley Books, 2007.

Levite, Ariel. "Never Say Never Again: Nuclear Reversal Revisited." *International Security* 27, No. 3 (Winter 2002/2003): 59–88.

Levy, Daniel. "Netanyahu Won't Attack Iran (Probably)." ForeignPolicy.com, March 2, 2012.

Lindsay, James, and Ray Takeyh. "After Iran Gets the Bomb." *Foreign Affairs* 89, No. 2 (March/April 2010): 33–49.

Lynch, Marc. "Upheaval: U.S. Policy Toward Iran in a Changing Middle East." Center for a New American Security, June 2011.

Majd, Hooman. *The Ayatollah's Democracy: An Iranian Challenge.* New York: Norton, 2010.

Maloney, Suzanne. "Thinking the Unthinkable: The Gulf States and the Prospect of a Nuclear Iran." Middle East Memo No. 27, Saban Center for Middle East Policy, Brookings Institution, January 2013.

McNally, Robert. "Energy Brief: Managing Oil Market Disruption in a Confrontation with Iran." Council on Foreign Relations, January 2012.

Menashri, David. "Iran's Regional Policy: Between Radicalism and Pragmatism." *Journal of International Affairs* 60, No. 2 (Spring/Summer 2007): 153–65.

———. *Post-Revolutionary Politics in Iran: Religion, Society, and Power.* London: Frank Cass, 2001.

Milani, Mohsen. "Tehran's Take: Understanding Iran's U.S. Policy." *Foreign Affairs* 88, No. 4 (July/August 2009): 46–62.

Morgan, Patrick M. *Deterrence Now.* Cambridge, U.K.: Cambridge University Press, 1999.

Murdock, Clark A., and Jessica M. Yeats. "Exploring the Nuclear Posture Implications of Extended Deterrence and Assurance." Center for Strategic and International Studies, November 2009.

Nader, Alireza, David E. Thaler, and S. R. Bohandy. *The Next Supreme Leader: Succession in the Islamic Republic of Iran.* Santa Monica, Calif.: RAND, 2011.

Nasr, Vali, and Ray Takeyh. "The Costs of Containing Iran." *Foreign Affairs* 87, No. 1 (January/February 2008): 85–94.

"Options for Deploying Missile Defenses in Europe." Congressional Budget Office, February 2009.

O'Sullivan, Meghan L. *Shrewd Sanctions: Statecraft and State Sponsors of Terrorism.* Washington, D.C.: Brookings Institution Press, 2002.

Ottolenghi, Emanuele. *The Pasdaran: Inside Iran's Islamic Revolutionary Guard Corps.* Washington, D.C.: Foundation for the Defense of Democracies, 2011.

Parsi, Trita. *A Single Roll of the Dice: Obama's Diplomacy with Iran.* New Haven, Conn.: Yale University Press, 2012.

———. *Treacherous Alliance: The Secret Dealings of Israel, Iran, and the United States.* New Haven, Conn.: Yale University Press, 2007.

Pascual, Carlos, and Jonathan Elkind, eds. *Energy Security: Economics, Politics, Strategies, and Implications.* Washington, D.C.: Brookings Institution Press, 2010.

Patrikarakos, David. *Nuclear Iran: The Birth of an Atomic State.* London: Tauris, 2012.

Paul, T. V. *Power Versus Prudence: Why Nations Forgo Nuclear Weapons.* Montreal: McGill-Queen's University Press, 2000.

Paul, T. V., Patrick M. Morgan, and James J. Wirtz. *Complex Deterrence: Strategy in the Global Age.* Chicago: University of Chicago Press, 1999.

Payne, Keith B. *The Fallacies of Cold War Deterrence and a New Direction.* Lexington: University Press of Kentucky, 2001.

Pedatzur, Reuven. "Israel Can Deter Iran." Translated by Sandy Bloom. Al-Monitor, October 9, 2012, available at http://m.al-monitor.com/pulse/security/01/10/the-iranian-threat-against-israe.html.

Peterson, Scott. *Let the Swords Encircle Me: Iran—A Journey Behind the Headlines.* New York: Simon & Schuster, 2010.

Pillar, Paul. *Terrorism and U.S. Foreign Policy.* Washington, D.C.: Brookings Institution Press, 2001.

———. "We Can Live with a Nuclear Iran." *Washington Monthly* (March/April 2012), available at http://www.washingtonmonthly.com/magazine/marchapril_2012/features/we_can_live_with_a_nuclear_ira035772.php.

Posen, Barry R. "Overkill." *Foreign Affairs* 89, No. 4 (July/August 2010): 160–63.

"The Price of Inaction: An Analysis of Energy and Economic Effects of a Nuclear Iran." Bipartisan Policy Center, October 10, 2012.

Raas, Whitney, and Austin Long. "Osiraq Redux: Assessing Israeli Capabilities to Destroy Iranian Nuclear Facilities." *International Security* 31, No. 4 (Spring 2007): 7–33.

Ramberg, Bennett. "Looking Back: Osirak and Its Lessons for Iran Policy." *Arms Control Today* 42, No. 4 (May 2012): 40–43.

Riedel, Bruce. "If Israel Attacks." *National Interest*, No. 109 (September/October 2010).

Rieger, René, and Markus Schiller. "Pre-Emptive Strike Against Iran: Prelude to an Avoidable Disaster?" *Middle East Policy* 19, No. 4 (Winter 2012): 127–39.

Robb, Charles, Dennis Ross, and Michael Makvosky. "The Economic Cost of a Nuclear Iran." *Wall Street Journal*, December 17, 2012.

Rubin, Barry. "The Right Kind of Containment." *Foreign Affairs* 89, No. 4 (July/August 2010): 163–66.

Russell, Richard. "A Saudi Nuclear Option?" *Survival* 43, No. 2 (Summer 2001): 69–79.

Saberi, Roxana. *Between Two Worlds: My Life and Captivity in Iran*. New York: HarperCollins, 2010.

Sadjadpour, Karim. "The Nuclear Players." *Journal of International Affairs* 60, No. 2 (Spring/Summer 2007): 125–34.

———. "Reading Khamenei: The World View of Iran's Most Powerful Leader." Carnegie Endowment for International Peace, 2008.

Sadjadpour, Karim, and Diane de Gramont. "Reading Kennan in Tehran." *Foreign Affairs* 90, No. 2 (March/April 2011).

Sagan, Scott D., and Kenneth N. Waltz. *The Spread of Nuclear Weapons: A Debate Renewed*. 2nd ed. New York: Norton, 2002.

Sagan, Scott D., Kenneth Waltz, and Richard K. Betts. "A Nuclear Iran: Promoting Stability or Courting Disaster?" *Journal of International Affairs* 60, No. 2 (Spring/Summer 2007): 135–50.

Sartori, Anne E. *Deterrence by Diplomacy*. Princeton, N.J.: Princeton University Press, 2005.

Schake, Kori. "Dealing with a Nuclear Iran." *Policy Review*, No. 142 (April/May 2007).

Sebenius, James K., and Michael Singh. "Is a Nuclear Deal with Iran Possible?" *International Security* 37, No. 3 (Winter 2012/2013): 52–91.

Seifzadeh, Hossein S. "The Landscape of Factional Politics and Its Future in Iran." *Middle East Journal* 57, No. 1 (Winter 2003): 57–75.

Sick, Gary. *All Fall Down: America's Fateful Encounter with Iran*. London: Tauris, 1985.

Slavin, Barbara. *Bitter Friends, Bosom Enemies: Iran, the U.S., and the Twisted Path to Confrontation*. New York: St. Martin's Press, 2007.

Smith, Jeffrey H., and John B. Bellinger III. "Providing a Legal Basis to Attack Iran." *Washington Post*, September 27, 2012.

"Spider Web: The Making and Unmaking of Iran Sanctions." Middle East Report No. 138, International Crisis Group, February 25, 2013.

Stephens, Bret. "Iran Cannot be Contained." *Commentary* 130, No. 1 (July/August 2010): 61–70.

Takeyh, Ray. "All the Ayatollah's Men." *National Interest*, No. 121 (September/October 2012): 51–61.

———. *Guardians of the Revolution: Iran and the World in the Age of the Ayatollahs*. Oxford: Oxford University Press, 2009.

———. *Hidden Iran: Paradox and Power in the Islamic Republic*. New York: Times Books, 2006.

Talmadge, Caitlin. "Closing Time: Assessing the Iranian Threat to the Strait of Hormuz." *International Security* 33, No. 1 (Summer 2008): 82–117.

Terrill, W. Andrew. *The Saudi-Iranian Rivalry and the Future of Middle East Security*. Carlisle, Pa.: U.S. Army War College Strategic Studies Institute, 2011.

Vaez, Ali, and Karim Sadjadpour. "Iran's Nuclear Odyssey: Costs and Risks." Carnegie Endowment for International Peace, April 2013.

Waltz, Kenneth N. "The Spread of Nuclear Weapons: More May Be Better." Adelphi Paper No. 171. London: International Institute for Strategic Studies, 1981.

Ward, Steven R. "The Continuing Evolution of Iran's Military Doctrine." *Middle East Journal* 59, No. 4 (Autumn 2005): 559–76.

———. *Immortal: A Military History of Iran and Its Armed Forces*. Washington, D.C.: Georgetown University Press, 2009.

Watman, Kenneth, Dean Wilkening, with John Arquila and Brian Nichiporuk. "U.S. Regional Deterrence Strategies." MR490, RAND Corporation, 1995.

Waxman, Matthew. "What the Cuban Missile Crisis Teaches Us About Iran." CNN.com, October 25, 2012.

Wehrey, Frederic, Jerrold D. Green, Brian Nichiporuk, Alireza Nader, Lydia Hansell, Rasool Nafisi, and S. R. Bohandy. "The Rise of the Pasdaran: Assessing the Domestic Roles of Iran's Islamic Revolutionary Guards Corps." RAND Corporation, 2009, available at http://www.rand.org/pubs/monographs/2008/RAND_MG821.pdf.

Wehrey, Frederic, David E. Thale, Nora Bensahel, Kim Cragin, Jerrold D. Green, Dalia Dassa Kaye, Nadia Oweidat, and Jennifer Li. *Dangerous but Not Omnipotent: Exploring the Reach and Limitations of Iranian Power in the Middle East*. Santa Monica, Calif.: RAND, 2009.

Wilkening, Dean, and Kenneth Watman. "Nuclear Deterrence in a Regional Context." MR 500, RAND Corporation, 1995.

Yadlin, Amos, and Avner Golov. "A Nuclear Iran: The Spur to a Regional Arms Race?" *Strategic Assessment* 15, No. 3 (October 2012): 7–26.

Yadlin, Amos, and Yoel Guzansky. "Iran on the Threshold." *Strategic Assessment* 15, No. 1 (April 2012): 7–14.

Zanotti, Jim, Kenneth Katzman, Jeremiah Gertler, and Steven A. Hildreth. "Israel: Possible Military Strike Against Iran's Nuclear Facilities." Congressional Research Service, R42443, March 27, 2012.

Zarif, M. Javad. "Tackling the Iran-U.S. Crisis." *Journal of International Affairs* 60, No. 2 (Spring/Summer 2007): 73–94.

Index

Page numbers beginning with 439 refer to end notes.

Love & Misadventure

Love & Misadventure

Written & Illustrated by

L A N G   L E A V

**Andrews McMeel
Publishing, LLC**

Kansas City · Sydney · London

Andrews McMeel Publishing, LLC
an Andrews McMeel Universal company
1130 Walnut Street, Kansas City, Missouri 64106

www.andrewsmcmeel.com

www.langleav.com

13 14 15 16 17 RR2 10 9 8 7 6 5 4 3 2

ISBN: 978-1-4494-5614-6

Library of Congress Control Number: 2013947184

ATTENTION: SCHOOLS AND BUSINESSES
Andrews McMeel books are available at quantity discounts
with bulk purchase for educational, business, or sales
promotional use. For information, please e-mail the Andrews
McMeel Publishing Special Sales Department:
specialsales@amuniversal.com